AF778496

Law-Making and Legitimacy in International Humanitarian Law

In memory of Robert Cryer
A brilliant scholar and beloved friend

Law-Making and Legitimacy in International Humanitarian Law

Edited by

Heike Krieger

Professor of Public and International Law, Freie Universität Berlin, Co-Chair Berlin Potsdam Research Group 'The International Rule of Law – Rise or Decline?', and Max Planck Fellow, Max Planck Institute for Comparative Public Law and International Law, Heidelberg, Germany

With Assistant Editor

Jonas Püschmann

Research Fellow, Max Planck Institute for Comparative Public Law and International Law, Heidelberg, Germany

Edward Elgar PUBLISHING

Cheltenham, UK • Northampton, MA, USA

© The Editor and Contributors Severally 2021

Cover image: Beth Macdonald on Unsplash

All rights reserved. No part of this publication may be reproduced, stored in a retrieval system or transmitted in any form or by any means, electronic, mechanical or photocopying, recording, or otherwise without the prior permission of the publisher.

Published by
Edward Elgar Publishing Limited
The Lypiatts
15 Lansdown Road
Cheltenham
Glos GL50 2JA
UK

Edward Elgar Publishing, Inc.
William Pratt House
9 Dewey Court
Northampton
Massachusetts 01060
USA

A catalogue record for this book
is available from the British Library

Library of Congress Control Number: 2021945101

This book is available electronically in the **Elgar**online
Law subject collection
http://dx.doi.org/10.4337/9781800883963

Printed on elemental chlorine free (ECF)
recycled paper containing 30% Post-Consumer Waste

ISBN 978 1 80088 395 6 (cased)
ISBN 978 1 80088 396 3 (eBook)

Printed and bound in the USA

Contents

Contributors

Jean d'Aspremont, Professor of International Law, Sciences Po School of Law; Chair in Public International Law, University of Manchester

William Boothby, Former Deputy Director of Legal Services for the Royal Air Force; Honorary Professor, Australian National University

Michael Bothe, Professor Emeritus of Public and International Law, Goethe University Frankfurt am Main; Former President of the International Humanitarian Fact-Finding Commission

Emily Crawford, Associate Professor, University of Sydney Law School; Associate, Sydney Centre for International Law

Robert Cryer, (1974–2021) Professor of International and Criminal Law, Birmingham Law School, University of Birmingham

Shane Darcy, Professor and Deputy Director, Irish Centre for Human Rights, School of Law, National University of Ireland Galway

Denise Garcia, Associate Professor of Political Science and International Affairs, Northeastern University in Boston; Former Fellow, Nobel Peace Institute

Robin Geiß, Director of the United Nations Institute for Disarmament Research (UNIDIR); Affiliate Professor at the University of Glasgow

Robert Heinsch, Associate Professor of Public International Law, Grotius Centre for International Legal Studies of Leiden Law School; Director of the Kalshoven-Gieskes Forum on International Humanitarian Law, Leiden University

Jean-Marie Henckaerts, Legal Adviser in the Legal Division of the International Committee of the Red Cross (ICRC) and head of the unit charged with updating the Commentaries on the 1949 Geneva Conventions and their 1977 Additional Protocols

Hyeran Jo, Associate Professor, Department of Political Science, Texas A&M University

Daniel Joyce, Senior Lecturer, Faculty of Law & Justice, UNSW Sydney; Affiliated Research Fellow, Erik Castrén Institute, University of Helsinki

Stefan Kadelbach, Professor of Public Law, Public International Law, and European Law, Goethe Universität Frankfurt am Main; Member of the Board of Directors, Cluster of Excellence 'Normative Orders' (2007–2019)

Balingene Kahombo, Dr., Associate Professor of Public Law and African International

Relations, University of Goma; Senior Expert – Coordinator of the Technical Secretariat of the PANEL to accompany the President of the Democratic Republic of Congo as the Chairperson of the African Union 2021–2022; Co-Founder and Member of the Center for Research and Studies on the Rule of Law in Africa (*Centre de Recherches et d'Etudes sur l'Etat de Droit en Afrique* – CREEDA)

Heike Krieger, Professor of Public and International Law, Freie Universität Berlin; Co-Chair, Berlin Potsdam Research Group 'The International Rule of Law – Rise or Decline?'; Max Planck Fellow at the Max Planck Institute for Comparative Public Law and International Law, Heidelberg

Philip Liste, Professor of Political Science and the Politics of Human Rights, Fulda University of Applied Sciences

Timothy Meyer, Professor of Law, Vanderbilt Law School; Director of the International Legal Studies Program

Georg Nolte, Professor of International Law, Humboldt University Berlin

Elvina Pothelet, Dr., Regional Legal Adviser for West Africa, International Committee of the Red Cross (ICRC)

Anni Pues, Lecturer in International Law (School of Law), University of Glasgow

Jonas Püschmann, Research Fellow at the Max Planck Institute for Comparative Public Law and International Law, Heidelberg; doctoral candidate, Freie Universität Berlin

Thomas Rauter, Judicial Expert for the Regional Government of Salzburg (Austria); former Research and Teaching Assistant as well as Lecturer at the Universities of Graz and Salzburg

Alejandro Rodiles, Associate Professor of International Law and Global Governance, ITAM, Mexico City; Senior Fellow, Berlin Potsdam Research Group 'The International Rule of Law – Rise or Decline?'

Tom Ruys, Professor of International Law, Ghent University; Ghent Rolin-Jaequemyns International Law Institute (GRILI)

Cedric Ryngaert, Professor of Public International Law, Utrecht Centre for Accountability and Liability Law, Utrecht University

Dale Stephens, Professor, University of Adelaide; Fellow, Australian Academy of Law; Director, Adelaide Research Unit on Military Law and Ethics (RUMLAE); Chair of SA Red Cross IHL Advisory Committee; Head of SA/NT Combined Navy Reserve Legal Panel

Wouter G. Werner, Professor of International Law, Centre for the Politics of Transnational Law, Vrije Universiteit Amsterdam; Extraordinary Professor of International Law, University of Curacao

Cindy Wittke, Leader of the Political Science Junior Research Group and the research project 'Between Conflict and Cooperation: The Politics of International Law in the post-Soviet Space' (PolVR 01UC1901, Federal Ministry of Education and Research) at the Leibniz Institute for East and Southeast European Studies (IOS), Regensburg

Preface

At the beginning of 2021, when this book was completed, the Treaty on the Prohibition of Nuclear Weapons entered into force. For many states, NGOs, and the ICRC its entry into force marked a 'victory for humanity'. For other observers, the treaty represents yet another example of international law's cynicism or lacking sense of realism, since none of the states possessing nuclear weapons ratified the treaty. However, even from a cynical or realist perspective, it is not farfetched to assume that the treaty will create an argumentative burden, at least for democratic states, to justify why they do not join it.

Law-making processes in international law are complex and full of different shades of grey. The present book seeks to contribute to an analysis of these law-making processes from the perspective of international humanitarian law. For this purpose, it brings together renowned experts and practitioners in the field of international humanitarian law with distinguished scholars from a general international or human rights law background. The project was birthed within the Collaborative Research Centre 700 'Areas of Limited Statehood' (SFB 700) at the Freie Universität Berlin – SFB 700 was a coordinated research programme funded by the German Research Foundation (DFG) – and profited from my Max Planck Fellowship at the Max Planck Institute for Comparative Public Law and International Law, for which I would like to thank the Max Planck Society for the Advancement of Sciences. The funding by the DFG allowed us to organize an author's meeting for an exchange of views in order to enhance the book's coherence.

Thanks are due to the authors of this volume for taking an interest in and engaging with the research questions of this book. I am also grateful to Luke Adams, Fiona Todd and David Fairclough from Edward Elgar Publishing for their advice and support. Many other people contributed to the editing process. In particular, I want to express my gratitude to my research fellows Anton Petrov (SFB 700), who prepared the author's gathering, Lars Müller (SFB 700), who supported the editing process before joining the Federal Foreign Office, and Jonas Püschmann (MPIL Heidelberg), who took over as assistant editor and helped to finalize the project vigorously and diligently. My student assistants Nathanael van der Beek, Valentina Chiofalo, Christina Jugel, Louisa Reutter, Teymina Saak, and Pia Wolski supported the editing process by adapting the manuscript to the style guide. Alicia de la Cour Venning helped to refine the English language. Thanks to you all!

The book is dedicated to the memory of Robert Cryer, who died on 3 January 2021 at the age of 46 years. I first met Rob in September 2003 when I came to the University of Nottingham under an Erasmus Teaching Mobility program. Rob met me at the station, took me to a flat on the beautiful Nottingham campus, which he had organized, and introduced me to many new aspects of the British way of life, including the faculty club (something unheard-of in Germany) and a legendary pub quiz night. In that quiz I mixed up the ways in which the characters of Robert de Niro and Bob Hoskins were killed in the movie *Brazil*. The group at the next table which checked our answers found my answer extraordinarily disgusting and Rob teased me about this answer ever since – actually until our last long talk in November 2020. After my five weeks in Nottingham we changed roles and Rob came to Göttingen, where I was based in those days writing my *Habilitation*. So now my family and I introduced him to the specifics of the German way of life, including Christmas markets (which he really liked). During these months we became close friends and remained so. Rob cared deeply about international law and its promises for a better and more peaceful world. He was an extraordinary international lawyer and basically knew everything about international law. Whenever I wanted to know 'what the law is' or needed a special quote, I could turn to him. One of my most favorite quotes that he himself coined is both funny and insightful: 'International law is neither God nor mummy – it can't make everything right.' His library was impressive; he had read practically everything that was published and his own outstanding work, in particular on international criminal law, has influenced scholars around the world. But above all, Rob was one of the kindest, funniest, and most caring persons I have ever met.

Heike Krieger

Abbreviations

ABM	anti-ballistic missile
ACtHPR	African Court of Human and Peoples' Rights
AI	artificial intelligence
AP I	Protocol Additional to the Geneva Conventions of 12 August 1949, and relating to the Protection of Victims of International Armed Conflicts (opened for signature 8 June 1977, entered into force 7 December 1978) 1125 UNTS 3
AP II	Protocol Additional to the Geneva Conventions of 12 August 1949, and relating to the Protection of Victims of Non-International Armed Conflicts (opened for signature 8 June 1977, entered into force 7 December 1978) 1125 UNTS 609
AP III	Protocol Additional to the Geneva Conventions of 12 August 1949, and relating to the Adoption of an Additional Distinctive Emblem (opened for signature 8 December 2005, entered into force 14 January 2007) 2404 UNTS 261
APRM	African Peer Review Mechanism
Art	Article
ASEAN	Association of Southeast Asian Nations
AU	African Union
AUCIL	African Union Commission on International Law
BCC	Belgian Criminal Code
CCC	Constitutional Court of Colombia
CCM	Convention on Cluster Munitions (adopted 30 May 2008, entered into force 1 August 2010) 2688 UNTS 39
CIL	Customary International Law
CNN	Cable News Network
CUP	Cambridge University Press
DRC	Democratic Republic of the Congo
ECCC	Extraordinary Chambers in the Courts of Cambodia
ECHR	European Convention on Human Rights (adopted 4 November 1950, entered into force 3 September 1953) 213 UNTS 221
ECtHR	European Court of Human Rights

e.g.	exempli gratia / for example
ELN	Ejército de Liberación Nacional
EU	European Union
FARC	Fuerzas Armadas Revolucionarias de Colombia
FCO	Foreign and Commonwealth Office
FLN	Algerian National Liberation Front
G7	Group of 7
GATT	1947 General Agreement on Tariffs and Trade (adopted 30 October 1947, entered into force 1 January 1948) 55 UNTS 187
GC I	Geneva Convention for the Amelioration of the Condition of the Wounded and Sick in Armed Forces in the Field (opened for signature 12 August 1949, entered into force 21 October 1950) 75 UNTS 31
GC II	Geneva Convention for the Amelioration of the Condition of Wounded, Sick and Shipwrecked Members of Armed Forces at Sea (opened for signature 12 August 1949, entered into force 21 October 1950) 75 UNTS 85
GC III	Geneva Convention relative to the Treatment of Prisoners of War (opened for signature 12 August 1949, entered into force 21 October 1950) 75 UNTS 135
GC IV	Geneva Convention relative to the Protection of Civilian Persons in Time of War (opened for signature 12 August 1949, entered into force 21 October 1950) 75 UNTS 287
HPCR-Manual	Humanitarian Policy and Conflict Research Manual on International Law Applicable to Air and Missile Warfare (Harvard-Manual)
HRC	United Nations Human Rights Council
IAC	International armed conflict
IACHR	Inter-American Court of Human Rights
Ibid	ibidem / in the same place
ICAN	International Campaign to Abolish Nuclear Weapons
ICC	International Criminal Court
ICCLA	Ius Constitutionale Commune in Latin America
ICCPR	International Covenant on Civil and Political Rights (adopted 16 December 1966, entered into force 23 March 1976) 999 UNTS 171
ICEM	International Commission of Enquiry on Mercenaries
ICESCR	International Covenant on Economic, Social and Cultural Rights (adopted 16 December 1966, entered into force 3 January 1976) 993 UNTS 3
ICGLR	International Conference on the Great Lakes Region
ICJ	International Court of Justice
ICL	international criminal law

ICRC/CICR	International Committee of the Red Cross / Comité international de la Croix-Rouge
ICRC DPH Study	Interpretative Guidance on the Notion of Direct Participation in Hostilities under International Humanitarian Law
ICTR	International Criminal Tribunal for Rwanda
ICTY	International Criminal Tribunal for the former Yugoslavia
IDP	internally displaced person
i.e.	id est / that is
IHL	international humanitarian law
IHRL	international human rights law
ILA	International Law Association
ILC	International Law Commission
ILM	International Legal Material
IR	International Relations
IRA	Irish Republican Army
ISIS	Islamic State of Iraq and Syria
LOAC	law of armed conflict
MAPROBU	African Prevention and Protection Mission in Burundi
MILF	Moro Islamic Liberation Front
MJP	Mouvement pour la Justice et la Paix
MLC	Mouvement de Libération du Congo
MTP	Movimiento Todos por la Patria
NATO	North Atlantic Treaty Organization
NEPAD	New Partnership for Africa's Development
NGO	non-governmental organisation
NIAC	non-international armed conflict
NPT	Treaty on the Non-Proliferation of Nuclear Weapon (adopted 1 July 1968, entered into force 5 March 1970) 729 UNTS 161
NSCN	National Socialist Council of Nagalim
NWFZ	Nuclear Weapon Free Zone
OAS	Organization of American States
OAU	Organization of African Unity
OPANAL	Agency for the Prohibition of Nuclear Weapons in Latin America and the Caribbean
OUP	Oxford University Press
PAC	Pan-Africanist Congress
PDKI	Democratic Party of Iranian Kurdistan

PKK	Kurdistan Worker's Party
PLO	Palestine Liberation Organization
PMSC	private military and security company
POW	prisoner of war
PSC	African Union Peace and Security Council
R2P	Responsibility to Protect
RCD	Rassemblement Congolais pour la Démocratie
RGIL	Rebel Groups and International Law
SCSL	Special Court for Sierra Leone
SDI	Strategic Defense Initiative
SG	United Nations Secretary-General
STL	Special Tribunal for Lebanon
SWAPO	South West Africa People's Organization
TAK	Kurdistan Freedom Hawks
UAV	unmanned aerial vehicle
UDHR	Universal Declaration of Human Rights
UK	United Kingdom
UN	United Nations
UNGA	United Nations General Assembly
UNSC	United Nations Security Council
US	United States of America
VCLT	Vienna Convention on the Law of Treaties (adopted 23 May 1969, entered into force 27 January 1980) 1155 UNTS 331
VCLTO	Vienna Convention on the Law of Treaties between States and International Organizations or between International Organizations
WMD	Weapons of Mass Destruction
WTO	World Trade Organization

PART I

Introduction

1. Law-making and legitimacy in international humanitarian law

Heike Krieger and Jonas Püschmann

1. THE AMBIGUOUS STATE OF INTERNATIONAL HUMANITARIAN LAW

International humanitarian law (IHL) seems to be in an ambiguous and sometimes even turbulent state. Since the 1990s, it developed from a niche subject primarily dealt with by a small group of military lawyers to a topic at the forefront of international legal discourse in academia and beyond. International organizations, international and domestic courts, semi-judicial bodies, expert groups, non-governmental organizations (NGOs), global public opinion and even armed groups bring forward interpretations of relevant treaties or rules of customary international law. However, the strong increase in legally relevant discourses and practices by these actors stands in stark contrast to two other developments: a certain absence of corresponding state-driven legal practices and a strong perception that 'IHL is more often violated than respected' – an observation which in turn results in 'discourses about the effectiveness of IHL and a tendency to question its impact'.[1]

In the twentieth century, IHL developed through a number of multilateral treaties ranging from the 1907 Hague Regulations to the 1949 Geneva Conventions and their 1977 Additional Protocols. In particular, major conflicts worked as a catalyst for change in IHL. However, since 1977, no major multilateral treaty has been concluded with the exception of select treaties in the field of weapons law. At the same time, informal and non-binding processes have collapsed at the inter-state level. Most significantly, the Intergovernmental Process on Strengthening Respect for IHL pursued within the framework of the Red Cross and Red Crescent Conferences has so far failed in establishing a voluntary, non-binding national reporting system or any comparable informal voluntary process. While states were apparently reclaiming their role in the law-making process at the 32nd International Conference of the Red Cross and Red Crescent in 2015, a 2019 International Committee of the Red Cross (ICRC) report sharply concluded: 'Despite efforts undertaken by delegations, it became clear that, in the current international environment, the time was not ripe for reaching a consensual

---

1 International Committee of the Red Cross, 'International Humanitarian Law and the Challenges of Contemporary Armed Conflicts – Recommitting to Protection in Armed Conflict on the 70th Anniversary of the Geneva Conventions' (October 2019) 76 <https://shop.icrc.org/international-humanitarian-law-and-the-challenges-of-contemporary-armed-conflicts-recommitting-to-protection-in-armed-conflict-on-the-70th-anniversary-of-the-geneva-conventions-pdf-en> accessed 31 January 2021.

agreement among states on ways to strengthen respect for IHL within the intergovernmental process.'[2]

However, this stagnation of the intergovernmental process does not mean that there has been or will be no need to develop the rules of IHL. The so-called 'new wars paradigm' has raised questions as to whether IHL sufficiently regulates non-international armed conflicts and to what extent it should be applied or modified in view of military encounters with armed groups or terrorist groups. Moreover, the swift development of new technologies, in relation to cyberspace, artificial intelligence (AI) or autonomous weapon systems, for example, challenges some of the traditional pillars of IHL, including the principle of distinction. Yet the need for the law to evolve is predominantly being met through informal methods of law-making, as this book will show, although, in the context of cyberspace regulation, states currently seem to reclaim the lead.[3]

2. THE RISE OF NON-STATE ACTORS

While informal methods of law-making are employed by both state and non-state actors, it is the rise of the latter in this realm that suggests a more foundational shift in the direction in which IHL will develop as well as in the law-making process itself. Non-state actors are apparently no longer exclusive law-takers,[4] but also 'law-shapers, law-influencers, law-interpreters, law-makers, law-enforcers, or a combination thereof'.[5] This has led scholars to even conclude that it 'is no exaggeration to say that jurists, NGOs, scholars and other non-State actors pres-

---

[2] ICRC and the Swiss Federal Department of Foreign Affairs, 'Factual Report on the Proceedings of the Intergovernmental Process on Strengthening Respect for IHL – Progress report' (October 2019) 11 <https://rcrcconference.org/app/uploads/2019/10/33IC-IHL-Compliance-factual-report-_en.pdf> accessed 31 January 2021.

[3] eg Germany, The Federal Government, 'On the Application of International Law in Cyberspace' (March 2021) <https://www.auswaertiges-amt.de/blob/2446304/32e7b2498e10b74fb17204c54665bdf0/on-the-application-of-international-law-in-cyberspace-data.pdf>; Iran, Armed Forces Cyberspace Center, 'Declaration of General Staff of the Armed Forces of the Islamic Republic of Iran Regarding International Law Applicable to the Cyberspace' (July 2020) <https://www.yjc.ir/en/news/47482/declaration-of-general-staff-of-the-armed-forces-of-the-islamic-republic-of-iran-regarding-international-law-applicable-to-the-cyberspace>; France, Ministère des Armées, 'International Law Applied to Cyberspace Operations' (October 2019) <https://www.defense.gouv.fr/content/download/567648/9770527/file/international+law+applied+to+operations+in+cyberspace.pdf>; The Netherlands, Ministry of Foreign Affairs, 'Letter to the Parliament on the International Legal Order in Cyberspace' (July 2019) <https://www.government.nl/ministries/ministry-of-foreign-affairs/documents/parliamentary-documents/2019/09/26/letter-to-the-parliament-on-the-international-legal-order-in-cyberspace>; United Kingdom Attorney General's Office and Jeremy Wright, 'Cyber and International Law in the 21st Century' (23 May 2018) <https://www.gov.uk/government/speeches/cyber-and-international-law-in-the-21st-century>; Commonwealth of Australia, Department of Foreign Affairs and Trade, 'Australia's International Cyber Engagement Strategy' (October 2017) <https://www.dfat.gov.au/sites/default/files/DFAT%20AICES_AccPDF.pdf> all accessed 18th July 2021.

[4] Math Noortmann and Cedric Ryngaert, *Non-State Actor Dynamics in International Law: From Law-Takers to Law-Makers* (Taylor and Francis 2016).

[5] Ezequiel Heffes and Marcos Kotlik, 'How Focusing on Non-State Actors Can Change the IHL Narrative' (*opinio juris*, 3 November 2020) <opiniojuris.org/2020/11/03/how-focusing-on-non-state-actors-can-change-the-ihl-narrative/> accessed 31 January 2021.

ently have greater influence on the interpretation and development of IHL than do States'.[6] This increasing impact non-state actors exert in relation to law-making stands in stark contrast to perceptions of their earlier role during the formative stage of the international rules governing warfare. Eyal Benvenisti and Doreen Lustig have argued that IHL law-making in the nineteenth century shut off non-state actors, in particular emerging civil society, on purpose. The role of non-state actors was largely reduced to that of 'agenda setter'. Any further involvement in actual law-creation was explicitly barred at conferences on early IHL treaties on the basis of states being eager to 'monopolize war'.[7]

Though the centrality of states still remains, as this book will show, non-state actor influence in law-creation appears to have become increasingly significant: the ICRC played a major role in convening expert meetings before the 1949 and 1974–77 diplomatic conferences, for example, by submitting drafts of the Conventions and Protocols.[8] Moreover, other non-state actors such as NGOs were influential in promoting and also influencing draft IHL treaties. For example, the Ottawa Process culminating in the Mine Ban Treaty in 1997 was an initiative involving several states and NGOs under the network 'International Campaign to Ban Landmines' outside of the traditional state-led UN framework. This achievement was regarded by the then Canadian Foreign Minister as 'the harbinger of the new multilateralism: new alliances among states, new partnerships with non-state actors, and new approaches to international governance'.[9] The process later served as a model for similar developments leading among others to Protocol IV to the Convention on Certain Conventional Weapons governing the use of blinding laser weapons, the influential Rome Statute establishing the International Criminal Court[10] and the 2013 Arms Trade Treaty.[11] Further, NGOs frequently take part in processes of compliance-monitoring and judicial proceedings in the field of IHL.[12] Beyond NGOs, the examination of the role of armed groups in law-making processes and their compliance with those rules has expanded alongside the increasing regulation of their conduct. While the question as to how this changes the way we perceive international law remains

---

6 Michael Schmitt and Sean Watts, 'The Decline of International Humanitarian Law *Opinio Juris*' (2015) 50 Texas International Law Journal 189, 209.

7 Eyal Benvenisti and Doreen Lustig, 'Monopolizing War: Codifying the Laws of War to Reassert Governmental Authority, 1856–1874' (2020) 31 European Journal of International Law 127, 168.

8 cf Anthea Roberts and Sandesh Sivakumaran, 'Law-Making by Nonstate Actors' (2012) 37 Yale Journal of International Law 107, 114 (fn 31).

9 Lloyd Axworthy, 'Towards a New Multilaterialism' in Maxwell Cameron, Robert Lawson and Brian Tomlin (eds), *To Walk Without Fear: The Global Movement to Ban Landmines* (OUP 1998) 452–53.

10 Kenneth Anderson, 'The Ottawa Convention Banning Landmines, the Role of International Non-Governmental Organizations and the Idea of International Civil Society' (2000) 11 European Journal of International Law 91, 109–10. See further also International Law Association, 'Non-State Actors, Final report, Johannesburg Conference' (2016) 9 <https://ila.vettoreweb.com/Storage/Download.aspx?DbStorageId=1206&StorageFileGuid=fd5b9048-2919-45dc-bcbe-bca53fd4c7a7> accessed 31 January 2021.

11 See Denise Garcia, 'Global Norms Governing the Protection of Civilians, Conflict, and Weapons: Formal or Informal Law-Making?', Chapter 5 in this book, 64.

12 See generally ILA (n 10).

subject to debate, the International Law Association (ILA) in its 2016 report on non-state actors and international law concluded that the rise of non-state actors:

> is problematic on many accounts including the growing gap between the theory of international law and the practice of international relations, the controversial legitimacy of the State monopoly over norm creation and the lack of incentives for some NSAs to abide by State-created rules. Consequently, commentators have proposed various alternatives to the State-centred view of international law that occasionally endow NSAs with an improved position.[13]

The diversification of relevant actors may therefore resemble 'a change in the structure of the law-making process that weakens or even undermines the primacy of State consent as the traditional foundation of positive international law-making in order to improve the law's legitimacy towards non-State actors'.[14] This book will examine the various alternatives that have been proposed to include non-state actors, from a legitimacy and methodological perspective of IHL.

As new methods and actors have entered the law-making process, the nineteenth century narrative of states monopolizing law-making in IHL has shifted: various norm interpreters, such as international courts, have opted to defy the original intentions of state-driven IHL documents for the sake of promoting humanitarian values.[15] A well-known example concerns the International Criminal Tribunal for the former Yugoslavia (ICTY) in its *Kupreškić* Judgment. The Tribunal found that the prohibition on reprisals against civilians amounts to a rule of customary international law. It based its findings, among others, on the demands of humanity in line with the Martens Clause.[16] In this regard, Meron has argued that 'robust efforts had [been] made to humanize the behaviour of States and fighting groups in armed conflicts' and to this end, 'Courts and tribunals have often ignored operational or battlefield practice (…) stretching the traditional meaning of customary law'.[17] He accredits '[p]ublic opinion, the media, the NGOs and the ICRC (…) a critical role in promoting such tendencies'.[18] This point had also

---

[13] ibid 16. On the question of whether the inclusion of certain non-state actors actually magnifies power asymmetries between the Global North and the Global South, see Heike Krieger and Jonas Püschmann, 'A Legitimacy Crisis of International Humanitarian Law?', Chapter 26 in this book.

[14] Heike Krieger, Björnstjern Baade and Linus Mührel, 'Introduction' in Björnstjern Baade, Linus Mührel and Anton O. Petrov (eds), *International Humanitarian Law in Areas of Limited Statehood* (Nomos 2018) 21, 24.

[15] Benvenisti and Lustig, 'Monopolizing War' (n 7) 169; idem, 'Beyond the "Sham" Critique and the Narrative of Humanitarianism: A Rejoinder to Jochen von Bernstorff' (2020) 31 European Journal of International Law 721, 725.

[16] *Prosecutor v Kupreškić* (Judgment) IT-95-16 (14 January 2000) para 527. For an evaluation of such an approach and divergent state practice, see Jean-Marie Henckaerts and Louise Doswald-Beck, *Customary International Humanitarian Law* (ICRC/CUP 2005) rule 146: 'Because of existing contrary practice, albeit very limited, it is difficult to conclude that there has yet crystallized a customary rule specifically prohibiting reprisals against civilians during the conduct of hostilities.'

[17] Theodor Meron, *The Humanization of International Law* (Brill 2006) 3.

[18] ibid 3.

been noted by NGOs themselves, for example, HRW's Executive Director in a speech in 2010 reflected that:

> military hated (...) intervention by human rights groups because suddenly they had lost their monopoly over the interpretation of humanitarian law (...). As a result, we now have a much more pluralistic environment in which these terms are interpreted. And that's all to the good in terms of defending human rights in warfare.[19]

These perspectives may have wide ramifications on the underlying consensus of IHL, which is based on a compromise between military necessity and humanitarian values: the legal regime rests on the assumption that in order to gain a military victory, states may target enemy combatants and military objectives in a proportionate pursuit of military advantage. As a consequence, and subject to specific conditions, the killing of civilians and destruction of civilian objects may be legally justifiable.[20] For some, a more pluralistic environment threatens to undermine this balance and is sometimes seen as a result of a methodologically flawed interpretation of the law: '[a] more pluralistic environment for legal interpretation is fine; but, at a minimum, all participants need to be talking about the same legal paradigm, and be willing to use its accepted modes of analysis and interpretation.'[21] For others, in particular human rights activists, engaging with IHL may challenge their self-perception and self-presentation as human rights defenders. For them, a 'humanitarian dilemma' may arise: human rights activists, may on the one hand, accept to 'participate in the production and implementation of norms that sought to mitigate the horrors and suffering of war'. On the other, they have to come to terms with a 'humanitarian deference to state authority [that] facilitate[s] and could be perceived as validating the actions of military men and diplomats'.[22]

3. THE NEED TO FOCUS ON THE LEGITIMACY OF LAW-MAKING PROCESSES

This book offers insight into the causes of this ambivalent state of IHL. It (re-)focuses attention on law-making processes and the actors involved against a legitimacy standard and thereby asks what contemporary law-making processes reveal about the overall state of this legal regime. Whereas the notion of legitimacy does exist within IHL scholarship in several different ways, none of this relates to the concept of legitimacy as a criterion for evaluating law-making processes.

---

[19] Kenneth Roth, 'Human Rights: From Practice to Policy' in Carrie Booth Walling and Susan Waltz (eds), Proceedings of a Research Workshop (University of Michigan, October 2010) 31–32 <http://humanrightshistory.umich.edu/files/2013/02/Roth.pdf> accessed 31 January 2021.

[20] Nicolas Lamp, 'Conceptions of War and Paradigms of Compliance: The "New War" Challenge to International Humanitarian Law' (2011) 16 Journal of Conflict and Security Law 225, 232; Meron (n 17) 8.

[21] Page Wilson, 'The Myth of International Humanitarian Law' (2017) 93 (3) International Affairs 563, 576.

[22] On this, see Pablo Kalmanovitz, *The Laws of War in International Thought* (OUP 2020) 144 with reference to the writings of the Swiss jurist and co-founder of ICRC and Institut de Droit International, Gustave Moynier.

This book conceptualizes approaches to law-making broadly. Accordingly, the concept is not only understood as covering traditional state-driven law-making processes, in line with Article 38 of the International Court of Justice (ICJ) Statute, in particular the adoption of treaties or the formation of customary international law.[23] Instead, it includes 'the whole spectrum of law-making and shaping activities, including the interpretation and application of international law, the identification of customary rules, the development of the law, and the adoption of soft law instruments and manuals'.[24] Such a perspective focuses on the interactions between different actors involved in shaping understandings and generating practices through which the law evolves.[25]

On the one hand, the diversity of actors involved in law-making may well enhance IHL's legitimacy, as these actors promote transparency and participation and often push for improving the normative aspirations of IHL. On the other hand, a number of challenges arise for both the state as the main actor in international law and the legal regime itself. Informal law-making processes provoke critical reflection upon the role of states in the creation of law. Do states remain the gate keepers since eventually no rule of international law can be created without a state's consent? Or does the evolution of law-making processes reflect a decreasing importance in the role of the state in international law? Another reading of contemporary developments may suggest that courts and experts help states evade necessary political decisions in relation to armed conflict, which may be politically wearisome to take responsibility for alone, especially when it comes to democratic states and post-heroic societies.[26]

From the internal perspective of the law, the question of whether such a law-making process can guarantee legally secure outcomes and coherent interpretations, arises. In a decentralized legal order where no central court or organ provides binding interpretations, the diversity of actors and their priorities might contribute to legal insecurities and ambiguities, instead of clearing them up. The proliferation of relevant actors in norm creation and application thereby challenges the structuring effect of the legal order and its coherence. Moreover, the plurality of entities brings along a plurality of agendas. Whereas legal methodology and process may limit ensuing tendencies of the law to drift apart, there is a danger that increasingly diverse agendas give rise to tensions between legal actors. As argued above, this may weaken a legal regime's underlying consensus.[27] In addition, informal ways of ascertaining and developing the law also give rise to the question of whether they are themselves seen as legitimate in the eyes of the main actors. Or – to the contrary – might those processes weaken the compliance-pull of IHL because their legitimacy is considered doubtful? The development of the North Atlantic

---

[23] For a more recent analysis of the traditional sources of international law see Curtis A. Bradley (ed), *Custom's Future: International Law in a Changing World* (CUP 2016); Samantha Besson and Jean d'Aspremont (eds), *The Oxford Handbook on the Sources of International Law* (OUP 2017).

[24] Sandesh Sivakumaran, 'Making and Shaping the Law of Armed Conflict' (2018) 71 Current Legal Problems 119, 120.

[25] Jutta Brunnée and Stephen Toope, *Legitimacy and Legality in International Law: An Interactional Account* (CUP 2010) 5, 63–65; on the role of actors in the law-making process see also Jean d'Aspremont (ed), *Participants in the International Legal System: Multiple Perspectives on Non-State Actors in International Law* (Routledge 2012).

[26] On post-heroic societies, see Herfried Münkler, 'Heroische und Postheroische Gesellschaften' (2007) 61 Merkur 742.

[27] Dana Burchardt, 'The Twilight of Legal Order? On the Current Challenges Faced by the Concept of a Legal System' (2018) 9 Transnational Legal Theory 110, 143.

Treaty Organization (NATO)-backed Tallinn Manual 1.0 is a case in point. The law-making process underpinning its establishment magnified the general challenge of navigating actor power asymmetries, demonstrating that informal processes may hide the political domination of certain actors whilst enabling insufficient participant representation, thereby undermining legal legitimacy.

The analytical lens of legitimacy used in the book allows us to engage normatively with these challenges. The concept of legitimacy is opaque, giving rise to a plethora of definitions, interpretative conceptions and theoretical debates. Studies on the legitimacy of international law also regularly draw criticism for being too subjective[28] or even for resembling a form of neo-naturalism.[29] At the same time, the legitimacy of law is useful to justify the binding force of the law.[30] In that respect, it provides 'useful indicators of the pull of projects of rehabilitation and reinvention of international law'.[31] For the purposes of the present book, a distinction is drawn between empirical and normative legitimacy. Empirical legitimacy refers to the actual acceptance of a legal regime as legitimate in the eyes of its addressees (legitimacy beliefs), whereas normative legitimacy describes the assessment of a legal order in the light of moral, ethical or legal criteria. Both elements play out in international law's standard accounts of legitimacy, which in its empirical variance is a prerequisite for the compliance pull of international law,[32] while its normative elements are the result of 'shared understandings created through communities of legality practices'.[33]

The present book therefore departs from discourses, both in academia and diplomatic practice, about the state of IHL, which often centre around issues of compliance and effectiveness (more precisely, the lack of).[34] The focus on accountability mechanisms in fora ranging from the International Fact-Finding Commission and the UN Human Rights Council to the International Criminal Court (ICC) and national criminal courts, prioritizes compliance and responsibility in relation to violations of the law, rather than the prevention of violations, dissemination and creation of IHL.[35] Debates about the application of IHL to new technologies are often driven by concern around IHL's effectiveness in protecting humanitarian interests. As Ian Clark and his co-authors stress, if questions around legitimacy are at all raised, they are

---

28 eg James Crawford, 'The Problems of Legitimacy-Speak' (2004) 98 American Society of International Law Proceedings 271.

29 cf Jean d'Aspremont, 'The Roles of Legitimacy in International Legal Discourses: Legitimizing Law vs Legalizing Legitimacy', Chapter 2 in this book, 29.

30 Cedric Ryngaert, 'Imposing International Duties on Non-State Actors and the Legitimacy of International Law' in Math Noortmann and Cedric Ryngaert, *Non-State Actor Dynamics in International Law* (Ashgate 2010) 71.

31 d'Aspremont, 'The Roles of Legitimacy in International Legal Discourses' (n 29) 28.

32 Thomas Franck, *The Power of Legitimacy Among Nations* (OUP 1990) 24.

33 Brunnée and Toope (n 25) 86–87.

34 For a criticism of this approach see Ian Clark and others, 'Crisis in the Law of War? Beyond Compliance and Effectiveness?' (2018) 24 European Journal of International Relations 319; Peter Heblij and Jean-Michel Cambron, 'The Challenges in the Implementation of International Humanitarian Law' (2015) 20 Recueils de la Societe Internationale de Droit Penal Militaire et de Droit de la Guerre 49, 51; Eve Massingham and Annabel McConnachie (eds), *Ensuring Respect for International Humanitarian Law* (Routledge 2020).

35 Thilo Marauhn, 'The International Rule of Law in Light of Legitimacy Claims' in Heike Krieger, Georg Nolte and Andreas Zimmermann (eds), *The International Rule of Law: Rise or Decline? Approaching current foundational challenges* (OUP 2019) 295.

considered symptomatic of a lack of the law's effectiveness, rather than its cause.[36] Finally, the legitimacy of certain actors involved in armed conflict and its regulation, in particular armed groups, has been a recurring subject within IHL literature. However, recent works tend to examine the accountability of these actors.[37] Their role within the process of humanitarian law-making is less explored and relevant contributions focus narrowly on compiling the respective practice a particular group has contributed to.[38] In contrast to these approaches, the present book aims to assess the overall state of IHL by (re-)focusing attention on law-making processes in light of legitimacy or a lack thereof. It thereby aims to offer an insight into the causes of the currently ambivalent state of IHL.

For this purpose, the work builds on three recent academic discourses. One is concerned with states' abstinence from the law-making process[39] and the increasing importance of expert manuals within the regulation of warfare.[40] The present book aims to relate these scholars' analysis to the broader subject of the overall state of IHL, by taking a comparative perspective of the various actors and practices we see present within the law-making process. A second strand in literature is concerned with perceptions of a deeper legitimacy crisis of IHL.[41] Such discourses often interact with an exploration into the normative legitimacy of IHL. They mostly refer to the general idea of humanitarianism as the raison d'être of the law of armed conflict[42] and connect this focus to the consideration of more specific questions, in particular related to the principles of necessity and proportionality in warfare[43] or the relationship between IHL and human rights.[44] A third approach increasingly focuses on contestations of IHL's codification and interpretation.[45] As opposed to viewing IHL as being in a state of crisis,

---

36 Clark and others (n 34) 324.

37 See eg Katharine Fortin, *The Accountability of Armed Groups under Human Rights Law* (OUP 2017); Carla Ferstman, *International Organizations and the Fight for Accountability* (OUP 2017).

38 See eg Robin Geiß, Andreas Zimmermann and Stefanie Haumer (eds), *Humanizing the Laws of War: The Red Cross and the Development of International Humanitarian Law* (CUP 2017); Alan Boyle and Christine Chinkin, *The Making of International Law* (OUP 2007); Shane Darcy, *Judges, Law and War: The Judicial Development of International Humanitarian Law* (CUP 2014).

39 Schmitt and Watts (n 6); Sivakumaran (n 24).

40 Sara Kendal, 'Inscribing the State: Constitution Drafting Manuals as Textual Technologies' (2020) 11 Humanity 101; Knut Dörmann, 'The Role of Nonstate Entities in Developing and Promoting International Humanitarian Law' (2018) 51 Vanderbilt Journal of Transnational Law 713; Anton Petrov, *Expert Laws of War: Restating and Making Law in Expert Processes* (Edward Elgar 2020); Terry Gill, Robin Geiß and Heike Krieger (eds), *Yearbook of International Humanitarian Law 23 (2020)* (Asser Press 2021) forthcoming.

41 Clark and others (n 34) 319.

42 See eg Dug Cubie, *The International Legal Protection of Persons in Humanitarian Crises: Exploring the Acquis Humanitaire* (Hart Publishing 2017); in the shape of 'second-generation human security' in Christine Chinkin and Mary Kaldor, *International Law and New Wars* (CUP 2017).

43 See eg Jens D. Ohlin, Larry May and Claire Finkelstein (eds), *Weighing Lives in War* (OUP 2017); Etienne Henry, *Le principe de nécessité militaire: Histoire et actualité d'une norme fondamentale du droit international humanitaire* (Pedone 2016).

44 See eg Jens D. Ohlin (ed), *Theoretical Boundaries of Armed Conflict and Human Rights* (CUP 2016).

45 Helen Kinsella and Giovanni Mantilla, 'Contestation before Compliance: History, Politics, and Power in International Humanitarian Law' (2020) 64 International Studies Quarterly 649; see also Benvenisti and Lustig, 'Monopolizing War' (n 7); Kalmanovitz (n 22).

scholars perceive IHL, from a broader historical perspective, as existing within a process of 'ongoing negotiation and contestation'.[46]

4. CONTENT AND STRUCTURE OF THE BOOK

The present book analyses how law-making processes play out in IHL and what they reveal about its overall status, based on considerations of legitimacy. Do developments examined in the chapters reflect that an underlying consensus within IHL frays, in particular in terms of its sphere of application, content, actors, and processes? Further, to what extent do these developments indicate that this legal regime is experiencing a deeper legitimacy crisis?

The book addresses these questions from different angles and is therefore divided into six parts: legitimacy as an analytical lens (Part II), informal law-making in international humanitarian law as a political choice (Part III), new law through practice? (Part IV), courts and manuals – decoupling law-making from states? (Part V), legitimacy and participation (Part VI) and legitimacy and norm entrepreneurs (Part VII).

Part II critically engages with the opaque concept of legitimacy. *Jean d'Aspremont* begins this enquiry by stressing the heterogeneity of pertinent scholarly legal debates and the various structuring roles legitimacy plays in such discourses. He differentiates between theoretical discourses which aim to legitimize the international legal order and those within IHL which aim to legalize the (il)legitimacy of actors. In the former case, legitimacy is used to reinvent and rehabilitate international law. In the latter, the focus lies on legitimizing or de-legitimizing the behaviours of actors engaged in armed conflict by passing legitimacy judgments through legal categories. While d'Aspremont favours a legal formalist point of view, he concludes that legitimacy arguments are nonetheless a means to guarantee the practical relevance of international law in the social world. *Stefan Kadelbach* and *Tom Ruys* comment on d'Aspremont's claims. Kadelbach stresses the ambiguous nature of legitimacy in IHL, given the law's obvious moral authority and a lack of input-legitimacy. Nevertheless, he concludes that d'Aspremont overstates the consequences of legitimist thinking on IHL and questions the utility of a strictly legal formalist point of view because it would not be able to respond to the problems surrounding the inclusion of non-state actors in the law-making process. *Tom Ruys* engages with d'Aspremont's latter claim in favour of formalism and demonstrates how legitimacy considerations already influence the interpretation of IHL. He depicts, inter alia, how considerations of actor legitimacy in non-international armed conflicts (NIACs) influence the possibility of allowing criminal prosecution of members of non-state armed groups and denying them belligerent equality, which leads to a worrisome disregard of IHL in NIACs. The latter observation is taken up in Part VI of the book, which analyses the role of armed groups in the law-making process.

Part III considers informal ways of law-making and the political choices involved. It questions whether the conclusion of treaties has indeed lost any relevance in the realm of IHL and whether this formal means of law-making has been replaced by informal processes including, perhaps counterintuitively, non-compliance. In her analysis of whether and why a trend towards informal law-making has reached the realm of IHL, *Denise Garcia* contends that a turn towards informality can indeed be observed in general IHL treaty-making. Nevertheless,

[46] Kinsella and Mantilla (n 45) 652.

recent developments also show that there is still formal law-making in the realm of disarmament and arms regulation treaties, which can often be traced back to the influence of actors beyond the state. *Philip Liste* addresses the challenges of informal law-making in IHL from the perspective of international relations theory. He argues that conceptualizing legitimacy within an international order of states is different from a normative endeavour which seeks to decouple it from the state. He argues that in such a constellation, 'international' humanitarian law will hardly function, and its development therefore faces legitimacy challenges. Finally, *Timothy Meyer*, by zooming in on an especially pertinent practice, asks under which circumstances non-compliance may constitute law-making (beyond mere cheating) and whether this practice is normatively desirable. He contends that the acceptance of the contribution of non-compliance to law-making may lead to a greater effectiveness of international law, but generally lacks procedural legitimacy as it favours powerful states.

The legitimacy of any effort to develop IHL will very much depend on whether this effort is in line with methodological exigencies of international law. Therefore, Part IV of the book is devoted to the methodological challenges that arise from law-making through treaty interpretation and customary international law. It inquires as to what extent methodology can secure legal coherence and stability. *Emily Crawford* explores the methodological space for developments in IHL by discussing treaty interpretation over time. By engaging in a case study on Common Article 3 of the Geneva Conventions and its lack of definition of the term 'non-international armed conflicts', she analyses how far a treaty can be stretched through an evolutive interpretation and under which circumstances one should consider interpretation as an amendment of a treaty. In his comment, *Shane Darcy* stresses the role of courts in the interpretation of treaties based on subsequent practice while admitting that the legal relevance of any court interpretation depends on states' consent. He thereby critically analyses the somewhat discretionary approaches states choose in this process and the contradictions inherent to the arguments raised. In addition to these perspectives, *Jean-Marie Henckaerts* and *Elvina Pothelet*, drawing on their practical experience, zoom in on how the ICRC applies the treaty interpretation methodology set out in the 1969 Vienna Convention on the Law of Treaties to interpretation of the Geneva Conventions. In doing so, they throw light on the challenges which arise when the practice of non-state actors, including judicial and quasi-judicial bodies as well as (academic) experts, is taken into account. In line with Crawford, they argue that where the adoption of new IHL treaties does not seem to be a realistic future prospect, the interpretation of existing treaties will be crucial to ensure that they continue to be applied 'over time'. Concluding this part, *Robert Heinsch* examines the adaptability of customary international law in light of recent challenges in IHL. Highlighting the special nature customary humanitarian law holds in terms of regulating the most extreme circumstance of humanity, Heinsch observes the acceptance of a quicker and modified law-creating process. Nevertheless, he warns that in order to not endanger the legitimacy of IHL, one should not stretch methodological approaches too far and disregard state practice completely in the pursuit of flexible or humanitarian solutions.

In light of the questions that arose in the previous part, Part V compares legitimacy challenges arising from law-making by state-empowered courts and expert processes as the two most important avenues for developing IHL in recent times. With regard to state-empowered courts, *Thomas Rauter* discusses the role of international criminal tribunal decisions for the determination of customary international law. He contends that while a sound methodological approach would enhance the perceived legitimacy of international criminal justice and serve the principle of *nullum criminen sine lege*, jurisprudence to date shows no common, unified approach to identifying customary law. Focusing on expert processes, *Wouter Werner* engages with the proliferation of expert manuals in the field of IHL from the perspective of critical legal studies. He adds a new approach to current debates by focusing on the specific concept of a 'manual'. According to him, an apparent tension lies within all manuals: the need to restate the law as it is and the desire to provide concrete, workable instructions for the users of the manual. In their comment, *Robin Geiß* and *Anni Pues* combine theoretical reflection with practical experience in expert processes. Their chapter argues that while manual processes that deal with longstanding issues may facilitate application of the body of law in practice, they may forestall a necessary broader political debate where novel challenges can be addressed. This is because in the latter case, expert-driven approaches to merely restate the law would necessarily entail a form of law-making and their perceived legitimacy may therefore depend on a transparent and inclusive process. *Georg Nolte* adds to this debate by linking the work of the International Law Commission on subsequent practice in the interpretation of treaties and on the identification of customary international law to the phenomenon of manuals. He conceives the drafting of manuals as a classic legal technique for interpreting the law and calls for a reasonable judgment as to whether times are ripe for a restraint or activist interpretation of the relevant rules. In conclusion, *Dale Stephens* pulls together the threads offered in the preceding chapters by comparing expert manuals with court decisions in terms of their legitimacy. He shows that despite being active in a legal realm that is characterized by ambiguities and blind spots, manuals still produce meaningful impact for the law's operation and continue to shape their audiences' expectations about this legal regime.

Part VI engages with further indicators of legitimacy, participation and procedural fairness, and examines the opportunities that exist for states and armed groups from the Global South to influence formal and informal law-making. With a focus on regional developments in the law-making from the Global South, *Alejandro Rodiles* explains the historical and often ignored role of Latin America in the making of IHL. In the course of his chapter, he explains how regional law-making began as a vehicle for independence and then later became part of a broader legal project for the region, basing its legitimacy on human dignity. *Balingene Kahombo* adds an African perspective and explores law-making efforts which reflect the regionalization of the law of armed conflicts in Africa. In pointing out that African states' participation in major IHL treaty-making was historically lacking, he analyses how contemporary regional law-making efforts may have led to a more legitimate and effective IHL in Africa. In his comment on both chapters, *Michael Bothe* draws on a long-durée perspective and questions the extent to which different historic positions of economic development and society determine the influence of states from the Global South in modelling the international legal order.

Taking a look at the involvement of non-state actors in law-making, especially of non-state armed groups, *Cindy Wittke* analyses contemporary ceasefire agreements for intra-state conflicts between state and non-state parties. Her contribution shows the potential of law-making by non-state armed groups. By comparing different kinds of ceasefire agreements, Wittke finds common characteristics that reflect trust and belief in the legitimacy of international law. At the same time, she also critically assesses the role of third parties in such processes, such as the United Nations Security Council. Her observations bring to the fore new perspectives on how and by whom law (especially IHL) can be created and enforced, within the grey zone between an ongoing conflict and an effective peace process. Taking a broader view on non-state armed groups, *Hyeran Jo* contributes to this latter observation by examining the role of armed groups in the general legitimacy discourse of IHL. Her chapter shows the active role that armed groups already play in IHL despite international law being largely state-driven. This calls, she argues, for a recognition of the participation of at least some armed groups as an enabling condition, but not a prerequisite, of IHL's legitimacy. Concluding, and commenting on the chapters by Wittke and Jo, *Cedric Ryngaert* engages with the legitimacy challenges the imposition of IHL on armed groups is confronted with. He contends that, while a more inclusive approach may result in IHL norms appearing more legitimate, where groups do not want to 'own' such norms, the imposition of those norms may still be legitimate and warranted due to their substantive value.

Various norm entrepreneurs foster the dissemination of IHL. Their authority, which may be based on the moral cause they pursue or on their specific legal expertise, is seen as an important element for a norm's legitimacy. However, the work of human rights NGOs has also been severely criticized by military lawyers[47] and other authors[48] for misstating IHL. Part VII of the book therefore deals with the role of human rights advocacy and public opinion in IHL as one possible indicator of a more fundamental shift in the underlying consensus of the law. In view of a widespread perception of increasing contestations in the interpretation of IHL, *Robert Cryer* discusses to what extent such contestations and polarizing debates have been informed by 'interested interpretations'. He asks whether IHL is particularly susceptible to this phenomenon and what sense of identity informs such interpretations of the law. He thereby offers a critique of the idea that any one identity can easily be attributed to any one particular interpreter, as it would be reductionist to ascribe one identity to any person. *Daniel Joyce* adds to this perspective, by taking a broader look at the historically influential and still present impact of the media and public opinion on law-making in IHL. He points towards the special role of the media and public opinion in IHL, as evidenced by the Martens Clause, and critically evaluates the more recent phenomena of the CNN effect and social media. According to him, these developments may eventually demand a new thinking about the relevant actors and shifting dynamics in law-making that may deliver the promises of a participatory international law. In his comment to this chapter, *William Boothby* deals with the current, pertinent role of social media in modern warfare. He cautions that while increased accountability caused by the increasing ability of civilians to become witnesses of war crimes is to be welcomed, there is also the risk that such broad coverage may generate undue expectations on the conduct of warfare and eventually limit the effectiveness of armed operations.

In their conclusion, *Heike Krieger* and *Jonas Püschmann* reflect upon the fraying consensus underlying IHL and argue that this regime is indeed experiencing a deeper legitimacy crisis. Instead of strengthening the legal regime, the multiplication of relevant actors in the law-making discourse of IHL has further contributed to and augmented the already existing ambiguities. While states eventually remain the gate-keepers for any formal change of IHL,

---

47 See among others Michael Schmitt, *Essays on Law and War at the Fault Lines* (Springer and TMC Asser Press 2012) 113ff; Charles Shotwell, 'Economy and Humanity in the Use of Force: A Look at the Aerial Rules of Engagement in the 1991 Gulf War' (1993) 4 United States Air Force Academy Journal of Legal Studies 15, 32ff and 44.

48 Gerald Steinberg and Anne Herzberg, 'NGO Fact-Finding for IHL Enforcement: In Search of a New Model' (2018) 53 Israel Law Review 261, 279ff; Marauhn (n 35) 298; Wilson (n 21).

discursive practices and interpretative processes by non-state actors shape IHL and gradually shift its underlying balance. There are indications that a process of decoupling between public moral considerations and the moral underlying IHL norms is prompting this shift.

PART II

Legitimacy as analytical lens

2. The roles of legitimacy in international legal discourses: Legitimizing law vs legalizing legitimacy

Jean d'Aspremont[1]

In international legal studies, legitimacy is commonly thought of as a multi-faceted concept as it most often refers to the acceptability of rules, actors, processes, or international law as a whole.[2] It is accordingly no surprise that scholarly legal works on legitimacy in the international legal literature are of an extreme variety, sometimes even bringing the debate to the brink of cacophony. That legitimacy is discussed in relation to a great range of objects is not the only factor that explains why scholarly legal debates on legitimacy are so heterogeneous. It is submitted here that the international legal discourse on legitimacy is also highly diverse given the variety of structuring roles which the concept of legitimacy simultaneously plays within that legal discourse. Indeed, legitimacy comes to shape international legal discourse in very different ways. The focus in this chapter surrounds two specific structuring roles of legitimacy. First, this chapter sheds light on how legitimacy is deployed as a tool of reinvention and rehabilitation of international law as a whole. Such endeavours are particularly witnessed in theoretical scholarly works when international lawyers inquire about the legitimacy of international law broadly. Second, this chapter shows how technical legal vocabularies and doctrines are deployed for the sake of the legitimization and delegitimization of behaviours of actors which are held to fall within their scope. This structuring role is particularly witnessed in the practice and scholarship in relation to fields like international human rights law or international humanitarian law (IHL). The former role of legitimacy is referred to as the 'legitimizing of international law' while the latter is called the 'legalizing of international legitimacy'.

Throughout the following sections, the discussion places an emphasis on IHL. Such a choice warrants a preliminary observation. It is acknowledged that IHL literature may, at first glance, not appear to provide the most appropriate scholarly material to discuss the function of legitimacy. Indeed, since its inception, IHL has been portrayed and taught as being immune to any legitimacy assessment. Instead, international lawyers have always presented the main structures of IHL as favouring vocabularies and doctrines alien to legitimacy-related appraisals,

---

1 The author wishes to thank Tom Ruys and Stefan Kadelbach for their useful comments on an earlier draft. The author is also grateful to Rosa Beets for her assistance. All the usual caveats apply.

2 Jean d'Aspremont and Eric De Brabandere, 'The Complementary Faces of Legitimacy in International Law: The Legitimacy of Origin and the Legitimacy of Exercise' (2010) 34 Fordham International Law Journal 101.

especially with respect to the determination of the applicability of the rules of IHL.[3] The reason thereof may simply be that the protection envisaged by IHL allegedly required an 'a-political' and 'universal' scope of application which could be jeopardized by legitimacy-based patterns of argument. And yet, as this chapter demonstrates, the notion of legitimacy continues to inform many argumentative constructions in IHL literature and practice, thereby making IHL illustrative of one of the key roles played by legitimacy in international legal discourse. In particular, it is shown that IHL operates as an omnipresent and highly influential technical vocabulary geared towards the legitimization and delegitimization of the behaviours of actors. Whilst legitimacy may operate simultaneously within the scholarship and practice surrounding international human rights law, this chapter's observations are limited to IHL.

After a brief outline of the various objects in relation to which legitimacy is discussed in international legal studies (1), this chapter reviews the role played by the concept of legitimacy in theoretical legal studies grappling with the question of the legitimacy of international law as a whole. On this occasion, the chapter sheds light on how legitimacy is used as an object of inquiry to reinvent and rehabilitate international law (2). The chapter then turns to the way in which legitimacy has been debated in relation to IHL and shows how, within this body of law, technical vocabulary and doctrine are mobilized as tools to (de-)legitimize the behaviour of international actors (3). This chapter ends with a few concluding remarks on the persistence of a common mindset among international lawyers in spite of the functional heterogeneity of international legal studies that is revealed by inquiry into legitimacy (4).

1. INTRODUCTORY REMARKS: THE MULTI-FACETED CONCEPT OF LEGITIMACY IN INTERNATIONAL LEGAL STUDIES AND THE RISK OF CACOPHONY

Within international legal literature on legitimacy, one finds a great variety of objects in relation to which legitimacy is examined. Although one should avoid versing into either over-simplification or overly sophisticated analysis, it seems necessary, at least for the sake of the argument made in this chapter, to distinguish between various objects of legitimacy which are subject to scholarly debate. It is specifically submitted here that, in international legal studies, legitimacy is approached in relation to four objects. One can distinguish the legitimacy of international law as a whole, the legitimacy of the rules of international law, the legitimacy of processes whereby actors come to power in their relevant constituencies or whereby rules are made, and the legitimacy of international actors, each of them being understood from different perspectives and tested by reference to a range of different standards. A few words must be said about each of these objects of legitimacy in international legal studies and the various standards of legitimacy that have been resorted to for each of them. On this occasion, attention is also paid to the way in which each of these objects of legitimacy has played out in both IHL literature and practice, the focus of this chapter.

[3] François Bugnion, 'Jus ad Bellum, Jus in Bello and Non-International Armed Conflicts' (2003) 6 Yearbook of International Humanitarian Law 167, 194. For a comprehensive overview of the question of the determination of the applicability of IHL, see Jean d'Aspremont and Jérôme de Hemptinne, *Droit International Humanitaire* (Pedone 2012) 45–79.

1.1 The Legitimacy of International Law

The field of international legal studies has witnessed intense – and sometimes very sophisticated – debate surrounding the legitimacy of international law as a whole. In relation to international law broadly, legitimacy is commonly discussed in relation to the authority and sense of obligation that may stem from international law.[4] Such debates are often foundational and delve into the historical and philosophical roots of international law.[5]

This 'turn' to legitimacy is however a rather recent phenomenon. For a long time, international lawyers paid little heed to the question of legitimacy of international law as they were traditionally only interested in the bi-dimensional and static questions of legality, be it the validity of obligations or responsibility for wrongful conduct.[6] At least according to a common narrative, questions of legitimacy were simply deemed irrelevant to the study of international law. Should the question of legitimacy of international law arise, most international lawyers assume that international law is legitimate because it was created via formal sources of international law.[7] The turn to discussions surrounding legitimacy in international legal studies is traditionally associated with the aftermath of the Cold War. This period saw a rise in the number of claims suggesting that consent by the actor allegedly bound by international law cannot perform any legitimizing function[8] and that new standards of legitimacy of international law should be designed. These new discourses have proven to be geared towards the reinvention or the rehabilitation of international law as a whole.[9] This approach to legitimacy is further examined in section 2 below. Section 2 demonstrates that such discourses surrounding legitimacy have recently lost their thrust and been supplanted by new grand frameworks which nonetheless continue to perform similar reinvention and rehabilitation related functions.

---

4 Jutta Brunnée and Stephen Toope, *Legitimacy and Legality in International Law – An Interactional Account* (CUP 2010) 53. For them, law is legitimate when 'it has the capacity to generate fidelity to the rule of law itself and not merely to specific rules' and 'only when law is produced through the interactional framework we describe can it be said that the law is "legitimate"'.

5 John Tasioulas, 'The Legitimacy of International Law' in Samantha Besson and John Tasioulas (eds), *The Philosophy of International Law* (OUP 2009) 97–118; Allen Buchanan, 'The Legitimacy of International Law' in Besson and Tasioulas, ibid 79–96.

6 According to this classical narrative, the South West Africa case epitomizes this fidelity to legal form. Indeed, in the South West Africa case the ICJ held that 'a court of law [could] take account of moral principles only in so far as these are given a sufficient expression in legal form'. It continued with the statement that '[l]aw exists, it is said [sic], to serve a social need; but precisely for that reason it can do so only through and within the limits of its own discipline. Otherwise, it is not a legal service that would be rendered.' See *South West Africa (Ethiopia v South Africa, Liberia v South Africa)* (Judgment, Second Phase) [1966] ICJ Rep 34 para 49. For critical remarks, see Jean d'Aspremont, 'Bindingness' in Jean d'Aspremont and Sahib Singh (eds), *Fundamental Concepts for International Law: The Construction of a Discipline* (Edward Elgar 2019) 67–82.

7 Brunnée and Toope (n 4) 52.

8 Rüdiger Wolfrum, 'Legitimacy in International Law from a Legal Perspective' in Rüdiger Wolfrum and Volker Röben (eds), *Legitimacy in International Law* (Springer 2008) 1, 7–19; Buchanan (n 5) 79, 90–94.

9 On the turn to legitimacy and compliance in Anglo-American legal scholarship, see Jean d'Aspremont, 'Send Back the Lifeboats: Confronting the Project of Saving International Law' (2014) 108 American Journal of International Law 680.

As this chapter's emphasis falls upon IHL, it must be highlighted here that, within this body of law there has been little appetite for discussion surrounding the legitimacy of IHL itself. As a result of the dominant pragmatism of the field, such foundational debates have commonly been kept at bay with attention focusing upon other objects of legitimacy, namely the legitimacy of rules and the legitimacy of actors. It may be that the very purpose of IHL, i.e. regulating the conduct of hostilities and protecting those involved in armed conflict, has been deemed a self-standing and self-legitimizing goal, something that is probably also witnessed within international human rights law. It is precisely because the legitimacy of IHL as a whole has never been a major source of concern for humanitarian professionals in the field that the concept of legitimacy has played a dramatically different role across IHL practice and scholarship, as is explained in section 3 below.

1.2 The Legitimacy of Actors

There is a prolific literature on the legitimacy of actors in general international law. When it comes to the legitimacy of governments and newly created states, much of this debate is channelled as a question of recognition.[10] But recognition is not the only perspective from which the legitimacy of actors has been debated. Whether or not the legitimacy of actors has been discussed from the perspective of their recognition, it is submitted here that the legitimacy of international, regional, and domestic actors has been appraised in a way that distinguished between the legitimacy of origin and the legitimacy of exercise.[11] This dichotomy points to a distinction between the legitimacy pertaining to the source of power and the legitimacy related to the exercise of power.[12]

Irrespective of this variety in vantage points, the legitimacy of actors has been extensively discussed in the literature and it is not necessary to revisit such debates. It matters more to highlight that the legitimacy of actors is a question which has significantly influenced IHL discourses, especially at three levels: the determination of the applicability of IHL; the contribution to international humanitarian law-making; and the imposition of obligations upon insurgents and other parties in armed conflict.

As far as the determination of the applicability of IHL is concerned, it is common to claim, at least since the move away from the practice of recognition of belligerency,[13] that IHL is

---

[10] For a classic – albeit contested – study, see Hersch Lauterpacht, *Recognition in International Law* (Clarendon 1947). More recently, see generally Jure Vidmar, 'Explaining the Legal Effects of Recognition' (2012) 61 International and Comparative Law Quarterly 361; Cedric Ryngaert and Sven Sobrie, 'Recognition of States: International Law or Realpolitik? The Practice of Recognition in the Wake of Kosovo, South Ossetia, and Abkhazia' (2011) 24 Leiden Journal of International Law 467; for an overview of the literature on the topic, see Jean d'Aspremont, 'Recognition in International Law' (2018) Oxford Bibliographies Online <http://www.oxfordbibliographies.com/view/document/obo-9780199796953/obo-9780199796953-0009.xml> accessed 31 January 2021.

[11] This distinction has been used by Jean d'Aspremont in 'Legitimacy of Governments in the Age of Democracy' (2006) 38 New York University Journal of International Law and Politics 877, 894ff.

[12] Though not addressing the issue of legitimacy, Friedrich A. Hayek offers a good explanation for the distinction between the exercise of power and the source of power, Friedrich A. Hayek, *The Road to Serfdom* (Routledge Classics 1976) 71.

[13] Konstantinos Mastorodimos, 'Belligerency Recognition: Past, Present and Future' (2014) 29 Connecticut Journal of International Law 301; Sasha Radin, 'The Current Relevance of the Recognition

averse to legitimacy acting as a mechanism to determine the applicability of the rules of this body of law.[14] The rationale often being that the protection envisaged by IHL requires a universal scope of application which could be jeopardized by legitimacy-based arguments. As is well known, such a legitimacy-free approach to the determination of the applicability of IHL has somewhat backfired, for fears to extend legitimacy to insurgents have led states to refuse to support the international legal regime designed for non-international armed conflicts.[15] One important exception to such legitimacy-averse approach to the applicability of IHL is however found in the qualification of conflicts[16] where peoples are fighting against colonial domination, alien occupation and racist regimes in the exercise of their right of self-determination, as international armed conflicts as is now formalized by Additional Protocol I.[17] Although the three categories of conflict falling under this notion are formally defined and restrictive,[18] the determination of those conflicts that would qualify as such remains a highly political notion whose application inevitably involves consideration regarding the legitimacy of actors.[19] Indeed, the extent to which those representing people fighting against colonial domination, alien occupation and racist regimes in the exercise of their right of self-determination are perceived as legitimate will inform the applicability of IHL. This being said, it seems that, in recent practice, this exception to the legitimacy-free approach to the applicability of IHL has lost some of its relevance.[20] And yet, another possible exception to the legitimacy-free

---

of Belligerency' in Mariëlle Matthee, Brigit Toebes and Marcel Brus (eds), *Search of the Human Face: Liber Amicorum in Memory of Avril McDonald* (Asser Press 2013) 115–52.

14 Bugnion (n 3) 194; Marko Milanovic and Vidan Hadzi-Vidanovic, 'A Taxonomy of Armed Conflict' in Nigel D. White and Christian Henderson (eds), *Research Handbook on International Conflict and Security Law* (Edward Elgar 2013) 256–314.

15 For an overview of the status of ratifications see the Protocol Additional to the Geneva Conventions of 12 August 1949, and Relating to the Protection of Victims of Non-International Armed Conflicts (Protocol II) of 8 June 1977 (adopted 8 June 1977, entered into force on 7 December 1978) 1125 UNTS 609. For a discussion of the reasons invoked by states not to ratify Protocol II, see Cherif Bassiouni, 'The New Wars and the Crisis of Compliance with the Law of Armed Conflict by Non-State Actors' (2008) 98 Journal of Criminal Law and Criminology 782.

16 On the classification of conflicts, see gen. Elizabeth Wilmshurst (ed), *International Law and the Classification of Conflicts* (OUP 2012). See also Milanovic and Hadzi-Vidanovic (n 14) 256–314.

17 Protocol Additional to the Geneva Conventions of 12 August 1949, and Relating to the Protection of Victims of International Armed Conflicts (Protocol I) of 8 June 1977 (adopted 8 June 1977, entered into force on 7 December 1978) 1125 UNTS 3 arts 1 (4), 96 (3). Before its formalization in Additional Protocol I, that claim had been vindicated by the UN General Assembly. See UNGA Res 2383 (XXIII) (7 November 1968). For a historical overview, see Georges Abi-Saab, 'Wars of national liberation in the Geneva Conventions and Protocols' (1979) 165 Recueil des Cours de l'Académie de Droit International 366.

18 Antonio Cassese, 'Wars of National Liberation and Humanitarian Law' in Christophe Swinarski (ed), *The Human Dimension of International Law* (OUP 2013) 313; Dietrich Schindler, 'The Different Types of Armed Conflicts according to the Geneva Conventions and Protocols' (1979) 165 Recueil des Cours 357.

19 See discussion in d'Aspremont and de Hemptinne (n 3) 61–63.

20 For Eric David, this category will soon be obsolete. See Eric David, *Principes de droit des conflits armés* (4th edn, Bruylant 2008) 197. See however the unilateral declaration by the Polisario Front on 21 June 2015 on behalf of the people of Western Sahara that it undertook to apply the 1949 Geneva Conventions and Additional Protocol I to the conflict between it and the Kingdom of Morocco <http://theirwords.org/media/transfer/doc/declarationofficielle_polisariofront_2015-f426d1a96a4465affd1f87e794374b06.pdf> accessed 31 January 2021.

approach to the applicability of IHL is sometimes invoked in relation to those – contested[21] – approaches[22] according to which the support which one foreign state may provide to insurgents leads to an internationalization of the conflict which would have otherwise remained of a non-international character. Irrespective of such possible exceptions, IHL has remained averse to appraisals of the legitimacy of actors.

It must be noted that, in IHL practice and scholarship, the legitimacy of actors may also bear upon debates about law-making. Indeed, following the growing attention paid to non-state actors in general[23] as well as landmark decisions by international courts,[24] the way in which rules of IHL are made has attracted more attention. Within that debate, both the descriptive claims about the state of law-making processes as well as the normative claims about the possibility of opening up such processes to insurgents have come to be informed by considerations of legitimacy. Fears of legitimizing insurgency have nurtured reservations against allowing non-state actors to play a role in international law-making.[25] This also explains why experts have resorted to the notion of 'hybrid treaties' to qualify agreements between states and non-state actors in order to avoid legitimizing non-state actor parties to the agreement.[26] The potential granting of legitimacy to non-state actors has also fuelled reservations as to the possibility of accepting the practice of non-state actors as contributing to the emergence of customary rules.[27]

Finally, the imposition of IHL obligations upon insurgents has also been informed by considerations pertaining to the legitimacy of actors. According to a routine argument, states are said to be fearful that the imposition of obligations on non-state actors brings about some formal recognition of the insurgents they are fighting against. The same fear of legitimizing insurgents can be said to have frustrated the success of the framework applicable to non-international armed conflicts. Unsurprisingly, the legitimizing effects of obligations imposed on non-state actors – and thus this common narrative – has been contested. Arguments have been made that

---

21 For criticisms of such approach as they reward insurrections, see CICR, *Rapport sur les travaux de la Conférence d'experts gouvernmentaux* (CICR 1971) para 301.

22 For some supporters of such an approach to the classification of armed conflicts, see David (n 20) 173; Ingrid Detter, *The Law of War* (CUP 2000) 49; Theodor Meron, 'War Crimes in Yugoslavia and the Development of International Law' (1994) 88 American Journal of International Law 81; Theodor Meron, 'Classification of Armed Conflict in the Former Yugoslavia: Nicaragua's Fallout' (1998) 92 American Journal of International Law 238.

23 See eg ILA Committee Resolution No. 6/2016 'Non-State Actors and International Law' (Johannesburg, 7–11 August 2016) <https://www.ila-hq.org/images/ILA/docs/No.6_Resolution_2016_NonStateActors.pdf> accessed 31 January 2021.

24 *Prosecutor v Sam Hinga Norman* (Decision on preliminary Motion Based on Lack of Jurisdiction (Child Recruitment)) SCSL-2004-14-AR72(E) (31 May 2004) (Special Court for Sierra Leone) para 22.

25 Julie Mertus, 'Considering Nonstate Actors in the New Millennium: Toward Expanded Participation in Norm Generation and Norm Application' (2000) 32 New York University Journal of International Law and Politics 537, 561–62.

26 See generally Christine Bell, *Peace Agreements and Human Rights* (OUP 2000); See also Anthea Roberts and Sandesh Sivakumaran, 'Lawmaking by Nonstate Actors: Engaging Armed Groups in the Creation of International Humanitarian Law' (2012) 37 Yale Journal of International Law 108, 143–49.

27 Cedric Ryngaert, 'Non-State Actors in International Humanitarian Law' in Jean d'Aspremont (ed), *Participants in the International Legal System* (Routledge 2011) 284–94.

granting non-state armed groups obligations does not come with any legitimizing effects[28] or that the legitimizing effects are offset by the benefits of the obligations imposed upon them.[29]

The foregoing should suffice to show that legitimacy appraisals, albeit not explicitly of an operative value, have informed discussions in IHL practice and scholarship. It will be shown below, however, that the role played by legitimacy in IHL may be far more fundamental than such preliminary observations lead us to believe.

1.3 The Legitimacy of Rules

Legitimacy can also be discussed in relation to specific rules of international law. Such a micro debate often manifests itself as a question of optimization of international law-making processes.[30] In such scholarly discussions, mention has commonly been made of particular standards of legitimacy organized around the distinction between input legitimacy and output legitimacy. Input legitimacy refers to the procedural and substantive criteria that make rules legitimate. Output legitimacy refers to the substantive quality of the rule concerned and the possible normative and regulatory outcome that it has the potential to generate. Among the criteria of input legitimacy which have been resorted to, participation of addressees of rules in the making of such rules, or the participation of NGOs, have usually ranked very high.[31]

As was noted above, this approach to legitimacy has been extensively discussed in relation to law-making. It is of no avail to revisit such literature here. It matters more to highlight that the debate about the legitimacy of rules has regularly surfaced in IHL literature and practice. Indeed, it is with a view to enhancing the legitimacy (and thus the compliance pull) of rules of IHL in the eyes of non-state actors, that pleas for a greater engagement with non-state actors including their inclusion in the making of rules, irrespective of considerations about the legitimacy of these actors, have been heard. In the same vein, the argument has been made that imposing obligations on non-state actors short of their consent[32] is not only a conceptual issue but also calls for some legitimacy justification.[33] In that sense, IHL debates have witnessed a discrepancy between arguments based on the legitimacy of rules (favouring an inclusion of insurgents in law-making processes) and the abovementioned arguments based on the legiti-

---

28 Roberts and Sivakumaran (n 26) 134–37.

29 ibid 134–37.

30 Jan Klabbers, Anne Peters and Geir Ulfstein, *The Constitutionalization of International Law* (OUP 2009) 39–43.

31 Buchanan (n 5) 85–87; Mattias Kumm, 'The Legitimacy of International Law: A Constitutionalist Framework of Analysis' (2004) 15 European Journal of International Law 907. For a discussion of the various bases of legitimacy in connection with procedure, substance, outcome, see Chris A. Thomas, 'The Use and Abuse of Legitimacy in International Law' (2014) 34 Oxford Journal of Legal Studies 729, 749–52.

32 For the argument that a unilateral commitment is the most natural source of obligations of insurgents, see Antonio Cassese, 'The Status of Rebels under the 1977 Geneva Protocol on Non-International Armed Conflicts' (1981) 30 International and Comparative Law Quarterly 416; Cedric Ryngaert, 'Human Rights Obligations of Armed Groups' (2009) 41 Revue Belge de droit international 355.

33 Jan Klabbers, '(I Can't Get No) Recognition: Subjects Doctrine and the Emergence of Non-State Actors' in Jarna Petman and Jan Klabbers (eds), *Nordic Cosmopolitanism: Essays in International Law for Martti Koskenniemi* (Brill Publishing 2003) 351, 354–55.

macy of actors (favouring an exclusion of non-state actors). The controversy does not seem to have been resolved.[34]

1.4 The Legitimacy of Processes

Legitimacy is sometimes approached in international legal studies in relation to processes. The legitimacy that is discussed in international legal studies may be that of the process whereby a rule is made, or, the process whereby an actor is empowered. Inquiries therefore usually comprise examination of either the legitimacy of rules or of actors. The same holds for IHL.[35]

Having distinguished between various aspects of the legitimacy discourse in international legal scholarship, this chapter now zeroes in more specifically on two roles of legitimacy in international legal studies. It particularly sheds light on how legitimacy contributes to the reinvention and rehabilitation of international law as well as how legitimacy proves to be the ultimate goal of resorting to technical legal vocabulary. On this occasion, it will be shown that the first function is particularly apparent when international legal scholarship enquires into the legitimacy of international law as a whole, while the second function is more often at work when international lawyers, for example within IHL literature, let their arguments be informed by considerations pertaining to the legitimacy of actors or the legitimacy of rules.

2. LEGITIMACY AT THE SERVICE OF LAW: THE REINVENTION AND REHABILITATION OF INTERNATIONAL LAW

This section sketches out some of the main features of scholarly works engaging with the question of the legitimacy of international law as a whole. It is argued here, in particular, that studies regarding the legitimacy of international law as a whole have traditionally been informed by projects of reinvention and rehabilitation of this body of law. This section starts with several observations on the success in the 1990s of legitimacy discourse, demonstrating how legitimacy was hailed as the beacon of a long-awaited methodological revolution in international legal studies said to liberate international lawyers from their formal straitjackets. The attention then turns to the role of the concept of legitimacy in post-1990 discourse and the reinvention and rehabilitation virtues associated with legitimacy. In conclusion it recalls how, despite the disrepute into which legitimacy discourse fell over the last decade, the projects of reinvention and rehabilitation that had accompanied them were left intact.

---

[34] This may have informed the very radical form of pragmatism that has come to dominate legal arguments on the imposition of obligations on non-state actors in recent years. It could also be said that it is the same pragmatism and scepticism about legitimacy-based arguments which has informed the practice of Geneva Call.

[35] International law being a process whereby authoritative decisions are made for the New Haven School of International Law, legitimacy inevitably plays a role therein. However, within the New Haven School of thought, legitimacy was rarely discussed as an autonomous concept, let alone as a vantage point for scholarly inquiry. See gen. Harold Dwight Lasswell and Myres Smith McDougal, *Jurisprudence for a Free Society* (Martinus Nijhoff 1992). See also Michael W. Reisman, Siegfried Wiessner and Andrew R. Willard, 'The New Haven School: A Brief Introduction' (2007) 32 Yale Journal of International Law 575.

Mundane accounts of contemporary international legal thought usually contend that it was in the wake of the end of the Cold War that legitimacy came to be hailed as a necessary saviour of international legal scholarship and the conduit for refreshing and unorthodox methodological approaches, although many such constructions came to be discredited in more recent international law scholarship. According to such narratives, with the end of the Cold War, international lawyers shed their legality-based conservatism and finally grasped the relevance of constructing, challenging, and reforming international law from the vantage point of legitimacy.[36] This revelation, it is said, was the consequence of a series of factors, including: international lawyers' fatigue associated with ontological questions about international law; their self-confidence following the end of the Cold War; the rise in power of international organizations; the expansion of the scope of international law; the emancipation from state control and thus the decline of domestic accountability mechanisms as legitimizing factors; the perception that international law was growing more effective and increasingly complied with.[37] In this narrative, Thomas Franck is commonly commended as having spearheaded this focus on legitimacy.[38] Franck's work, so the story goes, paved the way for a new generation of scholarship surrounding the legitimacy of international law which is meant to continuously grow in sophistication.[39] Although the framing of Franck as a pioneer of the legitimacy movement could prove bewildering as Franck's focus on legitimacy remained rather legalistic,[40] this narrative grants him the paternity for encouraging international lawyers to abandon their formal straitjacket and embracing the 'real questions' posed by international law.[41]

Three particular developments can be said to have been nurtured by this turn to legitimacy. First, the revelation of the early 1990s led to a greater embracing of empiricism (knowledge drawn out from experience) by international lawyers, especially in Anglo-American scholarship. Social practice and belief were turned into one of the main indicators of legality.[42] This is not to say that empiricism had never been explored – the turn to instrumentalism by the New Haven Law School in the 1950s and 1960s was accompanied by empiricist movements. Yet, it was Franck's unearthing of legitimacy that structurally rerouted the Anglo-American towards empirical inquiry. In doing so, considerations surrounding the legitimacy of international law allowed questions related to compliance (why do states comply with international law) to conveniently converge with definitional inquiries (what is international law).[43] It simultaneously brought about a move away from conceptual investigation of the self-validating nature

---

36 For illustrations of this common account of the rise of legitimacy in international legal studies, see Tasioulas (n 5) 97; Thomas (n 31) 729; Wolfrum (n 8) 1–2; Hilary Charlesworth, 'Conclusions' in Hilary Charlesworth and Jean-Marc Coicaud (eds), *Fault Lines of International Legitimacy* (CUP 2010) 389.

37 For a discussion of some of the driving forces behind the rise of legitimacy as a central topic of scholarly study, see Kumm (n 31) 907. See also Daniel Bodansky, 'The Concept of Legitimacy in International Law' in Wolfrum and Röben (n 8) 309–17.

38 See Thomas Franck, *Fairness in International Law and Institutions* (OUP 1995) 6.

39 For an example of recent refinement of Franck's theory, see Brunnée and Toope (n 4).

40 See the criticisms of Franck's theory of legitimacy by Brunnée and Toope (n 4) 52–53.

41 Thomas Franck, *The Power of Legitimacy among Nations* (OUP 1990) 5–7.

42 David Kennedy, 'The Mystery of Global Governance' (2008) 34 Ohio Northern University Law Review 829, 838 (commenting on the Manhattan School of International Law).

43 On this aspect of the turn to legitimacy, see David Bederman, *The Spirit of International Law* (Georgia University Press 2002) 3. On the turn to compliance in Anglo-American legal scholarship, see d'Aspremont (n 9) 680.

of international law by virtue of an audacious and unabashed presumption that there is an Archimedean vantage point from which international law can be simply observed, witnessed and analysed.[44] This turn to empiricism rests on an attempt to develop a new authoritative coding[45] which is not bound to be inductive[46] and which seems to be within the reach of international lawyers.

The second move fuelled by the turn to inquiry into the legitimacy of international law as a whole pertains to the way international lawyers understand the normativity of law. Indeed, studies of the legitimacy of international law as a whole have often been accompanied by a move away from formalistic modes of thinking. This aspect of the turn to legitimacy is more substantive. It refers to the return to methods based on the substantive validity of legal claims whereby the formal categories inherent in legality (validity-responsibility) are discredited for their failure to explain and make sense of the world[47] as well as why states and other actors feel a sense of duty to obey international legal rules. According to these legitimacy-based perspectives, international law should be construed in a way that is alien to existing formal categories and turned into a vocabulary for judgment and action.[48] De-formalization becomes then inevitable because legitimacy is a matter of degree, not a matter of binary structure.[49] Such a move is meant to release us 'from law's binary bind'[50] as it becomes possible to move from institutions to regimes, from rules to regulation, from government to governance, from responsibility to compliance, from legality to legitimacy, from legal expertise to international relations expertise.[51] A good illustration of this facet of the turn to legitimacy is the refinement of Franck's theory[52] that has recently been offered by Brunnée and Toope.[53] In the same vein, it has been proposed that we 'consider legitimacy not as a source of legal compliance or as a moral benchmark but rather as a process by which institutional or social inequalities can be justified'.[54] It should be noted, however, that not all scholars embracing the turn to legitimacy

---

44 On the Manhattan School of international law and especially Tom Franck's school, see the symposium in (2002) 13 European Journal of International Law 901. See also David Kennedy, 'Tom Franck and the Manhattan School' (2003) 35 New York University Journal of International Law and Politics 397.

45 Lee Epstein and Andrew D. Martin, 'Quantitatives to Empirical Legal Research' in Peter Cane and Herbert Kritzer (eds), *Oxford Handbook on Empirical Legal Research* (OUP 2010) 910, 911.

46 Developing the coding scheme can be inductive or deductive, cf ibid.

47 Franck, *The Power of Legitimacy among Nations* (n 41) 5.

48 David Kennedy, *Of War and Law* (Princeton University Press 2006) 45; idem, *International Legal Structures* (Nomos 1987); idem, 'When Renewal Repeats: Thinking Against the Box' (1999) 32 New York University Journal of International Law and Politics 335; idem, 'Challenging Expert Rule: The Politics of Global Governance' (2005) 27 Sydney Law Review 5; idem, 'The Disciplines of International Law and Policy' (1999) 12 Leiden Journal of International Law 9.

49 Franck, *The Power of Legitimacy among Nations* (n 41) 27.

50 ibid 36.

51 Jean d'Aspremont, 'The Politics of Deformalization in International Law' (2011) 3 Goettingen Journal of International Law 503, 510. The above typology of the broad, inclusive concept of de-formalization derives from the same article at 508–10.

52 Franck, when insisting on the need for symbolic validation, proved more formalist than those who succeeded him and whom he partially inspired. See Franck, *The Power of Legitimacy among Nations* (n 41) 92. This is a remark I owe to an exchange with Jan Klabbers.

53 See generally Brunnée and Toope (n 4).

54 Charlesworth (n 36) 398.

have sought to shed the use of formal legal categories as well as formalistic modes of thinking. The turn to legitimacy has led some scholars to propose major changes to the doctrine of sources, without espousing an all-out de-formalization of international law.[55]

Although this may be less obvious, a third consequence of the shift in focus towards legitimacy can be found in the revival of constitutionalist thinking of international law within European legal studies. Indeed, it seems difficult to deny that the – discovered or projected – constitutionalization of international law contemplated in such studies is meant to contribute to the legitimization of international law as a whole,[56] or, at least, create a demand for a certain type of legitimacy.[57] This quest for legitimacy in constitutionalist thinking also explains the attachment of its promoters to legal formal categories.[58] It is true that that constitutionalist thinking predates the 1990s turn to legitimacy.[59] Yet, it is submitted here that the post-Cold War turn to legitimacy in international legal studies is not alien to the resuscitation of constitutionalist legal thought.

Whatever the various consequences of the turn to legitimacy, it is argued here that the abovementioned legitimacy discourses have all been accompanied by a project of reinvention and rehabilitation of international law of some sort. Such reinvention and rehabilitation have manifested itself in various ways. In the following paragraphs, three specific expressions of the reinvention and rehabilitation of international law that lurk behind legal scholarship surrounding the legitimacy of international law as a whole are mentioned. First, it can be argued that studies of the legitimacy of international law as a whole have promoted a form of pragmatic reconstruction of international law. Indeed, from the perspective of legitimacy,

---

55 See eg Harlan Cohen, 'Finding International Law, Part II: Our Fragmenting Legal Community' (2012) 44 New York University Journal of International Law and Politics 1049, 1063 (seeking to revise the doctrine of sources to incorporate the internalized legitimacy rules of the system and make the legal framework more accurate and reflective of practice by replacing secondary rules with legitimacy rules); see also Matthias Goldmann, 'We Need to Cut Off the Head of the King: Past, Present, and Future Approaches to International Soft Law' (2012) 25 Leiden Journal of International Law 335 (arguing that the distinction hard-soft does not uphold legitimacy).

56 For some critical remarks, see Jan Klabbers, 'International legal positivism and constitutionalism' in Joerg Kammerhofer and Jean d'Aspremont (eds), *International Legal Positivism in a Postmodern World* (CUP 2014) 264–90. See also Jean d'Aspremont, 'International Constitutionalism, Legal Forms, and the Need for Villains' in Anthony F. Lang, Jr. and Antje Wiener (eds), *Handbook on Global Constitutionalism* (Edward Elgar 2017) 155–69.

57 Thomas Kleinlein, *Konstitutionalisierung im Völkerrecht* (Springer 2012) 703, 713. For an illustration, see Anne Peters, 'The Merits of Global Constitutionalism' (2009) 16 Indiana Journal of Global Legal Studies 397, 410; eadem, 'Compensatory Constitutionalism: The Function and Potential of Fundamental International Norms and Structures' (2006) 19 Leiden Journal of International Law 579.

58 Anne Peters, 'The Merits of Global Constitutionalism' (n 57) 397, 409; See eg Christian Tomuschat, 'International Law: Ensuring the Survival of Mankind on the Eve of a New Century: General Course on Public International Law' (1999) 281 Recueil des Cours 26. See the remarks Klabbers, 'International Legal Positivism and Constitutionalism' (n 56) 285.

59 On the history of constitutionalist thinking, see Thomas Kleinlein, 'Alfred Verdross as a Founding Father of International Constitutionalism' (2012) 4 Goettingen Journal of International Law 385; Ignacio de la Rasilla del Moral, 'The Unsolved Riddle of International Constitutionalism' (2010) 12 International Community Law Review 81; Ignacio de la Rasilla del Moral, 'At King Agramant's Camp – Old Debates, New Constitutional Times' (2010) 8 International Journal of Constitutional Law 580; see also the remarks of Richard Collins, 'Constitutionalism as Liberal-Juridical Consciousness: Echoes from International Law's Past' (2009) 22 Leiden Journal of International Law 251.

questions raised by international law ought no longer to be answered through technical vocabulary and paradigms about the distinction between law and non-law but, rather, through pragmatic inquiry into the fidelity of law. Legitimacy discourses allow international lawyers to move into a 'post-ontological' age where foundational questions about international law can be eluded.[60] For international lawyers who have grown tired of debates surrounding the foundations of international law[61] and the scepticism too often heard in regard to the contradictions which inform the main doctrines,[62] studies on the legitimacy of international law as a whole provides a comfort zone far away from foundational battlefields. Such pragmatism is buoyed by the descriptive virtues which the concept of legitimacy seems to offer and which outpaces traditional formal categories that are unable to capture more fully multi-layered dynamics.[63] In that sense, the turn to exploration of the legitimacy of international law as a whole allows international lawyers to feel they can make greater sense of the world thanks to this avenue of inquiry necessitating resort to a wide range of multidisciplinary tools.[64]

Second, inquiries into the legitimacy of international law as a whole have promoted a sort of rehabilitation of international law in spite of its enforcement deficiencies. Indeed, the turn to legitimacy came to assuage one of international lawyers' greatest challenges: the so-called Austinian imperatival handicap of the international legal system. Though international lawyers have developed powerful argumentative tools to diminish the ontologically devastating consequences of this fable, they never like to be reminded that international law suffers from an enforcement disability. A focus upon the legitimacy of international law encouraged lawyers to think that international law does not need enforcement mechanisms.[65] By improving the legitimacy of international law, international lawyers are led to believe that effectiveness is

---

[60] See eg the famous claim of Thomas Franck according to which we have entered a post-ontological era. See Franck, *Fairness in International Law and Institutions* (n 38) 6. For a contestation of the idea of a post-ontological era in international legal thought see Ronald Dworkin, 'A New Philosophy for International Law' (2013) 41 Philosophy and Public Affairs 2, 3.

[61] See eg Thomas Franck, *The Power of Legitimacy among Nations* (n 41) 32.

[62] Gerry Simpson, 'On the Magic Mountain: Teaching Public International Law' (1999) 10 European Journal of International Law 74: 'Is international law really? The pitiless refrain haunts us at every turn. When our Law School colleagues or skeptical students ask this question we search our bag of rhetorical tricks for answers. Few of these are sophisticated or illuminating as Thomas Franck's self-referential theory of legitimacy. Thus, we resort to false analogies between domestic legal institution and their international counterparts or make reference to murderers who remain un-apprehended (rather like the superpowers whose invasions go unpunished). We are perhaps slightly ashamed at these not quite accurate parallels.' In the same vein, see Martti Koskenniemi, 'International Legal Theory and Doctrine' (November 2007) in Rüdiger Wolfrum, *Max Planck Encyclopedia of Public International Law* (online edn) para 22: 'Unwilling to re-enter the terrain of positivism/naturalism, international lawyers turned to the social science vocabulary of legitimacy to address the normative force of international rules (…) The language of "legitimacy" goes some way towards resolving the dilemmas posed by purely external and purely internal explanations for international law's binding force.'

[63] Brunnée and Toope (n 4) 5, 47.

[64] The interdisciplinary agenda is not always explicit as most of these legitimacy discourses continued to be shrouded in legal veil. See Martti Koskenniemi, 'The Mystery of Legal Obligation' (2011) 3 International Theory 319.

[65] This is also the reading made by Daniel Bodansky, 'Legitimacy in International Law and International Relations' (2012) APSA 2011 Annual Meeting Paper (26 January 2012) 9 <http://ssrn.com/abstract=1900289> accessed 31 January 2021.

not dependent on enforcement.[66] If its legitimacy is upheld, international law can successfully lay down authoritative standards of conduct.[67] In that sense, legitimacy comes to play the same self-preserving and self-sustaining function[68] as reputation[69] or other so-called soft enforcement mechanisms.[70] In that sense, the turn to legitimacy can also be seen as allowing, not only as a rehabilitation of international law, but also its reinvention beyond the Austinian handicap.

Third, some variants of the shift towards a focus on the legitimacy of international law as a whole have supported a reinvention of international law in terms of law-ascertainment. Indeed, the turn to legitimacy seems to make possible an approach whereby international law is identified, not by virtue of the formal containers of international norms, but rather by virtue of the feeling that norms are binding. In other words, the turn to legitimacy has often materialized itself in a conflation between the creation of the *instrumentum* and the sense of obligation/reason for action.[71] As a result of such a reinvention of international law, what matters is more a feeling of fidelity to the law, rather than the ascertainment of a formally binding obligation.

It is submitted that, despite the functional appeal of the various abovementioned projects of reinvention and rehabilitation of international law that have accompanied the turn to the legitimacy of international law as a whole in the aftermath of the Cold War, the success of such inquiries abated as severe criticism of the turn to legitimacy has been raised. Such criticisms are often associated with the multidisciplinarity inherent to the turn to legitimacy.[72] Mention can be made here of the hegemonic move towards new vocabularies and the empowerment of new experts.[73] The turn to legitimacy has also been faulted for its evasiveness and inability to transcend the inner contradictions of international legal arguments.[74] Legitimacy-based per-

---

66 On the idea that illegitimate institutions can generate compliance through sanction mechanisms, see Buchanan (n 5) 79, 80–81.

67 Tasioulas (n 5) 97, 100.

68 See eg Franck, *The Power of Legitimacy among Nations* (n 41) 16; Kumm (n 31) 907.

69 Andrew Guzman, 'A Compliance-Based Theory of International Law' (2002) 90 California Law Review 1823.

70 For an interesting attempt to refute the Austinian handicap of international law by virtue of a conception of enforcement based on 'outcasting', see Oona Hathaway and Scott Shapiro, 'Outcasting: Enforcement in Domestic and International Law' (2011) 121 Yale Law Journal 252.

71 This is conspicuous in the work of Brunnée and Toope (n 4) 46.

72 For an acknowledgement that the turn to legitimacy calls for a turn to international relations, see Brunnée and Toope (n 4) 5; for criticism of inter- and multidisciplinarity, see Jan Klabbers, 'The Relative Autonomy of International Law and The Forgotten Politics of Interdisciplinarity' (2004) 1 Journal of International Law and International Relations 35; Martti Koskenniemi, 'Constitutionalism as Mindset: Reflections on Kantian Themes about International Law and Globalization' (2006) 8 Theoretical Inquiries in Law 14; see also idem, 'The Mystery of Legal Obligation' (2011) 3 International Theory 319.

73 Martti Koskenniemi, 'Miserable Comforters: International Relations as New Nature Law' (2009) 15 European Journal of International Relations 395. Martti Koskenniemi has also written that this is a pragmatism that sometimes 'involves an illegitimate naturalization of practitioner frameworks'. See idem, 'Doctrines of State Responsibility' in James Crawford, Alain Pellet and Simon Olleson (eds), *The Law of International Responsibility* (OUP 2010) 45 (citing Susan Marks, *The Riddle of All Constitutions* (OUP 2000) 66–67).

74 Martti Koskenniemi, 'Legitimacy, Rights and Ideology, Notes Towards a Critique of the New Moral Internationalism' (2003) 7 Associations 349, 363; On the instability of the concept of legitimacy, see also Jan Klabbers, 'Review of Fault Lines of International Legitimacy' (2011) 105 American Journal of International Law 394, 394.

spectives only seem to postpone difficult questions and, in that sense, constitute a short-lived problem-avoidance strategy. Others have bemoaned the inherently subjective character of any legitimacy determination.[75] It has also been argued that legitimacy is never achieved and thus in the end not something to be complacent about.[76] Likewise, objections have been raised against the constant ambiguity infusing legitimacy-based approaches and their oscillation between normative and descriptive legitimacy.[77] Related to that, legitimacy-based approaches have been criticized for promoting neo-naturalism[78] and presuming one type of universality.[79] The managerial and problem-solving dimension of the turn to legitimacy have been said to conceal its *a priori* and pre-reflective commitments.[80] Eventually, the revolution brought about by a focus upon the legitimacy of international law came to be seen as premised on a few strawmen, among which the claim that formalism has originally been conceptualized as an indicator of the idea of obligation.[81]

It is fair to say that the abovementioned charges have significantly dented the popularity of inquiries into the legitimacy of international law as a whole.[82] In 21st-century international legal thought, such inquiry has lost much of its lustre. That does not mean, however, that international lawyers have moved away from the anti-formalism, pragmatism, managerialism, empiricism, multidisciplinarity, and, above all the project of reinvention and rehabilitation of international law.[83] All those approaches and projects that have accompanied studies on the legitimacy of international law as a whole have relented. In other words, projects of reinvention and rehabilitation of international law keep on returning,[84] albeit through different frameworks or narratives. The question of legitimacy of international law as a whole does not seem to be the right angle to promote (or engage in) such projects of reinvention.[85] It remains that

---

75 See David Caron, 'The Legitimacy of the Collective Authority of the Security Council' (1993) 87 American Journal of International Law 552, 557.

76 See Nathaniel Berman, 'Intervention in a "Divided World": Axes of Legitimacy' in Charlesworth and Coicaud (n 36) 115–45.

77 Bodansky (n 65) 7.

78 Koskenniemi (n 64) 320.

79 ibid 323–24.

80 ibid 320.

81 On the idea that the legitimacy of state consent is alien to questions of legality addressed by the sources of international law, see Samantha Besson, 'Theorizing the Sources of International Law' in Besson and Tasioulas (n 5) 163.

82 For some remarks on the loss of confidence towards projects of reinvention, see Kennedy, 'The Mystery of Global Governance' (n 42) 829, 836.

83 The empiricism promoted by inquiries into the legitimacy of international law as a whole has, more recently, emancipated itself from the legitimacy agenda in which it originates. Indeed, it is noteworthy that in recent years, the empirical branch of the legitimacy school has gradually ceded pride of place to the empirical school of international law that more radically prioritized the study of the conditions under which international law is formed and produces effects, irrespective of questions of legitimacy. See Greg Shaffer and Tom Ginsburg, 'The Empirical Turn in International Legal Scholarship' (2012) 106 American Journal of International Law 1.

84 For a discussion of several recent projects of reinvention of international law, see gen. Kennedy, 'The Mystery of Global Governance' (n 42) 829. For some remarks on how constitutionalist European legal scholars have tried to combine these moves in another project of reinvention, see Mattias Kumm, 'On the Past and Future of European Constitutional Scholarship' (2009) 7 International Journal of Constitutional Law 401.

85 See generally David Kennedy, 'When Renewal Repeats: Thinking Against the Box' (n 48) 335.

inquiries into legitimacy of international law as a whole, although being no longer the flavour of the month, proved useful indicators of the pull of projects of rehabilitation and reinvention of international law.[86]

3. LAW AT THE SERVICE OF LEGITIMACY: INTERNATIONAL HUMANITARIAN LAW AS A TOOL FOR (DE-)LEGITIMIZING BEHAVIOURS

The attention now turns to IHL where the concept of legitimacy has not primarily functioned as a vehicle for a reinvention or rehabilitation of the discipline. The structuring role of legitimacy in IHL practice versus IHL scholarship has been very different. It is argued in this section that, in contrast to theoretical inquiries discussed in the previous section, IHL discourse has witnessed another role of legitimacy, on the basis that legitimacy has proved to be the very goal of the deployment of IHL legal doctrine and vocabulary. Indeed, legitimizing or delegitimizing the behaviours of actors engaged in armed conflicts as allegedly falling within the scope of IHL is the very reason why IHL doctrine and vocabulary is mobilized. All the key distinctions around which argument about IHL ought to be articulated are at the service of the production of a discourse about the (il)legitimacy of the conduct of the actors considered to fall within the realm of IHL.[87] In that sense, passing a judgment on the (il)legitimacy of actors involved in armed conflicts amounts to the very *raison d'être* of the use of doctrines and vocabularies of IHL by professionals and non-professionals.[88]

This specific role of the concept of legitimacy in IHL practice and scholarship calls for four remarks. First, the claim that IHL operates as a technical vocabulary that is mobilized to legitimize or delegitimize the behaviour of actors which are considered to fall within its purview is not new.[89] Second, such a finding can also be made with respect to other fields of international law, international human rights law providing similar examples. Third, and more importantly, this finding should not be interpreted as meaning that the legitimacy battle trumps the legality battle.[90] The instrumentalization of IHL for legitimizing purposes that is discussed here does not amount to a retreat of IHL.[91] On the contrary, the constant mobilization of IHL to legitimize or delegitimize the behaviours of actors reveals the impact and ubiquity of IHL doctrine

---

86 That does not mean that the need to rehabilitate or reinvent international law has remained unchallenged. See David J. Bederman, 'Constructivism, Positivism, and Empiricism in International Law' (2001) 89 Georgetown Law Journal 469, 471; see also d'Aspremont (n 9) 680.

87 Kennedy, *Of War and Law* (n 48) 96–97. It should be noted that the mobilizing of IHL vocabularies may also be for self-legitimizing purposes. This is well illustrated by Israel's contention that it applies the Geneva Conventions de facto. For a discussion of that position see Djamchid Momtaz, 'Israel and the Fourth Geneva Convention: on the ICJ Advisory Opinion concerning the Separation Barrier' (2007) 8 Yearbook of International Humanitarian Law 344. For some criticism of that position see UNGA Res ES-10/6 (9 February 1999) UN Doc A/RES/ES-10/6.

88 Bassiouni (n 15) 711, 781.

89 Kennedy, *Of War and Law* (n 48) 96–97; Dale Stephens, 'Blurring the Lines: The Interpretation, Discourse and Application of the Law of Armed Conflict' (2009) 12 Yearbook of International Humanitarian Law 85, 108–109.

90 contra Stephens (ibid) 85, 108–109.

91 Michael Schmitt, 'Targeting and International Humanitarian Law in Afghanistan' (2009) 85 International Law Studies 329.

and vocabulary. In fact, as a result of such constant mobilization, IHL is turned into a universal argumentative vocabulary used to discuss right and wrong within conflicts, even outside the professional community of international lawyers.[92] In that sense, we are seeing a rise to power of IHL rather than a decline. IHL doctrine and vocabulary is invoked all the time, everywhere and by a whole range of actors to legitimize and delegitimize behaviours in armed conflict. From such a perspective, accounts demoting IHL to irrelevance on the basis that it has limited impact on actors do not hold, for there can hardly be a more influential role for IHL than being the vocabulary of reference for any claim about the acceptability of the behaviours of actors engaged in armed conflicts. Fourth, shedding light on the mobilization of IHL to legitimize and delegitimize of the role of actors simultaneously recalls that IHL does not necessarily or ontologically side with the 'good' or with peace. Indeed, the legitimizing and delegitimizing role of IHL doctrine and vocabulary show that the latter, when used to legitimize a behaviour, also operates as a set of legal entitlements to kill.[93] In that sense, IHL doctrine and vocabulary empowers actors engaged in armed conflicts.[94] In contrast to inquiries into the legitimacy of international law as a whole, where the concept of legitimacy reveals virtuous projects of reinvention and rehabilitation, the concept of legitimacy in IHL divulges the dark side of the mobilization of IHL doctrine and vocabulary.[95]

Whether IHL provides a vocabulary that allows an intelligible argument about the rights and wrongs within armed conflict is another question. It cannot be excluded that international legal scholars have pushed the sophistication of IHL doctrine and vocabulary to a level where they can no longer act as a meaningful yardstick for the evaluation of the acceptability of the behaviours of actors engaged in armed conflicts.[96] The constant quest for sophistication and elaboration of new distinctions – which can sometimes be seen as the manifestation of a pathological obsession for taxonomies[97] – have exacerbated the ease with which IHL doctrine and vocabulary can be deployed as empowering argumentative tools. In that sense, the unquench-

---

[92] David Kennedy, *A World of Struggle: How Power, Law, and Expertise Shape Global Political Economy* (Princeton University Press 2016) 258: 'It is easy to understand the virtues of a powerful legal vocabulary, shared by elites around the world, which appears to distinguish legal from illegal war and wartime violence. It is exciting to see law become the mark of legitimacy as legitimacy has become the currency of power. It is more difficult to see the opportunities this opens for the military professional to harness law as a weapon, or for sovereigns to continue to exercise of power as right.'

[93] ibid 262.

[94] For an illustration in the case of Israel and Hamas, see Milanovic and Hadzi-Vidanovic (n 14) 256–314.

[95] This has sometimes been discussed through the lens of what has been called 'lawfare'. The concept of lawfare is said to have been coined by Charles J. Dunlap, 'Lawfare Today: A Perspective' (2008) 3 Yale Journal of International Affairs 146. On that concept, see Michael Kearney, 'Lawfare, Legitimacy and Resistance: The Weak and the Law' (2010) 16 Palestine Yearbook of International Law 79.

[96] Kennedy, *A World of Struggle* (n 92) 259: 'Lines are now harder to draw, both because the world of war has become more mixed up and because ambiguities, gaps, and contradictions in the materials used to draw the lines have become more pronounced.' Kennedy also writes that nowadays 'the experience of irresolvable debate (…) is ever more common'.

[97] See generally Jules Coleman, 'The Architecture of Jurisprudence' (2011) 121 Yale Law Journal 2.

able thirst of IHL scholars for sophistication and new taxonomies – which they paradoxically see as simplifying the world[98] – may not necessarily be serving virtue.[99]

4. CONCLUDING REMARKS: LEGITIMIZING INTERNATIONAL LAW VS. LEGALIZING INTERNATIONAL LEGITIMACY

If IHL can be construed as putting in place doctrines and vocabularies at the service of the legitimization and delegitimization of behaviours of belligerents as discussed in section 3, the contrast with theoretical studies on the question of the legitimacy of international law as a whole that were discussed in section 2 could not be greater. Whilst debates on the legitimacy of international law revolve around the reinvention and rehabilitation of international law, the IHL literature and practice are about legalizing the (il)legitimacy of actors and passing legitimacy judgments through the legal categories of IHL – thus, legitimizing of international law on the one hand and legalizing of legitimacy judgments on the other.

Does the foregoing mean that exploring the role of legitimacy in international legal studies inevitably confronts us with the immense functional pluralism at work in international legal discourse? Although the concept of legitimacy has been playing various structuring roles within international legal discourse, as is demonstrated in this chapter, the concept of legitimacy has simultaneously laid bare a common attitude among all international lawyers, namely the desire for their discourse to be taken seriously.[100] Indeed, whether they seek to reinvent or rehabilitate international law or want to pass judgment on the behaviours of actors, international lawyers want international law to count. Said differently, international lawyers, be it in inquiring about the legitimacy of international law as a whole or in invoking IHL to gauge the acceptability of actors in armed conflict, want their voices to be heard, not only by judicial authorities but also beyond courtrooms, as to allow international law to constitute a 'method of practical intervention in the social world'.[101] In that sense, behind the variety of projects which the previous sections have divulged, one can discern an overarching common inclination to ensure that international law remains relevant. At the end of the day, such a finding of shared sensibility seems to eclipse all contrasts that have been discussed throughout this chapter. Indeed, it is remarkable that exploring the role of legitimacy in international legal studies, as was attempted here, simultaneously demonstrates that international lawyers, despite letting legitimacy dictate their engagement with international law in dramatically divergent ways, are not disillusioned nor resigned cynics of some sort. In fact, they continue to reinvent international law or mobilize its doctrine and vocabulary in good faith and with the belief that their craft can matter in the world. This is no trivial conclusion.

---

98 See generally Anne Peters, 'Realizing Utopia as a Scholarly Endeavor' (2013) 24 European Journal of International Law 533 (stating that scholarship is all about the generation of theories to reduce complexity).

99 On this paradox, see gen. the remarks of d'Aspremont (n 9) 680.

100 Klabbers, 'The Relative Autonomy of International Law and The Forgotten Politics of Interdisciplinarity' (n 72) 35, 41.

101 The expression is from Neil Walker, 'Beyond Boundary Disputes and Basic Grids: Mapping the Global Disorder of Normative Orders' (2008) 6 International Journal of Constitutional Law 373, 374.

3. The role of legitimacy in international humanitarian law: A comment

Stefan Kadelbach

1. INTRODUCTION

The relationship between the notion of legitimacy and international humanitarian law (IHL) seems to be ambivalent. On the one hand, IHL touches the core of all law, the protection of the human being against illegitimate force, and thus has an obvious moral authority. On the other hand, it does not appear to fit with the notion of input-legitimacy, which equally derives from a (largely Kantian) concept of morality. This point can be made irrespective of the four reference points discerned in the chapter by Jean d'Aspremont regarding expectations of legitimacy: the international law framework of IHL in general, specific rules of international (humanitarian) law, single actors, or the process of international law-making.

First, as to international law in general. Its preconditions stem from a time in which most of the states which are today members of the United Nations either did not yet exist at all or have gone through radical metamorphoses so that they cannot necessarily be regarded the same as those which had participated in the formation of international law. The same holds true, second, of the core of humanitarian law which stems from the epoch preceding the First World War. Third, the legitimacy of actors which are supposed to abide by IHL is often contested, as is their position as subjects of international law. Last, as far as the parties participating in armed conflict are non-state actors, they do not have the capacity to create international law and to participate in the process of the making of IHL.

In spite of this seemingly contradictory relationship, this chapter shares the view expounded in the preceding chapter that IHL is a suitable field of law to test hypotheses of legitimacy in international legal theory. Criteria developed in international legitimacy discourse have a role to play in refining the argument in identifying applicable law, the application of IHL itself, and the recognition of non-state actors. However, this comment takes a less sceptical view with respect to the use of IHL arguments. It insists on what seems almost too obvious to state, namely that IHL derives its legitimacy from its very essence of aiming to protect human existence. This characteristic helps us understand various approaches attempting to respond to challenges that may be raised with respect to IHL's legitimacy.

This chapter's argument will be made across three sections. After shortly recapitulating the argument made in the preceding chapter (2), the ensuing section will address the general legitimacy discourse and its implications for IHL (3). The last section will expand on a number of reflections about the further impact of criteria of legitimacy on IHL (4).

2. LEGITIMIZING LAW AND LEGALIZING LEGITIMACY

The first argument proposed in the preceding chapter is that the objective of the scholarly legitimacy debate from the early 1990s onwards was to reinvent and rehabilitate international law as a whole, which meant providing a basis to international law and went beyond the legal form and consent in the legal order ('legitimizing international law'). The second claim is that technical legal vocabulary is used to legitimize or delegitimize the behaviour of actors in regard to IHL ('legalizing international legitimacy'). The argument advances in three steps.

First, the distinction is taken up between different points of reference for legitimacy discourse in international legal thought. Legitimacy considerations accordingly tend to modify purely formal techniques, like the ascertainment of a rule by a canon of sources of law, or the recognition of states, governments, and belligerents. This move, however, is said to be averse to the universality of the application of IHL, to wit, by infusing criteria alien to the black-letter of IHL conventions and by incurring the risk of advocating for dual standards. On the other hand, criteria of legitimacy may 'inform' the opening of IHL for non-state parties and contribute to the justification of imposing IHL obligations on them.

The second section goes a step backwards and comments critically on features of the legitimacy discourse, taking Thomas Franck as a point of departure. Accordingly, the intrinsic normativity of a rule and its pull towards compliance provide the ground for empiricism in that factual compliance itself gains indicative weight for ascertaining the law. Consequences are a de-formalization of law and a value-based approach infused by constitutionalist thinking. The shift is described as a reinvention of international law since it helps to newly address old problems like ontological questions about the foundation of international law, the lack of enforcement mechanisms and the establishment of empirical evidence for the ascertainment of law. Criticism aligned with this trend points to the empowerment of new experts, hegemonic use of their authority, and subjectivity of legitimacy criteria. Thus, the account defends the virtues of formalism against the influence of claims to normativity extraneous to the law.

Seen against this background, third, legitimacy is said to have an entirely different role to play in IHL, since it is the very point of the legal argument in this field to (de-)legitimize the behaviour of actors participating in armed conflict.

Thus, the concept of legitimacy has an ambiguous function to fulfil in IHL: it provides for arguments which reinforce the validity of IHL, but it also serves as a tool to undermine its normativity, even against the best intentions of its defenders.

3. LEGITIMACY IN INTERNATIONAL LAW

The account this approach gives of legitimacy theories overstates the consequences of their underlying assumptions for the stability of legal expectations. This conclusion is based on three observations.

To begin with, it is questionable whether Thomas Franck is the proper addressee to blame for deformalizing international law and preparing the ground for new types of power discourse. It is worth the effort to defend Franck against false friends. His theory deals with the reason why international law is law (its *Geltungsgrund*, to adopt a German word). It not only draws on Dworkin's moral realism and Habermas's discourse theory to enrich the explanation of the normativity of international law, but also on Herbert Hart by insisting on formal validation in order to draw the line between law and non-law.[1] The same holds true of the approach of Brunnée and Toope.[2]

Another point is whether fidelity to the forms of law alone offers more. No legal argument, be it of a traditional nature or of extra-legal normative descent, escapes the objection brought forward by deconstructing legal realism: that they are subject to strategic use and oscillate between 'apology and utopia'.[3] Adherents to legitimacy approaches could be tempted to reverse the argument: the merit of questioning mere legality as the sole category of conclusive reasoning might be that value judgments can be more openly addressed. Thus, the exhortation that both may not be conflated is well justified, but it applies to both approaches alike.

Last, the dichotomy of legality and legitimacy triggers the question: what is the relationship between legitimacy and positive law? Clearly, legitimacy is not in itself a legal norm. Obviously, it is not a rule in the sense that it applies in binary form. Rather, legitimacy is determined as a matter of degree, so that it can be realized like principles in a more-or-less fashion in the Dworkinian sense.[4] However, assuming that principles form part of positive law, legitimacy would be hard to verify via canonist methods adopted to identify international legal norms. Since legitimacy is conceived of as an underlying notion against which institutions of positive law are measured, one may speak of a *standard*, a category of norms overarching the concepts of policies and principles.[5] Legitimacy can therefore not plausibly function as an alternative to formal law. It does not pose a threat to formalism, but, as rightly stated in the first section of the preceding chapter, it may inform the deployment of legal argument. Legitimacy is a non-legal expectation, the fulfilment of which enhances compliance and thus, in theory at least, is meant as a tool to tame sheer power and to enrich political decision-making through normative criteria. As will be seen, it is power which thwarts legitimacy, not law.

4. THE LEGITIMACY OF INTERNATIONAL HUMANITARIAN LAW

The backdrop against which the argument that IHL is used to delegitimize actors is likely manifold. Jean d'Aspremont does not really elaborate on it. The contention brings arguments to mind which are brought forward to influence public opinion: techniques of disinformation used by the parties to armed conflict as a means of warfare. However, it also reminds us of the democratic intervention debate, the 'illegal combatant' quarrel, justifications of degrading treatment or torture for the sake of combating terrorism and the like. Whereas the former delegitimizing method relies upon a false representation of facts, the latter tends to withdraw

---

1 Thomas Franck, 'Legitimacy in the International System' (1988) 82 American Journal of International Law 705; idem, *The Power of Legitimacy Among Nations* (OUP 1990) 24, 41; idem, *Fairness in International Law and Institutions* (OUP 1995) 30; for the element of formal validation Herbert Lionel Adolphus Hart, *The Concept of Law* (Clarendon Press 1961) 97ff.

2 Jutta Brunnée and Stephen Toope, *Legitimacy and Legality in International Law – An Interactional Account* (CUP 2010) 52.

3 Martti Koskenniemi, *From Apology to Utopia* (Lakimiesliiton Kustannus 1989).

4 Ronald Dworkin, *Taking Rights Seriously* (5th edn, Duckworth 1987) 22–28.

5 cf ibid 22–28; see also Roscoe Pound, 'Hierarchies of Sources and Forms in Different Systems of Law' (1933) 7 Tulane Law Review 475; as for the application to international law see Hardy C. Dillard, 'Some Aspects of Law and Diplomacy' (1957) 91 Recueil des Cours de l'Académie de Droit International 477.

the protection expected of legal institutions by withholding recognition of subjects under the law as equal. In the present context, only this latter technique is of interest. Three forms of legitimacy can be distinguished: the legitimacy of rules, the legitimacy of their application and the legitimacy of actors.

4.1 Legitimacy of Rules

As to the rules of IHL, the detrimental effect of delegitimizing arguments on the efficacy of these norms is evident, as it is for international law in general. The question is, however, whether this effect is a consequence of legitimacy discourse as it is pursued in the theory of international law. It appears that concerns that international law loses its formal quality ought to be addressed rather to theories which advocate for a value-based strategic use of legal techniques, like the New Haven approach, the forerunner of later rational choice theories. For such a theory, which claims to defend 'world public order',[6] the rules of international law are merely 'past trends of decision-making', which are to be taken into account before acting on the international level, but do not constitute the limit of action.[7] It is against this way of thinking, which was prominent until the 1980s, that Franck's writings should be read.

Taking the symbolic validation requirement upon which Franck and his followers insist seriously, the shift away from black-letter law towards less clearly defined legitimacy criteria would have to pass the test outlining the modes of international law-making, commonly referred to as 'sources': democratic intervention would have to be ascertained positively as an exception to the prohibition of the use of force, be it by a change in the legal paradigm via the practice of the UN Security Council or as customary law.[8] Likewise, the notion of the 'illegal combatant', which was meant as an expansion of the undefined status of spies and guerrilla fighters to further categories and thereby to deny them the rights of prisoners of war, would have to be recognized as a ground to rebut the presumption in Article 5 of the Third Geneva Convention;[9] accordingly, in case of doubt, a person must be granted POW protection until their status is verified by a court.[10] Finally, no exception to the absolute prohibition of torture has been recognized by the international community of states so far.[11]

---

6 For a summary see Myres S. McDougal and W. Michael Reisman, 'International Law in Policy-Oriented Perspective' in Ronald St. John Macdonald and Douglas Millar Johnston (eds), *The Structure and Process of International Law* (Nijhoff 1986) 103ff.

7 Myres S. McDougal, Harold Lasswell and Lung-chu Chen, *Human Rights and World Public Order* (Yale University Press 1980) 423ff.

8 Jeremy I. Levitt, 'Pro-democratic Intervention in Africa' (2006) 24 Wisconsin International Law Journal 785; Simone van den Driest, 'Pro-democratic intervention and the Right to Political Self-determination' (2010) 57 Netherlands International Law Review 29.

9 cf Knut Dörmann, 'The Legal Situation of "Unlawful/Unprivileged Combatants"' (2003) 85 International Review of the Red Cross 45.

10 Geneva Convention Relative to the Treatment of Prisoners of War (Third Geneva Convention) (adopted 12 August 1949, entered into force 21 October 1950) 75 UNTS 135.

11 See Nigel Rodley, 'The Prohibition of Torture: Absolute Means Absolute' (2006) 34 Denver Journal of International Law and Policy 145.

4.2 Legitimacy of Application

Like the verification of rules, the application of IHL seems exposed to moves to delegitimize it. At first sight, to defend a formal approach looks like the best method to avoid such effects, since IHL encompasses intrinsic legitimacy based on 'elementary considerations of humanity', to use a phrase repeatedly used by the International Court of Justice echoing the Martens clause.[12] The 'fairness' aspect of those rules derives from their object and purpose, to protect persons *hors de combat* from violence not warranted by military exigency, the guiding principles being distinction, proportionality and necessity, as they are found, for instance, in Articles 48–58 of the First Additional Protocol to the Geneva Conventions (AP I).[13] This does not mean, however, that the application of these rules is immune to strategic arguments, some of which open space for the weighing of antagonistic interests, as it becomes apparent in the proportionality test which applies to ascertain whether an attack is 'indiscriminate' and therefore prohibited according to Article 51(5)(b) AP I. In that respect, arguments surrounding legitimacy do not add to justified concerns: if divergent interpretations between the parties to an armed conflict occur, which will almost unavoidably be the case, they follow typical patterns of strategic use of legal argument.

It deserves to be added that many rules of IHL are formulated in unequivocal terms, such as Common Article 3 of the four Geneva Conventions of 1949, which prohibit certain behaviour 'at all times and everywhere' or, for example, the rules regarding attacks on civilian objects in Articles 52–56 AP I, even if conducted as a reprisal. Hence, it appears that a technical approach to the application of IHL is to a certain extent inherent in the subject matter, which reduces the risk of reopening a debate on the minimum morals agreed upon within IHL conventions.

4.3 Legitimacy of Actors

4.3.1 The act of recognition

If neither the process of identifying the rules of armed conflict nor their application is particularly vulnerable to arguments designed to delegitimize this body of law's use, the question remains as to the nature of potential it has with respect to its subjects, the actors and victims of international armed conflict. As far as the actors are not states, but national liberation movements or other armed opposition groups describing themselves as a nation, people, tribe, belligerent or insurgent,[14] not only their status under IHL, but also the character of the conflict as one to which IHL applies, may depend on an act of recognition. As far as such recognition implies a judgment of legitimacy, and be it only with respect to the capacity to represent

---

[12] *Corfu Channel Case (UK v Albania)* (Merits) [1949] ICJ Rep 4, 22; *Case concerning Military and Paramilitary Activities in and against Nicaragua (Nicaragua v United States)* (Merits) [1986] ICJ Rep 14 para 215; *Legality of the Threat or Use of Nuclear Weapons* (Advisory Opinion) [1996] ICJ Rep 226 para 79; *Legal Consequences of the Construction of a Wall in the Occupied Palestinian Territory* (Advisory Opinion) [2004] ICJ 136 para 157.

[13] Protocol Additional to the Geneva Conventions of 12 August 1949, and Relating to the Protection of Victims of International Armed Conflicts (Protocol I) of 8 June 1977 (adopted 8 June 1977, entered into force on 7 December 1978) 1125 UNTS 3.

[14] For their status see Jordan J. Paust, 'Armed Opposition Groups' in Math Noortmann, August Reinisch and Cedric Ryngaert (eds), *Non-State Actors in International Law* (Hart 2015) 274ff.

a certain group, one might say that, from a humanitarian perspective, legitimacy-based value judgments run counter to the project of IHL.

Again, the point made addresses the use of power by legal terms. The act of recognition is sovereign and political in character and, as a consequence, does not have to follow criteria recognized in international law. However, this observation is not yet an argument against concerns to import additional legitimacy criteria into the requirements for recognition. What appears to be decisive from a Franckian perspective is that recognition entails the prospect of creating a sense of obligation on the part of armed groups which have not participated in the negotiation of IHL treaties and could not contribute to custom. The argument was made in the past, for instance, by groups in Vietnam, Colombia, and El Salvador.[15] This argument points to a dilemma between, on the one hand, including claims regarding participation, and, on the other hand, losing sight of the rights of protected persons. The latter risk may materialize by recognizing armed bandits with no intention to comply and by including unwelcome contributions. Both relate to each other and reflect the problem of potentially downgrading standards: actor recognition requires criteria which may be expressed in both legitimacy and legalistic terms, and rule recognition requires, according to legitimacy theory, the inclusion of relevant actors.

4.3.2 Criteria of recognition

Looking at the problem from the perspective of the (unjustifiably) non-recognized, a formal approach appears to promise more neutrality than a concept built on criteria extraneous to IHL. However, a formal approach would also not help us to evade the question as to which groups are eligible. In that respect, various concepts are suggested which range from the verification of state-like features and the characteristic of being an addressee of IHL (including criminal law) to a criterion of 'excluded voices'.[16] Some of these criteria are based on effective control of territory and people, others are purely normative, for example, criteria such as fairness and inclusiveness. Thus, legitimacy arguments might prove relevant to a decision between inclusion and exclusion. In that regard, the scepticism voiced in the preceding chapter appears to have a point; for the judgment on which 'voices' had been 'excluded' implies the acceptance of their cause being justified, which can be controversial, and such doubts should not go to the disadvantage of the persons whose rights are at stake.

In order to avoid such obstacles to the application of IHL, a mid-way approach appears to serve the object and purpose of IHL best. There is a difference between the recognition of belligerents and of other forms of recognition, for example, recognizing a state, a government or the acquisition of territory. The latter are exclusively political in nature and basically rely on elements of social legitimacy. It is true that the recognition of insurgents is not devoid of political connotation either. But the very reason for recognizing armed groups as belligerents is normative, namely to encourage their compliance with IHL.

Therefore, it is plausible to coordinate the recognition of belligerents with the prerequisites enabling their qualification as combatants, as opposed to armed bandits or terrorists. Both

---

15 See reference in Anthea Roberts and Sandesh Sivakumaran, 'Lawmaking by Nonstate Actors: Engaging Armed Groups in the Creation of International Humanitarian Law' (2012) 37 Yale Journal of International Law 107, 127.

16 ibid 107.

sets of criteria are not the same, but they do have some common features.[17] They comprise both factual and normative elements. The factual requirements for recognition would be the degree of organization, including command and control over personnel, and thus the possibility to enforce IHL. On the normative side, the express willingness to comply can be established objectively, for example via unilateral declarations and contractual commitments. The International Committee of the Red Cross or other non-governmental organizations can play a mediating role in this sense by encouraging armed groups to subscribe to standards,[18] as it is prominently done by the Deed of Commitment of Geneva Call.[19] Thus, recognition which follows normative criteria could contribute to the legitimacy of the group which in turn enhances the prospect of IHL being observed. The monitoring role of the international community, which is often necessary, may be taken up by the UN or by regional organizations as agents.

4.3.3 The problem of downgrading standards

Whether non-state actors have rights and obligations does not depend on their capacity to participate in law-making.[20] Nevertheless, to link the recognition of belligerents to their willingness to subscribe to IHL entails the problem that adherence to universal standards seems to become a matter of negotiation. Even though this objection does not affect the applicability of customary law, to which non-state actors are bound irrespective of their willingness to comply,[21] it is pertinent with respect to treaty obligations. On the other hand, apart from core conventional duties which are directed towards non-state armed groups that fulfil certain criteria,[22] non-state actors would otherwise rarely be bound by IHL at all. Thus, the matter is basically one of including those who are supposed to abide by norms, for example the protection of children from recruitment as soldiers, the protection of women from violence, or the ban of anti-personnel mines, which are all spelled out in treaty law, but only rudimentarily rooted in international custom. In theory at least, such an involvement and recognition as a subject of IHL should improve the prospect of mitigating or ending the conflict by agree-

---

[17] cf also Heike Krieger, 'A Turn to Non-State Actors: Inducing Compliance with International Humanitarian Law in War-Torn Areas of Limited Statehood' (2013) SFB-Governance Working Paper Series 62, 8 <https://www.sfb-governance.de/publikationen/sfb-700-working_papers/wp62/SFB-Governance-Working-Paper-62.pdf> accessed 31 January 2021.

[18] For the role of humanitarian NGOs see Hans-Joachim Heintze and Charlotte Lülf, 'Non-State Actors under International Humanitarian Law' in Noortmann, Reinisch and Ryngaert (n 14) 97ff.

[19] Geneva Call, 'Deed of Commitment' (*Geneva Call*, 1 July 2019) <http://genevacall.org/how-we-work/deed-of-commitment/> accessed 31 January 2021.

[20] This appears to be generally accepted, see, for instance, Jordan J. Paust, 'Responsibilities of Armed Opposition Groups and Corporations for Violations of International Law and Possible Sanctions' in Noemi Gal-Or, Cedric Ryngaert and Math Noortmann (eds), *Responsibilities of the Non-State Actor in Armed Conflict and the Market Place* (Brill 2015) 105.

[21] See *Prosecutor v Tadić* (Decision in Defence Motion for Interlocutory Appeal on Jurisdiction) ICTY-94-1-I (2 October 1995) para 119; on the concept of quasi-custom see Roberts and Sivakumaran (n 15) 107, 149ff.

[22] cf Geneva Convention Relative to the Treatment of Prisoners of War (Third Geneva Convention) (adopted 12 August 1949, entered into force 21 October 1950) 75 UNTS 135 common art 3 and the Protocol Additional to the Geneva Conventions of 12 August 1949, and Relating to the Protection of Victims of Non-International Armed Conflicts (Protocol II) of 8 June 1977 (adopted 8 June 1977, entered into force on 7 December 1978) 1125 UNTS 609.

ments on ceasefire, exchange of prisoners, peace talks, etc.[23] The idea fits with notions of the participation of those subject to the law in the process of its formation, which is an argument of input legitimacy and ownership.[24] The question as to whether such agreements can be referred to as international law in a technical sense or rather form a category of a hybrid nature is of second order.[25] Whether such a theory of engagement of private actors compliant with IHL is realistic[26] is yet another question. After all, some evidence suggests that engagement in IHL can be achieved and that further actors are encouraged to follow suit.[27]

5. CONCLUSIONS

It appears that the preceding chapter overstated the consequences of legitimist thinking on IHL. Arguments it presented relate to political utility – and blame a certain type of normative theory in order to favour their use. What is more, it has left crucial questions open: what would be the response of a strictly legal formalist point of view to the problems surrounding the inclusion of non-state actors in the law-making process? It seems that IHL so far still does not take the increasing relevance of non-state actors appropriately into account.[28] Does formalism have its own – and a better – answer? Furthermore, the defence of a legal formalist view implies that it would be immune to hidden value judgments. But is that possible at all? And where does the justification for choosing a 'formal' approach come from? Or is legal positivism in itself enough? If so, why is that so?

Some points raised here sound Franckian and as such they are subject to critical legal realist objections. Certainly, such critique contributes to refining legitimacy criteria where they have their place in international law. This place is where sovereign will is otherwise unbound. After all, for the project of IHL, there is hardly anything as practical as a good theory.[29]

---

23 Gauthier de Beco, 'Compliance with International Humanitarian Law by Non-State Actors' (2005) 18 Journal of International Peace and Armed Conflict 190, 193.

24 cf Robert McCorquodale, 'An Inclusive International Legal System' (2004) 17 Leiden Journal of International Law 477; Marco Sassòli, 'Taking Armed Groups Seriously: Ways to Improve Their Compliance with International Humanitarian Law' (2010) 1 Journal of International Humanitarian Legal Studies 5, 20ff.

25 cf Andrew Clapham, *Human Rights Obligations of Non-State Actors* (OUP 2006) 28ff.

26 Nicolas Lamp, 'Conceptions of War and Paradigms of Compliance: The "New War" Challenge to International Humanitarian Law' (2011) 16 Journal of Conflict and Security Law 225.

27 Roberts and Sivakumaran (n 15) 107, 130ff.

28 See Veronika Bílková, 'Ensuring Human Security in Armed Conflicts: The Role of Non-State Actors and Its Reflection in Current International Humanitarian Law' in Cedric Ryngaert and Math Noortmann (eds), *Human Security and International Law* (Intersentia 2014) 29ff.

29 cf Anne Peters, 'There is Nothing More Practical than a Good Theory: An Overview of Contemporary Approaches to International Law' (2001) 44 German Yearbook of International Law 25, alluding to Kurt Lewin, 'Problems of Research in Social Psychology' in Dorwin Cartwright (ed), *Field Theory in Social Science: Selected Theoretical Papers* (Harper & Row 1951) 169.

4. Actor legitimacy and the application of IHL: A rejoinder to d'Aspremont

Tom Ruys[1]

1. INTRODUCTION

When opening any random textbook on the law of armed conflict or international humanitarian law (IHL), it rapidly dawns upon the reader that references to legitimacy are at once omnipresent in IHL, while IHL simultaneously maintains a deafening silence when it comes to considerations of legitimacy. First, IHL treatises are replete with the language of 'legitimacy'. Indeed, even if the actual treaties avoid this terminology, legal doctrine has spent considerable energy on identifying what qualifies as a '*legitimate* military objective' or a '*legitimate* target'.[2] Similar language is employed in military manuals around the globe.[3] Depending on how the term is defined, however, speaking of a 'legitimate' target or attack is something of a misnomer, inasmuch as the term is used to denote 'accordance with the law' or the quality of being *legal*, rather the distinct quality of being *just* or *reasonable*, e.g., on moral grounds.[4]

Leaving aside the concept of 'legitimate military objectives', more interesting for present purposes is the common portrayal of IHL as a body of law that is immune to legitimacy considerations. Nothing illustrates this better than the uncoupling of the *jus ad bellum* and the *jus in bello*. Indeed, IHL does not seek to take a stance in any purported battle between 'good or evil', or to distinguish aggressors from victims. Rather, it creates a level playing field in which both sides are equally allowed to engage in the status-based killing of enemy combatants, and

[1] The present chapter was completed in February 2018, with a minor update undertaken in July 2018 and October 2020.

[2] See, for instance Janina Dill, *Legitimate Targets? Social construction, International Law and US Bombing* (CUP 2015) 113ff.

[3] See, for instance, the manifold references to 'legitimate military objectives' or 'legitimate targets' in the US General Counsel of the Department of Defence, 'Law of War Manual' (June 2015, updated December 2016) <https://dod.defense.gov/Portals/1/Documents/pubs/DoD%20Law%20of%20War%20Manual%20-%20June%202015%20Updated%20Dec%202016.pdf?ver=2016-12-13-172036-190> accessed 31 January 2021.

[4] Thus, a drone strike that kills a high-level enemy combatant together with his five under-age children may well be in accordance with the law (inasmuch as the collateral damage is not excessive in comparison to the (expected) military advantage resulting from the target's elimination). Opinions are more likely to differ, however, as to whether it is also morally defensible.

where each is conversely equally bound by the obligation to respect those that are *hors de combat* – irrespective of the justness of their cause.[5] As Oppenheim put it in 1912:

> Whatever may be the cause of a war that has broken out, and whether or not the cause be a so-called just cause, the same rules of International Law are valid as to what must not be done, may be done, and must be done by the belligerents themselves in making war against each other (…)[6]

The same fundamental premise is enshrined in the preamble of the First Additional Protocol to the Geneva Conventions (AP I), where it is asserted that the provisions of the Geneva Conventions and of AP I must be fully applied 'in all circumstances (…) without any adverse distinction based on the nature or origin of the armed conflict or on the causes espoused by or attributed to the Parties to the conflict'. Underlying this premise is the understanding that the equal treatment of belligerent parties is an indispensable requirement to create a workable environment for IHL to apply and for both sides to have a reciprocal interest in complying.[7]

And yet, IHL's purported immunity to legitimacy considerations is partly a façade. Upon closer scrutiny, the development and application of IHL is indeed strongly driven by legitimacy concerns, particularly – as d'Aspremont rightly and eloquently points out – the issue of actor legitimacy. As d'Aspremont explains, these concerns play out at various levels, including, for instance, in the debate as to whether non-state armed groups can contribute to the formation and development of IHL. They also surface at the level of the applicability of IHL and the dichotomy between international armed conflicts (IACs) and non-international armed conflicts (NIACs). It is the latter aspect which forms the focus of this short comment.

2. IHL'S PURPORTED AVERSITY TO CONSIDERATIONS OF ACTOR LEGITIMACY

In the past, the impact of considerations of actor legitimacy on the scope of application of the laws of war was obvious, and existed not only in respect of NIACs, but also for certain IACs.

It is recalled that until the early 20th century, the law of nations was deemed to apply only to the family of so-called 'civilized' states, membership of which *inter alia* presupposed the express or tacit consent of the existing members of the club.[8] The same held true for the sub-domain of the laws of war. Thus, the British were amenable to applying the laws of war in their conflict with the South African Republics of the Transvaal and the Oranje Vrijstaat in the Boer War (1899–1902). European powers were, however, far less inclined to apply the laws of war during hostilities with African tribes in their scramble for Africa. Whether European

---

5 eg Yoram Dinstein, *The Conduct of Hostilities under the Law of International Armed Conflict* (3rd edn, CUP 2016) 4ff.

6 Lassa Oppenheim, *International Law: A Treatise. Vol. 2 War and Neutrality* (2nd edn, Longmans 1912) para 61.

7 In this sense, see eg Johanna Friman, *Revisiting the Concept of Defence in the Jus ad Bellum* (Hart 2017) 9 ('The *jus in bello* has in the past succeeded in curbing excesses, notwithstanding the pervasive animosity towards the enemy that is characteristic of any war, only because it has generated mutual advantages for both sides. The *jus in bello* therefore only has a chance of being respected if it applies independently of the breach of the *jus ad bellum* and if both sides are compelled to follow the same rules.').

8 Oppenheim (n 6) 26ff.

powers could make use of 'barbarous forces' and whether the latter were covered by the application of the laws of war was a point of dispute.[9]

A fortiori, as war was seen as a contention *between states* for purposes of overpowering the other,[10] *intra*-state conflicts – whether in the form of a small-scale 'rebellion' or rather an 'insurgency' involving more sustained, large-scale violence – were not governed by the laws of war, but by domestic (criminal) law only. This situation was different only in the case of a 'recognition of belligerency' by the *de jure* authorities. Such recognition could take place against the background of a state of general hostilities, when an armed group, possessing a quasi-governmental administration, had taken control over a substantial part of the territory. The decision to recognize the armed group as a belligerent[11] effectively brought into play the laws of war (including, *mutatis mutandis*, the rules on prisoners of war (POW) treatment) as between the belligerents. Yet, the decision ultimately remained a discretionary one. Thus, Sivakumaran explains how actual instances of recognition of belligerency on the part of parent states remained infrequent, since such recognition was considered 'a sign of (...) weakness' and likely to enhance the 'prestige' of the armed group.[12] Recognition proved forthcoming only when deemed advantageous by the parent state. The scarce and inconsistent practice is amply illustrated by the refusal to proceed to any recognition of belligerency during the Spanish Civil War (1936–39).

And yet, with one important exception (*namely* the situation of wars of national liberation – see *infra*), IHL is said to have moved beyond this subjective approach and to have become – in the words of d'Aspremont – 'averse to legitimacy as a mechanism determinative of the applicability of the rules of IHL'. Reliance on the notoriously difficult and controversial concept of 'war' as a trigger of the *jus in bello* has been replaced by the factual concept of 'armed conflict'. As far as IACs are concerned, the decolonization era has led to a universalization of the 'family of nations', implying that the application of the laws of war is no longer contingent upon the supposed 'civilized' nature of the opponent.[13] Nor is it contingent on the formal recognition of the enemy entity as a state, or of a particular regime as the government of the enemy state.[14] Thus, the fact that the Taliban regime had failed to gain recognition from the United States (US) (and from most of the international community) did not prevent the US intervention in Afghanistan in 2001 from triggering an IAC. In the words of Dinstein, '[a]s

[9] ibid 82.

[10] ibid 58ff.

[11] Note that when affected by a civil war, third states could similarly proceed to a recognition of belligerency, thus bringing into play the rules of neutrality law in their relations with the belligerents. Such recognition by a third state did not, however, affect the legal relationship between the belligerents themselves.

[12] Sandesh Sivakumaran, *The Law of Non-International Armed Conflict* (OUP 2012) 16 (with further references).

[13] Even if, rather anachronistically, art 38 (1) (c) ICJ Statute still refers to the 'general principles of law recognized by *civilized* nations' (emphasis added). Note that, even if a group's non-compliance with international humanitarian law does not prevent the coming into being of an 'armed conflict', non-compliance may still influence to what extent combatants will enjoy protection as prisoners of war upon capture. See eg Dinstein (n 5) 59ff.

[14] Dinstein (n 5) 37. See also the United States Law of War Manual 2015 (n 3) para 3.3.2.

long as the enemy satisfies objective criteria of statehood under international law, the armed conflict between the two Belligerent Parties would be characterized as inter-State.'[15]

Furthermore, as far as NIACs are concerned, Common Article 3 of the 1949 Geneva Conventions has seemingly put an end to the idea that states can refuse to acknowledge the application of the *jus in bello* to intra-state armed conflicts (by withholding recognition of belligerency) and choose to regard them as a matter of domestic law only. Instead, an NIAC automatically comes into existence when there is 'protracted armed violence between governmental authorities and organised armed groups or between such groups within a State'.[16] Case law – particularly that of the International Criminal Tribunal for the former Yugoslavia (ICTY) – and legal doctrine confirm that two objective, factual criteria are determinative for the existence of an NIAC, namely (1) the intensity of the violence, and (2) the degree of organization of the armed group or groups.[17] Indicators of intensity include, for example, the frequency of the acts of violence and military operations, the nature of the weapons used, the number of victims, etc.[18] Indicative elements to assess whether a non-state armed group possesses the required degree of organization include *inter alia* the existence of an organizational chart indicating a command structure, the ability to recruit and train new combatants.[19]

The sole[20] crack then in this supposedly factual and legitimacy-averse approach to the application of IHL pertains to the idea that, at least in respect of states that have ratified AP I, so-called wars of 'national liberation' – by peoples 'fighting against colonial domination and alien occupation and against racist regimes in the exercise of their right of self-determination' – are regarded as IACs rather than NIACs (Article 1(4) AP I). The implication is that members of the non-state armed group are endowed with the combatant privilege and cannot be prosecuted for mere participation in hostilities, but must instead be treated as POWs upon capture (assuming at least that they meet the – highly controversial[21] – requirements of Article 44 AP I). Clearly, the application of Article 1(4) AP I is dependent on a legitimacy ordeal. This view is further reinforced by the fact that it also requires a declaration by the group 'representing' the people concerned, to be submitted to (and accepted by?) the Swiss authorities (as depository of the treaty) (Article 96(3) AP I). As d'Aspremont observes, with the end of the colonial era, the exception appears to have lost some – if not most – of its relevance. It is telling indeed

---

15 Dinstein (n 5) 37.

16 *Prosecutor v. Tadić* (Appeals Chamber, Decision on Jurisdiction) ICTY-94-1 (2 October 1995) para 70.

17 See eg *Prosecutor v. Boskoski* (Trial Chamber, Judgment) ICTY-04-82 (10 July 2008) paras 175ff.; *Prosecutor v. Haradinaj* (Trial Chamber, Judgment) ICTY-04-84-T (3 April 2008) paras 49, 60.

18 Sylvain Vité, 'Typology of armed conflicts in international humanitarian law: legal concepts and actual situations' (2009) 91 International Review of the Red Cross 69, 76.

19 ibid 77.

20 Note that in his contribution, d'Aspremont draws attention to 'another possible exception to the legitimacy-free approach to the applicability of IHL (…) according to which the support which one foreign state may provide to insurgents – which is itself based on considerations pertaining to the legitimacy of those insurgents – leads to an internationalization of the conflict which would have otherwise remained of a non-international character'. However, under these (contested) approaches, it would seem to be the factual element, in particular the degree of state support to the non-state group, that determines the nature of the conflict (as an IAC or an NIAC), rather than actual considerations of actor legitimacy proper.

21 Further, see eg Dinstein (n 5) 61–64.

that the first – and so far only – successful declaration pursuant to Article 96(3) AP I was not submitted until 2015, and moreover pertains to an essentially dormant conflict (between the Polisario Front and the Kingdom of Morocco). With widespread sympathy for national liberation movements of the 1960s and 1970s long having made way for the post-9/11 obsession with the fight against terrorism, a revival of Article 1(4) AP I appears doubtful. In all, Article 1(4) AP I strikes as the exception that confirms the rule, namely that the application of IHL operates regardless of considerations of actor legitimacy.

Of course, the above, and greatly simplified, synopsis tells only part of the story. First, as to inter-state conflicts, for instance, it is far from clear that the criteria of statehood can indeed be regarded as exclusively 'objective' in nature. Such thesis *inter alia* rests on the – rather blunt – premise that recognition of statehood is purely 'declaratory' in nature only. Yet, as the legal limbo confronting a variety of *de facto* regimes, as well as, for instance, the temporary advance of the so-called 'Islamic State' illustrate, it is altogether difficult to maintain that the notion of statehood is itself completely immune to considerations of actor legitimacy.[22] Of course this is a general international law conundrum, rather than one that is IHL-specific. Still, the problem trickles through with respect to the application of IHL. Thus, the classification of a hypothetical armed conflict between the People's Republic of China and Taiwan, between Spain and Catalonia, or between Serbia and Kosovo (as an IAC or an NIAC) would inevitably raise questions as to the latter entities' status under general international law.

Second, while Common Article 3 and *Tadić* tell us that states cannot unilaterally deny the application of IHL within their territory by refusing to recognize the existence of an NIAC, this should not blind us from the fact that the discretion of the parent state has been abandoned in part only. This is so because IHL does not extend the combatant privilege and the concomitant POW protection to NIACs, but instead permits states to prosecute members of non-state armed groups pursuant to domestic criminal law (e.g., for treason, terrorist offences or murder) – irrespective of whether or not the individuals comply with the prescriptions of IHL. What is often overlooked today is that this is not how the application of IHL to NIACs was originally envisaged in the aftermath of the Second World War. The International Committee of the Red Cross (ICRC) 1948 'Stockholm draft' indeed foresaw that the Geneva Conventions would apply *in their entirety* to NIACs, thus extending the belligerent equality in IACs to (large-scale) NIACs.[23] The ICRC's position was supported by several states, including, among others, the US. The US agreed specifically that '[i]t was necessary that the *de jure* government should

---

22 Consider eg Martti Koskenniemi, *From Apology to Utopia* (CUP 2005) 272–82 (holding that neither the 'constitutive' nor the 'declaratory' approach to recognition can be consistently held). In the margin, note also the increasing emphasis on considerations of legitimacy for purposes of identifying the entity competent to invite outside military intervention on behalf of a state. Further, see eg Erika De Wet, 'The Modern Practice of Intervention by Invitation in Africa and its Implications for the Prohibition of the Use of Force' (2015) 26 European Journal of International Law 979.

23 '*Final Record of the Diplomatic Conference of Geneva of 1949*' vol II section B (Geneva, 26 April 1949), 47 (draft GC I), 61 (draft GC II), 73 (draft GC III), 113 (draft GC IV) <www.loc.gov/rr/frd/Military_Law/pdf/Dipl-Conf-1949-Final_Vol-2-B.pdf> accessed 31 January 2021. Note, however, that art 2 (4) of the draft POW Convention (GC III) and the draft Civilians Convention (GC IV) additionally introduced a reciprocity requirement: High Contracting Parties were bound to the latter Conventions in non-international armed conflict 'subject to the adverse party likewise acting in obedience thereto' (ibid 73, 113).

treat insurgents as regular combatants.'[24] At the same time, the US proposed that the Geneva Conventions apply to insurgencies/civil wars only if several cumulative criteria were met. For instance, the insurgents ought to exercise *de facto* authority over persons within a determinate territory and possess an organization purporting to have the characteristics of a state.[25] Some suggested that, in case of disagreement as to the existence of a full-scale civil war, the decision on the application of the Conventions should be left to the International Court of Justice (ICJ), or to an arbitrator or fact-finding body.[26] Other states dismissed the automatic granting of belligerent equality to insurgents, as this would 'strike at the heart of State sovereignty',[27] denying states the possibility to punish insurgents in accordance with their penal laws, and possibly '[inciting] political opponents to take up arms against a legitimate government'.[28] In the end, it was decided that only a minimum core of humanitarian provisions would apply to NIACs. At the same time, the scope of application of Common Article 3 was broadened to encompass all NIACs, instead of being limited to certain cases of full-scale civil war. As the Swiss delegation put it: 'half a loaf [was] better than no bread.'[29]

It is commonly accepted that the lack of belligerent equality in NIACs and the exposure of members of non-state armed groups to criminal prosecution (possibly involving capital punishment) upon capture for mere participation in hostilities hardly creates an incentive for such individuals to comply with IHL, and explains at least partly the all too widespread disregard for IHL in NIACs.[30] In spite hereof, a more modest proposal by Sweden to put captured combatants in NIACs 'on more equal footing' with POWs in IACs and to refrain from criminal prosecution 'only by reason of a person's taking part in hostilities',[31] was given short shrift during the 1974–77 Diplomatic Conference. The Pakistani delegate, for one, simply observed that in his country, 'insurgents would be executed, and any attempt to impose international legislation (…) would (…) constitute interference with the sovereign rights of States'.[32] In a similar vein, Nigeria held that 'a rebel was a criminal, and there could be no question of protecting criminals'.[33] All that states could agree upon was the inclusion of a provision that would merely *recommend* granting amnesty to persons that participated in the armed conflict at the close of hostilities.[34]

In conclusion, the equality of belligerents that is deemed essential to ensure compliance with IHL in IACs remains completely absent in NIACs. The reason for this fundamental divide between the two regimes remains tied to considerations of actor legitimacy, in par-

24 ibid 84.

25 ibid 12.

26 See eg ibid 45, 78 (Norway), 45–46 (United States), 122 (United Kingdom).

27 ibid 98ff, 121 (France).

28 ibid 10ff (Greece).

29 ibid 335.

30 But see, for a more critical appraisal: Frédéric Mégret, 'Response to Claus Kreβ: Leveraging the Privilege of Belligerency in Non-International Armed Conflict Towards Respect for the *Jus in Bello*' (2014) 96 International Review of the Red Cross 44.

31 *Official Records of the Diplomatic Conference on the Reaffirmation and Development of International Humanitarian Law Applicable in Armed Conflicts* vol IV (Geneva, 1947–1977) 35 <https://www.loc.gov/rr/frd/Military_Law/RC-dipl-conference-records.html> accessed 31 January 2021.

32 ibid vol VIII 360.

33 ibid vol XI 343.

34 See art 6 AP II to the Geneva Conventions.

ticular, the – often reiterated, yet contestable[35] – concern that according belligerent status to non-state armed groups will enhance their legitimacy (and might, for instance, lead their ranks to swell), as well as understandable concerns that it robs states of the 'stick' of criminal prosecution. During the 1949 Conference, the hope was uttered that 'if civil war developed considerable proportions, there would be an inclination on both sides to introduce, by special agreements, as many as possible of the provisions of the Convention.'[36] A fair number of such agreements have indeed been concluded in various NIACs.[37] Still, practice remains limited and inconsistent, as everything depends on the discretion of the *de jure* authorities. Meanwhile, the quest for a balanced solution that would lift that discretion in large-scale NIACs subject to certain requirements has regrettably been all but abandoned.[38]

3. ESTABLISHING NIACS: NOT A PURELY OBJECTIVE TEST AFTER ALL?

Whereas the abovementioned (and legitimacy-inspired) divide between IACs and NIACs is well known, considerations of actor legitimacy also operate in a less perceptible manner in the context of the determination of an NIAC. Indeed, as a modest complement to the analysis of d'Aspremont, it is observed that the twin requirements of 'intensity' and 'organization' may not be as inherently 'objective' – or may not necessarily be applied in such a strictly objective and factual manner – as we are invited to believe. The official story is that 'under international humanitarian law the motivation of organised groups involved in armed violence is not a criterion for determining the existence of an armed conflict'[39] – although an *individual*'s motive may well be relevant to determine whether they are engaging in 'direct participation in hostilities'.[40] Furthermore, the majority view seems to be that, while the non-state group's *ability*

---

35 See eg Olivier Bangerter, 'Reasons why Armed Groups Choose to Respect International Humanitarian Law' (2011) 93 International Review of the Red Cross 353, 378 (fn 99) (noting that agreements concluded between the Philippine and Sudanese governments and their NSAG adversaries have not brought about some magic change of status that would confer legitimacy on the armed group).

36 'Final Record of the Diplomatic Conference of Geneva of 1949' vol II, section B (n 23) 98 (UK).

37 For an insightful overview of relevant unilateral and parallel declarations as well as agreements, see Sivakumaran (n 12) 113ff.

38 For the author's own modest attempt to balance the competing interests, see Tom Ruys, 'The Syrian Civil War and the Achilles' Heel of the Law of Non-International Armed Conflict' (2014) 50 Stanford Journal of International Law 247, 270–80. See also: Claus Kreß, 'The Regulation of Non-International Armed Conflicts: Can a Privilege of Belligerency Be Envisioned in the Law of Non-international Armed Conflicts?' (2014) 96 International Review of the Red Cross 29.

39 ICRC, 'International Humanitarian Law and the Challenges of Contemporary Armed Conflicts' Report to the 31st International Conference of the Red Cross and Red Crescent (October 2011) 11 <https://www.icrc.org/en/doc/resources/documents/report/31-international-conference-ihl-challenges-report-2011-10-31.htm> accessed 31 January 2021. Also Sivakumaran (n 12) 182 ('The reasons that motivate the fighting are irrelevant insofar as the existence of a [NIAC] is concerned.').

40 See ICRC, 'Interpretive Guidance on the Notion of Direct Participation in Hostilities under International Humanitarian Law' (May 2009) 58ff (concerning the requirement of a 'belligerent nexus') <www.icrc.org/eng/assets/files/other/icrc-002-0990.pdf> accessed 31 January 2021.

to apply IHL is a crucial element in determining whether it possesses the required 'degree of organization', the question as to whether or not they *effectively do so* is not.[41]

And yet, we struggle at times to uphold such an objective approach in connection, for instance, with so-called 'criminal wars' or violence by 'terrorist' groups. As to the former category, the Mexican drug war is a case in point.[42] In the six years of the Calderón administration, drug-related violence in Mexico resulted in an estimated casualty figure of between 50,000 and 125,000.[43] The situation involved a number of highly organized cartels, such as Los Zetas or the Sinaloa cartel, possessing military-grade weaponry. It involved the deployment of over 6,000 federal troops. In spite of the foregoing, the Mexican authorities, while occasionally referring to the 'war on drugs', have refrained from recognizing the existence of an NIAC. The ICRC in turn has been reluctant to employ IHL terminology in relation to the situation in Mexico.[44] Nor, it would seem, has an NGO such as 'Geneva Call' sought to engage with any of the cartels to obtain IHL-related commitments. Geneva Call's website clarifies that it focuses on 'organized armed entities that are involved in armed conflict, which are primarily motivated by *political* goals (…)'.[45]

Interestingly, some authors have explicitly questioned whether IHL is indeed 'completely "blind"' with regard to subjective elements such as a group's motivation.[46] It has been stressed that groups that have no objective beyond making money, lack one or more of the indicia of 'organization' identified by the ICTY in the *Haradinaj* case[47] (even though these indicia must not be confused for cumulative preconditions). In particular, these groups allegedly do not 'possess the ability to define a unified military strategy and use military tactics'.[48] Alternatively, they are said to lack the capacity – or should one say interest? – 'to conclude agreements such as cease-fire or peace accords'.[49] Crawford similarly concludes that 'certain situations of armed violence (…) are perhaps best kept out of the framework of IHL'.[50] The suggestion that armed groups that lack clear 'political' goals cannot possess the required degree of organization nonetheless poses important practical problems and creates a slippery slope. Surely, it is not difficult to think of examples of NIACs involving armed rebel groups that were driven by and large by a desire for private gain, for example, in the form of access to a state's natural resources (such as diamonds or oil reserves) – just as kleptocratic and authoritarian regimes may turn to violence with the sole purpose of securing profitable access to the state's coffers. And what to think of non-state armed groups that partially fund their pursuits by profitable criminal activities, for example hostage-taking, narcotics trade, etc. – and where

---

41 Emily Crawford, *Identifying the Enemy: Civilian Participation in Armed Conflict* (OUP 2015) 179; Sivakumaran (n 12) 189.

42 For an excellent analysis of the Mexican war on drugs from a law of the armed conflict perspective see Emily Crawford (n 41) 180ff.

43 ibid 181.

44 See ibid 188.

45 ibid (emphasis added). See the website of 'Geneva Call' (1 July 2019) <https://genevacall.org/how-we-work/armed-non-state-actors/> accessed 31 January 2021.

46 Pierre Hauck and Sven Peterke, 'Organized Crime and Gang Violence in National and International Law' (2010) 92 International Review of the Red Cross 407, 433.

47 ibid; Emily Crawford (n 41) 185.

48 ibid.

49 Haradinaj (n 17) para 60; Emily Crawford (n 41) 185.

50 Emily Crawford (n 41) 189.

the thirst for profit gradually overtakes the original, supposedly more 'political', aims? In the end, in the case of a 'criminal war' such as Mexico's 'war on drugs', the question as to whether an NIAC exists can for all practical purposes remain unanswered as long as the state does not seek to trade the law-enforcement approach for the more flexible regime on the use of lethal force under IHL.[51] It follows that – absent an interest on the part of the *de jure* authorities, the non-state armed group(s) and third states to (partly) replace the human rights framework by an IHL framework – the question as to whether criminal wars can exceptionally amount to NIACs has remained an essentially theoretical one, with no authoritative answer as of yet in case law.

Yet, similar questions have arisen in the context of large-scale hostilities involving groups that are labelled as 'terrorist' groups by the international community or by individual states. What is more, these questions have not remained purely theoretical in nature, as recent case law of the Belgian courts, for instance, illustrates. This is due in part to the fact that several international counterterrorism instruments contain a carve-out from their scope of application in respect of '[t]he activities of armed forces during an armed conflict, as those terms are understood under international humanitarian law, which are governed by that law'. Such carve-outs can be found *inter alia* in the 1997 International Convention for the Suppression of Terrorist Bombings (Article 19(2)) or the 2005 Nuclear Terrorism Convention (Article 4(2)). They can also be found in European instruments such as the 2005 Council of Europe Convention on the Prevention of Terrorism (Article 26(5)) or EU Directive 2017/541 on combating terrorism.[52]

A similar clause has found its way into the Belgian Criminal Code (BCC). Articles 137–141ter of the Belgian Criminal Code identify a variety of 'terrorist offences' and concomitant penalties that can be imposed upon offenders, including offences consisting of recruiting, issuing propaganda or funding activities in support of a terrorist group. Echoing the abovementioned carve-outs, Article 141bis BCC clarifies that the provisions do not apply to 'acts of armed forces during an armed conflict as defined in, and governed by, international humanitarian law, nor to the acts of the armed forces of a State in the exercise of their official duties, inasmuch as these acts are governed by other provisions of international law'.

Interestingly, the precise impact of this carve-out was put before the Belgian courts in two separate sets of cases. The first set of cases pertained to a range of offences, including terrorist offences, committed by members of the so-called 'Sharia4Belgium' group, a radical Islamic group active within Belgium.[53] Several members of Sharia4Belgium had joined armed groups operating in Syria, specifically Jabhat Al-Nusra and Majlis Shura Al Mujahideen.

---

[51] According to Crawford (ibid), it 'seems unlikely that the Mexican government would publicly embrace such an approach, that the loss of dozens, if not hundreds of civilians' lives would be acceptable if it meant destroying a major cartel production facility'.

[52] European Parliament and Council Directive 2017/541 of 15 March 2017 on combating terrorism and replacing Council Framework Decision 2002/475/JHA [2017] OJ 31 L88/6, preamble, para 37 (copying the language used in Council Framework Decision 2002/475 on combating terrorism [2002] OJ L164/3, preamble, para 11). On the distinction between terrorist offences in the context of EU Directive 2017/541 and Framework Decision 2002/475/JHA, on the one hand, in the context of the EU restrictive measures on the other hand, see Case C-158/14 *Liberation Tigers of Tamil Eelam (LTTE)* ECLI:EU:C:2017:202 [2007] paras 76ff.

[53] See in particular: Antwerp Court of First Instance, Correctional Chambers, FD35.98.47-12 – AN35.F1.1809-12, Judgment of 11 February 2015; Antwerp Court of Appeal, Correctional Chambers, 2015/FP/1 – FD 35.9847-12, Judgment of 27 January 2016; Court of Cassation (Belgium), Nr. P.16.0244.N, Judgment of 24 May 2016.

Accordingly, one of the issues that came up during the proceedings was whether the latter groups ought to be regarded as 'armed forces as defined in international humanitarian law', and whether that meant that the carve-out of Article 141bis BCC was applicable. The second case concerned criminal charges for terrorist offences against more than 30 suspected members of the Kurdistan Worker's Party (PKK).[54]

While an in-depth analysis of the judgments is beyond the scope of this brief comment, the similarities and dissimilarities between the two cases is noteworthy. Both cases pay lip service to the twin requirements of 'intensity' and 'organization' and the non-cumulative indicia identified in the case law of the ICTY. At the same time, the brevity of the analysis of the court of first instance and of the Antwerp Court of Appeal in the *Sharia4Belgium* case is striking. Thus, both with respect to Majlis Shura Al Mujahideen and with regard to Jabhat Al Nusra, the Court of Appeal cursorily lists a number of elements that led it to conclude that neither group possesses the required degree of organization to qualify as an organized armed group under IHL. Several of those elements – for example the alleged lack of a command structure or an internal disciplinary system – are properly aligned with the ICTY case law, but are not substantiated in any meaningful way. Other elements, for example the fact that a group leader is only known by his *nom de guerre*, or that a group regularly posts messages on jihadist internet forums, appear unrelated to the various indicia identified by the ICTY. Still other elements seem to flatly contradict the Court's findings. Thus, the Court acknowledges that Jabhat Al Nusra constituted a 'major group of armed rebels that strive to establish a global Islamic state', and that the group was 'responsible for nearly 600 attacks'.[55] In particular as far as Al-Nusra is concerned, a group that has been able to count on several thousand members and that has exercised control over significant parts of Syrian territory,[56] the brevity of the Court's analysis is flabbergasting. A renowned scholar such as Gill finds little difficulty in asserting that Al Nusra was 'sufficiently organized and in control of a significant enough portion of Syrian territory to be seen as a party in its own right'.[57] In all, it is difficult to escape the conclusion that the Court's position was inspired less by a meticulous application of established factual and objective indicia, as found in the case law of the ICTY, but more so by the subjective, and legitimacy-inspired, considerations surfacing in the surrounding paragraphs. Both the court of first instance and the Court of Appeal indeed place considerable and repeated emphasis on the fact that Majlis Shura Al Mujahideen and Jabhat al Nusra belonged to 'the international terrorist network of Al Qaeda, and [conducted] a sectarian violent struggle against Shiites, infidels, democratic values, human rights and humanitarian law'.[58] It was stressed moreover that, apart from conducting 'armed missions against the government army of the Syrian president Bashar

---

54 See in particular: Brussels Court of Appeal, *Chambre des mises en accusation*, Judgment of 14 September 2017.

55 Antwerp Court of Appeal, Correctional Chambers, 2015/FP/1 – FD 35.9847-12, Judgment of 27 January 2016, 53–54 (author's translation).

56 eg Erika Solomon, 'Fighters Flock Back to Resurgent al-Nusra' *Financial Times* (London, 30 March 2015) <https://www.ft.com/content/b0cc7652-d61b-11e4-b3e7-00144feab7de> accessed 31 January 2021.

57 Terry D. Gill, 'Classifying the Conflict in Syria' (2016) 92 International Law Studies 353, 374.

58 Antwerp Court of Appeal, Correctional Chambers, 2015/FP/1 – FD 35.9847-12, Judgment of 27 January 2016 para 37 (author's translation); Antwerp Court of First Instance, Correctional Chambers, FD35.98.47-12 – AN35.F1.1809-12, Judgment of 11 February 2015, F36–F38.

Al Assad', they were 'engaged in terrorist activities (decapitations, suicide attacks, sectarian murders, torture and large-scale looting), destabilizing the region and creating unrest with the civilian population'.[59] Several passages suggest that the courts were more concerned with the groups' lack of effective compliance with IHL, rather than with their *ability* to comply with IHL.[60]

In the end, it is difficult to escape the impression that, notwithstanding the explicit references to the case law of the ICTY and the acknowledgment that the ICTY indicia are not cumulative in nature,[61] the Belgian courts were adamant not to apply the carve-out of Article 141bis of the Criminal Code to a group lacking a legitimate cause and employing the most reprehensible of tactics. Understandably, Belgian courts were unwilling to create a loophole that would impede the effective criminal prosecution of so-called 'foreign terrorist fighters', save in respect of acts committed on Belgian soil and constituting criminal offences in their own right,[62] and save in respect of possible war crimes committed abroad.[63] Whether it is a wise, let alone convincing, way of construing said provision appears doubtful. Belgian courts may not have been fully cognizant of the ramifications of their findings under IHL. It seems unlikely indeed that they intended to suggest that the use of lethal force against Al Nusra fighters in Syria would be governed by human rights standards, rather than by IHL standards – all the more since Belgian F-16s have been actively involved in operation 'Inherent Resolve', which has occasionally conducted air strikes against Al Nusra.

In the *PKK* case, the Brussels Court of Appeal in a judgment dated 14 September 2017 held that Article 141bis BCC did apply to members of the PKK. As a result, various acts committed within Belgian territory, such as the spreading of propaganda and securing funding for the PKK, did not qualify as a criminal offence in the sense of Article 137 of the Criminal Code.[64] The PKK ruling (unsurprisingly) infuriated Ankara.[65] It moreover appeared to depart from

---

[59] Antwerp Court of Appeal, Correctional Chambers, 2015/FP/1 – FD 35.9847-12, Judgment of 27 January 2016 para 37 (author's translation). See also ibid 38 (referring to the groups' 'violent armed struggle against all infidels, against democracy, against human rights and humanitarian law').

[60] For a critique of the Sharia4Belgium judgments, see eg Rogier Bartels, 'Terrorist Groups as Parties to an Armed Conflict' (2016) 47 Collegium – Proceedings of the Bruges Colloquium 65 (finding 'an unjustifiably strict application of the ICTY factors and indicators, in which the Court of Appeal required all of them to be fulfilled (…)').

[61] Antwerp Court of Appeal, Correctional Chambers, 2015/FP/1 – FD 35.9847-12, Judgment of 27 January 2016 para 36.

[62] The judgment of the Court of Appeal notes that art 141bis BCC could not in any case be invoked in respect of criminal offences conducted on Belgian soil, since there was no 'armed conflict' within Belgium, cf ibid 33 (author's translation).

[63] Note that, for various reasons, for example the availability of evidence, it may be far more difficult for prosecutorial services to prove an individual's involvement in the commission of a war crime than to prove the commission of certain terrorist offences, such as recruiting, issuing propaganda or funding activities in support of a terrorist group.

[64] Brussels Court of Appeal, *Chambre des mises en accusation*, Judgment of 14 September 2017, 17. Note that the Court does indicate that if the persons would have, for instance, committed terrorist attacks on Belgian soil, such acts would have been covered by the provisions on terrorist offences in the Criminal Code. In turn, 'terrorist acts' committed in the context of an armed conflict and within the zone of actual hostilities would be regarded as possible war crimes, rather than as terrorist offences. ibid 16.

[65] eg 'Turkey rebukes Belgium over "unacceptable" court ruling on PKK' *Hürriyet Daily News* (Ankara, 15 September 2017) <https://www.hurriyetdailynews.com/turkey-rebukes-belgium-over-unacceptable-court-ruling-on-pkk-118030> accessed 31 January 2021.

earlier rulings of other national courts in Europe qualifying the PKK as a terrorist group (and contrasts to the inclusion of the PKK on the EU terrorist list[66]). Still, from an IHL perspective, the ruling was better substantiated and more convincing than the *Sharia4Belgium* ruling – even though this did not prevent the Belgian Court of Cassation from subsequently annulling the judgment for lack of adequate reasoning[67] – only to be reaffirmed by the Court of Appeals in a subsequent judgment dated 8 March 2019.[68]

In concluding that the hostilities between the HPG (the PKK's military wing) and the Turkish authorities qualify as an 'armed conflict' under IHL, the Court of Appeal in its 2017 judgment relied on a variety of elements that are clearly linked to the ICTY indicia, including for instance: the number of HPG fighters (between 3,000 and 5,000, down from possibly 50,000 in the 1990s); the number of casualties (40,000 since 1984) and the damage caused (including the destruction of more than 3,000 Kurdish villages); the intensity of the hostilities and the type of weaponry used (ground and aerial offensives by the Turkish army, use of heavy weaponry by the HPG); the use of uniforms; the HPG's complex command structure; the HPG's adoption of codes of conduct, commitment to comply with IHL, and its system of courts; the PKK's involvement in peace negotiations; the existence of training camps, etc.[69]

While the aforementioned elements might have been deemed sufficient to decide on the existence of protracted armed violence between a state and an organized armed group in the *Tadić* sense, more subjective elements, linked to the perceived (il)legitimacy of the PKK, also surface throughout the ruling. First, the public prosecution service, which on behalf of the Belgian government opposed the application of Article 141bis to the PKK, explicitly questioned the representative nature of the group:

> [T]he PKK (…) [counts between] 3,000 and 5,000 fighters. (…) According to the public prosecution service the militant PKK guerrilla accordingly represents barely 0,03% of the Turkish-Kurdish population in Turkey and barely 0,01% of the total Kurdish population in the region called Kurdistan. Accordingly, the public prosecution service finds that the PKK cannot be regarded as representative for the Kurdish question or as the legitimate representation of a people that would be in conflict with a state (…).[70]

And while the Court's own focus rests primarily with the factual parameters relating to 'intensity' and 'organization', in another striking passage the Court notes how 'the goal of the PKK

---

66 The Council of the European Union, 'EU Terrorist List' <https://www.consilium.europa.eu/en/policies/fight-against-terrorism/terrorist-list/> accessed 31 January 2021.

67 Court of Cassation, 13 February 2018, P.17.1023.N/1. In spite of the elaborate reasoning of the Court of Appeals with respect to the intensity of the conflict and the degree of organization of the PKK, the Court of Cassation (incomprehensibly) finds that the Court of Appeals failed to answer the argument of the public prosecutor 'that, as a non-State actor, the PKK is not subject to humanitarian law' (author's translation), and fails to explain how it concludes from the factual findings 'that the PKK is effectively subject to international humanitarian law' (author's translation). The position of the Court of Cassation is difficult to reconcile with the actual content of the ruling of the Court of Appeal and, more generally, with international humanitarian law.

68 Brussels Court of Appeal, *Chambre des mises en accusation*, Judgment 2019/939 of 14 September 2019.

69 Brussels Court of Appeal, *Chambre des mises en accusation*, Judgment of 14 September 2017, 13ff.

70 ibid 13 (author's translation).

does not consist of terrorizing the population but to establish an independent State, based on a Marxist-Leninist state theory and party model. It desires a free population (…) Civilians are no targets of the HPG, even if hostilities also result in civilian casualties.'[71]

Finally, a substantial part of the judgment is devoted to possible ties between the PKK/HPG and the 'Kurdistan Freedom Hawks' (TAK), a group that 'deliberately conducts terror attacks, including suicide attacks, whereby the killing of innocent civilians and children is accepted'.[72] Curiously, the underlying rationale appears to be that possible ties with such organization – which the Court ultimately found were not sufficiently proven – could somehow exclude the application of Article 141bis. Such argument, however, is difficult to reconcile with the ICTY's approach and/or with the idea that it is the group's *ability* to comply with IHL, rather than its *actual compliance*, that is relevant for purposes of determining the existence of an NIAC.[73]

In the end, both the *Sharia4Belgium* case and the *PKK* case reveal, in opposite directions, how considerations of actor legitimacy still influence appraisals concerning the application of IHL (and, in parallel, the application of counterterrorism instruments).

4. CONCLUSION

The present comment has sought to complement and further nuance d'Aspremont's observations pertaining to the purportedly legitimacy-averse nature of IHL. Especially in the context of debates over the applicability of IHL, claims that considerations of actor legitimacy play no role whatsoever must be taken with a grain of salt.

On a final note, the author subscribes to d'Aspremont's observation that there has overall been little appetite to directly challenge the legitimacy of IHL in itself. Indeed, notwithstanding fundamental changes in the way in which armed conflicts are being fought (with the advance of asymmetric and guerrilla warfare), IHL remains firmly entrenched as *the* legal framework against which the conduct of hostilities and the treatment of persons *hors combat* is tested and judged. As observed by d'Aspremont, IHL is often mobilized to legitimize or de-legitimize the behaviour of the warring parties. While it would go too far to say that this (de-)legitimizing function constitutes IHL's *raison d'être*, the centrality of IHL in the justificatory discourse at the national and international level undeniably constitutes a key component of its compliance pull.

The ICRC's 2016 'people on war' survey largely confirms IHL's resilience in the changing landscape of modern warfare.[74] Thus, 70 years after the adoption of the 1949 Geneva Conventions, a large majority continues to agree that it makes sense to impose legal limitations on war through IHL.[75] At the same time, and leaving aside its methodological underpinning

---

71 ibid 16.

72 ibid 19.

73 The subsequent judgment of the Brussels Court of Appeal of 14 September 2019, adopted after the annulment of the first judgment by the Court of Cassation, nonetheless explicitly affirms that the proper criterion is the 'capacity' to comply with IHL, rather than effective compliance. Brussels Court of Appeal, *Chambre des mises en accusation*, Judgment 2019/939 of 14 September 2019, 22.

74 ICRC, 'People on War: Perspectives from 16 Countries' (5 December 2016) 16 <www.icrc.org/en/document/people-on-war> accessed 31 January 2021.

75 ibid 7.

(or lack thereof), the survey does reveal a more worrisome trend, when compared to a similar survey conducted in 1999. There has, for instance, been a rather striking increase in the percentage of persons that agrees that a captured enemy combatant can be tortured to obtain important military information (from 28% to 36%). Conversely, opposition to attacks against populated areas that are likely to result in substantial civilian casualties has decreased considerably (from 68% to 59%).

It is beyond the aim of this short chapter to broach the possible explanations for this disturbing trend. The present author would, however, agree with d'Aspremont that IHL's relevance as the yardstick for evaluating the conduct of the actors engaged in armed conflict (and, with it, IHL's legitimacy as a body of law) is hardly being served by legal scholars' 'pathological obsession for taxonomies' and the 'constant quest for sophistication'. Whereas IHL derives its strength from the fundamental and universal principles of distinction, proportionality and humanity, IHL experts have for too long been bogged down in a trench war over classification questions concerning both the typology of armed conflicts and the status of individuals as civilians or (lawful or unprivileged) combatants. For IHL as a body of law to retain the unassailable legitimacy it has so long enjoyed, these questions must eventually be laid to rest, even if – more than 40 years after the adoption of the Additional Protocols – that may eventually require a new codification round.

PART III

Informal law-making in international humanitarian law as a political choice

5. Global norms governing the protection of civilians, conflict, and weapons: Formal or informal law-making?

Denise Garcia

1. INTRODUCTION

The questions raised in this book relate to the profound transformation international law has undergone this century and, ultimately, how international law may protect civilians caught in the worst conflicts of our time. This question is particularly relevant in areas where states cannot provide security to their citizens and the rule of law has broken down (such as in the eastern area of the Democratic Republic of the Congo) or new forms of security are illegitimate vis-à-vis the eyes of the local population or to the international community.

In this chapter, I will consider the circumstances under which states conclude new treaties to regulate armed conflict. Alongside this discussion, I will examine why and in which contexts states are interested in, and willing to conclude, treaties specifically within the realm of international humanitarian law (IHL), including weapons law. The arguments developed here seek to shed light on whether the more general discourse surrounding 'stagnation of international law' is applicable within the field of IHL. In light of this important framework, I will investigate the extent to which the 'turn to informality' has reached the realms of IHL. More broadly, I will consider the conditions under which issues are regulated by treaty and the areas where informal means of law-making are more prevalent. Finally, I seek to explore situations whereby states try to avoid any form of regulation at all.

These questions are all the more timely in light of the contemporary challenges IHL faces as a result of increasing complexity surrounding the nature of conflict and its dramatic humanitarian consequences. There are five major challenges that I contend are worth addressing in order to initially understand why states may turn to informal instruments of law-making – the central question this book attempts to illuminate.

The first challenge relates to the idea that IHL as a body of law is insufficient. In this sense, two questions are relevant: is IHL sufficient to protect civilians within the existing dizzying mosaic of different intra-state conflicts where fewer IHL rules apply than those which exist to address international armed conflict? Is existing IHL sufficient to address new challenges: new actors participating in conflict which use new technologies not yet explicitly regulated by international law? This sense of 'insufficiency' surrounding the existing law may lead states to turn to informal instruments in an attempt to remedy mounting problems. Second, the increasing intricacy of conflict situations – that almost all are non-international in character though comprise transnational dimensions and usually take place within densely populated civilian areas – may bear on the need for new law-making especially in two situations: (1) when there exists an extraterritorial use of force involving targeted killings; and (2) where one of the warring parties is a non-state armed group and labelled as a 'terrorist' group. In these circumstances, states may feel it is less necessary to abide by IHL (as often there is no consensus on whether violence is characterized as a non-international conflict) or to enable access to humanitarian provision. Typically, such situations would fall under a law-enforcement paradigm and therefore under human rights law. Along the same lines and as a result, there is a conflation in the nonobservance of IHL and human rights law. The relationship between IHL and human rights law may be useful for filling gaps in the rules that are much needed in the law-making surrounding internal armed conflict. Given the intricacies of applying a joint IHL–human rights law paradigm, states may opt to do so through informal means of law-making. This would be a new way to try to remedy intractable conflict in which vulnerable populations need protection. In other words, conflict situations are no longer clear-cut: there is an overlap between law enforcement situations and non-international armed conflict – informal law-making may enable states to fill in the gaps in order to protect the civilian population.[1] Third, in today's conflicts, non-state armed groups operate in densely populated civilian areas. Governments and non-state groups often target civilians with arguably excessive force (sometimes including the use of prohibited weapons) and without proper observance of the rules of proportionality (as demonstrated by the Syrian conflict). Such actions hinder the ability of IHL and aid groups to provide humanitarian relief and gain access to vulnerable populations caught in the conflict. Given the mounting situations where such challenges occur, states may turn to informal arrangements to remedy humanitarian emergencies and to counter the reality that IHL is failing to protect civilians.

The fourth challenge that may give rise to new (informal) law-making is the use of new technologies, many operated in the cyber domain, which is outpacing the capacity of international law and IHL to set rules of behaviour. Are new rules needed here? It is not yet clear how international law will apply to these emerging threats or whether existing global governance structures will be sufficient. The capacity to launch cyberattacks and use remote-controlled weapons systems and the possible development of lethal autonomous robots or autonomous weapons systems – known as killer robots – raise numerous critical questions for scholars and policymakers. In the case of cyberattacks, it will be necessary to determine exactly what constitutes an attack, if such an attack should be classified as an armed attack according to IHL, and how to distinguish between civilian and military infrastructure. While some say that these interconnected issues have not created a gaping legal hole or a new legal crisis, and that existing international law may suffice to deal with such situations, there are certainly questions that still need to be addressed. Cyberspace is digitized, which allows for greater anonymity, thus complicating the attribution of conduct. As the ability to enforce IHL depends on attribution of responsibility, if a perpetrator cannot be identified it is not clear how IHL can be applied.[2]

---

1 Kenneth Watkin, 'Controlling the Use of Force: A Role for Human Rights Norms in Contemporary Armed Conflict' (2004) 98 American Journal of International Law 1.

2 Gwendelynn Bills, 'LAWS unto Themselves: Controlling the Development and Use of Lethal Autonomous Weapons Systems' (2014) 83 George Washington Law Review 176; Daniel N. Hammond, 'Autonomous Weapons and the Problem of State Accountability' (2015) 15 Chicago Journal of International Law 652.

Thus an understanding must be reached regarding the level of attribution needed under the law. Remote-controlled weapons and cyberwarfare raise legal questions surrounding who would be considered the attacker in such circumstances and what constitutes a battlefield. Lethal autonomous robots give rise to many legal and ethical concerns that need to be addressed. It is not clear who can be held responsible for attacks by robots, for example, as one cannot hold a robot itself responsible. The programming of such robots raises concerns, as there needs to be agreement regarding the type of instructions they can receive. The international community additionally needs to decide if existing law allows for the replacement of human discretion in the decision to kill with programmed responses, and if so, under which circumstances.[3]

In sum, as technology is fast outpacing existing international law, states may opt for 'faster' approaches to law-making, i.e., engaging informal legal remedies rather than formal mechanisms, especially in areas which involve consensus. Many of the new complexities also necessitate the involvement of new actors, including those which are beyond the state. It is critical to determine how existing branches of international law apply to protect civilians from harm,[4] and whether regulation which currently exists is sufficient to address the challenges posed by the development of new weapons and technologies.[5] Some authors affirm that existing frameworks are in principle sufficient.[6] In addition, the fact that a particular means or method of warfare is not specifically regulated does not mean that it can be used without restriction.[7] This does not, however, mean that laws cannot be strengthened or that new laws do not need to be created in order to address future arms development and technologies.[8] The question of how to create governance frameworks which sufficiently take into account new technological developments within the domain of warfare, formal or informal, is not without complexity.

The fifth challenge relates to the view that global compliance is faltering or a sense that the 'toolbox' for the compliance with global IHL rules is uncertain and needs to be updated; this position comes alongside news of increasing violations of IHL across conflicts that are unacceptable to the conscience of humanity. Such uncertainties give rise to multiple pressing questions regarding international law in general and to IHL (and its increasingly complex relationship with human rights law) in particular. These uncertainties have to be understood in the broader context of the evolution of international law. To examine these challenges to law-making today, it is worth taking a look at how the world found itself with the current

---

3 Denise Garcia, 'Future Arms, Technologies, and International Law: Preventive Security Governance' (2016) 1 European Journal of International Security 94.

4 Kenneth Anderson, Daniel Reisner and Matthew Waxman, 'Adapting the Law of Armed Conflict to Autonomous Weapon Systems' (2014) 90 International Law Studies 386.

5 ICRC, 'International Humanitarian Law and the Challenges of Contemporary Armed Conflicts' (31 October 2011) <https://www.icrc.org/eng/assets/files/red-cross-crescent-movement/31st-international-conference/31-int-conference-ihl-challenges-report-11-5-1-2-en.pdf> accessed 31 January 2021.

6 Matthew Waxman and Kenneth Anderson, 'Law and Ethics for Autonomous Weapon Systems: Why a Ban Won't Work and How the Laws of War Can' (13 April 2013) Stanford University, The Hoover Institution (Jean Perkins Task Force on National Security and Law Essay Series) (2013), American University WCL Research Paper 2013-11, Columbia Public Law Research Paper 13-351 <https://ssrn.com/abstract=2250126> accessed 31 January 2021.

7 Sarah Kreps and John Kaag, 'The Use of Unmanned Aerial Vehicles in Asymmetric Conflict: Legal and Moral Implications' (2012) 44 Polity 260.

8 Marco Sassoli, 'Autonomous Weapons and International Humanitarian Law: Advantages, Open Technical Questions and Legal Issues to be Clarified' (2014) 90 International Law Studies 308.

global normative order based upon treaties and formal processes. Following this discussion, I will further reflect on the extent to which law-making is being challenged by pressing complexities and in turn favouring quicker law-making approaches that involve non-treaty making and require the presence of new actors.

2. THE FORMAL TREATY-BASED NORMATIVE ORDER: FOUNDATIONAL HUMANITARIAN NORMS

Without a doubt we live in an era where moral and ethical progress can be seen through centuries of formation of commonly agreed global norms of behaviour among states through formal treaty-making initiatives. Some behaviours that were once considered normal, such as piracy, torture, slavery, and imperial annexation, are now prohibited under international law.

The origins of international law can be traced back to two motivations and desires that drove state behaviour: (1) the regulation of states' long-distance communications and transportation networks across the seas, and (2) the regulation of unacceptable behaviour during war. The first regulations regarding freedom of the seas rose during the 17th century and the first multilateral regulations vis-à-vis the global governance of telecommunications and postal services appeared around 1865, with the formation of the International Telecommunications Union in Geneva. The establishment of the Universal Postal Union took place in 1874, also in Switzerland, but this time, in the capital, Bern. Concomitantly, also in Switzerland, the International Committee of the Red Cross (ICRC) was created in 1864. This simultaneous historic development marks the establishment of an organization of international character that oversaw the creation of the first multilateral constraints on the waging of war.

Two different desires then motivated states at the onset of the creation of international law: one was spurred by a logistical motivation to coordinate movement and communications flows. The other was an aspiration to create standards of legitimacy regarding actions committed during war aimed at reducing the horrors of conflict: for example the requirement to care for sick and wounded military personnel, regardless of nationality, and the recognition of the neutrality of medical personnel, hospitals, and ambulances.

The modest 'coordination' origins of international law were advanced a few decades later through the creation of the United Nations (UN) in 1945. This crucial episode in the history of humanity created the essential framework for peace and security that spawned new global norms for further restrictions on war and, in particular, for the humane treatment of the human being. The UN Charter, international law's foundation treaty in international law, contains the first mentions of 'human rights'. The UN Charter therefore contains some of the most fundamental new norms: the prohibition of the use of force; establishing the UN Security Council (UNSC) as the chief arbiter of peace and security (transforming international relations from being purely coordinating in nature to acquiring a subordination nature); and setting the initial contours for the protection of the dignity of the human being as being a basis for peace and prosperity in the world. This new legal framework gave rise to the 1948 Universal Declaration of Human Rights (UDHR) and the 1949 Geneva Conventions. These developments heralded a new era for humanity, now under the certainty and predictability of international law. It is noteworthy how further refinements in IHL brought by the Geneva Conventions coincided with the consolidation of the importance of the protections of human rights as a normative framework. It is worth exploring what this means and the significance of these contemporaneous developments.

A few years later, the 1966 International Covenant on Civil and Political Rights (ICCPR)[9] and the International Covenant on Economic, Social and Cultural Rights[10] furnished the legal codification of all human rights provisions initially contained in the UDHR that only had hortatory force. The implementation of IHL laid dormant until the Vietnam War provided the horrific shock necessary for political action. A conference convened in Tehran, under the auspices of the UN in 1968, provided the impetus for further regulation of internal conflicts with a resolution titled 'Human rights in armed conflicts', which requested that the General Assembly examine concrete ways to apply the Geneva Conventions to all armed conflicts.[11] As a result, the UN General Assembly adopted Resolution 2444 (XXIII) on 'Respect for human rights in armed conflicts'.[12] This combination of IHL and human rights law concerns paved the way for diplomatic conferences, under the sponsorship of the ICRC, which led to the 1977 Protocols.[13] These developments contributed to further regulation of the protection of civilians in war which used Common Article 3 of the Geneva Conventions as its basis.[14] This evolution solidified IHL as a central concern for the international community ever since.

The UNSC played an essential role in advancing IHL, also in its relationship with human rights law, a fact that is not often noted. It did so in two ways: (1) by considering large-scale human rights violations and resulting humanitarian tragedies as threats to peace and security through the adoption of legally binding resolutions; and (2) by establishing two ad hoc tribunals, the International Criminal Tribunal for the Former Yugoslavia (ICTY) and the International Criminal Tribunal for Rwanda. The UN has also been involved with the Special Court for Sierra Leone and the Extraordinary Chambers in the Courts of Cambodia, amongst others. The Security Council's first resolution 688, issued in 1991, in regards to the Kurds in Northern Iraq and explicitly referred to destabilization caused by flows of refugees as threats to international peace and security.[15] The Council's second resolution was 770 issued on 13 August 1992 in relation to the deteriorating situation in Bosnia-Herzegovina, based upon Chapter VII, which called upon all states to facilitate the delivery of humanitarian aid.[16] Several such resolutions followed on Somalia, Kosovo, Rwanda, Haiti, and Albania. Those

---

9 International Covenant on Civil and Political Rights (adopted 16 December 1966, entered into force 23 March 1976) 999 UNTS 171 (ICCPR).

10 International Covenant on Economic, Social and Cultural Rights (adopted 16 December 1966, entered into force 3 January 1976) 993 UNTS 3 (ICESCR).

11 International Conference on Human Rights, 'Res. XXIII on human rights in armed conflicts' (12 May 1968), UN Doc A/Conf.32/41.

12 Respect for human rights in armed conflicts, UNGA Res 2444 (XXIII) (19 December 1968) UN Doc A/RES/2444.

13 Protocol Additional to the Geneva Conventions of 12 August 1949, and Relating to the Protection of Victims of International Armed Conflicts (Protocol I) of 8 June 1977 (adopted 8 June 1977, entered into force on 7 December 1978) 1125 UNTS 3 and Protocol Additional to the Geneva Conventions of 12 August 1949, and Relating to the Protection of Victims of Non-International Armed Conflicts (Protocol II) of 8 June 1977 (adopted 8 June 1977, entered into force on 7 December 1978) 1125 UNTS 609.

14 Dietrich Schindler, 'International Humanitarian Law: Its Remarkable Development and its Persistent Violation' (2003) 5 Journal of the History of International Law 165.

15 UNSC Res 688 (5 April 1991) UN Doc S/RES/688.

16 UNSC Res 770 (13 August 1992) UN Doc S/Res/770.

relating to East Timor and Sierra Leone in 1999 authorized the use of force for humanitarian purposes.[17]

Seventy years into this formal treaty-based normative order, with its intense codification of global norms, there remain urgent challenges and complexities which need to be addressed. How to best protect the dignity of the individual from atrocities of the worst kind and to respond to disrespect of global norms of humanity remain of primary concern. It is uncertain whether or not states can tackle these problems with the historic treaty-making approach; whether they will also opt for informal methods of law-making; or whether they will privilege law-making in certain areas and interpret such alongside existing law and incorporate other branches of international law.

3. INITIAL EXPLANATIONS TO INFORMAL LAW-MAKING

International law has evolved in the last 70 years to include and privilege the individual as a subject with rights and obligations, i.e., individuals can appear in international courts and can be held accountable for their behaviour or claim compensation for wrongdoing. The individual has progressively gained legal personality. This development signifies a departure from the origins of international law, which premised the state as the sole actor and the only subject of legal rights and duties. With this premise in mind, undoubtedly, individuals who are part of non-state armed groups carry rights and responsibilities under international law.

The complexity of the application of a legal framework to such responsibilities may lead states to adopt informal approaches to codification that would typically require states to choose: will they apply a strict IHL paradigm? Or will they seek out creative ways to integrate the increasing interplay between IHL and human rights law? The ICJ has held that human rights law is applicable in situations of conflict: 'The Court observes that the protection of the International Covenant on Civil and Political Rights does not cease in times of war, except by operation of Article 4 of the Covenant whereby certain provisions may be derogated from in a time of national emergency.'[18] There is increasing acceptance that armed non-state actors are also bound by at least customary norms of international human rights law.

---

[17] See for the Res, Schindler (n 14) 165, 175.

[18] *Legality of the Threat or Use of Nuclear Weapons* (Advisory Opinion) [1996] ICJ Rep 226 para 25. cf the right to life: according to art 6 ICCPR: 'Every human being has the inherent right to life. This right shall be protected by law. No one shall be arbitrarily deprived of his life.' The rights to liberty and security: according to art 9 of the ICCPR: '1. Everyone has the right to liberty and security of person. 2. Anyone who is arrested shall be informed, at the time of arrest, of the reasons for his arrest and shall be promptly informed of any charges against him. 3. Anyone arrested or detained on a criminal charge shall be brought promptly before a judge or other officer authorized by law to exercise judicial power and shall be entitled to trial within a reasonable time or to release.' The prohibition of torture: according to art 7 of the ICCPR: 'No one shall be subjected to torture or to cruel, inhuman or degrading treatment or punishment.' According to art 2 of the UN Convention against Torture and Other Cruel, Inhuman or Degrading Treatment or Punishment: '1. Each State Party shall take effective legislative, administrative, judicial or other measures to prevent acts of torture in any territory under its jurisdiction. 2. No exceptional circumstances whatsoever, whether a state of war or a threat of war, internal political instability or any other public emergency, may be invoked as a justification of torture. 3. An order from a superior officer or a public authority may not be invoked as a justification of torture.'

However, the way in which international institutions are set up, with the ICRC as the guardian of IHL and the UN system overseeing human rights law, poses institutional challenges to law-making. Reflecting on these challenges, it is important to bear in mind that an increasing reliance on customary international law may explain the lack of development of any new IHL treaties. This fact is notable alongside the increasing prominence of the legal personality of individuals, including their legal responsibility within non-international armed conflicts, and the way in which certain norms codified in treaties have historically been considered *jus cogens*. The result is that these norms rank noticeably higher in the order of global norms and therefore cannot be ignored or derogated from. In this sense, it is important to note the effects such norms have on the behaviour of actors in situations of conflict.[19] One notable *jus cogens* norm is the prohibition of hostilities directed at civilian populations.[20] It is worth considering the effects these developments will have on law-making.

Individuals are duty-bound to respect such global norms regardless of whether or not their state or non-state armed group has acquiesced to a particular treaty.[21] This understanding has found favour in interpretations of the following: Common Article 3 to the Geneva Conventions, which confers obligations to all parties to a conflict; UNSC resolutions which call upon non-state armed groups to respect international law and protect civilians (S/2012/376);[22] and the ICJ, which has held that states and recipients may be in breach of international obligations when furnishing weapons to non-state armed groups.[23] If a prime area of concern for new treaties in IHL, namely the prohibition of hostilities directed against the civilian population, is already enshrined in customary law, then states may be disinclined to engage in further formal treaty-making.

In sum, two historic evolutions of the application of international law may pose one more difficulty to law-making today. The complexity surrounding the furnishing legal personality on individuals and the *jus cogens* nature of the prohibition of hostilities aimed at civilians, compounded with the customary nature of most IHL rules, may pose a disincentive to further formal treaty-making in IHL. It is worth further exploring the extent to which states may consider negotiating new treaties to regulate armed conflict.

---

[19] The effects of *jus cogens* were summarized by the International Criminal Tribunal for the former Yugoslavia (ICTY), *Prosecutor v Anto Furundžija* (Judgment) ICTY-95-17/1, T Ch II (10 December 1998): 'Because of the importance of the values it [the prohibition of torture] protects, this principle has evolved into a peremptory norm or *jus cogens*, that is, a norm that enjoys a higher rank in the international hierarchy than treaty law and even "ordinary" customary rules. The most conspicuous consequence of this higher rank is that the principle at issue cannot be derogated from by States through international treaties or local or special customs or even general customary rules not endowed with the same normative force.'

[20] UNGA 'Draft Articles on State Responsibility, Commentary on Article 40' (November 2001) 5th–6th Session (2001) UN Doc Supp No 10 (A/56/10) 283–84 paras 4–6.

[21] Sandesh Sivakumaran, 'Re-envisaging the International Law of Internal Armed Conflict' (2011) 22 European Journal of International Law 219.

[22] cf UNSC 'Report of the Secretary-General on the protection of civilians in armed conflict' (22 May 2012) UN Doc S/2012/376.

[23] Andrew Clapham, 'The Rights and Responsibilities of Armed Non-State Actors: The Legal Landscape & Issues Surrounding Engagement' (1 February 2010) <http://ssrn.com/abstract=1569636> accessed 31 January 2021.

4. WHEN DO STATES CONCLUDE NEW TREATIES AND WHEN DO THEY OPT FOR INFORMALITY?

It is worth elaborating on this idea of an increasing tendency towards informal law-making, including further explanation as to the nature of this tendency as well as the distinction between process and legal status of the results of any process thus far. An informal law-making process could lead to the development of a legally binding treaty. Conversely, a formal law-making process could result in the development of a non-legally binding text, for example, Geneva Call's Deed of Commitment for non-state armed groups engaged in conflict.[24] Another distinction to be made is that between soft law (for example: codes of conduct) and hard law (the body of IHL). It is important to recognize that a range of instruments exists to regulate the conduct of hostilities (political declarations, letters of intention, agreements, etc.).

Given the evolutionary process of law-making, it is important to take soft law and informal agreements into account in regards to their role in shaping the content of international law – in particular, to observe the nature of compliance with non-binding norms. A multidisciplinary project led by the American Society of International Law, called the *Soft Law Project*, explored the nature of compliance with environmental, human rights, arms control and finance laws. Soft law, in the form of non-binding instruments, has acted as a sufficient basis for legal obligation, or *opinio juris*, highlighting emerging custom; assisting in the establishment of the content of new norms; and demonstrating another form of state practice.[25]

The findings of the Soft Law Project reiterate the already commonly held view that states, international governmental organizations, NGOs, epistemic communities, and transnational corporations, among others, all contribute to the making of modern international law. The findings also pose the question: why the move towards soft law mechanisms over legally binding commitments? The choice to engage with instruments of soft law appears to relate to the nature of the problem being addressed, and is developed independently of expectations surrounding compliance. There are several concrete reasons why soft law commitments may often take precedence over legally binding treaties. Some are worth noting here:

1. The bureaucratization of international institutions and the accompanying necessity for rapid response and flexibility surrounding mandates to initiate norm creation make 'deformalized' responses through programmes of action and other such policy instruments more viable.
2. When a particular area of legal ambiguity arises and has yet to be fully understood or conceptualized, legally binding instruments may be deemed unsuitable as not enough is known yet to form appropriate conclusions and laws. The Soft Law Project authors suggest that soft law instruments may increasingly arise as in response to new international political and legal systems.

---

[24] Geneva Call, *Deed of Commitment* (1 July 2019) <http://genevacall.org/how-we-work/deed-of-commitment/> accessed 31 January 2021.

[25] Dinah Shelton (ed), *Commitment and Compliance: The Role of Non-Binding Norms in the International Legal System* (OUP 2003). See also Richard Price, 'From Politics to Law: Emerging Customary Norms and Anti-Personnel Landmines' in Christian Reus-Smit (ed), *The Politics of International Law* (CUP 2004) 106–30.

3. The new international political system is increasingly more transparent, participatory and accountable, with NGOs having become a major force in this context. Soft law mechanisms allow non-state actors to play a more prominent role than within the realm of traditional law-making.
4. Soft law can generally be enacted and adopted faster due to its generally less-restraining character.

Furthermore, soft law has been considered by some analysts as a stepping stone towards the creation of hard law, and by others as more than that: soft law often constitutes the first step in the formulation of effective responses to global problems – filling the normative vacuum and anticipating harder, more detailed regulation offered by treaties or international customary law. With the passage of time and the accumulation of state practice, 'soft laws' may develop into customary law and/or be translated into treaty form. Soft law is valuable on its own, not only as a stepping stone towards hard law. Soft law provides a basis for efficient international 'contracts', and it helps create normative 'covenants' and discourses that can reshape international politics. International regulation in all its forms must be considered one of the most significant institutional features of international relations.[26]

An illustrative case in point is as follows: since the mid-1990s, myriad regional and international legally and politically binding documents have been designed to establish standards and norms to deal with the problems associated with the spread of small arms. On an international level at that time, however, there was no broad-scope *international* legally binding agreement regulating the wide range of issues associated with this class of weapons. The first international conference to address the illicit arms trafficking convened in July 2001 under the auspices of the UN: the Conference on the Illicit Trade in Small Arms and Light Weapons in All Its Aspects, held in New York, 9–20 July 2001.[27] As a result, the politically binding *Program of Action on Small Arms* was issued and set up the first internationally agreed-upon set of norms and standards concerning most aspects surrounding the illicit trade in small arms.[28] The implementation and repeated practice of the *Program of Action* by a considerable number of states paved the way for the legally binding 2013 Arms Trade Treaty, which also includes small arms.

Customary international law has been defined as including state practice or widespread repetition by states of similar international acts over time. Such acts must occur out of a sense of obligation and be taken by a significant number of states, while also not being rejected by a significant number of states.[29]

Both conventional and customary rules are binding, or 'hard' law, as spelled out in Article 38(1) of the Statute of the International Court of Justice, constituting the main forms of interna-

---

26 Kenneth W. Abbott and Duncan Snidal, 'Hard and Soft Law in International Governance' (2000) 54 International Organization 421.

27 Denise Garcia, *Small Arms and Security – New Emerging International Norms* (Routledge 2006).

28 UNGA 'Report of the United Nations Conference on the Illicit Trade in Small Arms and Light Weapons in All Its Aspects' (9–20 July 2001) UN Doc A/CONF.192/PC/15.

29 George Washington Journal of International Law and Economics Staff, *Guide to International Legal Research* (4th edn, Butterworth Legal 2003); Shabtai Rosenne, *Practice and Methods of International Law* (Oceana Publications 1984); Morris L. Cohen and others, *How to Find the Law* (9th edn, West 1989) 450–95.

tional law. The complexity of the international legal and political system may have outgrown the paradigm established by Article 38(1), however. The question legal scholarship faces is whether this new rising paradigm brought about by new forms of law-making contributes to more cooperation and stability within the international system.[30] It is not yet clear if this is the case, especially within the realm of IHL, which is notably based upon formal treaty-making. Soft law may encompass several norms that are in effect observed by states even though technically they are not obliged to do so; however, the fact that they are generally observed, and are expected to be observed, gives this set of norms a predictable value similar to those norms expressed in hard law – which of course are also not always observed.

5. WHAT IS ACTUALLY HAPPENING IN LAW-MAKING TODAY? RISING GLOBAL NORMS

One of the goals of this chapter is to investigate the circumstances within which states are likely to conclude new treaties to regulate armed conflict. The questions why and when states conclude treaties in the realm of IHL and to what extent they opt for informal arrangements of law-making are essential for enabling us to grapple with the evolution of IHL today. A generally observed trend within international law is the resistance, on the part of states, to create such treaties, even through modest amendment, due to concerns regarding the loss of control over weapons including the ability of major powers to develop weapons. However, what is actually happening?

There are perhaps no abundant new formal law-making initiatives within IHL; however, I see two emerging global norms that may contribute to new arenas of law-making, be those informal or formal: (1) IHL applies to states and non-state actors engaged in international and non-international armed conflict; and (2) the utilization of disarmament and arms regulation as tools and mechanisms to protect civilians.

The first is an emerging global trend whereby the boundaries set by rules of restraint during war apply equally to international and non-international armed conflict. This is mainly due to two reasons: first, the foundational norms of protection within IHL are now considered customary and therefore bind all parties to a conflict.[31] Second, it is progressively accepted that human rights law and international criminal law are to be integrated in regards to the scope of protection offered to the individual by IHL in all types of conflict. It could be argued that this rising global norm is arising from two customary rules. The ICRC Customary Study contains 161 rules of customary IHL.[32] Among these, rules 70 and 71, which are applicable in both international and non-international armed conflict, are pertinent to our understanding of the

---

[30] Christine Chinkin, 'Normative Development in the International Legal System' in Shelton (n 25); Paul C. Szasz, 'International norm-making' in Edith Brown Weiss (ed), *Environmental Change and International Law: New Challenges and Dimensions* (United Nations University Press 1992) ch 2.

[31] The foundational norms of IHL are, as highlighted above: protection: the need to distinguish between civilians and combatants; precaution in attacks to ensure they are proportional and avoid unnecessary suffering; the limits on the choice of weaponry during conflict as not all weapons are legitimate or legal (ie weapons must be able to meet the requirements of the two abovementioned norms).

[32] Jean-Marie Henckaerts and Louise Doswald-Beck, *Customary International Humanitarian Law, Vol. 1: Rules* (ICRC/CUP 2005).

rising norm regarding the human costs of the availability, use, and misuse of weapons during armed conflict.

Rule 70 reads as follows: 'The use of means and methods of warfare which are of a nature to cause superfluous injury or unnecessary suffering is prohibited.' Practice that can be observed from states' behaviour and judgments of international tribunals shows that parties to conflicts tend to observe the prohibition of weapons ascribed to international conflict in non-international conflict as well. The International Criminal Court and ICTY have both affirmed the need for actors engaged in intra-state conflict to adhere to this principle. The ICTY, in the seminal 1995 *Tadić* case, held:

> Indeed, elementary considerations of humanity and common sense make it preposterous that the use by States of weapons prohibited in armed conflicts between themselves be allowed when States try to put down rebellion by their own nationals on their own territory. What is inhumane, and consequently proscribed, in international wars cannot but be inhumane and inadmissible in civil strife.[33]

Now, to rule 71: 'The use of weapons which are by nature indiscriminate is prohibited. Weapons that cannot be directed solely at military objectives are prohibited.' This proscription is underpinned by another customary rule: a general prohibition on indiscriminate attacks. In the *Nuclear Weapons* case, the ICJ stated that 'States must never make civilians the object of attack and must consequently never use weapons that are incapable of distinguishing between civilian and military targets.'[34]

A party's choice surrounding weapons during conflict is not unlimited – Additional Protocol I was the first treaty to articulate this prohibition on weapons that are by nature indiscriminate and cause unnecessary suffering or superfluous injury (cluster bombs or landmines, for instance).[35] Less clear in practice is whether further express prohibitions surrounding specific weapons systems are needed.

Compounding these factors is the point that since 1995, all new humanitarian law treaties apply to non-international armed conflict. This is an indication that the rising global norm of progressive application of IHL rules to non-state armed conflict is gaining momentum. These include:

- 1993 Convention on the prohibition of the development, production, stockpiling and use of chemical weapons;
- 1994 Convention on the safety of United Nations and associated personnel;
- 1995 Protocol IV to the 1980 Conventional Weapons Convention on blinding laser weapons;
- 1996 Protocol II to the 1980 Conventional Weapons Convention on the use of mines, booby-traps and other devices;

---

33 *Prosecutor v Duško Tadić aka "Dule"* (Decision on the Defense Motion for Interlocutory Appeal on Jurisdiction) ICTY-94-1-AR72, Appeals Chamber (2 October 1995) para 119.

34 *Legality of the Threat or Use of Nuclear Weapons* (Advisory Opinion) [1996] ICJ Rep 226 para 78.

35 Codified in Protocol Additional to the Geneva Conventions of 12 August 1949, and Relating to the Protection of Victims of International Armed Conflicts (Protocol I) (adopted 8 June 1977, entered into force 7 December 1978) 1125 UNTS 3, pt III, sec. I.

- 1997 Convention on the prohibition of the use, stockpiling, production and transfer of anti-personnel mines and their destruction ('Ottawa Convention' or the 'Mine Ban Treaty');
- 1998 Rome Statute of the International Criminal Court;
- 1999 Second Protocol to the Hague Convention of 1954 for the protection of cultural property in the event of armed conflict;
- 2000 Optional Protocol to the Convention on the rights of the child on the involvement of children in armed conflict;
- October 1980, amended on 21 December 2001, declaring the Convention on Prohibitions or Restrictions on the Use of Certain Conventional Weapons Which May Be Deemed to Be Excessively Injurious or to Have Indiscriminate Effects as amended on 21 December 2001 (CCW) referred to as the Convention on Certain Conventional Weapons. It is also known as the Inhumane Weapons Convention and all Protocols applicable also in non-international armed conflicts;[36]
- 2008 Convention on Cluster Munitions (CCM);
- 2013 Arms Trade Treaty.[37]

Therefore, one may ask whether the more general discourse surrounding the 'stagnation of international law' is applicable to IHL given the two recent additions to the IHL repertoire. There is a perception that currently states rarely rely on formal procedures to conclude new treaties, or amend existing ones, despite a widely shared belief that the rules of IHL must be adapted to the changing circumstances of warfare.

I would argue that there is no stagnation in IHL as it is built to last and to be resilient. Notwithstanding this view, new general treaty-making within IHL is improbable in the near future. In its place exists a more intense form of law-making activity, namely related to the second rising global norm of relevance here: the utilization of disarmament and arms regulation as a mechanism to protect civilians.

When the foundations of IHL were established, one was not able to foresee the nature of today's warfare technology, yet the law is still applicable and functional in regulating the use and development of weaponry. IHL has played a continuous role in either prohibiting or restricting new and existing weapons throughout history, and has been created, modified, and refined on several occasions (1864, 1899, 1907, 1929, 1949, and 1977) in order to enhance the protection of civilian populations, setting limits for conduct during war and limiting armaments (1868, 1907, 1925, 1972, 1980, 1993, 1995, 1996, 1997, 2001, 2003, 2008, and 2013), with clarifications and adaptations to reflect evolving customary law. One can therefore hardly speak of stagnation.

The question then arises: must IHL and other branches of international law be amended or modified in response to the evolving nature of warfare? Or do existing fundamental principles

---

[36] It reads as amended: 'In case of armed conflicts not of an international character occurring in the territory of one of the High Contracting Parties, each party to the conflict shall be bound to apply the prohibitions and restrictions of this Convention and its annexed Protocols.'

[37] For a complete list since 1864, please see International Committee of the Red Cross, 'What Treaties make up IHL? What is customary IHL?' (22 January 2015) <https://www.icrc.org/en/document/what-treaties-make-ihl-what-customary-ihl> accessed 31 January 2021. Many observers do not consider the Arms Trade Treaty an IHL document.

that place restrictions on arms remain valid and resilient? The guardian of IHL, the ICRC, takes the position that IHL applies to new weaponry and technological developments.[38] The problem of terminological clarity, however, arises in relation to the legal application of existent rules and norms to new weapons, in particular, in limiting and impeding the unwanted humanitarian consequences stemming from the use of such.

Despite the fact that informal methods of developing the law are on the rise, multilateral negotiations have not quite yet become the exception. It is interesting to see that courts, non-state groups, and NGOs now influence the making of politically binding agreements, codes of conduct, and more. It is important to observe how these processes are formed, if done through legitimate means, and how they fit into the evolution of international law. It is clear that informal processes have mushroomed, moving IL evolution away from its traditional sources.[39] Joost Pauwelyn and colleagues have examined this change utilizing a three-pronged framework: the first line of inquiry is the output that may result, for example the crystallization of norms or development of informal agreements; the second is the type of process which is adopted and whether it occurs beyond the framework of international organizations; and third is the composition of actors involved in the process, beyond the state. This new trend in law-making gives rise to a number of questions: does it mark an evolution or a retrogression of international law? And if so, what is the impact surrounding accountability of the law-making process? Most importantly for the current argument, *has this 'trend towards informal law-making processes' reached the realm of IHL?*

The straightforward answer is 'yes'. And indeed, the soft power norm approach has value, though it is seen as voluntary. It may pave the way for further commitments, it may build momentum for further refinements in thinking and action, and it may also provide more time for additional stakeholders to embrace the new development. Examples of informal agreements abound. One is the 2008 Montreux Document on Pertinent International Legal Obligations and Good Practices for States Related to Operations of Private Military and Security Companies during Armed Conflict.[40] This is the first document to specifically address private military security companies at the international level and outlines the applicable international law. In sum, the adoption of soft norms is viewed by some as an incremental approach to law-making. This approach may shape values, but it is not sufficient as it is seen as voluntary. The process may also carry ambiguities and compromises.

Even the Anti-Personnel Mine Ban Convention and the Convention on Cluster Munitions began with declarations of intent that aimed to avoid causing harm to civilians. Now such treaties have a wide impact not only on the high contracting parties but also on non-state parties. The influence of the increasing respect of such norms leads to major changes in the behaviour of parties and non-parties alike, which are based not only on legal obligations, but also on the

---

38 ICRC, 'International Humanitarian Law and the Challenges of Contemporary Armed Conflicts' (22 November 2019) 26ff <https://shop.icrc.org/international-humanitarian-law-and-the-challenges-of-contemporary-armed-conflicts-recommitting-to-protection-in-armed-conflict-on-the-70th-anniversary-of-the-geneva-conventions-pdf-en> accessed 31 January 2021.

39 Joost Pauwelyn, Ramses Wessel and Jan Wouters (eds), *Informal International Lawmaking* (OUP 2012) 640.

40 UNGA 'The Montreux Document: On pertinent international legal obligations and good practices for States related to operations of private military and security companies during armed conflict' (6 October 2008) UN Doc A/63/467–S/2008/636, 7.

power of new normative interpretations. Interestingly, both treaties encountered enormous reticence from the major powers, especially the United States.

Opportunities to develop IHL are highly dependent on the political context. It appears that at this time, the current political climate is not in favour of reforming the law of IHL. This is mainly due to the fact that the international system is still accommodating the rise of new powers which seek to wield military and political influence in regards to maintaining peace and security. This is in contrast to the failure to reform global governance structures which are currently responsible for upholding security, in particular the UNSC. Maybe as a result of this conjuncture, informal law-making processes have reached the domain of IHL indeed. Many view this process more as a confidence-building measure rather than something which would manifest in a radical rehaul of IHL. A political declaration on the use of explosive weapons in a densely populated area is illustrative. In connection with the explosive weapons issue, Human Rights Watch published a report on various types of political commitments.[41]

Evolution of law also depends on purpose. Sometimes the development of new legal rules may not be appropriate as one may fear that launching negotiations on new legal rules would lower existing standards rather than strengthen them – though in some cases political commitments may act as a sufficient fallback when the time is not right for the development of new legal rules. The explosive weapons issue is a good example. Also, sometimes a political commitment may be seen as a step in the right direction and create the foundation for legally binding commitments to evolve at a later stage.

The second rising global norm that is worthy of discussion here is the utilization of disarmament and arms regulations as a mechanism to protect civilians. This rising practice must be examined in light of one of the foundational humanitarian norms, that which sets limits on the choice of weaponry used during conflict on the basis that not all weapons are seen as legitimate or legal – thus, the choice to use a particular weapon becomes the mechanism through which to carry out the core obligations of IHL aspirations. The IHL Rule 'The Choice of Weapon', where prohibitions on the use of weapons that cause superfluous injury or unnecessary suffering and weapons that are by nature indiscriminate, are part of the body of customary law in any armed conflict. There are limits on the choice of weapons which can be used during conflict as not all weapons are legitimate or legal (i.e., weapons must be able to meet the requirements of the norms mentioned above). Weapons use, therefore, becomes the mechanism to carry out the core obligations of compliance with IHL norms and aspirations.

This rising norm can be observed through the changing role of the ICRC. The starting point can be traced to the Intergovernmental Group of Experts for the Protection of War Victims (January 1995) and the 26th International Conference of the Red Cross and Red Crescent (December 1995), entrusted at the time by 135 states party to the Geneva Conventions of 1949, mandating the ICRC 'to examine, on the basis of first-hand information available to it, the extent to which the availability of weapons is contributing to the proliferation and aggravation of violations of IHL in armed conflicts and the deterioration of the situation of civilians'.[42]

---

41 Bonnie Docherty, 'Making a Commitment: Paths to Curbing the Use of Explosive Weapons in Populated Areas' (*Human Rights Watch and IHRC*, June 2015) <https://www.hrw.org/sites/default/files/supporting_resources/ewipa_paper_final.pdf> accessed 31 January 2021.

42 'Meeting of the Intergovernmental Group of Experts for the Protection of War Victims (Geneva, 1995), Recommendation VIII, as endorsed by Resolution 1 of the 26th International Conference of the

Providing the impetus for this new study was the recognition of new disturbing trends: (1) the growing number of new actors within the realms of warfare with increasing access to lethal weapons. The end of the Cold War resulted in the availability of arms surpluses for sale (or for looting), trafficked by arms merchants operating on the fringes of international law; (2) the difficulty in ensuring these new actors complied with IHL after gaining access to extremely lethal weapons surpluses.

Before the 1995 Protocol on Blinding Lasers, the ICRC was less active in terms of weapons law, only addressing nuclear weapons. In recent years, the changing global environment has required that all actors understand the effects weapons have on the increasingly integrated and interconnected world. Weapons contamination and risk reduction were not issues before. However, as a result of these new treaties being developed and the resulting norms, these issues have become a major focus regarding both weapons of mass destruction and conventional arms.

The ICRC's 1999 Study was essential in bringing about a new norm because it asked the important research question: 'Are violations of international humanitarian law or civilian injuries more likely to occur as a function of the availability of weapons in a society?'[43] The ICRC's findings suggest that arms accessibility can negatively impact already vulnerable civilian populations during conflict, leading to protracted suffering and violations of IHL. In addition, the study departs from the premise that IHL is the most relevant branch of international law in regards to considering how limitations on weapons availability may have a role in protecting civilians. In terms of the control of conventional arms, the new norm embodied recognition from the outset of two important elements: (1) that increased controls and transparency surrounding arms transfers should exist; and (2) that the impact on compliance with IHL provisions should constitute a fundamental criterion for the transfer of weapons. Since the 1999 Study, the ICRC proposed that arms transfer standards should include a criterion as to whether the arms recipient is likely to breach IHL obligations using the weapons being transferred.

This growing norm regarding the human cost associated with the availability, use and misuse of weapons in armed conflict was reiterated at the 28th International Conference of the Red Cross and Red Crescent, in its Agenda for Humanitarian Action (adopted by consensus on 6 December 2003). Further contours from this emerging normative understanding were put forward: including the idea to strengthen the protection of civilians from the indiscriminate use and effects of both legal weapons and prohibited weapons in order to limit unnecessary suffering through controls on weapons development, proliferation, and use. Following these developments, the ICRC began to play an influential role in promoting the integration of IHL criteria in the much-needed codification of international law on arms transfers.[44] The rationale behind regulation was that when states transfer weapons, they are making the means to wage war available to more players. The preliminary legal tenet rests on Common Article 1 (to all Geneva Conventions) that reminds states of their obligation to carry out warfare according

---

Red Cross and Red Crescent, Geneva, 1995' reprinted in (1996) 310 International Review of the Red Cross 58 and 88 respectively.

43 ICRC, *Arms Availability and the Situation of Civilians in Armed Conflict* (ICRC 1999) 15 <https://www.icrc.org/en/doc/resources/documents/publication/p0734.htm> accessed 31 January 2021.

44 Camilla Waszink, *Arms Transfer Decisions: Applying International Humanitarian Law Criteria, Practical Guide* (ICRC 2007).

to the rules of IHL. As a corollary, it is seen that arms transfers that are likely to violate IHL should not occur.

The 'Weapons: ICRC statement to the United Nations, 2015' is unequivocal in confirming this idea and may set the path for further consolidation of this emerging norm. It states:

> This compelling evidence of the tremendous human costs of nuclear weapons led the International Movement of the Red Cross and Red Crescent to conclude that it is difficult to envisage how any use of nuclear weapons could be compatible with international humanitarian law. On this basis, the Red Cross and Red Crescent Movement has called on States to negotiate a legally binding international agreement prohibiting the use of and completely eliminating nuclear weapons, based on existing commitments and international obligations.[45]

During times of international instability, it may be tempting for some states to view nuclear weapons as a tool that enhances their security. But weapons that risk catastrophic and irreversible humanitarian consequences cannot seriously be viewed as useful in protecting civilians or humanity as a whole. A large majority of states today recognize that the potential humanitarian impact of nuclear weapons can no longer be ignored and must underpin all nuclear disarmament efforts.

In 2015, the ICRC President, Peter Maurer, appealed to all states to establish a time-bound framework for negotiating a legally binding agreement that would prohibit the use of nuclear weapons and lead to their eventual elimination – and to consider the form that such an agreement could take. He additionally called on nuclear-armed states, in the meantime, to reduce the role that nuclear weapons play in their military doctrines and to reduce the number of nuclear weapons systems placed on high alert, in accordance with existing commitments, so as to diminish the risks of intentional or accidental use of nuclear weapons.[46] Along the same lines, the ICRC, in the ground-breaking statement to the United Nations, also stated that the use of explosive weapons in densely populated areas is inherently indiscriminate. The ICRC calls on all states to explain how states intend to abide by IHL through their choice of weapons.

As a result of the critical role played by the ICRC as the guardian of IHL, it is essential to determine this organization's influence on new law-making, through both formal and informal mechanisms.

6. THE UNIQUE ROLE OF THE ICRC

The role of the ICRC as the guardian of IHL is unique and means this branch of international law holds an unusual position compared to others. The ICRC distinguishes IHL from other branches of international law. The ICRC influences state behaviour with its moral clout. The ICRC maintains neutrality and takes action only in regards to credible humanitarian challenges according to both its mandate and experience. Therefore, the opinion of the ICRC is usually taken seriously by states.

---

45 ICRC, 'Weapons: ICRC Statement to the United Nations, 2015' (15 October 2015) <www.icrc.org/en/document/weapons-icrc-statement-united-nations-2015> accessed 31 January 2021.

46 ICRC, 'Nuclear Weapons: Ending a Threat to Humanity' (18 February 2015) <https://www.icrc.org/en/document/nuclear-weapons-ending-threat-humanity> accessed 31 January 2021.

States and other parties to an armed conflict have an obligation to 'respect and ensure respect for' IHL 'in all circumstances' (Article 1 common to the Geneva Conventions). They must attempt to prevent and end violations of IHL by all parties taking part in the conflict. However, it is the ICRC that carries out this role most actively the majority of the time.

The ICRC plays an important role, whereas the UN High Commissioner for Human Rights would not have the same freedom nor be considered as neutral, meaning the latter is not as well suited to taking on initiatives to create new law.

Yves Sandoz wrote about the ICRC as the guardian of IHL and discerned five central functions of the body.[47] The first is the 'monitoring' function, which involves the continuous assessment of the effectiveness of IHL rules and efforts to adapt and revise them when needed. The second is the 'catalyst' function, which involves engaging experts and non-governmental organizations to contribute their expert knowledge to the understanding and application of IHL, its evolution, and its interpretation (the commissioning of the Customary Law study[48] being an example here). The third is the 'promotion' function, which includes advocacy efforts for the dissemination and teaching of IHL. An indicator of the success of this function is how widely IHL is adhered to by countries around the world. In addition, the Swiss government is the depository of the IHL treaties and has assumed some responsibility for the promotion of these instruments. This function importantly includes the education of armed forces across the world as well as non-state actors. The ICRC assists and also reminds states that they are treaty-bound to abide by IHL and it is in their interest to do so. Armies that respect IHL are more efficient due to increased unity and consistency. The fourth function is that of 'guardian angel'. This task is to defend IHL from the development of new rules or laws which would weaken or disregard its existence. The fifth is the 'direct action' function, which is the most important as it relates to the direct and practical application of the law to conflict. The ICRC is able to carry out this function via accessing conflict areas around the world, conducting prison visits, and through the provision of health care to the wounded as well as water and sanitation services.

The ICRC uses its access to gain a concrete understanding of the situation, which enables it to execute this function in two ways. First, it reminds parties of their obligations vis-à-vis civilians and the means through which they wage war; and signals failures to observe these obligations. The second is by protecting victims by giving them direct assistance. Further, sometimes the ICRC is the last remaining link between the conflicting parties. Therefore it can act as a neutral mediator and facilitate negotiations between parties. Finally, the 'watchdog' function the ICRC serves allows it to raise the profile of the most serious violations ('sounding the alarm'). However, the ICRC must show restraint in such actions in order to continue to have access to conflict zones and to be able to protect victims from further violations. All these functions energize the processes of law-making. However, one must note: the ICRC must be cautious and often has to act deliberately and 'slowly'.

---

47 Yves Sandoz, 'The International Committee of the Red Cross as a Guardian of International Humanitarian Law' (31 December 1998) <https://www.icrc.org/en/doc/resources/documents/misc/about-the-icrc-311298.htm> accessed 31 January 2021.

48 Jean-Marie Henckaerts and Louise Doswald-Beck (n 32).

7. WITH OR WITHOUT THE ICRC: WHEN IS REGULATION INFORMAL, FORMAL, OR ABSENT?

Now that the role of the ICRC as a guardian has been examined, questions remain as to when states may engage with treaty regulation and in regards to which issues. When and why do they opt to pursue informal means of law-making? When do they try to avoid any form of regulation at all? The realist theory in international relations answer to these questions is: states only conclude new treaties when there is public outcry over a weapons system (landmines, cluster bombs), or when powerful states feel it is in their best interest (such as in the case of the United Kingdom's leadership regarding the Arms Trade Treaty in which the UK acted as the champion state and led the negotiations towards the Treaty). Predictability, stability, and security (both strategic/state-level security and human security) are the main drivers for treaty regulation.

States try to avoid formal regulation when major players are not on board. Politically binding agreements may act as trust- and confidence-building measures that can pave the way for legally binding initiatives. One such example is the agreement between states not to place weapons in outer space, which lead to the ongoing discussions on a Treaty on Prevention of the Placement of Weapons in Outer Space and of the Threat or Use of Force against Outer Space Objects.

However, to create a more nuanced complementary answer to these key questions, one may look at the last IHL formal treaties, which all share a strong characteristic: they are all people-centred treaties; they not only served the interests of their patrons (states) but reflected strong intent to assist vulnerable civilians and victims. The law-making processes associated with these treaties were also distinct in the sense that they resulted from the influence of many other actors beyond the state. Therefore one may ask instead, when states engage in 'humanitarian security regime' law-making that aims to protect civilians or control or restrict certain weapons systems, what shape do such law-making efforts take and how do they impact world politics? Elsewhere I have defined humanitarian security regimes as those driven by altruistic imperatives aiming to prohibit and restrict behaviour, impede lethal technology, or ban categories of weapons through disarmament treaties; and those which centrally embrace humanitarian perspectives which seek to prevent civilian casualties, preclude harmful behaviour, and protect and guarantee the rights of victims and survivors of armed violence. Thus, the chief goals of humanitarian security regimes are to reduce human suffering, to prohibit harm, and to protect victims.[49]

The relevance of humanitarian security regimes in terms of law-making rests on three factors. Law-making in areas that were previously considered to be the exclusive domain of states have now been successfully modified by non-state actors aiming to protect potential and actual victims and survivors of conflict and to reduce human suffering. There was some civil society engagement in conferences at The Hague in 1899; however, not to the same extent as has occurred since the process which led to the 1997 Ottawa Convention. Throughout that campaign civil society groups were vital actors. More recent campaigns have benefited from new technologies that help activists, in particular the internet and social media, which have exponentially increased civil society's capacity to stimulate change. The Nobel Peace Prize of

---

49 Denise Garcia, 'Humanitarian Security Regimes' (2015) 91 International Affairs 55.

1997 was awarded to Jody Williams and the International Campaign to Ban Landmines (ICBL) in recognition of the new role played by civil society in terms of influencing international law.

States have initiated law-making in domains closely related to national security (such as armaments), largely in acknowledgement of humanitarian concerns. It is argued that three conditions influence the emergence of law-making by humanitarian security regimes and which may shed light on the circumstances under which states regulate in general, or specifically by treaty, including for which purposes:

1. *Marginalization and delegitimization*: Delegitimization refers to a progressive change in the values attached to certain behaviours, technologies, or weapons systems: whereby values slide from the lofty position of prestige and authority, towards being marginalized and seen as illegal. This process is crucial for building regime momentum and usually precedes other steps. If particular behaviours, technologies, or weapons systems are considered legitimate, it is because they assumed authority under a legal or political framework which gradually influenced the practice of states. These norms therefore come to be part of the fabric of international security and, at least to some extent, deemed legitimate. Delegitimization is the reverse of this process.
2. *Multilevel agency*: State and non-state actors alike initiate processes of marginalization and delegitimization. These processes are accompanied by a generation of credible and authoritative knowledge which shows that a problem exists or may materialize in the future and therefore requires a change in the status quo. At first, one 'champion state' may adopt the idea; this is often followed by a process of multiregional 'core group' formation, bringing together other countries that espouse the same idea. These states will then engage in peer-to-peer pressure on other states to create momentum for regime emergence. These efforts are supported by advocates comprising non-state actors. The core group may jointly draft a resolution to be submitted to the UN General Assembly (UNGA) and sponsor workshops and gatherings to further generate momentum at various levels. *Throughout these stages, synergies between the state and non-state realms are markedly significant.* Through 'multilevel agency', actors at various levels act cohesively to develop new norms and establish a political cost associated with violating them.
3. *Reputational concerns*: States do care about their reputations, and try to maintain their image as normal, accepted members of the international community, which abide by the commonly accepted framework of values agreed upon in international law. These values constitute humanitarian motivation and stem from the body of norms and ideas of the two branches of international law: human rights law and IHL. The latter has been instilled within state practice for over a century; the IHL Geneva Conventions are now universal and their rules considered customary.

In addition, three distinguishing characteristics define law-making here:

1. 'Effects-based goals': the principle characteristic underlying all humanitarian security regimes is the goal to reduce human suffering. The objective is to create frameworks that protect the most vulnerable and underprivileged, the victims of armed violence, and the civilian population at large – to benefit the security of the individual.

2. The 'constituent source of agency', namely, an exceptional constellation of actors in multilevel agencies, in which the ICRC, as the guardian of IHL, has an integral constituent function.
3. A 'humanitarian law framework',[50] provided by the compelling force of the previously existing IHL normative framework, the aim of which is to ensure human security, in particular the rights of survivors and victims of conflict.[51] For instance, the Ottawa Convention, an IHL treaty, has had a definitive impact on the behaviour of states that are not party to the treaty. This new framework has fundamentally altered how states relate not only to this weapons system but also to others, such as cluster munitions.

Historically, humanitarian concerns initiated law-making processes but were not the predominant motivation leading states towards formal treaty-making. In other words, the motives were mixed between considerations of humanitarian law and national security. This can be seen with the 1968 Nuclear Non-Proliferation Treaty; the 1972 Convention on the Prohibition of the Development, Production and Stockpiling of Bacteriological (Biological) and Toxin Weapons and on Their Destruction; the 1980 Convention on Prohibitions or Restrictions on the Use of Certain Conventional Weapons Which May Be Deemed to Be Excessively Injurious or to Have Indiscriminate Effects; and the Chemical Weapons Convention of 1992.

The key humanitarian principles, now customary, have been driving law-making in the last century. In sum, humanitarian concerns have always been part of the equation in regards to new IHL formal law-making. It is only in recent years, however, that these norms have assumed centre stage and become the driving force behind regulation, as seen regarding the 1997 Ottawa Convention and the 2008 CCM. This reasoning can also be said to have been the core driver of overwhelming support for the Arms Trade Treaty.[52] The landmine and cluster munitions bans are the first instruments in IHL not only to ban a weapon, but also to mandate the high contracting parties to assist present and future victims, while the Arms Trade Treaty is the first treaty to expressly state, as its purpose, the aim of reducing human suffering.

The significance of the Arms Trade Treaty for the current discussion is relevant. The treaty is the culmination of a decades-long process that was started more than 20 years ago by a group of Nobel Peace laureates led by Oscar Arias. The laureates outlined principles regarding what should be legal and illegal vis-à-vis arms transfers and the founding normative tenor for the treaty – that arms transfer restraints should centre around two core groups of principles: (1) the foundational obligations set out in the UN Charter, and (2) considerations around the risks

---

50 Ruti G. Teitel, *Humanity's Law* (OUP 2011) 3–18.

51 The framework of 'victim assistance' is very well established and developed in the Mine Ban Convention, which serves as a model for other processes: 'Victim assistance is a process aiming to ensure that landmine survivors can participate fully and effectively in their societies. The injuries caused by anti-personnel mines often result in the amputation of one or more limbs and in other permanent disabilities, with serious social, psychological and economic consequences for the victims, their families and their communities' (ICRC, *The Mine Ban Convention: Progress and Challenges in the Second Decade* (ICRC 2011) 20).

52 Denise Garcia, *Disarmament Diplomacy and Human Security: Regimes, Norms, and Moral Progress in International Relations* (Routledge 2011).

of undertaking an arms transfer, i.e., if the weapons will likely be used for the commission of serious violations of international human rights law or IHL.[53]

The treaty represents a new multilateral framework to address arms transfers. The treaty is intended to prevent arms flows to destabilizing regions and help to prevent arms diversions. It creates express prohibitions on the transferring of arms that strengthen the existing mechanism of arms embargoes; elicits state responsibility vis-à-vis existing obligations, including human rights law commitments, such as prohibition against torture and genocide; and connects arms transfer obligations to a duty to refrain from the commission of crimes against humanity and grave breaches of the Geneva Conventions (war crimes). Lastly, the Treaty is the first global agreement to apply the existing rules of IHL and human rights law to arms transfers, with concrete criteria for the assessment of transfers.

The Arms Trade Treaty's larger significance rests on three factors. First, it is a concerted response to help reduce the human cost of conflict. As stated by the ICRC, the Treaty is a historic step towards reducing human suffering.[54] Further, it is the first time this has been explicitly stated as a goal in an arms treaty. Second, the Treaty is a global mechanism for levelling the playing field in regards to export controls. The United States considered the Treaty as a way to bring other countries up to its own export control standards. Third, the Treaty is unique in the sense that it sets standards on behaviour specifically concerning arms transfers that could facilitate the commission of atrocities during war and peace. In a larger sense, the Treaty is part of a long process, occurring in the last hundred years or more, of creating global humanitarian norms. The process that led to this outcome has been both audacious and innovative.[55]

8. CONCLUSIONS: LAW-MAKING, TREATY CONCLUSION AND INFORMALITY

This book is timely as we live in an era of fragmentation of international law. There are many challenges that arise from the diversification and expansion of international law.[56] This book is about the profound transformation in the making of international law. It concretely examines new mechanisms of law-making in the critical area of the regulation of war – IHL.

Therefore, specifically in terms of new law-making within IHL, the goal is to improve the situation of civilians caught in armed conflict. I argue that new formal treaty-making, specifically within the realm of IHL, is unlikely to eventuate for now. However, there have been important formal and informal law-making developments in one area of IHL, namely restric-

---

53 Nobel Peace Laureates' International Code of Conduct on Arms Transfers released by Oscar Arias, former President of Costa Rica, and other Nobel Laureates, on May 29 1997 <http://www.internationalhumanrightslexicon.org/hrdoc/docs/armsnobel.htm> accessed 31 January 2021.

54 ICRC, 'Arms Trade Treaty: A Historic Step Towards Reducing Human Suffering' (2 April 2013) <https://www.icrc.org/en/doc/resources/documents/news-release/2013/02-04-weapons-arms-trade-treaty.htm> accessed 31 January 2021.

55 Denise Garcia, 'Disarming the Lords of War, A New International Treaty to Regulate the Arms Trade' (2014) 91 Foreign Affairs 55.

56 UNGA 'Fragmentation of International Law: Difficulties arising from the Diversification and Expansion of International Law, Report of the Study Group of the International Law Commission' (4 April 2006) UN Doc A/CN.4/L.682.

tions on the choice of weapon and the use of regulation to disarm and control certain weapons as a mechanism to protect civilians. I also observe that new formal and informal law-making in IHL integrates human rights law. It is well established in state practice and jurisdiction that both human rights law and IHL apply in all conflict, irrespective of its nature or gravity.[57] Human rights law has progressively grown to be considered relevant to the behaviour of non-state armed actors during conflict.[58] This is mainly due to new law-making by the UNSC, which requires non-state armed groups to obey human rights law.[59]

It is promising, then, that new law-making assimilates human rights law, given the complex overlapping in conflict situations today (law enforcement and conflict). The integration of human rights law and IHL can be seen most notably in two areas. The first is the 2010 International Code of Conduct for Private Security Service Providers (PMSCs), which seeks to ensure respect for human rights and IHL in regions where the rule of law has been undermined. Along the same lines, the Montreux Document, a parallel initiative of Switzerland and the ICRC, aims to improve the compliance by PMSCs with IHL and human rights law. The second area of regulation is arms control: the Arms Trade Treaty, which the ICRC had a sizeable influence in bringing to fruition, is based in both IHL and human rights law.

Two factors which may be dissuading states from pursuing formal law-making in IHL in general were discussed: (1) a turn to customary law. Most rules of IHL are considered custom and are formally adhered to, despite the many violations. Many customary norms are considered *jus cogens*. Therefore, perhaps, instead of engaging in new law-making, states would be best served to focus on compliance mechanisms. (2) The other is a blurring of the lines between conflict and law-enforcement situations, namely in the fight against terrorism and the increasing use of targeted killings.

Respect for human rights law and IHL, as they are broadly codified, serves as a parameter for judging progress towards law-making that protects civilians given the nature of conflicts today. It seems then that the most fruitful areas for new law-making – formal and informal – lie at this intersection. Obviously, institutionally, law-making in these areas may be complex. The UN oversees the human rights law regime and the ICRC administers IHL. Human rights law and IHL-based norms may, in fact, generate stigmatization effects even before they are internalized in state law and practice. The 1997 Ottawa Convention, for instance, has a fundamental ethical standard-setting function. Stigma against the use of certain weapons may occur faster if the norms upon which it is grounded are founded on human rights law and IHL.

---

[57] *Legality of the Threat or Use of Nuclear Weapons* (Advisory Opinion) [1996] ICJ Rep 226; *Legal Consequences of the Construction of a Wall in the Occupied Palestinian Territory* (Advisory Opinion) [2004] ICJ Rep 136; *Armed Activities on the Territory of the Congo (Democratic Republic of the Congo v. Uganda)* [2005] ICJ Rep 168.

[58] Christian Tomuschat, 'The Applicability of Human Rights Law to Insurgent Movements' in Horst Fischer and others (eds), *Krisensicherung und Humanitärer Schutz – Crisis Management and Humanitarian Protection: Festschrift für Dieter Fleck* (Berliner Wissenschafts-Verlag 2004) 573–91; Dieter Fleck, 'Humanitarian Protection Against Non-State Actors' in Jochen A. Frowein and others (eds), *Verhandeln für den Frieden – Negotiating for Peace: Liber Amicorum Tono Eitel* (Springer 2003) 69–94.

[59] UNSC Res 1193 (1998) UN Doc S/RES/1193; Res 1213 (1998) UN Doc S/RES/1213; Res 1214 (1998) UN Doc S/RES/1214; Res 1216 (1998) UN Doc S/RES/1216; Res 1471 (2003) UN Doc S/RES/1471; Res 1479 (2003) UN Doc S/RES/1479; Res 1509 (2003) UN Doc S/RES/1509; and Res 1528 (2004) UN Doc S/RES/1528.

Further integration of human rights law and IHL in non-international armed conflicts is happening and could help advance the two emerging norms that I argued are developing and could lead to new formal law-making (informal law-making is definitely occurring under this rising normative framework):

1. IHL applies to states and non-state actors in international and non-international conflict;
2. Utilization of disarmament and arms regulation as a tool and mechanism to protect civilians (the IHL Rule 'The Choice of Weapon' as a Restraint Paradigm and a Mechanism for IHL Enforcement).

Many new and challenging violations of IHL continue to emerge, and the glaring complexities of current conflicts, which are often fought in densely populated urban areas and which feature the increasing use of new technologies (with extra-judicial components), mean it is important to keep in mind the integration of other branches of international law, such as human rights law and international criminal law, in the search for new law-making that offers solutions to protect civilians.

Even though informal mechanisms are concomitantly flourishing in IHL law-making, one cannot yet maintain that there has been a straightforward turn to informality or stagnation. This is mainly because of the unique role of the ICRC in ensuring that IHL persists and evolves. In addition, restrictions and prohibitions on new and existing weapons throughout history have served to enhance the protection of civilian populations, setting limits for conduct during war and limiting the range of armaments available to conduct war (1868, 1907, 1925, 1972, 1980, 1993, 1995, 1996, 1997, 2001, 2003, 2008, and 2013).

The sense of stagnation perhaps arises out of the fact that multilateral negotiations take many years to unfold, for example, the Arms Trade Treaty took over 20 years to come to fruition. It is essential, therefore, to place the questions posed in the context of the formation of the larger frameworks within the context of the current challenges to IHL, namely: the creation of the main overarching norms of peace and security and the non-use of force; human rights as enshrined in the UN Charter; and the rise in importance of IHL since 1864, which was concomitant with the codification and consolidation of human rights law after 1945.

Finally, it is essential to note that global rule-making, which once was fundamentally anchored on consensus, may be indeed in decay.[60] It is simply very hard to find solutions to global problems adopting the means of consensus, because many countries feel that they have a legitimate stake in dealing with complex global issues, ranging from climate change, to IHL, to the protection of civilians, and seek to raise their voice in this regard. The Arms Trade Treaty, as the newest IHL treaty, abandoned 'consensus' negotiations due to frustrations surrounding the inability to agree upon a legally binding document covering legal arms transfers in the small arms meetings from 2001–2006, due to objections from a small number of nations, including the US. The Arms Trade Treaty represents a significant shift in negotiation tactics as it broke free from the constraints of 'consensus' negotiations and instead was adopted by a vote in the UNGA, where approval of such treaties requires only a majority. This path can

---

60 Nico Krisch, 'The Decay of Consent: International Law in an Age of Global Public Goods' (2014) 108 American Journal of International Law 1; see also Ian Hurd, 'The International Rule of Law and the Domestic Analogy' (2015) 4 Global Constitutionalism 365.

serve as a model for law-making that addresses many other pressing matters concerning the protection of civilians that is the urgent focus of the discussion carried out here.

6. Post-international humanitarian law?

Philip Liste

1. LEAVING THE LAW'S COMFORT ZONE

Law-making has long been a political endeavour and continues to be so. It has been political in its contribution to the contemporary regime of knowledge[1] but also for challenging such regimes, perhaps pushing them towards their limits. In the mid-19th century, Henri Dunant promoted a new form of international humanitarianism as well as a form of the very organization of what, in retrospect, appears to be an important step in the development of international law. However, this putative advance in the politico-legal knowledge of the time built upon a co-emergence of the individual as a socially relevant (legal) subject and the very concept of the 'international' as a relevant framework for the relation between sovereigns.[2] Moreover, the creation of this new regime of 'humanity's law',[3] the application of the corresponding norms, as well as the ongoing shaping and reshaping of the regime allowed for the concepts' ongoing co-existence. Today, this co-existence is still subject to socio-legal practice, though under different circumstances, that is, a perhaps changing normative ecology. Questions for the development and/or stagnation of international humanitarian law (IHL) will thus hardly be answered by turning only to the interplay of old and new actors within the 'international' realm. We have, also, to account for the changing normative ecology of legal practice.

While an international constellation of sovereign states and individuals was established during the 19th century and by way of IHL, this constellation has become subject to severe reproduction during the 20th century's 'move to institutions'[4] – perhaps even a constitutionalization of international politics.[5] The momentum of this normative development also comes to the fore in the United Nations (UN) Charter. Its Preamble, especially, plays some constitutional tunes in that it circumscribes a semantic circle. This is not unusual. In fact, constitutional documents establish the very entity in whose name they are signed. 'The signature', as Jacques

---

1 For the concept, see Michel Foucault, 'The Subject and Power' (1982) 8 Critical Inquiry 777.

2 Friederike Kuntz, *Aporias: The International Relation, Interrelated Sovereigns, the Human Individual, and Power-Knowledge* (University Bielefeld 2018) (on file with the author).

3 Ruti Teitel, *Humanity's Law* (OUP 2011).

4 David Kennedy, 'The Move to Institutions' (1987) 8 Cardozo Law Review 841.

5 Jeffrey L. Dunoff and Joel P. Trachtman (eds), *Ruling the World? Constitutionalism, International Law, and Global Governance* (CUP 2009); Jan Klabbers and others (eds), *The Constitutionalization of International Law* (OUP 2009); Anthony F. Lang and Antje Wiener (eds), *Handbook on Global Constitutionalism* (Edward Elgar 2017).

Derrida puts it, 'invents the signer'.[6] In a gesture of 'We, the Peoples', the UN Charter, at first sight, seems to replicate such constitutional semantics. By closer inspection, however, we recognize that the Preamble consists of two sentences – the first starting from the famous 'We, the Peoples of the United Nations'; however, only the second leads into the establishment of 'an international organization to be known as the United Nations'. A certain break consists in the fabulous emergence of 'our respective Governments'. What starts as a somewhat liberal constitution of a body politic, in actual fact, leans towards state internationalism.[7] Against this backdrop, we may not want to draw the conclusion that the Peoples have been created 'through representatives assembled in the city of San Francisco, who have exhibited their full powers'. We may nonetheless find global humanity and 'fully powered' state-based internationalism to exist within a complex and somewhat dialectical relationship. In this contribution, I argue that this dialectic continues to have an effect and that this effect finds expression in the current developments also described by Denise Garcia (in this book) – that is, current developments in IHL, as well as the wider field of 'humanity's law'.[8]

With respect to the legitimacy of certain international legal regimes, I will briefly draw on some of the insights in the field of international relations (IR). While, indeed, scholarship in this field has a strong tradition of asking for the state's willingness to establish – or not to establish – certain international legal regimes,[9] this focus has also become subject to critique.[10] I argue that an analysis of the development and/or stagnation of international law (and IHL in particular) can benefit from consideration of the 'social life' of international norms,[11] the embeddedness of power in norms-related practice, and a wider orientation towards normativity as it has been established during IR's 'sociological turn'.[12] It is this strand of work in which the interrelated claims on power and legitimacy relate to the construction of elements like 'humanity', 'globality', or the 'international', which are of major importance for the everyday reproduction of the normative order.[13] Legitimacy thus corresponds with the type of normative order in which – and for which – it is thought. To conceptualize legitimacy within an international order of states is different from a normative endeavour, which seeks to relocate it, in other words to make sense of legitimacy within a 'post-international', 'transnational', or 'global' order. Coming to terms with recent normative developments in IHL presents exactly

---

6 Jacques Derrida, 'Declaration of Independence' (1986) 7 New Political Science 7, 10.

7 See Katja Freistein and Philip Liste, 'Organisation-im-Kommen. Intertextualer Institutionalismus in der Analyse von Weltorganisationen' in Martin Koch (ed), *Weltorganisationen* (Springer VS 2012) 89; Friederike Kuntz, '"We the Heads of State ...": Pitfalls of Global Constitutional Practice' (2020) 9 Global Constitutionalism 437.

8 Teitel (n 3).

9 Stephen David Krasner (ed), *International Regimes* (Cornell University Press 1983); Kenneth Abbott and others, 'The Concept of Legalization' (2000) 54 International Organization 401.

10 Martha Finnemore and Stephen John Toope, 'Alternatives to "Legalization". Richer Views of Law and Politics' (2001) 55 International Organization 743; Andreas Fischer-Lescano and Philip Liste, 'Völkerrechtspolitik. Zu Trennung und Verknüpfung von Politik und Recht der Weltgesellschaft' (2005) 12 Zeitschrift für Internationale Beziehungen 209; Friedrich Kratochwil, 'The Force of Prescriptions' (1984) 38 International Organization 685.

11 Kratochwil, 'The Force of Prescriptions' (n 10).

12 Stefano Guzzini, 'A Reconstruction of Constructivism in International Relations' (2000) 6 European Journal of International Relations 147.

13 Jens Bartelson, 'The Social Construction of Globality' (2010) 4 International Political Sociology 219.

this challenge, for it is this field of international regulation that represents but a shift from a state mode of legitimacy to 'humanity's law'.[14] But wait! Haven't humanitarian and modern state internationalism co-emerged, perhaps as two sides of the same coin? Can we really conceive of the process in terms of a normative shift within an 'international' constellation and thus pit one against the other? Or do we already talk about a wider transformation, for example from an 'international' to a 'transnational' or 'post-international' constellation?

It is a matter of dialectics that while a multiplicity of actors has entered onto international battlefields thus challenging the normative scope of IHL, state actors perform but a continuation of war not only by new technical means but also in different and seemingly new spaces, in other words, spaces no longer easily addressed as 'international'. As Friederike Kuntz has demonstrated the dialectical relationship between humanity and the international starts rather early, earlier than with the creation of the UN. Rather, the two concepts can be understood as having co-emerged during the 19th century.[15] To be sure, IHL has contributed to the production of the 'international' as a normative space. However, inasmuch as IHL is currently facing a new historical constellation of violence (as Garcia also points out[16]), this nexus between IHL and the reproduction of the 'international' may have become problematic. The plight of IHL may consist in the problem that as 'international' humanitarian law, it will hardly work in a *post-international constellation*. At the same time, a semantic shift to humanity law will not necessarily do the trick because the very idea of safeguarding humanity in the international arena has also come under pressure.

Today, the normative boundaries of the international order appear to be blurred. For Teitel, '[t]he reinvigorated humanitarianism of humanity law sparks a rethinking of the prevailing basic categories and distinctions in international legal and political order – such as the international/national, public/private, and war/peace divisions.'[17] It is important that the moment of humanity alone is misconceived as being a cause for these boundaries to blur. While humanity has become an element in the constellation of order, protecting human beings within the post-international constellation may differ from what it meant to do the same within an international constellation.

2. THE SOCIAL LIFE OF LAW AS PRACTICE

In the introduction to this book, Heike Krieger and Jonas Püschmann stress two aspects of current normative developments: a 'positive' and a 'negative' side.[18] While a proliferation of new actors in the interpretative discourses of IHL may enhance legitimacy, this may also contribute to insecurity and ambiguity. While we may want to agree that broader participation in the reproduction of a regime enhances its legitimacy, this may also stimulate indeterminacy, that is, indeterminacy of what is already indeterminate.[19] Moreover, where there is light, there

---

14 Teitel (n 3).

15 Kuntz (n 2).

16 Denise Garcia, 'Global Norms Governing the Protection of Civilians, Conflict and Weapons: Formal or Informal Law-Making?', Chapter 5 in this book, 57.

17 Teitel (n 3).

18 Heike Krieger and Jonas Püschmann, 'Law-Making and Legitimacy in International Humanitarian Law', Chapter 1 in this book, 7.

19 David Kennedy, *Of War and Law* (Princeton University Press 2006).

will also be shadow. The aim to protect individuals from harm goes hand in glove with new opportunities to govern. While individuals can understand themselves to be bearers of international human rights, they may also find themselves sentenced under international criminal law. While the UN Security Council has taken steps as to the international protection of civilians,[20] as Garcia (in this book) acknowledges, it has also established a procedure to globally surveil and govern individuals while attempting to counter transnational terrorism.[21] In addition, and more generally, while discourses on 'human security' have been furthered to protect individuals, these discourses have also served the purposes of broadening 'security' concerns beyond the state and thus helped to legitimize new forms of state intervention on various scales.[22]

It is here that the social sciences and especially the field of IR may contribute to a better understanding of the normative processes under study. While for quite a period of its existence the academic field of IR has been rather disinterested in international (legal) norms, this began to change significantly from the 1980s onwards. In retrospect, two strands of theoretical work can be said to have furthered this reorientation towards international law and international legal norms indeed as a core object of inquiry. First, rationalist regime theory discussed the role that international regimes would play for state actors' opportunities to cooperate under the inhospitable conditions of international anarchy. Yet, while Stephen Krasner's oft-cited definition of a regime is wide enough to entail an international legal character,[23] questions regarding the *legal* status of regimes, as well as the willingness of state actors to grant such a status, were put on hold. In fact, it took until the new millennium when Kenneth Abbott and his colleagues launched a successful research programme on the 'legalization of world politics'.[24] Instead of asking 'do regimes matter?', the focus had now shifted to the legal form of regimes. Moreover, this research interest also allowed questions regarding a state's willingness to opt for a more or less legal formalization of international regulation.

Second, an increased interest in international law has been stimulated by what has eventually become the most important theoretical reorientation in the field, in other words, its 'sociological' turn. In a critique on rationalist regime theory, Friedrich Kratochwil asked for an understanding of the 'social life' of international norms and,[25] in so doing, paved the way for an increasingly vibrant avenue of IR norms research,[26] which after a while also started to

---

20 UNSC 'Report of the Secretary-General on the Protection of Civilians in Armed Conflict' (22 May 2012) UN Doc S/2012/376.

21 See eg UNSC Res 1267 (15 October 1999) UN Doc S/RES/1267; UNSC Res 1373 (28 September 2001) UN Doc S/RES/1373.

22 David Chandler, *Hollow Hegemony: Rethinking Global Politics, Power and Resistance* (Pluto 2009) 80–105.

23 Stephen David Krasner, 'Structural Causes and Regime Consequences. Regimes as Intervening Variables' (1982) 36 International Organization 185, 186 ('Regimes can be defined as sets of implicit or explicit principles, norms, rules, and decision-making procedures around which actors' expectations converge in a given area of international relations'). For an interesting discussion of the concept in legal studies, see Andreas Fischer-Lescano and Gunther Teubner, *Regime-Kollisionen. Zur Fragmentierung des globalen Rechts* (Suhrkamp 2006).

24 Abbott and others (n 9).

25 Kratochwil, 'The Force of Prescriptions' (n 10).

26 Martha Finnemore and Kathryn Sikkink, 'International Norm Dynamics and Political Change' (1998) 52 International Organization 887; Thomas Risse and others (eds), *The Power of Human Rights: International Norms and Domestic Change* (CUP 1999).

take serious norms-related practice as legal practice.[27] Work on the 'contestation' of international norms stresses that norms are invoked in various sites of social interaction and studies how actors contest the established meaning of norms. Norms are thus conceived as parts of a 'structure of meaning in use'.[28] This structure can always change corresponding to the socially constructed meaning of the norms.[29] Arguably, this variation in IR norms research comes close to the everyday working experience of lawyers – understood as a particular type of social practice. In so doing, it also shares certain features with the international strands of critical legal scholarship, even though these similarities are still rarely acknowledged.[30] In the remainder of this chapter, I build upon this second strand of theoretical work in IR to explore a perspective on legitimacy in the sense of a normative ecology of IHL as a regime of humanity law. I will also draw upon insights in law and society studies, especially critical legal studies and law and geography, which, I think, have a lot in common with IR after this sociological re-orientation.

In her contribution, Garcia raises several questions that apparently parallel the direction taken in the legalization approach.[31] 'When do states regulate which issue by what treaty' and, as she adds, 'when do they opt for rather informal modes of law-making?' In so doing, the explanation of *stagnation/transformation* and *formality/informality* finds its vantage point in the state.[32] By no means is this research interest to be marginalized. However, I argue that formulating the research question in this way implies at least two assumptions that are not made subject to further reflection: an assumption on *what the state is able to do* in its normative context and an assumption on *what the state is*. First, while constructivists in IR have thought about how state agency and international normative structure are co-constitutive,[33]

---

27 Antje Wiener, 'Contested Compliance. Interventions on the Normative Structure of World Politics' (2004) 10 European Journal of International Relations 189. For an in-depth acknowledgement in international law, see Jutta Brunnée and Stephen Toope, *Legitimacy and Legality in International Law* (CUP 2010).

28 Jutta Weldes and Diana Saco, 'Making State Action Possible: The United States and the Discursive Construction of "The Cuban Problem", 1960–1994' (1996) 25 Millennium: Journal of International Studies 361.

29 Jan Klabbers, 'The Meaning of Rules' (2006) 20 International Relations 295; Antje Wiener, *Theory of Contestation* (Springer 2014). For the further debate, see Maren Hofius, 'Community at the Border or the Boundaries of Community? The Case of EU Field Diplomats' (2016) 42 Review of International Studies 939; Holger Niemann and Henrik Schillinger, 'Contestation "All the Way Down"? The Grammar of Contestation in Norm Research' (2017) 43 Review of International Studies 29; Jonas Wolff and Lisbeth Zimmermann, 'Between Banyans and Battle Scenes. Liberal Norms, Contestation, and the Limits of Critique' (2016) 42 Review of International Studies 513.

30 But see Klabbers (n 29); Friedrich Kratochwil, 'How Do Norms Matter' in Michael Byers (ed), *The Role of Law in International Politics: Essays in International Relations and International Law* (OUP 2000) 35–68; Philip Liste, 'The Workings of Power in Transnational Law' (2020), TLI Think! Paper 24/2020, Transnational Law Institute Research Paper Series, Transnational Law Institute, The Dickson Poon School of Law, King's College London <https://papers.ssrn.com/sol3/papers.cfm?abstract_id=3756985> accessed 15 July 2021; Nicholas Onuf, *International Legal Theory: Essays and Engagements, 1966–2006* (Routledge 2011); Nikolas Rajkovic and others (eds), *The Power of Legality: Practices of International Law and their Politics* (CUP 2016).

31 Garcia (n 16), 73.

32 ibid.

33 Alexander Wendt, *Social Theory of International Politics* (CUP 1999).

practice-oriented norms researchers have been interested in 'structures of meaning in use',[34] that is, in how norms-related practice – as in the field of diplomacy[35] – contributes to the practices' normative ecology. While, arguably, these studies have not yet fully exhausted the argument – for example in arguing that the state itself is practice[36] – they have nonetheless relocated the vantage point from the state to *state practice*.

Second, the argument is easily pushed to the point that we may see state practice even where not 'practised' by what we traditionally acknowledge as state agents.[37] Yet, there is no need to push the argument that far, since even more conventional studies suggest that the state we thought to know has changed its form throughout the course of globalization[38] or transgovernmental network governance.[39]

3. THE ZERO-SUM NARRATIVE OF MODERN INTERNATIONAL LAW

The multiplicity of actors involved in practices like both *doing war* and *doing international humanitarian law* does not leave untouched the normative background in which a potential furthering of humanity law takes place. To be sure, the proliferation of new groups of actors, both on the side of civilians to be protected from various forms of 'international' violence as well as on the side of non-state actors which participate in such acts of violence, suggests that a practice-oriented approach that considers a normative dimension is needed. How does practice contribute to social reproduction of the normative ecology of IHL? Considering the mentioned encounters of state and non-state actors – on the battlefields and elsewhere – does it still make sense to speak about 'international' encounters,[40] or should we better use terms like 'transnational' or 'post-international'? And what is the role of IHL – or humanity law – in the reproduction of such encounters, as well as the normative spheres in which they take place?

States have played and continue to play a dominant role in such normative processes. Not only do regimes of humanity law come into being through state consent. They are also – and continuously, as I would hold – reproduced by way of state practice, and Garcia is in fact acknowledging such processes,[41] for example by describing the role of international custom in

---

34 Weldes and Saco (n 28); Antje Wiener, 'Enacting Meaning-in-Use: Qualitative Research on Norms and International Relations' (2009) 35 Review of International Studies 175.

35 Vincent Pouliot, 'The Logic of Practicality. A Theory of Practice of Security Communities' (2008) 62 International Organization 257; Hofius (n 29).

36 For the argument in anthropology, see Akhil Gupta, 'Blurred Boundaries: The Discourse of Corruption, the Culture of Politics and the Imagined State' in Aradhana Sharma and Akhil Gupta (eds), *The Anthropology of the State: A Reader* (Wiley-Blackwell 2006); James Scott, *Seeing like a State: How Certain Schemes to Improve the Human Condition Have Failed* (Yale University Press 1998).

37 See Annelise Riles, *Collateral Knowledge. Legal Reasoning in the Global Financial Markets* (University of Chicago Press 2011). For a radical argument on the transnational state, see William I. Robinson, *Global Capitalism and the Crisis of Humanity* (CUP 2014).

38 Saskia Sassen, 'Neither Global nor National. Novel Assemblages of Territory, Authority and Rights' (2008) 1 Ethics & Global Politics 61.

39 Anne-Marie Slaughter, *A New World Order* (Princeton University Press 2004).

40 For a feminist account to the concept of 'international encounters' see Cynthia Enloe, *Bananas, Beaches and Bases: Making Feminist Sense of International Politics* (2nd edn, University of California Press 2014).

41 Garcia (n 16), 77.

the potential furthering of IHL. The problem with such a view – in other words assuming the state to be the vantage point – is that we tend to neglect how the state and IHL are interrelated. The usual assumption seems to be that the state, in fact, possesses the power to wage war, and that IHL is an attempt to limit the states' 'war power'. As a result, we easily end up with a zero-sum narrative – the more IHL, the less sovereign is the state. It is against this backdrop that the complexity increases through a proliferation of 'new' actors, which, interestingly, appear on both sides – those actors waging war and those attempting to limit the somewhat proliferated 'war powers'.

However, it is perhaps attractive to attempt a thought experiment in which – against the zero-sum narrative of modern international law – IHL is not limiting but enabling the international conduct of states. Let us imagine! Somewhat paradoxically, the 19th-century idea of IHL can also be understood as bringing to the fore a normative demarcation between sovereign state spheres, though in the name of humanity.[42] While war usually takes place on the territory of a state, it is obvious that the use of military force puts the territoriality of the place in question. Through international humanitarianism, the battlefields were made subject to a certain type of regulation of violence. Thus, it is by way of IHL that a formerly domestic space becomes international with the result that the domestic regulation of violence no longer applies. Where a space is in a state of war, interaction is governed by IHL. In turn, it is the application of IHL that renders this space an international space. War is but a spatio-temporal suspension of territorial state sovereignty. Hence, the battlefield is a prototype of an 'international' space not only because states interact in this space but, and more importantly, because this very interaction finds expression in the normative discourse of IHL. By normatively turning state space into war space, IHL abandons the validity of, say, domestic criminal law. IHL is thus 'spatio-generative' for it contributes to the demarcation of space as international space.[43] At the end of the day or, as it were, at the end of the war situation, domestic regulation – old or new – will be revalidated, the war-ridden space be rendered domestic. In other words, the shifting validities of domestic and international law collaborate in the production of space as either domestic or international space.[44]

However, it is questionable whether this 'international' mode of a production of space survives the mentioned proliferation of actors on all sides. On the one hand, it is civilians who have come to threaten humanity 'internationally', whereas, on the other hand, it is state actors who have come to threaten it rather 'transnationally' (for example via drone warfare). Hence, in the post-international constellation, a Tolstoyian interplay of war and peace has come to

---

42 For an in-depth historical study on the co-emergence of the 'international' and the 'individual' see Kuntz (n 2).

43 For the theoretical debate, see Nicholas K. Blomley and others (eds), *The Legal Geographies Reader. Law, Power, and Space* (Blackwell Publishers 2001); Irus Braverman and others (eds), *The Expanding Spaces of Law. A Timely Legal Geography* (Stanford University Press 2014); David Delaney, *The Spatial, the Legal and the Pragmatics of World-making. Nomospheric Investigations* (Routledge 2010); Richard Thompson Ford, 'Law's Territory (A History of Jurisdiction)' (1999) 97 Michigan Law Review 843; Andreas Philippopoulos-Mihalopoulos, 'Law's Spatial Turn: Geography, Justice and a Certain Fear of Space' (2010) 7 Law, Culture and the Humanities 187. For IR, see Philip Liste, 'Geographical Knowledge at Work: Human Rights Litigation and Transnational Territoriality' (2016) 22 European Journal of International Relations 217.

44 Philip Liste, 'Colliding Geographies: Space at Work in Global Governance' (2016) 19 Journal of International Relations and Development 199.

an end. The contemporary pitfalls of 'humanitarian' regulation of violence pose questions for 'where' today's battlefields are. Put differently: what is the adequate scale of humanitarian law in a 'post-national constellation'?

Perhaps, and this is where my thought experiment leads me to, the practice of informality is shifting the scales that help us in understanding problems in a changing world. By way of an informal reproduction of IHL (for example in the work of military handbooks, etc.),[45] the regime has been transformed. This transformation is far-reaching in that it is not limited to the reinterpretation of particular norms but affects the regime's geographic knowledge. While it has traditionally contributed to the production of 'international' space, IHL, in being subject to transgovernmental network governance,[46] has seemingly overcome its 'internationalist' geographical disposition. Practices like drone warfare, targeted killings, or cyber warfare no longer take place in a space necessarily understood as 'international'. Applying IHL to these practices or approving IHL so that it can be applied, also changes the geographical effect of it. To be sure, the zero-sum narrative is less convincing where the spatio-generative force of law has become more indeterminate. It is here that the category of power must be taken into consideration. The critical insight that law structures bargain[47] and, furthermore, that law contributes to the social reproduction of the very subjects whose bargaining power it structures,[48] can be taken at face value, also with respect to IHL and the wider field of humanity law. Law also structures or at least takes part in structuring the space in which social interaction takes place.

4. HUMANITARIANISM IN A NEW NORMATIVE CONSTELLATION

In sum, throughout my consideration of IHL's normative ecology, two main arguments have been made. First, the relation between humanity and the international is dialectical. The two concepts are co-emergent and thus deeply interrelated so that the usual assumption that humanity law transcends state internationalism becomes problematic. Second, IHL has a role to play in the production of space. It has contributed, and arguably continues to contribute, to the production of 'international' space. However, new normative developments as described by Garcia may be interpreted as bringing to the fore shifts in the geographical *(spatio-generative)* capabilities of IHL and, eventually, even a transformation from international to post-international space.

As a result, post-international humanitarian law could be understood in at least two different ways – first, as *post*-international humanitarian law, that is, as giving way to a normative order that has overcome any attempts to legally protect humanity; and second, as *post-international* humanitarian law, that is, as an ongoing attempt to further humanitarianism, though under the conditions of a new normative constellation. To opt for the latter necessitates reflecting

45 Wouter Werner, 'Godot was Always There. Repetition and the Formation of Customary International Law' (2019) Global Cooperation Research Papers 22 <https://doi.org/10.14282/2198-0411-GCRP-22> accessed 31 January 2021.

46 Slaughter (n 39).

47 Robert Lee Hale, 'Coercion and Distribution in a Supposedly Non-Coercive State' (1923) 38 Political Science Quarterly 470.

48 Duncan Kennedy, 'The Stakes of Law, or Hale and Foucault!' (1991) XV Legal Studies Forum 350.

upon the power mechanisms at work within IHL and international humanitarian legal practice. There is thus still hope that the 'invisible college'[49] of international humanitarian lawyers still has a game to play.

49 Oscar Schachter, 'The Invisible College of International Lawyers' (1977) 72 Northwestern University Law Review 217.

7. Noncompliance as law-making

Timothy Meyer

1. INTRODUCTION

Michael Reisman once wrote that 'international lawyers frequently respond to the appearance of a discrepancy between existing and emerging legal arrangements by heatedly rejecting the new with a fury of virtuous unanimity against the evil whose name is Change'.[1] This quote is never more true than when international lawyers consider the role of lawbreaking in law-making. While civil disobedience has a safe – and in some countries revered – legacy as a means of prodding governments to make laws more consonant with modern notions of justice, commenters are not similarly sanguine in discussing noncompliance as a law-making device in international law. Lawbreaking is often viewed as antithetical to the values underlying the law of nations and a challenge to the enterprise of international law.

Yet, as I explain below, in certain circumstances it makes perfect sense to talk about noncompliance as law-making. Indeed, far from representing a challenge to international law, recognizing the juris-generative role of noncompliance reveals that some violations demonstrate a state's commitment to international law's collective endeavor. States sometimes violate the law in order to improve it, just as those who engage in civil disobedience do so in order to change it for the better. Moreover, allowing noncompliance to play a law-making role may be essential to the long-term viability of the international legal enterprise. While states cannot really exit their relationships with each other, they can effectively exit their legal obligations by persistently violating the law. Given this reality, turning some violations into constructive acts of law-making may enhance the viability of the international legal system, rather than undermine it.

At the same time, the role of noncompliance is fraught. In most cases, noncompliance can only effectively be used to change the law by a handful of states. Those states use noncompliance to circumvent the traditional multilateral law-making process, thereby reducing the procedural legitimacy of the resulting law. Moreover, states that use noncompliance will typically do so because the changes in the law are in their own interest. Sometimes the changes may also increase overall welfare, but not always. Noncompliance can thus also produce laws that are inequitable relative to the status quo. This downside is inextricably bound up with noncompliance's function as a safety valve – it allows law to adapt to political realities in a way that formal multilateral law-making can prevent. The United States' (US) conduct in regards

[1] W Michael Reisman, 'Assessing Claims to Revise the Law of War' (2003) 97 American Journal of International Law 82, 83 (internal quotations and citations omitted).

to the laws of war and use of force during the 21st century highlight the double-edged sword of noncompliant law-making. On the one hand, the US has challenged, expanded, and shifted the boundaries of legality, making clear that the law does not constrain states equally. On the other hand, using noncompliance to change the law has constrained the US in ways different from those that commentators normally discuss.

This chapter proceeds as follows. Part 2 unpacks the notion of noncompliance as law-making. Noncompliance is frequently seen as an act that sets the lawbreaker at odds with the community of nations that have enacted the law broken. Denying noncompliance law-making power is, on this view, essential to safeguarding the collective values embodied in multilateral law. Yet noncompliance as law-making is different in kind from noncompliance designed only to cheat on a state's obligations. As such, it has different ends and employs different means than mere cheating. Nor is noncompliance binary. States often take action that is only arguably noncompliant, or which some states view as noncompliant and others do not. Although these instances might be framed as matters of interpretation, they can give rise to the same costs as noncompliance and states can take the arguably unlawful action with an eye to changing the kinds of conduct other states consider compliant. For these reasons, I use 'noncompliance' to refer to both outright noncompliance and to arguable noncompliance that might raise questions of interpretation. I also treat reinterpreting an existing legal obligation as similar to renegotiating an obligation. Interpretation and negotiation are different legal skills. However, reinterpretation and renegotiation often have the same practical effect and can therefore be used for the same end – shifting expectations about what counts as compliance.[2]

Part 3 sets forth a descriptive theory of law-making through noncompliance. I argue that for noncompliance to be an effective law-making technique, it must 1) be public; 2) carry with it a credible threat to continue the violation indefinitely; 3) the normative content of the violation must be acceptable to other states as an alternative rule; and 4) the violator's relative costs of law-making through noncompliance are less than they would be through conventional multilateral law-making channels. Although this theory is a general theory of when noncompliance will work as a law-making vehicle, throughout the chapter my discussion focuses primarily on international humanitarian law (IHL).

Part 4 assesses the normative desirability of law-making through noncompliance. I argue that a limited role for law-making through noncompliance is necessary for the international legal system to function effectively. Noncompliance as law-making can thus be justified on systemic grounds. Having said that, law-making through noncompliance injects the power and self-interest of the violating state into the law-making process to a much greater extent than multilateral law-making. It thus raises distributional concerns. These concerns, while serious, are ameliorated by features of law-making through noncompliance and the more active role taken by non-governmental organizations (NGOs) such as the International Committee of the Red Cross (ICRC) to safeguard the collective interest in the content of the law.

---

[2] Monica Hakimi, for example, has argued that the process of customary international law identification is inextricably bound up with the process of customary international law-making. Monica Hakimi, 'Custom's Method and Process: lessons from Humanitarian Law' in Curtis A Bradley (ed), *Custom's Future: International Law in a Changing World* (CUP 2016).

2. WHAT DO WE MEAN BY 'NONCOMPLIANCE AS LAW-MAKING'?

2.1 Noncompliance as Cheating

At first blush, the notion of noncompliance as law-making may seem like an oxymoron. Lawmakers are engaged in a juris-generative act. As such, they are committed to the legal regime they are creating. Lawbreakers are attempting to evade the law's strictures to their own advantage. They reject judgments about common objectives embodied in the legal regime. Jean-Marie Henckaerts reflected this view in his response to the US government's comments on the ICRC's report on customary IHL: 'But when an operational practice is generally considered to be a violation of existing rules – for example, civilian installations are targeted – that is all it is, a violation. Such violations are not of a nature to modify existing rules; they cannot dictate the law.'[3]

Commenting later on the 'large mix of official practice supporting [customary international humanitarian law rules in non-international armed conflicts] and their outright violation' of those rules, Henckaerts goes further. To suggest that widespread violations of purported customary international humanitarian law rules means that there is not enough practice to support the rule 'confound[s] the value of existing "positive" practice with the many violations of the law in non-international armed conflicts. This would mean that we let violators dictate the law or stand in the way of rules emerging.'[4]

This view is quite sensible. It reflects the fact that international law embodies the values that the international community has endorsed through treaties and custom. It prevents what Michael Glennon has urged, namely 'that the excessive violation of a rule, whether embodied in custom or treaty, causes the rule to be replaced by another rule that permits unrestricted freedom of action'.[5] Cautious international lawyers may well fear the anarchy that might come from adopting such a view.

It also deals with the moral hazard problem to which Henckaerts alludes. To recognize violations as more than violations risks opening the door to letting bad actors establish the rules. This problem is most famously captured with references to the rules against torture. Unfortunately, many nations have in the not-too-distant past engaged in behavior that might be considered torture. The use of waterboarding by the US during the Bush Administration represents the most salient example. Yet, despite this activity, all nations and commentators continue to state that international law prohibits torture. The torturers' noncompliance is just that – a violation that has not changed the law.

Beyond simply denying violations' law-making force, many commentators through the years have invoked noncompliance as evidence that international law is ineffective at chang-

---

3 Jean-Marie Henckaerts, 'Customary International Humanitarian Law: A Response to US Comments' (2007) 89 International Review of the Red Cross 473, 477.

4 ibid 486.

5 Michael J Glennon, 'How International Rules Die' (2005) 93 Georgetown Law Journal 939, 940.

ing state behavior[6] or not 'law' in some relevant sense.[7] This claim has had particular purchase in IHL. No less an authority than Hersch Lauterpacht wrote that: 'if international law is (...) the vanishing point of law, the law of war is even more conspicuously the vanishing point of international law (...). The very idea of the legal regulation of a condition of mere force has appeared to many incongruous to the point of absurdity.'[8] The place of noncompliance in international law is thus fraught. Denying or limiting the law-making role of noncompliance preserves the fundamentally collective nature of the international legal enterprise. It ensures that the worst elements of our behavior are not captured in the content of the law.

But international law may not be able to bear the weight of stigmatizing noncompliance in such a black-and-white way. Although IHL's status as law is beyond question today, Lauterpacht's claim surrounding its 'absurdity' touches on a suspicion that many have had over the years. If noncompliance is too frequent, or if the law cannot constrain certain (usually powerful) states, of what value is international law in general, and laws governing how force is used in particular? If noncompliance is simply unlawful conduct, one can be forgiven for thinking that compliance is an important metric by which we should judge international law's effectiveness.[9] Insisting that noncompliance is nothing more than bad behavior, in other words, can create a legitimacy problem if too much practice appears to occur with disregard for formal legal rules.

2.2 How Noncompliance Influences Law-Making

The view that noncompliance is or should be viewed as mere unlawful conduct – and the resulting risk that compliance will become the primary metric by which international law is judged – misunderstands the relationship between state behavior and law-making.[10] It assumes that law and behavior relate to each other sequentially. First, states act as lawmakers. They write the laws that will govern their future conduct, or they produce them through the amalgam of state practice and *opinio juris* that leads to customary international law (CIL). Here, states bargain with each other over treaty terms in the shadow of power and interest, as well as in light of the moral considerations that have driven so much law-making in the human rights and

---

6 Peter Spiro has referred to the notion that individual acts of noncompliance demonstrate that international law is ineffective generally as the Perfect Compliance Fallacy. See Peter Spiro, 'Ukraine, International Law, and the Perfect Compliance Fallacy' (*Opinio Juris,* 2 March 2014) <opiniojuris.org/2014/03/02/ukraine-international-law-perfect-compliance-fallacy/> accessed 31 January 2021.

7 See eg Jack L Goldsmith and Eric A Posner, *The Limits of International Law* (OUP 2005) 3: 'International law has long been burdened with the charge that it is not really law'.

8 Hersch Lauterpacht, *International Law, Collected Papers*, vol 2 (CUP 1975) 37.

9 Effectiveness is a distinct notion from compliance. Effectiveness asks how much a state has changed its behavior in response to an international obligation, regardless of whether it has achieved compliance. Compliance asks whether a state has satisfied the legal standard. A law might be highly effective without producing compliance if the legal standard is very demanding. Alternatively, compliance rates might be very high but effectiveness low if the law only directs states to do what they would have done in the absence of the law. Despite these difficulties, studies of international law's effectiveness often use compliance as a proxy. See Lisa L. Martin, 'Against Compliance' in Jeffrey L Dunhoff and Mark A Pollack (eds), *Interdisciplinary Perspectives on International Law and International Relations: The State of the Art* (CUP 2013) 591–610.

10 Timothy Meyer, 'How Compliance Understates Effectiveness' (2014) 108 Proceedings of the 108th Annual Meeting (American Society of International Law) 168, 170.

humanitarian areas in the last century. They weigh the effect of their statements and actions on the formation of custom. Indeed, even though custom is not traditionally understood to involve an element of bargaining, many of the interactions between states that produce custom look a lot like implicit bargaining.[11] This element of bargaining is especially clear today, when states regularly use negotiated acts, such as UN General Assembly Resolutions and treaties that codify or crystallize custom, as a way to deliberately create custom.[12]

At the second stage, states are international citizens. Like individual citizens of a nation, states are treated as if they have no power over the content of the rules governing them at this stage. Instead, they are passive recipients of the law who must choose whether or not to behave.

While this model captures important aspects of how states relate to each other, it fails to capture the fundamentally dynamic nature of international law-making and its relationship with compliance. International law (like all law) is uncertain in many of its applications. States can thus use arguably noncompliant acts as a way to advance claims about how the law should be interpreted. Monica Hakimi has argued, for example, that possibly unlawful efforts to boost enforcement against Iran for violating the Nuclear Nonproliferation Treaty are best understood as law-making activity, rather than simple enforcement.[13] More aggressively, states can openly violate the law in a bid to renegotiate its content.[14]

Law-making thus exists side by side with (non)compliance. Noncompliant acts may be merely violations. Or they may be tacit proposals to treat the conduct in question as legal. This raises a doctrinal problem: how can the law of treaties and customary international law accommodate law-making through noncompliance? It also raises a conceptual problem. Henckaerts is surely correct that not all noncompliance, nor indeed most noncompliance, is or should be treated as law-making activity. How, then, do we distinguish run-of-the-mill noncompliance from noncompliance as law-making?

With respect to the doctrinal question, the law-making role of violations has long been recognized in the context of custom. In 1971, Anthony D'Amato wrote that '[t]he only way customary international law can change (...) is by giving legal effect to departures from preceding customary norms.'[15] Perhaps the famous example is the expansion of the territorial sea to twelve miles, a shift in customary law brought about in part by widespread violation of

---

11 Harlan Cohen has written that '[c]ustom is the paradigmatic negotiated law'. Harlan Grant Cohen, 'International Law's Erie Moment' (2013) 34 Michigan Journal of International Law 249, 293. To be fair, as Ingrid Wuerth and Laurence Helfer note, custom is not formally negotiated in the way treaties are, although it does reflect a 'struggle for law reflected in exchanges of signals, cues, bids, and responses'. Ingrid Wuerth and Laurence R Helfer, 'Customary International Law: An Instrument Choice Perspective' (2016) 37 Michigan Journal of International Law 563, 575 (quoting David Bederman and Thomas Franck).

12 Timothy Meyer, 'Codifying Custom' (2012) 160 University of Pennsylvania Law Review 995.

13 Monica Hakimi, 'Unfriendly Unilateralism' (2014) 55 Harvard International Law Journal 105, 108.

14 Timothy Meyer, 'Power, Exit Costs, and Renegotiation in International Law' (2010) 51 Harvard International Law Journal 379.

15 Anthony D'Amato, *The Concept of Custom in International Law* (Cornell University Press 1971).

the traditional three-mile limit. The International Court of Justice (ICJ) recognized the potential law-making role violations of CIL can play in its *Nicaragua* decision.[16]

Yet at the same time that it recognized the law-making role of noncompliance in theory, the ICJ minimized that role in practice. The Court wrote 'that instances of State conduct inconsistent with a given rule should generally have been treated as breaches of that rule, not as indications of the recognition of a new rule', otherwise violations would undermine the consistent state practice necessary to support the continued existence of a rule of CIL.[17] In short, a preference for the status quo tends to prevail over efforts to use noncompliance to change CIL.[18]

Treaties present a more difficult doctrinal problem. Unlike custom, treaty law does not formally have a role for law-making through noncompliance. Nevertheless, noncompliance can still drive changes to treaties in several different ways. First, states can use persistent noncompliance as a threat to effectively withdraw from a treaty if it is not explicitly renegotiated. The US followed this tactic when it took itself off the gold standard in violation of the Articles of Agreement of the International Monetary Fund. This violation – effectively a withdrawal – prompted five years of renegotiation leading to amendments to the Articles of Agreement.[19]

Second, states can use violations, or arguable violations, to drive implicit renegotiations. These implicit renegotiations typically take the form of shifting interpretations of legal requirements. For instance, during the 1980s the US decided to proceed with its Strategic Defense Initiative (SDI), a missile defense program that appeared to violate the Anti-Ballistic Missile (ABM) Treaty with the Soviet Union.[20] Despite protesting SDI's illegality, the Soviet Union ultimately acquiesced in the US reinterpretation of the agreement, and the ABM Treaty operated for almost another two decades. Doctrinally, states can sometimes use the doctrine of subsequent state practice to accommodate arguably unlawful conduct as consistent with an existing treaty.[21] Technically, the use of subsequent state practice is a question of interpretation. My point, however, is that the interpretation of the treaty – states' expectations as to what counts as compliance – can shift in response to actions that states would have considered unlawful when they created the treaty and perhaps at the time a state first took the action in question.

Conceptually, noncompliance as cheating can be distinguished from noncompliance as law-making by the kinds of benefits noncompliance creates for the violator. The violator may be trying to get immediate benefit by cheating on its obligations while other states continue

---

16 *Case Concerning Military and Paramilitary Activities in and Against Nicaragua* (*Nicaragua v United States*) (Merits) [1986] ICJ Rep 14 para 186.

17 ibid.

18 This status quo bias is strongest in the case of *jus cogens* norms, where no violation could change the rule unless the violation gave birth to a new *jus cogens* rule.

19 Dominique Carreau, 'Why Not Merge the International Monetary Fund (IMF) with the International Bank for Reconstruction and Development (World Bank)?' (1994) Fordham Law Review 1989.

20 Gary M. Buechler, 'Constitutional Limits on the President's Power to Interpret Treaties: The Sofaer Doctrine, the Biden Condition, and the Doctrine of Binding Authoritative Representations' (1990) 78 Georgetown Law Journal 1983.

21 See Vienna Convention on the Law of Treaties (adopted 23 May 1969, entered into force 27 January 1980) 1155 UNTS 331 art 31 (3); ILC, 'First report on subsequent agreements and subsequent practice in relation to treaty interpretation' (6 May–7 June & 8 July–9 August 2013) UN Doc A/CN.4/660.

to comply. Analyses of compliance problems in international law usually assume that states violate their obligations in order to seek short-term benefits. The prisoner's dilemma, the game most commonly used to understand compliance problems, involves states cheating on their obligations to get an advantage today at the expense of long-term cooperation. Only by making long-term cooperation sufficiently valuable can states overcome the incentive to cheat in a prisoner's dilemma.[22] Moreover, when a state cheats on its obligations without seeking to change the law, it will likely seek to hide its violation. Hiding cheating maximizes the benefit a state gets. It engages in its preferred activity without incurring the costs of noncompliance other states might impose should they discover the violation.

The calculus is reversed for a violator seeking to change the law. The majority of the gains do not stem directly from its own noncompliance. The gains it hopes to achieve are through shifting the expectations and conduct of other states in the medium to long term. Because its aim is to change other states' behavior, the violator will make its own noncompliance public. That publicity, in turn, guarantees that the violator will pay short-term costs. In some situations, of course, the violator may also receive short-term benefits from violation, as in the prisoner's dilemma. The key idea, though, is that a violator seeking to change the law has happily decided to incur the costs of noncompliance today in order to secure benefits tomorrow – the opposite of the ordinary noncompliance model.

3. UNDER WHAT CONDITIONS CAN NONCOMPLIANT ACTS EFFECTIVELY MAKE LAW?

To say that noncompliance can be a form of law-making is not, of course, to say that it will be effective as such. In this section, I set forth four conditions that I posit are necessary for noncompliance to make law effectively: 1) the violation must be public; 2) it must carry with it a credible threat to continue the violation indefinitely; 3) the normative content of the violation must be acceptable as an alternative rule to other states; and 4) the violator's costs of law-making through noncompliance are less than they would be through multilateral law-making efforts.

3.1 Public Violations

Noncompliance intended to change the law must be public. If it is not, other states cannot adjust their future expectations and conduct in response to the violation. As discussed above, this feature distinguishes law-making through noncompliance from cheating on one's legal obligations. Moreover, as I explain in section 4, this necessity provides a critical safeguard in limiting the misuse of noncompliance as a law-making technique. Because the violation must be public, the violating state must be willing to incur the costs of violation in order to change the law.

As a result, standard techniques for deterring violations will be less effective at deterring noncompliance aimed at law-making. In the context of cheating, states frequently employ monitoring techniques or other forms of transparency as a way to reduce violations. For

---

[22] Of course, violations can also be unintentional, but I put such violations to one side and focus on violations that the relevant actors intend to commit.

example, the Red Cross might inspect prisoner of war (POW) camps to ensure that the treatment POWs receive is consistent with the Geneva Conventions. An increased risk of detection may deter states from committing violations by raising the expected costs of violation. You are more likely to be sanctioned if your breach is more likely to be discovered.

But discovery is the entire point of law-making through noncompliance. A state using noncompliance in this way will therefore treat sanctions as guaranteed. Monitoring mechanisms are useless because the state itself has an incentive to self-report. All else equal, this means that violations aimed at changing the law will be costlier in expectation than simple cheating.[23] Cheating, after all, may go undiscovered and therefore unsanctioned. But it also means that conventional legal methods will be less effective at dissuading a state from engaging in noncompliance as law-making once it is set on that course.

Put differently, states have two levers they can pull to deter cheating. They can raise the risk of discovery through monitoring and transparency, and they can raise the sanction for violation through means such as dispute resolution procedures. But where noncompliance aims to change the law, states can only use the second lever.

3.2 Credible Threat

Noncompliance works as a law-making technique when it creates the expectation in other states that the violating state will no longer cooperate under existing rules. The state must, in other words, create a credible threat that it will permanently walk away from prevailing rules. If states believe that the violating state will in the future revert to cooperation if they only wait it out, other states need not change their behavior. Put differently, states must assess whether the violating state is prepared to implement its unlawful policy unilaterally even if other states do not agree to changes in the law. If other states believe the violating state is so prepared, they are faced with a decision as to whether to acquiesce to changes in the law or forsake cooperation with the violating state.

The existence of a credible threat to engage in long-term violation or outright exit also distinguishes noncompliance as law-making from ordinary cheating. Cheating states ordinarily seek short-term gains. They will come back into compliance in the future if pressure is sufficiently great. Likewise, a violating state may trumpet its violation as a form of law-making even if it will revert to compliance if other states call its bluff. In cases of both cheating and bluffing, the status quo rule with compliance by all sides remains an option. But where a state can make a credible threat to continue its violation indefinitely, the state has effectively removed the status quo as an option for other states. Other states can either continue cooperating under the status quo rule without the violating state's participation, or they can change the rule to accommodate the violating state.

In reality, of course, states will often be unsure of the credibility of a violating state's threat. In practice, then, law-making through noncompliance may often become a game of brinksmanship. Instead of jumping to commit serious breaches of an obligation (which would be the most costly action for it to take), the violating state may take increasingly costly action to persuade other states that its threat is indeed credible.

---

23 The expected penalty for a violation is equal to the probability of discovery multiplied by the sanction in the event of discovery.

As a consequence, a state using noncompliance for law-making must demonstrate its resolve to continue an ongoing violation. One thing that can make demonstrating resolve easier is if other states follow suit quickly. If they quickly declare their support for the new rule, this reduces the pressure on the violating state to capitulate because it can now cooperate with some other states. Likewise, it increases pressure on status quo states as they shrink in number.

States have a number of other ways that they can demonstrate their resolve. Implementing a sustained program predicated on the new understanding of the law can demonstrate that the violating state is committed to its course of conduct. The US's program for detaining 'unlawful enemy combatants' at Guantanamo Bay, Cuba, illustrates how states may assess resolve. The Bush Administration maintained that a range of protections arguably applicable to the detainees under IHL did not apply.[24] For a variety of reasons beyond the scope of this chapter, many disagreed with the Bush Administration's position and viewed the US as violating IHL.[25] Yet the Bush Administration's commitment to its position was made clear by its consistent backing of the operation of the facility at Guantanamo Bay and its efforts to work with the US Congress to establish a domestic legal framework that would satisfy requirements set forth by the US Supreme Court, most notably in *Hamdan v. Rumsfeld*.[26]

Yet while the Bush Administration's own resolve may have been clear, many may have suspected that the next administration would walk back from some of the Bush Administration's more aggressive legal justifications for its action. In this way, nations may have doubted the US's long-term commitment to its position, even if they did not doubt the Bush Administration's determination.

Another example of how states demonstrate credibility comes from a debate over when the sinking of a neutral merchant vessel is permitted under the laws of war. As Isabel Hull recounts, until 1869 neither international law nor any European country permitted the sinking of such vessels under any conditions. In 1869, however, Russia adopted naval rules that would have permitted such vessels to be sunk under some conditions. Japan and the US changed the rules in their naval manuals in the decades that followed, but none of the three took action consistent with their new position. Thus, while they staked out a position at odds with the prevailing interpretation of the laws of war, the credibility of their commitment to the position was questionable due to the lack of concrete action.

In 1904, Russia took more aggressive action. It sank a British steamship during the Russo-Japanese War, a destruction that its prize court ultimately upheld as legal. Russia later partially retreated from the legal consequences of its actions by explaining a second neutral sinking as an accident. Yet these policy changes and outright violations set the table for a rethinking of rules regarding the sinking of neutral merchant vessels in the 1909 Declaration of London.[27]

---

24 See eg John Bellinger, 'Unlawful Enemy Combatants' (*Opinio Juris,* 17 January 2007) <opiniojuris.org/2007/01/17/unlawful-enemy-combatants/> accessed 31 January 2021.

25 See eg Johan Steyn, 'Guantanamo Bay: The Legal Black Hole' (2004) 53 International & Comparative Law Quarterly 1; Derek Jinks and David Sloss, 'Is the President Bound by the Geneva Conventions?' (2004) 90 Cornell Law Review 97, 101.

26 548 US 557 (2006).

27 Isabel V Hull, *A Scrap of Paper: Breaking and Making International Law During the Great War* (Cornell University Press 2014) 213.

This example highlights how states may dip their toes in the water of noncompliance. Early policy changes by Russia, the US, and Japan lacked indicia of credibility, since they were merely written policies. At the same time, changes to naval manuals are much less costly than the arguable wrongful sinking of a vessel. Russia's later actions, on the other hand, spurred legal change, ultimately leading Britain – the primary proponent of an absolute ban on the destruction of neutral merchant vessels – to accept exceptions to the rule permitting the destruction of the vessel where, among others, bringing the vessel into port for a determination of the validity of capture 'would involve danger to the safety of the warship or to the success of the operations in which she is engaged at the time'.[28] Even then, though, Russia's claim that its second sinking was an accident left it room to retreat from its position if it had encountered too much resistance. The incident reflects, in effect, Russia's desire to demonstrate resolve to change the law without incurring overly high costs for its actions.

3.3 Acceptability

Even if states view a noncompliant act as a credible threat, in order to be a successful law-making technique other states must still prefer to cooperate with the violating state on new terms rather than continue to cooperate among themselves under the existing legal rule. For some states, this calculus will be easy. They may, for example, also dislike the prevailing legal rule and prefer changes advocated by the violating state. Alternatively, they may be closely allied with the violating state and feel obligated to follow its lead. For example, the US has articulated an 'unwilling or unable' standard governing the use of force against non-state actors in a non-consenting state.[29] Some scholars have vehemently rejected that test,[30] however, and states have worried about when the standard is properly invoked.[31] Others, notably close US allies like the United Kingdom,[32] Australia,[33] Canada,[34] and Turkey,[35] have openly embraced the doctrine in the context of justifying the use of force against the Islamic State in Syria. The more states that follow the violating state's lead, the easier the violating state will find it to use noncompliance to change the law. As more states flock to its cause, the gravitational pull of the existing rule weakens in favor of the alternative.

---

28 ibid 214.

29 See Ashley S Deeks, '"Unwilling or Unable": Towards a Normative Framework for Extraterritorial Self-Defense' (2012) 52 Virginia Journal of International Law 483.

30 Kevin Jon Heller, 'Do Attacks on ISIS in Syria Justify the "Unwilling or Unable" Test' (*Opinio Juris*, 13 December 2014) <opiniojuris.org/2014/12/13/attacks-isis-syria-justify-unwilling-unable-test/> accessed 31 January 2021.

31 For example, the Dutch government appears to accept the 'unwilling or unable' test in principle but did not believe it justifies the use of force against the Islamic State in Syria as of 2014–15. See the Dutch Government's decision to get involved: Kamerstukken II 2014–15, 27925, nr. 506, 5–6.

32 The United Kingdom's embrace of the doctrine dates back to the *Caroline* incident. *See* Abraham D Sofaer, 'On the Necessity of Preemption' (2003) 14 European Journal of International Law 209, 214–17.

33 UNSC 'Letter from the Permanent Representative of Australia to the United Nations addressed to the President of the Security Council' (9 September 2015) UN Doc S/2015/693.

34 UNSC 'Letter from the Charge d'affairs a.i. of the Permanent Mission of Canada to the United Nations addressed to the President of the Security Council' (31 March 2015) UN Doc S/2015/221.

35 UNSC 'Letter from the Charge d'affairs a.i. of the Permanent Mission of Turkey to the United Nations addressed to the President of the Security Council' (24 July 2015) UN Doc S/2015/563.

For other states, however, the prevailing legal rule may be preferable to the alternative. These states may prefer to coordinate, all else equal, but have diverging preferences about the specific rule on which they coordinate.[36] Critically, however, these states can no longer weigh the value of cooperating on existing terms against any proposed change to the law. Assuming it can credibly threaten to violate its obligations indefinitely, the violating state has taken the status quo off the table. Instead, other states have to weigh up decisions to cooperate on existing terms without the violating state's participation against cooperating on new terms with the violating state.

In these situations, the success of noncompliance hinges on whether status quo states prefer cooperation on second-best terms to a failure to cooperate at all. As the disagreements over which rule to choose become greater, states may prefer to let the violating state (and any allies) go its own way. When this happens, noncompliance through law-making can cause agreement on legal rules to unravel. Alternatively, if the violating state was not committed to going it alone under its new policy, it may revert to cooperating under pre-existing legal rules.

Two examples illustrate the point. First, under both the Bush and Obama Administrations, the United States has made extensive use of drones to target non-state actors such as Taliban or al-Qaeda members in Afghanistan and the tribal regions of Pakistan. Leading public figures, such as Philip Alston, the UN Special Rapporteur on Extrajudicial, Summary, or Arbitrary Executions, have expressed concern that the US use of drones does not comply with the laws of war, specifically the principles of distinction and proportionality.[37] In response to these criticisms, the US took steps to justify its conduct, most notably through a 2010 speech by State Department Legal Adviser Harold Hongju Koh.[38] Despite these efforts, however, many have continued to decry the US drone program as unlawful.[39] Similarly, in 1922 and again in 1930 nations rejected Germany's view during the First World War – on which it had acted – that submarines could sink merchant vessels without attempting to save passengers and crew.[40]

In other cases, states may prefer an accommodation. Such cases will typically be situations in which the value states get from cooperation stems primarily from coordinating their policies, regardless of the specific rule on which they coordinate. In these situations the violating state acts as a catalyst. Changing international rules typically requires costly action of some kind, even if that action is simply bearing the diplomatic and political costs of generating a consensus. These costs give international law a status quo bias. This bias is especially strong in treaty law, where the consent of each state is necessary before it can be bound by any change. It also applies to custom, however, where replacing an existing customary rule

---

[36] This kind of strategic situation is often referred to as a Battle of the Sexes game. In the standard Battle of the Sexes game, players prefer coordination but have diverging preferences about which rule they coordinate on.

[37] 'US warned on deadly drone attacks' (*BBC News*, 28 October 2009) <news.bbc.co.uk/2/hi/8329412.stm> accessed 31 January 2021.

[38] Harold Hongju Koh, Legal Advisor, U.S. Department of State, 'The Obama Administration and International Law', Speech at Annual Meeting of the American Society of International Law (Washington, DC, 25 March 2010) <https://2009-2017.state.gov/s/l/releases/remarks/139119.htm> accessed 31 January 2021.

[39] See eg Avery Plaw, 'Counting the Dead: The Proportionality of Predation in Pakistan' in Bradley Jay Strawser (ed), *Killing by Remote Control: The Ethics of an Unmanned Military* (OUP 2013) 126–29 (reviewing reports alleging that US drone strikes in Pakistan kill a disproportionate number of civilians).

[40] Hull (n 27) 197, 209.

requires widespread state practice and *opinio juris* in favor of the new rule. This status quo bias can prevent changes in the law that most states would accept. Noncompliance can allow states collectively to overcome this status quo bias by offering the violating state's conduct as a focal point for cooperation.

The use of a single distinctive symbol to the medical services of a country's armed forces provides an illustrative example. Article 38 of the first Geneva Convention of 1949 provides that the red cross shall be 'the emblem and distinctive sign of the Medical Service of armed forces'. This rule reflects the great gains that come from having a single easily identifiable symbol that all nations use and hence can protect. Article 38 also included an exception for original parties to the Geneva Convention that already used a different symbol, such as the red crescent or red lion. As the 2016 ICRC commentaries explain, this provision was intended as a limited exception; new member states would all use the red cross in order to promote uniformity.[41] The commentaries go on, however, to note that in practice new members did not adhere to this rule. Instead, they 'adopted the emblem most suitable for their national circumstances. Today, all of the distinctive emblems enjoy equal status.'[42] In short, state practice inconsistent with the initial understanding of the original parties to the Geneva Convention drove this change. Yet because each nation would itself adopt a single symbol that other parties could identify, the rule still achieved its key coordinating function.[43]

Even in situations in which state opinions about the ideal rule diverge to a greater degree, states may ultimately come to accept the violating state's conduct. During the First World War, for example, Britain engaged in a de facto blockade of Germany. The blockade involved a number of techniques difficult to justify under pre-war international law, including the seizure of German-origin products regardless of ownership being shipped between two neutral ports. Britain worried greatly about the reaction of neutrals to its policies. It nevertheless proceeded to act first, rather than negotiate with other countries (including neutrals). The British action occasioned some discomfort from neutrals and its own ally, France. Ultimately, though, the San Remo Manual, negotiated after the war under the auspices of the International Institute of Humanitarian Law, 'judged Britain's blockade to have been on the whole a reasonable modern adaptation of the principles of maritime warfare'.[44]

3.4 Forum Selection

Noncompliance as law-making can be contrasted with multilateral law-making, either through express negotiations in the treaty context or implicit negotiation in the context of customary law. In the latter case, the change in the law precedes the (previously unlawful) conduct; with noncompliance, the change in the law is subsequent to the conduct. States wishing to advocate changes to the law must choose between these two methods: violate first, or negotiate? In

---

41 Geneva Convention (I) for the Amelioration of the Condition of the Wounded and Sick in Armed Forces in the Field (adopted 12 August 1949, entered into force 21 October 1950), 75 UNTS 85. ICRC, *Commentary on the First Geneva Convention: Convention (I) for the Amelioration of the Condition of the Wounded and Sick in Armed Forces in the Field* (CUP 2016) art 38 – Emblem of the Convention, para 2.

42 ibid.

43 I thank Jean-Marie Henckaerts for this example.

44 Hull (n 27) 210.

practice, of course, noncompliant acts that become the basis for subsequent law are typically negotiated at some point. The question is thus not whether to completely forego multilateral negotiations; rather, the decision is whether to table an initial proposal in diplomatic fora or through a noncompliant act.

States make this choice based on the relative costs of the two techniques. The primary costs associated with noncompliance are any sanctions flowing from the violation itself, as well as the costs of foregone cooperation during the period in which the state is in violation. Multilateral law-making comes with a set of diplomatic and political costs. Treaty development requires diplomatic conferences and sometimes cumbersome domestic ratification procedures. States advocating new rules also may have to lobby other nations. This lobbying can take the form of disbursing foreign aid or making concessions to other nations in an effort to win their support.

In the end, though, the primary cost associated with both models may be delay and the risk of failure.[45] If all states would willingly accept a change to the law, violation is likely not necessary as a means to advance the proposal. Multilateral law-making may reach the same result with relative speed. Unfortunately, though, a small number of determined states can usually defeat changes to the law through multilateral law-making. In the treaty context, they can simply refuse to agree to an amendment. Using violations to create pressure for change can thus speed up negotiations and make a successful outcome more likely.

To be sure, the customary law context – as well as the process of interpretation and use of subsequent practice in the treaty context, which bears some resemblance to the process through which customary law is formed[46] – is more flexible than treaty-making. Perhaps for this reason, these techniques have gained ground in recent years, especially in areas of the law like IHL. The ICRC's 2016 commentaries on the Geneva Conventions illustrate the point. As the Geneva Conventions already have commentaries, including an earlier set of commentaries issued by the ICRC itself,[47] the key reason for issuing new commentaries was to shift expectations about what constitutes compliance with the Conventions in light of evolving practices and views.

Yet even in customary law and related contexts, states' persistent objections or refusals to characterize arguably legal actions as lawful can prevent an existing rule of custom from changing. Indeed, even in situations in which a change makes no state worse off, states may fail to adopt changes to the law. Holdout states that would otherwise accept a particular rule may refuse to agree if they think that they can achieve an even better outcome by linking agreement on one issue to concessions from other states on another issue.

---

45 In the context of trade negotiations between the United States and the European Union, for instance, US Secretary of Commerce Penny Pritzker has emphasized that there is 'a cost to waiting' to complete a free trade agreement, 'Pritzker, Gabriel Blame Each Other for Lack of Progress in TTIP talks' (*Inside U.S. Trade*, 26 April 2016) <https://insidetrade.com/daily-news/pritzker-gabriel-blame-each-other-lack-progress-ttip-talks> accessed 31 January 2021.

46 Monica Hakimi, 'Law and the Universal Human Rights Treaties' (2013) <https://web.law.duke.edu/cicl/pdf/opiniojuris/panel_4-hakimi-law_and_the_universal_human.pdf> accessed 31 January 2021. Hakimi notes that '[w]hen a treaty does not delegate law-making authority, its interpretive space is filled – ie, its precise content is established – by something akin to custom.'

47 eg Jean Pictet, *Commentary on the Geneva Conventions of 12 August 1949* (ICRC 1952).

Holdout states can thus derail welfare-enhancing changes to the law. In economic parlance, so-called Kaldor-Hicks changes to the law increase overall welfare, although some states may be made worse off. Multilateral law-making makes it relatively easy for those states to prevent Kaldor-Hicks improving changes to the law.[48] In theory, transfers among states should be able to compensate those states, thereby transforming Kaldor-Hicks improvements into Pareto improvements – changes to the law that make no state worse off and make at least one state better off.[49] In reality, holdouts and transaction costs can make these transfers difficult to achieve.[50]

Violations can be particularly useful as a way to jumpstart negotiations bogged down by these difficulties. They can short-circuit some of these multilateral costs by forcing states to respond to the credible threat that another state will simply cease abiding by existing rules. Negotiating around violations can also delink issues. Rather than allow holdout states to use potentially unrelated issues to hijack diplomatic talks, as treaty negotiations permit, violations (and customary processes) allow states to consider issues in relative isolation.[51] Moreover, even if multilateral law-making of some form occurs subsequently, a state's unilateral violation of a rule can weaken the incentive to delay and hold out. Violation indicates a state is willing to act unilaterally, thus encouraging other states to take what accommodations they can get from the violating state in subsequent negotiations.

The US's somewhat undeserved reputation for 'going it alone' during the war on terror is a clear example of this kind of forum selection calculus, although, as mentioned above, decisions by organizations such as the ICRC to use custom and custom-like processes evince a similar decision. American views on the correct application of the doctrine of self-defense are a case in point. The US considered using the United Nations Security Council (UNSC) as a means of legalizing its use of force against Iraq in 2003. Failing to achieve the necessary votes in the UNSC, the US proceeded to use force in arguable violation of the prohibition on the use of force in the UN Charter. It did so while advancing the view that the law justified its actions. Similarly, the 'unwilling or unable' test has been used to justify the use of force in countries like Pakistan (vis-à-vis the raid that killed Osama bin Laden) and Syria, rather than consent or multilateral authorization.

Within *jus in bello*, the US's use of drones and its increasing use of cyber-attacks demonstrate the American preference for negotiating against the backdrop of an existing policy and pattern of arguably unlawful conduct. In these areas, technological change and practice have outstripped the law. States and commentators thus dispute both how the law should be applied

---

48 Andrew T Guzman, 'Against Consent' (2012) 52 Virginia Journal of International Law 747, 758–59.

49 ibid.

50 ibid.

51 Wuerth and Helfer (n 11) 576. Although linkages are commonly thought of as a boon to negotiations by creating more possible trades, linkages can also cause cooperation to unravel. Timothy Meyer, 'From Contract to Legislation: The Logic of Modern International Lawmaking' (2014) 14 Chicago Journal of International Law 559, 585–87; Oren Perez, 'Multiple Regimes, Issue Linkage and International Cooperation: Exploring the Role of the WTO' (2005) 26 University of Pennsylvania Journal of International Economic Law 735.

to these new technologies,[52] and also the legality of American conduct.[53] In both of these cases, adopting its preferred policy before that policy's legality is clear enables the United States to obtain a double benefit. It can pursue its preferred policy (although perhaps at some cost due to any repercussions it suffers), while at the same time pressuring other states to adopt its views.

4. GENERAL WELFARE VERSUS DISTRIBUTIONAL CONSIDERATIONS

The theory of noncompliance predicts that states will only engage in noncompliance when they expect doing so will make them individually better off. The conditions set forth in Part 3 describe when that will be true. They say nothing, however, about when such changes will increase overall welfare as measured against the status quo. As explained above, states may acquiesce to changes in the law because cooperating with the violating state – even under less favorable rules – is better than forgoing cooperation. But those states might still be made worse off than they were under pre-existing rules. Worse, the changes to the law could actually reduce overall welfare. That is, the gains to the violator from changing the law might be outweighed by the losses to states more generally. Law-making through noncompliance could be, in other words, simply a game of redistribution, one that the procedural safeguards of multilateral law-making would prevent.

These questions about the overall welfare effects of noncompliance through law-making have never been more important than they are today. Within both *jus ad bellum* and *jus in bello*, the US has in recent years led a coalition of states that pushed the limits of what many nations and commentators believe international law allows. Other nations such as Israel have used tactics in armed conflicts in Lebanon and Gaza that have drawn considerable scrutiny and criticism. These nations argue that international law does and/or should permit their actions, while opponents vigorously and persistently object lest those actions come to be accepted as legal through silence.

We thus must ask: under what conditions might we expect that what is in the violating state's best interest will also be in the general interest? In these circumstances, we may be less suspicious of arguably noncompliant acts that come with claims that the law should accommodate them. Part 4.1 offers three conditions under which noncompliance as law-making is likely to produce rules that increase overall welfare. Parts 4.2 and 4.3, respectively, discuss two possible objections: that legitimizing law-making through noncompliance may weaken international law's compliance pull, and that noncompliance's distributive consequences may delegitimize international law. Ultimately, I argue that – apart from the welfare effects of individual rulemaking efforts – noncompliance as law-making provides an important safety valve that boosts international law's effectiveness.

---

[52] eg Marco Roscini, *Cyber Operations and the Use of Force in International Law* (OUP 2014); Oona Hathaway and others, 'The Law of Cyber-Attack' (2012) 100 California Law Review 817.

[53] See above n 37–38.

4.1 Noncompliance and General Welfare

Below I consider three conditions under which law-making through noncompliance is likely to produce individual results that increase the overall welfare of the international community. To be clear, I am not arguing that in these situations welfare increases when any noncompliant act is accepted as lawful. Rather, I am arguing that in these circumstances the process of law-making described above is more likely to lead to beneficial results. International law tries to balance the competing interests of states and, especially in the case of IHL, vulnerable individuals. An initial violation by a state may often not strike the balance in the right way. Over time, however, noncompliance is more likely to strike a good balance in the three situations outlined below.

First, overall welfare is more likely to increase when a handful of especially interested states are the primary beneficiaries of cooperation. Not all states, after all, benefit equally from cooperation on every issue. Rules governing naval warfare, for example, are especially important to states with large navies, such as the United States or Russia. They are relatively unimportant to states with only small navies and largely irrelevant to landlocked states. Rules on naval warfare are thus a particularly good example of where we might expect noncompliance to usefully spur law-making efforts. Indeed, as Hull recounts, the patterns of deliberate noncompliance by Britain and Germany during the First World War had just this effect, prompting revisions to naval warfare rules.[54]

States that use force more frequently are also likely to benefit more from having their preferred laws of war than are those states that rarely use force. The application of rules on proportionality and discrimination to conflicts with non-state actors illustrates the point. The US's military action in Iraq and Afghanistan and Israel's in Lebanon and the Gaza Strip gave rise to difficult decisions about how to target militants embedded in civilian populations. Few other countries regularly face these kinds of decisions. Many disagree with how the US and Israel apply targeting rules in their various conflicts. The fact remains, however, that the US and Israel benefit far more than non-combatant states from exercising their preferred rules.[55]

This same line of reasoning suggests that noncompliance is more likely to produce welfare gains when the regulated activity is uncommon. In these situations, states that do engage in the activity have a much greater interest in having their preferred rules than do other states. Yet the multilateral treaty-making process can enable relatively inactive states to hold up decision-making. CIL, of course, does give some special weight to the views and practices of especially affected states.[56] Even in regards to CIL, however, a small group of states actively engaged in a particular practice can be overwhelmed by the strong objections of states that only infrequently engage in the relevant practice. In these situations, noncompliance offers a way to generate changes to the law that benefit those states most central to cooperation, and therefore increase overall welfare.

---

54 Hull (n 27) 207–10.

55 Of course, IHL rules are not only for the benefit of other states; they also exist to protect individuals, especially civilians in the case of targeting rules. Law-making is still, however, a predominantly state-centric exercise, which is why I focus here on states. I discuss the role of non-state actors in greater detail in Part 5.

56 *North Sea Continental Shelf Cases (Federal Republic of Germany v Denmark; Federal Republic of Germany v Netherlands)* (Judgment) [1969] ICJ Rep 3 para 73.

Second, noncompliance may boost general welfare when many states have similar preferences over legal rules. In these situations, the violator may 'speak' for a silent majority of states that prefer to change a legal rule but have been stymied either by resistance from another group of states or simply by the costs of generating change in the multilateral system. In these situations, a large number of states benefitting from a rule change translates into general welfare gains. The example discussed above of the distinctive emblems for medical personnel under the first Geneva Convention, in which states' overriding preference is to have identifiable emblems, illustrates this type of noncompliance.

Legal issues where states face uncertainty, such as areas where technology changes quickly, offer a third situation in which states might benefit from noncompliance.[57] Technological changes can render international law quickly inadequate to govern situations or technological capabilities that did not exist when a particular rule was formulated. Yet states will often be reluctant to wait for multilateral law-making processes to clarify the appropriate uses of new technologies. Instead, they will push the boundaries of legality in an effort to ensure that their preferred uses are permitted. In many instances, this kind of aggressive action can increase general welfare. States that are familiar with new technologies, for example, are often best positioned to understand its limits and uses. Debates over the legality of an individual state's use of a new technology can thus provide a fruitful debate about what the law should look like generally.

The use of drones by the US once again provides a useful illustration. In principle, drones are no different from other weapons systems, such as missiles fired from aircraft. They can be used consistent with targeting rules and thus are not per se unlawful in the way that cluster munitions, for instance, might be.[58] On the other hand, much of the criticism about drones seems to stem from concerns that an unmanned vehicle, or its operators who are removed from the actual scene of combat, cannot comply with the principles of distinction and proportionality to the same degree as a pilot in a cockpit.[59] A serious debate about this concern, and sensible legal rules on the use of drones for targeting combatants, requires a familiarity with drone technological capabilities. Those countries in possession of new technologies are best positioned to discover its uses and limits and educate others about its use. In the drone context, the US military has held public fora aimed at doing just this.[60] Moreover, as Laurie Blank and others have pointed out, in principle drones allow operators to make even better decisions than a live pilot.[61] Drones tend to be operated remotely by larger crews than piloted aircraft.[62] Moreover, because drones do not put operators at risk, they can remain in the combat theater longer than

---

[57] Uncertainty combined with common interests will make noncompliance as law-making particularly effective. By contrast, noncompliance will be less desirable when states face deep distributional tension over the resolution of uncertain issues. See Timothy Meyer, 'Shifting Sands: Power, Uncertainty, and the Form of International Legal Cooperation' (2016) 27 European Journal of International Law 161.

[58] Laurie Blank, 'After Top Gun: How Drone Strikes Impact the Law of War' (2012) 33 University of Pennsylvania Journal of International Law 675, 684.

[59] See 'Report of the Special Rapporteur on extrajudicial, summary or arbitrary executions, Philip Alston' (28 May 2010) Human Rights Council 14th Session, UN Doc A/HRC/14/24/Add.6 para 80.

[60] See eg Charles Blanchard, Gen. Counsel, U.S. Air Force, 'Drones, Remote Targeting and the Promise of Law' (New America Foundation Conference, Panel II, 24 February 2011) <www.ustream.tv/recorded/12909598> accessed 31 January 2021 (describing the drone targeting and acquisition process).

[61] Blank (n 58) 677.

[62] ibid.

manned aircraft. They can therefore collect better intelligence that can be used to make better targeting decisions.[63] For these reasons, technological improvements to drones may actually have the effect of raising the bar for compliance with IHL. A 'reasonable commander' with drones at their disposal may be expected both to have and make use of more information in applying targeting principles.[64]

In this way, technological advances can lead to IHL becoming more effective at achieving its purpose of balancing states' use of force to achieve military objectives with the protections owed to vulnerable populations.[65] These gains, however, rest on those nations that can develop and deploy those innovations actually doing so. The use of arguably noncompliant action as a way to shape the use of new technologies is thus vital to moving the law forward. Similar arguments can be deployed in other areas of technological innovation, such as cyber warfare.

4.2 Does Legitimizing Noncompliance as Law-Making Increase or Reduce the Compliance Pull of International Law?

Although noncompliance as law-making can produce rules that increase welfare, it has at least two possible downsides. First, the possibility of noncompliance as law-making may increase noncompliance, including noncompliance that has no redeeming benefits. States that might otherwise have complied with the law may be tempted to violate it, not to cheat, but in order to move the law in the direction of their preferred rules. On this view, legitimizing noncompliance as a law-making tactic encourages some violations that would otherwise not have occurred. These violations may lead to rules that reduce welfare relative to the status quo. Moreover, breaches of international legal obligations risk undermining the obligation in question, and potentially the broader family of obligations to which the breached obligation belongs.[66] Where noncompliance is used as a law-making technique, the violating state intends this breakdown as a means to facilitate the formation of an alternative rule. If states fail to coalesce around the new rule, however, the result may be a long-term decline in cooperation. Disruption carries risks.

Accepting noncompliance as legitimate in at least some contexts also carries with it the risk of undermining a culture of compliance among states.[67] Literature on compliance with international law suggests that states often comply not out of a rational calculus that compliance is optimal in individual circumstances, but rather because government officials have absorbed the norm that compliance with international law is important.[68] For government officials, especially the lower-level officials who make the great majority of decisions that affect compliance with the great majority of international laws, compliance becomes a bureaucratic

---

63 ibid 697.

64 Christopher Drew, 'Human Rights Group Says 29 Civilians Were Killed by Israeli Air Attacks in Gaza' (*The New York Times*, 30 June 2009) <www.nytimes.com/2009/07/01/world/middleeast/01gaza.html> accessed 31 January 2021.

65 The development and use of the submarine during the First World War offers an historic example of the same phenomenon.

66 Jacob Katz Cogan, 'Noncompliance and the International Rule of Law' (2006) 31 Yale Journal of International Law 189, 203.

67 ibid 204.

68 See Harold Hongju Koh, 'Transnational Legal Process' (1996) 75 Nebraska Law Review 181.

imperative. In the IHL context, training manuals that set forth a nation's understanding of the laws of war become the relevant set of rules for soldiers in the field making judgments, often under extraordinary pressure, as to how to conduct themselves. Legitimizing noncompliance as a tool in certain circumstances risks blurring the organizational culture that promotes compliance in complex organizations under often difficult circumstances.

The difficulties posed by an increased incentive to violate the law are likely overstated for three reasons, however. First, international law has a weak system of sanctions. Without a centralized enforcer, noncompliance – either to cheat or as a way to push for changes to the law – will occur anyway. Recognizing this fact is not likely to significantly increase the amount of noncompliance as law-making, although in marginal cases the legitimacy of the technique might make a difference in whether a state decides to use noncompliance as a law-making technique.

More generally, trying to eliminate noncompliance is likely a foolhardy endeavor. In the domestic regulatory context, commentators have observed that the optimal amount of noncompliance is usually non-zero.[69] Eliminating noncompliance is costly. In economic terms, the marginal cost of preventing the next violation should be justified by marginal benefits from deterring that violation. Under this economic framework, it will rarely be cost-effective to eliminate all noncompliance, or the risk thereof. Instead, the risk of some noncompliance will persist because the costs of preventing it are greater than the benefits.

Consider nuclear weapons. In its *Nuclear Weapons Advisory Opinion*, the ICJ expressed doubt that the use of nuclear weapons could ever comply with rules of proportionality, distinction, or necessity.[70] That nine of the most militarized nations in the world remain in possession of nuclear weapons thus creates the risk of grave breaches of targeting rules. Yet, as disarmament efforts have shown, the cost of eliminating nuclear stockpiles is incredibly high. Nations have taken on proliferation risks posed by nations like Iran, but more aggressive action to eliminate existing nuclear weapons in the hands of major military powers, and therefore the risk of noncompliance by those states, would have prohibitive costs.

If noncompliance cannot be eliminated, there is a benefit to directing noncompliance towards a constructive purpose. Noncompliance as cheating serves no redeeming collective purpose. Such noncompliance deprives other parties of the benefits of the violating state's cooperation purely to benefit the individual party. Noncompliance as law-making, however, offers the possibility of a collective benefit: a change in the law that increases nations' welfare. Beyond the offsetting benefit of positive changes to the law, noncompliance as law-making is, as discussed above, necessarily public, reducing somewhat the costs associated with monitoring legal commitments. The possibility of noncompliance as law-making can thus serve to funnel what might otherwise be undeterrable efforts at cheating into productive efforts to change the law.

Second, law-making through noncompliance cannot easily be confined only to those situations in which it produces beneficial results. Its legitimacy and effects must therefore be judged on the whole. For example, you cannot have the benefits of a 12-mile territorial sea and

---

[69] See eg Kevin M. Stack and Michael P. Vandenberg, 'The One Percent Problem' (2011) 111 Columbia Law Review 1385.

[70] *Legality of Threat or Use of Nuclear Weapons* (Advisory Opinion) [1996] ICJ Rep 1996 226 paras 42, 95.

200-mile exclusive economic zone – rules that emerged from a process initiated by unilateral challenges to the traditional 3-mile limit on the territorial sea – without also having the US push the boundaries on what constitutes self-defense. Either noncompliance can be used for law-making or it cannot. This is not to say, of course, that one cannot object to the substance of changes to the law brought about by noncompliance. But just as we do not say that treaties as instruments are bad simply because we disagree with the substance of individual treaties, so too we should not judge noncompliance as law-making as a technique simply because we disagree with individual outcomes.

Third, the features of effective law-making through noncompliance will serve as safeguards to reduce the moral hazard associated with purely redistributive law-making. Noncompliant states must incur the costs of violation in order to advance a 'proposal' – a proffered new rule – through noncompliance. These costs are likely higher than advancing such a proposal through multilateral negotiations. While negotiations give rise to transaction costs, merely making a proposal is relatively cheap. By contrast, noncompliance subjects a state to sanctions. Other states may withdraw reciprocal compliance, the violating state may suffer reputationally, and it may even be subject to sanctions. These costs are also more certain when noncompliance is a law-making act because in order to be effective as such, the act must be public. States that engage in law-making through noncompliance thus attest, through their costly actions, to the desirability of the new rule and their willingness to push for it. While hardly a sure-fire indication of the rule's desirability, such a filter is more reliable than diplomatic cheap talk.[71] It indicates that the proffered change in the rule has attained elevated importance for the violating state that may justify closer consideration from other states. These features should limit somewhat the possibility that states will casually violate the law in the hopes of changing it in a way that is not systemically valuable.

States can also calibrate the odds that noncompliance will be used for law-making by increasing the sanction for violations. Making rules legally binding, as opposed to using a non-binding vehicle such as the ICRC's commentaries on the Geneva Conventions or manuals such as the Talinn Manual on the International Law Applicable to Cyber Warfare, increases the reputational penalty associated with violation.[72] Increasing the sanctions for violations will deter some instances of law-making through noncompliance. On the other hand, using non-binding instruments such as commentaries or military manuals acts as a delegation to particularly motivated states to use noncompliance as a form of law-making.[73] Making an instrument binding deters such actions, although it cannot prevent them. More precise obligations have a similar effect. By carefully delineating what counts as noncompliance, precise obligations increase reputational penalties for noncompliance. States cannot as easily push the boundaries of what counts as noncompliance while maintaining a fig leaf of good faith compliance.

71 Goldsmith and Posner (n 7) 172–73.
72 Timothy Meyer, 'Soft Law as Delegation' (2009) 32 Fordham International Law Journal 888.
73 ibid.

4.3 Distributive Considerations and Law-Making through Noncompliance as a Safety Valve

Furthermore, despite the fact that law-making through noncompliance can produce general welfare gains, over time it will lead to legal rules that tend to favor those states most able and willing to engage in noncompliance. In other words, even if overall welfare increases, the gains from changing the law will flow disproportionally to those states willing to violate the law to change it.

These distributive consequences of law-making through noncompliance may themselves represent a challenge for the legitimacy of international law, even if law-making through noncompliance does increase welfare. Law-making through noncompliance implicitly weighs the views of powerful or especially interested states more heavily than the views of weaker or peripheral states, or civil society. This concern may be especially important in areas of the law like IHL. To be sure, only a few states regularly engage in hostilities. These states, most notably the US in recent years, thus receive the lion's share of the benefits from having their preferred rules. As I explain above, this suggests that noncompliance as law-making is likely to increase welfare.

But to focus on the interests of those states is to misunderstand the values underlying IHL rules. Rules on the use of force and the conduct of hostilities implicate both humanity's larger interest in regulating how governments treat foreign citizens, as well as the interests of third party states. Like human rights law, IHL seeks in part to ensure that foreign governments do not abuse a position of power in terms of how they treat individuals subject to their influence or control.

Procedurally, noncompliance as law-making also reduces the importance of multilateral law-making, which less powerful states may resent. From a welfare standpoint, multilateral processes have primarily instrumental value – they are useful to the extent that they produce good results. From a broader legitimacy standpoint, however, multilateral law-making embodies important participatory values that are lacking in law-making through noncompliance.

Not only do the small number of states that regularly participate in hostilities benefit the most from having their preferred rules; they also are the only states in a position to regularly make use of noncompliance as a law-making technique. This fact – along with the US's willingness to seriously engage with legal criticism of its actions – explains why so many debates in IHL focus on the legality of US actions and policies. The US deploys military force overseas with much greater frequency than virtually any other nation. For most other states, their direct involvement in hostilities is episodic and uncertain at the time they engage in law-making. These states may resent having to react to law-making proposals that are motivated by the self-interest of violators engaged in a specific conflict in which the violation occurs. They may be unable to foresee how the proposed change will affect them, putting them at a disadvantage relative to those states that more regularly engage in conflict.

Indeed, IHL rules are multilateral in part because rules on how force will be used are best negotiated in the abstract, before the exigencies of individual conflicts tempt states to propose rules designed to achieve self-serving aims. Law-making through noncompliance thus not only changes who the law favors by permitting some states to more actively push for changes to the law; it also ensures that law-making occurs around proposals that are more self-serving than they might otherwise be.

This concern – that noncompliance as law-making delegitimizes international law – cannot be easily dismissed. Law-making through noncompliance clearly expands the role of power at the expense of principle in shaping the content of the law. At the same time, however, the possibility of using noncompliance as an end-run around the multilateral system is a critical safety valve for international law. Without such mechanisms that allow powerful states to assert their interests in situations in which they would violate the law anyway, international law risks obsolescence. Powerful states will not tolerate the slow pace of change through multilateral processes when their key interests are threatened. A place for noncompliance as law-making thus balances the interests of powerful states whose participation is critical for international law to function with the interests of less powerful states and civil society more broadly. Put differently, the possibility of noncompliance as an alternative to multilateral law-making preserves the multilateral law-making system, even if noncompliance sometimes produces results that reduce welfare or risk delegitimizing the law in the eyes of some.

To see how noncompliance can actually preserve the multilateral system, consider that exiting the system or engaging in persistent violation always remains an option if a state is willing to bear the costs. Powerful states, on whom international law's sanctions tend to work the least well and who tend to suffer the least when international cooperation breaks down, are therefore the freest to walk away. Other states may be hesitant about imposing retaliatory sanctions on powerful states, and powerful states may be the least in need of reciprocal cooperation from weaker states. Powerful states acting rationally will thus ignore or exit from legal obligations that no longer serve their needs.[74] As British Foreign Secretary Jack Straw put it, '[i]f you have a set of rules which conflict with reality, then reality normally wins.'[75]

Yet both history and international relations theory suggest that cooperation is difficult to sustain without the participation of particularly powerful states. The ultimate failure of the League of Nations without US participation is perhaps the best-known example of this phenomenon. One might also include the withdrawal of the US and European nations from the General Agreement on Tariffs and Trade 1947 (GATT) and simultaneous accession to the World Trade Organization (WTO) at the close of the Uruguay Round of trade negotiations. The US and the European Union's (EU) forerunner took this action as a means of inducing smaller countries that wished to maintain favorable market access to the two largest economies in the world to accept a host of additional trade rules not obviously to their benefit.[76] Other countries calculated that the original GATT regime could not be sustained without the participation of the world's largest markets.

In this way, powerful states are different from other states. They sustain international cooperation, either through their willingness to sanction violations by others or by providing benefits – such as military alliances, foreign aid, or preferential market access – to others who comply with their preferred rules. These benefits require, however, that the law cannot stray too far from the key interests of the powerful. Oftentimes, sustaining cooperation means

---

[74] Meyer (n 14) 379; Lloyd Gruber, *Ruling the World: Power Politics and the Rise of Supranational Institutions* (Princeton University Press 2000).

[75] George Parker, 'EU Pact Dispute Blights Foreign Minister Meeting' *Financial Times* (London, 23–30 November 2003) 6.

[76] See Richard Steinberg, 'In the Shadow of Law or Power? Consensus-Based Bargaining in the GATT/WTO' (2002) 56 International Organisations 339.

adapting legal rules to benefit powerful states whose participation is necessary to support international law.

Multilateral institutions are often poorly suited to this task. They are notoriously slow moving, especially when they operate by consensus, as they usually do. Negotiations over amendments to rules can be held hostage by holdout states that prefer status quo rules or simply want something (often unrelated) in exchange for support.[77] Institutions such as the UNSC expressly provide a veto to states that often sit on opposite sides of an issue, paralyzing the institution's ability to formulate legal obligations in response to evolving circumstances. And while the possibility of instant custom theoretically exists,[78] CIL can be slow to adapt to new circumstances when not coupled with explicit codification efforts.

Noncompliance as a law-making technique offers a way out of this conundrum. It provides a lower-cost alternative to more formal multilateral law-making. Powerful states can announce their intention to abide by a particular understanding of an international rule going forward. Other states can then acquiesce in that understanding or reject it. In either case, however, powerful states get the opportunity to see how states as a whole react to the new rule without having the rule tabled at the whim of a few holdouts. Indeed, rejecting a rule proffered by way of noncompliance may be more difficult for other states precisely because the noncompliance may make the proposal seem like a fait accompli. Noncompliance thus allows powerful states to update legal rules when the multilateral system becomes congested. And in designing rules to suit themselves, powerful states will, at least some of the time, preserve the multilateral enterprise for all states by remaining within the system.[79]

Randall Stone has described this phenomenon as the coexistence of formal and informal governance.[80] Critics of using noncompliance to push the law forward tend to view actions taken outside the formal multilateral legal system as antithetical to the legal system itself. Influential scholars such as Jean d'Aspremont have called for a return to formalism as a means of shoring up the normativity of the legal system.[81]

Pitting informal and formal means of governance against each other in this way mistakes the nature of the legal system, however.[82] The two systems exist side by side. The informal mechanisms provide a critical safeguard that allows great powers to agree to a multilateral system that vests veto power in states that are considerably weaker. They allow powerful or particularly interested states to intervene to influence the content of the law when doing so is

---

[77] Meyer (n 51) 559.

[78] See Bin Cheng, 'Custom: The Future of General State Practice in a Divided World' in Ronald St John MacDonald and Douglas M Johnston (eds), *The Structure and Process of International Law: Essays in Legal Philosophy Doctrine and Theory* (Martinus Nijhoff Publishers 1983).

[79] Joost Pauwelyn makes a similar argument about why WTO dispute resolution has been widely accepted, while investor–state dispute settlement has come under increasing criticism. According to Pauwelyn, part of the WTO's success is that politically sensitive diplomats administer its dispute process. Investment arbitrators, by contrast, are professional lawyers too far removed from the politics of the disputes they are adjudicating to be effective in the long run. See Joost Pauwelyn, 'The Rule of Law Without the Rule of Lawyers: Why Investment Arbitrators Are from Mars, Trade Adjudicators from Venus' (2016) 109 American Journal of International Law 761.

[80] Randall W Stone, *Controlling Institutions: International Organizations and the Global Economy* (CUP 2011) 13.

[81] Jean d'Aspremont, *Formalism and the Sources of International Law* (OUP 2011).

[82] Stone (n 80) 13.

especially important to them. Doing so has negative distributional consequences – the powerful become more powerful. But this reality also preserves the formal system. Powerful states would have greatly diminished incentives to join a legal system if doing so meant forgoing the pursuit of critical state interests in order to satisfy the demands of the slow-moving multilateral system. Noncompliance as law-making thus is one of a larger set of informal governance tools, such as the rise of soft law, that states have come to increasingly rely on in recent years.[83]

None of this is to say that international law leaves powerful states unconstrained. Rather, the possibility of noncompliance as law-making constrains states that use it in different ways. The primary constraint (apart from any sanctions that stem from noncompliance) is the drive to be successful. When a state uses noncompliance as a form of law-making, it wants to attract other states to its position. While the state might be willing to 'go it alone', the violating state benefits as more states adopt its position. Those states will no longer sanction the violating state or view the violating state as having a bad reputation. Those states will also conform their conduct to that of the violating state, a major benefit for the latter.

Attracting support, however, means that the violating state will often have to moderate its position. The state will not necessarily be able to obtain its most preferred rule. Instead, it will have to make concessions to make the proposed rule more palatable to other states, just as it would have to in treaty negotiations. Such nations must weigh their own interests in implementing their policies (in the language of the theory of noncompliance as law-making, the credibility of the threat of persistent noncompliance) against what other nations will accept (acceptability). This need to make the normative content of a violation acceptable to other nations provides an important constraint on the use of noncompliance as law-making.

Efforts by the US to justify the legality of its actions underscore how this constraint operates. For at least the last ten years the US has used an aggressive policy of legal diplomacy to engage its allies on IHL issues. Legal advisers such as John Bellinger, Harold Hongju Koh,[84] and Brian Egan[85] have become public figures, making legal policy statements justifying when and how the United States uses force abroad. Indeed, following his confirmation as Legal Adviser in early 2016, Brian Egan's first public speech, to the American Society of International Law, was entitled 'International Law, Legal Diplomacy, and the Counter-ISIL Campaign', and discussed how the United States approaches compliance with the laws of war in its conflict with the Islamic State.[86] Similarly, following the leak of the so-called Torture Memo – the US Justice Department document that laid out a legal argument that 'enhanced interrogation techniques' such as waterboarding do not constitute torture and are therefore legal – the US responded to pressure from other states and civil society, by withdrawing the

[83] Eyal Benvenisti, 'Towards a Typology of Informal International Lawmaking Mechanisms and their Distinct Accountability Gaps' in Joost Pauwelyn, Ramses A Wessel and Jan Wouters (eds), *Informal International Lawmaking* (OUP 2012).

[84] Koh (n 38).

[85] Brian Egan, 'Keynote Address: International Law, Legal Diplomacy, and the Counter-ISIL Campaign' (110th American Society of International Law Annual Meeting, Washington, DC, 1 April 2016) <https://www.justsecurity.org/wp-content/uploads/2016/04/Egan-ASIL-speech.pdf> accessed 31 January 2021.

[86] ibid.

memo and stopping waterboarding, as well as other means of interrogation that used physical pressure.[87]

Both of these instances demonstrate efforts by the US to explain its conduct to other nations and show that the United States responds to criticism, moderating its legal position and its real-world actions in order to make its views more palatable to other nations. 'Legal diplomacy', it seems, and international legal discourse more generally, constrained the US even as it pushed the boundaries of legality.

The practice of legal diplomacy that states use to persuade others to accept their arguably unlawful conduct also rebuts another claim: that noncompliance shows that powerful states disregard the international legal system. Although tribunals have become increasingly important in recent years, international law remains fundamentally a negotiated system of law.[88] As such, it has both dynamic and static features. One can ask whether a state has complied with the law at a moment in time, as tribunals do. Or one can ask whether states generally comply with the law over time, taking into account that states use their compliance decisions to try and shape the law. States that may not be committed to strict compliance with prevailing rules may nevertheless be committed to the dynamic project of international law. Recognizing that noncompliance can fuel law-making may open the door to greater dialogue with countries that have historically remained on the outskirts of international law.

Russia provides a case in point. In recent years, Russia has taken a variety of actions that many view as clearly unlawful, most notably its annexation of Crimea. Yet Russia has proven itself considerably more adept at deploying legal arguments to justify its position than it might have been in the past. Russian President Vladimir Putin justified Russian action in Crimea as legal under the emerging doctrine of the responsibility to protect (R2P).[89] This argument represents an effort to use noncompliance as law-making. Russia's actions violated most nations' understanding of rules on the use of force, yet Russia attempted to persuade them that the emerging R2P doctrine should permit its actions.[90]

Russian actions have taken many by surprise. This reaction reflects in part the view of many that Russia's actions are illegal. But it also reflects unease with the entrance of a new major power into the international legal arena. Russia has shown that it is capable of deploying legal tools in service of its interests in the same way as other major powers. To be sure, that ability promises to shape the content of international law and legal debate going forward. At the same time, it also offers a restraint on Russian action, however modest. If Russia wishes for other nations to take it seriously when it makes legal arguments, it must in turn make efforts to conform its actions in accordance with broader international legal discourse. In trade law, China has learned this lesson in the 15 years since its accession to the WTO, and the result has

---

[87] Wilson Andrews and Alicia Parlapiano, 'A History of the CIA's Secret Interrogation Program' (*New York Times*, 9 December 2014) <https://www.nytimes.com/interactive/2014/12/09/world/timeline-of-cias-secret-interrogation-program.html> accessed 11 January 2021.

[88] Cohen (n 11) 293.

[89] Meg Sullivan, 'Justifying Crimea: President Putin Invokes R2P' (*Brown Political Review*, 11 April 2014) <https://brownpoliticalreview.org/2014/04/justifying-crimea-president-putin-invokes-r2p/> accessed 31 January 2021.

[90] Outside of the military context, Russia joined the WTO in 2012 and has immediately gone on the offensive, launching a WTO dispute against the European Union over restrictions contained in the EU's Third Energy Package.

been significant trade liberalization. Russia's engagement offers similar promise. The process of using arguably noncompliant action to shape the law will act as a restraint on Russia as it goes forward.

Finally, while informal governance empowers strong or especially interested states to take action outside the formal channels for law-making, it also has another effect – it empowers NGOs, experts, and civil society to play a more direct role in law-making. Once the formal, mostly state-centric multilateral law-making process becomes no longer exclusive, procedures more favorable to non-state actors become viable.

The recent exposition of customary IHL illustrates how a focus on CIL can be combined with another technique: delegation of law-drafting to expert bodies. Organizations such as the ICRC, or in other contexts the International Law Commission,[91] have significant credibility in the eyes of both state and non-state stakeholders. When these entities expound the content of CIL, they provide a juris-generative activity that occurs outside the direct control (although not indirect influence) of states. Just as noncompliance can act as an agenda-setting device, so too do the actions of these organizations. In both cases, states are called upon to respond and no single state or even necessarily a small group of states can use procedural devices to bottle the proposal up. The ICRC's role in developing (some would say clarifying) the content of customary IHL rules illustrates the point. The ICRC is equally adept at marshaling evidence of state practice and *opinio juris*, both in the CIL sense of those terms as well as their treaty interpretation commentaries. The ICRC's database of new state and international law practice allows it to counterweight states that might be inclined to use noncompliance to push the law in self-serving directions. The ICRC is also in a position to engage in debate about the content of IHL with states themselves, as evidenced by the public back-and-forth between the ICRC and officials from the US.[92]

Informal governance, such as noncompliance as law-making, thus comes with its own set of checks and balances. They are not the same as the procedural checks that come from the consensus procedures of multilateral law-making. In this sense, they may lack the participatory legitimacy that attaches to bodies such as the United Nations. Nor do they operate in the same way that international law's weak system of sanctions do to deter violations by most states. At the same time, however, they provide counterbalance to a necessary aspect of the international system. They ensure that powerful states that use noncompliance to move the law in their preferred direction cannot do so unchecked.

5. CONCLUSION

While law-making through noncompliance has long been controversial, it is also a reality with which we must contend. Recognizing the occurrence of noncompliance need not be done grudgingly, however. A descriptive theory of when noncompliance is an effective law-making technique, coupled with an account of the systemic values served by such noncompliance, can

---

91 See Laurence R Helfer and Timothy Meyer, 'The Evolution of Codification: A Principal-Agent Theory of the International Law Commission's Influence' in Curtis Bradley (ed), *Custom's Future: International Law in a Changing World* (CUP 2016).

92 See John B Bellinger, II and William J Haynes II, 'A US government response to the International Committee of the Red Cross study *Customary International Humanitarian Law*' (2007) 89 International Review of the Red Cross 443; Henckaerts (n 3) 477.

lead to useful prescriptions. Providing an incentive to channel noncompliance into law-making – to make noncompliance public and the noncompliant acts acceptable to other states, as the theory here describes – can lead to better compliance outcomes over time and to greater effectiveness for international law. Rather than disparage law-making through noncompliance, states and commentators would thus do well to consider how noncompliance might be incorporated into law-making activity.

PART IV

New law through practice?

8. Interpreting the Geneva Conventions: Subsequent practice instead of treaty amendments? A case study of 'non-international armed conflicts' under Common Article 3

Emily Crawford

1. INTRODUCTION

Treaty-making in international humanitarian law (IHL), as in international law more generally, has always been a complex process – how does one produce an instrument of suitable specificity to address a particular ill without compromising consensus among those for whom the treaty addressed? Does one choose a generally worded treaty in the hope that the provisions can be interpreted broadly and thus induce more states to participate in the treaty regime? Or does one favour more focused and specific treaty terms but in doing so run the risk of fewer states becoming party? Adopting a generally worded treaty creates the possibility of the provisions being too vague to apply, thus rendering the treaty regime essentially powerless. However, if a treaty is generally worded, the generality of the provisions may allow for practice more in line with what was envisaged by the drafters of the treaty. Equally, such generally worded provisions may allow for subsequent practice to stretch the intent of the drafters beyond what was anticipated.

These issues of treaty intention, interpretation, and longevity were among those faced by the international community in Geneva in 1949, when it met to debate and adopt the new conventions on the protection of persons in situations of armed conflict. One of the most contentious issues was the inclusion of the category of 'non-international armed conflict' within the protection regime of the new conventions. Debate at the Diplomatic Conference was divided between those who felt that non-international armed conflicts should receive the full protection of the conventions, to those who argued that non-international armed conflicts deserved no such international recognition.[1] When it was eventually accepted that non-international armed conflicts *would* be included in the treaty regime in Common Article 3, debate was then divided over how exactly to define 'non-international armed conflict'. Ultimately, a non-definition approach was taken, with Common Article 3 stating its applicability to 'armed conflicts not of

[1] See below for the discussion of the Diplomatic Conference at Geneva in 1949.

an international character'. Nowhere in Common Article 3 was any indication given as to the interpretive scope intended for the Article.

In the years following the adoption of Common Article 3, the lack of a specific definition proved to be both advantageous and disadvantageous, with state practice showing both a wide and narrow application of the Article to situations of armed conflict. Nearly 70 years after the adoption of Common Article 3, it is thus interesting to look back at state practice in relation to the Article and ask: in the absence of clear treaty rules on the scope of the term 'armed conflict not of an international character', how did states interpret this term? Did it accord with what the drafters at Geneva in 1949 were aiming for? The drafting history of Common Article 3 strongly suggests that Common Article 3 was only meant to apply to medium- to high-level intensity internal armed conflicts. However, state practice since the Article's adoption demonstrates a moving away from the higher threshold arguably envisaged by the international community in 1949, to a more generous and liberal application of the rules to many kinds of internal and non-international armed conflict. Has state practice thus amounted to a form of treaty amendment, broadening the scope of applicability of the Article beyond what states at Geneva in 1949 likely envisaged? Or is it merely an example of how a more than 70-year-old treaty provision has evolved over time?

Questions such as these raise issues of treaty interpretation, as well as the relationship between treaties, subsequent practice, and customary international law – do treaties remain products of their time, or are they adaptive instruments? In order to examine these questions, this chapter will use Common Article 3 as a case study, looking at the drafting history of Common Article 3 as well as how Common Article 3 has been applied in practice. This chapter will also examine the rules of treaty interpretation, and the recent work of the International Law Commission (ILC) on treaties over time, to better understand the text and practice of Common Article 3, and explore whether State practice in relation to Common Article 3 amounts to an amendment of the scope of Common Article 3, or rather shows the Geneva Conventions to have an evolutive character.

2. COMMON ARTICLE 3 AND THE DRAFTING HISTORY OF 'ARMED CONFLICT NOT OF AN INTERNATIONAL CHARACTER'

The reasons behind updating and expanding the 1929 Geneva Conventions following the Second World War have been well documented,[2] but it is useful to mention a few salient points. The International Committee of the Red Cross (ICRC) had, for some years, been trying

---

[2] There have been numerous accounts of the motivations and processes behind the development of the law of armed conflict in the post-Second World War era; for a sample of such works, see generally Sandesh Sivakumaran, *The Law of Non-International Armed Conflict* (OUP 2012) 30–37; David Elder, 'The Historical Background of Common Article 3 of The Geneva Convention of 1949' (1979) 11 Case Western Reserve Journal of International Law 37; Anthony Cullen, *The Concept of Non-International Armed Conflict in International Humanitarian Law* (CUP 2010); Laura Perna, *The Formation of the Treaty Law of Non-International Armed Conflicts* (Martinus Nijhoff 2006) 49–52; Geoffrey Best, *Humanity in Warfare: The Modern History of the International Law of Armed Conflicts* (Methuen 1980) specifically ch 5; Geoffrey Best, *War and Law Since 1945* (Clarendon 1994) specifically ch 3.

to secure state approval to accept ICRC services during times of civil conflict, to no avail.[3] However, the events of the previous decade, including the destruction wreaked during the Spanish Civil War during the 1930s, contributed to a growing sense that, at the very least, the ICRC should play some role in assisting those affected by conflicts that occurred within state borders. Thus, among the discussions held prior to the Diplomatic Conferences at Geneva in 1949, the suggestion was forwarded by the ICRC that civil wars should be regulated by the new Geneva Conventions. At the Seventeenth International Red Cross Conference, held in Stockholm in 1948,[4] a proposal was adopted that the new Geneva Conventions include the following provision:

> In all cases of armed conflict not of an international character which may occur in the territory of one or more of the High Contracting Parties, each of the adversaries shall be bound to implement the provisions of the present Convention. The Convention shall be applicable in these circumstances, whatever the legal status of the Parties to the conflict and without prejudice thereto.[5]

When this draft – known at the time as Article 2 – came before the Geneva Diplomatic Conference, it was, unsurprisingly subject to considerable debate. The term 'armed conflict not of an international character' had 'never been used in an instrument of international law prior to 1949'.[6] However, once it was accepted that *some* regulation of non-international armed conflict would be included in the final Conventions,[7] the focus of delegates and the

---

[3] Proposals to states that National Red Cross and Red Crescent societies might be permitted to offer assistance in times of civil strife were first discussed on the international level at the Ninth International Conference of the Red Cross, held in Washington in 1912. However, the suggestion was strongly repudiated by the European states, with Russian delegate General Alexei Yermelov stating that the Russian government 'would under no circumstances, and in no form whatever, become a party to, or even discuss, any agreement or recommendation on this subject (…) Red Cross societies have no duty whatsoever towards bands of insurgents or revolutionaries who cannot be considered by the laws of my country as anything other than criminals' *Neuvième Conférence international de la Croix-Rouge tenue à Washington du 7 au 17 mai 1912, Compte rendu* (The American Red Cross, Washington 1912) 45; see further François Bugnion, *The International Committee of the Red Cross and the Protection of War Victims* (Macmillan 2003) 248–50. The issue was again raised at the Tenth Red Cross Conference in 1921 and at the Sixteenth Conference in 1938 – see further Elder (n 2) 37, 41–43.

[4] A revision of the 1929 Geneva Convention was tabled by the ICRC in 1938 at the Sixteenth ICRC Conference, with an aim to debate the revision at a Diplomatic Conference in 1940. The outbreak of the Second World War delayed the Conference. The 1937 Draft Convention provided in art 1 that 'in case of civil war, in any part of the home or colonial territory of a Contracting Party, the principles of the Convention shall be equally applied by the said Party, subject to the adverse Party also conforming thereto.' Indeed, attempts to introduce treaty regulation of non-international armed conflicts was on the ICRC agenda as far back as 1921, at its Tenth Conference – see Perna (n 2) 49–50.

[5] Text of the Draft International Conventions for the Protection of War Victims as Approved by the Seventeenth International Red Cross Conference at Stockholm, August 1948 (Taken as the Basis for Discussion at the Diplomatic Conference), reprinted in 'Final Record of the Geneva Diplomatic Conference 1949' (Geneva 1949) vol I, 47 <https://www.loc.gov/rr/frd/Military_Law/pdf/Dipl-Conf-1949-Final_Vol-1.pdf> accessed 31 January 2021 (hereinafter *Final Record*).

[6] Cullen (n 2) 28–29.

[7] See further the debates during the Diplomatic Conference in 1949 as to whether non-international armed conflicts should be included in the Conventions at all – at 'Final Record of the Diplomatic Conference of Geneva of 1949' (Geneva, 26 April 1949) vol IIB, 121 <www.loc.gov/rr/frd/Military_Law/pdf/Dipl-Conf-1949-Final_Vol-2-B.pdf> accessed 31 January 2021.

Special Committee at the Conference tasked with considering what would become Common Article 3 was on the definition of a non-international armed conflict.

The first approach suggested that the Conventions in their entirety would apply to non-international armed conflicts, but only if certain minimum criteria could be met by the non-governmental party to the conflict. France suggested that applicability of the Conventions should only be triggered if the non-state party to the conflict possessed 'organised military forces belonging to a responsible authority capable of respecting, or enforcing respect for the Convention, in a given territory'.[8] Spain took the approach that the Conventions should only 'be applied in cases where the legal government was obliged to have recourse to the regular military forces against insurgents organised as military and in possession of a part of the national territory'.[9] The US and China took a stricter view, stating

> that the insurgents, must have an organisation purporting to have the characteristics of a State; that the insurgent civil authority must exercise de facto authority over persons within a determinate territory; the armed forces must act under the direction of an organized civil authority and be prepared to observe the ordinary laws of war; [and] the insurgent civil authorities must agree to be bound by the provisions of the Convention.[10]

Australia forwarded its own proposal, suggesting that the Conventions could apply in a few separate instances – one where the *de jure* government has recognized the insurgents as belligerents; or two, where the *de jure* government has claimed for itself the rights of belligerent and recognized the insurgents as belligerents solely for the purposes of the Convention.[11] The Australian representative also suggested that a non-international armed conflict could be considered as existing where the situation was referred to the UN Security Council or the General Assembly of the United Nations as being a threat to international peace, a breach of the peace, or an act of aggression.[12]

The question was eventually handed to a working party of the Special Committee, which devised two proposals. The first proposal stated that the Conventions would apply to non-international armed conflicts provided that the *de jure* government recognizes the status of belligerency of the adverse party, that the adverse party present the characteristics of a state (i.e., possessing an organized military force, possessing an organized civil authority exercising de facto governmental functions over the population of a determinate portion of the national territory), and that the adverse party has a means of enforcing the Convention and complying with the laws and customs of war.[13] Some revisions were suggested – the removal of the phrase 'presents the characteristics of a State' was one; however, the ICRC criticized the proposal as imposing requirements so onerous that the provision 'could never have been applied in any recent case of civil war'.[14] Also a source of concern was that the proposed criteria were 'lacking an objective basis for determining whether or not they had been fulfilled, with the consequence

---

8 ibid 10.
9 ibid 11.
10 ibid 12–13.
11 ibid 15.
12 ibid 15.
13 ibid 124.
14 ibid 48; Russia was also of the opinion that the Working Party proposal was too demanding (ibid 48).

that the matter would essentially be left to the discretion of the de jure government'.[15] In order to adopt an acceptable provision, the working party reconvened and took a different approach – rather than define what amounted to a non-international armed conflict, they would instead leave the term undefined, and delineate the minimum standards to be observed.[16]

Draft Article 2A, as it was then being called, went to the plenary for debate, and a number of different opinions were forwarded. The Soviet delegate was of the opinion that the Article did not go far enough, and that the Conventions in totality 'must be implemented in all cases of armed conflict, whatever their character may be'.[17] In contrast, the representative from Burma, General Oung, sought to have Article 2A removed outright from the Conventions, arguing that 'inclusion of this Article in the Convention is a very serious danger to sovereignty and civilian rights. To give international recognition to insurgency would certainly be as grave an error as recognition of aggression.'[18]

In between these two polar positions, other concerns about Article 2A were voiced. The Danish and United Kingdom (UK) delegations stated that the use of the term 'parties to the conflict' might allow anyone to invoke the protections of the Conventions. As the Danish delegate, Georg Cohn noted, 'we must recognise that all these "Parties to the conflict", however small and insignificant they may be (for example, a gang of ordinary criminals engaged in armed conflict), will have the benefit of all the rights recognised by the Convention.'[19] Similar concerns were raised by the UK delegate, who said:

> The word 'belligerent', I need hardly remind the Conference, has a well understood meaning in international law and is used in particular in relation to questions of neutrality. Certain rights are accorded in international law to belligerents, and the wholesale replacement of the word 'belligerent' in these Conventions by the expression 'Parties to the conflict', the wholesale replacement of one expression in an international treaty by another expression can lead to legal consequences which I am certain are not intended by the framers of these humanitarian Conventions.[20]

Ultimately, the Diplomatic Conference adopted Article 2A as Common Article 3, which set down a number of minimum standards to be observed 'in situations of armed conflict not of an international character'.

---

[15] Sivakumaran (n 2) 159. See also *Final Record*, vol IIB, 123 (Report of the Special Committee to the Joint Committee).

[16] See comments made by the Italian delegate Adolfo Maresca, Comments in Seventh Meeting of the Special Committee of the Joint Committee, 19 May 1949, in *Final Record*, vol IIB, 50.

[17] Platon Morosov, Comments in Eighteenth Plenary Meeting, 28 July 1949, *Final Record*, vol IIB, 325.

[18] General Tun Hla Oung, Comments in Eighteenth Plenary Meeting, 28 July 1949, *Final Record*, vol IIB, 327.

[19] Georg Cohn, Comments in Nineteenth Plenary Meeting, 29 July 1949, *Final Record*, vol IIB, 332.

[20] Joyce Gutteridge, Comments in Nineteenth Plenary Meeting, 29 July 1949, *Final Record*, vol IIB, 333.

3. THE INTENDED SCOPE OF COMMON ARTICLE 3 AND THE RULES ON TREATY INTERPRETATION UNDER INTERNATIONAL LAW

Common Article 3, as adopted, provided no guidance as to what criteria were to be met for the existence of an 'armed conflict not of an international character'. What then was the intended scope of Common Article 3? What criteria needed to be met before an 'armed conflict not of an international character' could be deemed to exist? There are two salient issues that arise here. The first, which will be examined in more detail later in this chapter, is the question of how much merit we can attach to the intended scope of Common Article 3. That is to say, nearly 70 years after the adoption of Common Article 3, to what extent are the intentions of the drafters still relevant, and can we look to subsequent practice in relation to Common Article 3 to either confirm the intentions of states in 1949, or has an alternative interpretation of the Article emerged out of nearly seven decades of practice? This issue relates to the question of treaties over time – and whether the interpretation of provisions must be primarily informed by the contemporary environment in which the treaty was adopted, or whether a treaty is a dynamic, evolutive instrument. As mentioned above, this issue will be explored in more detail later in this chapter.

The second relevant issue is one of treaty interpretation. In attempting to ascertain the meaning of Common Article 3, to what extent are we permitted, under the rules of treaty interpretation, to look to factors beyond the plain and ordinary meaning of the text? Are discussions at the 1949 Diplomatic Conference a useful, permissible source, for making meaning of the term 'armed conflict not of an international character'? It is here that we must look to the rules on treaty interpretation, as outlined in the Vienna Convention on the Law of Treaties (VCLT).[21] Article 31 is the starting point, stating that:

> 1. A treaty shall be interpreted in good faith in accordance with the ordinary meaning to be given to the terms of the treaty in their context and in the light of its object and purpose.
> 2. The context for the purpose of the interpretation of a treaty shall comprise, in addition to the text, including its preamble and annexes:
>   (a) any agreement relating to the treaty which was made between all the parties in connection with the conclusion of the treaty;
>   (b) any instrument which was made by one or more parties in connection with the conclusion of the treaty and accepted by the other parties as an instrument related to the treaty.
> 3. There shall be taken into account, together with the context:
>   (a) any subsequent agreement between the parties regarding the interpretation of the treaty or the application of its provisions;
>   (b) any subsequent practice in the application of the treaty which establishes the agreement of the parties regarding its interpretation;
>   (c) any relevant rules of international law applicable in the relations between the parties.
> 4. A special meaning shall be given to a term if it is established that the parties so intended.

While the rules of treaty interpretation are by no means straightforward, it is possible to outline some general approaches to Article 31 and its application. The 'ordinary meaning' of the terms

---

21 Vienna Convention on the Law of Treaties (adopted 23 May 1969, entered into force 27 January 1980) 1155 UNTS 331.

of the treaty refers to the regular, normal, or customary meaning of the words or phrases used in the treaty.[22] This regular, normal, or customary meaning may be found through recourse to dictionaries,[23] or other specialist works.[24] The context of the treaty refers to both reading the words in their immediate surroundings – i.e., the context of words in particular sentences[25] – as well as the context of the terms in a more macro sense: how are the words contextualized in relation to the title of the treaty, or headings within the treaty?[26] The preamble of a treaty, for example, also comprises the context.[27] Context is also connected to the 'object and purpose' of the treaty – both function as a way to understand the ordinary meaning of the treaty terms. This final element of the interpretation matrix, 'object and purpose', has been stated as meaning 'the substantial content of the norm, the provisions, rights and obligations created by the norm. The object of a treaty is the instrument for the achievement of the treaty's purpose, and this

---

[22] Richard Gardiner, *Treaty Interpretation* (2nd edn, OUP 2015) 183.

[23] The WTO has had recourse to the dictionary meaning of words in several instances – such as in WTO, *Canada–Measures Affecting the Export of Civilian Aircraft* (2 August 1999) WT/DS70/AB/R, 39, para 154; see also Chang-Fa Lo, 'Good Faith Use of Dictionary in the Search of Ordinary Meaning under the WTO Dispute Settlement Understanding' (2010) 1 Journal of International Dispute Settlement 431; David Pavot, 'The Use of Dictionary by the WTO Appellate Body: Beyond the Search of Ordinary Meaning' (2014) 4 Journal of International Dispute Settlement 29. Note, however, comments made by Sir Humphrey Waldock, at the Vienna Conference on the law of treaties, who, in his capacity as former Special Rapporteur, made it clear that in approaching the term 'ordinary meaning', it was not the intention of the International Law Commission to suggest that 'words have a "dictionary" or intrinsic meaning on themselves' and reemphasized the tripartite approach that treaties must be interpreted in good faith, in accordance with the ordinary meaning of the words in their context (Comments by Sir Humphrey Waldock, 'Official Records: Summary Records of the Plenary Meetings and of the Meetings of the Committee of the Whole' UN Conference on the Law of Treaties, First Session (Vienna 26 March-24 May 1968) UN Doc A/CONF.39/11, 185, para 70.

[24] See, for example, the International Court of Justice (ICJ) in the decision of *Kasikili/Sedudu Island (Botswana v Namibia)* (Judgment) [1999] ICJ Rep 1045 paras 20 and 30, where the Court states 'In order to illuminate the meaning of words agreed upon in 1890, there is nothing that prevents the Court from taking into account the present day state of scientific knowledge, as reflected in the documentary material submitted to it by the Parties' (para 20), going on to look at definitions contained in several works including the *Dictionnaire français d'hydrologie de surface avec équivalents en anglais, espagnol, allemande* and the *Water and Wastewater Control Engineering Glossary* (at para 30 of the decision).

[25] For an example of the ICJ applying a contextual approach to a term in a treaty provision, see the *Case concerning the Land, Island And Maritime Frontier Dispute (El Salvador/Honduras: Nicaragua intervening)* [1992] ICJ Rep 351, 582–84 paras 373–74: 'it is difficult to see how one can equate "delimitation" with "determination of a legal situation" (…) no doubt the word "determine" in English (and, as the Chamber is informed, the verb "*determinar*" in Spanish) can be used to convey the idea of setting limits, so that, if applied directly to the "maritime spaces" its "ordinary meaning" might be taken to include delimitation of those spaces. But the word must be read in its context; the object of the verb "determine" is not the maritime spaces themselves but the legal situation of these spaces.'

[26] See further *Case Concerning Oil Platforms (Islamic Republic of Iran v United States of America)* (Preliminary Objection) [1996] ICJ Rep 803, 819 para 47, for an example of how the ICJ used the title of a treaty to assist in interpretation of the treaty – 'it should also be noted that, in the original English version, the actual title of the Treaty of 1955 (…) refers, besides "Amity" and "Consular Rights", not to "Commerce" but, more broadly, to "Economic Relations".'

[27] See *Border and Transborder Armed Actions (Nicaragua v Honduras)* (Jurisdiction and Admissibility) [1988] ICJ Rep 69, 106 para 97, for an example of the Court looking at a preamble for the purposes of treaty interpretation.

purpose is, in turn, the general result which the parties want to achieve by the treaty.'[28] In practice, courts have used the preamble as well as treaty's substantive provisions to come to a decision on interpretation.[29]

Article 31 should be read and applied in its entirety – the Article should not be subject to 'excessive molecularization'.[30] Rather, as noted by the *Aguas del Tunari v Bolivia*:

> Interpretation under Article 31 of the Vienna Convention is a process of progressive encirclement where the interpreter starts under the general rule with (1) the ordinary meaning of the terms of the treaty, (2) in their context and (3) in light of the treaty's object and purpose, and by cycling through this three step inquiry iteratively closes in upon the proper interpretation.[31]

Thus, ascertaining the ordinary meaning of a term must not be done in the abstract, but rather it is 'immediately and intimately linked with context, and then to be taken in conjunction with all the relevant elements of the Vienna Rules'.[32]

Note must also be made of Article 32 VCLT, which outlines that, in addition to Article 31:

> Recourse may be had to supplementary means of interpretation, including the preparatory work of the treaty and the circumstances of its conclusion, in order to confirm the meaning resulting from the application of Article 31, or to determine the meaning when the interpretation according to Article 31:
> (a) leaves the meaning ambiguous or obscure; or
> (b) leads to a result which is manifestly absurd or unreasonable.

In having recourse to Article 32, one must not use the provision as means to begin the interpretive process anew; rather, Article 32 can only be used to confirm any interpretation originally found through application of Article 31. As noted by the ILC in a commentary on an early draft of Article 32, the provision is designed as supplemental to Article 31: 'the text of the treaty must be presumed to be the authentic expression of the intentions of the parties, and that the elucidation of the meaning of the text rather than an investigation *ab initio* of the supposed intentions of the parties constitutes the object of interpretation.'[33] Both Articles 31 and 32 are considered as having customary status.[34]

---

28 Isabelle Buffard and Karl Zemanek, 'The "Object and Purpose" of a Treaty: An Enigma?' (1998) 3 Austrian Review of International & European Law 326.

29 In *Sovereignty over Pulau Litigan and Pulau Sipadan (Indonesia/Malaysia)* [2002] ICJ Rep 625, 652 para 51. See also Judge Weeramantry in *Case Concerning the Arbitral Award of 31 July 1989 (Guinea-Bissau v Senegal)*, (Dissenting Opinion) [1991] ICJ Rep 53, 142: 'the preamble is a principle and natural source from which indications can be gathered of a treaty's objects and purposes even though the preamble does not contain substantive provisions.'

30 Gardiner (n 22) 162.

31 International Centre for the Settlement of Investment Disputes *Aguas del Tunari S.A. v Bolivia* (2005) ICSID Case No ARB/02/03 para 91.

32 Gardiner (n 22) 181.

33 ILC, 'Report of the International Law Commission on the Work of its 18th Session' (1966) Yearbook of the International Law Commission (vol. II) 223, commentary to art 28, para 18.

34 This has been stated by the ICJ in *Territorial Dispute (Libyan Arab Jamahiriya/Chad)*, (Judgment) [1994] ICJ Rep 6, para 41; *Kasikili/Sedudu Island (Botswana v Namibia)* (Judgment) [1999] ICJ Rep 1045 para 18, and *Case Concerning Oil Platforms (Islamic Republic of Iran v United States of America)* (Preliminary Objection) [1996] ICJ Rep 803 para 23.

In applying the rules of treaty interpretation, the aim is to ensure that the meaning ascribed to the treaty and its provisions accords with the 'shared intentions, expectations and objectives of the parties'.[35] As outlined in Articles 31 and 32, achievement of this aim is done through a tripartite process of examining the text of the provision, the object and purpose of the treaty, and the context (that is, any other agreements or instruments made by parties to the treaty and related to the conclusion of the treaty). Article 31 does not prescribe a hierarchy of norms[36] – rather they are 'a logical progression (…) one naturally begins with the text, followed by the context, and then other matters, in particular, subsequent material'.[37] Finally, mindful that interpretation of the terms of the treaty must be done in good faith, even if the text of the treaty is clear, if applying such a textual interpretation would lead to a result which is ambiguous, obscure, manifestly absurd, or unreasonable, recourse may be had to supplementary means of interpretation, including documents such as the *travaux préparatoires*.[38]

With such instruction in mind, what then can be said about how to interpret the term 'armed conflict not of an international character'? What is the ordinary meaning of the term in its context and in light of the object and purpose of the Geneva Conventions in their entirety? It should be noted that a detailed textual analysis of the Geneva Conventions (or indeed a detailed analysis of the law of treaty interpretation) is beyond the scope of this chapter; however, a few cogent points about treaty interpretation and Common Article 3 are worth noting. First, there is little in Common Article 3 to provide guidance on how to interpret the term 'armed conflict not of an international character' – indeed, as Farer notes, 'one of the most assured things that might be said about the words "armed conflict not of an international character" is that no one can say with assurance precisely what meaning they were intended to convey.'[39]

The phrase 'not of an international character' would, on its face, suggest that any conflict not between states would be captured under this term. However, it is evident, when one looks at the *travaux préparatoires* from the Diplomatic Conference at Geneva in 1949, it was clearly *not* the intention of the majority of states to have Common Article 3 apply to *all* situations of conflict not involving two or more states at war with one another.[40] Thus, the determinative term to define is 'armed conflict'. What is meant in Common Article 3 by 'armed conflict'? Again, there is nothing in Common Article 3 that would suggest a threshold for when a purely domestic situation of violence – such as a riot or violent protest – can be properly considered an armed conflict. Common Article 3 sets no explicit minimum threshold requirements, such as the intensity or duration of hostilities, or the degree of organization of participants in the conflict.

However, it may be possible to extrapolate some potential threshold requirements if one considers the inclusion in Common Article 3 of the sentence which provides that the parties to

[35] Oliver Lissitzyn, 'Treaties and Changed Circumstances (Rebus Sic Stantibus)' (1967) 61 American Journal of International Law 896.

[36] Anthony Aust, *Modern Treaty Law and Practice* (3rd edn, CUP 2013) 208.

[37] ibid 208.

[38] Supplementary materials are also permitted to confirm the meaning resulting from the application of art 31 VCLT, cf art 32.

[39] Tom Farer, 'Humanitarian Law and Armed Conflicts: Toward the Definition of "International Armed Conflict"' (1971) 71 Columbia Law Review 43.

[40] See above regarding the position of states at Geneva in 1949 on the scope of applicability of Common Article 3.

the conflict 'should further endeavour to bring into force, by means of special agreements, all or part of the other provisions of the present Convention'.[41] The 'special agreements' provision foresees the possibility that parties to a conflict might agree to apply the Conventions, in whole or in part, to their conflict. Indeed, many of the provisions of the Geneva Conventions are based on the presumption that the parties to the conflict possess state-like facilities, such as the exclusive control of territory, the possession of organized governmental bodies including administrative, executive and judicial systems, and organized military forces under responsible command. Geneva provisions for the administration of occupied territory, and the establishment and management of prisoner of war and internship camps, for example, suggest a reasonably high baseline of organization will be possessed by parties to the conflict. Therefore, if Common Article 3 encourages parties to a non-international armed conflict to adopt special agreements to apply the Conventions in their entirety, it seems reasonable to assert that those parties are expected to possess an above-average degree of administrative and military organization, if not near para-statal characteristics.[42] This approach would appear to be confirmed by comments made by the ICRC's Frédéric Siordet, who noted in 1950, 'Article 3, even if it has the appearance of a miniature Convention, is not in itself a separate agreement relating to non-international armed conflicts. It is only one provision, amongst others, of four Conventions which have a very definite object: to protect the victims of war.'[43]

This interpretation of the text – that Common Article 3 was intended to apply to high-level non-international armed conflicts – also seems confirmed if one looks to the *travaux préparatoires* from the Diplomatic Conference. Based on the statements made by states during the Diplomatic Conference, there were more states in favour of a higher threshold for what would become Common Article 3. The US,[44] Australia,[45] the UK,[46] Spain,[47] Venezuela,[48]

---

41 Geneva Convention Relative to the Protection of Civilian Persons in Time of War (adopted 12 August 1949, entered into force 21 October 1950) 75 UNTS 287, art 3.

42 Farer (n 39) 47–48.

43 Frédéric Siordet, 'The Geneva Conventions and Civil War' (1950) 3 Revue Internationale de la Croix-Rouge Supplement 201, 211.

44 Leland Harrison, Comments in the Second Meeting of the Joint Committee, 27 April 1949, *Final Record*, vol IIB, 12.

45 William R. Hodgson, Comments in the Second Meeting of the Joint Committee, 27 April 1949, *Final Record*, vol IIB, 15.

46 Sir Robert Craigie, Comments in the First Meeting of the Joint Committee, 26 April 1949, *Final Record*, vol IIB, 10.

47 The Marquis of Villobar, Comments in the First Meeting of the Joint Committee, 26 April 1949, *Final Record*, vol IIB, 11.

48 Pedro Falcon Briceno, Comments in the Nineteenth Plenary Meeting, 29 July 1949, *Final Record*, vol IIB, 333.

France,[49] China,[50] Italy,[51] Canada,[52] Monaco,[53] and Greece[54] all, at one point or other during the Conference, voiced the opinion that the application of the laws of war to *all* non-international armed conflicts would be a step too far, or otherwise suggested that the threshold for application of the Conventions be set somewhere near or equivalent to that of recognition of belligerency – namely, that the adverse party 'possesses an organised military force, an authority responsible for its acts acting within a defined territory and having means of observing and enforcing the Convention'.[55] Only a few states – the USSR,[56] Romania,[57] Norway,[58] Hungary,[59] Mexico,[60] Czechoslovakia[61] – were on the record that what would become Common Article 3 should be applied broadly.

Thus, in adopting Common Article 3, it appears that the intended scope of the Article and of the term 'armed conflict not of an international character' was to be limited to conflicts of a relatively high level. Indeed, as Anthony Cullen has noted, during the Diplomatic Conference, no delegates

> contested or objected to the use of the term 'civil war' as synonymous with 'armed conflict not of an international character' (…) it appears that there was broad agreement that the threshold required for the application of international humanitarian law would be similar to that traditionally assumed for the recognition of belligerency.[62]

---

[49] Albert Lamarle, Comments in the First Meeting of the Joint Committee, 26 April 1949, *Final Record*, vol IIB, 10.

[50] Nan-Ju Wu, Comments in the Second Meeting of the Joint Committee, 27 April 1949, *Final Record*, vol IIB, 12.

[51] Adolfo Maresca, Comments in the Second Meeting of the Joint Committee, 27 April 1949, *Final Record*, vol IIB, 13.

[52] Max Wershof, Comments in the Second Meeting of the Joint Committee, 27 April 1949, *Final Record*, vol IIB, 13.

[53] Paul de Geouffre de la Pradelle, Comments in the Second Meeting of the Joint Committee, 27 April 1949, *Final Record*, vol IIB, 14.

[54] Michel Pesmazoglou, Comments in the First Meeting of the Joint Committee, 26 April 1949, *Final Record*, IIB, 10–11.

[55] Proposed French Amendment to the Stockholm version of common article 2 on non-international armed conflicts, 26 April 1949, *Final Record*, vol III, Annex 12, 27.

[56] General Nikolai Slavin, Comments in the Second meeting of the Joint Committee, 27 April 1949, *Final Record*, vol IIB, 14.

[57] Victor Dimitriu, Comments in the First Meeting of the Joint Committee, 26 April 1949, *Final Record*, vol IIB, 11.

[58] Frede Castberg, Comments in the First Meeting of the Joint Committee, 26 April 1949, *Final Record*, vol IIB, 11.

[59] Andor Falus, Comments in the First Meeting of the Joint Committee, 26 April 1949, *Final Record*, vol IIB, 11.

[60] Pedro de Alba, Comments in the First Meeting of the Joint Committee, 26 April 1949, *Final Record*, vol IIB, 11.

[61] Pavel Winkler, Comments in the Nineteenth Plenary Meeting, Comments in the Nineteenth Plenary Meeting, 29 July 1949, *Final Record*, vol IIB, 334.

[62] Cullen (n 2) 42. That states wanted to limit the scope of Common Article 3 was also noted by Tom Farer, who remarked in 1971 that 'it is improbable that the "founding fathers" of the Geneva Conventions intended to hold all civil conflicts within the limits of Article 3.' (Farer (n 39) 45).

As such, Common Article 3, at least as envisaged in 1949, would apply to conflicts only where the insurgent group had:

> won for itself a territorial existence by taking possession of a given part of the national territory (…) fulfil[ed] the conditions which must be met to constitute a regular government de facto exercising in that part of the territory the ostensible rights belonging to sovereignty (…) [and that the] struggle waged in its name is (…) conducted by organised forces subject to military discipline and complying with the laws and customs of war.[63]

However, as outlined in the VCLT, textual analysis, even if supported by supplementary means of interpretation, is not the only factor to consider when analysing and interpreting treaty provisions. As provided in Article 31(3)(b) VCLT, subsequent practice in relation to the treaty is also relevant in interpreting its terms.[64] As such, one should look to how Common Article 3 was applied in practice – does the conduct of states in their own internal and non-international armed conflicts confirm a restrictive reading of Common Article 3? Was the use of non-specific language in Common Article 3 a mechanism to allow for the provision to evolve and expand in scope and applicability over time? Has state practice in relation to Common Article 3 amounted to an amendment to its original scope? The next section of this chapter begins to examine these questions.

4. COMMON ARTICLE 3 IN PRACTICE

If we accept that the intention of the drafters of Common Article 3 was to limit the operation of the provision to comparatively high-level internal armed conflicts, state practice after 1949 would suggest that this intention was soon ignored, as IHL principles started to be applied more broadly and in more situations than would meet the strict criteria of recognition of belligerency. Indeed, the first inklings that the narrower approach would not endure were seen in the actions of Portugal in 1949. When it came time to sign the Conventions, Portugal stated:

> As there is no actual definition of what is meant by a conflict not of an international character, and as, in case this term is intended to refer solely to civil war, it is not clearly laid down at what moment an armed rebellion within a country should be considered as having become a civil war, Portugal reserves the right not to apply the provisions of Article 3, in so far as they may be contrary to the provisions of Portuguese law, in all territories subject to her sovereignty in any part of the world.[65]

---

63 As outlined by the Institute of International Law's Regulations for Civil War (1900), under art 8; see (1900) 18 Annuaire IDI 227, 229. For a more exhaustive analysis of recognition of insurgency and belligerency, see further Robert Wilson, 'Recognition of Insurgency and Belligerency' (1937) 31 ASIL Proceedings 136; Hersch Lauterpacht, *Recognition in International Law* (CUP 1947) specifically ch 12–17.

64 Aust (n 36) 215, calling art 31(3)(b) VCLT 'a most important element in the interpretation of any treaty (…) however precise a text appears to be, the way in which it is actually applied by parties is usually a good indication of what they understand it to mean.'

65 *Final Record*, vol I, 351. Interestingly, while this statement was made at the time of signing, Portugal did not lodge a reservation to this effect upon ratification.

Additional indications that a broader approach to Common Article 3 might prevail came with the publication, in 1952, of the Pictet Commentaries to the First Geneva Convention.[66] In the Commentary to Common Article 3, the drafting history of the Article and the Conference's attempts to define the term 'armed conflict not of an international character' are examined.[67] The Commentary commends the drafters of Common Article 3 as 'wisely'[68] eschewing a definition of non-international armed conflict, going on to list a number of 'convenient criteria'[69] to indicate the existence of a non-international armed conflict. Those convenient criteria are the same criteria suggested by states during the drafting phase at Geneva – the criteria akin to recognition of belligerency. Such an approach would seem to suggest that the ICRC supported a narrow approach to Common Article 3. However, these 'convenient criteria' were drawn from discussions during the Diplomatic Conference at a time when the Conventions in their entirety were still to be applied to non-international armed conflicts.[70] Moreover, any such assessment is quickly put aside by the following comments in the ICRC Commentary on the Conventions:

> The above criteria are useful as a means of distinguishing a genuine armed conflict from a mere act of banditry or an unorganized and short-lived insurrection. Does this mean that Article 3 is not applicable in cases where armed strife breaks out in a country, but does not fulfil any of the above conditions (which are not obligatory and are only mentioned as an indication)? We do not subscribe to this view. We think, on the contrary, that the Article should be applied as widely as possible. There can be no reason against this. For, contrary to what may have been thought, the Article in its reduced form does not in any way limit the right of a State to put down rebellion. Nor does it increase in the slightest the authority of the rebel party. It merely demands respect for certain rules, which were already recognized as essential in all civilized countries, and enacted in the municipal law of the States in question, long before the Convention was signed.[71]

With this entreaty from the ICRC in mind, how did states receive Common Article 3? Did states accept that 'armed conflict not of an international character' was a reference to situations similar to recognition of belligerency only? Or did state practice after 1949 demonstrate that Common Article 3 armed conflicts could include conflicts at a lower threshold? For a notably long time, it was difficult to discern, through an examination of state practice alone, what the constituent elements of a non-international armed conflict actually were. Following the adoption of Common Article 3, the international community found itself with a provision to be applied in all situations of conflict not of an international character, but with no explicit definition of what a non-international armed conflict was. Indeed, since the adoption of Common Article 3 very few states have been prepared to acknowledge that they consider themselves engaged in a Common Article 3 conflict.[72]

---

66 Jean Pictet (ed), *Commentary to Geneva Convention I for the Amelioration of the Condition of the Wounded and Sick in Armed Forces in the Field* (ICRC 1952).

67 ibid 37–48.

68 ibid 49. See also Siordet (n 43) 211.

69 Pictet (n 66) 49.

70 See Siordet (n 43) 201–202.

71 Pictet (n 66) 50.

72 For example, the United Kingdom did not accept that Common Article 3 applied to their conflicts in Kenya, Cyprus, and Malaya. The reluctance to apply Common Article 3 in these cases was, as GIAD Draper noted, 'determined by political considerations and not by any objective assessment of

However, there have been examples of states drawing on the provisions of Common Article 3 in their conflicts. For example, during the conflict in Nigeria against the Biafran separatists, the Nigerian army issued an 'Operational Code of Conduct for Nigerian Armed Forces',[73] in which the provisions of Common Article 3 were deemed to be applicable. The Code included prohibitions on the ill treatment of pregnant women,[74] children,[75] hospital workers,[76] and captured or other fighters rendered *hors de combat*.[77] Indeed, the Nigerian code of conduct seemed to go beyond the minimum requirements of Common Article 3, by granting prisoner of war status and treatment to captured enemy personnel.[78] In the civil conflicts that took place in the Congo following its independence from Belgium, the central government in Leopoldville declared in a 1961 letter sent to the Swiss authorities that they would abide by the Conventions in their conflict with the Katanga province.[79] Similar statements regarding the applicability of Common Article 3 or the fundamental principles contained therein were also made by state authorities in the conflicts in Yemen,[80] Cuba,[81] Bosnia,[82] and Algeria.[83] Instances of application of Common Article 3 vary from *ad hoc* agreements by all parties to the conflict to apply either

---

the facts' (GIAD Draper, *The Red Cross Conventions* (Stevens 1958) 15 (at n 47)). It should be noted that these conflicts would now be classified as wars of national liberation; however, at the time, there was no Additional Protocol I to regulate such conflicts as international conflicts. As such, the only relevant treaty law was Common Article 3. In the conflict against the armed opposition group RENAMO in Mozambique, the government characterized the armed group as a 'disorganised movement of thieves' (See Jeremy M. Weinstein, *Inside Rebellion: The Politics of Insurgent Violence* (CUP 2007) 230). An American delegate to the Diplomatic Conferences that debated and adopted the Additional Protocols commented that non-observance of Common Article 3 appeared to be 'an almost universal phenomenon' (Comments by Walter Reed, *Official Records of the Diplomatic Conference on the Reaffirmation and Development of International Humanitarian Law Applicable in Armed Conflicts, Geneva (1974–1977)*, CDDH/III/SR.32, vol XIV, 313).

73 General Yakubu Gowon, Directive to all Officers and Men of the Armed Forces of the Federal Republic of Nigeria on Conduct of Military Operations, Operational Code of Conduct for Nigerian Armed Forces, issued by General Yakubu Gowon, Commander-in-Chief of the Armed Forces of the Federal Republic of Nigeria (July 1967) <https://casebook.icrc.org/case-study/nigeria-operational-code-conduct> accessed 31 January 2021 (Operational Code of Conduct for Nigerian Armed Forces).

74 ibid, art 4(a).

75 ibid, art 4(b)–(c).

76 ibid, art 4(d).

77 ibid, art 4(e).

78 ibid.

79 ICRC, 'The Red Cross in Action in the Congo' (1962) 10 International Review of the Red Cross 3, 7–8.

80 See Kathryn Boals, 'The Relevance of International Law to the Internal War in Yemen' in Richard Falk (ed), *The International Law of Civil War* (Johns Hopkins University Press 1971) 315–16.

81 David Forsythe, 'Legal Management of Internal War: The 1977 Protocol on Non-International Armed Conflicts' (1978) 72 American Journal of International Law 274.

82 Bosnia and Herzegovina, Agreement No. 1, 22 May 1992 <https://casebook.icrc.org/case-study/former-yugoslavia-special-agreements-between-parties-conflicts> accessed 31 January 2021, art 2(1) – (6).

83 Elden Greenberg, 'Law and the Conduct of the Algerian Revolution' (1970) 11 Harvard International Law Journal 37. See also the discussion of the French position on Algeria in Lindsay Moir, *The Law of Internal Armed Conflict* (CUP 2002) 68–74; Mohammed Bedjaoui, *Law and the Algerian Revolution* (International Association of Democratic Lawyers 1961) 142–52.

the Conventions in totality (or at least the basic principles embodied in Common Article 3);[84] to explicit acceptance of the applicability of Common Article 3 by state parties (as well as by non-state parties to the conflict);[85] to instances where ICRC visits to detainees were accepted or facilitated by authorities.[86] Arguably, it was the adoption of Common Article 3 – with its scaffold of minimum humanitarian standards, its encouragement of *ad hoc* agreements, and its provision for acceptance of ICRC assistance – that was instrumental in facilitating these state activities in armed conflict.

In looking at these armed conflicts, the crucial question to ask is: were these high-intensity non-international armed conflicts, essentially similar to civil wars or situations of belligerency, or were they lower-intensity conflicts, ones that would not meet the criteria for recognition of belligerency? If all situations of application of Common Article 3 were only to high-intensity armed conflicts, it would seem that state practice in relation to Common Article 3 was in accordance with the intentions of the drafters in 1949. However, if Common Article 3 was being applied more widely, in more situations of violence, state practice would seem to be moving away from a narrow reading of 'armed conflicts not of an international character'.

There are certainly examples of the application of Common Article 3 to situations of high-level internal violence, violence of a type that would seem to meet the recognition of belligerency criteria of an organized armed force which has

> won for itself a territorial existence by taking possession of a given part of the national territory (…) fulfil[ed] the conditions which must be met to constitute a regular government de facto exercising in that part of the territory the ostensible rights belonging to sovereignty (…) [and that the] struggle waged in its name is (…) conducted by organised forces subject to military discipline and complying with the laws and customs of war.[87]

The conflict in Algeria in the 1950s would certainly seem to meet those criteria: the Algerian National Liberation Front (FLN) possessed a notable degree of internal organization[88] and territorial control.[89] Moreover, the conflict itself was of significant duration and intensity.[90] Likewise, the conflict in Nigeria against the Biafran secessionists was, in essence, a civil war

---

84 In the Congo, Yemen, and Nigeria – see Forsythe (n 81) 275. See also Sivakumaran (n 2) 200–204, who also discusses examples of recognition or application of Common Article 3 in the post-1949 era.

85 In Guatemala, France, Lebanon, Cuba, Yemen, Vietnam, the Dominican Republic, Uruguay, and Chile, see Forsythe (n 81) 275.

86 In Algeria, Cyprus, Hungary, Malaysia, Kenya, South Vietnam, Rhodesia, Laos, Indonesia, Aden, Bolivia, Northern Ireland, Guinea-Bissau, Mozambique, Burundi, the Philippines, Angola, Thailand, Iraq, Ethiopia, and Lebanon, see Forsythe (n 81) 276.

87 Institute of International Law (n 63) art 8, translation in Yves Sandoz, Christophe Swinarski and Bruno Zimmerman (eds), *Commentary on the Additional Protocols of 8 June 1977 to the Geneva Conventions of 12 August 1949* (ICRC/Martinus Nijhoff 1987) 1322–23.

88 See Bedjaoui (n 83) 46–52 for a description of the internal administrative structure of the FLN.

89 See Bedjaoui (n 83) 38–44, describing the scope of territory under FLN control, as well as the administrative systems in place in those liberated areas.

90 The conflict took place between 1954 and 1962; the French maintained troop numbers at over 400,000 during the conflict, with estimates placing the number of FLN troops at the time of ceasefire at over 50,000. See further Moir, *The Law of Internal Armed Conflict* (n 83) 68–69.

giving rise to a state of belligerency: both sides of the conflict 'were well equipped, with substantial organised armies under responsible authorities, in control of territory'.[91]

However, there have also been examples of Common Article 3 being deemed applicable to armed conflicts that did not meet (or had not yet, at the time of the statement) the high threshold of recognition of belligerency. For example, the UN,[92] the UN Commission on Human Rights,[93] and the International Court of Justice (ICJ),[94] have all affirmed the applicability of Common Article 3 to situations that would seem to fall short of the recognition of belligerency test.[95] Indeed, in perhaps one of the most controversial[96] examples of this broader applicability approach to Common Article 3, the Inter-American Commission on Human Rights in their 1997 decision of *Abella v Argentina* (also known as the *La Tablada* case)[97] held that a Common Article 3 armed conflict was deemed to have existed in 1989, as a result of a 30-hour-long assault by 42 members of an organized armed group known as Movimiento Todos por la Patria (MTP), against the 3rd Mechanized Infantry Regiment barracks in La Tablada, in Buenos Aires, Argentina. In its report, the Commission affirmed the applicability

---

91 Moir, *The Law of Internal Armed Conflict* (n 83) 79. See also Edward Nwogugu, 'The Nigerian Civil War: A Case Study in the Law of War' (1974) 14 Indian Journal of International Law 13; Michael Bothe, 'Article 3 and Protocol II: Case Studies of Nigeria and El Salvador' (1982) 31 American University International Law Review 899, 901–902.

92 In UNSC Res 794 (3 December 1992) UN Doc S/RES/794 and UNSC Res 814 (26 March 1993) UN Doc S/RES/814 on the situation in Somalia; UNSC Res 1213 (3 December 1998) UN Doc S/RES/1213 on Angola; and UNSC Res 993 (12 May 1993) UN Doc S/RES/993 on Georgia. See also UNGAR 50/193 on Croatia; the UNCHR Res 70 (1998) UN Doc E/CN.4/RES/1998/70, UNCHR Res 68 (1992) UN Doc E/CN.4/RES/1992/68, UNCHR Res 53 (1990) UN Doc E/CN.4/RES/1990/53, UNCHR Res 74 (1995) UN Doc E/CN.4/RES/1995/74, UNCHR Res 75 (1996) UN Doc E/CN.4/RES/1996/75 and UNCHR Res 65 (1997) UN Doc E/CN.4/RES/1997/65 on Afghanistan; the UNCHR (Sub-Commission) Res 9 (1989) UN Doc E/CN.4/Sub.21989/9 on El Salvador; and the Report of the UN Secretary General, 'Causes of Conflict and the Promotion of Durable Peace and Sustainable Development in Africa' (1998) UN Doc A/52/871-S/1998/318.

93 UNCHR Res 18 UN Doc E/CN.4/RES/1999/18, at para 17 (23 April 1999) on Kosovo; UNCHR Res 59 (1997) UN Doc E/CN.4/RES/1997/59 at para 7 (15 April 1997) on Sudan; and UNCHR Res 67 UN Doc E/CN.4/RES/1998/67 at para 6 (21 April 1998) on Sudan.

94 *Military and Paramilitary Activities in and against Nicaragua (Nicaragua v United States)* (Merits) [1986] ICJ Rep 14 para 218, referring to *Corfu Channel Case (UK v Albania)* (Merits) [1949] ICJ Rep 4, 22.

95 Forsythe also argues that several situations of conflict short of full-scale belligerency were relevant for application of Common Article 3, including Guatemala in 1954, Lebanon in 1958, Cuba in 1959, Yemen in 1962, the Dominican Republic in 1965, Uruguay in 1972, and Chile in 1973. See further Forsythe (n 81) 275.

96 There are a range of views as to whether the Inter-American Commission was correct in their application of IHL to the incident at La Tablada – see further Liesbeth Zegveld, 'The Inter-American Commission on Human Rights and International Humanitarian Law: A Comment on the Tablada Case' (1998) 38 International Review of the Red Cross 505; Lindsay Moir, 'Law and the Inter-American Human Rights System' (2003) 25 Human Rights Quarterly 182; Sivakumaran (n 2) 169.

97 *Juan Carlos Abella v Argentina*, Case 11.137, Inter-American Court of Human Rights Report No. 55/97, OEA/Ser/L/V/II.97, doc. 38 (October 30 1997).

of Common Article 3 to the assault, distinguishing the attack on the barracks as different from internal tensions,[98] and stating:

> Common Article 3 is generally understood to apply to low intensity and open armed confrontations between relatively organized armed forces or groups that take place within the territory of a particular State. Thus, Common Article 3 does not apply to riots, mere acts of banditry or an unorganized and short-lived rebellion. Article 3 armed conflicts typically involve armed strife between governmental armed forces and organized armed insurgents (…) It is important to understand that application of Common Article 3 does not require the existence of large-scale and generalized hostilities or a situation comparable to a civil war in which dissident armed groups exercise control over parts of national territory.[99]

The Commission went on to note that:

> the violent acts at the La Tablada military base on January 23 and 24, 1989 can be properly characterized as a situation of internal disturbances. What happened there was not equivalent to large scale violent demonstrations, students throwing stones at the police, bandits holding persons hostage for ransom, or the assassination of government officials for political reasons – all forms of domestic violence not qualifying as armed conflicts. What differentiates the events at the La Tablada base from these situations are the concerted nature of the hostile acts undertaken by the attackers, the direct involvement of governmental armed forces, and the nature and level of the violence attending the events in question. More particularly, the attackers involved carefully planned, coordinated and executed an armed attack, i.e., a military operation, against a quintessential military objective – a military base.[100]

Thus, the Inter-American Commission demonstrated a wide application of Common Article 3, with the requirement of control of some degree of territory clearly not considered as being definitive for the application of Common Article 3.[101]

A similar approach was demonstrated by the ICTY in the *Tadić* decision, where the Court stated that for a non-international armed conflict to exist, there must be 'protracted armed vio-

---

[98] Quoting the 1973 Commentary to the Draft Additional Protocols, the Commission identified internal disturbances as 'riots, that is to say, all disturbances which from the start are not directed by a leader and have no concerted intent; isolated and sporadic acts of violence, as distinct from military operations carried out by armed forces or organized armed groups; other acts of a similar nature which incur, in particular, mass arrests of persons because of their behavior or political opinion' (*Abella v Argentina* (n 97) 149).

[99] ibid 152.

[100] ibid 154–56.

[101] The *Abella* decision was controversial, with commentators challenging the competence of the Inter-American Commission – a human rights body – to apply IHL; the Inter-American Court of Human Rights later held that the Court only had the competence to apply human rights law, and not IHL (in *Las Palmeras v Colombia* (Judgment) Inter-American Court of Human Rights Series C No 90, 33 (6 December 2001)). However, in *Bámaca-Velásquez v Guatemala* (Judgment) Inter-American Court of Human Rights Series C No 70 (25 November 2000) the Inter-American Court held that lack of competence to apply IHL did not limit the Court from having recourse to IHL for the purposes of interpretation of the American Convention on Human Rights (adopted 22 November 1969, entered into force 18 July 1978) 1144 UNTS 123, 209. For critiques of *Abella*, see further Zegveld (n 96) 505; Moir, 'Law and the Inter-American Human Rights System' (n 96) 182; Christine Byron, 'A Blurring of the Boundaries: The Application of International Humanitarian Law by Human Rights Bodies' (2006-2007) 47 Virginia Journal of International Law 839.

lence between governmental authorities and organised armed groups or between such groups within a State.'[102] While the Chamber in *Tadić* did not expound on what constituted 'protracted armed violence' at that time, several other cases in the ICTY did – including *Limaj*[103] and *Haradinaj*.[104] When examining what might be considered relevant indicia to indicate the existence of a non-international armed conflict, the ICTY stated that such indicia could include:

> the number, duration and intensity of individual confrontations; the type of weapons and other military equipment used; the number and calibre of munitions fired; the number of persons and type of forces partaking in the fighting; the number of casualties; the extent of material destruction; and the number of civilians fleeing combat zones. The involvement of the UN Security Council may also be a reflection of the intensity of a conflict.[105]

Notably, the *Tadić* formula does not suggest that territorial control is in any way a prerequisite for the application of the law of non-international armed conflict.[106] A word of caution is useful here: the *Tadić* formula for determination of an existence of an armed conflict is not, *per se*, state practice – it is the decision of an international tribunal.[107] Moreover, in coming to their definition of armed conflict, the ICTY gave no indication or evidence as to how it came to such a conclusion, citing no supporting state practice or opinio juris to suggest the methodology of how the definition was arrived at.[108] That being said, the *Tadić* formula has, since its first enunciation, been widely utilized by a number of different organizations and institutions, including in reports of special rapporteurs,[109] international commissions of enquiry including those

---

[102] *Prosecutor v Tadić* (Decision on the Defence Motion for Interlocutory Appeal on Jurisdiction) IT-94-1 (2 October 1995) 70.

[103] *Prosecutor v Limaj et al* (Trial Judgment) IT-03-66-T (30 November 2005) paras 135–67.

[104] *Prosecutor v Haradinaj et al* (Trial Judgment) IT-04-84 (3 April 2008).

[105] *Prosecutor v Haradinaj et al* (Trial Judgment) IT-04-84 (3 April 2008).

[106] See further Claus Kreß, 'The 1999 Crisis in East Timor and the Threshold of the Law on War Crimes' (2002) 13 4 Criminal Law Forum 403, 417, comparing and contrasting the Tablada and *Tadić* tests.

[107] Sivakumaran is particularly cautious regarding courts and tribunals that have applied Common Article 3 widely, finding it 'difficult to agree with the exhortation in the ICRC Commentaries (…) that common Article 3 should be applied "as wide[ly] as possible" including in situations of banditry' (Sivakumaran (n 2) 162). Sivakumaran here references *Abella*, as well as the ICTY in *Prosecutor v Milošević* (Judgment) IT-98-29/1-T (12 December 2007) and *Prosecutor v Boškoski and Tarčulovski*, (Judgment) IT-04-82-T (10 July 2008). Note however the ILC's report 'Ways and Means for Making the Evidence of Customary International Law More Readily Available' (*Yearbook of the International Law Commission*, vol II, 1950, 369–70), which includes decisions of both national and international courts as evidence of state practice. James Crawford also considers decisions of national and international courts as evidence of state practice (James Crawford, *Brownlie's Principles of Public International Law* (8th edn, OUP 2012) 24).

[108] *Prosecutor v Tadić*, (Decision on the Defence Motion for Interlocutory Appeal on Jurisdiction) IT-94-1 (2 October 1995) 70.

[109] UNCHR 'Report of the Special Rapporteur on the Human Rights Situation in the Sudan, Sima Samar' (11 January 2006) UN Doc E/CN.4/2006/111, para 8; UNCHR 'Report of the Special Rapporteur of the Commission on Human Rights on the Situation of Human Rights in Palestinian Territories' (6 March 2002) UN Doc E/CN.4/2002/32, para 18.

relating to Darfur,[110] Lebanon,[111] and Timor-Leste,[112] other courts such as the Special Court for Sierra Leone,[113] the International Criminal Tribunal for Rwanda,[114] and the International Criminal Court,[115] and in national legislation,[116] as well as in state military manuals,[117] and subsequent treaties on the law of armed conflict.[118] Indeed, the fact that the *Tadić* formulation was accepted by states during the adoption of the Rome Statute of the International Criminal Court suggests that states have accepted the *Tadić* definition of armed conflict as the definitive statement on the existence of an armed conflict.[119]

This wealth of varying kinds of state practice has thus led some commentators to note that Common Article 3 now clearly operates at a lower level than was originally planned in Geneva in 1949.[120] The question now arises: does this state practice in relation to Common Article 3 represent a departure from what was agreed in Geneva in 1949? Has state practice amounted to an amendment of the scope of Common Article 3? Or is this more accurately characterized as the natural evolution of a treaty provision over time? Is the practice of states and tribunals regarding Common Article 3 thus to be considered a form of treaty amendment, or is it more likely an example of subsequent practice as part of the process of treaty interpretation, as

---

110 Report of the International Commission of Inquiry on Darfur to the United Nations Secretary-General Pursuant to Security Council Resolution 1564 of 18 September 2004, 25 January 2005, para 74.

111 UNHRC 'Report of the Commission of Inquiry on Lebanon pursuant to Human Rights Council Resolution S-2/1' (23 November 2006) UN Doc A/HRC/3/2, para 51.

112 Report of the Commission for Reception, Truth, and Reconciliation Timor-Leste, 31 October 2005, para 141.

113 *Prosecutor v Sesay et al*, (Judgment) SCSL-04-15-T (2 March 2009) para 95.

114 *Prosecutor v Akayesu*, (Judgment) ICTR 96-4-T (2 September 1998), 621; *Prosecutor v Rutaganda*, (Judgment) ICTR-96-3 (6 December 1999) para 93.

115 *Prosecutor v Lubanga* (Decision on the Confirmation of Charges) ICC-01/04-01/06 (29 January 2007) para 233.

116 A significant number of pieces of national legislation dealing with non-international armed conflicts have been adopted in the wake of the adoption of the Rome Statute of the International Criminal Court. The Rome Statute sets the threshold for applicability as the *Tadić* test (in art 8(2)(d) and (f)); as such, domestic legislation that gives effect to the Rome Statute in relation to non-international armed conflicts would thus seem to accept the *Tadić* test as the threshold for non-international armed conflicts. The ICRC lists numerous pieces of domestic legislation implementing the Rome Statute – these can be found at <https://www.icrc.org/customary-ihl/eng/docs/v2_rul_rule156> accessed 31 January 2021.

117 The ICRC lists numerous military manuals that have adopted the art 8(2)(f) definition of armed conflict – these can be found at <https://www.icrc.org/customary-ihl/eng/docs/v2_rul_rule156> accessed 31 January 2021.

118 See, for example, Second Protocol to The Hague Convention of 1954 for the Protection of Cultural Property in the Event of Armed Conflict 1999 (adopted 26 March 1999, entered into force 9 March 2004) 2253 UNTS 172, art 22; and Protocol on Prohibitions or Restrictions on the Use of Mines, Booby-Traps and Other Devices as amended on 3 May 1996 (Protocol II to the 1980 CCW Convention as amended on 3 May 1996) (adopted 10 October 1980, entered into force 3 December 1998) 2048 UNTS 93, art 1(2).

119 See further the debate regarding the drafting and adoption of art 8 of the Rome Statute, as discussed in William Schabas, *The International Criminal Court: A Commentary on the Rome Statute* (OUP 2010) 196–207, Eve la Haye, *War Crimes in Internal Armed Conflicts* (CUP 2008) 138–44.

120 See Sivakumaran (n 2) 162; Cullen (n 2) 60.

envisaged in Article 31(a) and (6) VCLT? During the trials at Nuremberg, the judges commented that:

> The law of war is to be found not only in treaties, but in the customs and practices of states which gradually obtained universal recognition, and from the general principles of justice applied by jurists and practice by military courts. This law is not static, but by continual adaptation follows the needs of a changing world.[121]

In order to begin to address these questions, the next part of this chapter looks at the debate as to treaty interpretation and subsequent practice, and the related questions of whether treaties should be considered products of their time, or whether one should take an evolutive approach to treaty interpretation.

5. COMMON ARTICLE 3, SUBSEQUENT PRACTICE, AND TREATIES (AND TREATY INTERPRETATION) OVER TIME: A CASE OF AMENDMENT, INTERPRETATION, OR EVOLUTION?

As has been explored in this chapter, practice in relation to Common Article 3 has demonstrated that states, as well as other international bodies, have tended to define a Common Article 3 armed conflict as existing when there is protracted armed violence between governmental authorities and organized armed groups (or between such organized groups). The requirement of territorial control by the organized armed group has not generally been considered a prerequisite for the applicability of Common Article 3. This lower threshold of applicability for Common Article 3 would seem to be at odds with the intentions of states at Geneva in 1949, as evidenced in the official records of the diplomatic conference. We are thus presented with something of a conundrum. The majority of states at the Diplomatic Conference at Geneva in 1949 were of the opinion that Common Article 3 should only apply to armed conflicts of a character similar to that required for recognition of belligerency. However, Common Article 3, as eventually adopted, provided no threshold criteria for application; consequently, in practice, Common Article 3 came to be applied to a much wider variety of non-international armed conflicts. Should we therefore conclude that state practice in relation to Common Article 3 has amounted to a form of treaty amendment? Is this more accurately characterized as part of the process of treaty interpretation? Or is this a case of approaching treaties from an evolutive interpretation perspective?

The question of subsequent practice and its effect on treaty interpretation is a complex one. The starting point for such an analysis brings us back to Article 31 VCLT, specifically Article 31(3)(b), which provides that, in interpreting a treaty, and in addition to questions of ordinary meaning of terms in context in light of their object and purpose, one must also take into account 'any subsequent practice in the application of the treaty which establishes the agreement of the parties regarding its interpretation'. Subsequent practice is of importance to the process

---

[121] *Judgment of the Nuremberg International Military Tribunal 1946* (1947) 41 American Journal of International Law 172, 219.

of interpretation, because, as the ICJ stated in the *Kasikili/Sedudu Island* case, 'it constitutes objective evidence of the understanding of the parties to the meaning of the treaty.'[122]

With this in mind, how do we reconcile what seems to have been the intention of states regarding Common Article 3, with the subsequent practice of states in relation to Common Article 3? An initial reading of state practice when contrasted with what states professed to have intended in 1949 would seem to suggest that the ambit of Common Article 3 has been modified, and that non-international armed conflicts under Common Article 3 are more broadly defined than what was envisaged by states in 1949. Indeed, it is theoretically possible that a treaty can be modified by subsequent practice.[123] However, it must be noted that declaring a treaty modified by examining state practice is controversial: as Kohen notes, treaties are formal manifestations of the will of states, often requiring protracted and complicated procedures to come to fruition:

> the long and arduous international and internal legal processes that must be followed for a treaty to be concluded and enter into force cannot be reversed by the sudden modification of a treaty simply by virtue of the conduct of state agents who would likely not have the modification of the treaty in mind when going about their business.[124]

Proving amendment through subsequent practice is a notably difficult process;[125] the likelihood that one could prove that state practice in relation to Common Article 3 – variable as it has been – amounted to amendment seems an unlikely prospect.

A more probable conclusion is that state practice in relation to Common Article 3 amounts instead to an example of evolutive interpretation.[126] As Georg Nolte has noted, 'treaties are not just dry parchments. They are instruments for providing stability to their parties and to fulfil the purposes which they embody. They can therefore change over time, must adapt to new situations, evolve according to the social needs of the international community'.[127] Evolutive

---

[122] *Kasikili/Sedudu Island (Botswana v Namibia)* (Judgment) [1999] ICJ Rep 1045, 1076 para 49. As Gardiner notes, 'treaties embody the common understanding of the parties to them. Hence concordant practice of the parties is best evidence of their correct interpretation' (Gardiner (n 22) 253).

[123] The possibility was admitted by the European Court of Human Rights, in *Al-Saadoon and Mufdhi v United Kingdom*, App No. 61498/08 (2 March 2010) para 119; see also *Öcalan v Turkey*, App No. 46221/99 (12 May 2005) paras 162–65.

[124] Marcelo Kohen, 'Keeping Subsequent Agreements and Practice in Their Right Limits' in Georg Nolte (ed), *Treaties and Subsequent Practice* (OUP 2013) 36.

[125] ibid 37, 44. See also Campbell McLachlan, 'The Evolution of Treaty Obligations in International Law' in Georg Nolte (ed), *Treaties and Subsequent Practice* (OUP 2013) 71–72.

[126] See further Eirik Bjorge, *The Evolutionary Interpretation of Treaties* (OUP 2014); Malgosia Fitzmaurice, 'Dynamic (Evolutive) Interpretation of Treaties, Part I' (2008) *Hague Yearbook of International Law* 101; Julian Arato, 'Subsequent Practice and Evolutive Interpretation: Techniques of Treaty Interpretation over Time and Their Diverse Consequences' (2010) 9 *The Law and Practice of International Courts and Tribunals* 443; Christian Djeffal, *Static and Evolutive Treaty Interpretation: A Functional Reconstruction* (CUP 2016).

[127] Georg Nolte, 'Report of the International Law Commission on the Work of its 60th Session' (5 May–6 June, 7 July–8 August 2008) UN Doc A/63/10, Annex A, para 1.

interpretation has been defined by the ICJ in the *Dispute regarding Navigational and Related Rights* case as referring to situations

> in which the parties' intent upon conclusion of the treaty was, or may be presumed to have been, to give the terms used – or some of them – a meaning of content capable of evolving, not one fixed once and for all, so as to make allowance for, among other things, developments in international law.[128]

Determining whether an evolutive approach may be taken can be achieved by, among other things, looking to the choice of words and terms in the treaty. As the ICJ noted in *Navigational and Related Rights*:

> Where the parties have used generic terms in a treaty, the parties necessarily having been aware that the meaning of the term was likely to evolve over time, and where the treaty has been entered into for a very long period, or is 'of continuing duration', the parties must be presumed, as a general rule, to have intended those terms to have an evolving meaning.[129]

What then can we say about the use of the term 'armed conflict' in 1949? While most states in Geneva in 1949 spoke of non-international armed conflict as synonymous with recognition of belligerency, the fact remains that Common Article 3, as adopted, did *not* include an explicit mention of recognition of belligerency, nor was any attempt made to include in the Article an explicit definition of what 'armed conflict not of an international character' was meant to encompass. The community of states intentionally chose to keep the term undefined. What then can we draw from the use of such a non-specific term? Arguably, the choice of the essentially generic term 'armed conflict' can be seen as demonstrative of an intention to allow the term to be broadly interpreted, in light of developments in the field.

The ICJ decision in the *Navigational and Related Rights* case is also significant for this analysis, as it draws the connections between evolutive interpretation, subsequent practice, and subsequent agreements. As Nolte has argued, the *Navigational and Related Rights* case:

> demonstrates that subsequent agreements and subsequent practice of the parties can have (…) a supportive (…) effect on the possibility of an evolutive interpretation. The supportive effect consists in confirming that an evolved understanding of a treaty can be based on subsequent practice as an authentic means of interpretation.[130]

In this respect, it is pertinent to examine one of the most significant examples of subsequent agreement to the Geneva Conventions, its Additional Protocols of 1977, specifically, Additional Protocol II (AP II).[131] AP II, like Common Article 3, also regulates non-international armed conflicts, and states that it 'develops and supplements Article 3 (…) without modifying

---

[128] *Dispute regarding Navigational and Related Rights (Costa Rica v Nicaragua)* (Judgment) [2009] ICJ Rep 213, para 64.

[129] ibid, para 66.

[130] Georg Nolte, 'First Report on Subsequent Agreements and Subsequent Practice in Relation to Treaty Interpretation' (19 March 2013) UN Doc A/CN.4/660, 25 para 60.

[131] The Additional Protocols comprise Protocol Additional to the Geneva Conventions of 12 August 1949, and relating to the Protection of Victims of International Armed Conflicts of 8 June 1977 (8 June 1977, entered into force 7 December 1978) 1125 UNTS 3 (hereinafter AP I), and Protocol Additional to the Geneva Conventions of 12 August 1949, and relating to the Protection of Victims of

its existing conditions of application'.[132] However, AP II goes on to specify a threshold of applicability – to non-international armed conflicts:

> which take place in the territory of a High Contracting Party between its armed forces and dissident armed forces or other organised armed groups which, under responsible command exercise such control over a part of its territory as to enable them to carry out sustained and concerted military operations and to implement this Protocol.[133]

AP II thus sets a higher threshold for application than Common Article 3, an Article which does not explicitly include territorial control as a prerequisite for application. Therefore, in adopting AP II, states essentially confirmed that Common Article 3 was considered as applying to situations considerably below the threshold for recognition of belligerency.[134] This subsequent agreement of states would thus seem to confirm a broad, rather than narrow, reading of Common Article 3. Indeed, such an approach is consistent with decisions by the ICJ and other tribunals, which have taken evolutive approaches to treaty interpretation, but have remained close to the text 'and from the determinable intention of the parties to the treaty, as they have also been expressed in their subsequent agreements and subsequent practice'.[135] As such, evolutive interpretation 'does not seem to be a separate method of interpretation but rather the result of a proper application of the usual means of interpretation'.[136] Thus, limiting oneself to treating Common Article 3 non-international armed conflicts as fixed in what some states in 1949 understood non-international armed conflicts to be would stand in contradiction to subsequent practice, subsequent agreement, and the general support of tribunals, courts and 'leading writers today for evolutive interpretation of treaties'.[137]

Non-International Armed Conflicts of 8 June 1977 (8 June 1977, entered into force 7 December 1978) 1125 UNTS 609 (hereinafter AP II).

[132] Art 1(1) AP II.

[133] ibid.

[134] See Sandoz, Swinarski and Zimmerman (n 87) 1348–50. However, this is not to say that the threshold for Additional Protocol II is equivalent for that of belligerency; indeed, as Sivakumaran points out, historically recognition of belligerency required the additional element of civil administration, supplementary to armed hostilities carried out by an organized armed group with some degree of territorial control (Sivakumaran (n 2) 190–92). As such, the spectrum of conflict intensity would thus be Common Article 3 armed conflicts, followed by AP II armed conflicts, and then armed conflicts warranting recognition of belligerency.

[135] Georg Nolte, 'First Report on Subsequent Agreements and Subsequent Practice in Relation to Treaty Interpretation' (19 March 2013) UN Doc A/CN.4/660, 26 para 62, citing decisions in *Aegean Sea Continental Shelf (Greece v Turkey)* (Judgment) [1978] ICJ Rep 3, 31 para 74; *Case Concerning the Delimitation of Maritime Boundary Between Guinea-Bissau and Senegal* (1989), Report of International Arbitral Awards, vol XX, pt II, 119, 151–52 para 85; *Legal Consequences for State of the Continued Presence of South Africa in Namibia (South West Africa) notwithstanding Security Council resolution 276 (1970)*, [1971] ICJ Rep 16, 30 para 51.

[136] Georg Nolte, 'First Report on Subsequent Agreements and Subsequent Practice in Relation to Treaty Interpretation' (19 March 2013) UN Doc A/CN.4/660, 26 para 62. See also James Crawford, *State Responsibility: The General Part* (CUP 2013) 247, who stated evolutive interpretation of treaties is 'essentially one of the correct application of VCLT Article 31'.

[137] *Arbitration regarding the Iron Rhine ("Ijzeren Rijn") (Belgium v Netherlands)* (2005) 27 RIAA 35 para 81.

6. CONCLUSIONS

Treaties are fundamental to the successful functioning of the international legal system; they are the clearest expression of the intention of states regarding their international relations. As such, it is important that the correct meaning be ascribed to the terms used in treaties, to ensure that the meaning is consonant with the intentions of those who drafted and adopted the instrument. The treaty laws of armed conflict have been among the most successful in the modern history of international law, with all states in the world party to the Geneva Conventions of 1949, and similarly high levels of participation in other IHL treaties, such as the Additional Protocols, and the various weapons treaties.[138] However, as the years pass, these treaties age – conventions and protocols that may have appeared forward-looking are quickly eclipsed by social, political, and technological developments. It is thus important to ensure that these documents of state agreement remain useful and viable instruments, capable of addressing contemporary issues. However, it is also equally important to ensure that these instruments are not stretched beyond their terms of reference. An evolutive approach to treaty interpretation presents a logical and feasible means by which a treaty such as the Geneva Conventions, adopted in an era beginning to embrace the jet engine, can still be relevant for a world accustomed to unmanned aerial vehicles and cyber warfare.

---

[138] See further the ICRC website at <https://www.icrc.org/ihl> accessed 31 January 2021 for a listing of the IHL treaties and their state parties.

9. A subtle yet significant influence: Judicial decisions and the development of international humanitarian law

Shane Darcy

1. INTRODUCTION

While it is no longer the case that treaties and custom are the only two sources of international law, as was stated in the first edition of Oppenheim's *International Law*,[1] these two sources have tended to loom the largest in the field of international humanitarian law. In the engaging and thought-provoking contributions of Emily Crawford and Timothy Meyer, both authors consider how international treaties and the rules of customary international humanitarian law are being or might be developed, with each highlighting either implicitly or explicitly the limits of the treaty-making process. In the course of their analyses of the methods of law-making, both also have occasional recourse to judicial decisions as an important but formally subsidiary source of international humanitarian law.[2]

The judgments of international courts are frequently used as an authoritative source to support legal claims being made or to suggest the direction of developments in this field. Oppenheim had foreseen the value of judgments in the context of law-making, and wrote in 1905 that the decisions of prize courts and national judicial bodies could, like scholarly writings, 'influence the growth of International Law by creating usages which gradually turn into custom, or by inducing the members of the Family of Nations to conclude such treaties as stipulate legal rules for future international conduct'.[3] The judges at Nuremberg, keenly aware of the relatively limited nature of the existing law on the use of force and for regulating warfare, emphasized its evolving nature, and the role of judges in that context:

> The law of war is to be found not only in treaties, but in the customs and practices of states which gradually obtained universal recognition, and from the general principles of justice applied by jurists and practiced by military courts. This law is not static, but by continual adaptation follows the needs of a changing world.[4]

---

[1] Lassa Oppenheim, *International Law* (Longmans, Green, and Co. 1905) 21–22.

[2] Statute of the International Court of Justice (adopted 26 June 1945, entered into force 24 October 1945) 33 UNTS 993 (ICJ Statute) art 38(1)(d).

[3] Oppenheim (n 1) 24.

[4] *Judgment of the Nuremberg International Military Tribunal 1946* (1947) 41 American Journal of International Law 172, 219.

The question of international humanitarian law's adaptation lies at the heart of the Crawford and Meyer chapters, and the role of judicial bodies in this process has garnered greater attention in recent years in view of the increased application of international humanitarian law by judicial bodies.[5] Judgments of international and national courts have played a subtle yet significant role in the advancement of the laws of armed conflict.

2. NON-INTERNATIONAL ARMED CONFLICT

The influence of judicial bodies on the development of international humanitarian law is amply demonstrated in Crawford's chapter, which provides an exposition of the interplay between various sources of international law and the authorities that interpret and apply them, through the specific example of the definition of an armed conflict not of an international character under Common Article 3 of the 1949 Geneva Conventions. The hesitant first steps by states to regulate internal armed conflicts under international law were not aided by the absence of a definition.[6] The drafters of Additional Protocol II elaborated on the law applicable to such conflicts, but also laid down an exacting threshold which emphasized organization on the part of armed groups, responsible command, control over a territory and the capacity for sustained and concerted military operations, as well as implementation of the instrument.[7] The Protocol, as it makes clear from the outset, 'develops and supplements' Common Article 3, but 'without modifying its existing conditions of application'.[8] Crawford examines the very question of Common Article 3's application and assesses whether subsequent state practice in relation to the Article can be considered as a form of treaty amendment or an example of reasonable evolution over an extended period of time. The resort to the *travaux préparatoires* of the 1949 Conventions, as provided for by the Vienna Convention on the Law of Treaties (VCLT),[9] illuminates the origins of the concept of an armed conflict not of an international character, while also prompting consideration of whether international treaties should remain products of their time.

Judges at the International Criminal Tribunal for the Former Yugoslavia (ICTY) have taken the view that international humanitarian law must evolve and, moreover, that the judiciary has an important role to play in that regard. Former ICTY President Gabrielle Kirk McDonald stressed that the law of war needs to keep pace with war itself: 'We must understand the evo-

---

5 See for example Derek Jinks, Jackson Nyamuya Maogoto and Solon Solomon (eds), *Applying International Humanitarian Law in Judicial and Quasi-Judicial Bodies* (T.M.C. Asser Press 2014); Sharon Weill, *The Role of National Courts in Applying International Humanitarian Law* (OUP 2014); Shane Darcy, *Judges, Law and War: The Judicial Development of International Humanitarian Law* (CUP 2014); Alessandro Spadaro, 'International Humanitarian Law in the Jurisprudence of International Criminal Courts and Tribunals' in Dražan Djukić and Niccolò Pons (eds), *The Companion to International Humanitarian Law* (Brill 2018) 135.

6 See generally Anthony Cullen, *The Concept of Non-International Armed Conflict in International Humanitarian Law* (CUP 2010).

7 Protocol Additional to the Geneva Conventions of 12 August 1949, and relating to the Protection of Victims of Non-International Armed Conflicts (adopted 8 June 1977, entered into force 7 December 1978) 1125 UNTS 609 art 1(1).

8 ibid.

9 Vienna Convention on the Law of Treaties (adopted 23 May 1969, entered into force 27 January 1980) 1155 UNTS 331 (VCLT) art 32.

lutionary history of war and strive to ensure that the rules governing its conduct address those realities.'[10] She described the Tribunal as a 'drill' that could be applied to 'the immovable rock of State sovereignty'.[11] Antonio Cassese, who also served as ICTY President, felt that as a judge at an international tribunal, 'you have to create a new law, and you have to say something new'.[12] He put it that '[i]nternational courts, under cover of applying or interpreting law, actually set new legal standards, either by proclaiming what the general principles of international law are or through *obiter dictum*.'[13] While such a view was not shared by all members of the bench,[14] certain judgments of the ICTY have had a significant influence on the development of international humanitarian law, including in relation to the definition of non-international armed conflict. The key decision is the landmark 1995 Interlocutory Appeal Decision on Jurisdiction by the ICTY Appeals Chamber in *Prosecutor v Tadić*, wherein the judges put forward a simple yet highly influential definition: 'an armed conflict exists whenever there is a resort to armed force between States or protracted armed violence between governmental authorities and organized armed groups or between such groups within a State.'[15] Cassese, who sat on the Appeals Chamber, later described this definition as 'an interesting contribution to the clarification of an area of international humanitarian law which is badly in need of judicial refinement'.[16]

Prior to considering such acts of judicial creativity in her chapter, Crawford looks to state practice regarding Common Article 3 to assess if this amounts to an amendment of the Article's original scope or an evolving interpretation. While the VCLT specifies that 'any subsequent practice in the application of the treaty' can be taken into consideration in interpreting the instrument, the provision makes it clear that this is both the subsequent practice of the parties to the treaty, as opposed to that of international courts or organizations, as well as practice 'which establishes the agreement of the parties regarding its interpretation'.[17] As to amendment, Ian Brownlie has highlighted the distinction between treaty modification and interpretation by subsequent practice, while noting that 'the distinction is often rather fine'.[18] Given the absence of a definition of armed conflict in Common Article 3, Crawford focuses more on interpretation than formal amendment. This throws up a conundrum concerning the impact of subsequent practice *between* states parties to a treaty, as the practice tends to relate

10 Gabrielle Kirk McDonald, 'The Changing Nature of the Laws of War' (1998) 156 Military Law Review 30.

11 ibid.

12 Robert Badinter and Stephen Breyer (eds), *Judges in Contemporary Democracy* (New York University Press 2004) 214.

13 ibid 32.

14 See Rafael Nieto-Navia, 'Do International Courts and Tribunals have the Power to "Create" Law?' (2006) 6 The Global Community: Yearbook of International Law and Jurisprudence 75.

15 *Prosecutor v Tadić* (Decision on the Defence Motion for Interlocutory Appeal on Jurisdiction) IT-94-1 (2 October 1995).

16 Antonio Cassese, 'The International Criminal Tribunal for the Former Yugoslavia and the implementation of international humanitarian law' in Luigi Condorelli, Anne Marie La Rosa and Sylvie Scherrer (eds), *The United Nations and International Humanitarian Law* (Editions Pedone 1996) 235.

17 VCLT art 31(3)(b).

18 Ian Brownlie, *Principles of Public International Law* (7th edn, OUP 2008) 630.

to the application of Common Article 3 by a state party itself on its own territory. However, as Brownlie notes, '[s]ubsequent practice by individual parties has some probative value'.[19]

In her review of state practice since 1949, Crawford finds some clear examples of the application of Common Article 3 to conflicts which entailed a high level of violence, akin to the recognition of belligerency standard that previously prevailed.[20] There are, however, examples offered of Common Article 3 being applied to conflicts that would not meet this threshold, not by states individually, but by the United Nations and judicial bodies, such as the International Court of Justice (ICJ). Recourse is also made to other judicial bodies which have 'affirmed' the applicability of Common Article 3, including the Inter-American Commission on Human Rights in the 'controversial' *La Tablada* case, and the ICTY in a series of cases, including the above-mentioned *Tadić* decision.[21] However, Crawford rightly includes a word of caution:

> the *Tadić* formula for determination of an existence of an armed conflict is not, *per se*, state practice – it is the decision of an international tribunal. Moreover, in coming to their definition of armed conflict, the ICTY gave no indication or evidence as to how it came to such a conclusion, citing no supporting state practice or *opinio juris* to suggest the methodology of how the definition was arrived at.[22]

That being said, the definition of an armed conflict in *Tadić* was subsequently relied upon by various international organizations, judicial bodies and by states themselves, when drafting the Rome Statute of the International Criminal Court. Crawford notes that the latter in particular 'suggests that states have accepted the *Tadić* definition of armed conflict as the definitive statement on the existence of an armed conflict'. Curiously, Article 8 of the Rome Statute does not directly apply the ICTY's definition of an armed conflict to all of the war crimes it contains, and uses a different and partly negative definition of armed conflict for those war crimes deriving specifically from common Article 3.[23] However, jurisprudence from the International Criminal Court has largely minimized the distinction and applied the *Tadić* formulation to both categories of war crimes applicable to non-international armed conflicts.[24]

Crawford's conclusion that '[t]his wealth of varying kinds of state practice' points towards an 'evolutive interpretation' of the armed conflict requirement in Common Article 3 also draws on judicial opinion.[25] The idea of evolving interpretation was alluded to by the ICJ as arising in a situation where 'the parties' intent upon conclusion of the treaty was, or may be presumed to have been, to give the terms used – or some of them – a meaning or content capable of evolving, not one fixed once and for all, so as to make allowance for, among other

---

19 ibid 634.

20 Emily Crawford, 'Interpreting the Geneva Conventions: Subsequent Practice Instead of Treaty Amendments? – A Case Study of "Non-International Armed Conflicts" under Common Article 3', Chapter 8 in this book, 131–32.

21 ibid, 131–34.

22 ibid, 134.

23 Compare art 8(2)(c) and art 8(2)(e) Rome Statute of the International Criminal Court (adopted 17 July 1998, entered into force 1 July 2002) 2187 UNTS 90.

24 See for example *Prosecutor v Bemba* (Judgment pursuant to Article 74 of the Statute) ICC-01/05-01/08-3343 (21 March 2016) paras 127–41. See also Roger Bartiels, 'The Classification of Armed Conflicts by International Courts and Tribunals' (2020) 20 International Criminal Law Review 595, 619–20.

25 Crawford (n 20), 135–36.

things, developments in international law'.[26] This is not dissimilar to the 'living instrument' concept that has informed judicial interpretation at the European Court of Human Rights.[27] Crawford finds this understanding by the ICJ of treaty interpretation to be especially apt in the case of Common Article 3, especially given the high threshold of applicability for Additional Protocol II:

> This subsequent agreement of states would thus seem to confirm a broad, rather than narrow, reading of Common Article 3. Indeed, such an approach is consistent with decisions by the ICJ and other tribunals, who have taken evolutive approaches to treaty interpretation, but have remained close to the text (…).[28]

For Crawford's analysis, judicial decisions provide a valuable supplementary source to consider when assessing the practice of states vis-à-vis a specific treaty provision. The caveat which she laid down, that judicial decisions are not an example of state practice *per se*, points towards their limitations as subsidiary sources of international law, even though they were especially influential in this context. Moreover, it would seem counterintuitive that a decision such as *Tadić* would carry such weight here given that it offered a definition of armed conflict without providing any evidence of its legal basis. Arguably, it is the subsequent endorsement of the Appeals Chamber's finding, especially by states, which affirms the judges' claim rather than the holding in and of itself.

The legal value to be ascribed to judgments would logically depend on the quality of the reasoning given and the evidence provided, particularly where claims regarding the status of customary international law are being made.[29] Morris Greenspan wrote that 'the intrinsic merits of a judgment lend it authority, not just the standing of the tribunal which issued it'.[30] In the case of the ICTY, however, it is clear that the subsequent acceptance or rejection of its decisions has often not exclusively or even largely been based on the quality of the Tribunal's reasoning or evidence.[31] It has tended to be the case that if judicial decisions align with the views or interests of a sufficient number of states, then they are more likely to be endorsed. While similar criticism regarding the treatment of customary international law as has been made of the *Tadić* decision can also be made of the *Kupreškić* judgment of the ICTY on the question of belligerent reprisals,[32] the reaction from states has been notably different, as will be discussed in the next section. As well as offering an example of an inherent limitation of judicial decisions as a vehicle for the development of international humanitarian law, the doctrine of reprisals, which involves resort to violations of international humanitarian law for

---

[26] *Dispute regarding Navigational and Related Rights (Costa Rica* v *Nicaragua)* (Judgment) [2009] ICJ Rep 213 para 64.

[27] See for example Kanstantin Dzehtsiarou, 'European Consensus and the Evolutive Interpretation of the European Convention on Human Rights' (2011) 12 German Law Journal 1730.

[28] Crawford (n 20), 139.

[29] Benjamin N. Cardozo, *The Nature of the Judicial Process* (Yale University Press 1921) 178.

[30] Morris Greenspan, *The Modern Law of Warfare* (University of California Press 1959) 7–8.

[31] Alexander Zahar, 'Civilizing Civil War: Writing Morality as Law at the ICTY' in Bert Swart, Alexander Zahar and Göran Sluiter (eds), *The Legacy of the International Criminal Tribunal for the Former Yugoslavia* (OUP 2011) 469–507.

[32] *Prosecutor v Kupreškić et al* (Judgment) ICTY-95-16-T (14 January 2000).

the purpose of enforcement, also offers a cautionary tale for Meyer's theory of noncompliance as law-making.

3. LAW-BREAKING AND LAW-MAKING

In his provocative chapter, Meyer draws less on judicial decisions than Crawford did to support the theory of noncompliance as law-making. This may be a reflection of the controversial nature of the concept, although he does rely upon an oft-cited paragraph from the judgment of the ICJ in *Nicaragua v United States* on the elements of customary international law to support his argument. Meyer posits that the Court 'recognized the potential law-making role violations of [customary international law] can play' in the following paragraph:

> It is not to be expected that in the practice of States the application of the rules in question should have been perfect, in the sense that States should have refrained, with complete consistency, from the use of force or from intervention in each other's internal affairs. The Court does not consider that, for a rule to be established as customary, the corresponding practice must be in absolutely rigorous conformity with the rule. In order to deduce the existence of customary rules, the Court deems it sufficient that the conduct of States should, in general, be consistent with such rules, and that instances of State conduct inconsistent with a given rule should generally have been treated as breaches of that rule, not as indications of the recognition of a new rule. If a State acts in a way prima facie incompatible with a recognized rule, but defends its conduct by appealing to exceptions or justifications contained within the rule itself, then whether or not the State's conduct is in fact justifiable on that basis, the significance of that attitude is to confirm rather than to weaken the rule.[33]

Meyer's claim that the Court acknowledged 'the law-making role of noncompliance in theory' would seem to be based on the reference in the paragraph to breaches that could amount to 'indications of the recognition of a new rule'. This seemingly thin support from the Court was accompanied by the assertion that the judges minimized the role of noncompliance in law-making in practice, because 'a preference for the status quo tends to prevail over efforts to use noncompliance to change customary international law'.[34] In any event, the theory of noncompliance as law-making put forward does not seem to be limited to changes in customary international law that may be brought about by state practice which violates existing rules (and presumably by a sufficient number of states and accompanied by the necessary *opinio juris*), but rather serves also as a means of flagging up a state's desire for a change in the law.

While deliberate law-breaking would fundamentally be at odds with the object and purpose of international humanitarian law, it has had a place in this legal regime, as a permissible though problematic response to the unlawful acts of one's opponent via the doctrine of belligerent reprisals.[35] Reprisals were considered as having a legitimate law enforcement role, but their use has become increasingly restricted by specific prohibitions on reprisals against protected persons and objects in most of the major treaties of humanitarian law.[36] Where not

---

[33] *Case Concerning Military and Paramilitary Activities in and Against Nicaragua, (Nicaragua v United States of America)* (Merits) [1986] ICJ Rep 14 para 186.

[34] Timothy Meyer, 'Noncompliance as Law-Making', Chapter 7 in this book, 94.

[35] See generally Frits Kalshoven, *Belligerent Reprisals* (Nijhoff 2005).

[36] See Jérôme de Hemptinne, 'Prohibition of Reprisals' in Andrew Clapham, Paolo Gaeta and Marco Sassòli (eds), *The 1949 Geneva Conventions; A Commentary* (OUP 2015) 575–97; Shane Darcy, 'The Evolution of the Law of Belligerent Reprisals' (2003) 175 Military Law Review 184.

outlawed, any resort to belligerent reprisals must accord with certain requirements under customary international law, including last-resort, high-level authorization and proportionality.[37] There are notable similarities between both these conditions and criticisms of the doctrine of reprisals, and those of Meyer's theory of noncompliance as law-making. Before considering judicial attempts to expand the scope of the existing treaty prohibitions on belligerent reprisals, it is worth considering these parallels.

Noncompliance as law-making, according to Meyer, is not about cheating to gain an immediate advantage, but rather is aimed at changing the law by shifting other states' behaviour and their expectations over the medium to long term.[38] Belligerent reprisals likewise are not simply law-breaking, but are *prima facie* violations for the purpose of law enforcement, although the expectation is for an immediate change in enemy behaviour. Law enforcement is the underlying rationale for reprisals, rather than revenge or punishment. These loftier aims necessitate that both noncompliance as law-making and reprisals have a public element. For the former, the theory put forward is that the violation must be public in order to make clear its purpose and to prevent misuse of this law-making technique. For the latter, a public declaration is considered an essential component. The United Kingdom *Manual of the Law of Armed Conflict* requires that '[r]easonable notice be given that reprisals will be taken',[39] while the ICTY considered that reprisals could be taken 'only after a prior and formal warning has been given, which has failed to put an end to the violations committed by the adversary'.[40] For noncompliance as law-making, it is not clear whether the rationale underlying the unlawful act also needs to be publicly announced, although this is perhaps implicit.

A characteristic of both belligerent reprisals and noncompliance as law-making is that they both would involve unilateral action and a course of action that would tend to favour more powerful states. Law-making through noncompliance 'expands the role of power at the expense of principle in shaping the content of the law', Meyer concedes.[41] Colonel Daniel Reisner, the former head of the International Law Department of the Israeli Defence Forces, controversially advocated for changing international law through its violation:

> What we are seeing now is a revision of international law (...) If you do something for long enough, the world will accept it. The whole of international law is now based on the notion that an act that is forbidden today becomes permissible if executed by enough countries (...). International law progresses through violations. We invented the targeted assassination thesis and we had to push it. At first there were protrusions that made it hard to insert easily into the legal moulds. Eight years later it is in the center of the bounds of legitimacy.[42]

---

37 Jean-Marie Henckaerts and Louise Doswald-Beck, *Customary International Humanitarian Law, Volume I: Rules* (CUP 2009) 515–18.

38 Meyer (n 34), 95.

39 United Kingdom Ministry of Defence, 'The Joint Service Manual of the Law of Armed Conflict' JSP 383, 2004, 421 <www.gov.uk/government/collections/jsp-383> accessed 31 January 2021.

40 *Prosecutor v Martić* (Judgment) ICTY-95-11-T (12 June 2007) para 466.

41 Meyer (n 34), 110.

42 Yotam Feldman and Uri Blau, 'Consent and Advise' (*Haaretz*, 29 January 2009) <www.haaretz.com/consent-and-advise-1.269127> accessed 31 January 2021.

Belligerent reprisals have also been criticized as a law of the strongest, which favours parties of greater military power.[43] States which have opposed aspects of the restrictions on reprisals in Additional Protocol I include the United States and the United Kingdom, while France, Germany, Italy, and Egypt also raised some concerns regarding aspects of these most recent prohibitions.[44] For both belligerent reprisals and noncompliance as law-making, there are also questions about their relevance for non-state armed groups.[45]

The clearest concerns with belligerent reprisals and noncompliance as a method of law-making is that they seek to legitimize violations of a body of law that is aimed at protecting the victims of armed conflict and they may even contribute to further law-breaking. Meyer points out that acceptance of noncompliance as law-making carries with it the risk of increasing noncompliance and 'undermining a culture of compliance among states', although he considers that these concerns are overstated.[46] No less an authority than Oppenheim's *International Law* has put it that belligerent reprisals 'instead of being a means of securing legitimate warfare may become an effective instrument of its wholesale and cynical violation in matters constituting the very basis of the law of war'.[47] In addition to offering a potential justification for unlawful behaviour, questions have also been raised about the effectiveness of belligerent reprisals as a sanction for the laws of armed conflict.[48] The *Commanders Handbook on the Law of Naval Operations* notes the United States' reluctance to resort to reprisals as a means of law enforcement due to the risk that they 'will trigger counter-reprisals by the enemy',[49] although it has not foregone the right to resort to these 'extreme measures of coercion'.[50] Nevertheless, these concerns have led to the progressive restriction on the use of belligerent reprisals under treaties of international humanitarian law. The International Committee of the Red Cross rightly observes that 'there is a trend to outlaw belligerent reprisals altogether'.[51] The ICTY has sought to advance the law in this regard, especially as it relates to reprisals against civilians.

As far back as the post-Second World War trials, judicial bodies have grappled with the doctrine of belligerent reprisals.[52] The ICTY has been forthright in addressing the doctrine,

---

43 See for example *Official Records of the Diplomatic Conference on the Reaffirmation and Development of International Humanitarian Law Applicable in Armed Conflicts in Geneva, 1974–1977*, vol IX, 62, 71, 79 <https://www.loc.gov/rr/frd/Military_Law/RC-dipl-conference-records.html> accessed 31 January 2021.

44 See Henckaerts and Doswald-Beck (n 37) 521.

45 In relation to non-state actors and reprisals see de Hemptinne (n 36) 590; Henckaerts and Doswald-Beck (n 37) 526–29.

46 Meyer (n 34), 106–108.

47 Hersch Lauterpacht (ed), *International Law: Disputes, War and Neutrality* (7th edn, Longman 1952) 565.

48 Kalshoven (n 35) 25.

49 Department of the Navy Office of the Chief of Naval Operations and Headquarters, US Marine Corps, Department of Homeland Security and US Coast Guard, 'Naval Commanders Handbook on the Law of Naval Operations' (July 2007) ch 6.2.4.3 <www.jag.navy.mil/documents/NWP_1-14M_Commanders_Handbook.pdf> accessed 31 January 2021.

50 United States Department of Defense, *Law of War Manual 2015* (US Department of Defense 2015) 1093 <archive.defense.gov/pubs/law-of-war-manual-june-2015.pdf> accessed 31 January 2021.

51 Henckaerts and Doswald-Beck (n 37) 513.

52 See for example *In re Rauter,* Holland [4 May 1948] Special Criminal Court, Case No. 193 (1949) 16 Annual Digest and Reports of Public International Law Cases 543.

claiming first that a rule outlawing reprisals against all civilians 'is an integral part of customary international law and must be respected in all armed conflicts'.[53] The *Kupreškić* trial judgment provides a more detailed treatment of the subject, in which Judge Cassese and his colleagues provide a compelling argument against reprisals, but an ultimately unconvincing claim that the relevant rules in Additional Protocol I have become customary international law.[54] The judgment had dismissed a number of reservations to the Additional Protocol I on the matter, prompting the United Kingdom to state in its *Manual on the Laws of Armed Conflict* that it rejects the findings in *Kupreškić* on customary international law, as it 'flies in the face of most of the state practice that exists'.[55] While the International Committee of Red Cross considers these cases as valuable indications of the growing body of authority 'condemning or outlawing reprisals',[56] it is clear that this jurisprudence has had nowhere near the same impact as *Tadić*, even though it too was criticized for its treatment of customary international humanitarian law.[57] Extending the concept of war crimes to non-international armed conflicts as *Tadić* did, was acceptable to states, including members of the Security Council, whereas the claimed right to resort to belligerent reprisals, even against civilians in enemy territory, is something which a handful of powerful states have not been willing to yet relinquish. Although almost extinct in practice, belligerent reprisals are not yet completely outlawed under international humanitarian law.

4. CONCLUSION

Legitimizing noncompliance with international humanitarian law whether for purposes of law-making or law enforcement is at odds with the obligation of all states parties to the 1949 Geneva Conventions 'to respect and ensure respect' for those treaties 'in all circumstances'. While international humanitarian law is addressed to states (and armed opposition groups), its rules, as the ICTY has argued, are not aimed at protecting state interests, but rather are 'primarily designed to benefit individuals *qua* human beings'.[58] Judicial bodies have played an important role in interpreting, applying, and occasionally developing the content of humanitarian law, even if its treaty content is primarily decided upon by states. Although an international court has 'no purely legislative competence', as former ICJ President Robert Jennings put it, and decides cases using 'the building materials available in already existing law',[59] there are times where judicial decisions have used such materials creatively and proven to be an influential vehicle for the development of international humanitarian law. As the ICTY jurisprudence also demonstrates, however, the international legal system confers on states the ultimate but not absolute authority for deciding the law's trajectory.

---

[53] *Prosecutor v Martić* (Decision) ICTY-95-11-R61 (8 March 1996) paras 16–17.

[54] *Prosecutor v Kupreškić et al.* (Judgment) ICTY-95-16-T (14 January 2000) paras 515–36.

[55] United Kingdom Ministry of Defence, 'The Joint Service Manual of the Law of Armed Conflict', JSP 383, 2004, 421 <https://www.gov.uk/government/collections/jsp-383> accessed 31 January 2021.

[56] Henckaerts and Doswald-Beck (n 37) 523.

[57] See however *Prosecutor v Mbarushimana* (Decision on the Confirmation of Charges) ICC-01/04-10/10 (16 December 2011) para 143.

[58] *Prosecutor v Kupreškić et al.* (Judgment) ICTY-95-16-T (14 January 2000) para 518.

[59] Robert Y. Jennings, 'The Role of the International Court of Justice' (1997) 68 British Yearbook of International Law 43.

10. The interpretation of IHL treaties: Subsequent practice and other salient issues

Jean-Marie Henckaerts and Elvina Pothelet[1]

The International Committee of the Red Cross (ICRC) is an impartial, neutral and independent organization whose exclusively humanitarian mission is to protect the lives and dignity of victims of armed conflict and other situations of violence and to provide them with assistance. The ICRC also endeavours to prevent suffering by promoting and strengthening international humanitarian law (IHL).[2] The implementation of this mission implies *inter alia* to work for the faithful application of IHL, for its understanding, dissemination and development.[3] To this end the ICRC has been engaged for over 150 years in efforts to disseminate, clarify and develop IHL. In the context of its work for the clarification of IHL, in 2011 the ICRC embarked on an interpretation exercise of the main IHL treaties: the 1949 Geneva Conventions and their Additional Protocols of 1977.[4] More specifically, the project consists in updating the original Commentaries issued by the ICRC in the wake of the adoption of these treaties.[5] These Commentaries aimed to clarify the scope and content of the then newly adopted texts, and to provide practical guidelines for their application. The so-called 'Pictet Commentaries' (named after ICRC lawyer, Jean Pictet, under whose general editorship the Commentaries on the four 1949 Conventions were drafted) became, over time, a source of interpretation widely seen as authoritative, being cited by military lawyers, international and national judges and scholars around the world. However, the Pictet Commentaries were drafted in the 1950s and those on the 1977 Additional Protocols in the 1980s. The drafters of these Commentaries were obviously not in a position to reflect the legal and operational developments of the past 70-plus

1 The authors would like to thank Prof. Georg Nolte of the Humboldt University Berlin, and Kubo Mačák and Iris Müller, Legal Advisers in the ICRC Legal Division, for their helpful comments on earlier drafts. All errors and omissions remain the sole responsibility of the authors. The views expressed in this chapter are personal and do not necessarily reflect those of the ICRC.

2 'The ICRC's mandate and mission' <www.icrc.org/en/mandate-and-mission> accessed 31 January 2021.

3 Statutes of the Red Cross and Red Crescent Movement, adopted by the 25th International Conference of the Red Cross at Geneva in 1986, amended in 1995 and 2006, art 5(2)(c) and (g).

4 The ICRC Commentary on the third Protocol additional to the Geneva Conventions of 12 August 1949, and relating to the Adoption of an Additional Distinctive Emblem (2005), was published in 2007 and thus did not require an update. See Jean-François Quéguiner, 'Commentary on the Protocol additional to the Geneva Conventions of 12 August 1949, and relating to the Adoption of an Additional Distinctive Emblem (Protocol III)' (2007) 89 International Review of the Red Cross 175.

5 See Jean S. Pictet (ed), *Commentary on the Geneva Conventions of 12 August 1949*, vol I–IV (ICRC 1952–1960).

years (or over 40 years in case of the Additional Protocol Commentaries). With the update of these original commentaries, the ICRC intends to provide up-to-date legal guidance that takes into account the issues and challenges witnessed in contemporary armed conflicts, as well as developments in technology and in international and national law.

This chapter aims to share the authors' experience in applying the treaty interpretation methodology set out in the 1969 Vienna Convention on the Law of Treaties (VCLT) to the interpretation of the Geneva Conventions. It highlights how treaty interpretation rules operate in relation to IHL treaties, with a particular emphasis on the role of 'subsequent practice' and some difficulties associated with the identification of such practice. The chapter first highlights the importance of treaty interpretation, including in the field of IHL, and clarifies the nature of the process and the rules that apply to it. It then explains how treaty interpretation rules have been applied in the updated Commentary on the First Geneva Convention, with a focus on some of the difficulties encountered.

1. TREATY INTERPRETATION: DEFINITION AND IMPORTANCE

> Interpretation is the alpha and omega of the life of any treaty. No time spent on this crucial issue is lost.[6]

1.1 On the Importance and Difficulties of Treaty Interpretation

All laws, no matter how detailed they are, have to be interpreted when being applied. International treaties are no different, quite the contrary: as they are the result of lengthy negotiations between states with often competing interests, their phrasing regularly requires special interpretative efforts. As noted by Aust, 'there is no treaty that cannot raise some question of interpretation'.[7] In addition, there may be several interpretations of the same provision with a concomitant risk for potential conflicts between these interpretations.

That being said, when it comes to the Geneva Conventions, the drafters succeeded in adopting reasonably clear and practice-oriented phrasing, so as to make them easily comprehensible by anyone having to apply their provisions, first and foremost, military personnel and their commanders. Yet, they have given rise to interpretative efforts, by military commanders and their lawyers, international and national judges and academics alike. One may advance two main reasons for this. First, IHL treaty provisions need to be interpreted before they are translated into operational standards; this is true of the detailed provisions such as those governing the protection of prisoners of war in the Third Geneva Convention, and of those phrased in general terms, such as the obligation to collect and care for the wounded and sick,[8] or the

---

6 Robert Kolb, *The Law of Treaties: An Introduction* (Edward Elgar Publishing 2016) 164.

7 Anthony Aust, *Modern Treaty Law and Practice* (3rd edn, CUP 2013) 205.

8 The obligation is expressed in these general terms in art 3 common to the four Geneva Conventions applicable to non-international armed conflicts. The updated Commentary provides a detailed interpretation of this phrase, including obligations implicit in collecting and caring for the wounded and sick. See ICRC, *Commentary on the First Geneva Convention: Convention (I) for the Amelioration of the Condition of the Wounded and Sick in Armed Forces in the Field* (2nd edn, ICRC/CUP 2016), art 3, paras 729–78. The obligation is expressed in more detail with regard to international armed conflicts. See First Geneva Convention, art 12.

prohibition of inhumane treatment.[9] Second, the Geneva Conventions were drafted more than 70 years ago (more than 40 years for their two 1977 Additional Protocols), which is a very significant amount of time for any treaty. Operational realities have changed since 1949 and new issues concerning the interpretation of the geographical, temporal and personal scope of application of IHL have arisen. This is the case for example with regard to the geographical scope of application of Common Article 3 in the context of so-called 'spillover', 'cross-border' or 'transnational' non-international armed conflicts.[10] While it is only normal that the drafters could not foresee these developments, they nonetheless adopted a wording that allows sufficient flexibility to ensure that the rules remain relevant to evolving forms of armed conflicts. This adaptation process, however, demands continuous and meticulous interpretative efforts.

Interpreting a treaty is the process by which practitioners and academics seek to clarify and explain the meaning of treaty provisions – in other words, to 'make sense' of treaty rules.[11] The interpretative process has been described as 'an intellectual operation aiming to extract the legal solution that stands out at a given moment in time'.[12] It consists of providing a picture of how the law is to be understood at the moment of interpretation.

The difficulties attached to explaining the scope and content of legal rules beyond the letter of the treaty are self-evident. This led the International Law Commission (ILC) to opine in 1966 that treaty interpretation 'is to some extent an art, not an exact science'.[13] Nonetheless, the stakes are high: how one interprets a treaty provision will determine the extent and modalities of its application. Any serious interpretative attempt must therefore follow established rules.[14]

---

9 The Geneva Conventions contain several articles that prohibit inhumane treatment under various denominations: see art 3 common to the four Geneva Conventions; First Convention, arts 12(2) and 15(1); Second Convention, arts 12(2) and 18(1); Third Convention, arts 13, 17(4) and 87(3); Fourth Convention, arts 27, 32 and 37(1); Additional Protocol I, arts 10 and 75(1) and (2); and Additional Protocol II, arts 4(1) and (2) and 7. The ICRC's updated Commentary develops on what these prohibitions entails. See eg on sexual violence or the prohibition of non-refoulement, in ICRC (n 8), art 3, paras 696–707 and 708–16.

10 See ICRC (n 8) art 3, paras 471–82.

11 Some have described treaty interpretation as the process resulting in 'releasing the exact meaning and the content of the rule of law that is applicable to a given situation', Nguyen Quoc Dinh, Patrick Daillier and Alain Pellet, *Droit international public* (7th edn, Librairie générale de droit et de jurisprudence 2002) 253, no. 162, unofficially translated and cited in Jean-Marc Sorel and Valérie Boré Eveno, 'Article 31 General rule of interpretation' in Olivier Corten and Pierre Klein (eds), *The Vienna Conventions on the Law of Treaties – A Commentary*, vol I (OUP 2011) 806. For introductions on treaty interpretation see also Serge Sur, *L'interprétation en droit international public* (Librairie générale de droit et de jurisprudence 1974); Maarten Bos, 'Theory and Practice of Treaty Interpretation' (1980) 27 Netherlands International Law Review 3; Aust (n 7) 205–207; Richard Gardiner, *Treaty Interpretation* (2nd edn, OUP 2015) 7–9; Georg Nolte (ed), *Treaties and Subsequent Practice* (OUP 2013) 1–2.

12 Sorel and Boré Eveno (n 11) 806.

13 ILC, 'Report of the International Law Commission on the Work of its eighteenth Session: Draft Articles on the Law of Treaties with Commentaries' (4 May–19 July 1966) UN Doc A/6309/Rev.1, 218. Some have been further asserting that 'Interpretation is an art, not a science' (getting rid of the qualifiers 'to some extent' and 'exact'), see Sir Michael Wood, 'Preface' in Gardiner, *Treaty Interpretation* (n 11) xv.

14 As Roberto Ago put it, in reaction to the ILC's famous statement which he describes as 'too glibly', the question 'was whether there were any rules for practicing that art', ILC, 'Summary Records of the Sixteenth Session' (11 May–24 July 1964) UN Doc A/CN.4/SERA/1964, 23 para 34.

The importance of treaty interpretation explains why specific rules governing treaty interpretation have been developed.[15] They are codified in Articles 31–33 VCLT[16] and are accepted as reflecting customary international law.[17] Before addressing the method of interpretation in the updated Commentary on the First Geneva Convention, it is important to locate treaty interpretation in the normative fabric of international law. More specifically, it must be distinguished from identification of international law rules.

1.2 Distinguishing Between Law Creation, Custom Identification and Treaty Interpretation

International law is created mainly through the adoption of treaties and the formation of customary law.[18] Treaties and customary law are among the main sources of international law, the most authoritative enumeration of which is found in Article 38(1) of the Statute of the International Court of Justice.[19] Contrary to treaty provisions, customary law is by definition unwritten. As a result, its exact scope and content can be uncertain. Efforts to *identify* customary law are therefore crucial. Based on a mandate by the 26th International Conference of the Red Cross and Red Crescent to 'prepare (…) a report on customary rules of IHL applicable in international and non-international armed conflicts', the ICRC released a study in 2005 which aimed to identify customary international humanitarian law rules.[20] In doing so, the ICRC had to carefully examine the two constituent elements of customary international law: 'general practice' that is 'accepted as law' (*opinio juris*).[21]

---

15 For more on the development of rules of interpretation, see Gardiner, *Treaty Interpretation* (n 11) 57–80.

16 Vienna Convention on the Law of Treaties 1969, art 31–33.

17 See eg *Libya v Chad* (Judgment) [1994] ICJ Rep 6 para 41; *Kasikili/Sedudu Island* (Judgment) [1999] ICJ Rep 1045 paras 18–20; *Application of the Genocide Convention* (Judgment) [2007] ICJ Rep 43 para 160; *Question of the Delimitation of the Continental Shelf between Nicaragua and Colombia beyond 200 Nautical Miles from the Nicaraguan Coast (Nicaragua v Colombia), Preliminary Objections* (Judgment) [2016] ICJ Rep 116 para 33; ILC, 'Report of the International Law Commission – Seventieth session (30 April–1 June and 2 July–10 August 2018)' UN Doc A/73/10, Text of the draft conclusions on subsequent agreements and subsequent practice in relation to the interpretation of treaties adopted by the Commission (on second reading), conclusion 2(1); Gardiner, *Treaty Interpretation* (n 11) 13–14; Aust (n 7) 207.

18 See eg Hugh Thirlway, *The Sources of International Law* (2nd edn, OUP 2019) 14 ('treaties and international custom are the two main sources of law').

19 The Article in fact defines the law to be applied by the Court. Art 38(1) Statute of the International Court of Justice reads: '1. The Court, whose function is to decide in accordance with international law such disputes as are submitted to it, shall apply: a. international conventions, whether general or particular, establishing rules expressly recognized by the contesting states; b. international custom, as evidence of a general practice accepted as law; c. the general principles of law recognized by civilized nations; d. subject to the provisions of Article 59, judicial decisions and the teachings of the most highly qualified publicists of the various nations, as subsidiary means for the determination of rules of law.'

20 Jean-Marie Henckaerts and Louise Doswald-Beck, *Customary International Humanitarian Law* (ICRC/CUP 2005).

21 ILC (n 17) 124, conclusion 2 ('To determine the existence and content of a rule of customary international law, it is necessary to ascertain whether there is a general practice that is accepted as law (*opinio juris*).')

Treaty provisions, on the other hand, are strictly defined by the language adopted by the drafters. As such, they are in principle less ambiguous than custom. Yet, as highlighted above, the very nature of treaty-making as well as the passing of time require that treaty provisions are explained and clarified, through treaty interpretation. This is the purpose of the ICRC's updated Commentaries, like other commentaries: to clarify the meaning of the Geneva Conventions and of their 1977 Additional Protocols in order to facilitate their understanding and implementation. Neither the ICRC's Study on Customary International Humanitarian Law nor the updated Commentaries create new law. The former merely 'put into words' already existing customary law, formed by existing practice and *opinio juris*, whereas the latter seeks to explain and clarify the content of already existing treaty provisions.

Although the distinction between law-making, identification of custom and treaty interpretation is clear, the lines between these categories may at times appear blurred. For example, interpretation may involve identifying a rule which is not explicitly stated in the relevant treaty text. For example, the updated Commentary on Common Article 3 includes a section on sexual violence, although this type of violence is not explicitly mentioned in the Article.[22] However, in so doing the ICRC Commentary does not create new law. It reflects the developments in law and practice which recognize that sexual violence is a type of conduct which may constitute prohibited 'violence to life and person, in particular murder of all kinds, mutilation, cruel treatment and torture' or 'outrages upon personal dignity, in particular humiliating and degrading treatment', which are explicitly included in Common Article 3. In particular, although Common Article 3 does not mention rape, international case law has nonetheless recognized rape as an act of torture.[23] It would not be realistic, nor desirable, that treaty provisions mention all foreseeable types of prohibited or required conduct. Thus the Commentary clarifies and illustrates which specific conduct may fall under the broad categories of conduct identified in the treaty.

In addition, while the ILC in its draft conclusions on subsequent agreements and subsequent practice highlights that treaty interpretation cannot amount to the modification of a treaty (which requires a formal process regulated by distinct rules of the VCLT),[24] in practice, interpretation following the VCLT rules may still lead to a result approaching modification. For example, Common Article 8 (Article 9 of the Fourth Geneva Convention) provides that the Conventions '*shall* be applied with the co-operation and under the scrutiny of the Protecting Powers' (emphasis added). However, practice of states parties since 1949 led the ICRC to conclude that states came to a change of understanding of this provision, now viewing the appointment of Protecting Powers as optional rather than mandatory.[25] Similarly, Article 38(2) of the

---

22 See ICRC (n 8) art 3, paras 696–716.

23 For case law, see ibid, paras 637 and 703.

24 See ILC (n 17), conclusion 7(3): 'It is presumed that the parties to a treaty, by an agreement or a practice in the application of the treaty, intend to interpret the treaty, not to amend or to modify it. The possibility of amending or modifying a treaty by subsequent practice of the parties has not been generally recognized. The present draft conclusion is without prejudice to the rules on the amendment or modification of treaties under the Vienna Convention on the Law of Treaties and under customary international law.'

25 'Over the decades since 1949, however, States have come to a different understanding of this provision. (…) [T]he appointment of Protecting Powers since 1949 has been the exception rather than the rule in international armed conflicts. Absent any protest, therefore, it would seem that the failure to appoint a Protecting Power is not, at least in the eyes of most States, seen as a violation of their treaty

First Geneva Convention provides that the only states able to use the red crescent emblem or the red lion and sun emblem were those already doing so at the time the 1949 Geneva Conventions were adopted. But the fact that a number of states chose to use one of these two emblems upon or subsequent to their adherence to the Convention without formal objection by other parties to the Convention, led the ICRC to 'conclude that a practice or custom at variance with the rule set out in Article 38 has thus been allowed to take root'.[26]

Despite these areas of intersection, it is important to keep the processes of treaty-making, identification of customary law norms and interpretation of treaties clearly separate. They are governed by distinct sets of rules: Article 38 of the ICJ Statute for the first two processes and Articles 31–33 VCLT for the third one. What are the rules governing treaty interpretation then?

1.3 The VCLT Interpretation Regime

The 1969 VCLT interpretation regime rests on a general rule expressed under Article 31, and on supplementary means of interpretation, under Article 32. These two articles reflect a mix between the 'literal' approach (where the text is the main factor of interpretation) and the 'effectiveness' or 'teleological' approach (where the supposed intention of the parties is the most important factor of interpretation).

Although the two articles may give the impression of strictly phrased rules corresponding to a carefully ordered process, the VCLT interpretation regime actually offers some flexibility in the application of these rules as well as in the sources used for the interpretive exercise – essentially via the open list of supplementary means (see below). Thus, Articles 31 and 32 should be understood as codifying general principles guiding interpretation.[27]

Taking into account these rules as a whole, the interpreter retains an important role in determining how they should be applied.[28] The interpretive task necessarily involves the interpreter's own judgment, carried out in good faith.[29] As Gardiner states: 'In any particular instance, the difficult part of the art of treaty interpretation involves going beyond the [interpretation] rules themselves, that is the evaluation and judgment required in applying the rules to a particular treaty to produce an actual interpretation.'[30] In other words, 'rules [of interpretation]

---

obligations. At the same time, there is no indication that the High Contracting Parties consider that Article 8 has fallen into desuetude', ICRC (n 8), art 8, para 1045. For another example, see ILC (n 17) 54, para 12 (with regard to the obligation to display the distinctive emblem in Article 12 of Additional Protocol II).

26 ICRC (n 8) art 38, para 2548.

27 '[The VCLT rules'] content and (…) proper interpretation show a nature which is more akin to principles than rules', Richard Gardiner, 'The Vienna Convention Rules on Treaty Interpretation' in Duncan Hollis (ed) *The Oxford Guide to Treaties* (2nd ed, OUP 2020) 487.

28 'As a set of principles ancillary to the instruments whose interpretation they assist, and as provisions which are themselves set out in a treaty, these rules require interpretation', ibid 460.

29 On good faith, see eg Mark Villiger, *Commentary on the 1969 Vienna Convention on the Law of Treaties* (Nijhoff 2009) 426 and Ulf Linderfalk, 'What Are the Functions of the General Principles? Good Faith and International Legal Pragmatics' (2018) 78 Zeitschrift für ausländisches öffentliches Recht und Völkerrecht 1, 9.

30 Gardiner, 'The Vienna Convention Rules' in Hollis (n 27) 460.

can assist judgment but cannot replace it'.[31] So how were these rules interpreted and applied in the framework of the update of the Commentary on the First Geneva Convention?

2. THE GENERAL RULE OF INTERPRETATION APPLIED TO INTERNATIONAL HUMANITARIAN LAW TREATIES (ARTICLE 31 VCLT)

Pursuant to Article 31 VCLT, a treaty must be interpreted 'in good faith in accordance with the ordinary meaning to be given to the terms of the treaty in their context and in the light of its object and purpose'. Although this rule of interpretation has different elements, which are examined under separate headings below, the interpretation itself must combine all the elements.[32]

2.1 The Ordinary Meaning of the Text

The 'ordinary meaning of the terms' in the case of the Geneva Conventions did not raise many major issues since the Conventions were precisely worded with a view to make them easily comprehensible by those who have to apply them and those who benefit from their protection. Where necessary, the Commentaries refer to authoritative, standard English dictionaries.[33] The French version of the Conventions, which is equally authentic, has also been consistently used.[34]

In order to determine their ordinary meaning, the terms of the treaty must be placed 'in their context'. In this sense, context is 'an aid to selection of the ordinary meaning'.[35] Elements pertaining to the context are briefly discussed in the next section (Article 31(2) VCLT).

The meaning of the treaty terms must also be determined in light of the object and purpose of the treaty. The 'object' can be understood as referring to the rights and obligations enshrined in the treaty,[36] and 'purpose' as the aim to be achieved by the treaty provisions.[37] However, the terms 'object' and 'purpose' are used as 'a combined whole'.[38] Thus, a treaty's object and purpose is said to refer to its 'raison d'être',[39] its 'fundamental core',[40] or 'its essential con-

---

31 ibid 462.

32 See ILC (n 13) 220, paras 9–10; ILC (n 17), conclusion 2(5); Gardiner, *Treaty Interpretation* (n 11) 31–32; Aust (n 7) 208.

33 Such as the *Concise Oxford English Dictionary* or legal dictionaries such as *Black's Law Dictionary*.

34 See First Geneva Convention, art 55 and its commentary, ICRC (n 8).

35 Gardiner, *Treaty Interpretation* (n 11) 197.

36 Paul Reuter, *Introduction to the Law of Treaties* (2nd edn, Graduate Institute of International Studies 1995) 186, para 283.

37 Isabelle Buffard and Karl Zemanek, 'The "Object and Purpose" of a Treaty: An Enigma?' (1998) 3 Austrian Review of International & European Law 331–32.

38 Villiger, *Commentary* (n 29) 427, with further references; Gardiner, *Treaty Interpretation* (n 11) 212–13 ('a composite item'); David S. Jonas and Thomas N. Saunders, 'The Object and Purpose of a Treaty: Three Interpretive Methods' (2010) 43 Vanderbilt Journal of Transnational Law 565, 578 ('a unitary concept').

39 *Reservations to the Genocide Convention* (Advisory Opinion) [1951] ICJ Rep 15 para 23.

40 Alain Pellet, 'Article 19. Formulation of reservations' in Corten and Klein (n 11) 450–51.

tent'.[41] A usual place to look for the object and purpose of a treaty is its preamble. However, in the case of the Geneva Conventions, the preambles are very short and provide only limited guidance,[42] contrary to the Additional Protocols, which have more substantial preambles. Essentially, a treaty's object and purpose refers to its 'fundamental core' or 'its essential content'. Thus, for example, the object and purpose of the First Convention is 'to ensure respect for and protection of the wounded and sick, as well as the dead, in international armed conflict'.[43] All the rules of the Convention are geared towards this purpose: the obligation to search for the wounded and sick, to respect and protect medical and religious personnel, units and transports, and the rules governing the use of the protective emblem. Of note, Common Article 3 – which is often considered a mini treaty within the Conventions – can be said to have a distinct purpose, that of protecting persons not or no longer participating in hostilities in situations of non-international armed conflict. Further, the Geneva Conventions regime (and international humanitarian law more generally) rest on a balance between humanitarian considerations and military necessity. These elements have served as an interpretive compass throughout the drafting of the updated Commentary.

2.2 The Context

Article 31(3) VCLT identifies which elements constitute the 'context' of the treaty in the sense of paragraph 1. These elements include the whole text of the treaty, its annexes and preambles. As noted above, the preamble of each of the 1949 Conventions is very limited and the annexes are more operational.[44] They have thus been of less relevance than other elements of context, such as the title of the Convention, its structure and chapter headings.[45]

In addition, the context comprises 'any agreement relating to the treaty which was made between all the parties in connection with the conclusion of the treaty', as well as 'any instrument which was made by one or more parties in connection with the conclusion of the treaty and accepted by the other parties as an instrument related to the treaty' (Article 31(2)(a) and (b) VCLT). There is no such agreement or instrument in connection with the conclusion of the Geneva Conventions or their Additional Protocols.

2.3 Subsequent Developments

The interpretation of treaty terms may evolve over time, especially when they regulate subject matters which themselves evolve. This is undeniably the case with warfare and its humanitar-

---

41 Jonas and Saunders (n 38) 576.

42 The preamble of the First Geneva Convention reads: 'The undersigned Plenipotentiaries of the Governments represented at the Diplomatic Conference held at Geneva from April 21 to August 12, 1949, for the purpose of revising the Geneva Convention for the Relief of the Wounded and Sick in Armies in the Field of July 27, 1929, have agreed as follows (…)'.

43 ICRC (n 8), Introduction, para 30.

44 For example, the two annexes of the First Geneva Convention are a 'Draft agreement relating to hospital zones and localities' and a model 'Identity card for members of medical and religious personnel attached to the armed forces'.

45 It should be noted that the marginal titles for each article are neither part of the text nor of the context because these were established after the Diplomatic Conference by the depositary, the Swiss Federal Council.

ian consequences. The Vienna Convention recognizes the need to take into account the passing of time, through subsequent agreements, subsequent practice and other rules of international law (Article 31(3) VCLT). The ILC considers that subsequent agreements and practice 'may assist in determining whether or not the presumed intention of the parties upon the conclusion of the treaty was to give a term used a meaning which is capable of evolving over time'.[46]

While 'subsequent agreements' did not prove relevant for the updated Commentary on the First Geneva Convention,[47] subsequent practice and other rules of international law have been particularly important when interpreting the Convention.

2.3.1 Subsequent practice in the application of the treaty which establishes the agreement of the parties regarding its interpretation (Article 31(3)(b))

Subsequent practice is an important source of interpretation.[48] As explained by Aust, '[h]owever precise a text appears to be, the way in which it is actually applied by the parties is usually a good indication of what they understand it to mean, provided the practice is consistent and is common to, or accepted, expressly or tacitly, by both or all parties'.[49]

The ILC defines subsequent practice as follows: 'subsequent practice as an authentic means of interpretation under article 31, paragraph 3 (b), consists of conduct in the application of a treaty, after its conclusion, which establishes the agreement of the parties regarding the interpretation of the treaty.'[50]

The threshold for subsequent practice to qualify as authentic means of interpretation under Article 31(3)(b) is fairly restrictive. The said practice must establish 'the agreement of the parties'. According to the ILC, this requires 'a common understanding regarding the interpretation of a treaty which the parties are aware of and accept'.[51] This is generally understood as implying agreement of *all* parties to the treaty.[52] Agreement of all parties does not mean that

---

46 ILC (n 17), conclusion 8.

47 The Additional Protocols to the Geneva Conventions do not as such constitute 'subsequent agreements between the parties regarding the interpretation of the treaty or the application of its provisions'. They are separate treaties which have not been ratified by all Parties of the Geneva Conventions, as art 31(3)(a) VCLT would require. This does not exclude, however, that the provisions of the Additional Protocols – which complement the Geneva Conventions – may be taken into account for the interpretation of the Geneva Conventions under art 32 VCLT.

48 According to the ILC, '[s]ubsequent agreements and subsequent practice under article 31, paragraph 3 (a) and (b), being objective evidence of the understanding of the parties as to the meaning of the treaty, are authentic means of interpretation, in the application of the general rule of treaty interpretation reflected in article 31', ILC (n 17), conclusion 3.

49 Aust (n 7) 215. Or in the words of Yasseen: 'Appliquer le traité, cela suppose l'avoir compris, donc interprété. La pratique suivie dans l'application du traité a, par conséquent, pour fondement un certain sens accepté par ceux qui la suivent.' ('Applying a treaty implies that it has been understood, and therefore that it has been interpreted. Practice in the application of the treaty is, therefore, based on a specific understanding accepted by the authors of the practice', our translation), Mustafa Kamil Yasseen, 'L'interprétation des traités d'après la convention de Vienne sur le droit des traités' (1976) 151 Collected Courses of the Hague Academy of International Law 47.

50 ILC (n 17), conclusion 4(2).

51 ILC (n 17), conclusion 10(9).

52 For an explanation why art 31(3)(b) should be understood as such despite the absence of an explicit reference to the agreement of 'all' parties, see ILC (n 17), conclusion 10(2), para 13. In doctrine, see Gardiner, *Treaty Interpretation* (n 11) 266 and 270; Aust (n 7) 216. Gerhard Hafner, 'Subsequent

there must be practice by all parties: 'Silence on the part of one or more parties can constitute acceptance of the subsequent practice when the circumstances call for some reaction.'[53] Yet, identifying evidence of such endorsement may prove difficult, in particular for specific points of interpretation. A meeting of state parties could produce evidence of such agreement but there are no regular meetings held within the framework of the Geneva Conventions.[54] This being said, state parties to the Geneva Conventions normally do meet every four years on the occasion of the International Conference of the Red Cross and Red Crescent, with members of the International Movement of the Red Cross and Red Crescent.[55] Resolutions of this Conference have contributed to strengthening IHL and its implementation – some of them are referenced in the updated Commentary on the First Geneva Convention.

It is important to note that agreement by all parties would be precluded if there are conflicting positions. However, the ILC draws a distinction between conflicting interpretations and diverse forms of application of a given rule:

> The fact that parties apply a treaty differently does not, as such, permit a conclusion that there are conflicting positions regarding the interpretation of the treaty. Such a difference may indicate a disagreement over the one correct interpretation, but it may also simply reflect a common understanding that the treaty permits a certain scope for the exercise of discretion in its application.[56]

The ILC cites human rights treaties as leaving a margin of appreciation in their application, and this may also be the case for some IHL treaty provisions. For example, the updated Commentary on the First Convention has identified several aspects of the treaty where the implementation is left to the discretion of the state.[57] Rather than suggesting that there is only one correct interpretation, this diverse practice provides examples endorsed by different states on the various ways to implement the Convention's rules.

Agreements and Practice: Between Interpretation, Informal Modification, and Formal Amendment' in Nolte (n 11) 112–13.

[53] ILC (n 17), conclusion 10(2). See also Gardiner, *Treaty Interpretation* (n 11) 270 ('it is sufficient if there is practice of one or more parties and good evidence that the other parties have endorsed the practice.').

[54] There has been an International Conference for the Protection of War Victims, Geneva, 1993, as well as Conferences of High Contracting Parties to the Fourth Geneva Convention, Geneva, 15 July 1999, 5 December 2001, and 17 December 2014.

[55] These as the National Societies of the Red Cross or Red Crescent, the International Federation of Red Cross and Red Crescent Societies and the ICRC.

[56] ILC (n 17), commentary on draft conclusion 10(1), para 4.

[57] See eg ICRC (n 8) para 1968 (who qualifies as religious personnel), para 2005 (decision whether or not to arm military medical and religious personnel) and paras 2566 and 2579 (whether to display the distinctive emblem).

Absent conflicting positions, agreement over a given practice may be expressed explicitly. It has also been argued that agreement may be deduced from absence of reaction.[58] The ILC most recently reasserted this view,[59] although with a dose of caution:

> The relevance of silence or inaction for the establishment of an agreement regarding interpretation depends to a large extent on the circumstances of the specific case. Decisions of international courts and tribunals demonstrate that acceptance of a practice by one or more parties by way of silence or inaction is not easily established.[60]

Importantly, the ILC accepts silence as agreement of a practice only 'when the circumstances call for some reaction'. Based on the case law mentioned by the Commission, such 'circumstances' seem to mostly involve cases where the *affected* state was silent.[61] Applied to practice related to IHL treaties, states affected by (mis)application of IHL rules are most likely to be enemy belligerents. As such, it is foreseeable that they will not hesitate to voice their disagreement. In these circumstances, their silence may well demonstrate agreement on a given practice by their enemy belligerents. The same logic may, depending on the circumstances and the rule concerned, extend to third states not party to the conflict as all states have an interest in the correct application of IHL.[62] For example, the fact that states generally did not object to the absence of the appointment of Protecting Powers in recent decades can be taken as tacit agreement of this practice, and hence the ICRC concluded that the obligation expressed in Common Article 8 (Article 9 of the Fourth Geneva Convention) should today be interpreted as an option.[63]

Nevertheless, subsequent practice as understood under Article 31(3)(b) is not easy to establish in relation to IHL treaties. Other subsequent practice – i.e., that which does not, or not clearly, establish the agreement of the parties regarding the interpretation of a treaty – did play a key role in drafting the Commentary, as a supplementary means of interpretation under Article 32. We will therefore develop further on the notion of 'subsequent practice' in the interpretation of IHL treaties in Part 3 below.

2.3.2 'Relevant rules of international law applicable in the relations between the parties' (Article 31(3)(c))

The principle enshrined in Article 31(3)(c) aims to achieve coherence amongst different parts of international law.[64] While this provision has attracted growing attention only recently, the

---

58 See eg *Kasikili/Sedudu Island (Botswana v Namibia)* (Judgment) [1999] ICJ Rep 1045, Dissenting opinion of Judge Weeramantry, 1153, 1159–60. In doctrine, see Gardiner, *Treaty Interpretation* (n 11) 267 and Aust (n 7) 216.

59 See ILC (n 17), conclusion 10(2): 'The number of parties that must actively engage in subsequent practice in order to establish an agreement under article 31, paragraph 3 (b), may vary. *Silence on the part of one or more parties may constitute acceptance of the subsequent practice when the circumstances call for some reaction*' (emphasis added).

60 ILC (n 17), commentary on draft conclusion 10(2), para 18.

61 ibid paras 14–17.

62 See ICRC (n 8), art 1, para 119.

63 ibid, art 8, paras 1114–1119.

64 For more on the meaning and history of this rule see Gardiner, 'The Vienna Convention Rules' in Hollis (n 27) 469–70.

European Court of Human Rights has had recourse to this interpretive method for a long time.[65] This provision has proved instrumental in interpreting the First Geneva Convention.

There is general agreement that Article 31(3)(c) does not merely refer to the law as it stood at the moment of the adoption of the treaty, but also to the law as it stands at the moment of the interpretation.[66] This seems particularly obvious when it comes to treaties regulating warfare, a matter subject to continuous operational and legal developments.[67]

In the framework of the interpretation of the Geneva Conventions, 'relevant rules of international law' include not only the Additional Protocols, but also customary IHL, international criminal law, human rights law and refugee law.[68] The latter three distinct branches of international law were still in their infancy when the Pictet Commentaries were being drafted but they have grown significantly in the meantime. This new legal environment has inevitably resulted in evolutions in the ICRC Commentary. To give but one example, in 1952, Pictet's recommendation that Common Article 3 'should be applied as widely as possible' was based on the fact that there was, at the time, no other clearly defined bodies of international law protecting those affected by situations of violence short of armed conflict. Since 1949, however, the protection provided by human rights law in such situations has considerably developed. The updated Commentary reflects today's prevailing interpretation that international humanitarian law should apply only to the situations it was intended to regulate: armed conflicts, but not beyond.[69] This interpretation is, furthermore, more loyal to the terms of the treaty itself.

An important caveat is that only other treaty rules 'applicable in the relations between the parties' can inform the interpretation of a given treaty. When interpreting the Geneva Conventions, this has meant, for example, that reliance on the Additional Protocols has to be very carefully considered since they are not, contrary to the Conventions, universally ratified. However, they can be referred to as a matter of general interpretation when they reflect customary IHL, such as the definition of wounded and sick in Article 8 of Additional Protocol I or the definition of military objectives in Article 52(2) of the Protocol. Other rules are referred to in the updated Commentaries on the understanding that, in principle, they only apply to parties to the Protocols.

---

[65] ibid 487.

[66] *Legal Consequences for States of the Continued Presence of South Africa in Namibia (South West Africa) notwithstanding Security Council Resolution 276 (1970)* (Advisory Opinion) [1971] ICJ Rep 16 para 53; Kolb (n 6) 158; Gardiner, 'The Vienna Convention Rules' in Hollis (n 27) 469–70; Aust (n 7) 216.

[67] As Kolb puts it '[the UN Charter and ECHR] tend to be interpreted in the light of the law as it stands at the moment of interpretation. These treaties are intended to inform social life as it evolves. Their purpose could not be fulfilled if they were to be construed in an "obsolete" surrounding. The same is true for IHL treaties and for a series of other subject matters,' Kolb (n 6) 158.

[68] For an argument that the drafting history of art 31(3)(c) suggests that the 'relevant rules' are not restricted to customary rules but also include treaty rules, see Gardiner, 'The Vienna Convention Rules' in Hollis (n 27) 470.

[69] See ICRC (n 8), art 3, para 390.

In addition, there have been important developments in general international law. For example the articulation of the rules on state responsibility by the ILC[70] has to be taken into account when discussing the responsibility of states to ensure respect for IHL.[71]

3. SUPPLEMENTARY MEANS TO INTERPRET INTERNATIONAL HUMANITARIAN LAW TREATIES (ARTICLE 32)

The general rule of interpretation in Article 31 is complemented by the rule in Article 32 on supplementary means of interpretation, which include – but are not restricted to – the 'preparatory work of the treaty and the circumstances of its conclusion'.

3.1 The Importance of Supplementary Means

Although Article 32 suggests that supplementary means are optional – 'recourse *may* be had' (emphasis added) – and thus of secondary importance, experience suggests otherwise.

According to the text of Article 32, supplementary means of interpretation may be used for two purposes: 'confirming' the meaning of a term resulting from the application of Article 31, or 'determining' the meaning, when the application of Article 31 left the meaning ambiguous or obscure or led to a manifestly absurd or unreasonable result.[72] Whether a given interpretation needs 'confirmation' implies some discretion for the interpreter to decide whether or not to have recourse to supplementary means.[73] In fact, the preparatory work (or *travaux préparatoires*) is used almost routinely by interpreters, and not only in cases where the general rule of interpretation yielded an unsatisfactory result.[74] Most interpretations, including many

---

[70] ILC, 'Report of the International Law Commission – Fifty-third session (23 April – 1 June and 2 July – 10 August 2001)' UN Doc A/56/10, Draft articles on Responsibility of States for Internationally Wrongful Acts, with commentaries.

[71] ICRC (n 8), art 1, paras 118–91.

[72] For a view that art 32 means could also be used to 'correct' the meaning of a treaty provision see Stephen M. Schwebel, 'May Preparatory Work be Used to Correct Rather than Confirm the "Clear" Meaning of a Treaty Provision?' in Jerzy Makarczyk (ed), *Theory of International Law at the Threshold of the 21st Century* (Kluwer Law International 1996) 173–81.

[73] This was even acknowledged by the principal architect of the Vienna rules, Sir Humphrey Waldock: 'This formulation [the precursor to art 32] seemed to the Commission about as near as it is possible to get to reconciling the principle of the primacy of the text (…) with frequent and quite normal recourse to *travaux preparatoires* without any too nice regard for the question whether the text itself is clear. Moreover, the rule (…) is inherently flexible, since the question whether the text can be said to be "clear" is in some degree subjective.' ILC, 'Sixth Report on the Law of Treaties' (1966) II Yearbook of the ILC 99 [20], cited in Gardiner, 'The Vienna Convention Rules' in Hollis (n 27) 463.

[74] See eg *Application of the Genocide Convention* (Judgment) [2007] ICJ Rep 43 paras 162–65. Aust notes that international tribunals, and the parties arguing before them, have for long had recourse to the preparatory work, Aust (n 7) 217–18, citing *Lockerbie (Libya v UK)* (Preliminary Objections) [1998] ICJ Rep 9 paras 4.17–4.18; Lord McNair, *The Law of Treaties* (Clarendon Press 1961) 413 and 422, and examples given in Martin Mennecke and Christian Tams, 'The Right to Consular Assistance under International Law' (1999) 42 German Yearbook of International Law 192, 223–24; see also Martin Ris, 'Treaty Interpretation and ICJ Recourse to Travaux Préparatoires: Towards a Proposed Amendment of Articles 31 and 32 of the Vienna Convention on the Law of Treaties' (1991) 14 Boston College International and Comparative Law Review 111, 131.

commentaries on other treaties, systematically examine the preparatory work and not only in cases where the meaning is ambiguous or obscure or leads to a result which is manifestly absurd or unreasonable.[75]

In addition, recourse to the preparatory work helps to understand 'the terms of the treaty in their context' which is a requirement under the general rule (see Article 31(1) and (2)). Recourse to the preparatory work may also be particularly important when no recent practice on a topic can be found, such as for Articles 33 and 34 of the First Convention dealing with buildings and material of medical units of the armed forces and aid societies which have fallen into enemy hands.[76]

In our experience, subsequent practice as a supplementary means of interpretation is particularly useful in the interpretation of IHL treaties because, as highlighted above, it is difficult to identify subsequent practice meeting the requirements of Article 31(3)(b).[77] Thus, the interpretation of IHL treaties highlights the practical importance of Article 32. This has also been pointed out in doctrine. According to Gardiner, the meaning of the verb to 'determine' in Article 32 'is very much to fulfil a primary role in treaty interpretation'.[78] He even challenges the idea of a sequential order between Articles 31 and 32.[79] We now turn to the question: which supplementary means are relevant for the interpretation of IHL treaties specifically?

3.2 Preparatory Work

Preparatory work should be understood broadly, as including successive drafts of the treaty, conference records and explanatory statements made in drafting committees.[80] During treaty negotiations, important discussions may also occur outside of any formally recorded arena. However, in the case of the Geneva Conventions and their Additional Protocols, an important amount of documentation has been collected, ranging from drafts and reports preparatory to the 1949 and 1974–1977 Diplomatic Conferences to the stenographic notes (minutes) of the Conferences and their Final/Official Records.[81] These documents have been helpful to the authors of the original and updated Commentaries, in clarifying the meaning of certain provisions.

---

75 ICRC (n 8), Introduction, para 48.

76 See ibid, commentary on arts 33 and 34.

77 See section 3.1. above.

78 Gardiner, *Treaty Interpretation* (n 11) 354.

79 According to Gardiner, 'Just as the "crucible" approach does not see the elements of the general rule as hierarchical or sequential (…) so too the distinction between the general rule and supplementary means was not slotted into any particular sequence,' 'The Vienna Convention Rules' in Hollis (n 27) 474. Gardiner also reports that 'McDougal [the US representative at the Vienna Conference] proposed that supplementary means should have the same engagement in the interpretative process as all the elements in the general rule,' ibid 471. See also 464 and 484. Schwebel in Makarczyk (n 72) 173–81.

80 For more on preparatory work as supplementary means of interpretation, see Aust (n 7), 218, Gardiner, 'The Vienna Convention Rules' in Hollis (n 27) 470–74.

81 For a full list of (and access to) the documents constituting the *travaux préparatoires* to the 1949 Geneva Conventions and their Additional Protocols, see '1949 Geneva Conventions: *travaux préparatoires* and final records', ICRC Library website <https://library.icrc.org/library/Default.aspx> accessed 31 January 2021.

3.3 'Subsequent Practice' as a Supplementary Means

As stated above, state practice which does not fulfil the requirements of 'subsequent practice' under Article 31 – i.e., practice for which it is not possible to identify the agreement of all parties – may be examined as supplementary means. This is recognized by the ILC,[82] which explains that 'any practice in the application of the treaty that may provide indications as to how the treaty is to be interpreted may be a relevant supplementary means of interpretation under article 32' (this is what the ILC calls 'subsequent practice in the broad sense').[83]

Save for the element of the agreement of the parties, the meaning of 'subsequent' practice under Article 32 should be the same as 'subsequent practice' under Article 31. 'Subsequent practice' is generally understood as being limited to practice of the parties to the treaty, usually states.[84] Thus any act attributable to the state[85] constitutes 'state practice', amongst which only the practice carried out in application of the treaty would be a valid source of interpretation under Article 31(3)(b). The act must constitute official practice, and 'an act of a subordinate organ, which is not supported by superior organs, is not able to constitute adequate practice'.[86] The weight of such practice may depend on its clarity and specificity, as well as whether and how it is repeated.[87] Thus in case of conflicting positions between various state organs or between different instances of a state's practice, that practice is considered internally inconsistent and its weight may be diminished.

Physical acts relevant to the interpretation of IHL treaty rules include conduct on the battlefield; the use of weapons, means and methods of warfare; the treatment of persons in the power of a party to the conflict; or the actual display of the emblem. However, such acts are rarely documented in official and public sources, especially as far as the conduct of hostilities is concerned. Hence, evidence of the actual implementation of the law during armed conflicts – official practice – is more easily found in documents such as national legislation, military manuals, instruction to armed and security forces, communiqués during armed conflicts, national case law, diplomatic protests, opinions of state military and civilian legal advisers, official state pronouncement on the drafts of subsequent IHL treaties, executive decisions

---

82 ILC (n 17), conclusion 2(4): 'Recourse may be had to other subsequent practice in the application of the treaty as a supplementary means of interpretation under article 32.' For references to case law and doctrine supporting this see ILC (n 17), commentary on draft conclusion 2(4), para 9 (footnotes 36–37), and commentary on draft conclusion 4(3), paras 25–32. Practice not accompanied by an agreement of all parties is examined by Georg Nolte in ILC, 'Fourth report on subsequent agreements and subsequent practice in relation to the interpretation of treaties', Sixty-eighth session (2 May–10 June and 4 July–12 August 2016) UN Doc A/CN.4/694, paras 107–109.

83 ILC (n 17), commentary on draft conclusion 4, para 24.

84 See ILC (n 17), conclusion 5 on attribution of subsequent practice: '1. Subsequent practice under articles 31 and 32 may consist of any conduct of a party in the application of a treaty, whether in the exercise of its executive, legislative, judicial or other functions; 2. Other conduct, including by non-State actors, does not constitute subsequent practice under articles 31 and 32. Such conduct may, however, be relevant when assessing the subsequent practice of parties to a treaty.' On the practice of non-state actors, see Part 3.4.

85 See ILC Articles on State Responsibility for Internationally Wrongful Acts.

86 Hafner in Nolte (n 52) 112.

87 ILC (n 17), conclusion 9.

and regulations, pleadings before international tribunals, and official statements made within international organizations and at international conferences.

Subsequent practice under Article 31(3)(b) must be 'in the application of the treaty'. The same should be true of subsequent practice as supplementary means. It can prove difficult to determine whether conduct occurs in the application of a treaty or, for example, in the application of a related treaty or of customary law. However, it seems that because all states are parties to the Geneva Conventions, it can be assumed that states act in the application of the Conventions, possibly alongside other sources of IHL, when their conduct relates to issues regulated by the Conventions.

In addition, violations of a treaty rule cannot count as practice informing the interpretation of that rule. The ILC's Commentary on the Draft Conclusions specifies that: 'an element of good faith is necessary in any subsequent practice in the application of the treaty.' A manifest misapplication of a treaty, as opposed to a *bona fide* application (even if erroneous), is therefore not an 'application of the treaty' in the sense of Articles 31 and 32.[88]

Interpretation is concerned with clarifying the meaning and extent of a legal obligation or prohibition; conduct which is not carried out in application of the rule cannot inform how it must be applied. However, in practice, it may be difficult to make such distinction, as noted above with respect to the use of the red crescent as protective emblems (Article 38 of the First Convention).

Sources of subsequent practice mentioned above are available in the public domain, notably through the ICRC databases on customary IHL and national implementation.[89] The ICRC archives have also been a valuable resource. States communicate with the ICRC in the context of its mandate 'to work for the faithful application of international humanitarian law applicable in armed conflicts and to take cognizance of any complaints based on alleged breaches of that law'.[90] Thus, the ICRC archives contain documents in which states have clarified their understanding of the Geneva Conventions. The Commentaries draw on research in the archives, while respecting their confidential nature.[91]

The ILC carefully nuances the value of subsequent practice not fulfilling the requirement of Article 31(3)(b): 'In any case, the distinction between agreed subsequent practice under article 31, paragraph 3 (b), as an authentic means of interpretation, and other subsequent practice (in a broad sense) under article 32, implies that a greater interpretative value should be attributed to the former.'[92]

While we agree with this remark, it is noteworthy that the lower interpretive value of practice under Article 32 is only *relative* to that of subsequent practice under Article 31(3)(b), on the assumption that the latter is available. Yet, as highlighted above, in the field of IHL, agreement of third states vis-à-vis the practice of parties to an armed conflict cannot always be

---

[88] ILC (n 17), commentary on draft conclusion 4(2), para 19.

[89] See ICRC, 'IHL database search' <https://ihl-databases.icrc.org/applic/ihl/ihl-search.nsf/home.xsp?lang=EN> accessed 31 January 2021.

[90] Movement's Statute (n 3), art 5.

[91] The fact that practice is communicated only to a limited extent, eg in a bilateral context, may be sufficient to make it a means of interpretation. In this vein, communications to the ICRC in the framework of its role as guardian and promoter of the Geneva Conventions, even if confidential, are not purely private acts and count as practice that may contribute to the interpretation of the Conventions.

[92] ILC (n 17), commentary on draft conclusion 4(3), para 33.

easily established, in particular for specific points of interpretation. Therefore, 'other subsequent practice' in the broad sense, falling under Article 32, may be the only practice available to the interpreter. Its weight in confirming or determining the meaning of IHL rules should therefore not be underestimated.

3.4 Practice of Other Actors

That 'subsequent practice' under Article 31(3)(b) refers only to state practice is largely uncontroversial. Similarly, when the ILC refers to 'subsequent practice' as a supplementary means under Article 32, it clearly designates state practice only.[93] Yet when other, non-state, actors are involved in the application of a treaty, the question of the relevance of their practice arises.

Different approaches on this issue are possible. According to a first approach the practice of non-state actors is considered only to the extent that it casts light on state practice. This is the approach adopted by the ILC: 'Other conduct, including by non-State actors, does not constitute subsequent practice under articles 31 and 32. Such conduct may, however, be relevant when assessing the subsequent practice of parties to a treaty.'[94]

Under this approach, practice or 'conduct' of non-state actors is looked at only to the extent that it can inform state practice which itself is a source of treaty interpretation – under Article 31 if it reflects the agreement of other state parties, or under Article 32 if it does not. This approach is also evoked by Judge Simma when he asks whether states' silence in relation to interpretations by implementing human rights supervisory bodies could constitute state practice.[95] However, the ILC has concluded that such silence cannot be so interpreted.[96]

Another approach would consist in analysing the practice (or conduct) of non-state actors in itself, not only through the prism of state practice. Some authors consider that subsequent practice extends to that of other actors, such as organs of international organizations, under certain circumstances.[97]

---

93 ILC (n 17), conclusion 5(1).

94 ibid, conclusion 5(2).

95 'Another issue arises in regard to the reactions of states parties to a treaty to views or activities of supervisory bodies established by these treaties. For instance, could we say that a lack of opposition by states parties to the International Covenant on Civil and Political Rights to a view of the Human Rights Committee considering the interpretation and application of the Covenant could lead to some sort of acquiescence vis-à-vis that view, and, in that sense, would constitute state practice, consisting of not doing anything?', Bruno Simma, 'Miscellaneous Thoughts on Subsequent Agreements and Practice' in Nolte (n 11) 47–48.

96 ILC (n 17), conclusion 13(3).

97 See eg Laurence Boisson de Chazournes, 'Subsequent Practice, Practices and "Family Resemblance": Towards Embedding Subsequent Practice in its Operative Milieu' in Nolte (n 11) 57–59; Gabrielle Marceau and Clément Marquet, 'Practices and Ways of Doing Things in the World Trade Organization (WTO) Law' in Hélène Ruiz-Fabri (ed), *International Law and Litigation: A Look into Procedure* (Nomos & Hart Publishing 2018) 519–21; Djemila Carron, *L'acte déclencheur d'un conflit armé international* (Collection Genevoise/Zurich: Schulthess Éditions Romandes/Paris: Librairie générale de droit et de jurisprudence 2016) 21. Marcelo Kohen acknowledges that the practice of implementing bodies 'will certainly be of particular importance in the interpretation of the treaties concerned', see Marcelo Kohen, 'Keeping Subsequent Agreements and Practice in Their Right Limits' in Nolte (n 11) 41.

There may be good reasons to accept such practice as a supplementary means of interpretation, when the actor in question is part of the institutional machinery set up under the treaty. In that vein, the commentaries refer to ICRC practice in the application of the Geneva Conventions, in particular for those provisions that give a role to the ICRC, such as Common Articles 3, 9 and 10, and Articles 123 and 126 of the Third Geneva Convention and its equivalent provisions in the Fourth Geneva Convention.[98] The experience gained as guardian of the Geneva Conventions stems from a mandate given to it by states – in the Conventions themselves as well as in the Statutes of the International Red Cross and Red Crescent Movement, adopted by all states parties to the Geneva Conventions. Whatever view is taken on the role and weight of practice of other actors, this practice has informed state practice to the extent that it has been accepted or acquiesced by states themselves and therefore should be taken into account in interpreting the Conventions.

3.5 Interpretative Efforts by Others

3.5.1 Interpretation by judicial and quasi-judicial bodies

As mentioned above, other 'relevant rules of international law applicable in the relations between the parties' comprise another important source of interpretation under Article 31(3)(c). The work of judicial and quasi-judicial bodies interpreting and applying these distinct legal rules may also be relevant when interpreting IHL.[99] In particular, these interpretive efforts may be relevant as supplementary means of interpretation. International criminal tribunals and human rights bodies have conducted substantial interpretative work in relation to IHL norms. These interpretative pronouncements prove particularly important in confirming or determining the meaning of the Geneva Conventions. For example, the definitions of torture, cruel or degrading treatment or hostage-taking under the Geneva Conventions are largely informed by those developed by such bodies.[100] This being said, in relation to international criminal case law, the ICRC's Commentary underscores:

> the humanitarian treaty obligation may be broader than the criminalized parts of it in a rule contained in an instrument of international criminal law. The humanitarian treaty obligation exists independently of the rule of international criminal law on which the case law is founded. The content of the obligation may therefore not be identical in both bodies of law and differences are pointed out wherever they exist.[101]

---

[98] On the role of the ICRC, see also ILC (n 17), commentary on draft conclusion 5, para 15.

[99] International criminal tribunals have jurisdiction over war crimes, the primary rules of which are IHL rules. As to human rights law bodies, they may be called to interpret notions which are similar under IHRL and IHL (eg the prohibition of ill treatment); or, when applying human rights law in times of armed conflict, they may interpret human rights law in the light of IHL rules, or apply IHL rules directly.

[100] For example, the updated commentary largely refers to the ICTY case law for the definition of torture under Common Article 3, see ICRC (n 8), art 3, paras 626–45. Similarly, when defining 'hostage taking', the ICRC's updated Commentary refers to case law from the Special Court for Sierra Leone (*Sesay*, Appeal Judgment, 2009, para 598), see ICRC (n 8), art 3, para 648.

[101] ICRC (n 8), Introduction, para 38.

3.5.2 Interpretation in legal writings

Commentaries and academic reports or writings have been recognized as valid supplementary means of interpretation[102] and are often used by interpreters such as courts and tribunals. A subsidiary source of international law,[103] doctrine is logically a relevant means of interpretation, notably because it may itself consist in collecting and interpreting state practice. However, it does not carry in itself the same weight, as a means of interpretation, as the actual practice of the parties themselves.

IHL-related doctrine has expanded considerably in the last decades. In the case of the ICRC's updated Commentary, significant time and effort has been invested to collect and analyse relevant publications in order to be able to reflect the diversity of legal interpretations, to the extent they are legally sound and faithful to the object and purpose of the Conventions. Peer reviewers have proved very helpful in this process, signalling doctrine from their regions and/or fields of expertise.

Finally, the legal writings of the ICRC itself can prove important when interpreting the Geneva Conventions, as it reflects 150 years of interaction with primary addressees of the Conventions.[104]

4. CONCLUSION

The interpretation of treaties will always be an inherent, essential part of treaty regulation.[105] IHL treaties are no exception to this rule. In a context where the adoption of new IHL treaties does not seem to be a realistic prospect in the near future, it is expected that the interpretation of existing treaties will be crucial to ensure that they continue to be applied over time in a manner that is consistent with their object and purpose. A challenge linked to relatively older treaties is that the societal and operational realities reflected in certain aspects of the language of the treaty may not be in touch with current realities of the application of the treaty. In the case of the Geneva Conventions, there are also rules which have been the object of little practice since the Second World War.[106] Thus, while the substantive rules remain valid and relevant, there is a real need to adapt our understanding of the treaty text to today's armed conflicts and their humanitarian consequences.

The VCLT interpretation regime offers a coherent legal framework for the interpretation of treaties, including IHL treaties. More than 70 years after the adoption of the Geneva Conventions, subsequent practice has become an important source of their interpretation. However, identifying subsequent practice meeting the requirements of Article 31(3)(b) proves

102 Gardiner, *Treaty Interpretation* (n 11) 401–404.

103 '[T]he teachings of the most highly qualified publicists of the various nations are subsidiary means for the determination of rules of law', see art 38(1)(d) of the ICJ Statute.

104 On the role of the ICRC in this respect, see also ILC (n 17), commentary on draft conclusion 5, para 15.

105 For the reasons why we need treaty interpretation see Panos Merkouris, 'Introduction: Interpretation is a science, is an art, is a science' in Malgosia Fitzmaurice, Olufemi A. Elias and Panos Merkouris (eds), *Treaty Interpretation and the Vienna Convention on the Law of Treaties: 30 Years on* (Brill, Nijhoff 2010) 5–7.

106 See eg rules on Protecting Powers, national society medical personnel incorporated into armed forces' medical services, and conciliation and enquiry procedures in arts 8, 10, 11, 26–27 and 52 of the First Geneva Convention.

challenging, especially in relation to specific points of interpretation – the main tenets of the Conventions have been universally recognized as evidenced by the universal adherence to the treaties. We submit that the conditions for recourse to subsequent practice under the supplementary rule of interpretation should therefore be understood broadly. The open list of supplementary means in Article 32 allows for sufficient flexibility to incorporate sources specifically relevant to IHL treaties: subsequent practice of states, as well as interpretations by international courts and tribunals and doctrine.

The Commentaries' update confirms that the Geneva Conventions are living instruments that remain as relevant as ever to regulate contemporary armed conflicts. In that sense they are a primary example of how treaties apply over time, an indispensable condition for treaties to remain relevant.

11. Methodological challenges in ascertaining customary international humanitarian law: Can customary international law respond to changing circumstances in warfare?

Robert Heinsch

'Tis well said again; And 'tis a kind of good deed to say well: And yet words are no deeds. (William Shakespeare, *Henry VIII*, Act 3, Scene 2)

1. INTRODUCTION: CHANGING CIRCUMSTANCES IN WARFARE AND THE NEED FOR A WELL-FOUNDED METHODOLOGY TOWARDS CUSTOMARY INTERNATIONAL LAW

From the 1990s onwards – since the end of the Cold War and even more so after the terrorist attacks on the World Trade Center on 9/11 – there have been substantial changes in warfare, especially in relation to 1) the predominant means and methods of warfare with regard to the use of new technologies like drones, autonomous weapons and cyber warfare, 2) the types of conflict that occur, with a predominance of asymmetrical conflict situations, and 3) the character of the main actors engaged in hostilities tending towards a rising number of non-state actors that have never signed or ratified an international humanitarian law (IHL) treaty or other document.

These new developments give rise to the everlasting question whether IHL is able to deal with the challenges raised by them.[1] As an old saying in the world of IHL goes: 'The law of armed conflict is always one conflict behind.'[2] Is this really true? Does IHL lag behind the current developments in warfare, and is therefore not able to adequately regulate modern conflicts? This scenario would have a serious impact on the protection of protected persons, i.e. civilians, prisoners of war, and other people *hors de combat*, on the one hand, and the application of the regulations limiting the conduct of hostilities, like the prohibition to cause unnecessary suffering, on the other hand.

1 In general on the topic of IHL dealing with the challenges of modern warfare, see Robin Geiss, Terry Gill and Robert Heinsch, 'Final Report ILA Study Group on the Conduct of Hostilities, The Conduct of Hostilities Under International Humanitarian Law: Challenges of 21st Century Warfare' (2016) 19 Yearbook of International Humanitarian Law 287.

2 Andrew Clapham and Paolo Gaeta (eds), *The Oxford Handbook of International Law in Armed Conflict* (OUP 2015) 52.

However, we also know that change in the way armed conflicts are conducted is a constant phenomenon, and that it is not the first time that IHL has to adapt to new developments. In the end, international law in general – and in the widest sense every national legal system – knows three ways to deal with substantial change to factual circumstances: a) adopting a modern and progressive interpretation of the legal provision(s),[3] b) the creation of new rules through the passing of new legislation, or, in our case, new international treaties, or c) the development of new *customary* law rules that are able to give an answer to the challenges mentioned above.[4]

This chapter will focus on the last option and examine the question of whether *customary* IHL is able to deal with recent developments, and what the methodological challenges are that we have to face. In this context, we will put forward our main hypothesis, namely that customary IHL is crucial for adapting IHL to new developments in modern warfare, but that a methodological approach well founded in the theory of international sources is pivotal in order to ensure acceptance and legitimacy of any newly developing rule. In order to show the importance of a sound approach to customary IHL, a three-step approach will be followed, presenting the following: 1) a short overview of the developments in modern warfare which customary IHL has to deal with, 2) a detailed look at the special methodology used in order to determine a rule of customary IHL, and 3) a critical evaluation of the results of the examination and suggestions as to how to approach customary IHL in the future.

2. THE CHANGES IN MODERN WARFARE

What are these new developments that prompt us to discuss whether customary IHL can deal with the changing circumstances in warfare? The ensuing section will give a short overview of these changes in order to be able to later judge whether customary IHL is actually able to deal with them.

2.1 New Technologies

First of all, it is important to note that the last few decades have seen rapid changes in warfare, especially due to huge technological advances in this area. Some of the same technological advancements that have changed our daily lives, like the overwhelming reliance on computers and the Internet, have also affected the way military operations are conducted. These technologies present situations that could not have been envisaged at the time that key IHL conventions were drafted, such as the 1899/1907 Hague Conventions, the 1949 Geneva Conventions, or

---

[3] For an overview on methodology with regard to the interpretation of international treaties, see Anthony Aust, *Modern Treaty Law and Practice* (CUP 2007); Malgosia Fitzmaurice, 'The Practical Working of the Law of the Treaties – General Principles of Interpretation' in Malcolm Evans (ed) *International Law* (OUP 2010) 183–88; Malcolm Shaw, *International Law* (CUP 2008) 932–39.

[4] For an in-depth analysis see the extensive monographs on the topic by Birgit Schlütter, *Developments in Customary International Law – Theory and Practice of the International Court of Justice and the International Ad Hoc Criminal Tribunals for Rwanda and Yugoslavia* (Martinus Nijhoff Publishers 2010); Brian D. Lepard, *Customary International Law – A New Theory with Practical Applications* (CUP 2010); Shane Darcy and Joseph Powderly (eds), *Judicial Creativity at the International Criminal Tribunals* (OUP 2010); Theodor Meron, 'Revival of Customary Humanitarian Law' (2005) 99 American Journal of International Law 817.

even the 1977 Additional Protocols. To give just a few examples of 'new military technologies' and the challenges they present to existing IHL, here is a short overview:

2.1.1 Remote-controlled weapons

An unmanned aerial vehicle (UAV, commonly known as a 'drone') can target a suspected terrorist installation in the mountains of Pakistan while being controlled by a person looking at a computer screen in Nevada. The person controlling the drone does not need to be a member of the military, but instead might be a member of the intelligence service of a country.[5] The building on the screen, which looks like a military barracks, may in reality be a school in a former military barracks, but due to the difficulties of checking the use of the building through intelligence gathered on the ground, the controller of the drone may target the object in the belief that they are hitting a military target.[6]

2.1.2 Lethal autonomous weapons

Although weapons that are completely autonomous when deciding which object to target are still in the process of being developed, this is a fast-growing area, since every commander probably dreams of the day when they can send a robot into the battlefield instead of a soldier who might come back in a coffin. A lethal autonomous weapon will be programmed to target certain objects, and – in contrast to remote-controlled weapons – will launch the final attack itself, with no human interference apart from the input given by the algorithm of the programmer and the decision of the commander to use the weapon in the first place. This might raise serious questions with regard to responsibility for the respective actions as well as the accuracy when complying with the general IHL principles applicable to the conduct of hostilities.[7]

2.1.3 Cyber and information warfare

The growing dependency on the Internet and computer networks also in the area of warfare have made states and their authorities more and more vulnerable to so-called cyber attacks. This raises serious challenges surrounding the application of IHL.[8] For example, one can

5 See William Boothby, 'The Law Relating to Unmanned Aerial Vehicles, Unmanned Combat Air Vehicles and Intelligence Gathering from the Air' (2011) 24 Journal of International Law of Peace and Armed Conflict 81.

6 Protocol Additional to the Geneva Conventions of 12 August 1949 and Relating to the Protection of Victims of International Armed Conflicts (adopted 8 June 1977, entered into force 7 December 1978) 1125 UNTS 3, art 52(3); Dan Saxon (ed), *International Humanitarian Law and the Changing Technology of War* (Martinus Nijhoff Publishers 2013) 5–6; Anthony D'Amato, 'International Law, Cybernetics and Cyberspace' in Michael Schmitt and Brian O'Donnell (eds), *International Law Studies Vol. 76 Computer Network Attacks and International Law* (U.S. Naval War College 2002) 59–71; Tony Gillespie and Robin West, 'Requirements for Autonomous Unmanned Air Systems Set by Legal Issue' (2010) 4 The International C2 Journal 4.

7 See ICRC, *Report on Autonomous Weapon Systems: Technical, Military, Legal and Humanitarian Aspects* (ICRC 2014) 1–43; Michael Schmitt, 'Autonomous Weapon Systems and International Humanitarian Law: A Reply to the Critics' (2013) 9 Harvard National Security Journal 14, 17, 18; ICRC, *A Guide to the Legal Review of New Weapons, Means and Methods of Warfare* (ICRC 2006) 4.

8 See Michael Schmitt, *Tallinn Manual on the Law Applicable to Cyber Warfare: prepared by the International Group of Experts at the Invitation of NATO Cooperative Cyber Defence Center of Excellence* (CUP 2013); David Turns, 'Cyber War and the Concept of "Attack"' in Dan Saxon (ed), *International Humanitarian Law and the Changing Technology of War* (Martinus Nijhoff Publisher

imagine the (fictitious?) example that a civilian computer expert programs a virus for a cyber attack against a state-owned nuclear power plant, shutting down the control systems and leading to a meltdown and the emission of nuclear radiation affecting thousands of civilians.

2.2 New Forms of Conflict

Another challenge for IHL surrounds the new forms of conflict we are currently witnessing.

2.2.1 Increase in non-international armed conflicts

Since the end of the Cold War there has been a rise in non-international armed conflicts. For example, the early phase of war in the Balkans, the civil wars in Rwanda, the Democratic Republic of the Congo (DRC), Uganda, and Darfur, Sudan. Partly because of a lack of stability in a world dominated by the bipolarity of the East–West conflict, the last almost 30 years have witnessed a growing number of 'identity wars' or 'ethnic wars' in which tensions which had been suppressed before by the East–West divide have come to the forefront.

2.2.2 Transnational armed conflicts

A special form of non-international armed conflict that has recently grown in frequency includes the so-called 'transnational armed conflict', where a non-state armed group is engaged in protracted armed violence with a state. However, in this situation it is not operating from the territory of said state, but from across an international border.[9] Usually the respective neighboring state either tolerates the actions of the non-state actor or does not have complete control over its own territory. The actions of ISIS in Syria and Iraq are an example.

2.2.3 Low-level conflicts and anti-terrorism measures

Maybe one of the biggest challenges we face in today's world is the increase in low-level conflicts. These tend to have fewer casualties compared to traditional armed conflicts, but last over a longer period of time. They will often be characterized by an 'asymmetrical warfare' scenario, i.e. a situation where the relative military power, strategies, and tactics of the belligerents differ significantly. Examples include where a state with overwhelming military and technological force fights a weaker non-state party that is forced to resort to non-conventional tactics, such as terrorism and guerilla warfare. We have seen this kind of conflict, e.g. in Chechnya, Darfur, Afghanistan, Iraq, and many more. Since 9/11 there has also been a tendency – by politicians and the general public – to frame anti-terrorism measures as armed conflicts, as part of the so-called 'Global War on Terror'. However, the 'War on Terror' itself – starting on 11 September 2001 and continuing until the last terrorist cell has been eliminated – in general does not fit well into the existing categories of armed conflict, missing either the international armed conflict component of the use of armed force between two sovereign states, and the 'protracted armed violence' requirement for non-international

---

2013) 211–15; Herbert Lin, 'Cyber Conflict and International Humanitarian Law' (2010) 94 International Review of the Red Cross 515, 518–19; ICRC, *International Humanitarian Law and the Challenges of Contemporary Armed Conflict*, 32nd International Conference of the Red Cross and the Red Crescent (ICRC 2015).

[9] See Constantin von der Groeben, *Transnational Conflicts and International Law* (Institute for International Peace and Security Law 2014).

armed conflict. However, armed activity in the context of counter-terrorist operations can pass the threshold of an international armed conflict, for example in the case of the coalition military operations against Afghanistan and Iraq. However, there seems to be the need to assess this on a case-by-case basis.[10]

2.3 The Rise of Non-State Actors

The last important key feature of all these 'new' forms of conflict is that they involve a growing number of non-state actors, as demonstrated in the context of current civil wars. For example, the Sudan People's Liberation Army in Sudan, or in transnational conflicts, for example ISIS in Syria, and finally in the 'War on Terror' against al-Qaeda. This rise of non-state actors raises serious issues, including the question of how non-state actors are bound by IHL, since they usually have not given explicit 'consent' to the respective conventions, as states do through ratification of international treaties, or when state practice is taken into account in the context of customary law rules.[11] As already mentioned above, in asymmetrical conflicts with states, these non-state actors may be tempted to use means and methods of warfare that are prohibited under IHL. In addition, problems arise like the direct participation of civilians in hostilities: if a civilian carries out an attack, they lose their protection as a civilian and become a legitimate military target. But how does one deal with this when the non-state actor is in principle using civilians in order to carry out their attacks?

3. THE ROLE OF CUSTOMARY INTERNATIONAL HUMANITARIAN LAW

3.1 The Recent Resurgence of Custom in International Humanitarian Law

For a long time, especially after the Second World War, the role of customary law was not the prime focus of international (humanitarian) lawyers, simply because there was greater willingness amongst states to codify international law in multilateral treaties – as exemplified by the 1949 Geneva Conventions and their 1977 Additional Protocols, the 1980 Weapons Convention, and the 1997 Anti-Personnel Landmines Convention. It was only with the rise of international criminal law at the beginning of the 1990s and the establishment of the ad hoc International Criminal Tribunals for the Former Yugoslavia (ICTY) and Rwanda (ICTR) that

---

10 See ICRC, *International Humanitarian Law and the Challenges of Contemporary Armed Conflicts*, 30th International Conference of the Red Cross and the Red Crescent (ICRC 2007) 8: 'each situation of organized armed violence must be examined in the specific context in which it takes place and must be legally qualified as armed conflict, or not, based on the actual circumstances. (…) The law of war was tailored for situations of armed conflict (…) it is both dangerous and unnecessary, in practical terms, to apply international humanitarian law to situations that do not amount to war'; ICRC, *International Humanitarian Law and the Challenges of Contemporary Armed Conflict*, 32nd International Conference (n 8) 16–19.

11 See Marco Sassoli, 'Taking Armed Groups Seriously: Ways to Improve their Compliance with International Humanitarian Law' (2010) 8 Journal of International Humanitarian Legal Studies 13–14; Sandesh Sivakumaran, 'Implementing Humanitarian Norms through Non-State Armed Groups' in Heike Krieger (ed), *Inducing Compliance with International Humanitarian Law, Lessons from the African Great Lake Region* (CUP 2015) 125–33.

this changed. The increased necessity to apply IHL during the trials of the ad hoc Tribunals, especially with regard to violations committed in non-international armed conflicts, triggered a new devotion to the use and examination of customary international (humanitarian) law. In its landmark 1995 Decision concerning Jurisdiction, the ICTY Appeals Chamber in the *Tadić* case embarked on a pages-long journey through existing customary IHL with a particular focus on the rules applicable in non-international armed conflict. The background for this was the fact that the ICTY Statute did not expressly mention in either Article 2 or 3 that the ICTY would also have jurisdiction for war crimes committed in a non-international armed conflict. However, the Appeals Chamber interpreted Article 3 in a way that the mentioned violation of the 'laws or customs of war' would also encompass jurisdiction over violations of customary IHL – ignoring in a way the following list of 'Hague Law' rules, which seemed to indicate that Article 3 was actually dealing with the rules governing the traditional means and methods of warfare.[12]

The rest is (legal) history. The ICTY and the ICTR confirmed the existing customary IHL rules in the following years of their jurisprudence in various decisions,[13] and in 1998, states embraced a lot of the stated customary law rules via adoption of the Rome Statute which established a permanent International Criminal Court (ICC). At the same time, and with the mandate of the International Red Cross and Red Crescent Conference, the International Committee of the Red Cross (ICRC) initiated a process of collecting and documenting the existing customary rules of IHL in the context of the ICRC Study on Customary International Law. After a ten-year process and with the help of researchers and experts in nearly 50 states, the ICRC published the Customary International Humanitarian Law Study in 2005.[14] While some of the results and part of the methodology received criticism from academics[15] as well as states, the ICRC Study had an important impact on the use of customary IHL in international and national courts and tribunals, as well as by political decision-makers.[16] It showed the need for a consensus on the methodology used to establish the rules of customary IHL in order to give legitimacy to the decisions of international (criminal) courts and tribunals, not only because of the principle of legality (*nullum crimen sine lege*), but also to ensure that the respective IHL rules are applied by state and non-state actors on the battlefield. This is particularly important

---

[12] *Tadić Case* (Appeals Chamber Decision on Jurisdiction) ICTY-94-1 (2 October 1995), para 99; with regard to the results see paras 100–101.

[13] For an overview of the jurisprudence, see Larissa van den Herik, *The Contribution of the Rwanda Tribunal to the Development of International Law* (Martinus Nijhoff Publisher 2005); Schlütter (n 4).

[14] See Jean-Marie Henckaerts and Louise Doswald-Beck (eds), *Customary International Humanitarian Law, Vol 1: Rules* (CUP 2005).

[15] Daniel Bethlehem, 'The Methodological Framework of the Study' in Elizabeth Wilmshurst and Susan Breau (eds), *Perspectives on the ICRC Study on Customary International Humanitarian Law* (CUP 2007) 3–14 and Ian Scobbie, 'The Approach to Customary International Law in the Study' in Elizabeth Wilmshurst and Susan Breau (eds), *Perspectives on the ICRC Study on Customary International Humanitarian Law* (CUP 2007) 15–49.

[16] For an in-depth justification of the methodology of the ICRC study, Jean-Marie Henckaerts, 'Study on Customary Rules of International Humanitarian Law: A Contribution to the Understanding and Respect for the Rule of Law in Armed Conflict' (2005) 87 International Review of the Red Cross 175; idem, 'Customary International Humanitarian Law: A Rejoinder to Judge Aldrich' (2006) 76 British Yearbook of International Law 525; idem, 'Customary International Humanitarian Law: A Response to US Comments' (2007) 89 International Review of the Red Cross 473.

since some of the traditional rules governing the conduct of hostilities were codified in the 1977 Additional Protocols I and II of the Geneva Conventions, but have not been universally ratified.[17] The most important aspect to consider within this current examination, however, is that new customary IHL rules might develop vis-à-vis the use of modern technologies or ways warfare is conducted in modern conflict situations.

3.2 The Benefits of Customary International Law in Addressing Recent Developments

Before we take a closer look at the methodology used to determine existing customary international law, it is important to recall the benefits of using customary IHL to overcome the challenges posed by changes in modern warfare mentioned above.

3.3 In Relation to New Military Technologies

Like most legal systems, IHL makes use of certain general principles – codified in treaty law – which should also provide guidance as to how to deal with new military technologies such as drones or cyber warfare. Therefore, one way of addressing new means and methods of warfare is to apply the general principles and rules governing the conduct of hostilities as laid down in international conventions, especially in Additional Protocol I. These principles include the principle of distinction, the principle of proportionality, the principle of necessity, the principle to take precautions in attack, and the prohibition against unnecessary suffering. Applying *existing* treaty law and finding the correct interpretation of the treaty provisions is the method used in the *Tallinn Manual on International Law Applicable to Cyber Warfare.* The Manual explicitly states in its introduction to the 2nd edition that 'it is difficult to definitely identify any cyber-specific customary international law'.[18] Nevertheless, the Tallinn experts obviously agreed, 'that, as formulated, [the rules] reflect customary international law (unless they expressly reference a treaty) as applied in the cyber context'.[19] This seems to be a very ambitious endeavor, given the quite restrictive public information on state practice in this area. From the current author's perspective, it would probably be more honest to say that the Tallinn rules are general IHL principles, which have been 'transferred' to the cyber domain. In this context, it is important to state that some of the principles mentioned must often be seen as *too general* to deal with the challenges which arise from the use of new weapons technologies, and therefore it would be helpful to see whether there are actually specific new (customary) international rules developing in this area.

This argument obtains added value when one takes into account that not all states are party to the relevant IHL treaties. While the 1949 Geneva Conventions have been universally ratified, the Additional Protocols still lack universal ratification status. For example, the US is not party to Additional Protocol I, in which we find most of the rules regulating the conduct

---

17 For an overview of the current ratification status of both Additional Protocol I as well as Additional Protocol II, please refer to the ICRC's Treaty Database <https://ihl-databases.icrc.org/applic/ihl/ihl.nsf/vwTreaties1949.xsp> accessed 31 January 2021.

18 Michael Schmitt, *Tallinn Manual 2.0 on the International Law Applicable to Cyber Operations* (2nd edn, CUP 2017) 3.

19 ibid.

of hostilities applicable in international armed conflict. This means that in the case of the use of UAVs ('drones'), which are predominantly used by the US, we can rarely apply Additional Protocol I directly.

When it comes to the advantages of customary international law in the context of the development of new technologies of warfare, one crucial aspect might be that customary international law is able to develop faster than international treaty law. While the International Court of Justice (ICJ) has stated in the *North Sea Continental Shelf* cases that it usually will take some time until a rule of customary international law develops, it has not excluded the scenario whereby rules can also develop in a rather short period of time, as long as the respective practice is general and consistent, but not universal.[20] Customary international law might therefore adapt quicker to new challenges since it does not need the explicit consent of all parties as would be required by a new treaty.

3.4 In Relation to New Forms of Conflict

Customary international law has already played an important role in the assimilation of the legal regimes for international and non-international armed conflict. Due to its historical development, there is still a clearcut distinction between the applicable IHL in international and non-international armed conflicts in treaty law:[21] the majority of IHL treaties were drafted when most wars were taking place between sovereign states. However, the distinction also exists due to the hesitancy of states to let other international actors judge them if they face allegations of IHL violations in cases where government troops are fighting against rebel groups in non-international armed conflict. As a result, there are far fewer treaty rules that apply to non-international armed conflict: In the four Geneva Conventions, there is only Common Article 3, compared to several hundred other articles that relate to international armed conflict. Even Additional Protocol II, which expands the number of rules applicable to non-international armed conflict, has only 28 articles compared to 102 articles in Additional Protocol I (dealing with international armed conflict). However, through an extensive study of state practice and *opinio juris*, the ICTY and ICTR, and later the ICRC, were able to extend many of the IHL rules traditionally applicable to only international armed conflict to non-international armed conflict.[22] Here we can clearly see the effect which customary IHL can have in terms of adapting the legal regime to respond to new challenges: The 2005 ICRC

---

[20] *North Sea Continental Shelf cases* (Federal Republic of Germany v Denmark; Federal Republic of Germany v the Netherlands) (Judgment) [1969] ICJ Rep 43 para 74; Maurice Mendelson, 'The Formation of Customary International Law' (1998) 272 Recueil des Cours de l'Académie de Droit International 211.

[21] On this distinction, please see Dapo Akande, 'Classification of Armed Conflicts: Relevant Legal Concepts' in Elizabeth Wilmshurst (ed), *International Law and the Classification of Conflicts* (OUP 2012) ch 3, Oxford Legal Studies Research Paper No 50/2012 <https://ssrn.com/abstract=2132573> accessed 31 January 2021.

[22] For an extensive examination of this process, please refer to Robert Heinsch, 'Judicial "Law-Making" in the Jurisprudence of the ICTY and ICTR in Relation to Protecting Civilians from Mass Violence: How Can Judge-Made Law Be Brought into Coherence with the Doctrine of the Formal Sources of International Law?' in Philipp Ambach, Frédéric Bostedt, Grant Dawson and Steve Kostas, *The Protection of Non-Combatants During Armed Conflict and Safeguarding the Rights of Victims in Post-Conflict Society* (Brill Nijhoff 2015) 297–330.

Study on Customary International Humanitarian Law made clear that only 16 (10%) of the 161 customary legal rules identified in the study are solely *applicable in international armed conflicts*. That means that 90% of the identified customary IHL rules are applicable in *both international and non-international armed conflict*.

3.5 In Relation to New (Non-State) Actors

Customary IHL can, however, also have a decisive advantage with regard to the tendency of modern conflicts to involve a high number of non-state actors. Non-state actors are usually not part of the international law-making process when it comes to treaty law. An exception are those moments when non-governmental organizations participate in diplomatic conferences which lead up to the passing of a new IHL treaty, or when they exert influence on national governments. However, the practice of certain rebel groups in non-international armed conflict, as well as the pronouncements of organizations like the ICRC, have been taken into account when determining 'state' practice and *opinio juris*.[23] This should be, however, mentioned with a word of care. The Special Rapporteur of the International Law Commission has clarified in his Second Report on Identification of Customary International Law that 'general practice' refers to the fact 'that it is primarily the practice of States that contributes to the creation, or expression, of rules of customary international law'.[24] And going even one step further, he stated in the Third Report on Identification of Customary International Law that '[c]onduct by other non-State actors [other than international organizations] is not practice for the purposes of formation or identification of customary international law.'[25] This approach found its way finally into paragraph 3 of the Conclusion 4 of the 2018 Draft Conclusions on Identification of Customary International Law, in which it is clarified that 'Conduct of other actors is not practice that contributes to the formation, or expression, of rules of customary international law, but may be relevant when assessing the practice referred to in paragraphs 1 and 2'.[26] While this traditional approach towards the formation of customary international law is understandable from the perspective of the Special Rapporteur of the International Law Commission, it nevertheless begs the question: In the area of armed conflict, do we not need a modified process for the determination of customary IHL rules?

---

[23] *Tadić Case* (n 12) para 109.

[24] ILC, 'Second report on identification of customary international law' (22 May 2014) UN Doc A/CN.4/672, 18 <http://legal.un.org/docs/?symbol=A/CN.4/672> accessed 31 January 2021.

[25] ILC, 'Third report on identification of customary international law' (27 March 2015) UN Doc A/CN.4/682, 54 <http://legal.un.org/docs/?symbol=A/CN.4/682> accessed 31 January 2021.

[26] ILC, 'Draft conclusions on identification of customary international law, with commentaries', adopted by the International Law Commission at its seventieth session, in 2018, and submitted to the General Assembly as a part of the Commission's report covering the work of that session (A/73/10). The report is also available in *Yearbook of the International Law Commission, 2018*, vol. II, Part Two <https://legal.un.org/ilc/texts/instruments/english/draft_articles/1_13_2018.pdf> accessed 31 January 2021.

4. HOW CUSTOMARY LAW CAN RESPOND TO CHALLENGES OF MODERN WARFARE: DO WE NEED A MODIFIED PROCESS OF CUSTOMARY INTERNATIONAL LAW IN THE FIELD OF INTERNATIONAL HUMANITARIAN LAW?

As we have seen in the previous section, customary international law can have several advantages with regard to the area of IHL. The question that remains is whether we need a modified process with regard to the formation and/or determination of customary IHL. The reason for this might come from the fact that IHL regulates one of the most extreme circumstances of human society: war. As Sir Hersch Lauterpacht once famously said: 'If international law is, in some ways, at the vanishing point of law, the law of war is, perhaps even more conspicuously, at the vanishing point of international law.'[27] We will now take a closer look at whether or not this is really true, and whether this is justification enough to modify the law-creating process for customary law in the area of IHL.

In general, Article 38 of the ICJ Statute is rather clear on the requirements which are necessary in order to determine customary international law: It states that international custom is to be seen as 'general practice accepted as law'. From this principle, the ICJ, other tribunals, as well as commentators have derived that the traditional method requires two elements: a) one objective element (state practice), and b) one subjective element (*opinio juris*).[28] This has been confirmed by the ICJ (among others) in the *North Sea Continental Shelf Cases*, the *Continental Shelf Case (Libya v Malta), the Nicaragua Case*, as well as the *Nuclear Weapons Advisory Opinion.*[29] This two-pronged approach was also confirmed by the Special Rapporteur of the International Law Commission, Sir Michael Wood, in his *Second Report on Identification of Customary International Law*, and resulted in Conclusion 2 ('Two constituent elements') of the 2018 Draft Conclusions, which reads: 'To determine the existence and content of a rule of customary international law, it is necessary to ascertain whether there is a general practice that is accepted as law (opinio juris)'.[30]

However, since the 1995 *Tadić* decision by the Appeals Chamber of the ICTY, there has been extensive debate about the formation of custom in IHL.[31] In particular, there have been

---

[27] Hersch Lauterpacht, 'The Problem of the Revision of the Law of War' (1952) 29 British Yearbook of International Law 360.

[28] See the 1945 Statute of the International Court of Justice (ICJ) (adopted 26 June 1945, entered into force 24 October 1945) 39 AJIL Supp. 215, art 38 (1) lit. b); representing the opinion of many: Ian Brownlie, *Principles of International Law* (OUP 2003) 4–6. For a more detailed discussion of the creation of customary international law see Mendelson, 'The Formation of Customary International Law' (n 20) 159–60; Patrick Daillier and Alain Pellet, *Droit International Public* (LGDJ 2002) paras 207–208.

[29] North Sea Continental Shelf cases (n 20) para 74; Continental Shelf Case (Libya v Malta) (Judgment) (1985) ICJ Rep 29–30 para 27; Case Concerning the Military and Paramilitary Activities in and against Nicaragua (Nicaragua v United States of America) [1986] ICJ Rep 97 para 183; Legality of the Threat or Use of Nuclear Weapons (Advisory Opinion) [1996] ICJ Rep 253 para 64.

[30] ILC, 'Draft conclusions on identification of customary international law' (n 26).

[31] See, for example Nirmala Chandrahasan, 'The Continuing Role of Customary International Law in the Development of International Humanitarian Law' (2009) 21 Sri Lanka Journal of International Law 55; George Aldrich, 'Customary International Law – An Interpretation on behalf of the International Committee of the Red Cross' (2006) 76 British Yearbook of International Law 503; Michael Bothe, 'Customary International Humanitarian Law: Some Reflections on the ICRC Study' (2005) 8 Yearbook

arguments in favor of a process of customary international law in IHL in which the role of 'state practice' is reduced, while more emphasis is put on the subjective requirement of *opinio juris.*

4.1 Benefits of Reducing the 'State Practice' Criterion of Customary Law Formation in the Realm of International Humanitarian Law

In order to evaluate whether there is a need to modify the requirements for customary law in IHL, we will have a look at the arguments in favor of reducing the importance of the objective criterion with regard to customary IHL. One of the most important arguments put forward when discussing the law-creation process with regard to customary law in IHL are the practical difficulties in determining actual state practice on the battlefield. As was stated by the ICTY Appeals Chamber in the *Tadić* case: 'when attempting to ascertain State practice [...] it is difficult, if not impossible, to pinpoint the actual behavior of the troops in the field for the purpose of establishing whether they in fact comply with, or disregard, certain standards of behavior.'[32]

This is still a very valid point, and has recently been reaffirmed in the context of cyber warfare by Mike Schmitt and Sean Watts in their article on the decline of *opinio juris* in the field of customary IHL.[33] Even the ICRC does not always have access to the (normal) battlefield, and if it does, it usually does not publish reports on what is happening there. In addition, the parties to the conflict will sometimes withhold information deliberately or false information will be distributed.

This problem can also be seen in relation to the use of new means and methods of warfare: for example, with regard to cyber warfare, due to the anonymity of the Internet it is almost an inherent characteristic that an attack as such is invisible, while only the effects of such an attack can be seen. Another illustration comes from the use of remote-controlled weapons – they may be used in remote areas of a country, for example in the mountains of Pakistan, where there is hardly any supervision by neutral agencies. This makes it very difficult to find reliable information on the practice of states in this area. The states themselves would usually have this information, but they are unlikely to share the data with other actors due to secrecy issues.

Another important aspect of determining customary international law in the field of IHL is the fact that most respective state practice needs to be found in relation to prohibitive norms. That means that a positive example for complying with a respective IHL norm would be an omission. In IHL, the majority of norms are *prohibitive norms*,[34] like, for example, the

of International Humanitarian Law 143; Yoram Dinstein, 'The ICRC Customary International Law Study' (2006) 36 Israel Yearbook on Human Rights 1; Dieter Fleck, 'International Accountability for Violations of the Jus in Bello: The Impact of the ICRC Study on Customary International Humanitarian Law' (2006) 11 Journal of Conflict and Security Law 179; Jean-Marie Henckaerts, 'Study on Customary Rules of International Humanitarian Law: Purpose, Coverage and Methodology' (1999) 81 International Review of the Red Cross 660; David Turns, 'Weapons in the ICRC Study on Customary International Humanitarian Law' (2006) 11 Journal of Conflict and Security Law 201.

32 *Tadić Case* (n 12) para 99.

33 Michael Schmitt and Sean Watts, 'The Decline of International Humanitarian Law *Opinio Juris* and the Law of Cyber Warfare' (2015) 50 Texas International Law Journal 189–90.

34 Sonja Boelaert-Suominen, 'Grave Breaches, Universal Jurisdiction and Internal Armed Conflicts: Is Customary International Law Moving Towards a Uniform Enforcement Mechanism for All Armed Conflicts?' (2000) 5 Journal of Conflict and Security Law 66.

prohibition against indiscriminate attacks. As a consequence, a positive affirmation of one of these norms would be reflected not through an active behavior but through an *omission*[35] (i.e. not launching an indiscriminate attack). That this is a valid point is proven by the currently ongoing 'IHL-in-Action' project between the ICRC and four IHL clinics: Leiden Law School, Emory Law School, Radzyner Law School, and Roma Tre University are examining conflict situations with the aim of finding positive examples which demonstrate respect for IHL.[36] The researchers involved in this project are encountering daily challenges in finding reliable information on examples for compliance with IHL, also because media reports usually concentrate on violations, and states label the relevant information classified.[37]

Finally, some voices claim that because of the devastating effect of today's military activities in the context of the law of armed conflict, humanitarian concerns demand that certain IHL norms might have become customary international law before the respective requirements are actually put into (state) practice. They justify this approach by relying on the famous Martens Clause.[38]

4.2 Different Approaches to Customary International Law in Order to Adapt International Humanitarian Law to Modern Warfare

As we have seen, customary IHL provides decisive advantages when responding to challenges posed by modern warfare, especially because the norm-creating process in customary international law is less formal than that of international treaty law. The main question is, however, how strictly the two requirements of state practice and *opinio juris* have to be fulfilled in order to give rise to a new norm of international (humanitarian) law. In this regard, different approaches have been put forward in order to reflect the current system of law-making in a realistic way. Not all of the theoretical approaches are necessarily directly related to the area of IHL. They should nevertheless be taken into account in order to find the best way to make IHL responsive to the challenges created by modern conflicts.

---

35 With regard to the question of omissions and the development of customary law, see Heike Spieker, *Völkergewohnheitsrechtlicher Schutz der natürlichen Umwelt im internationalen bewaffneten Konflikt* (Universitätsverlag Dr. N. Brockmeyer 1992) 80–81. In general, see Maurice Mendelson, 'State Acts and Omissions as Explicit Claims' in Michel Virally (ed), *Le Droit International au Service de la Paix, de la Justice et du Developement: Melanges* (Pedone 1991) 373.

36 For details on this project, please refer to <www.kalshovengieskesforum.com/ihl-in-action/> accessed 31 January 2021 and Juliane Garcia Ravel and Vincent Bernard, 'Changing the narrative on international humanitarian law' (*ICRC*, 24 November 2017) <https://blogs.icrc.org/law-and-policy/2017/11/24/changing-the-narrative-on-international-humanitarian-law/> accessed 31 January 2021.

37 For a summary of what leads to respecting IHL, please refer to Juliane Garcia Ravel and Madalena Vasconcelos Rosa, 'IHL in action: seven patterns of respect' (*ICRC*, 19 November 2020) <https://blogs.icrc.org/law-and-policy/2020/11/19/ihl-in-action-seven-patterns-respect/> accessed 31 January 2021.

38 See Antonio Cassese, 'The Martens Clause: Half a Loaf or Simply Pie in the Sky?' (2000) 11 European Journal of International Law 187.

4.2.1 *Opinio juris* being more important[39] (Cheng 1983)

One of the most extreme theoretical approaches to customary international law is that promulgated by Bin Cheng, who, in 1983, put forward the view that *opinio juris* should be given decisive weight when determining customary international law. From his perspective, the objective element of state practice could be completely neglected: 'As international law is a horizontal legal system in which states are both the law-makers and the subjects of the legal system, *opinio juris* can arise or change instantaneously.'[40] This also makes it possible to witness the creation of 'instant customary international law'.[41] While his theory was originally developed in the context of international space law, it seems not too far-fetched to transfer the approach to IHL, because of the difficulties of ascertaining actual state practice on the battlefield. This difficulty was later elaborately discussed in the 1995 *Tadić* Jurisdiction decision,[42] but instead of choosing the approach brought forward by Cheng, to base the development of customary IHL solely on *opinio juris*, the ICTY chose a more indirect approach, by labeling selected documents expressing governments' and other state actors' views as 'verbal' practice.[43] While this *prima facie* circumvents the criticism that the Tribunal would ignore the second 'practice' requirement, in the end it is not as 'honest' as Cheng's theory, and leads to the problem that it might be that the same action is counted as state practice as well as *opinio juris*.

4.2.2 Sliding scale theory (Kirgis 1987)

One approach which takes into account the fact that state practice and *opinio juris* will not always be available in the same density, is Kirgis's so-called 'sliding scale theory'. While acknowledging the general validity of the two-element requirement as laid down in Article 38 of the ICJ Statute, he is of the opinion that the subjective and objective elements can be handled in a more flexible manner.[44] According to his view, the more proof of coherent state practice that can be found, the less evidence of the subjective element is necessary.[45] And this can also be applied vice versa, meaning that if there is a dominant *opinio juris* one can almost completely neglect the search for respective state practice.[46] In this regard, Kirgis's theory bridges in some ways the two extremes of Cheng's 'only-opinio-juris' approach on the one hand, and Mendelson's emphasis on the objective element, on the other. Because of its flexibility, Kirgis's approach could have various benefits for the realm of IHL. His theory is able to take into account situations where, the acquisition of information on 'hard' state practice is difficult to obtain due to the specific circumstances on the battlefield, but nevertheless, there is clear proof of a coherent and dominant *opinio juris*, creating the ability to prove the existence of a customary law norm, while still maintaining the two-element approach.

---

39 Bin Cheng, 'Custom: The Future of General State Practice in a Divided World' in Ronald Macdonald and Douglas Johnston (eds), *The Structure and Process of International Law: Essays in Legal Philosophy Doctrine and Theory* (Martinus Nijhoff Publisher 1983) 515.

40 ibid 532, 536.

41 Bin Cheng, 'United Nations Resolutions on Outer Space: "Instant" International Customary Law' (1965) 23 Indian Journal of International Law 46.

42 *Tadić Case* (n 12) para 99.

43 ibid.

44 Frederic Kirgis, 'Custom on a Sliding Scale' (1987) 81 American Journal of International Law 146.

45 ibid 149.

46 ibid.

4.2.3 Use of verbal practice (*Tadić* 1995)

The 1995 ICTY Appeals Chamber decision on jurisdiction in the *Tadić* case is probably one of the most important decisions by an international court or tribunal with regard to the existence of customary international law in the area of IHL. The background of this decision was that the Tribunal's jurisdiction had been challenged by the defendant and the Tribunal needed to find a way to justify that it had jurisdiction over war crimes committed in non-international, as well as international, armed conflict. Using Article 3 of the ICTY Statute, which in the view of the Appeals Chamber also conferred jurisdiction for war crimes under customary international law onto the ICTY, the judges established that indeed there was established customary international law which penalized serious violations of IHL as war crimes also in non-international armed conflict. In order to prove this, they relied heavily on so-called 'verbal practice' that they derived from: official pronouncements of states, military manuals, as well as judicial decisions.[47] They justified reliance on 'verbal practice' on the basis that first-hand information from the battlefield is usually very hard to get hold of.[48] The Appeals Chamber held that

> when attempting to ascertain State practice with a view to establishing the existence of a customary rule or general principle, it is difficult, if not impossible, to pinpoint the actual behavior of the troops in the field for the purpose of establishing whether they in fact comply with, or disregard, certain standards of behaviour.[49] [Therefore it concluded that] reliance must primarily be placed on such elements as official pronouncements of States, military manuals and judicial decisions.[50]

On the other hand, it clarified that due to the fact that IHL mainly consists of prohibitions, positive practice supporting the existence of a customary IHL rule in most cases would constitute an omission. For example, demonstrating that the torturing of prisoners of war (POWs) is illegal would need to be proven by the fact that POWs were *not* tortured. Therefore, it would be much more indicative of the existence of a respective customary norm if it was contained in military manuals distributed to states' armed forces. The ICRC used a similar approach in its 2005 Customary Law Study,[51] as did the ICJ in the *Nicaragua* case.[52]

However, these decisions raised the problem as to whether those examples of 'verbal practice' could also constitute proof of *opinio juris* and whether this 'double-counting' would be acceptable according to the two-element approach of Article 38 of the ICJ Statute.[53] Although

---

47 *Tadić Case* (n 12) para 118, see also Gerhard Werle, *Völkerstrafrecht* (Mohr Siebeck 2003) 132 confirms that in the context of International Criminal Law, verbal practice as expressed through official declarations, plays an important role; Edward Kwakwa, *The International Law of Armed Conflict: Personal and Material Fields of Application* (Kluwer 1992) 29, however, sees verbal practice as less important than the actual combat practice on the battlefield.

48 *Tadić Case* (n 12) para 99.

49 ibid.

50 ibid.

51 Henckaerts and Doswald-Beck (n 14) xxv, xxviii, xxxii; Henckaerts, 'Study on Customary Rules of International Humanitarian Law: A Contribution to the Understanding and Respect for the Rule of Law in Armed Conflict' (n 16); Henckaerts, 'Customary International Humanitarian Law: A Rejoinder to Judge Aldrich' (n 16).

52 Case Concerning the Military and Paramilitary Activities in and against Nicaragua (n 29) paras 187–88; Theodor Meron, 'The Geneva Conventions as Customary Law' (1987) 81 American Journal of International Law 362.

53 Mendelson, 'The Formation of Customary International Law' (n 20) 206–207.

this approach does not explicitly change the two-element approach of requiring both state practice and *opinio juris*,[54] it does, however, give rise to the possibility of the same statement being used as evidence of state practice *and opinio juris*.[55] States indirectly accepted the ICTY's method by agreeing to the Rome Statute's (ICC) codification of war crimes in such a way that most of the war crimes for non-international armed conflict codified in Article 8 of the ICC Statute, were previously considered international crimes under customary law according to the 1995 *Tadić* decision.[56] The validity of this approach was finally also confirmed by the International Law Commission, since their Conclusion 6 ('Forms of Practice') of the Draft Conclusions on Customary International Law states that 'Practice may take a wide range of forms. It includes both physical and *verbal* acts. It may, under certain circumstances, include inaction.'[57]

4.2.4 State practice being more important, *opinio juris* only in doubtful cases (Mendelson 1998)[58]

While Cheng had (over)emphasized the overwhelming importance of *opinio juris*, Maurice Mendelson, who at the same time was the first Rapporteur and later Chairman of the International Law Association's (ILA) Committee dealing with the formation of customary international law, chose the opposite approach, by emphasizing the importance of the objective element of customary international law. The subjective element would only be necessary to consider in problematic cases where state practice is not conclusive nor contradictory. Nevertheless, for Mendelson, the decisive element – state practice – has to be confirmed in a context that gives rise to the 'legitimate expectation of similar conduct in the future'.[59] Picking up on the Shakespeare quote at the beginning of this chapter: For Mendelson, deeds are more important than the words, because it is easy to say something in the quiet room of a government office or in the teaching room of a military barracks, but much more difficult to follow through with appropriate behavior. This might be especially true with regard to behavior on the battlefield. Mendelson's approach was later more or less completely confirmed by the 2000 London final report of the ILA Committee,[60] which is not surprising considering the

---

54 Theodor Meron, 'The Continuing Role of Custom in the Formation of International Humanitarian Law' (1996) 90 American Journal of International Law 238, 239, states that 'the Appeals Chamber at least formally adhered to the two elements'.

55 Many academics do not see it as double-counting in the strict sense, since they see verbal practice as sufficient evidence of the objective element, and from this State practice can induce the respective *opinio juris*.

56 See Claus Kreß, 'War Crimes Committed in Non-International Armed Conflict and the Emerging System of International Criminal Justice' (2000) 30 Israel Yearbook on Human Rights 109, with the statement that the acceptance by the Rome Statute of the results found through this method by the ICTY indicates that states obviously agreed with the Tribunal's approach with regard to identifying war crimes in non-international armed conflicts.

57 See ILC, 'Draft conclusions on identification of customary international law' (n 26) [italics by author].

58 Mendelson, 'The Formation of Customary International Law' (n 20) 197, 292.

59 ibid 188.

60 Committee on Formation of Customary (General) International Law, 'Statement of Principles Applicable to the Formation of General Customary International Law' in ILA (ed), *Final Report of the Committee* (ILA 2000) 29–30 <http://www.ila-hq.org/en/committees/index.cfm/cid/30> accessed 31 January 2021.

crucial role Mendelson played in this committee. However, one has to admit that the emphasis on actual state practice has a certain appeal for people who take a positivist approach to international law, as it avoids the danger which arises from approaches which put an emphasis on the subjective element or even on principles of public conscience and humanity, reflecting a more natural law approach.

4.2.5 'Modern positivism' (Simma/Paulus 1999)[61]

Mendelson's (and the ILA report's) emphasis on the objective element has to be seen as a step back to a more traditional view of customary international law, strengthening also the role of the main actors in this area, the state. However, only a year after the publication of Mendelson's article, another influential essay was published by Simma and Paulus describing a more liberal theory of customary international law. This theory would apply especially in the area of human rights law and IHL, and was coined as 'modern positivism'. It denotes a method – especially in the areas of international humanitarian and human rights law – in which the behavior of states, which lies at the border between actual state practice and *opinio juris*, is deemed to be particularly important.[62] It reflects a shift towards a 'softer approach' to evidence of state practice.[63] Picking up on the statements, which we found in the *Tadić* Appeals Decision on Jurisdiction, Simma and Paulus clarified that 'verbal practice' would also fall into this category. According to their view, a partial and slow observance of the norms is seen as evidence of state practice, while contrary practice is downplayed. They also promulgate an apparently 'softer approach' to *opinio juris*. In this context, they look at pronouncements that were previously considered internal affairs, but now have impact on the international level. In addition, in coherence with the statements of the ICJ in the *North Sea Continental Shelf* cases and the *Nuclear Weapons* advisory opinion,[64] it seems possible to derive *opinio juris* of states also from international treaties[65] or voting behavior in international organizations.[66] This scenario reaches a point where it becomes very difficult to clearly distinguish state practice from *opinio juris*. This reminds one of Rein Müllerson's observation from two years earlier, in which he stated that the two elements of customary international law are more or less two sides of the same coin, and therefore 'may be separated for analytical purposes but (…) cannot exist

---

[61] Bruno Simma and Andreas Paulus, 'The Responsibility of Individuals for Human Rights Abuses in Internal Conflicts: A Positivist View' (1999) 93 American Journal of International Law 306.

[62] Kreß (n 56) 108.

[63] Simma and Paulus (n 61) 306.

[64] *North Sea Continental Shelf cases* (n 20) para 74; Legality of the Threat or Use of Nuclear Weapons (n 29) paras 64, 70–73.

[65] Richard Baxter, 'Treaties and Custom' (1970) 129 Recueil des Cours 25; Gary Scott and Craig Carr, 'Multilateral Treaties and the Formation of Customary International Law' (1996) 25 Denver Journal of International Law and Policy 71; Spieker (n 35) 50–51; Mark Villinger, *Customary International Law and Treaties: a case study of their interactions and interrelations with special consideration of the 1969 Vienna Convention on the law of treaties* (Martinus Nijhoff Publishers 1985); Karol Wolfke, 'Treaties and Custom: Aspects of Interrelation' in Jan Klabbers and Rene Lefeber (eds), *Essays on the Law of Treaties: A Collection of Essays in Honour of Bert Vierdag* (Martinus Nijhoff Publishers 1998) 31–32.

[66] Simma and Paulus (n 61) 306–307; Case Concerning the Military and Paramilitary Activities in and against Nicaragua (n 29) para 183; Legality of the Threat or Use of Nuclear Weapons (n 29) paras 160–61, 188–89; Robert Jennings and Arthur Watts, *Oppenheim's International Law* (OUP 1992) 26; Scott and Carr (n 65); Villinger (n 65).

independently from each other'.[67] More than 15 years after Bin Cheng's approach, which is famous for creating instant customary international law through *opinio juris* by decisive state actors in a certain area of international law, Simma and Paulus observe that there have been developments, especially in the area of human rights, where treaties and customary law have been created 'instantly' and have led to overlapping conventional as well as customary law. In the context of IHL, Simma and Paulus in their article state that the international criminal tribunals frequently refer to general principles of IHL, which they deduce from the Geneva Conventions, the Hague Conventions, and other IHL treaties. In the end, this 'strategy' of deriving customary international law from treaty law is nothing new, as it had elaborately been stated in the *North Sea Continental Shelf* cases by the ICJ, affirming that international treaties could a) codify existing customary international law, b) crystalize emerging customary international law, and c) provide the decisive impetus for a new rule of customary international law.[68] This had been equally stated in the 2000 ILA Committee report on the formation of customary international law,[69] and was finally also laid down in the 2018 ILC Draft Conclusions in Paragraph 1 of Conclusion 11, which reads:

> A rule set forth in a treaty may reflect a rule of customary international law if it is established that the treaty rule: (a) codified a rule of customary international law existing at the time when the treaty was concluded; (b) has led to the crystallization of a rule of customary international law that had started to emerge prior to the conclusion of the treaty; or (c) has given rise to a general practice that is accepted as law (opinio juris), thus generating a new rule of customary international law.[70]

4.2.6 The Martens Clause approach (*Kupreškić* trial judgment 2000)

With the impetus created by the jurisprudence of the first truly international criminal tribunals, the ICTY and the ICTR, the end of the 1990s and the beginning of the 2000s represent the time when new progressive theories with regard to the development of customary international law in the area of IHL, were developed on a regular basis. Going a step further than the 'verbal' practice approach of the 1995 *Tadić* Appeals Chamber, and also more progressive than the 'modern positivism' put forward by Simma and Paulus, was the method used by the ICTY Trial Chamber in the 2000 *Kupreškić* Trial Judgment. The Martens Clause has been seen as modifying customary law in IHL in two ways: On the one hand, it is argued that the Clause allows for putting the 'laws of humanity' as well as the 'demands of public conscience' on the same level as customary international law (i.e. the 'established usages') and uses these as historical sources of principles of international law.[71] Concurrently, the requirement of *opinio juris sive necessitatis* assumes an especially important role when determining the existence of a humanitarian rule. However, if one reads the judgment carefully, the Trial Chamber (again with Judge Antonio Cassese presiding over the case) in the *Kupreškić case* did not go as far as some of the academic commentators had suggested – the ICTY Trial Chamber rather used the Martens Clause in order to compensate for the lack of consistent state practice with regards to

---

67 Rein Müllerson, 'On the Nature and Scope of Customary International Law' (1997) 2 Austrian Review of International and European Law 344.

68 North Sea Continental Shelf cases (n 20) para 71.

69 Committee on Formation of Customary (General) International Law (n 60) 46.

70 ILC, 'Draft conclusions on identification of customary international law' (n 26).

71 *Prosecutor v Kupreškić et al* (Judgment) ICTY-95-16-T (14 January 2000) para 527.

the prohibition of reprisals against civilians. It is important to note that the Chamber did not find that the Clause elevated the 'principles of humanity and the dictates of public conscience' to the rank of *independent* sources of law.[72] However, it did find that the Clause attenuated the criterion of state practice, while increasing the importance of *opinio necessitatis*, 'crystalizing as a result of the imperatives of humanity or public conscience'.[73]

4.2.7 Custom through national decisions reflecting *opinio juris* (Special Tribunal for Lebanon 2011)[74]

Most likely one of the latest developments regarding the methodology surrounding sources of IHL was the confirmation by the Special Tribunal for Lebanon of the customary law status of the crime of terrorism. Although this decision does not directly refer to IHL, it reflects an interesting additional approach to the theory of customary international law, as it (again) highlights the importance of an existing *opinio juris.* In this context, it bases the evidence of *opinio juris* very much on reference to national jurisprudence. As described in paragraphs 100 and 101 of the decision:

> 100. In sum, those judgments, viewed in combination with national legislation and the international attitude of States as taken in international fora, evince that the courts thereby intend to apply at the domestic level a notion that is commonly accepted at the international level. In other words, those decisions reflect a legal opinion (*opinio juris*) as to the fundamental elements of the crime of terrorism. Those decisions aim to safeguard national and international exigencies, and are therefore predicated on the notion that there exists an international obligation to prosecute and punish terrorism as a crime based on commonly accepted legal ingredients.
>
> 101. We shall add *ad abundantiam* another argument to support the Appeals Chamber's finding based on convergent national judgments. Even if the view were taken that those national judgments do not advert, not even implicitly, to a customary international rule nor explicitly note that they neither reflect an international obligation of the State nor express a feeling of international legal obligation, nevertheless our conclusion stands. It is supported by the legal criteria suggested on the basis of careful scrutiny of international case law by a distinguished international lawyer, Max Sørensen. According to him one should assume as a starting point the *presumption of the existence of opinio juris whenever a finding is made of a consistent practice*; it would follow that *if one sought to deny in such instances the existence of a customary rule, one must point to the reasons of expediency or those based on comity or political convenience that support the denial of the customary rule.*[75]

This approach in some ways resonates with that of Maurice Mendelson in 1998, namely that *opinio juris* is only necessary in doubtful cases, and seems to switch the burden of proof onto those who do not believe that the respective rule exists.

---

[72] ibid, para 525.

[73] ibid, para 527.

[74] Special Tribunal for Lebanon, Interlocutory Decision on the Applicable Law: Terrorism, Conspiracy, Homicide, Perpetration, Cumulative Charging, Decision of 16 February 2011, STL-II-O 1111 AC/R 176 bis.

[75] ibid, paras 100–101 [italics by author].

5. THE APPROACH REFLECTED IN THE 'DRAFT CONCLUSIONS ON IDENTIFICATION OF CUSTOMARY INTERNATIONAL LAW' OF THE INTERNATIONAL LAW COMMISSION (2018)

The level of importance surrounding the identification of customary international law in today's relations between states can be seen by the fact that in 2012, during its 64th session, the International Law Commission put the topic of 'Formation and evidence of customary international law' (renamed in 2013 to 'Identification of customary international law') on its current agenda, and appointed Sir Michael Wood as the Special Rapporteur.[76] Since May 2013, the Special Rapporteur presented five different reports, dealing with various aspects of the identification of customary international law, and presented detailed draft conclusions with regard to this topic. These 16 Draft Conclusions were passed by the International Law Commission in May 2018 together with the respective commentaries.[77] In this context it is important to note that the first report gave an overview of the different approaches towards customary international law as put forward by a) states and other intergovernmental actors, b) the case law of the ICJ, c) the case law of other courts and tribunals, and d) the work of other bodies.[78] Especially important for the current chapter is the fact that the Commission highlighted the 'need to address (…) whether there are different approaches to the formation and evidence of customary international law in different fields of international law, such as international human rights law, international criminal law and international humanitarian law'.[79] This question, however, was not as explicitly answered in the subsequent reports or the final commentaries as one might have assumed from this starting point. However, throughout the first report one finds some interesting statements that relate to observations which were made during the description with regard to the main approaches towards the development of customary IHL. The first report of the Commission observes that certain commentators have suggested that the ICJ has 'a marked tendency to assert the existence of a customary rule more

[76] ILC, 'Provisional summary record of the 3132nd meeting' (22 May 2012) A/CN.4/SR.3132, 16; ILC, 'Formation and evidence of customary law, Note by Michael Wood Special Rapporteur' (7 May–1 June and 2 July–3 August 2012) <http://legal.un.org/docs/?symbol=A/CN.4/653> accessed 31 January 2021.

[77] See ILC 'Draft Conclusions on Identification of Customary International Law' (n 26).

[78] ILC, 'First report on formation and evidence of customary international law' (17 May 2013) UN Doc A/CN.4/663.

[79] ibid 7–8 with reference among others to Jean d'Aspremont, 'An autonomous regime of identification of customary international humanitarian law: do not say what you do or do not do what you say?' in Raphaël van Steenbergh (ed), *Droit international humanitaire: un régime spécial de droit international?* (Bruylant, 2013) 67–95; Meron, 'The Continuing Role of Custom in the Formation of International Humanitarian Law' (n 54) 238.

than to prove it';[80] what might be even more important is that the report observes that the Court follows 'a rather flexible approach'.[81]

Furthermore, the International Law Commission confirmed in its First Report the observation that while the ICTY in general has confirmed the necessity of establishing both elements of customary international law, state practice and *opinio juris*,[82] the Trial Chamber in *Prosecutor v Kupreškić* used the Martens Clause to overcome situations in which state practice is scant or inconsistent, and therefore the subjective element would become the decisive element.[83] It also took note of the special approach of the Special Tribunal for Lebanon with regard to *opinio juris* being reflected by national judicial decisions,[84] the 2000 London Statement of Principles Applicable to the Formation of (General) Customary International Law,[85] and the ICRC Customary International Law Study.[86] In addition, the First Report also described briefly the existence of 'other approaches to customary international law, sometimes referred to as "modern", that have sought to reinterpret the constitutive elements of customary international law and, consequently, to reframe it as a source of international law',[87] especially those two forms of relaxing either the importance of the objective element,[88] or reducing the role of *opinio juris*.[89] The report highlighted that there is currently a tendency to employ a deductive methodology, deducing 'new customary international law', in order to make customary international law into a 'more rapid and flexible source of international law, one that is able to fulfil a "utopian potential" and "compensate for the rigidity of treaty law", particularly in the fields of human rights, humanitarian and environmental law'.[90] At the same time, the International Law Commission also highlighted that these 'modern' approaches have met 'some fierce criticism',[91] including the 'claim that "modern custom" is, in fact, not customary

---

80 ILC, 'First report on formation and evidence of customary international law' (n 78) 25 with reference to Alain Pellet, 'Shaping the Future of International Law: The Role of the World Court in Law-Making' in Mahnoush H. Arsanjani (ed), *Looking to the Future: Essays on International Law in Honor of W. Michael Reisman* (Brill 2011) 1065, 1076.

81 ILC, 'First report on formation and evidence of customary international law' (n 78) 26 with multiple references in footnote 123.

82 ibid 29, with reference to the cases *Prosecutor v Hadzihasanovic* (Decision on Interlocutory Appeal Challenging Jurisdiction in Relation to Command Responsibility) IT-01-47-AR72 (16 July 2003) para 12; *Prosecutor v Delalic* (Judgment) IT-96-21-T (16 November 1998) paras 302, 256; *Prosecutor v Aleksovski* (Judgment) IT-95-14/1-A (24 March 2000) para 23; *Tadić Case* (Judgment) IT-94-1 (15 July 1999) paras 287–92.

83 ILC, 'First report on formation and evidence of customary international law' (n 78) 29–30.

84 ibid 34.

85 ibid 42.

86 ibid 43.

87 ibid 49.

88 ibid 50.

89 ibid 50.

90 ibid 51; Jörg Kammerhofer, 'Orthodox Generalists and Political Activists in International Legal Scholarship' in Matthew Happold (ed), *International Law in a Multipolar World* (Routledge 2012) 138, 147; Jan Wouters and Cedric Ryngaert, 'Impact on the Process of the Formation of Customary International Law' in Menno Kamminga and Martin Scheinin (eds), *The Impact of Human Rights Law on General International Law* (OUP 2009) 111, 129, 130; David Hunter, James Salzmann and Durwood Zaelke, *International Environmental Law and Policy* (Foundation Press 2002) 312–13.

91 ILC, 'First report on formation and evidence of customary international law' (n 78) 53.

international law at all'.[92] However, the report closes its overview of the different academic approaches with the remark that 'several authors stress that it is precisely its flexibility that makes it a valuable source of international law'.[93]

The ensuing reports of the International Law Commission on the identification of customary international law as well as the final draft conclusions then take a stand on what is actually required in the context of the formation and evidence of customary international law and suggests 16 'conclusions'. Not surprisingly, the committee takes a more traditional view regarding this process, although one can see that at the same time it speaks favorably of certain new developments that have been described above. Without wanting to go through all the subtleties of these five reports which describe the process of identifying customary international law across hundreds of pages, a couple of important statements which are especially relevant for the area of IHL shall be highlighted.

First of all, the International Law Commission follows a rather state-centered approach with regard to the actors that can influence the creation of customary international law. As reflected in Conclusion 4 (1) of the Draft Conclusion, for the objective element, 'The requirement of a general practice, as a constituent element of customary international law, refers primarily to the practice of States that contributes to the formation, or expression, of rules of customary international law',[94] which needs to be read together with Draft Conclusion 4 (3), which elaborates that 'Conduct of other actors is not practice that contributes to the formation, or expression, of rules of customary international law, but may be relevant when assessing the practice referred to in paragraphs 1 and 2'.[95] The only concession made is that according to paragraph 2 of this Conclusion, 'In certain cases, the practice of international organizations also contributes to the formation, or expression, of rules of customary international law.' According to the Special Rapporteur, this last sentence alludes especially to the role the ICRC has played with regard to influencing the development of customary IHL.[96] As specifically stated in the respective commentary to Conclusion 4,

> Official statements of the International Committee of the Red Cross (ICRC), such as appeals for and memorandums on respect for IHL may likewise play an important role in shaping the practice of States reacting to such statements; and publications of the ICRC may assist in identifying relevant practice. Such activities may thus contribute to the development and determination of customary international law, but they are *not* practice as such.[97]

However, the approach taken by the ICTY in the 1995 *Tadić* case to include also practice of rebel groups, i.e. of non-state actors, would be rejected by the International Law Commission's

---

92 ibid with further references in fn 252.

93 ibid 56; Jeremy Pearce, 'Customary International Law: Not Merely Fiction or Myth' (2003) 125 Australian International Law Journal 31; David Bederman, 'Acquiescence, Objection and the Death of Customary International Law' (2010) 21 Duke Journal of Comparative & International Law 41, 42–43.

94 ILC, 'Draft Conclusions on Identification of Customary International Law' (n 26).

95 ibid.

96 ILC, 'Fourth report on the identification of customary international law' (8 March 2016) UN Doc A/CN.4/697, 22 <http://legal.un.org/docs/?symbol=A/CN.4/695> accessed 31 December 2020.

97 ILC, 'Draft Conclusions on Identification of Customary International Law' (n 26) 132 [italics by author].

conclusion.[98] Also, the International Law Commission makes clear that the practice of international organizations will not 'create' the law, but only 'contributes to' the law.[99]

A second major point with regard to the elements necessary to create a new rule of customary international law is that two elements are always required. As laid down in Draft Conclusion 2 [entitled 'Two constituent elements']: 'To determine the existence and content of a rule of customary international law, it is necessary to ascertain whether there is a general practice that is accepted as law (*opinio juris*).'[100] Also in the accompanying commentary to the Special Rapporteur's Second Report, he makes it clear that the approach followed, especially in the area of human rights law, IHL, and international criminal law, according to which only *opinio juris* suffices as the constituting element, should be rejected.[101] Although the Special Rapporteur admits that depending on the area of law there might be a 'difference in the application of the two-element approach in different fields',[102] the important statement is that 'both elements are required'.[103] This would undermine all the approaches mentioned above which either concentrate only on practice (Mendelson and the ILA Report), or give prominence to *opinio juris* (Cheng, Meron, and *Kupreškić*).

However, and this is very important, with regard to the forms which state practice and *opinio juris* can take, the International Law Commission Draft Conclusions allow a certain flexibility, especially with regard to the form of practice. Draft Conclusion 6 clarifies that 'Practice includes both physical and verbal actions'.[104] What might be even more revolutionary is that paragraph 2 of Draft Conclusion 6 lists the possible manifestations of practice, on the one side, and paragraph 2 of Draft Conclusion 10, while listing the possible forms of evidence of *opinio juris*, refers partly to the *same* examples. This includes 'decisions of national courts', and 'conduct in connection with treaties' as well as 'conduct in connection with resolutions adopted by an international organisation or at an intergovernmental conference'.[105] In this regard, one of the most important developments in the area of IHL, which was primarily initiated by the ICTY jurisprudence in the area of war crimes, the use of verbal practice, has been confirmed by the International Law Commission.[106] The only limitation can be found in Draft Conclusion 3 (2), stating that 'Each of the two constituent elements is to be separately ascertained. This requires an assessment of evidence for each element.' In this regard the admission of verbal practice does generally not allow for double-counting as explained by the

---

98 ILC, 'Third report on identification of customary international law' (n 26) 54.

99 ibid.

100 ILC, 'Second report on identification of customary international law' (n 24) 7.

101 ibid 12, stating 'the better view is that this is not the case'.

102 ibid.

103 ibid.

104 ILC, 'Draft Conclusions on Identification of Customary International Law' (n 26).

105 ibid.

106 Which is not completely surprising given the fact that this had been already previously practiced, see *Tadić Case* (Separate Opinion of Judge Sidhwa) ICTY-94-1 (26 January 2000) para 114. Judge Sidhwa uses almost the same list of sources as evidence for state practice when he observes: 'State practices may consist of treaties, decisions of international and national courts, national legislation, diplomatic correspondence (…)'. In this context, he is referring to the enumeration of Brownlie; Mendelson, 'The Formation of Customary International Law' (n 20) 204, who also refers to Brownlie's list, and obviously sees this mainly as a way for the material element (ie state practice) to be reflected. Along the same lines, see Malanczuk, *Akehurst's Modern Introduction to International Law* (Routledge 1997) 39–40.

Special Rapporteur in the Third Report.[107] The interesting formulation here is that the Special Rapporteur uses the words 'should therefore *generally* not serve as evidence of *opinio juris* as well'. This could indicate that under special circumstances it might nevertheless be admitted.

6. EVALUATION AND CONCLUSION

Overall, one can see that throughout the last 30 years a more flexible approach has increasingly been applied to the methodology surrounding the development of customary international law, especially in the area of IHL. This development comprised different aspects; however, the common denominator is that while officially all approaches try to maintain the two-element requirement of Article 38 of the ICJ Statute, the importance – especially of the objective element – is usually downplayed. At the same time, the subjective element – be it in the form of 'verbal practice' or *opinio juris* alone, which under the demands of public conscience and the principles of humanity gives rise to a new rule of customary IHL – is highlighted. Decisive in this development has been the jurisprudence of the ad hoc Tribunals for the Former Yugoslavia as well as for Rwanda and most recently the Special Tribunal for Lebanon. This is partly due to the influence of the late Judge Antonio Cassese, who was involved in three of the landmark decisions dealing with customary international law (1995 *Tadić* Appeals Chamber Decision on Jurisdiction, 2001 *Kupreškić* Trial Chamber Judgment, and 2011 STL Applicable Law Decision). In some ways, one can observe that the results of the methodology applied were accepted with varying degrees of consent. While the results of the ICTY Appeals Chamber with regard to war crimes in non-international armed conflict made their way to a substantial degree into Article 8 of the ICC Statute, and into rules 151–161 of the ICRC Customary Law Study, the finding of the *Kupreškić* Trial Chamber[108] relying on the Martens Clause to reach the conclusion that belligerent reprisals against civilians were part of customary international law, was encountered with more reluctance. Equally controversial was the finding of the Special Tribunal for Lebanon with regard to the customary law status of the crime of terrorism.

While these reactions were especially directed against the existence or non-existence of specific rules, there were also comments with regard to the approach of the ICTY in its decisions and the ICRC in its customary law study, the latter being subject to substantial criticism. For example, the US government criticized the methodology of the ICRC Customary Law Study[109] in various ways: on the one hand, the then US Secretary of State Bellinger criticized in a letter to the ICRC that the study uses insufficiently dense state practice to meet the 'extensive and

[107] ILC, 'Third report on identification of customary international law' (n 25) 6: 'When seeking to identify the existence of a rule of customary international law, evidence of the relevant practice should therefore generally not serve as evidence of *opinio juris* as well: such "double counting" (repeat referencing) is to be avoided'; ILC, 'Second report on identification of customary international law' (n 24) 59: 'Acceptance as law should thus generally not be evidenced by the very practice alleged to be prescribed by customary international law. This provides, moreover, that the same conduct should not serve in a particular case as evidence of both practice and acceptance of that practice as law.'

[108] *Prosecutor v Kupreškić et al* (Judgment) ICTY-95-16-T (14 January 2000) paras 521–22; Antonio Cassese, *International Criminal Law: Cases and Commentary* (OUP 2011) 17.

[109] John Bellinger III and William Haynes II, 'A US government response to the International Committee of the Red Cross study Customary International Humanitarian Law' (2007) 89 International Review of the Red Cross 444–71.

virtually uniform' standard required by the ICJ with regard to the objective element, and that at the same time it puts too much emphasis on written materials (instead of 'real' state practice).[110] Furthermore, the US criticized the fact that undue weight was to be given to statements by non-governmental organizations and the ICRC itself, and that negative practice would be given inadequate weight.[111] Moreover, the US claimed that the method used in the study would fail to pay due regard to the practice of specially affected states, which is crucial, as pointed out by the ICJ in the *North Sea Continental Shelf* cases, and that the use of 'verbal practice' would merge state practice and *opinio juris*.[112]

There are other points which can be put forward to criticize the methodology used by the ICTY and the ICTR. The heavy reliance on military manuals raises the question as to how valid the respective rules are in the heat of the battle. Taking recourse to rules and principles which have been formulated during times of peace, under much easier conditions, i.e. without the stress which comes during the participation in an armed conflict, could be problematic. However, while this argument appears to raise a good point at first glance, one has to keep in mind that the same argument could be held against IHL rules contained in international conventions. These provisions are also drafted and negotiated in the quietness of a government office or by the drafting committee of a Diplomatic Conference. In this regard, the usefulness of military manuals should neither be underestimated as proof of customary IHL.[113] While it might be true that these manuals are drafted during times of peace, one needs to keep in mind that they are written by the best experts in the field, usually by members of the Ministry of Defence in collaboration with experienced military commanders and sometimes with the advice of highly regarded academics. Further, since they are issued by an organ of a state, there is a clear case for giving military manuals high importance within the process of ascertaining a rule of customary IHL.

However, there has been particular criticism regarding the use of the Martens Clause.[114] While the use of verbal practice or the strong reliance on *opinio juris* still takes into account that states are responsible for creating customary IHL, the use of the 'dictates of public conscience' and 'principles of humanity' leads to the danger of customary IHL being developed in alignment with the moral persuasions of the observer or the judge sitting on the bench of an (international) criminal tribunal. This process obviously overlaps with a natural law approach. And while the principles of humanity play an especially important role in the area of IHL, acting as the counterbalance to military necessity, it is doubtful whether such a vague concept should be included in the law-creating realm of international law. There are especially issues with regard to compliance with the principle of legality in relation to international criminal law where the rights of the accused may be compromised.

Nevertheless, customary international law has emerged as one of the most effective ways for IHL to adapt to changing circumstances in warfare. Customary international law allows IHL to adapt to new means and methods of warfare in a way that may be quicker than conventional law. It has also played a significant role in developing the law regulating

---

[110] ibid 444–45.

[111] ibid.

[112] ibid.

[113] See Michael Wood, 'The Evolution and Identification of the Customary International Law of Armed Conflict' (2018) 51 Vanderbilt Journal of Transnational Law 727.

[114] See Antonio Cassese, 'The Martens Clause: Half a Loaf or Simply Pie in the Sky?' (n 38) 187.

non-international armed conflict. Furthermore, a flexible approach to the requirements of state practice and *opinio juris* is required by the special circumstances which surround the battlefield – for example invisible practice, the formation of prohibitive norms through omission, and the need to develop IHL before certain means and methods of warfare are put into practice. Nevertheless, despite these special circumstances, the core of Article 38 of the ICJ Statute cannot and should not be changed. An approach which more or less completely disregards state practice cannot be tolerated because it would give those who apply the law the power to create their own rules (and would take us back to a 'natural law' approach – which gives rise to the danger of abuse of the discretion exercised by the law applier). Although other legal personalities have appeared on the international platform, it is still the states who set the rules.

If one does not want to endanger the legitimacy of IHL, one is well advised to stick to a – slightly amended – two-element approach. Thus, the idea of using the Martens Clause as a catch-all provision in order to 'create the law' according to the principles of humanity and the dictates of public conscience is leading us one step too far; from the perspective of this author one should also be very careful to solely rely on judicial decisions of national courts in order to prove *opinio juris*, as was done by the Special Tribunal for Lebanon in 2011. However, the methodology used by the ICTY in its 1995 *Tadić* Decision as well as the ICRC in its Customary Law Study heads into the right direction in order to find a balance between the requirements of the theory of sources as well as the special situation posed by the nature of armed conflict. Nevertheless, we should never forget the words of William Shakespeare quoted at the beginning of this chapter: *''Tis well said again; And 'tis a kind of good deed to say well: And yet words are no deeds.'*

PART V

Courts and manuals – decoupling law-making from states?

12. Judicial practice in international criminal law: Law-making in disguise?

Thomas Rauter[1]

1. INTRODUCTION

In the modern era of international criminal law, starting with the UN *ad hoc* tribunals, the predominant role of customary international law as the legal basis for international criminal convictions has been highlighted by the reports of the Secretary General on the international criminal tribunals. He linked the legality of the proceedings before international criminal tribunals to customary international law, in order to adhere to the *nullum crimen sine lege* principle.[2] The International Criminal Tribunal for Yugoslavia (ICTY) determined that its mandate obliged it to apply legal principles that are 'beyond doubt part of customary international law' and thus made criminal convictions dependent on the existence of customary international criminal norms.[3] Other international criminal tribunals followed suit, determining that the legal basis for convictions for committing international crimes generally must be found in customary international law.[4]

At the outset, however, there appears to be a clear contradiction between the demand that international criminal tribunals should only apply criminal norms that are beyond any doubt part of customary law, and the appraisal of the judges of international criminal tribunals in

1 For a comprehensive analysis see Thomas Rauter, *Judicial Practice, Customary International Criminal Law and Nullum Crimen Sine Lege* (Springer 2017). The author would like to thank the Austrian National Bank's 'Jubiläumsfonds' for funding this research. The views contained in this contribution are his own.

2 See with regard to the ICTY: UNGA 'Report of the Secretary-General Pursuant to Paragraph 2 of Security Council Resolution 808' (3 May 1993) UN Doc S/25704 para 34.

3 See for example *Prosecutor v Hadžihasanović* (Decision on Interlocutory Appeal Challenging Jurisdiction in Relation to Command Responsibility) IT-01-47-AR72 (16 July 2003) para 44; *Prosecutor v Blaškić* (Judgment) IT-95-14-A (29 July 2004) paras 139–41; *Prosecutor v Strugar* (Decision on Interlocutory Appeal) IT-01-42-AR72 (22 November 2002) paras 10–14; *Prosecutor v Kordić* (Judgment) IT-95-14/2-T (26 February 2001) para 20.

4 See for the ICTR *Prosecutor v Akayesu* (Judgment) ICTR-96-4-T (2 September 1998) paras 611–17; see for the SCSL *Prosecutor v Fofana* (Judgment) SCSL-04-14-T (2 August 2007) para 94; *Prosecutor v Brima* (Judgment) SCSL-04-16-T (20 June 2007) paras 636–39. The role of general principles of law in international criminal law will not be discussed in this contribution. See in that regard Fabián O. Raimondo, *General Principles of Law in the Decisions of International Criminal Tribunals* (Brill 2008).

the legal literature for their 'judicial creativity' or 'judicial activism'[5] when determining customary international criminal law. Indeed, doubts have been expressed as to whether the way in which customary international law has been determined by international criminal tribunals is reconcilable with the *nullum crimen sine lege* principle. The methods judges have applied when identifying customary international criminal law have been the point of considerable criticism in the legal literature. Judges at international criminal tribunals have been criticized for their selectivity,[6] and for making generalizations on the basis of a handful of cases.[7] It has been argued that the way customary law has been applied by the tribunals provided a 'convenient licence for judicial law-making'[8] or as stretching, according to Nollkaemper, 'the procedural requirements for the identification of customary international law, and thereby the requirements for procedural legitimacy, to its breaking point'.[9] In order to be able to assess whether such criticism is just or exaggerated, it is indispensable to understand the doctrinal confusion that surrounds customary international law as a source of law.

2. CUSTOMARY INTERNATIONAL LAW AND ITS METHODOLOGICAL CHALLENGES

Developing a methodological underpinning for customary international law has been a constant challenge. Indeed, customary law has become an inspiring source for innovative legal theories. Lacking a coherent theoretical basis, critics have suggested that customary international law has an 'identity crisis',[10] or is 'situated in a theoretical minefield'.[11] Indeed, there appears to be no common consensus, on either a catalogue of specific rules that have attained the status of customary law, or on the doctrinal and methodological approaches required to establish and determine customary international law as a source of law. The legal doctrine has elaborated different approaches to customary international law, which have been classified into so-called 'traditional' and 'modern' approaches.[12]

---

[5] See eg the contributions in Shane Darcy and Joseph Powderly (eds), *Judicial Creativity at the International Criminal Tribunals* (OUP 2010).

[6] Ilias Bantekas, 'Reflections on Some Sources and Methods of International Criminal and Humanitarian Law' (2006) 6 International Criminal Law Review 121, 130.

[7] Alexander Zahar and Goran Sluiter, *International Criminal Law* (OUP 2008) 105; André Nollkaemper, 'The Legitimacy of International Law in the Case Law of the International Criminal Tribunal for the Former Yugoslavia' in Thomas Vandamme and Jan-Herman Reestman (eds), *Ambiguity in the Rule of Law* (Europa Law Publishing 2001) 17.

[8] William Schabas, 'Customary Law or "Judge-Made" Law: Judicial Creativity at the UN Criminal Tribunals' in José Doria and others (eds), *The Legal Regime of the International Criminal Court* (Martinus Nijhoff Publishers 2009) 100.

[9] Nollkaemper (n 7) 18.

[10] Bruno Simma and Philip Alston, 'The Sources of Human Rights Law: Custom, Jus Cogens, and General Principles' (1988–1989) 12 Australian Yearbook of International Law 82, 88. See also J. Patrick Kelly, 'The Twilight of Customary International Law' (2000) 40 Vanderbilt Journal of International Law 449, 450.

[11] Martti Koskenniemi, 'The Pull of the Mainstream' (1990) 88 Michigan Law Review 1946, 1947.

[12] Anthea Roberts, 'Traditional and Modern Approaches to Customary International Law: A Reconciliation' (2001) 95 American Journal of International Law 757.

2.1 Traditional Customary International Law

State practice is generally seen as the key element of customary international law according to the traditional line of thinking. Schwarzenberger, for example, describes custom as a 'superstructure of a comparative analysis of state practice'.[13] This argument follows an inductive approach by proving the existence of a customary norm on repetitive instances of state practice with a clear focus on positive state actions,[14] while purely verbal claims by states do not suffice.[15] Customary international law thus crystallizes through a pattern of state practice by an abstraction from facts.[16] State practice is evaluated by its duration, consistency (uniformity) and generality,[17] making customary international law detectable through empirical analysis. According to the 'traditional view' on *opinio iuris*, it represents the subjective conviction of states that their acts (i.e., state practice) are required by an existing rule of international law. In other words, states believe in the legality of their state practice.[18] Another theory would equate *opinio iuris* with consent or acquiescence, thus requiring some form of state consent, either directly or implicitly.[19] To adhere to the perception that international law is consensual in nature, various writers do not perceive *opinio iuris* as a belief that state practice is required by law, but understand custom as a 'tacit agreement', rather than an agreement in written form, that places state consent at the centre of attention.[20] This voluntarist conception has the advantage of solving the so-called *opinio iuris* paradox, because it recognizes the legislative will of states and thus the constitutive nature of custom.[21]

Following the conception of the International Court of Justice (ICJ) that both elements are necessary for the formation of customary international law, it is argued that customary interna-

---

13 Georg Schwarzenberger, *The Inductive Approach to International Law* (Stevens & Sons 1965) 35.

14 cf Roberts (n 12) 758; Simma and Alston (n 10) 88.

15 Anthony D'Amato, *The Concept of Custom in International Law* (Cornell University Press 1971) 88ff. See also *Fisheries (United Kingdom v Norway)* (Merits) (Dissenting Opinion of Judge J.E. Read) [1951] ICJ Rep 116, 191: 'Customary international law is the generalization of the practice of States. This cannot be established by citing cases where coastal States have made extensive claims, but have not maintained their claims by the actual assertion of sovereignty over trespassing foreign ships. (…) The only convincing evidence of State practice is to be found in seizures, where the coastal State asserts its sovereignty over the waters in question by arresting a foreign ship.' See also Hugh W.A. Thirlway, *International Customary Law and Codification* (Sijthoff 1972) 51.

16 Niels Petersen, 'Customary Law without Custom? Rules, Principles, and the Role of State Practice in International Norm Creation' (2008) 23 American University Law Review 275, 301.

17 Alain Pellet, 'Article 38' in Andreas Zimmerman and others (eds), *The Statute of the International Court of Justice – A Commentary* (OUP 2012) 817–18 para 221; *North Sea Continental Shelf Cases (Federal Republic of Germany v Denmark, Federal Republic of Germany v the Netherlands)* (Merits) [1969] ICJ Rep 3 para 74 determining that state practice shall be 'extensive and virtually uniform'.

18 D'Amato (n 15) 73; Thirlway (n 15) 54, goes further claiming that *opinio iuris* could also include 'that if the practice in question was not required by the law, it was in the process of becoming so'.

19 D'Amato (n 15) 68.

20 Most prominently Grigoriĭ I. Tunkin, 'Co-Existence and International Law' (1958) 95 Collected Courses of the Hague Academy of International Law 1, 13.

21 Raphael M. Walden, 'The Subjective Element in the Formation of Customary International Law' (1977) 12 Israel Law Review 344; Alfred Verdross, 'Entstehungsweisen und Geltungsgrund des universellen völkerrechtlichen Gewohnheitsrechts' (1969) 29 Zeitschrift für ausländisches öffentliches Recht und Völkerrecht 636–37 with further references; Jörg Kammerhofer, *Uncertainty in International Law – A Kelsenian Perspective* (Routledge 2011) 77.

tional law is best described as a 'form of organic law-making'.[22] It involves a mixture of both a material element, in the form of state practice, and a subjective element, *opinio iuris*. The second element is construed either as a belief that the practice is required by law, or a legislative will element by states giving either individual consent or establishing common consensus in order to prove the existence of a customary norm.[23]

However, under such a traditional understanding, the development of customary international law is necessarily a slow process. The requirements of uniformity, generality and duration of state practice prevent it from partaking in legal advances. The tension between the cumbersome process of a traditional customary law creation and the need for a speedy legal adaption to new challenges has been expressed by the ICJ in its Advisory Opinion on the *Legality of the Threat or Use of Nuclear Weapons*. Referring to the *Continental Shelf Cases*, the Court adhered to the requirement of actual practice and *opinio iuris* of states,[24] but not without regret: 'The emergence, as *lex lata*, of a customary rule specifically prohibiting the use of nuclear weapons as such is hampered by the continuing tensions between the nascent *opinio juris* on the one hand, and the still strong adherence to the practice of deterrence on the other.'[25]

2.2 Modern Customary International Law

It was the conviction that a traditional understanding of customary international law could not adequately respond to pressing moral and global challenges that generated other theories surrounding the development of customary law, which have been labelled under the term 'modern customary law'.[26] In that regard some authors argue that the element of state practice has to be broadened, embracing not only physical acts of states but also their verbal practice; written expressions, such as policy statements and press releases; and their conduct within the forum of international organizations, including the resolutions for which they vote.[27] The International Committee of the Red Cross (ICRC) in its study on customary international humanitarian law (IHL), while accepting the traditional dichotomy between state practice and *opinio iuris*, included both physical and verbal acts within the element of state practice.[28] The

---

22 Robert Kolb, 'Selected Problems in the Theory of Customary International Law' (2003) 50 Netherlands International Law Review 119, 144.

23 ibid.

24 *Legality of the Threat or Use of Nuclear Weapons* (Advisory Opinion) [1996] ICJ Rep 253 para 64.

25 ibid 73.

26 Roberts (n 12) 757.

27 Committee on Formation of Customary (General) International Law, 'Statement of Principles Applicable to the Formation of General Customary International Law, Part II: The Objective Element: State Practice' in ILA, *Final Report of the Committee* (International Law Association 2000) 13–20, the ILA, however, opens up the possibility that verbal practice, while being able to evince state practice, could be attributed less weight than 'actual' practice; Malcolm N. Shaw, *International Law* (6th edn, CUP 2008) 82; Ian Brownlie, *Principles of Public International Law* (7th edn, OUP 2008) 6; Simma and Alston (n 10) 89 referring to a 'dubious metamorphosis' of state practice.

28 See Jean-Marie Henckaerts, *Customary International Humanitarian Law, vol I: Rules* (CUP 2005) xxxviii. However, the ICRC has been criticized by the US, which expressed its concern about the methodology stating that the state practice included in the ICRC Custom Study is 'insufficiently dense to meet the "extensive and virtually uniform" standard generally required to demonstrate the existence of a customary rule' and that it 'places too much emphasis on written materials, such as military manuals and

ICRC caveats its classification with the reminder that the separation of practice and *opinio iuris* is 'very difficult and largely theoretical'.[29] It is evident that expanding the scope of state practice to instances that were traditionally used to establish *opinio iuris* comes at the expense of the *opinio iuris* element.[30] Indeed, the element loses significance if the state's verbal claim of a right forms state practice and at the same time *opinio iuris*.[31] Mendelson tries to solve the problem by means of prohibiting the dual exploitation of one instance as both state practice and *opinio iuris*.[32] This remedy, however, smacks of a frantic adherence to the traditional two-element theory of customary law. A modern understanding of state practice may result in a 'purposive (subjective) concept' of state practice as the psychological element is already incorporated within the instance of state practice.[33]

Another modern interpretation of customary international law suggests that *opinio iuris* be the dominant element. Cheng's notion of 'instant custom' reduces the role of state practice to a purely evidentiary function: no usage is required in the sense of repeated practice as long as the belief or will of states (*opinio iuris*) is clearly established.[34] Through general statements, proclamations, and incantations deduced from the international *fora* by reference to multilateral treaties or resolutions of international organizations – that is, by means of a deductive approach – international customary law can be instantly established by voiced *opinio iuris*.[35] That approach sits uneasily with the very notion of customary law, since, when supplanting the element of repetitive state practice through *opinio iuris*, very little custom is left within

---

other guidelines published by States, as opposed to actual operational practice by States during armed conflict'. See further John B. Bellinger and William J. Haynes, 'A US Government Response to the International Committee of the Red Cross Study Customary International Humanitarian Law' (2007) 89 Review of the Red Cross 444, 445.

29 Henckaerts (n 28) xlvi.

30 See for instance De Witte in relation to the discussion 'The Classical "Sources" of International Law Revisited' in Antonio Cassese and Joseph Weiler (eds), *Change and Stability in International Law-Making* (de Gruyter 1988) 14.

31 Rein Müllerson, 'The Interplay of Objective and Subjective Elements in Customary Law' in Karel Wellens (ed), *International Law: Theory and Practice: Essays in Honour of Eric Suy* (Martinus Nijhoff Publishers 1998) 162; see also Brownlie (n 27) 8, who does not differentiate between state practice and *opinio iuris* in his list of evidence for customary international law.

32 Maurice H. Mendelson, 'The Formation of Customary International Law' (1998) 272 Collected Courses 161, 206–207, who considers however that *opinio iuris* needs to be established only in cases of doubt, see ibid 292.

33 Kammerhofer (n 21) 66–67.

34 Bin Cheng, 'United Nations Resolutions on Outer Space: "Instant" International Customary Law' in Bin Cheng (ed), *International Law: Teaching and Practice* (Stevens & Sons 1982) 251; see also Simma and Alston (n 10) 89.

35 Roberts (n 12) 758; Simma and Alston (n 10) 89.

customary international law.[36] It appears revolutionary in the light of the ICJ's mantra-like emphasis on both *opinio iuris* and state practice.[37]

Furthermore, some authors argue that from a structural hierarchical perspective, norms and rules derived from the constitutional foundations of the international community are subject to a different law-ascertaining method than 'ordinary' customary international law.[38] Similarly, other writers argue that a modern and thus less rigid approach for the determination of customary international law might be indicated for specific issues such as human rights or humanitarian law,[39] which are human-centred and not state-centred. Such approaches reveal a value-oriented ascertainment of customary law: the greater the moral pull, the easier contrary state practice is neglected, and it is assumed that noble humanitarian principles and human rights ideals are positive norms of customary law. Morality is the reason why many academics are willing to apply less strict requirements for the formation of customary international law when the fundamental values of the international community are concerned. Most eloquently, Kirgis proposed the sliding scale theory: 'The more destabilizing or morally distasteful the activity – for example, the offensive use of force or the deprivation of fundamental human rights – the more readily international decision makers will substitute one element for the other, provided that the asserted restrictive rule seems reasonable.'[40]

2.3 A Multiplicity of Custom-Creative Processes?

In conclusion, it can be said that these different approaches to customary international law suggest uncertainty with regard to the doctrinal foundations of customary international law and the methods for identifying it. Taking into consideration these different theoretical approaches, it is suggested that there is probably no single approach to the formation of

---

36 Robert Jennings, 'The Identification of International Law' in Bin Cheng (ed), *International Law: Teaching and Practice* (Stevens & Sons 1982) 5: '[W]hat we perversely persist in calling customary international law is not only *not* customary law: it does not even faintly resemble a customary law'; Karol Wolfke, *Custom in Present International Law* (Martinus Nijhoff 1964) 40–41: 'Without practice (*consuetudo*), customary international law would obviously be a misnomer, since practice constitutes precisely the main *differentia specifica* of that kind of international law' (emphasis in original).

37 However, it needs to be emphasized that also the ICJ in certain cases showed a rather flexible approach to customary international law, see Special Rapporteur Michael Wood ILC, 'First Report on Formation and Evidence of Customary International Law' (65th Session, 6 May–7 June and 8 July–9 August 2013) UN Doc A/CN.4/663 para 64.

38 See the differentiation of 'consuetudine-fondamento' (fundamental custom) and 'consuetudine-fonte' (custom as a source) in Giuseppe Sperduti, *La fonte suprema dell'ordinamento internazionale* (A. Giuffre 1946) 155ff; Christian Tomuschat, 'Obligations Arising for States without or against Their Will' (1993) 241 Collected Courses 195, 310.

39 Arguing for a modern approach to customary human rights law: Oscar Schachter, 'International Law in Theory and Practice' (1982) 178 Collected Courses 21, 334; Roozbeh B. Baker, 'Customary International Law in the 21st Century: Old Challenges and New Debates' (2010) 21 European Journal of International Law 173, 180; Roberts (n 12) 759; see also Theodor Meron, *Human Rights and Humanitarian Norms as Customary Law* (OUP 1989).

40 Compare further Frederic L. Kirgis, 'Custom on a Sliding Scale' (1987) 81 American Journal of International Law 146, 149. See also Theodor Meron, 'International Law in the Age of Human Rights' (2003) 301 Collected Courses 24, 388.

customary law, but a 'multiplicity of custom-creative processes'.[41] Indeed, Verdross already indicated such a possibility in 1968.[42] However, if customary international law is a 'dance floor where (almost) anything goes',[43] there seems to be no limit for the ascertainment of customary international law. On the other hand, the International Law Commission (ILC), which included the topic 'formation and evidence of customary international law' in its 'long-term programme of work' in 2011,[44] seems to backpedal from such multiple processes. The discussions of the ILC implied broad support for a two-element approach to customary international law that includes state practice and *opinio iuris* as necessary elements for the identification of customary international law.

3. METHODOLOGICAL APPROACHES BY INTERNATIONAL CRIMINAL TRIBUNALS

3.1 A Word of Caution

Since international criminal tribunals generally avoid disclosing the way they find customary international law, a word of caution is required. A methodological analysis can only be considered sufficient to the extent that case law is susceptible to examination and classification. One could argue that the role of international criminal tribunals is to deliver judgments and that – to draw on Pellet's comments on the ICJ – they are only judicial bodies and not teachers or scholars in relation to the underlying methodology.[45] Nevertheless, it is maintained here that the issue is different with regard to criminal proceedings. An accused is entitled to know the exact underlying jurisdictional legal basis of the charges against them, whether they form part of conventional or customary international criminal law,[46] and similarly a convicted criminal is entitled to comprehend the legal basis of their conviction. Part of the fair trial guarantee is that the rationale of a trial judgment shall be explained, accompanied by a reasoned opinion.[47] The disclosure of how the respective chamber arrived at a customary international criminal norm is a necessary element therewith an individual can comprehend the legal reason and normative basis of their conviction, and as such be able to challenge possible methodological shortcomings on the part of the judges.[48] The non-disclosure practice of international criminal tribunals

41 Kammerhofer (n 21) 204.

42 Verdross (n 21) 636: 'Because it is probable that each of the different theories [on customary law] contain some correct element, the presumption of one mode of creation for all norms of customary international law is probably not correct.'

43 Jean d'Aspremont, 'Customary International Law as a Dance Floor: Part I' (*EJIL Talk!*, 14 April 2014) <http://www.ejiltalk.org/customary-international-law-as-a-dance-floor-part-i/> accessed 31 January 2021.

44 ILC, 'Report of the Planning Group' (63rd Session, 26 April–3 June and 4 July–12 August 2011) UN Doc A/CN.4/L.796. See also ILC, 'Report of the International Law Commission, Supplement No. 10' (66th Session) A/66/10 paras 365ff.

45 Pellet (n 17) 761 para 236.

46 See eg *Strugar* (n 3) para 13.

47 See art 23(2) ICTY Statute; see also art 23(2) ICTR Statute; art 74(5) Rome Statute; art 18 SCSL Statute; Rule 101 Extraordinary Chambers in the Court of Cambodia, Internal Rules (Rev. 8) (2011).

48 Similar Guénaël Mettraux, *International Crimes and the ad hoc Tribunals* (OUP 2005) 14–15, argues that a 'court must carefully reason and explain its conclusion as to the customary or non-customary

with regards to the applied method(s) is thus problematic. But also researchers must seek to interpret which method(s) the tribunals were in fact applying. Lacking clear clarifications from the bench, such interpretation is necessarily contestable.

3.2 The Traditional Two-Elements Approach

The jurisprudence of international criminal tribunals reveals that when they elaborate on customary international law in the abstract, the various chambers share the prevailing view that customary international law consists of two constituent elements, state practice and *opinio iuris*.[49] However, when determining the concrete underlying customary international criminal norm or mode of liability, they generally spare themselves the cumbersome task of establishing lasting, uniform and widespread state practice accompanied by *opinio iuris*, or they do not assign the listed evidence to the two elements. Thus, in relation to the methodological underpinnings of their decisions and judgments, international criminal tribunals are merely paying lip service to the traditional 'two-element' requirement for customary law formation, and they generally do not explicitly or implicitly specify which elements they consider adequate to establish state practice and which elements are proof of *opinio iuris*.

In the 40 ICTY Trial Chamber judgments that have been analysed, only 11 make explicit reference to state practice and/or *opinio iuris*.[50] In those 11 judgments, the ICTY Trial Chambers explicitly referred to state practice 22 times and to *opinio iuris* 16 times.[51] Only in four instances has state practice been allocated to specific evidence. *Opinio iuris* has been allocated to specific evidence in 12 instances. An analysis of the ICTY Appeals Chamber judgments does not improve this situation. In the 37 ICTY Appeals Chamber judgments that have been analysed, only seven Appeals Chambers make explicit reference to state practice and/or *opinio iuris*.[52] Those seven judgments explicitly referred to state practice 22 times and

---

status of a norm [as it is] an element of the fair trial guarantee and the rationale of a judgment must therefore be "clearly explained".'

[49] See eg for the ICTY, *Prosecutor v Hadžihasanović* (Judgment) IT-01-47-T (15 March 2006) para 254; *Hadžihasanović* (n 3) para 12; *Prosecutor v Furundžija* (Judgment) IT-95-17/1 (21 July 2000) para 281. See for the SCSL: *Prosecutor v Norman* (Decision on Preliminary Motion Based on Lack of Jurisdiction (Child Recruitment)) SCSL-2004-14-AR72(E) (31 May 2004) para 17. For the ECCC see *Co-Prosecutors' Request to Exclude Armed Conflict Nexus Requirement from the Definition of Crimes Against Humanity* (Decision) 002/10-09-2007/ECCC/TC (26 October 2011) para 12.

[50] The 11 ICTY Trial Chamber judgments are the following: *Prosecutor v Delalić (Ĉelebici)* (Judgment) IT-96-21-T (16 November 1998); *Prosecutor v Furundžija* (Judgment) IT-95-17/1-T (10 December 1998); *Prosecutor v Jelisić* (Judgment) IT-95-10-T (14 December 1999); *Prosecutor v Kupreškić* (Judgment) IT-95-16 (14 January 2000); *Prosecutor v Kunarac* (Judgment) IT-96-23-T & IT-96-23/1-T (22 February 2001); *Prosecutor v Krstić* (Judgment) IT-98-33-T (2 August 2001); *Prosecutor v Vasiljević* (Judgment) IT-98-32-T (29 November 2002); *Prosecutor v Simić* (Judgment) IT-95-9-T (17 October 2003); *Prosecutor v Galić* (Judgment) IT-98-29-T (5 December 2003); *Hadžihasanović* (n 49); *Prosecutor v Boškoski* (Judgment) IT-04-82-T (10 July 2008).

[51] The search terms included 'State practice', 'national practice', 'practice', 'opinio juris' and 'opinio iuris'. Instances when trial chambers merely used quotations of previous judgments that contained these phrases have not been counted.

[52] The seven ICTY Appeal Chamber judgments are the following: *Prosecutor v Tadić* (Appeal Judgment) IT-94-1-A (15 July 1999); *Prosecutor v Delalić (Ĉelebici)* (Appeal Judgment) IT-96-21-A (20 February 2001); *Prosecutor v Aleksovski*, (Appeal Judgment) IT-95-14/1A (24 March 2000); *Blaškić*

to *opinio iuris* seven times. In only five instances has the Appeals Chambers allocated the element of state practice with specific evidence, and they have allocated specific evidence to *opinio iuris* four times.

It is astonishing to see that the chambers of the International Criminal Tribunal for Rwanda (ICTR) also did not allocate specific evidence to state practice and/or *opinio iuris* in their judgments, nor explicitly even refer to state practice and/or *opinio iuris* as elements for the establishment of customary international law.

At the Special Court for Sierra Leone (SCSL), two Trial Chambers and two Appeals Chambers explicitly mention state practice and/or *opinio iuris* in their judgments,[53] while only in four instances has the element of state practice been allocated with specific evidence, and in three instances has *opinio iuris* been allocated with specific evidence.

With regard to the Extraordinary Chambers in the Courts of Cambodia (ECCC), in the three judgments available at the time of writing, the two trial chambers have explicitly referred to state practice four times and to *opinio iuris* two times, whereas state practice has been allocated two times to specific evidence.[54] The ECCC Supreme Court Chamber in its *Duch* judgment has referred to state practice eight times and to *opinio iuris* seven times. Both elements have been allocated to specific evidence only once.[55]

It is interesting to note that in the cases where state practice has been allocated to specific evidence, the international criminal tribunals did not analyse actual 'battlefield' practice by states during armed conflict, but focused on 'official pronouncements of States, military manuals and judicial decisions'.[56] The ICTY *Tadić* Appeals Chamber denounced the quality of actual state conduct by troops as untrustworthy, dismissing its value for determining customary international law.[57] It thus focuses on 'verbal' or 'paper' practice. This 'modern positivistic'[58] conception of state practice has been adequately described by Kress as being on the borderline between actual state practice and *opinio iuris*.[59] The jurisprudence of international criminal tribunals is thus in line with a modern conception of customary international law that broadens the scope of state practice. However, widening the scope of the element of 'state

---

(n 3); *Prosecutor v Krnojelac* (Appeal Judgment) IT-94-I-A (17 September 2003); *Prosecutor v Kordić* (Appeal Judgment) IT-95-14/2-A (17 December 2004); *Prosecutor v Đorđević* (Appeal Judgment) IT-05-87/1-A (27 January 2014).

53 The SCSL judgments are: *Prosecutor v Fofana* (n 4); *Prosecutor v Sesay* (Judgment) SCSL-04-15-T (2 March 2009); *Prosecutor v Fofana* (Appeal Judgment) SCSL-04-14-A (28 May 2008); *Prosecutor v Taylor* (Appeal Judgment) SCSL-03-01-A (26 September 2013).

54 *Prosecutor v Kaing alias Duch* (Judgment) 001/18-07-2007/ECCC/TC (26 July 2010); *Prosecutor v Nuon* (Judgment) 002/19-09-2007/ECCC/TC (7 August 2014).

55 *Prosecutor v Kaing Guek Eav (Duch)* (Appeals Judgment) 001/18-07-2007-ECCC/SC (3 February 2012).

56 *Prosecutor v Tadić* (Decision on the Defence Motion for Interlocutory Appeal on Jurisdiction) IT-94-1 (2 October 1995) para 99. See also *Prosecutor v Strugar* (Judgment) IT-01-42-T (31 January 2005) fn 754; *Boškoski* (n 50) fn 1273; *Prosecutor v Đorđević* (Judgment) IT-05-87/1-T (23 February 2011) fn 5779; *Prosecutor v Stanišić and Župljanin* (Judgment) IT-08-91-T (27 March 2013) fn 86.

57 *Prosecutor v Tadić* (n 56).

58 A term coined by Bruno Simma and Andreas L. Paulus, 'The Responsibility of Individuals for Human Rights Abuses in Internal Conflicts: A Positivist View' (1999) 93 American Journal of International Law 302, 306.

59 Claus Kress, 'War Crimes Committed in Non-International Armed Conflict and the Emerging System of International Criminal Justice' (2001) 30 Israel Yearbook on Human Rights 103, 108.

practice' to include verbal and paper practice renders the exact contours and delimitation of the two elements rather unclear.[60]

The approach chosen by the ICTY *Tadić* Appeals Chamber in relation to the determination of criminal responsibility for war crimes committed in non-international armed conflict under customary international law is problematic. Whereas one could also question the qualitative value of the instances of state practice quoted by the Appeals Chamber, that is, whether or not they could actually qualify as proof for the criminalization of war crimes committed in non-international armed conflict,[61] at this point I will focus on the quantity of quoted state practice: one domestic case, four military manuals and two pieces of national legislation.[62] These references to state practice leave much to be desired when applying the high frequency and high consistency test as established by the ICJ in the *North Sea Continental Shelf Cases*, which requires that state practice should be both 'extensive and virtually uniform'.[63] The Appeals Chamber has rightly been criticized by scholars who question whether it could have made greater effort in its search for instances of state practice.[64]

Despite this criticism, the findings of the *Tadić* Appeals Chamber with regard to criminal responsibility for war crimes committed in non-international armed conflict are settled jurisprudence.[65] Subsequent jurisprudence has placed a favourable gloss on the sheer quantity of the quoted state practice of the *Tadić* Appeals Chamber.[66] Whereas the ICTY *Tadić* Appeals Chamber itself did not explicitly elaborate on the ICJ's high frequency and high consistency test of state practice, it is safe to conclude that it tacitly ignored it. The Appeals Chambers of other international criminal tribunals were more expressive concerning the non-applicability of the high frequency and high consistency test of state practice.

---

60 See section 2.2 Modern Customary International Law.

61 The ICTY *Tadić* Appeals Chamber appeared not to be overconfident in its proof: the military manuals of the US and Great Britain only 'lend themselves to the interpretation' non-international armed conflict situations could give rise to war crimes and also the norms of the Criminal Code of the Federal Republic of Yugoslavia only 'seem[ed] to imply that they also apply to internal armed conflicts'. See *Prosecutor v Tadić* (n 56) paras 131–32.

62 ibid paras 128–32.

63 See *North Sea Continental Shelf Cases (Federal Republic of Germany v Denmark, Federal Republic of Germany v the Netherlands)* (Merits) [1969] ICJ Rep 3 para 74.

64 Wolff Heintschel von Heinegg, 'Criminal International Law and Customary International Law' in Andreas Zimmerman (ed), *International Criminal Law and the Current Development of Public International Law* (Duncker und Humblot 2003) 35ff; Kress (n 59) 107; Theodor Meron, 'The Continuing Role of Custom in the Formation of International Humanitarian Law' (1996) 90 American Journal of International Law 238, 240. Cassese himself in that regard admitted that 'we came up with a lot of evidence (…) *well some evidence* [laughter].' See 'Nino – In His Own Words' (Editorial) (2011) 22 (4) European Journal of International Law 931, 942.

65 See eg for the ICTY: *Prosecutor v Tadić* (Opinion and Judgment) IT-94-1-T (7 May 1997) para 614; *Prosecutor v Delalić (Ĉelebici)* (n 52) paras 153ff; see for the ICTR: *Prosecutor v Akayesu* (n 4) para 613; *Prosecutor v Rutaganda* (Judgment) ICTR-96-3-T (6 December 1999) para 87; see for the SCSL: *Prosecutor v Fofana* (Decision on Preliminary Motion on Lack of Jurisdiction Materiae: Nature of Armed Conflict) SCSL-2004-14-AR72(E) (25 May 2004) para 24: 'Any argument that these norms [CA 3 and art 4 (2) AP II] do not entail individual criminal responsibility has been put to rest in ICTY and ICTR jurisprudence.'

66 In the *Delalić* case it has been stated that the *Tadić* Appeals Chamber 'illustrate[d] that there are many instances of penal provisions for violations of the laws applicable in internal armed conflicts', see *Prosecutor v Delalić (Ĉelebici)* (n 50) para 307; *Prosecutor v Delalić (Ĉelebici)* (n 52) paras 175ff.

The Appeals Chamber of the SCSL, when concerned with a preliminary motion alleging that it lacks jurisdiction in relation to child recruitment – a war crime according to Article 4 of the SCSL Statute – looked into state practice demonstrating 'few examples of national legislation criminalizing child recruitment prior to 1996',[67] the total amount of national legislation being five. These instances of state practice would hardly pass the high frequency and high consistency test. However, the SCSL Appeals Chamber circumvents this issue by reference to Akehurst, stating that 'a practice followed by a very small number of states can create a rule of customary law if there is no practice which conflicts the rule'.[68] Judge Robertson filed a dissenting opinion criticizing the Appeals Chamber for not differentiating between forced recruitment, which he considered to be a war crime, and voluntary enlisting. He considered that under customary international law as it stood by the end of 1996, voluntary enlisting of children or involving them in hostilities was prohibited by humanitarian law, triggering state responsibility, but that this prohibition did not entail individual criminal responsibility.[69] Despite this cutting critique by Judge Robertson, the findings of the Appeals Chamber have been followed in subsequent judgments of the SCSL,[70] and the International Criminal Court (ICC) has used the SCSL case law as a source for interpretation of the Rome Statute.[71] It is indeed stunning to see the SCSL Appeals Chamber circumventing the high frequency and high consistency test with reference to one single legal scholar, thereby conveniently avoiding the task of searching for an adequate number of instances of state practice.

In addition, the Supreme Court Chamber of the ECCC elaborated on the frequency and consistency of state practice for the determination of customary international criminal law. It plainly stated that in this particular field of law 'the traditional requirement of "extensive and virtually uniform" state practice may actually be less stringent than in other areas of international law'.[72]

---

67 *Prosecutor v Norman* (Decision on Preliminary Motion Based on Lack of Jurisdiction (Child Recruitment)) SCSL-2004-14-AR72(E) (31 May 2004) para 45. The Appeals Chamber refers to the UNICEF Amicus Brief that lists five instruments of national legislation that explicitly criminalized the recruitment of children (Colombia's national law, the Code of Military Justice of Argentina, Spain's Penal Code, Ireland's Geneva Conventions Act and Norway's Military Penal Code).

68 *Prosecutor v Norman* (n 67) para 49, referring to Michael Akehurst, 'Custom as a Source of International Law' (1977) 47 British Yearbook of International Law 1.

69 *Prosecutor v Norman* (n 67) (Dissenting Opinion of Justice Robertson) para 60: 'what had emerged, in customary international law, by the end of 1996 was a humanitarian rule that obliged states, and armed factions within states, to avoid enlisting under fifteens or involving them in hostilities, whether arising from international or internal armed conflict. What had not, however, evolved was an offence cognisable by international criminal law which permitted the trial and punishment of individuals accused of enlisting (ie accepting for military service) volunteers under the age of fifteen. It may be that in some states this would have constituted an offence against national law, but this cannot be determinative of the existence of an international law crime.' Judge Robertson refers to the difference of forcible recruitment and enlistment in paras 8–10.

70 SCSL, *Prosecutor v Fofana* (n 4) para 184; *Prosecutor v Brima* (n 4) para 728; *Prosecutor v Sesay* (Judgment) SCSL-04-15-T (2 March 2009) para 184.

71 Situation in the Democratic Republic of the Congo in the Case of the *Prosecutor v Thomas Lubanga Dyilo* (Judgment) ICC-01/04-01/06 (14 March 2012) para 603: 'The SCSL's case law therefore potentially assist in the interpretation of the relevant provisions of the Rome Statute.'

72 *Prosecutor v Kaing Guek Eav (Duch)* (n 55) para 93.

It appears that the non-applicability of the high frequency and high consistency test with regards to state practice has met common agreement before international criminal tribunals. The ICTY *Tadić* Appeals Chamber in its Jurisdiction Decision opened the possibility of establishing customary international law merely on 'trace elements' of state practice, but remained silent with regard to its doctrinal problems. However, the highest chambers of other international criminal tribunals, the SCSL Appeals Chamber and the ECCC Supreme Court Chamber, did not shy away from proclaiming that the traditional method of establishing customary international law on the basis of 'extensive and virtually uniform' state practice is not applicable when determining customary international criminal law. This is in line with a modern understanding of customary international law: in certain fields of law the context is relevant for ascertaining different requirements when establishing customary international law.[73] As the existence of a norm of customary international criminal law is desirable, requirements for the ascertainment of customary international law are less stringent, resulting in the omission of the high frequency/consistency test of state practice.

3.3 The Non-Allocation to Elements Method

It is evident that the identification of concrete evidence for (lasting, consistent, widespread) state practice and *opinio iuris* is a cumbersome task. Rather than applying a meticulous analysis of customary international criminal law by establishing concrete evidences for state practice and *opinio iuris*, international criminal tribunals generally prefer not to allocate the listed evidence to the elements of state practice or *opinio iuris*.[74] It allows the chambers the comfortable position of simply enumerating all instances of evidence for the determination of customary international criminal law, without being required to ascertain the legal relevance attached to these instances. The conception of sources is wide, comprising international conventions, resolutions of international organizations, the work of the ILC and the ICRC, international and domestic case law, official pronouncements of states or other international actors, national legislation, and the writings of legal scholars. Mere enumeration of these sources allows the chambers of international criminal tribunals to avoid the task of classifying the listed elements as instances of state practice, *opinio iuris*, or both, or as mere subsidiary means for the determination of a rule of law. Such a 'non-allocation' approach is by far the most commonly applied 'method' for the determination of customary international criminal law and has been applied by all international criminal tribunals.

The non-allocation of evidence to the concrete elements of state practice and *opinio iuris* is a recurring theme through the entire jurisprudence of the ICTY. It has been applied in relation to specific crimes, including the crime of genocide,[75] imprisonment,[76] other inhumane acts,[77]

---

[73] See above section 2.2 Modern Customary International Law.

[74] See also Birgit Schlütter, *Developments in Customary International Law* (Martinus Nijhoff 2010) 187, naming such an approach to customary international law the 'sources based approach'.

[75] *Prosecutor v Jelisić* (n 50) paras 59ff, that excepting national case law does not allocate evidence to specific instances of state practice or *opinio iuris*.

[76] *Prosecutor v Jelisić* (n 50) paras 295ff.

[77] *Prosecutor v Blaškić* (Judgment) IT-95-14-T (3 March 2000) paras 237ff.

enslavement[78] and deportation[79] as crimes against humanity, as well as modes of liability such as command responsibility.[80]

The SCSL also applied the 'non-allocation to elements' approach in its case law. It was used in relation to specific crimes, such as the crime of acts of terrorism[81] and pillage,[82] both being charged as war crimes under Article 3 of the SCSL Statute, enlisting children[83] charged under Article 4 of the SCSL Statute, and to other inhumane acts[84] and enslavement[85] as crimes against humanity.

Since there is no allocation of evidence to the elements of state practice and *opinio iuris*, the reader of these judgments is left uninformed as to the value of particular evidence for the determination of customary international criminal law. Thus, the chambers of international criminal tribunals, when applying the non-allocation approach to the determination of customary international criminal law, fail to indicate the value of the listed evidence as either proving state practice and/or *opinio iuris* or as subsidiary means for the determination of a rule of law. One reason for such a non-allocation approach might be seen in the focus on 'verbal' or 'paper' practice instead of actual state behaviour. It seems that without a clear demarcation between evidence that may be used to indicate state practice and evidence that may be used to indicate *opinio iuris*, international criminal tribunals prefer to remain silent.

3.4 The Value-Based Deductive Approach

In some way or other, in the early phase of the ICTY, all chambers took recourse to a purposive elaboration of customary international criminal law in accordance with the general spirit of IHL, which is said to safeguard *human dignity* or *human treatment/protection*.[86] Other

---

78 *Prosecutor v Kunarac* (n 50) paras 518ff.

79 *Prosecutor v Stakić* (Appeals Judgment) IT-97-24-A (22 March 2006) paras 274ff establishing that deportation requires that individuals are transferred across a state border or *de facto* border, referring to post-Second World War jurisprudence, international conventions, the ILC Draft code, the ICRC Custom Study, and ICTY jurisprudence, but not explicitly referring to state practice or *opinio iuris*.

80 *Prosecutor v Aleksovski* (Judgment) IT-95-14/1 (25 June 1999) paras 66ff; *Prosecutor v Delalić (Ĉelebici)* (n 50) paras 333ff; *Prosecutor v Delalić (Ĉelebici)* (n 52) paras 228ff.

81 *Prosecutor v Brima* (n 4) paras 660ff inter alia referring to AP II, ICTY case law, the report of the United Nations War Crimes Commission, and domestic military manuals.

82 ibid, paras 184 and 204ff.

83 *Prosecutor v Fofana* (n 4) paras 182ff inter alia referring to AP I and AP II, the 1989 Convention on the Rights of the Child, the Rome Statute.

84 *Prosecutor v Brima* (n 4) paras 697ff referring to ICTY case law, the IMT Nuremberg Charter, Control Council Law No. 10, the Rome Statute and national case law.

85 ibid, paras 739ff.

86 See eg *Prosecutor v Furundžija* (n 50) para 162 when elaborating and defining torture under art 3 ICTY Statute; ICTY, *Prosecutor v Aleksovski* (n 80) paras 49ff elaborating and defining 'outrages upon personal dignity' under art 3 ICTY Statute, paras 49ff; *Prosecutor v Delalić (Ĉelebici)* (n 50) para 263 eliminating a strict nationality requirement in order to determine a broad category of protected persons under the grave breaches regime based on ethnicity; *Prosecutor v Blaškić* (n 77) paras 167ff stating that common art 3 expresses the fundamental principle underlying the Geneva Conventions, humane treatment, and that it covers acts of AP I relating to unlawful attacks upon civilian targets. The *Prosecutor v Aleksovski* (n 52) para 146 defended the 'overall control' test against the 'effective control' test of the ICJ as the former 'provides for greater protection of civilian victims of armed conflicts'; this different

chambers apply the Martens Clause,[87] which refers to the *principles of humanity* and the *dictates of public conscience.*[88]

Such an 'object and purpose' approach on the basis of the underlying humanitarian values has met only little resistance in the jurisprudence. The ICTY *Krnojelac* Trial Chamber notably sought to curb such a deductive approach when criticizing previous trial chambers that expanded the crime of torture with a *mens rea* requirement of 'humiliation' of the torture victim. It stated that:

> [i]n light of the principle of legality, the proposition that 'the primary purpose of humanitarian law is to safeguard human dignity' is not sufficient to permit the court to introduce, as part of the *mens rea*, a new and additional prohibited purpose, which would in effect enlarge the scope of criminal prohibition against torture beyond what it was at the time relevant to the indictment under consideration.[89]

Interestingly, fundamental humanitarian principles have also been used to challenge the traditional requirements for the formation of customary international law. The ICTY *Kupreškić* Trial Chamber did not 'merely' use the Martens Clause as an interpretative guideline of rules of customary norms of IHL. Although it stated that the Martens Clause is not an autonomous source of law,[90] when analysing the customary rules of reprisals against civilians it utilized the clause as a justification for a differentiated methodology when determining customary international humanitarian rules. The Trial Chamber was faced with the problem that the treaty provisions that prohibit reprisals, as contained in Articles 51(6) and 52(1) of AP I, had not been ratified by powerful states, such as the US, France, India, Indonesia, Israel, Japan, Pakistan, and Turkey. Therefore, it could not be argued that the treaty norms were a codification of existing customary norms or crystallizing new customary norms. It also admitted that it could

---

and less rigorous standard is wholly consistent with the fundamental purpose of Geneva Convention IV, which is to ensure 'protection of civilians to the maximum extent possible'.

87 *Prosecutor v Tadić* (n 65) para 618 referring to the Martens Clause to determine that crimes against humanity was not a 'novel concept' of the IMT Nuremberg Charter; *Prosecutor v Furundžija* (n 50) inter alia referring to the Martens Clause to determine that 'a general prohibition against torture has evolved in customary international law' (para 137) and that 'the prohibition of rape and serious sexual assault has also evolved in customary international law' (para 168); *Prosecutor v Kupreškić* (n 50) paras 525ff elaborating on the customary rules of precaution in attacks on military objectives causing damage to civilians.

88 The original Martens Clause was contained in the preamble to the 1899 Hague Convention concerning the laws or customs of war on land: 'Until a more complete code of the laws of war is issued, the High Contracting Parties think it right to declare that in cases not included in the Regulations adopted by them, populations and belligerents remain under the protection and empire of the principles of international law as they result from the usages established between civilized nations, from the laws of humanity, and the requirements of the public conscience.' A modern version of the Martens Clause is found in art 1(2) AP I and the preamble of AP II referring to 'the principles of humanity' and 'the dictates of public conscience'.

89 *Prosecutor v Krnojelac* (Judgment) IT-97-25-T (15 March 2002) para 186.

90 *Prosecutor v Kupreškić* (n 50) para 525. See also the position of the UK with regard to the ICJ's Nuclear Weapons Advisory Opinion as quoted in Theodor Meron, 'The Martens Clause, Principles of Humanity, and the Dictates of Public Conscience' (2000) 94 American Journal of International Law 78, 85; see also Thilo Rensmann, 'Die Humanisierung des Völkerrechts durch das *ius in bello* – Von der Martens'schen Klausel zur Responsibility to Protect' (2008) 68 Zeitschrift für ausländisches öffentliches Recht und Völkerrecht 111, 114.

not detect adequate recent state practice to establish customary international law through a traditional method. Despite this apparent deadlock, the ICTY *Kupreškić* Trial Chamber pushed for a methodological *coup d'état* when determining customary IHL:

> This is however an area where *opinio iuris sive necessitatis* may play a much greater role than *usus*, as a result of the aforementioned Martens Clause. In the light of the way States and courts have implemented it, this Clause clearly shows that principles of international humanitarian law may emerge through a customary process under the pressure of the demands of humanity or the dictates of public conscience, even where State practice is scant or inconsistent. The other element, in the form of *opinio necessitatis*, crystallizing as a result of the imperatives of humanity or public conscience, may turn out to be the decisive element heralding the emergence of a general rule or principle of humanitarian law.[91]

The following conclusions can be drawn from the ICTY *Kupreškić* Trial Chamber's approach to customary IHL: first, it is indifferent to state practice as a necessary element for the formation of customary international law. The Trial Chamber even quotes state practice in the form of military manuals that allow reprisals against civilians but does not take them into account for its determination of customary international law.[92] Second, the *Kupreškić* Trial Chamber made a deliberate distinction between *opinio iuris* and *opinio necessitatis*.[93] It did not require that customary law is based on a 'legal conviction', but contented itself with the existence of extra-legal convictions based on social, moral, or political necessity in order to establish the prevailing psychological element for the determination of customary international law.[94] The ICTY *Kupreškić* Trial Chamber explicitly based its customary law finding on the prohibition of reprisals entirely on the existence of *opinio necessitatis*. This was, it claimed, manifested in UN General Assembly Resolution 2675 (1970), the number of states that have ratified AP I, and the fact that states generally refrained from claiming to have a right to use reprisals against civilians.[95] While these manifestations might very well be used to prove a legal conviction, i.e., *opinio iuris*, the wording used by the ICTY *Kupreškić* Trial Chamber suggests that customary law can be based on *opinio necessitatis* alone, that is to say, out of social, moral, or political necessity. This methodological artifice is, according to the ICTY *Kupreškić* Trial Chamber, made possible by the Martens Clause, the demands of humanity, and the dictates of public conscience.

In his legal writing Cassese considered the Martens Clause to be 'an ingenious blend of natural law and positivism'.[96] The Martens Clause, being itself enshrined in positive law, in

---

91 *Prosecutor v Kupreškić* (n 50) para 527.

92 ibid 532.

93 ibid 531.

94 See also Cassese, the presiding judge in the *Kupreškić* Trial Chamber, in his scholarly writing: Antonio Cassese, 'The Martens Clause: Half a Loaf or Simply Pie in the Sky?' (2000) 11 European Journal of International Law 187, 214: 'Put differently, the requirement of *opinio iuris* or *opinio necessitatis* may take on a special prominence. As a result, the expression of legal views by a number of states and other international subjects concerning the binding value of a principle or a rule, *or the social and moral need for its observance by states*, may be held to be conductive to the formation of a principle or a customary rule, even when those legal views are *not backed up by widespread and consistent state practice, or even by no practice at all*' (emphasis added).

95 *Prosecutor v Kupreškić* (n 50) paras 532–33.

96 Antonio Cassese (n 94) 189.

IHL conventions, could be viewed as providing a bridge between the polarizing positions of positivism and naturalism. However, it is more appropriate to say that such use of the Martens Clause for the determination of customary international law conceals the re-invocation of naturalism in positivistic clothing.[97] It is evident that the way the Martens Clause has been applied by the ICTY *Kupreškić* Trial Chamber is nothing less than the equation of moral, social, or political necessity with customary international law.[98] It has to be noted that the ICTY *Kupreškić* Trial Chamber's finding – that reprisals against civilians are absolutely prohibited under customary international law – has been criticized in the legal literature.[99] It has not been followed by subsequent ICTY jurisprudence and national state practice.[100] Despite this renunciation of the absolute prohibition of reprisals under customary IHL, the ICTY *Kupreškić* Trial Chamber's methodological approach to the determination of customary international law has left its mark in the case law of another international criminal tribunal. At the ECCC the Supreme Court Chamber has held that when 'evaluating the emergence of a principle or general rule concerning conduct that offends the laws of humanity or the dictates of public conscience (…) the requirement of *opinio juris* may take pre-eminence over the *usus* element of custom'.[101] While the ECCC Supreme Court Chamber was not following the ICTY *Kupreškić* Trial Chamber's conception that *opinio necessitatis* can be considered as forming an adequate basis of customary international law, it was willing to declare that the *opinio iuris* element may trump state practice as the prevailing element for its determination.

---

[97] See also Robert Cryer, 'The Philosophy of International Criminal Law' in Alexander Orakhelashvili (ed), *Research Handbook on the Theory and History of International Law* (Edward Elgar 2011) 250, stating in regard to the ICTY *Kupreškić* Trial Chamber reasoning that 'the argumentation is notionally, or presentationally, positivist. The argument of the Chamber was that custom accepted the position, and, again some state practice was (mis)quoted. It is clear, though, that the underlying ideal of the opinion is naturalist.'

[98] See also Tamás Hoffmann, 'The Gentle Civilizer of Humanitarian Law' in Carsten Stahn and Larissa van den Herik (eds), *Future Perspectives on International Criminal Justice* (TMC Asser Press 2010) 76.

[99] See eg Frits Kalshoven, 'Reprisals and the Protection of Civilians' in Lal C. Vohrah and others (eds), *Man's Inhumanity to Man: Essays in Honour of Antonio Cassese* (Kluwer 2003) 481ff.

[100] See *Prosecutor v Martić* (Judgment) IT-95-11-T (12 June 2007) paras 465ff arguing that reprisals can be considered lawful under international humanitarian law subject to strict conditions. That finding has been accepted by the Appeals Chamber, *Prosecutor v Martić* (Appeals Judgment) IT-95-11-A (8 October 2008) paras 263ff. Concerning state practice see for example the explanatory note regarding the German draft law for the German Code of Crimes against International Law, Bundesratsdrucksache 29/02 (15 January 2002) 33 considering that reprisals subject to strict conditions may constitute a justification for the commission of international crimes. The UK Joint Service Manual of the Law of Armed Conflict (2004) JSP 383, 423 explicitly criticizes the ICTY *Kupreškić* Trial Chamber, stating that 'the court's reasoning is unconvincing and the assertion that there is a prohibition in customary law flies in the face of most of the state practice that exists. The UK does not accept the position as stated in this judgment.' <https://www.gov.uk/government/publications/jsp-383-the-joint-service-manual-of-the-law-of-armed-conflict-2004-edition> accessed 31 January 2021.

[101] *Prosecutor v Kaing Guek Eav (Duch)* (n 55) para 93. Note, however, that in that regard the ECCC Supreme Court Chambers referred to Cassese's legal writing and not to the ICTY *Kupreškić* Trial Chamber over which he presided.

3.5 A Multiplicity of Custom-Creative Processes!

This short treatise is by no means complete. The case law referred to above, however, shows that international criminal tribunals, in terms of the determination of customary international criminal law, do not adhere to a 'common, unified approach to the identification of rules of customary international law'[102] – as has been proclaimed by the ILC. This finding might surprise, since in the abstract international criminal tribunals do consider that customary international law must be established on the basis of the traditional method of state practice and *opinio iuris*. However, international criminal tribunals generally fail to establish proof of these elements *in concreto* when elaborating on specific crimes and modes of liability. Indeed, there are only a handful of cases in the jurisprudence of international criminal tribunals that seek to adhere to the traditional requirements of state practice and *opinio iuris* for the determination of customary international criminal law. The reluctance of international criminal tribunals to refer to state practice and *opinio iuris* explicitly, or to allocate specific evidence to these elements in their judgments, is indeed eye-catching.

4. THE ROLE OF JUDGES WHEN DETERMINING CUSTOMARY INTERNATIONAL LAW

The rich jurisprudence of international criminal tribunals has woken international criminal law up from a long sleep. Indeed, beginning with the ICTY, the international community *via* the UN Security Council set up an international criminal tribunal for the first time since the Nuremberg era and stopped turning a blind eye to the enforcement of international criminal law at the international level. The ICTY paved the way for a 'proliferation'[103] of various international criminal tribunals, such as the ICTR, SCSL, and ECCC, finally resulting in the creation of a permanent institution, the ICC. As stated above, the doctrinal foundation of certain findings of customary law by international criminal tribunals has been the point of heavy critique in the literature.[104] Whether one considers this critique as just depends on one's dogmatic and philosophical concept of the foundations of customary international law and consequently is also dependent on the role ascribed to judges in that process.

The SCSL *Taylor* Appeals Chamber held that international criminal tribunals merely 'act as the instruments of States'[105] and that their mandate authorized them only to 'apply customary international law as it stands'.[106] Similarly, Judge Schomburg at the ICTY held that the:

> Tribunal is not acting as a legislator; it is under an obligation to apply only customary international law applicable at the time of the criminal conduct, (…) the International Tribunal is required to adhere strictly to the principle of *nullum crimen sine lege praevia* and must ascertain that a crime was 'beyond any doubt part of customary law'.[107]

---

102 See above section 2.3 A Multiplicity of Custom-Creative Processes.
103 Pellet (n 17) 860 para 320.
104 See section 1. Introduction.
105 *Prosecutor v Taylor* (Appeal Judgment) SCSL-03-01-A (26 September 2013) para 463.
106 ibid 464.
107 Separate and Partially Dissenting Opinion of Judge Schomburg to *Prosecutor v Galić* (Appeal Judgment) IT-98-29-A (30 November 2006) para 21.

However, such an assessment is hardly consistent with reality. The judges at international criminal tribunals have been forced to adjudicate in a legal sphere in which they did not necessarily find clear legal norms.[108] As has been suggested by Shahabuddeen, '[t]he state of international criminal law was meager at the time of the establishment of the ICTY'.[109] Due to the meagre state of international criminal law, international criminal tribunals were given no other choice in certain cases but to fill a void in international legislation, assuming in that regard the responsibility of states. States, as the principal law-creators in the international legal sphere, neglected the task of equipping them with precise international criminal norms adequate to fulfil their task to deliver justice. Therefore, the international criminal tribunals turned to the flexibility and doctrinal confusion surrounding customary international law as a source of law. Relying on modern approaches, according to Meron, '[t]he "ought" merges with the "is", the *lex ferenda* with the *lex lata*'[110] and the legislative process of customary law that is determined by noble ideas is exposed. Consequently, international criminal judges have certainly been much more than just 'the mouth that reproduces the meaning of the law' as demanded by Montesquieu.[111]

As has aptly been held by Mettraux:

> In the history of international criminal law, international tribunals have done more than merely give jural *imprimatur* to norms in waiting and have been much more than mere 'evidential sources' of customary law. In effect, taking advantage of the plasticity and indeterminacy of customary law, international courts and tribunals, not least the *ad hoc* Tribunals, have often acted as 'customary midwives', 'des accoucheurs de norms coutumières', so that international criminal law may owe more to judges than any other part of international law.[112]

The lines between a mere application, a development, and the creation of customary international criminal law are blurred. The development of customary international criminal law through the jurisprudence of international criminal tribunals is in line with the so-called 'judicialization' of international law.[113] One could even argue that contemporary judicial law-making by international tribunals is a political and legal reality in the international legal sphere.[114] The notion of a clear dividing line between a mere application and the creation of law is probably more a myth than reality. However, judicial law-making at the international level is generally concealed: as Jennings argued, one essential function of the judiciary is to

---

[108] Robert Heinsch, *Die Weiterentwicklung des humanitären Völkerrechts durch die Strafgerichtshöfe für das ehemalige Jugoslawien und Ruanda* (Berliner Wissenschafts-Verlag 2007) 371.

[109] Mohamed Shahabuddeen, 'Judicial Creativity and Joint Criminal Enterprise' in Darcy and Powderly (n 5) 187.

[110] Theodor Meron, 'The Geneva Conventions as Customary Law' (1987) 81 American Journal of International Law 348, 361.

[111] C. de Secondat, Baron de Montesquieu, *De l'Esprit des lois,* Livre XI, Chapitre 6 (1748), in the original language: 'la bouche, qui prononce les paroles de la loi' (as translated by the author).

[112] Mettraux (n 48) 14.

[113] Gleider I. Hernandez, 'The Judicialization of International Law: Reflections on the Empirical Turn' (2014) 25 European Journal of International Law 919.

[114] See for example Armin von Bogdandy and Ingo Venzke, 'Beyond Dispute: International Judicial Institutions as Lawmakers' in idem (eds), *International Judicial Lawmaking* (Springer 2012) 3ff.

give the impression that it is merely applying existing rules of law, even if in reality a court creates law.[115] For such concealed law-making, Shapiro even brands judges as liars.[116]

While at the international level progressive determinations of customary international law are generally unproblematic when states are in the dock, the situation could be different in international criminal proceedings. The relationship between the human rights of the accused and the progressive determination of customary international criminal law is a fraught one. The obligation to maintain a clear distinction between *de lege lata* and *de lege ferenda* is owed, in particular, to the dual nature of international criminal law. While it is embedded in public international law it must simultaneously adhere to fundamental principles of criminal law. For this reason Meron considers that progressive approaches to customary international law by international criminal tribunals could not be reconciled with criminal law principles such as *nullum crimen sine lege*.[117] However, the application of law includes declaring, formulating, clarifying, interpreting, and developing the law and, as such, the difference between establishing a mere determination of existing law and rule-creation is one of degree.[118] According to the ICTY Appeals Chambers, the *nullum crimen sine lege* principle 'does not prevent a court from *interpreting and clarifying* the elements of a particular crime',[119] even going so far as to claim that it does not 'preclude *the progressive development* of the law'.[120] When taking a closer look at the judgments, the *nullum crimen sine lege* principle in general has not gained much attention in the jurisprudence of international criminal tribunals. This is particularly true with regard to the question as to what the concrete requirements of its *praevia* and *certa* components in relation to customary international criminal law as a legal basis in international criminal proceedings are.

Generally, it seems as if international criminal tribunals avoid the task of establishing whether accessibility and foreseeability of the concrete international criminal norm have been given in particular cases. The jurisprudence of the UN *ad hoc* tribunals implies that if criminal responsibility is given under customary international law, the criteria of accessibility and foreseeability can be assumed.[121] A customary criminal norm is based on a plurality of sources from the international and various national legal orders: state practice in the form of physical and verbal acts and paper practice, such as policy statements and press releases as well as the conduct of states in international organizations, including the resolutions they vote for; domestic law; military manuals; and national and international case law. It seems dubious,

---

115 As quoted by Tom Ginsburg, 'Bounded Discretion in Judicial Lawmaking' (2004) 45 Virginia Journal of International Law 631, 636.

116 Martin Shapiro, 'Judges as Liars' (1994) 17 Harvard Journal of Law & Public Policy 155.

117 Theodor Meron, 'Editorial Comment, Revival of Customary Humanitarian Law' (2005) 99 American Journal of International Law 817, 825.

118 Robert Y. Jennings, 'General Course on Principles of International Law' (1967) 121 Collected Courses 11, 341.

119 *Prosecutor v Delalić (Ĉelebici)* (n 52) para 173 (emphasis added); see also *Prosecutor v Aleksovski* (n 52) para 126.

120 *Prosecutor v Milutinović* (Decision on Dragolub Ojdanić's Motion Challenging Jurisdiction – Joint Criminal Enterprise) IT-99-37-AR72 (21 May 2003) para 38 (emphasis added).

121 See for *Prosecutor v Stakić* (n 79) para 101; this critique in relation to ICTY case law has been raised by the ECCC, *Prosecutor v Ieng* (Public Decision on the Appeals Against the Co-Investigative Judges Order on Joint Criminal Enterprise (JCE)) 002/19-09-2007-ECCC/OCIJ (PTC38) (20 May 2010) para 45.

therefore, how a customary criminal norm can ever be accessible and its punishment foreseeable.[122] When the knowledge of criminal statutes by individuals on the domestic level is a legal fiction, it follows that the knowledge of customary international criminal law is a fiction of a legal fiction.

The argument against applying stringent requirements in relation to accessibility and foreseeability generally focuses on the nature of international law, and the lack of a central legislator, in particular.[123] Therefore, due to uncertain factors in the creation and determination of customary law, it is suggested that the requirements of accessibility and foreseeability need to be loosened. Critics, however, argue that, instead, it is the relativization of the *nullum crimen sine lege* principle that comes at the expense of precision when determining customary international criminal law.[124] Concerns in relation to accessibility of the law and foreseeability of punishment have been sweepingly denied. For example, the ICTY *Delalić* Trial Chamber in relation to *nullum crimen sine lege* held that:

> The purpose of this principle is to prevent the prosecution and punishment of an individual for acts which he reasonably believed to be lawful at the time of their commission. It strains credibility to contend that the accused would not recognize the criminal nature of the acts alleged in the Indictment.[125]

In the few cases where the European Court of Human Rights (ECtHR) had to elaborate on the questions of foreseeability and accessibility under Article 7 of the European Convention on Human Rights (ECHR) in relation to the commission of international crimes, the court rather took the 'flagrantly unlawful nature of the ill-treatment' into consideration. The ECtHR did not discuss whether, on basis of the available material, the concrete underlying international criminal norm was accessible to the individual.[126] According to Schabas, the moral blame-

---

122 Ward N. Ferdinandusse, *Direct Application of International Criminal Law in National Courts* (TMC Asser Press 2006) 239. See also Jos Verhoeven, 'Article 21 of the Rome Statute and the Ambiguities of Applicable Law' (2002) 23 Netherlands Yearbook of International Law 2, 22, asking how could an individual 'be satisfactorily informed of the existence or exact content of a customary international rule (...), which the states themselves very often remain largely ignorant of'. Similarly, Susan Lamb, 'Nullum Crimen, Nulla Poena Sine Lege in International Criminal Law' in Antonio Cassese and others (eds), *The Rome Statute of the International Criminal Court: A Commentary, Volume I* (OUP 2002) 743, stating that the NCSL principle, which 'is based explicitly upon the value of legal certainty, sits uneasily with the very nature of customary international law, which is unwritten and frequently difficult to define with precision.'

123 See already the US Military Tribunal, *United States of America v Josef Altstötter and Others Case* ('The Justice Case'), Trials of War Criminals Before the Nuremberg Military Tribunal under Control Council Law No. 10 ('the Green Series') vol III, 41 <https://www.loc.gov/rr/frd/Military_Law/NTs_war-criminals.html> accessed 31 January 2021.

124 See Pierre Hauck, 'The Challenge of Customary International Crimes to the Principle of Nullum Crimen Sine Lege' (2008) 21 (2) Humanitäres Völkerrecht 58, 59.

125 *Prosecutor v Delalić (Ĉelebici)* (n 50) para 313: 'The purpose of this principle is to prevent the prosecution and punishment of an individual for acts which he reasonably believed to be lawful at the time of their commission. It strains credibility to contend that the accused would not recognize the criminal nature of the acts alleged in the Indictment.' This conception was accepted and fully shared by *Prosecutor v Delalić (Ĉelebici)* (n 52) paras 179–80.

126 *Kononov v Latvia* App no 36376/04 (ECtHR, 17 May 2010) para 238; see also *Jorgić v Germany* App no 74613/01 (ECtHR, 12 July 2007) para 113 referring to 'acts of a considerable severity'.

worthiness of the underlying conduct is also the reason why the ECtHR has 'eschewed an excessive positivism accepting that the principle *nullum crimen* is respected even by unwritten or judge-made rules'.[127]

5. CONCLUDING REMARKS

The analysis of the jurisprudence of modern international criminal tribunals shows that there is no detectable common, unified approach to the identification of rules of customary international law. Instead, international criminal tribunals have used, very well, the flexibility and doctrinal confusion surrounding customary international law as a source of law, when determining customary international law, and in certain cases they have even created it. The reluctance of international criminal tribunals to refer to state practice and *opinio iuris* explicitly, or to allocate specific evidence to these elements in their judgments, is indeed blatant. The delimitation between a mere application and interpretation of existing legal principles and the creation of new law is particularly difficult when judges refer to modern and progressive approaches to customary international law. In particular, in international criminal proceedings, theoretically, the human rights of the accused (the *nullum crimen sine lege* principle, *in dubio pro reo*) should bar judges from creating law. A more conscious and probably more restrictive approach of using and establishing customary international law would not only ensure that a judgment is considered as being based on a well-founded reasoning therewith the individual can comprehend the basis of their conviction, but would enhance the perceived legitimacy of international criminal justice. Consequently, sound methodological approaches for the determination of customary international criminal norms are not only crucial for abstract legal theory, but enable us to determine whether the human rights of individual defendants have been infringed. That is the case when international criminal tribunals have created law retroactively, or have excessively interpreted the contours of a crime or mode of liability under customary international criminal law. This is, due to the manifest immorality of the underlying conduct, hard to assert. One might even argue that too stringent *nullum crimen sine lege* requirements would have impeded the entire development of international criminal law. In the words of the US Military Tribunal in the Justice Case, international criminal law would have been 'strangled' at birth.[128] It is for this reason that even the ECtHR, when analysing whether the *nullum crimen sine lege* requirements were met, has not been overly positivistic when international core crimes are at stake.

---

[127] William Schabas, *The International Criminal Court. A Commentary on the Rome Statute* (OUP 2010) art 22, 404.

[128] US Military Tribunal, *Altstötter and Others Case* (n 123) 974–75.

13. The law at hand: Paratext in manuals on international humanitarian law

Wouter G. Werner

1. INTRODUCTION

By now, international humanitarian lawyers have become accustomed to the idea that they can look up applicable law in a 'manual'. Whoever has questions about the relevant rules on, say, air and missile warfare, non-international armed conflicts, warfare at sea or cyber warfare has the option of picking up a manual to find some practical answers. Manuals in the field of international humanitarian law (IHL) have grown in importance, partly due to the lack or slowness of formal mechanisms of international law-making. In order to deal with novel and complex issues in areas such as cyber-war, non-international armed conflicts or air warfare, experts are called in to articulate the law at hand in a 'manual'. However, what it means to lay down (humanitarian) law in the specific form of a 'manual' has not been explored so far. Until now, debates on 'manuals' in IHL have focused on their content, the composition of the group of experts developing the manual, the manuals' status in law, or on their possible impact. As far as I know, the somewhat peculiar form of the 'manual' itself has not been subject to further reflection or discussion yet. This is what I set out to do in my chapter. I will do so on the basis of a study of a family of manuals in the field of international (humanitarian) law: the 1880 and 1913 Oxford Manuals (on war on land and war at sea respectively), the 1994 San Remo Manual on International Law Applicable to Armed Conflicts at Sea, the 2006 San Remo Manual on the Law of Non-International Armed Conflict, the 2009 Harvard Manual on International Law Applicable to Air and Missile Warfare (HPCR), and the Tallinn Manual 2.0 on the International Law Applicable to Cyber Operations. Although the scope of these manuals is often broader than only IHL (in particular the Tallinn Manual covers many more fields), I will nevertheless sometimes refer to them as 'IHL manuals'. The reason is that the manuals in question either predominantly or originally deal with problems in the field of the law of armed conflict. The reader should keep in mind, however, that more fields than IHL are covered in several of the manuals I discuss.

Before I move to the central argument of the chapter, I will briefly delineate the concept of an 'international manual' in section 2. Section 3 discusses a tension that runs through all modern international manuals in the field of (humanitarian) law: the need to restate the law as it is and the desire to provide concrete, workable instructions to the users of the manual. Based on a comparison between manuals in the field of humanitarian law and consumer product manuals, I hope to show how and why this tension emerges. Section 4 focuses on a few ways in which modern manuals seek to manage this tension. In this context, I will focus specifically on the *form and presentation* of the rules contained in modern manuals. Based on the work of the French literary scholar Gérard Genette I analyse a few so-called 'paratextual elements' of manuals: their titles, their prefaces and the use of bold to accentuate the rules they present.

2. THE CONCEPT OF AN INTERNATIONAL MANUAL

The manuals analysed in this chapter share three combined characteristics that set them apart from other forms of legal advice or from domestic military manuals.

In the first place, they are what Boothby has called 'international manuals'. International manuals are 'prepared by a group of international experts working in their personal capacity', whereas 'the text of the manual, or at least the rules identified in the Manual represent the collective and agreed view of the participating experts'.[1] The fact that the manuals are produced by an international group of experts sets them apart from domestic military manuals, as well as from legal advice produced by national committees or individual experts. The fact that manuals represent the views of an international group of experts also matters for their legitimacy and impact. Manuals such as the San Remo, Tallinn, and Harvard Manual have been widely discussed in academic circles, as well as by professionals and policy-makers working in the area of conflict and security law. This also explains why the composition of the group of experts for international manuals is generally much more of an issue than the composition of national advisory bodies or the background of authors writing domestic military manuals.[2]

Second, the manuals under discussion in this chapter take the form of 'restatements' of law. This means that they come in a particular form, whereby the results are presented – a form that is markedly different from most other forms of legal advice.[3] International manuals are organized in the form of a set of 'rules' that reflect existing international law, and accompanied by a commentary or explanation that spells out the precise meaning of the rule, possible points of disagreement among the experts, etc. The 1994 San Remo Manual, for example, contains a list of 'provisions' that read almost like a treaty. Each provision is numbered and formulated as if it were an article in an international convention, even though the introduction to the manual clearly states that most of its 'provisions' are merely restatements of already applicable law. The 2006 San Remo Manual, as well as the Harvard and Tallinn Manual, adopt a language closely related to that used in so-called 'US Restatements of Law' as produced by the American Law Institute. Their main conclusions are formulated in what the manuals themselves call 'black letter rules', and are correspondingly printed in bold. The term 'black letter

1 William H. Boothby, *Conflict Law, The Influence of New Weapons Technology, Human Rights and Emerging Actors* (Springer and Asser Press 2014) 65.

2 See for example Roscini's critical remarks on the overrepresentation of Western experts in the Tallinn Manual: Marco Roscini, *Cyber Operations and the Use of Force in International Law* (OUP 2014) 31.

3 A document that somewhat resembles a 'manual' is the *ICRC Interpretative Guidance on the Notion of Direct Participation of Hostilities Under International Humanitarian Law*. However, the ICRC guidance is not a restatement of applicable rules in a broader sub-field of humanitarian law, but rather a document indicating how a rather specific term is to be interpreted. In addition, its conclusions are not formulated as 'black letter rules' or treaty-like 'provisions' but instead as a series of 'recommendations'.

rules' is closely related to the 'black letter principles' that can be found in US Restatements as well as to the 'black letter law' that those restatements claim to represent.[4]

Third, the manuals are meant to 'instruct' its users on how to deal with legal rules and how to act in accordance with existing rules. In that sense they resemble manuals in fields such as consumer product manuals. In other words, their aim is not to restate existing law as such, but to do so with the aim of instructing the reader how they should read and apply the law. The focus on 'instructions' implies that manuals have a practical orientation, which is reflected in the ambition to formulate (seemingly) straightforward 'black letter rules' that decision-makers can take up when faced with a concrete problem.

3. BETWEEN RESTATEMENT AND INSTRUCTION

3.1 Manuals as Restatements

Modern manuals present themselves as restatements of existing law. Take for example the 1994 San Remo Manual on Naval Warfare. Although the Manual acknowledges that 'a few provisions (…) might be considered progressive developments in the law', it is quick to emphasize that it should primarily be considered as a *restatement* of already existing law.[5] In similar fashion, the 2009 *Harvard Manual on Air and Missile Warfare* is introduced as 'the most up-to-date restatement of existing international law applicable to air and missile warfare',[6] while its main objective is phrased as producing a 'restatement of existing law applicable to air or missile operations in international armed conflict'.[7] The idea of a restatement implies, according to the authors, that 'existing international law is presented with no attempt to conceal any blemishes or inadequacies'. The 2013 *Tallinn Manual on Cyber Warfare* (which is now integrated in the Tallinn Manual 2.0), in its turn, says it 'identifies international law applicable to cyber warfare',[8] while in subsequent speeches and publications its chair consistently referred to the Manual as a restatement of international law.[9]

The idea that manuals in the field of IHL are 'restatements' is interesting in light of the overarching topics of this book as a whole, law-making and legitimacy. To 'restate' a valid rule

---

4 According to Harvard Law School, one of the law schools that has been involved in several restatements, the aim of the 'restatements' is to 'distill the "black letter law" from cases, to indicate a trend in common law, and, occasionally, to recommend what a rule of law should be'. Catherine Biondo, 'Secondary Sources: ALRs, Encyclopedias, Law Reviews, Restatements, & Treatises' (Harvard Law School, 9 October 2016 <http://guides.library.harvard.edu/c.php?g=309942&p=2070280> accessed 31 January 2021.

5 Introductory note to the San Remo Manual <https://www.icrc.org/ihl/INTRO/140?OpenDocument> accessed 31 January 2021.

6 Harvard Manual on International Law Applicable to Air and Missile Warfare 2009 (HPCR) <http://ihlresearch.org/amw/HPCR%20Manual.pdf> accessed 31 January 2021.

7 ibid 6.

8 Michael N. Schmitt (ed), *Tallinn Manual on the International Law Applicable to Cyber Warfare* (CUP 2013).

9 See for example, Michael N. Schmitt, 'In Defense of Due Diligence in Cyberspace' (2015–2016) 125 The Yale Law Journal Forum 68, 70 <http://www.yalelawjournal.org/forum/in-defense-of-due-diligence-in-cyberspace> accessed 31 January 2021, where Schmitt describes the Tallinn Manual as 'a restatement of law consisting of ninety-five "black letter" rules and accompanying commentary'. Note that also pages such as Wikipedia or the internet archive refer to the Tallinn Manual as a restatement.

implies that it has been authoritatively 'stated' earlier. In this way, the question of law-making can be delegated to agents outside the circle of experts who have produced the manual. The legitimacy of the manual then hinges upon the correct restatement of rules whose validity has been secured in other ways already. This logic is spelled out most clearly (and radically) in the 2009 Harvard Manual, which takes as its starting point that 'the authors of the HPCR Manual have no power to legislate'. As a consequence, the manual argues, their job is not to make law appear more coherent, morally acceptable or logical than others have made it: 'the emerging restatement must be evaluated not on the basis of logic, expediency or policy considerations. The only test is whether the text of the HPCR Manual is an "accurate mirror-image of existing international law".'[10] Where the 1880 Oxford Manual spoke freely about 'the progress of juridical science' as one of the driving forces behind the rules it presented, the 2009 Harvard Manual shies away from any pretension to law-making. Instead it portrays itself in terms of a direct representation of existing rules, irrespective of their possible shortcomings.

By presenting their content primarily in terms of 'restatements' of already existing rules, manuals in humanitarian law hark back to the etymological origins of the concept of legitimacy. Etymologically speaking, 'legitimacy' springs from a family of concepts all circling around 'lawfulness': 'make lawful, declare to be lawful, (…) fixed by law, in line with the law'.[11] While the latter meaning may be too narrow for those interested in rational, normative assessments of existing rules and institutions, it is an almost perfect fit for the claims to legitimacy made in modern manuals in humanitarian law. After all, claims to legitimacy made in those manuals are about exactly this: engendering a belief in the acceptability of the manual because its arguments are fixed by and in line with existing international law. Manuals (rightly) claim that they cannot be understood as forms of law-making according to most of the traditional understandings of the law-making process. The development of manuals cannot be regarded a formal act of law-making because the experts involved are not empowered by a rule of positive law to come up with new rules or even novel interpretations of international law. At best, they could claim that they represent 'teachings of the most highly qualified scholars', as mentioned in Article 38 of the ICJ Statute. However, even if this interpretation would be accepted, the 'teachings' contained in international manuals predominantly claim that they reflect law that is already validated through (other) forms of formal law-making. Not surprisingly, therefore, international manuals themselves explicitly deny that they are engaged in law-making in the formal sense. Nor can manuals be understood as a form of informal law-making, if this is taken to mean the production of alternative normative guidelines that seek to replace or co-exist with rules of formal international law. The purpose of the manuals is quite the opposite: to stay firmly within the confines of traditional, formal law. The idea is to strengthen and clarify formal law, and to come up with a restatement of what formal law in a particular field requires. Manuals in humanitarian law are characterized by a very strong commitment to formal, public international law, not by an attempt to bypass it through the creation of alternative forms of regulation. In a way, producing a manual is an attempt to rescue formal law from its own shortcomings. Increasingly, formal law (domestic as well as

---

[10] HPCR (n 6) 2.

[11] Online Etymology Dictionary <http://www.etymonline.com/index.php?term=legitimate> accessed 31 January 2021.

international) has difficulties coping with the acceleration of time[12] and the rapid rise of new problems such as cyberwar, drone warfare, automated weapon systems, etc. Processes of formal law-making often simply take too long to adapt to changing social and technological realities. One way of dealing with this problem is calling in experts to spell out if and how already existing legal frameworks are able to reduce socio-political complexity and provide guidance for behaviour in new contexts. Or, to put it differently, one way of dealing with this is to ask experts to transform the new and the unfamiliar, into the unstructured familiar – essentially to rephrase uncertainties in terms of laws that have been around for decades or centuries.

The notion of a 'restatement' of the law echoes US legal practice. According to the Harvard Law School Library, the aim of restatements in US law is to 'distill the "black letter law" from cases to indicate trends in common law, and occasionally to recommend what a rule of law should be. In essence, they restate existing common law into a series of principles or rules.'[13] Restatements of the law are prepared by the American Law Institute and are often considered authoritative because of their content as well as the prestige of the Institute and the experts involved. Not surprisingly, the dual aim of 'distilling' and 'recommending' makes restatements also vulnerable to critiques from two sides: either they are regarded too conservative (adding little to what is already out there) or they are regarded as too activist (producing rules beyond positive law).[14] In similar fashion, manuals in the field of IHL unavoidably run the risk of being critiqued from both sides: for some, the manuals will move too far beyond what they consider to be existing international law, whereas for others the manuals will not contribute sufficiently to the development of international law.[15] It is impossible to foreclose such critiques completely, because the point of manuals is to do two things at the same time. Manuals first and foremost are designed to restate the law that is already out there. However, if this were a matter of simply registering what can be found objectively, there would be no need for years of research, deliberation and decision-making among a group of international experts. Manuals are drafted by people who have the capacity to prioritize, to reimagine, to apply old rules to new phenomena, to come up with suggestions how to amend the law, etc. In other words: the end product of the experts' deliberations is not just a series of neutral reproductions of what already exists. The publication of the manuals hopes to change the symbolic order through which lawyers make sense of the world. In order to do that, manuals have to operate in between the idea of restatements as 'mirrors of existing law' and manuals as 'contributing to the development of international law'. Just like the Roman God Janus, they look with one face into the past (mirroring the law already out there) and with one face towards the future

---

[12] Hartmut Rosa, *Social Acceleration: A New Theory of Modernity* (Columbia University Press 2013).

[13] LibGuides Community <https://guides.library.harvard.edu/c.php?g=309942&p=2070280> accessed 31 January 2021. For similar characterizations see, among others, the University of Texas, Tarlton Law Library <http://tarltonguides.law.utexas.edu/restatements> accessed 31 January 2021; the Case Western Reserve Database <http://lawlibrary.case.edu/research-guides/restatements-of-the-law/> accessed 31 January 2021; or the Brooklyn Guide <http://guides.brooklaw.edu/c.php?g=330883&p=2222651> accessed 31 January 2021.

[14] For a discussion see Kristen David Adams, 'Blaming the Mirror: The Restatements and the Common Law' (2007) 40 Indiana Law Review 206.

[15] Although, of course, a very common response has also been to agree with the positions adopted in manuals.

(how law is to be developed and applied in future cases). This brings me to the second aspect of international manuals: their character as 'manuals'.

3.2 Manuals as Instructions

Manuals in IHL not only seek to restate the law. Their purpose is also to instruct readers how they should apply existing legal provisions to problems in the field of conflict and security. The term 'manual' captures quite nicely what is at stake here. On the one hand the term points to an activity that is done 'manually' rather than, for example, 'mechanically', to an activity that involves human agency, often in the form of an art or craftsmanship.[16] The practical, hands-on aspect of the term 'manual' is echoed in IHL manuals' insistence on the need to provide information that is useful for those who have to take decisions on the battlefield, or in legislative or judicial procedures. Although often hotly debated in academic circles, the aim of manuals in IHL is not primarily academic, but rooted in and directed towards those who practise law in a variety of contexts. On the other (yet related) hand, the term refers to information that is 'ready at hand', for example in the form of a handbook or a booklet containing instructions. The aim here is to reduce complexity for decision-makers and to provide them with concrete instructions on how to act in accordance with the law. The term 'instructions' is key here, as it combines the different elements that can be found in manuals: giving knowledge, providing authoritative information or advice, teaching and ordering, or commanding.[17]

The typical context for the existence of 'manuals' has been in relation to the use of consumer products, where small instructional guides accompany items such as lawnmowers, microwaves, vacuum cleaners, etc. Consumer product instructions have grown in importance, partly due to the increasing complexity of many modern consumer goods, and partly due to the rules on product liability.[18] The growing importance of consumer product instructions is reflected in the rise of books, guidelines, journals,[19] papers, etc., that discuss specific aspects of designing 'manuals'. The topics covered in this literature vary from the articulation of clear objectives,[20] to the need to address specific target groups,[21] risk communication and issues sur-

---

16 See for example the definition contained in The Free Dictionary <http://www.thefreedictionary.com/manual> accessed 31 January 2021.

17 For a definition, see for example: Merriam-Webster Dictionary <http://www.merriam-webster.com/dictionary/instruction> accessed 31 January 2021.

18 For an overview of the rules in the context of the US see the restatement (sic) issued: American Law Institute, *3rd Restatement of the Law* <https://www.ali.org/meetings/show/restatement-law-third-conflict-laws-oct2015/> accessed 31 January 2021. The rules of the restatement have informed instructions on how to develop product instructions. See for example: Kenneth Ross, 'The Role of Product Instructions in Product Liability Prevention' (*Incompliance*, 30 April 2015) <http://incompliancemag.com/article/the-role-of-product-instructions-in-product-liability-prevention/> accessed 31 January 2021.

19 In this context, it is worth mentioning specifically the *Journal of Technical Writing and Communication* (published by Sage).

20 Gerald Cohen and Donald H. Cunningham, *Creating Technical Manuals: A Step by Step Approach to Writing User Friendly Instructions* (McGraw-Hill 1984).

21 For an example see the opening parts of the 1998 UK Writing Safety Instructions for Consumer Products, where different target groups are identified: Consumer Affairs Directorate, *Writing Safety Instructions for Consumer Products 1998*, DTI <http://www.humanics-es.com/saftyins.pdf> accessed 31 January 2021.

rounding liability,[22] or typographical aspects of manual design.[23] Different aspects of manual design have been put together in the US Consumer Product Safety Comission *Manufacturer's Guide to Developing Consumer Product Instructions*, which reads like a manual-manual, setting out how to develop proper guidance handbooks for consumers.[24] Just like consumer product manuals, manuals in the field of IHL need to identify the foreseeable users of the manual. The 1880 *Oxford Manual on Laws of War on Land* already contained the outspoken ambition to guide domestic legislators.[25] Some modern IHL manuals are also quite explicit about their objectives and foreseeable users. For instance, the *Harvard Manual on Air and Missile Warfare* contains a rather extensive section on the goals and potential users of the instructions, where it sets out that the manual seeks to influence domestic military training, rules of engagement, military manuals, legal advisors, and the actual conduct of troops on the ground, including officers who have to take rapid decisions. The San Remo *Manual on Non-International Armed Conflict* goes even beyond the identification of its main users and objectives. In its foreword the chair of the International Institute of Humanitarian Law not only identifies designers and teachers of military courses as one of the main foreseeable users, but also calls upon 'users of the Manual to come up with suggestions to further elucidate the law and improve both the black letter rules as well as the commentary in future editions of the text'. This resonates well with the recommendations for product manuals to solicit feedback of potential and actual users in order to improve the quality of the instructions.[26] The focus on their eventual 'users' also implies that manuals in the field of humanitarian law have to pay attention to elements that have been spelled out in instructional guides for product manuals, including the need to capture the attention of the reader (see also the analysis of the use of bold letters in section 4) or the use of authorities to enhance the credibility of the manuals.

However, the analogy regarding product instructions and manuals in the field of IHL should not be taken too far. There are some important differences between IHL manuals and their consumer product counterparts. Most of all, manuals in law and consumer product manuals have different referent objects. Consumer product manuals contain instructions on how to use something: the item purchased by the consumer. One of the major challenges for consumer product manuals is to ensure that customers actually read the instructions before they start using the product they have bought. Designers of product manuals 'cannot assume that all customers will seek the instructions (…). After buying a new product, consumers often want to use it immediately, so written items accompanying the product may seem like a distraction.'[27] In the case of manuals in the field of IHL the relationship between manual and product is more complicated. At first sight, it seems as if the law applicable to a particular field is the

---

22 For an example see Michael S. Wogalter and Kenneth R. Laughery (eds), *Warnings and Risk Communication* (Taylor & Francis Inc. 1999).

23 For an example see Gerald G. Alred, Charles Brusaw and Walter E. Oliu, *Handbook of Technical Writing* (St. Martin's Press 2000).

24 Manufacturer's Guide to Developing Consumer Product Instructions 2003, U.S. Consumer Product Safety Commission <https://www.cpsc.gov/PageFiles/103077/guide.pdf> accessed 31 January 2021. The examples from literature mentioned above are largely taken from this Guide.

25 ICRC, 'Preface to the Manual' <https://www.icrc.org/applic/ihl/ihl.nsf/Article.xsp?action=openDocument&documentId=B06FB334DC14CBD1C12563CD00515767> accessed 31 January 2021.

26 Manufacturer's Guide to Developing Consumer Product Instructions 2003 (n 24) 58.

27 ibid 15.

equivalent of the 'product' in consumer manuals. Manuals in the field of IHL would then be instructions on how to read and apply the law. However, as we saw in the previous sections, IHL manuals are at the same time 'restatements' of the law applicable in a particular field. In that sense, they are meant to both identify and clarify the applicable law in the first place and to reformulate that law in terms of a set of instructions, accompanied by a commentary. The assumption underlying IHL manuals is not that its users go back to the original legal sources themselves on the basis of the instructions provided by the experts. This would defy the purpose of the manuals, to provide instructions that can be taken up by, for example, executives or commanders in the field who have to make real-time decisions. IHL manuals are (also) meant to save its users the difficult task of using primary sources that are often ambiguous and not readily applicable to the problems at hand. Experts have done the complicated work for the users and provided them with a series of rules and commentaries that are easier to access and read. Whereas consumer product instructions face the challenge that consumers tend to skip reading them and start using the product immediately, IHL manuals are more likely to be used *instead* of primary legal sources. In this context it is not surprising to see that IHL manuals themselves are often referred to as 'products' produced by a group of experts.

The different referent objects of the two types of manuals helps explain the diverging status and nature of the rules they contain. Consumer product manuals contain instructions on how to use or maintain a product properly, how users need to behave if they want to make the product work according to its purposes. Yet, such manuals are not normative in the sense that they put readers under an *obligation* to behave in certain ways. After all, customers are, within the limits of the law, free to ignore the rules of the manual and to use products in any way they see fit. In other words, a product manual is concerned with the way in which 'normal', responsible users behave. A product manual is much more about doing what is *necessary* to achieve an established end goal than it is about doing what is *normatively required.* Normativity only comes in when consumers act irresponsibly because they ignored basic safety instructions. Otherwise, however, if they damage the product they have just bought because they failed to follow the product instructions, their conduct may be criticized as 'stupid', but not as a violation of the obligations contained in the manual. The picture looks quite different when we turn to manuals in the field of IHL. Here, manuals do not instruct readers how to properly use an independently existing product, but rather try to make sense of an interpretative practice organized around legal sources. Often, there is an ongoing interpretative struggle over the functions and proper use and interpretation of legal rules and institutions. Of course it is possible to participate in this interpretative practice and to come up with intersubjectively shared readings as to what that practice requires in concrete circumstances. This is exactly what manuals do: set out how an internationally constituted group of experts has agreed on specific rules and their application. However, that is quite different from the way product manuals spell out how one should behave to make a product work according to its functions and purposes. Manuals in the field of IHL cannot escape taking a position on issues that are normally taken for granted in consumer product manuals: how to identify the 'product' and what its proper use and function is. After all, the longing for answers to these more foundational questions is often the very reason why experts were called in.

This is reflected in the set-up of IHL manuals. As I explained in the previous section, manuals consist of a series of specific 'rules', which are presented as reflective of existing international law (a claim that is often reinforced by the use of terms such as 'black letter rules'). However, as with all rules, they cannot speak for, interpret or apply themselves; they need authoritative articulation in order to function. The point of manuals in IHL is precisely to come up with such authoritative articulations, based on the knowledge, experience and skills of the experts involved. However, this means that the rules contained in IHL manuals are not only restatements of the law, but also representations of the consensus that could be reached among the experts involved. Thus, while the *Harvard Manual on Air and Missile Warfare* claims to be a 'mirror-image of existing law', its black letter rules are also presented as reflecting 'the overall consensus among the group of experts'.[28] In similar fashion, the *Tallinn Manual* presents itself as a restatement of law and at the same time states that the formulation of its black letter was the result of 'consensus among the International Group of Experts'.[29] Since manuals in IHL deal with an interpretative legal practice that contains many different and often competing interpretations, there is sometimes a mismatch between the aim to restate law in the form of instructions and the aim to reach consensus among experts. The ambition to formulate 'manual like' instructions calls for precise and concrete rules that leave little room for interpretation, whereas the need to reach consensus may call for more general rules that accommodate different positions. Manuals in the field of IHL therefore need to constantly balance these two desiderata. Sometimes this leads to rather general 'black letter rules', followed by an explanation in the commentary that is more precise, but also demonstrates the different positions that could be taken. As Michael Schmitt argued in relation to the Tallinn Manual:

> (…) and so you, as users in a State, or a Ministry, or a scholar, this is not a Manual that gives you one answer. It's a Manual that says 'here's a broad Rule that everyone agrees on, but in terms of the interpretation of this Rule, you can kinda go through and say, "you know, that may have been the majority, minority view, among that group of scholars, but we in Israel think the minority view is an accurate reflection of law".'[30]

This once more shows that the material contained in IHL manuals makes them quite different from consumer product manuals. It would, for example, be difficult to imagine a manual on the use of a microwave that contains instructions such as 'some experts advise you to press this button; others disagree and suggest another button' or 'whether the microwave will keep functioning properly if used in X manner is as of yet uncertain'. However, in IHL manuals this is quite common and hardly surprising given the argumentative practice that international manuals seek to restate.

4. THE PRESENTATION OF INTERNATIONAL HUMANITARIAN LAW MANUALS

In this section, I will explore how the tensions inherent in IHL manuals are made visible in their physical appearance, in the way they are presented to the reader. In order to do this,

---

28 HPCR 2009 (n 6) 3.

29 Schmitt (n 8) 6.

30 Michael N. Schmitt, 'Tallinn Manual Part I', Presentation at CyCon 2012 <https://www.youtube.com/watch?v=wY3uEo-Itso> accessed 31 January 2021 (at 18:35).

I will first introduce the concept of 'paratext' (section 4.1) and then discuss some paratextual elements in IHL manuals (section 4.2).

4.1 Paratext

The term 'paratext' was coined by the French literary scholar Gérard Genette.[31] Genette came up with the concept of a 'paratext' in order to make sense of the multitude of elements that appear in printed works, although they do not belong to the story of the book in the strict sense. Examples include the title of a book, a preface, the name of the author, acknowledgements or the blurbs. Paratextual elements are crucial for understanding the nature and meaning of the written document. Without paratextual elements, it would become (more) difficult to situate a text, recognize its genre and to find out how to read it. As Genette has put it in relation to literary novels:

> the paratext is what enables a text to become a book and to be offered as such to the public (…). To indicate what is at stake, we can ask one simple question as an example: limited to the text alone and without a guiding set of directions, how would we read Joyce's *Ulysses* if it were not entitled *Ulysses*?[32]

Paratext belongs to the same material product as the rest of the text (the physical book, article, law, manual).[33] At the same time, paratextual elements are generally treated as something that is different from the text they present or refer to. If people talk about a novel, for example, they generally refer to the story that is contained in the pages after the title, the preface, the name of the author, etc. – although sometimes authors play with these conventions, for example by including a preface written by the main character of the novel.[34] Paratexts are 'para'-texts in the literal sense of the word, texts existing side by side with the rest of the text, while at the same time presenting the text to the reader. In this context, Genette refers to Borges' characterization of the preface as a 'vestibule', the part between the house and its surroundings, which allows visitors to enter or turn back.[35] Paratextual elements therefore 'surround and prolong [the text], precisely in order to *present* it, in the usual sense of this verb, but also in its strongest meaning: to *make it present*, to assure its presence in the world, its "reception" and its consumption (…)'.[36]

---

31 Gérard Genette, *Paratexts: Thresholds of Interpretation*, (Jane E. Lewin tr, CUP 1997). See also Kevin Jackson's lucid application and illustration of paratext in: *Invisible Forms: A Guide to Literary Curiosities* (St. Martin's Press 2000).

32 Genette (n 31) 1, 2.

33 An exception to this would be what Genette calls the 'epitext', which consists of elements that appear separately from the book, such as interviews with the author. In the context of IHL Manuals, an interesting example of epitext would be the explanations offered by Michael Schmitt on how to read the Tallinn Manual. See for example Michael Schmitt, 'The Tallinn Manual 2.0: What It Is and What It Is Not' (*Just Security*, 9 February 2017) <https://www.justsecurity.org/37559/tallinn-manual-2-0-international-law-cyber-operations/> accessed 31 January 2021.

34 A classical example is Vladimir Nabokov's *Lolita* (Olympia Press 1955).

35 Genette (n 31) 2.

36 Gérard Genette and Marie Maclean, 'Introduction to the Paratext' (1991) 22 New Literary History 261.

Genette's analysis of paratexts was limited to literary works. However, there is no reason to confine the study of paratexts to this form of writing. Paratextual elements occur in all forms of writing, including academic publications[37] or the packaging and promotion of medical products.[38] Paratexts matter a great deal in the field of law as well. In law, the status and authority of a document is of particular importance and paratextual elements help the reader to recognize what kind of text they encounter. Take for example the difference between the layout of judgment of the International Court of Justice and the summary of that very same judgment. The summary is presented to the reader with contact information, as well as information on the Twitter and YouTube account and the LinkedIn page. Interestingly, the summary also contains a disclaimer: 'not an official document'.

INTERNATIONAL COURT OF JUSTICE

2018
1 October
General List
No. 153

YEAR 2018

1 October 2018

OBLIGATION TO NEGOTIATE
ACCESS TO THE PACIFIC OCEAN

(BOLIVIA *v.* CHILE)

Figure 13.1 *ICJ Judgment in the case Obligation to Negotiate Access to the Pacific Ocean (Bolivia v Chile) (Merits) [2018] ICJ Rep 507*

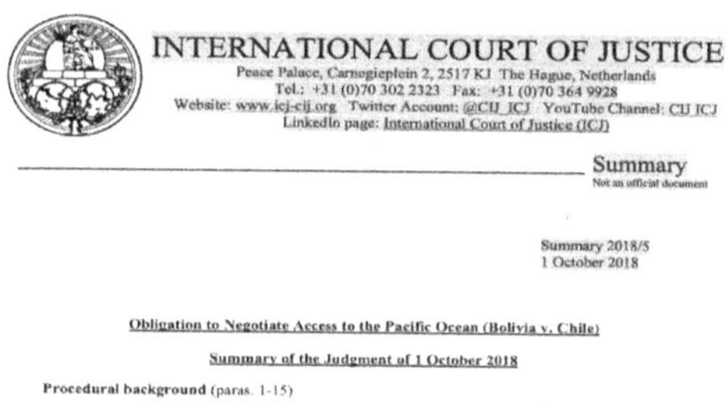

INTERNATIONAL COURT OF JUSTICE
Peace Palace, Carnegieplein 2, 2517 KJ The Hague, Netherlands
Tel.: +31 (0)70 302 2323 Fax: +31 (0)70 364 9928
Website: www.icj-cij.org Twitter Account: @CIJ_ICJ YouTube Channel: CIJ ICJ
LinkedIn page: International Court of Justice (ICJ)

Summary
Not an official document

Summary 2018/5
1 October 2018

Obligation to Negotiate Access to the Pacific Ocean (Bolivia v. Chile)

Summary of the Judgment of 1 October 2018

Procedural background (paras. 1-15)

Figure 13.2 *ICJ Summary of the Judgment in the case Obligation to Negotiate Access to the Pacific Ocean (Bolivia v. Chile) (Merits) [2018] ICJ Rep 507*

4.2 Paratextual Elements in International Humanitarian Law Manuals

I have selected three paratextual elements of IHL manuals: (1) titles; (2) prefaces; and (3) the layout of the restated rules. All these elements, I argue, reflect some of the tensions that IHL manuals have to deal with, in particularly the tension between neutrally restating rules and instructing the reader how to interpret and apply the same rules.

---

[37] Ken Hyland, *Disciplinary Discourses: Social Interactions in Academic Writing* (University of Michigan Press 2004).

[38] Hannah C. Tweed and Diane G. Scott (eds), *Medical Paratexts from Medieval to Modern: Dissecting the Page* (Palgrave Macmillan 2018).

4.2.1 Titles

Titles can fulfil at least two different functions in relation to the work they (re)present.[39] The first is to indicate, name or cover the topic of the text. Sometimes this is all that titles do, as in 'The Brothers Karamazov' or 'The Law of Armed Conflict: International Humanitarian Law in War'. The second function is to indicate the genre or subgenre to which the book belongs, as in 'The *Tragedy* of Hamlet, Prince of Denmark', 'The Law of War *Handbook*', or '*Introduction* to International Law' (emphases are mine). By including an indication of the genre, the author situates the book in a longer tradition and directs the expectations of the reader: in an introduction, do not expect too much complexity, in tragedy don't be disappointed if a happy ending is missing. By steering the reader in this way, the author also takes a certain risk: the written work may now be critiqued not only because of its content, but also because it fails to live up to the laws of a specific genre.

Titles of IHL manuals fulfil both functions. The use of the very term 'manual' in the title indicates the genre to which it belongs. As I set out before, the term 'manual' has a specific meaning in the law of armed conflict since at least the 1880s. The reader may expect a set of rules that instruct them how to deal with possible practical problems in a specialized area. The area concerned is designated in the second part of the title, as in the Tallinn Manual on the international law applicable to cyber operations or the San Remo Manual on international law applicable to armed conflicts at sea. The function of this part of the title is to indicate the topic of the manual, not its specific form. However, a title that covers 'the international law (…)' already hints at the difficulties of simultaneously restating the law and distilling clear-cut, easily applicable rules to concrete problems. International law is an interpretative practice that comes with uncertainties and controversies – exactly the reasons why there is need for a 'manual'. Another recurring aspect of titles in IHL manuals is the reference to concrete places and the mention of concrete dates directly after the title. The place is often directly incorporated in the title, as in the Oxford, San Remo or Tallinn Manual. The HPCR Manual on air and missile warfare does not formally contain such a reference, but is still often referred to as the 'Harvard Manual'. The use of such titles sets manuals apart from other genres of legal writing, such as academic articles or case notes. While by now it is common to include the place in titles of manuals, the same practice would look preposterous in academic legal writing. If I would entitle this chapter 'The Amsterdam Chapter on Paratext in Manuals', readers would take this as an ironical wink at best. In this respect, manuals look more like formal treaties or declarations than they resemble Article 38's 'teachings of qualified publicists'. However, in the very same title they immediately claim to be something else than formal law: they are 'manuals' that restate already valid rules.

4.2.2 Prefaces

A preface is an introductory text that guides the reader towards a text that follows. By contrast to the 'introduction', the preface does not belong to the main text itself, as illustrated by the practice of using roman page numbers, and by its often different, more personal style. However, it is not always easy to distinguish introductions from prefaces. The manuals

---

39 Genette (n 31) 76. Genette here refers to the work done in the sub-discipline of 'titology', in particular the work of Leo Hoek, *La marque du titre; Dispositifs sémiotiques d'une pratique textuelle* (De Gruyter 1981).

discussed in this chapter are a case in point. The HPCR manual, for example, is preceded by a foreword (preface) written by the director of the Harvard research programme that led the six-year-long drafting process. The foreword is followed by an 'introduction' written by the expert group itself. However, just like the prefaces described by Genette, this part of the text is separated from the main part of the text in different ways: the format of the page numbers differs, the tone, style and typography differ, and the introduction is a meta-text about the main text that follows a similar pattern as can be found in the Tallinn Manual and the San Remo Manuals. Below I will focus on the 'introduction' of the HPCR, as this is the most extensive, containing many examples of the functions traditionally fulfilled by prefaces.

So what are the functions of a preface? In the most general sense, prefaces seek 'to ensure that the text is read properly'.[40] This phrase combines two elements: to ensure that the text is *read*, and to ensure that it is read *in the proper way*. Prefaces, in other words, combine promotional and instructive elements. In order to convince the reader to continue, prefaces use a mix of rhetorical strategies, including an indication of the importance of the topic. An example can be found in Montesquieu's 'The Spirit of Laws', whose preface assures the reader modestly 'If this work meets with success, I shall owe it chiefly to the grandeur and majesty of the subject.'[41] In the manuals I study in this chapter, the importance of the subject is linked to another classical function often to be found in prefaces: to convince the reader of the usefulness of the text that follows. In a way, both elements already follow from the nature and purpose of manuals themselves. Manuals are drafted because international law is in need of an update, because there is a sense that international rules are somehow lagging behind new developments. Typically, therefore, manuals start out by explaining how new, important developments have created uncertainty and controversy about the application of existing law. The HPCR Manual does so by referring back to the Hague Rules of Aerial Warfare of 1923, followed by the following observation:

> The exponential changes brought about in air and missile technology in the last few decades have transformed the face of the modern battlefield, revolutionized military strategy, and created a series of distinct challenges to the protection of civilians in time of armed conflict. Over the course of the recent decades, the challenge of applying existing law to the use of aircraft and missiles in time of hostilities has amply demonstrated that there are bones of contention regarding the scope and content of the international legal rules pertaining to air and missile warfare.[42]

However, the invocation of the 'bones of contention' raises further questions: if existing law is so uncertain and contested, how is it possible to come up with 'rules' that restate the law as it is? If the manual restates the law as it is, should it not also restate its uncertainties and contested elements? At the same time, if it would do so, would it still be a 'manual'?

This takes me to a second function of prefaces: to convince the reader that the text is trustworthy and sincere. In academic publications, this is typically done in that part of the main text that deals with methods and sources. However, the format of the manual leaves no room

---

40 Genette (n 31) 197.

41 Charles Louis de Secondat and Baron de Montesquieu, *The Complete Works of M. de Montesquieu*, vol 1 (T. Evans 1777) <https://oll.libertyfund.org/titles/837> accessed 31 January 2021. The quote was used by Genette (n 31).

42 HPCR 2009 (n 6) ix.

for a separate methodological section in the main text. Instead, this is done in the preface (or preface-like introduction), in combination with the list of authorities and sources that is printed before the main text of the manual starts. Prefaces to manuals in the field of international (humanitarian) law typically describe the process leading up to the end product, and often informing the reader about the recurring consultation rounds among the experts themselves, but also with external experts and states. In addition, they sometimes tell the reader about the procedures that have been followed in order to arrive at the consensus-based rules that make up the main text of the manual. Although these parts of the text read like descriptions of what happened, they also fulfil a different function: they show the reader the thoroughness of the process, and thus the trustworthiness of the outcomes. At the same time, however, these parts of the text once more show that manuals are most of all restatements of the consensus among experts that have followed lengthy rounds of discussion, research and consultation.

In the HPCR manual, the retelling of the genesis of the end product is linked to yet another function of prefaces: the identification of the reader. The involvement of states, it argues, hopefully will enhance the chances that 'the *HPCR Manual* will be put to actual use by their respective armed forces'.[43] This is further specified in the section on the purposes of the manual, which seeks to provide legal advisors in armed forces with a 'pragmatic and cogent text', military commanders a 'practical tool' while making officers in the field 'confident of themselves at a time when decisions have to be made rapidly'.[44] In order to achieve this, the manual spells out how it is to be read properly by explaining the status of the rules and the relation between these rules and the commentary that follows them.

4.2.3 The presentation of rules on the page

Manuals literally present rules to the reader: the rules are put on paper and designed and formatted in a particular way. The Oxford Manuals, for example, contain rules that are drafted and formatted like provisions in a treaty, albeit with brief commentaries that one would not normally find in treaties.[45] The restatements are presented as 'articles' and the 1913 Oxford Manual is preceded by a 'preamble'. Both Oxford Manuals are included in the ICRC database with the heading 'Treaties, State Parties and Commentaries'.[46] Later manuals such as the San Remo manual on non-international armed conflicts, the HPCR manual or the Tallinn Manual use a different way to present their rules. These manuals refer to their restatements as 'black letter rules' and illustrate their status by printing them in bold. In this way, the rules are typographically set apart from the commentaries, which are printed in normal font. The aesthetic distinction between bold rules and ordinary commentaries underlines their different status and function. The rules stand out, immediately drawing attention. They are bold in more than one

---

43 Harvard Manual on International Law Applicable to Air and Missile Warfare 2009 (n 6) Introduction at xii.

44 ibid, Introduction at xiii.

45 The 1880 manual on laws of war on land starts with the following restatement: 'Article 1. The state of war does not admit of acts of violence, save between the armed forces of belligerent States. Persons not forming part of a belligerent armed force should abstain from such acts. "This rule implies a distinction between the individuals who compose the 'armed force' of a State and its other 'ressortissants'. A definition of the term 'armed force' is, therefore, necessary."'

46 ICRC, 'IHL Database, Treaties, State Parties and Commentaries' <https://ihl-databases.icrc.org/applic/ihl/ihl.nsf/vwTreatiesHistoricalByDate.xsp> accessed 31 January 2021.

sense: they appear thicker on the page, but also more resolute and straightforward. The black letter rules fit the idea of a manual as a book of practical instructions, although these instructions often turn out to be rather general (as a result of the need to reflect consensus among the experts). The rules are brief and eye-catching, whereas the commentary leaves more room for uncertainties and controversy inherent in any field of law.

The use of bold to emphasize the nature of rules taps in to a longer tradition of legal typography. As Kasia Solon Cristobal has shown, the term 'black letter law' used to refer to exactly that: law that appeared black on the page. The term arose when Italian humanists rediscovered the ancient Roman letter shapes that looked markedly different from the Gothic letters that were in use until then. In England, she argues, it became common to refer 'to Gothic as "blackletter" and Roman as "white letter" from the perception that more black than white appeared on a page and vice versa'.[47] Whereas Roman letter types gradually became the standard, lawyers for long persisted in using Gothic, also referred to as 'court hand'. This style of writing made the law increasingly inaccessible to most others, who had not been trained in reading 'court handwriting'. It was not until the late 19th century that the term 'black letter law' obtained its modern meaning of 'the basic principles of a subject in the law'.[48] In the context of the restatements of the law, carried out by the American Law Institute, the term also signifies rules that can be distilled from a variety of cases. The 'black letter' nature of these rules thus refers to their ability to reduce the complexity of legal developments and to distil relatively clear-cut rules. Where originally the term 'black letter' was used to criticize the inaccessibility of legal writing, it is now used to do the opposite: to clarify in a user-friendly way how rules are to be interpreted and applied.

5. CONCLUSION

This chapter has analysed an aspect of international humanitarian law manuals that is often overlooked in legal writing: its specific form and mode of presentation. Manuals literally look different from other forms of legal text, such as treaties, judgments, academic publications, or decisions. Their specific form and outlook, I have argued in this chapter, reflects the way in which they can and cannot claim legitimacy. In the first part of the chapter I have set out how manuals are always torn between their ambition to restate the law and their ambition to provide workable instructions for the readers (who are, quite tellingly, often referred to as 'users'). Both ambitions come with different claims to legitimacy and authority. In the second part I have illustrated how this tension is reflected in some so-called paratextual elements of manuals, in particular in the chosen titles, the prefaces and the layout of the core rules of the manuals. Through this analysis, I hope to have done more than to analyse some aspects of manuals in international humanitarian law. My chapter is also an invitation to look more closely at legal writing, to go beyond the content of what is written and to include the form, presentation and format of what is produced in international law.

---

[47] Kasia Solon Cristobal, 'From Law in Blackletter to "Blackletter Law"' (2016) 108 Law Library Journal 181, 188.

[48] ibid 212, quoting the Wolters Kluwers Law Dictionary.

14. International manuals in international humanitarian law: A rejoinder to Wouter G. Werner

Robin Geiß and Anni Pues[1]

1. INTRODUCTION

Manuals have become an increasingly popular choice in responding to the challenges of evolving technologies and the changing nature of war and conflict. Key features of manual development include: a process of research among an (often) close circle of international humanitarian law (IHL) scholars and military experts; institutionalized debate during the drafting process with the goal of achieving consensus on the rules suggested in the manuals and an accurate reflection of the spectrum of diverging views in the commentary to these rules; the explicit aim of creating impact through influence on the training and practice of military state actors (impact on state practice); and the potential use of formulated rules in domestic military manuals (impact on state practice and *opinio iuris*). These aims are achieved either through a broad and inclusive drafting process and/or through the close cooperation of states and those delivering training courses, in particular to military personnel.

Manuals have increased in number and in terms of thematic substance. Stagnating norm development processes in the area of war and conflict, despite the rapid development of new technologies potentially necessitating legislative adaptation, partially explain this trend.[2] When manuals plug into the void that develops because of this disparity, their importance and impact may be enhanced. After all, it seems safe to say that the Tallinn Manual – in light of states' reluctance to clarify their views and legal position on issues pertaining to cyber security[3] – has become 'the' reference for legal discussions about cyber warfare and cyber security more generally. Against this backdrop, reflection on the nature and role of manuals and experts (groups) is ever more important. So, too, is the legitimacy and transparency of the

1 The views expressed in the article are the sole responsibility of the individual authors. They do not necessarily reflect the views or opinions of the United Nations, UNIDIR, its staff members or sponsors.

2 See Wouter G. Werner, 'The Law at Hand – Paratext in Manuals on International Humanitarian Law', Chapter 13 in this book, 217, 220–221.

3 See Group of 7 (G7), 'G7 Declaration on Responsible States Behavior in Cyberspace' (Lucca, Italy: G7, 11 April 2017) <https://www.mofa.go.jp/files/000246367.pdf> accessed 31 January 2021, calling on states 'to publicly explain their views on how existing international law applies to States' activities in cyberspace to the greatest extent possible (…) giv[ing] rise to more settled expectations of State behavior'.

processes that bring them about, including how they are 'injected' and 'filtered' into international norm development processes. Especially in areas where there is a perceived 'knowledge gap', such as in the as yet not fully understood domain of cyber space. In these circumstances, the information contained in manuals is in high demand and quickly finds its way into law development processes more broadly. In that way a 'non-binding' expert manual can have significant influence on the formation of international law. So much so that some authors have recently called on states to reclaim their law-making role and to engage more assertively with normative development in the cyber domain.[4]

From the 1880 Oxford Manual to recent and forthcoming international manuals in the making, for example the Woomera Manual on the International Law of Military Space Operations[5] and the Manual on International Law applicable to Military Uses of Outer Space,[6] history allows for a broad-brush categorization of international manuals according to three distinct generations. Beginning with the 1880 Oxford Manual on the Law of War on Land, the first generation coincides with the early period of codification of IHL. The second generation of manuals starts with the 1994 San Remo Manual on International Law Applicable to Armed Conflicts at Sea (hereafter 1994 San Remo Manual) and reflects the need for IHL to be adjusted to changing conflict structures and new technologies. Recently, arguably a new generation of manuals has started to emerge, leaving the narrow realm of the laws of war behind and addressing broader questions pertaining to military operations generally. The projects addressing outer space, together with the Tallinn 2.0 Manual, mark what might loosely be categorized as a new generation of more holistic international manuals, i.e., a category of manuals in the military/security domain addressing legal questions pertaining to military operations in times of peace as well as during armed conflict.

2. THE FINE LINE – RESTATING, INTERPRETING, AND DEVELOPING

Are manuals a restatement of existing law, a technical description as one can find in 'product manuals',[7] or simply a distinct category of scholarly (group) writing? Or do they entail an element of genuine norm development? Contemporary manuals typically address areas in which international law suffers or is perceived to suffer from a lack of clarity, caused in particular by rapid technological advancement and by the changing nature of armed conflict itself. However, as Lauterpacht critically remarked in 1952, 'the radical change in the character of war in scope and method, the creation of new law is substantially a matter of political decision not necessarily related to any existing generally recognized legal principles.'[8] Thus, although

---

[4] Kubo Macak, 'From Cyber Norms to Cyber Rules: Re-Engaging States as Law-Makers' (2017) 30 Leiden Journal of International Law 877.

[5] 'The Woomera Manual' (*The University of Adelaide*, 13 February 2019) <https://www.law.adelaide.edu.au/woomera/the-woomera-manual> accessed 31 January 2021.

[6] 'Manual on International Law Applicable to Military Uses of Outer Space' (*McGill*) <https://www.mcgill.ca/milamos/> accessed 31 January 2021.

[7] See Werner (n 2) 219, 222–225.

[8] Hersch Lauterpacht, 'The Problem of the Revision of the Law of War' (1952) 29 British Yearbook of International Law 360, 379.

generally understood as restatements of the law, international manuals inherently tread the fine line between interpretation and law-making.[9]

Repetition and restating the law are meant to consolidate our understanding of a given rule. These techniques, however, can also lead to a blurring of our understanding of what the underlying (restated) rule actually is, namely when different restatements (manuals) feature small and competing textual differences. There is at least a risk that the ongoing inflation of such 'restatements', in light of the growing corpus of international manuals seeking to present the 'correct' or at least an agreed interpretation of contemporary law, means the underlying rules become blurred and contested. Increasing complexity and nuanced divergences from one manual to the other might defy the drafters' intention to facilitate our understanding of the law as it applies in new contexts. Indeed, with the ever-growing number of existing manuals and guidebooks on a diverse range of topics such as non-international armed conflicts, aerial and missile warfare as well as naval and cyberwarfare, it is hard not to lose sight of the forest for the trees. Another potential risk is that if the legal system lacks sufficiently clear distinctions between law and non-law, or between law and 'other normative prescriptions', the actors within the international community may invoke the most convenient position as 'law' in support of their interests.[10] This would lead to the inevitable result of a 'decline in the authority and normative power of the law'.[11]

Against this backdrop, it is important to reflect on the nature of the 'offering' made by manuals. Gustave Moynier, the drafter of the 1880 Oxford Manual, described it up front as an 'offering' to governments to progressively develop the law. Such an offering necessarily entails something new, something that has not yet been framed in the way that it is being offered now. The drafters of any of the second-generation manuals, however, have been cautious to avoid any claims of law-making. Indeed, they have adamantly emphasized the restatement character of manuals. The 'offering' towards governments reverberates in claims that these manuals serve as 'assistance to legal advisers and operators as to the current state of the law' and 'set forth a useful framework against which any inadequacy in the law can sensibly be assessed and addressed'.[12]

Wouter Werner offers an insightful analysis for what it means to restate the law. According to him, it necessarily includes the claim that rules already exist that are fit to address the identified challenge and it includes reshaping the law through repetition in a novel context.[13] The communicative processes at the core of manual-making contain an exercise of applying old rules to new challenges and contexts. Such repetition is not neutral but inherently contains selection processes, as an act of emphasis, of what is remembered and taken into account. This selective element inherent in the drafting process of manuals runs alongside the process changing the meaning of the repeated material.[14] Furthermore, transposing existing laws to new contexts inherently entails a law-making and developing element. An offering can be

---

[9] William H. Boothby, *Conflict Law: The Influence of New Weapons Technology, Human Rights and Emerging Actors* (T.M.C. Asser Press 2014) 65.

[10] Gennady M. Danilenko, *Lawmaking in the International Community* (Martinus Nijhoff 1993) 16–17.

[11] ibid.

[12] Boothby (n 9) 94.

[13] Werner (n 2) 218.

[14] ibid 221.

concealed as a restatement, but if the law is set or transposed ('restated') into new contexts, any such restatement will also contain an offering. Manual drafters therefore continuously walk a fine line between restatement, reinterpretation, and law-making. A clearer recognition of these inherent tensions – instead of futile attempts to conceal them – would support the drafters' cause.

These dimensions of new offerings are not problematic as such. Any private actors, writers or groups of writers are free to engage in a straightforward norm development exercise outlining progressively developed norms or develop and propose entirely new norms. A competition of ideas and suggestions is important for progress in democratic processes and precisely one of the tasks that legal academics should contribute to. Such propositions might come in the form of a manual, a handbook or something else. In addressing new spheres, groups of writers could, for example, devise entirely new rules from scratch and present a manual on what the law governing cyber space should ideally be instead of asking how existing (old) laws apply in this novel context. What is problematic, however, is that potential law-making contributions are often, intentionally or unintentionally, concealed – hidden behind the claim of mere restatement. The underlying incentive for this concealment presumably relates to simple marketing. A restatement of the existing law or, more precisely, the branding of a product as a restatement of existing law is likely to appeal to states. Suggestions of new rules and overt assumptions by non-state groups regarding their role as 'progressive norm developers' are more likely to provoke resistance and counter-reactions from states. International actors may be inclined to use such offerings as if this were the law as it stands without following established law-making procedures. Manuals appeal to and are directed towards a broad audience, including actors 'on the ground', legal advisers, and military personnel. The crucial point is that they appear as authoritative sources of law capable of conveying normative expectations. Bringing to light the inherent law-making elements in the drafting processes of international manuals is therefore important, as Wouter Werner has done in his contribution.

3. NORMATIVE PROCESSES AT WORK (POST-PUBLICATION) – INJECTION INTO THE SYSTEM

The content offered by manuals is injected into the 'system' through citation and referencing, by courts and other relevant actors, and through the inclusion in training materials for military personnel. Through these different routes, international manuals intrinsically – whether intended or unintended – shape state practice. Indeed, states play multiple roles in the normative processes triggered through the development of manuals. States may provide direct or more indirect sponsorship for the development of manuals and participate in the drafting process, signalling at least some form of approval of the process without implicating 'ownership' or endorsement of the end product, i.e., the manual. Such approval may, for example, be expressed through direct interaction between scholars and governmental experts who take on observer roles or through international organizations, as is the case regarding the Tallinn Manuals that were produced under the auspices of the NATO Cyber Defence Centre without being official NATO documents. Additionally, and more importantly, states play a key role by utilizing, endorsing, ignoring and/or explicitly rejecting parts of the regulatory framework offered in manuals. For example, Attorney General Jeremy Wright in his speech on 'Cyber and International Law in the 21st Century' delivered on 23 May 2018 implicitly engaged and rejected the position expressed in Tallinn 2.0 on sovereignty as a principle prohibiting certain cyber operations even if they do not meet the requirements of a prohibited intervention.[15] Apart from implicit or explicit engagement with the positions laid out in a manual, utilization of international manuals can take various forms, such as referencing and adoption of international manuals in domestic military manuals or the commissioning and design of tailor-made training courses for the military and other government officials based on international manuals. States may of course also decide to explicitly reject or tacitly ignore the formulated normative expectations in the proposed rules. In one assessment of state practice in relation to cyber space, a recent study argues that the Tallinn Manuals seem to have had only limited normative pull so far.[16] At the same time, important speeches by former US legal advisers Koh and Egan were clearly informed by discussions underlying the Tallinn Manuals and the mere existence of these drafting processes and expert discussions may have contributed to state perceptions of a need to position themselves on certain (contested) cyber issues that the Tallinn processes brought to light. Therefore, discussions triggered by manual development may inform legal debate, state practice and subsequent norm development. It is noteworthy that the Tallinn Manuals are frequently invoked and have quite likely acquired a relevance and prominence exceeding that of any other international legal manual.

4. THE LEGITIMACY OF EXERTING LAW-MAKING INFLUENCE THROUGH INTERNATIONAL MANUALS

Undermining the political process of norm-creation through the suggestion that old rules are fit to address new challenges could ultimately undermine law itself. If it is difficult to distinguish law from non-law, international actors might pick and choose convenient positions as law, a process that can lead to a loss of normative power and authority of international law.[17] This would contradict the entire exercise of manual-making, as this is aimed at strengthening the legal framework and the rule of law. The role of manuals in law-making therefore calls into question the rightfulness and legitimacy of such projects, a central theme in this book, and speaks directly to the issue of why the legitimacy of international manuals matters.[18] However, legitimacy is a multidimensional notion; there is not one simple answer to the question of when and under what circumstances a specific project might be legitimate. Questions at the heart of the legitimacy debate are: what is the authority that allows a circle of experts to act as (quasi)lawmakers in international law?[19] Does it matter how the outcome of these informal

---

15 Attorney General Jeremy Wright, 'Cyber and International Law in the 21st Century', speech delivered on 23 May 2018 <https://www.gov.uk/government/speeches/cyber-and-international-law-in-the-21st-century> accessed 31 January 2021.

16 Dan Efrony and Yuval Shany, 'A Rule Book on the Shelf? Tallinn Manual 2.0 on Cyberoperations and Subsequent State Practice' (2018) 112 American Journal of International Law 583.

17 Danilenko (n 10).

18 Thomas Franck, 'Legitimacy in the International System' (1988) 82 American Journal of International Law 705 has provided some key insights into the importance of legitimacy, such as the interconnection between legitimacy in a legal order and its normative pull or power to persuade.

19 Ruediger Wolfrum, 'Legitimacy in International Law from a Legal Perspective' in Ruediger Wolfrum and Volker Roeben (eds), *Legitimacy in International Law* (Springer 2008) 1, 6ff; Jean d'Aspremont and Eric De Brabandere, 'The Complementary Faces of Legitimacy in International Law: The

processes of law-making are injected into the system? Are the resulting legal rules satisfactory, or can they produce unsatisfactory results?[20]

5. EXPERTS, AUTHORITY AND LEGITIMACY

The authority of manual drafters is mainly based on their status as scholars. Authority, of course, is not the same as legitimacy. But both entail an element of external acknowledgement. The authority of legal scholarly writing can normatively be derived from Article 38(1)(d) of the ICJ Statute that assigns 'teachings of the most highly qualified publicists of the various nations' a role 'as subsidiary means for the determination of rules of law'. However, those publicists might not necessarily have to be lawyers or academics. International manuals of the second and third generation strongly emphasize the expert status of their authors, which implies the claimed authority to restate the law. The emphasis on the 'expert' status is striking and suggests a form of self-assertive authority. But it seems unlikely that Article 38 of the ICJ Statute envisaged the inclusion of technical experts in a specific field who, through their position in the armed forces, *de facto* represent the interests of individual states.[21] The striking argument for the participation of military experts is IHL's intrinsic requirement to function on the battlefield. This area of law needs to be particularly user-friendly to increase the potential for compliance in the inherently dire circumstances of armed conflict. Groups of specific experts in the field 'might even induce legitimacy because of their expertise that is being brought into the law-making process'.[22] The combination of legal scholars and technical experts in the drafting of manuals can offer the potential to a rightful claim to authority that receives external acknowledgement because of the specific combination of different, yet complementary, forms of expertise.

Manuals that propose rules for activities in entirely new and possibly still incompletely understood environments such as cyber space or outer space are confronted with a specific problem: the novelty of space and related activity entails that there will be very few who can claim to be experts in the field as experience can only be very limited. In contrast, drafters of manuals in long-established fields can more easily claim authority and produce respected results. To illustrate the point: the 1994 San Remo Manual was drafted by lawyers and naval experts as part of a seven-year project on the modernization of the law of armed conflict at sea, attempting to 'apply the principles and basic rules of international humanitarian law to modern

---

Legitimacy of Origin and the Legitimacy of Exercise' (2011) 34 Fordham Journal of International Law 190, 192 propose the concept 'legitimacy of origin' with which this question resonates.

[20] Mattias Kumm, 'The Legitimacy of International Law: A Constitutionalist Framework of Analysis' (2004) 15 European Journal of International Law 907 proposes a framework of analysis that includes outcome legitimacy as one pillar.

[21] It seems fictitious that military experts, who as part of their work, participate in the drafting of manuals leave any state's interests behind. Such interests might be internalized through years of service for one country. The disclaimer that expert views do not represent that of governments or international organizations needs to be understood in this light. See the example of the Tallinn Manuals: 'The expanded edition of the Tallinn Manual, like its predecessor, represents the views of its authors, and not of NATO, the NATO CCD COE, its Sponsoring Nations, or any other entity.' <https://ccdcoe.org/research/tallinn-manual/> accessed 31 January 2021.

[22] Wolfrum (n 19) 18 provide examples from the law of the seas and groups of experts in other areas of law.

naval warfare'.[23] It was aimed at the promotion of the 'comprehension of contemporary law', the coherent development of the law, and the promotion of respect for that law.[24] This manual had considerable impact on state military manuals – the UK, for example, drawing heavily on its text.[25] It also triggered a broader development that saw attempts to progressively restate IHL in the form of manuals in areas in which contemporary law was lacking because of the changing nature of conflict as well as the means and methods used. Naval warfare, although it has changed drastically, enjoys a long history that allows the development of genuine expertise and experts who are knowledgeable regarding the challenges through evolution within the field.

In contrast, it is more difficult for lawyers and military personnel alike to claim authority as experts in fields only recently inhibited with human activity.[26] Whether states actively reject the proposed rules, accept them but decide not to comply, do not apply them because of technical problems such as the timely attribution of responsibility, or policy considerations such as the quest not to escalate conflicts are the decisive factors at play in this context, is yet to be seen. The lack of established practice can therefore produce more controversial results. The claim to authority – 'we are the experts and can show you how to apply the rules' – therefore is less persuasive in new contexts.

But does it matter for the legitimization process if the drafting process is a 'one-man-show', involves a small group of experts with military backgrounds, or, larger – potentially even global – groups of experts that might include stakeholders from different backgrounds?[27] The more international manuals venture into new spaces and contexts, the more they unavoidably venture into the political domain. The legitimacy derived from the level of personal expertise combined in the drafters is less strong. Hence, projects such as the MILAMOS project on military operations in outer space are seeking legitimization through their claim to inclusivity, fairness, and the truly global nature of the project.[28] In spite of an existing regulatory framework for outer space, in many ways and especially in relation to various aspects of military

---

23 Louise Doswald-Beck, 'The San Remo Manual on International Law Applicable to Armed Conflicts at Sea' (1995) 89 American Journal of International Law 192, 194. Doswald-Beck had a central role in the drafting process of the manual; her article provides a comprehensive overview over the making of the San Remo Manual.

24 ibid 208.

25 UK Ministry of Defence, *Manual on the Law of Armed Conflict* (OUP 2004) para 13.2; Sandesh Sivakumaran, 'Making and Shaping the Law of Armed Conflict' (2018) 71 Current Legal Problems 119, 128. See also Boothby (n 3) 75–76 tracing the San Remo Manual's influence on UK, Canadian, Australian and German manuals and handbooks.

26 Efrony and Shany (n 16).

27 Naz K. Modirzadeh, 'Folk International Law: 9/11 Lawyering and the Transformation of the Law of Armed Conflict to Human Rights Policy and Human Rights Law to War Governance' (2014) 5 Harvard National Security Journal 225, 235–36 analyses: '[T]he military discipline of the field discourages entering into intellectual and professional projects that are not obviously and immediately linked to reality. The macho nature of IHL stems not so much from its predilection for violence or its interest in war, but rather from the pride the discipline takes in its perceived rigor, form, method, clarity of argumentation, and what all of that means in terms of shaping a particular kind of legal discourse.'

28 See the description of the project on its website <https://www.mcgill.ca/milamos/our-people> accessed 31 January 2021: '[The] impressive list of persons involved in the Project, each of whom enjoy a distinguished career and carry a wealth of experiences, is testament to the fair, inclusive, and interdisciplinary and truly global nature of MILAMOS Process and the McGill Manual.'

operations, this particular context remains legally unregulated. The project is therefore more politically loaded and an inclusive process with a more internationalized group of contributors can enhance its legitimacy. The process can on that basis appear less interest-driven and allows room for perspectives from a diverse range of backgrounds. This can increase the value as an offering to states of what the relevant interpretation of international law could be in relation to military operations in outer space.

Inclusivity of the drafting process is linked to outcome legitimacy, which questions the satisfactory nature of rules. Measuring such satisfactory results is a near-impossible task and strongly depends on perspective. Having said that, international law struggles with considerable hegemonic historical ballast – particularly in IHL, whereby, historically, state practice of a few dominant states in the field has contributed to the formation of custom.[29] The Tallinn Manuals with their close affiliation to one particular political alliance feed into this perception of a few select states having assumed a dominant role also in projects of informal law-making. Beyond this perception, can IHL's unique mission of safeguarding humanity in warfare produce outcome legitimacy because of the deeply moral impetus to alleviate and limit human suffering in times of armed conflict? Whenever international manuals aim to give (better) effect to IHL in the field, this reliance and promotion of the humanitarian claim can arguably indeed induce and affirm outcome legitimacy. For manual projects venturing beyond this exclusively humanitarian objective, aiming to regulate military conduct in times of armed conflict, e.g., for strategic reasons, this source of outcome legitimacy – albeit not necessarily blocked entirely – is significantly less relevant.

6. BLOCKADE OR PROGRESS?

International manuals tread a fine line between progressive (interpretative) development and the potential blockade of genuine normative progress through established, state-driven law-making processes. The increasing number and substantive scope of manuals is often explained by the slowness and stagnation of contemporary international norm-setting processes. However, it is up for debate whether international manuals actually remedy normative stagnation or contribute to its perpetuation. Manuals as ready-made application facilitators – in analogy to Werner's comparison with product manuals – focus on how to make existing law fit to challenges which arise – for example as a result of new technologies. Inherently and in line with their overriding aims and objectives, therefore, manuals do not necessarily search for or seek to explore areas in which the law may not fit and where different (new) rules may be more adequate to deal with the actual challenges posed. In this regard they may help to conceal genuine gaps in the existing body of law and obfuscate normative demands for further development of the law. The suggestion that with the help of a manual all relevant issues and challenges can be adequately addressed is very much the tenor of the Tallinn Manuals and largely

---

[29] Charles J. Dunlap, Jr., 'Law of War Manuals and Warfighting: A Perspective' (2012) 47 Texas International Law Journal 265, 273 diagnosing that 'in the area of air and missile warfare especially, the U.S. view will doubtless be authoritative if not controlling.' See Yoram Dinstein, *The Conduct of Hostilities under the Law of International Armed Conflict* (CUP 2010) 4, 6 similarly emphasizes the overriding importance of state practice of those states that are among the few that dominate a specific area, in particular in the 'more esoteric areas of state activities'. See generally Michael Byers, *Custom, Power and the Power of Rules* (CUP 1999).

in line with Western states' views on how international law regulates cyber space. Even though the Tallinn Manuals comprehensively address all central controversies regarding the interpretation of international law, a greater openness to critically interrogate whether central principles and rules are still fit to fulfil their actual purpose when applied to cyber space would have been desirable. Thus, while the Tallinn Manuals reflect every view and possible permutation regarding the application of the principle of distinction in cyber space and – in spite of the alarming insight that '[i]n theory, the application of the definition of military objectives could lead to the conclusion that the entire Internet can become a military objective, if used for military purposes'[30] – no further reflection is devoted to the central question of whether the principle of distinction can still embody the humanitarian protection it was originally designed to uphold when applied in the specific context of cyber space. In this regard, and precisely because the Tallinn Manual goes into such detail in its exploration of how the principle of distinction applies in cyber space, considered as a whole it does send a clear message that the existing rules of the *ius ad bellum* and *ius in bello* are fit to address all relevant cyber security issues. Such a message may inhibit initial discussions about potential gaps in the law and normative needs for future development, thereby forestalling normative evolution.[31] In addition, states may not feel the need to clearly position themselves if the general message is that the law as it stands is still fit for purpose. In light of the absence of a clear positioning of states on cyber issues, in a rather unusual step the G7 in their declaration on 'Responsible Behaviour in Cyberspace' called on states 'to publicly explain their views on how existing international law applies to states' activities in cyberspace'.[32]

Indeed, where human activity poses entirely new security challenges, normative expectations might better develop through a broad debate between a variety of stakeholders rather than being left to a group of experts. This resonates with Lauterpacht's words cited above, reminding jurists that the radical change in the nature and methods of conflict might require political decisions rather than attempting to apply existing rules. Lauterpacht continues in his analysis:

> [I]t may not be conducive to the progressive international regulation, on a humanitarian basis, of [radical changes] to represent them as being governed by any recognized rules of international law. The law on these subjects must be shaped – so far as it can be shaped at all – by reference not to existing law but to more compelling considerations of humanity, of the survival of civilization, and of the sanctity of the individual human being.[33]

---

30 Michael Schmitt (ed), *Tallinn Manual on the International Law Applicable to Cyber Warfare* (CUP 2013) 136.

31 Theodore Christakis and Karine Bannelier, 'Reinventing Multilateral Cybersecurity Negotiation after the Failure of the UN GGE and Wannacry: The OECD Solution' (*EJIL Talk!*, 28 February 2018) <https://www.ejiltalk.org/reinventing-multilateral-cybersecurity-negotiation-after-the-failure-of-the-un-gge-and-wannacry-the-oecd-solution/> accessed 31 January 2021, document the failure of UN mechanisms. Russia has been a long-standing proponent of a cyber security treaty, whereas the US is opposed to such a treaty. Ido Kilovaty and Itamar Mann, 'Towards a Cyber-Security Treaty' (*Just Security*, 3 August 2016) <https://www.justsecurity.org/32268/cyber-security-treaty/> accessed 31 January 2021.

32 G7 Declaration on Responsible States Behavior in Cyberspace (n 2).

33 Lauterpacht (n 8) 379.

7. OUTLOOK

Manuals dealing with long-standing issues such as naval or air and missile warfare can indeed serve as a useful inventory helping to facilitate the application of a largely agreed body of law in practice. The manuals, however, that have come to the forefront of recent legitimacy debate are primarily manuals dealing with novel contexts and technologies such as cyber space or outer space. These manuals have proved to be helpful in addressing new pressing issues and changing social realities at a time when states and other relevant actors are, for various reasons, still reluctant to do so. They can help to identify novel challenges and issues of controversy, chart and thereby influence the formation of new research fields, and provide a basis and impetus for further discussions. Scholars and groups of experts are of course free to engage in whatever kind of manual – interpretative or law – developing exercise they wish to engage in, but in light of the various direct and indirect ways in which the increasing number of manuals are filtered into the complex system of international law-making and shaping, critical analysis and reflection on the nature and impact of international manuals is a most timely undertaking. When dealing with entirely novel contexts and potentially sea-changing technologies, the very format of a manual as a ready-made tool aiming to facilitate the application of the law in practice may be at odds with some of the greater challenges posed: in particular, a naturally required reconsideration as to whether the law as it stands still reflects an adequate balancing of interests and the demands and considerations at play in this novel context. The main problem is not that these manuals are in a way mono-dimensional, focusing only on the question of how existing law will play out in new contexts rather than on the question of which kind of rules would be optimal to regulate these contexts. Nevertheless, and as Wouter Werner has rightly shown, manuals are designed and promoted as a mere restatement of the law. A manual, however, is never just that, and the very act of restating the law in novel contexts inherently and unavoidably entails a certain law-making element that should be acknowledged more openly. In our view, however, the main problem is that in light of the unique format of a manual, which inherently suggests that overall the law is clear and that simplified application possible, its content may be perceived and/or promoted as a comprehensive and conclusive assessment of regulatory needs, thereby forestalling broader political debate, (re-)consideration of regulatory objectives, and the most adequate legal mechanisms to deliver these. With two new manuals currently in the making, namely the MILAMOS and WOOMERA Manuals on the international legal framework applicable to military operations in outer space, it seems safe to say that international manuals in the *ius ad bellum* and *ius in bello* field will continue to play a role in the coming years. To do justice to the very objective of these manuals and to contribute to the clarification of international law, continuous critical debate about the nature and functionalities of international manuals as well as recognition and reflection about the potential shortcomings of the manual format – not least on behalf of their drafters – is certainly called for. Wouter Werner's skilful analysis provides an inspiring contribution to this important debate.

15. Interpretation and identification of international humanitarian law: Responses of the International Law Commission

Georg Nolte

1. INTRODUCTION

The Report of the Study Group of the International Law Commission (ILC) on Fragmentation of International Law is a response to the concern that international law is being developed in different directions by various international courts and lawyers concentrating within their respective fields of specialization.[1] The Fragmentation Report was released in 2006. Ten years later a book was published with the title *A Farewell to Fragmentation: Reassertion and Convergence in International Law*.[2] Perhaps this publication is an indication that the concerns about possible fragmentation of international law have partly given way to a broader awareness of the unity of international law as a legal system.

One aspect of the tension between fragmentation and convergence in international law is the debate about the relevance of the practice and legal opinions of different actors in international humanitarian law (IHL), and in particular about the relevance of manuals and commentaries which have been elaborated in this field.[3] What is the significance of such forms of guidance? The recent work of the International Law Commission may contribute to such an assessment.

---

1 ILC, 'Fragmentation of International Law: Difficulties Arising from the Diversification and Expansion of International Law – Report of the Study Group of the International Law Commission' (13 April 2006) UN Doc A/CN.4/L.682, as corrected (11 August 2006) UN Doc A/CN.4/L.682/Corr. (finalized by Martti Koskenniemi) 10–14 paras 6–15.

2 Mads Andenas and Eirik Bjorge (eds), *A Farewell to Fragmentation: Reassertion and Convergence in International Law* (CUP 2015).

3 Jean-Marie Henckaerts and Louise Doswald-Beck, ICRC, *Customary International Humanitarian Law: Volumes I and II* (CUP 2005); ICRC, *Commentary on the First Geneva Convention: Convention (I) for the Amelioration of the Condition of the Wounded and Sick in Armed Forces in the Field* (2nd edn, CUP 2016); Nils Melzer, 'Interpretive Guidance on the Notion of Direct Participation in Hostilities under International Humanitarian Law' (2008) 90 International Review of the Red Cross 57; idem, ICRC, *Interpretive Guidance on the Notion of Direct Participation in Hostilities Under International Humanitarian Law* (2009) <https://www.icrc.org/eng/assets/files/other/icrc-002-0990.pdf> accessed 31 January 2021; Louise Doswald-Beck, ICRC, *San Remo Manual on International Law applicable to Armed Conflicts at Sea* (CUP 1995); Michael N Schmitt, *Tallinn Manual on the International Law Applicable to Cyber Warfare* (CUP 2013).

The ILC is a subsidiary body of the UN General Assembly. It consists of 34 international lawyers who are elected by the General Assembly on the basis of regional representation. Thus, in its composition as a body, the Commission is more representative than most other non-judicial legal bodies. The Commission is also legitimate in the sense that its procedures ensure participation of its members and all UN member states, and that it provides ample time for consideration and debate. Further, the Commission operates almost exclusively on the basis of consensus.[4]

Particularly since the turn of the century the ILC has not concentrated as much on drafting treaties, but instead on producing 'paralegal' outputs which have functions similar to those of the well-known manuals or commentaries in the field of IHL.[5] Here I want to focus on two recently completed ILC projects which are significant for IHL because they concern methodological issues. They relate to the questions of how to interpret treaty law ('Subsequent agreements and subsequent practice in relation to the interpretation of treaties'[6]) and how to identify customary international law ('Identification of Customary International Law'[7]). By working on these projects, the ILC has attempted to rethink and reorient the practice regarding the interpretation of treaties and the determination of customary international law. The outcomes of this work provide certain standards which also permit assessment of the authoritativeness of manuals and other 'paralegal' materials.

The purpose of both ILC projects is, however, modest. They do not provide new theories of treaty interpretation, nor prescribe hard-and-fast rules concerning the role of practice in the determination of customary international law. They rather synthesize how subsequent agreements and subsequent practice, as means of interpretation, and the elements of customary international law have developed and been applied in the practice of states and judicial organs. This should provide some guidance for practitioners, in particular for domestic judges, who are less familiar with the usages and understandings in international law.[8] By looking at the interpretative practice within different treaty regimes and with respect to different rules of customary international law, the work of the Commission should also contribute to identifying common elements in the process of treaty interpretation across regimes and of the identification of customary international law. By identifying patterns, the Conclusions of the Commission, together with their Commentaries, give some guidance without imposing a straitjacket. The Commentaries on the Conclusions are almost as important as the Conclusions themselves since they give life and illustration to the Conclusions.

The following observations do not aim to provide a comprehensive overview of the work of the Commission on those topics. They merely highlight several aspects which are relevant

---

4 See Statute of the International Law Commission (adopted by the UN General Assembly (UNGA) 21 November 1947, UN Doc A/RES/174(II), amended by UNGA 12 December 1950 UN Doc A/RES/485(V), 3 December 1955 UN Doc A/RES/985(X), 18 November 1981 UN Doc A/RES/36/39) arts 16–24; compare 'Organization, programme and methods of work' (Codification Division, Office of Legal Affairs 11 January 2019) <http://legal.un.org/ilc/methods.shtml> accessed 31 January 2021.

5 Georg Nolte, 'International Law Commission Facing the Second Decade of the Twenty-first Century' in Ulrich Fastenrath and others (eds), *From Bilateralism to Community Interest – Essays in Honour of Judge Bruno Simma* (OUP 2011) 781, 787, 791.

6 ILC, 'Report of the International Law Commission on the 70th session' (30 April – 1 June and 2 July – 10 August 2018) UN Doc A/73/10 ch IV.

7 ibid ch V.

8 ibid ch V, 122, para 66; ch IV, 17 para 52.

for the interpretation and identification of international humanitarian law. The contribution by Henckaerts and Pothelet in this book offers an in-depth assessment on related aspects.

2. WHOSE PRACTICE COUNTS?

One aspect of the Commission's work which is important for IHL concerns the question of what counts as relevant practice for the purpose of the interpretation of treaties and the identification of customary international law. In international law rules are traditionally established and their interpretation or identification are generated by way of comparatively formal procedures between relatively few actors and with an emphasis on consent.

Thus, traditionally, as far as practice as a means of interpretation is concerned, only the subsequent practice of the parties themselves in the application of a treaty counts for the purpose of interpretation.[9] For another approach, states and international organizations, while remaining important, are increasingly supplemented by other actors (NGOs, transnational corporations, epistemic communities). These other actors are said to play an increased role and to emancipate themselves somewhat from states.[10] They would engage in practices which often exercise a strong compliance pull, both for formal international law as well as for informal arrangements. For this vision of international law, inter-governmental international organizations and other traditional forms of international law-making, are slow and inflexible, and often do not attain necessary substantive problem-solving capacity.[11] Optimists are confident that this vision produces 'thicker' forms of legitimacy than the traditional state-centred world. They assume that most affected actors will be part of the process of rule-making which takes place through procedures which are inclusive in the sense of taking relevant interests into account, but without being hampered by formalist consent requirements.[12] Sceptics identify selective power techniques, club structures, and other forms of domination therein.[13] But both optimists and sceptics among those who see an alternative international law emerging assume that states and formal international organizations are playing a more limited role, and in which the significance of the law that emanates from the traditional sources of international law is being reduced.

---

9 See in particular Vienna Convention of the Law of Treaties (VCLT) (adopted 23 May 1969, entered into force 27 January 1980) 1155 UNTS 331, art 31(3)(b).

10 Eyal Benvenisti, 'Towards a Typology of Informal International Lawmaking Mechanisms and their Distinct Accountability Gaps' in Joost Pauwelyn, Ramses A. Wessel and Jan Wouters (eds), *Informal International Lawmaking* (OUP 2012) 297, 298–305; Kal Raustialia, 'The Architecture of International Cooperation: Transgovernmental Networks and the Future of International Law' (2002) 43 Virginia Journal of International Law 1, 11; Anne-Marie Slaughter, *A New World Order* (Princeton University Press, 2004) 12ff.; Kenneth W. Abbott and Duncan Snidal, 'Hard and Soft Law in International Governance' (2009) 54 International Organization 421, 423.

11 Joost Pauwelyn, Ramses A. Wessel and Jan Wouters, 'When Structures Become Shackles: Stagnation and Dynamics in International Lawmaking' (2014) 25 European Journal of International Law 733, 743.

12 ibid 749–51.

13 Nico Krisch, 'The Decay of Consent: International Law in an Age of Global Public Goods' (2014) 108 American Journal of International Law 1, 31; Philip Alston, 'The Myopia of the Handmaidens: International Lawyers and Globalization' (1997) 8 European Journal of International Law 435, 441.

However, there are signs that the traditional world of states and international organizations, while often using instruments which the alternative approach offers, is reluctant to fully recognize them as part of the international legal system. The ILC has recently reinforced this reluctance in the context of its work whereby it also addressed the role of non-state actors. In 2018, the Commission adopted Conclusion 5 of the topic *Subsequent agreements and subsequent practice in relation to the interpretation of treaties*:

> *Conclusion 5*
> *Attribution of subsequent practice*
> 1. Subsequent practice under articles 31 and 32 may consist of any conduct of a party in the application of a treaty, whether in the exercise of its executive, legislative, judicial or other functions.
> 2. Other conduct, including by non-State actors, does not constitute subsequent practice under articles 31 and 32. Such conduct may, however, be relevant when assessing the subsequent practice of parties to a treaty.[14]

This Conclusion does not make a statement regarding the significance of conduct by non-state actors for purposes other than for the interpretation of treaties. It does, however, send a signal about hierarchy. It recognizes that conduct of non-state actors may be relevant for treaty interpretation, thereby taking a new reality into account. At the same time, however, it insists on the primary role of the parties to treaties when it comes to the relevance of subsequent conduct for the interpretation of treaties. The Commission thereby recognizes a threshold for an approach to treaty interpretation which emphasizes the 'shared understanding' of all actors that are involved in, and affected by, the application of the treaty, including non-governmental organizations.[15] This threshold frames the way in which community interests are identified in the context of treaty interpretation. As long as the states parties remain 'masters of the treaty'[16] it is difficult, even for a court, to interpret or identify a rule in a way which would lie beyond what the parties can reasonably have meant.

Also, the Commission adopted a parallel Conclusion regarding the topic *Identification of customary international law*:

> *Conclusion 4*
> *Requirement of practice*
> 1. The requirement of a general practice, as a constituent element of customary international law, refers primarily to the practice of States that contributes to the formation, or expression, of rules of customary international law.
> 2. In certain cases, the practice of international organizations also contributes to the formation, or expression, of rules of customary international law.

---

14 ILC, 'Report of the International Law Commission on the 70th session' (30 April – 1 June and 2 July – 10 August 2018)' UN Doc A/73/10 ch IV, 14 para 51.

15 See for a broader approach Laurence Boisson de Chazournes, 'Subsequent Practice, Practices, and 'Family-Resemblance': Towards Embedding Subsequent Practice in its Operative Milieu' in Georg Nolte (ed), *Treaties and Subsequent Practice* (OUP 2013) 62.

16 ILC, 'Commentaries to the draft conclusions on subsequent agreements and subsequent practice in relation to the interpretation of treaties in ILC "Report of the International Law Commission on the 70th session" (30 April – 1 June and 2 July – 10 August 2018)' UN Doc A/73/10 ch IV, 39 para 52; 134 BVerfGE 267, 349–350, 368, 381, 398; 89 BVerfGE 155, 190 (German Federal Constitutional Court).

3. Conduct of other actors is not practice that contributes to the formation, or expression, of rules of customary international law, but may be relevant when assessing the practice referred to in paragraphs 1 and 2.[17]

This Conclusion was intensely debated within the Commission.[18] Not so much because the Conclusion relegates the 'conduct of other actors' to a position of secondary importance, but, going even further, because some members would have preferred not to recognize that the practice of international organizations may play a role in the formation or expression of rules of customary international law at all.[19] From that perspective, the Commission insists on a traditional, state-centred approach to customary international law which leaves little room for other actors to play a role in setting the legally relevant practice for the articulation and specification of community interests. This does not exclude, of course, that some states are losing some of their political autonomy to national and transnational social forces which would then give such social forces relevant influence and turn such states into merely formally competent actors.

The Conclusions of the Commission respond to the widespread narrative according to which more and more relevant actors need to be taken into account and to play a role in the common process of interpretation. For example, the proposal to recognize the social practice or the practice of non-state actors as a means of interpretation was not admitted by the Commission.[20]

This does not mean, however, that the Commission considers that the conduct of actors other than states is irrelevant. Indeed, the Commission has emphasized in the context of both projects that such conduct 'may be relevant when assessing the practice' of the parties to the treaties. The Commission thereby requires that interpreters must carefully take into account the relationship between such actors and the parties to a treaty. The following quotation from the Commentaries of the Commission concerns precisely the role of the ICRC and of NGOs in international humanitarian law:

> (15) Other non-State actors may also play an important role in assessing subsequent practice of the parties in the application of a treaty. A pertinent example is the International Committee of the Red Cross (ICRC).[21] Apart from fulfilling a general mandate conferred on it by the Geneva Conventions for the protection of war victims and by the Statutes of the International Red Cross and Red Crescent

---

17 ILC, 'Report of the International Law Commission on the 70th session (30 April – 1 June and 2 July – 10 August 2018)' UN Doc A/73/10 ch V, 119 para 65.

18 The debate is not reflected in the report of the Commission or the commentaries to the adopted Draft Conclusions; but in the ILC, 'Summary record of the 3397th meeting' (8 May 2018) UN Doc A/CN.4/SR.3397; ILC, 'Summary record of the 3398th meeting' (9 May 2018) UN Doc A/CN.4/SR.3398; ILC, 'Summary record of the 3399th meeting' (10 May 2018) UN Doc A/CN.4/SR.3399; ILC, 'Summary record of the 3400th meeting' (11 May 2018) UN Doc A/CN.4/SR.3400; ILC, 'Summary record of the 3401st meeting' (11 May 2018) UN Doc A/CN.4/SR.3401; ILC, 'Summary record of the 3402nd meeting' (14 May 2018) UN Doc A/CN.4/SR.3402.

19 See eg Statement by Mr Murphy, ILC, 'Summary record of the 3397th meeting' (8 May 2018) UN Doc A/CN.4/SR.3397, 7–8; Statement by Mr Rajput, ILC, 'Summary record of the 3401st meeting' (11 May 2018) UN Doc A/CN.4/SR.3401, 3–4.

20 ILC, Report on the 65th session (2013) UN Doc A/68/10 Draft Conclusion 5 (2) and Commentaries 45–47.

21 Hans-Peter Gasser, 'International Committee of the Red Cross (ICRC)' (2014) in Rüdiger Wolfrum (ed), *Max Planck Encyclopedia of Public International Law* (online edn) para 20.

Movement,[22] ICRC occasionally provides interpretative guidance on the 1949 Geneva Conventions[23] and the Additional Protocols[24] on the basis of a mandate from the Statutes of the Movement.[25] Article 4, paragraph 2 (g), of the Statutes provides:

> 'The role of the International Committee, in accordance with its Statutes, is in particular: (…) (g) to work for the understanding and dissemination of knowledge of international humanitarian law applicable in armed conflicts and to prepare any development thereof.'

On the basis of this mandate, ICRC, for example, published in 2009 an *Interpretative Guidance on the Notion of Direct Participation in Hostilities under International Humanitarian Law*.[26] The Interpretative Guidance is the outcome of an 'expert process' based on an analysis of State treaty and customary practice and it 'reflect[s] the ICRC's institutional position as to how existing [international humanitarian law] should be interpreted'.[27] In this context it is, however, important to note that States have reaffirmed their primary role in the development of international humanitarian law. Resolution 1 of the 31st International Conference of the Red Cross and Red Crescent (2011), while recalling 'the important roles of the [ICRC]', 'emphasiz[es] the primary role of States in the development of international humanitarian law'.[28]

(16) Another example of conduct of non-State actors that may be relevant for assessing the subsequent practice of States parties is the Monitor, a joint initiative of the International Campaign to Ban Landmines and the Cluster Munitions Coalition. The Monitor acts as a *de facto* monitoring regime[29] for the 1997 Convention on the Prohibition of the Use, Stockpiling, Production and Transfer of Anti-Personnel Mines and on their Destruction (Ottawa Convention)[30] and the 2008 Convention on

---

[22] ibid para 25.

[23] Geneva Convention for the Amelioration of the Condition of the Wounded and Sick in Armed Forces in the Field (adopted 21 August 1949, entered into force 21 October 1950) 75 UNTS 31 (GC I), Geneva Convention for the Amelioration of the Condition of Wounded, Sick and Shipwrecked Members of Armed Forces at Sea (adopted 21 August 1949, entered into force 21 October 1950) 75 UNTS 85 (GC II), Geneva Convention relative to the Treatment of Prisoners of War (adopted 12 August 1949, entered into force 21 October 1950) 75 UNTS 135 (GC III), Geneva Convention Relative to the Protection of Civilian Persons in Time of War (adopted on 12 August 1949, entered into force 21 October 1950) 75 UNTS 287 (GC IV).

[24] Additional Protocol of the Geneva Convention of 12 August 1949, and relating the Protection of Victims of International Armed Conflicts (adopted 8 June 1977, entered into force 7 December 1978) 1125 UNTS 3 (AP I), Additional Protocol of the Geneva Convention of 12 August 1949, and relating the Protection of Victims of Non-International Armed Conflicts (adopted 8 June 1977, entered into force 7 December 1978) 1125 UNTS 609 (AP II).

[25] ICRC, Statute of the International Committee of the Red Cross (adopted by the 25th International Conference of the Red Cross at Geneva in 1986, amended in 1995 and 2006) <https://www.icrc.org/en/doc/resources/documents/misc/icrc-statutes-080503.htm> accessed 31 January 2021.

[26] Melzer and ICRC (n 3) 10.

[27] Melzer and ICRC (n 3) 9.

[28] ICRC, 'Draft Resolution on Strengthening legal protection for victims of armed conflicts 31st International Conference of the Red Cross and Red Crescent' (28 November – December 2011) EN 31IC/11/5.11.

[29] See Landmine & Cluster Munition Monitor <www.the-monitor.org> accessed 31 January 2021.

[30] Convention on the Prohibition of the Use, Stockpiling, Production and Transfer of Anti-Personnel Mines and on their Destruction (adopted 18 September 1997, entered into force 1 March 1999) 2056 UNTS 211 (Ottawa Convention).

Cluster Munitions (Dublin Convention).[31] The Monitor lists pertinent statements and practice by States parties and signatories and identifies, *inter alia*, interpretative questions concerning the Dublin Convention.[32]

(17) The examples of ICRC and the Monitor show that non-State actors can provide valuable information about subsequent practice of parties, contribute to assessing this information and even solicit its coming into being. However, non-State actors can also pursue their own goals, which may be different from those of States parties. Their documentation and their assessments must thus be critically reviewed.[33]

One important reason why the ILC has taken up methodological issues like treaty interpretation and the identification of customary international law is that there are still other 'new actors' which need to be taken very seriously. These actors are domestic courts.[34] Domestic courts are not just parties to an informal discussion. They want to know how to apply international humanitarian law and who to recognize as authoritative. It should therefore be helpful to determine and to differentiate the weight of the contributions of different actors, including manuals and commentaries, for the interpretation of treaties and for the identification of customary international law.

It is, of course, possible to criticize the Commission and to say that it is itself an epistemic community that is trying to defend its prerogatives which result from a state-centred world. Regardless of the merit of this doubtful argument, however, the position of the Commission has advantages in terms of determinacy. We know that we cannot have complete determinacy in law and in legal interpretation. But it is also true that if more and more actors had a recognized role and status in the process of interpretation or identification of international law, it would more likely become a forum for fruitless contestation rather than provide an avenue for convergence.

3. INTERPRETATION OR MODIFICATION?

Perhaps the most difficult question in the area of treaty interpretation is whether a certain treaty-related practice can still be considered an 'interpretation' of that treaty, or whether it goes beyond. The International Court of Justice articulated the problem in the 2009 Dispute Regarding Navigational and Related Rights case (*Costa Rica v Nicaragua*) where it held, in an *obiter dictum*, that 'subsequent practice of the parties, within the meaning of article 31 (3) (b) of the Vienna Convention, can result in a departure from the original intent on the basis of a tacit agreement'.[35] It is not entirely clear whether the Court thereby wanted to recognize that subsequent practice under Article 31(3)(b) VCLT may also have the effect of amending

31 2008 Convention on Cluster Munitions (adopted 30 May 2008, entered into force 1 August 2010) 2688 UNTS 39 (Dublin Convention).

32 See, for example 'Cluster Munition Monitor 2011' (Landmine & Cluster Munition Monitor October 2011) 24–31 <http://www.the-monitor.org/media/1641755/Cluster_Munition_Monitor_2011.pdf> accessed 31 January 2021.

33 ILC, 'Report of the International Law Commission on the 70th session' (30 April – 1 June and 2 July – 10 August 2018) UN Doc A/73/10 ch IV, 42 para 17.

34 ibid ch V, 122 para 66; ch IV, 17 para 52.

35 *Dispute regarding Navigational and Related Rights (Costa Rica v Nicaragua)* (Merits) [2009] ICJ Rep 213, 242 para 64.

or modifying a treaty, or whether it was merely making a point relating to the interpretation of treaties.[36]

The question as to whether subsequent practice can have the effect of modifying a treaty has been debated since the elaboration of the Vienna Convention. The Commission, in the 1960s, originally proposed that the Vienna Convention should recognize that agreed subsequent practice can have the effect of modifying the treaty, yet the Vienna Convention then rejected this proposal.[37] However, state practice, courts, and writers have continued to debate the question. Most writers seem to recognize the possibility of a modification or amendment of a treaty by agreed practice. Courts and states, however, tend to avoid taking a clear position and rather recognize a wide scope for the interpretation of a treaty by agreed subsequent practice.[38] The International Court of Justice and most other international courts and tribunals have preferred to give a particular treaty an interpretation which strains the 'ordinary meaning of the terms' of the treaty, rather than to openly recognize the possibility of an informal modification of the treaty by the subsequent practice of the parties. The most notable exception to this is the ECHR.[39]

As a result, Conclusion 7, para 3, only formulates a presumption that the parties to a treaty, by their common subsequent practice, do not intend to modify a treaty, but to interpret it. The additional statement according to which 'the possibility of modifying a treaty by subsequent practice of the parties has not been generally recognized' strengthens the presumption in favour of interpretation, but only somewhat ambiguously. The Commission thereby attempts to walk a fine line between the reluctance to recognize the possibility of the parties modifying a treaty by informal practices, and the experience from many cases that the common practice of the parties needs to be accommodated. The solution is that interpreters are encouraged to regard subsequent agreements and agreed subsequent practice as efforts by the parties to interpret a treaty rather than as efforts to modify or break out of a treaty.

4. SUBSEQUENT PRACTICE WHICH DOES NOT ESTABLISH THE AGREEMENT OF THE PARTIES

The generally restrictive approach of the Commission manifests itself with regard to the questions of *who* may generate subsequent practice for the purpose of treaty interpretation, who may generate practice for the purpose of the identification of customary international law, as well as with regard to the possibility of *modifying* a treaty even by the agreed practice of all the parties. This restrictive approach is also reflected in its treatment of practice by a number of parties to a treaty which does not amount to an agreed practice.

The Vienna Convention, in Article 31(3)(b), only speaks of subsequent practice which establishes the agreement of the parties, which means the agreement (but not necessarily the subsequent practice) of *all* states parties. The text of the Vienna Convention does not

36 ILC, 'Report of the International Law Commission on the 70th session' (30 April – 1 June and 2 July – 10 August 2018) UN Doc A/73/10 ch IV, Commentary on Draft Conclusion 7 (3), 60 para 27.

37 ILC, 'Report of the International Law Commission on the Work of its 66th Session' (5 May – 6 June and 7 July to 8 August 2014) UN Doc A/69/10, 187–88 paras 22–23.

38 ILC, 'Report of the International Law Commission on the Work of its 66th Session' (5 May – 6 June and 7 July to 8 August 2014) UN Doc A/69/10, 191–92 paras 32–35.

39 *Al-Saadoon and Mufdhi v the United Kingdom* App no 61498/08 (ECHR, 2 March 2010) para 119.

explicitly recognize that the practice which only establishes the agreement of a large majority of the states regarding their interpretation of a treaty can be a means of interpretation.[40] Such practice, however, is the rule in IHL.[41] The relevance of such practice has, however, been recognized by the Commission as a supplementary means of interpretation under Article 32 of the Vienna Convention:

> *Conclusion 2*
> *(General rule and means of treaty interpretation)*
> (4) 'Recourse may be had to other subsequent practice in the application of the treaty as a supplementary means of interpretation under article 32.'

For practising lawyers, the distinction between subsequent practice which establishes the agreement of all parties under Article 31(3)(b) and 'other subsequent practice' which does not establish such agreement under Article 32 may sometimes appear to be artificial. The legitimacy of the distinction as such is, however, difficult to contest.[42] The distinction serves to emphasize the value of the agreement of the parties as an 'authentic' primary means of interpretation.[43] This emphasis does not call into question the possible (and frequent) relevance of 'other subsequent practice' in other situations in which the meaning of a treaty (provision) is not entirely clear. It is, after all, always possible that the 'weight' of 'other subsequent practice' as a supplementary means of interpretation is considerable under the circumstances given the absence of similarly persuasive indications from other means of interpretation.

In its Commentary, the Commission has provided examples in which 'other subsequent practice' was considered relevant but where the practice of (certain) states had not established the agreement of (all) the parties regarding the interpretation of the pertinent provisions of the Geneva Conventions.[44]

5. GENERAL REFLECTIONS

The methodological perspective of the Commission provides some guidance for the interpretation of treaties and the identification of customary international law. The work of the Commission does not, however, explain the exact doctrinal significance of manuals and commentaries, and of the practice of non-state actors more generally. It rather provides standards by which the quality of commentaries and manuals and the significance of such practice may be assessed.

---

40 See ILC, 'Report of the International Law Commission on the 70th session' (30 April – 1 June and 2 July – 10 August 2018) UN Doc A/73/10 ch IV, Commentary on Draft Conclusion 2 (4), 20 para 8.

41 Jean-Marie Henckaerts and Elvina Pothelet, 'The Interpretation of IHL Treaties: Subsequent Practice and Other Salient Issues', Chapter 10 in this book, 160.

42 See note 16: ILC, Commentaries to the draft conclusions on subsequent agreements and subsequent practice in relation to the interpretation of treaties in ILC, 'Report of the International Law Commission on the 70th session' (30 April – 1 June and 2 July – 10 August 2018) UN Doc A/73/10 ch IV, 45; 134 BVerfGE 267, 349–350, 368, 381, 398; 89 BVerfGE 155, 190 (German Federal Constitutional Court).

43 ILC, 'Report of the International Law Commission on the 70th session' (30 April – 1 June and 2 July – 10 August 2018) UN Doc A/73/10 ch IV, 1, 3, para 51, Conclusion 3.

44 ILC, 'Report of the International Law Commission on the 70th session' (30 April – 1 June and 2 July – 10 August 2018) UN Doc A/73/10, ch IV, Commentary on Draft Conclusion 4 (3), 33–37, paras 23–35.

The question of Heike Krieger and Jonas Püschmann remains: does the fact that we are living in an 'age of manuals', and are seeing a rise in paralegal methods more generally, represent signs of a crisis of international law?[45] Yet manuals and other commentaries are a classic legal technique. The code of Justinian was a collection of rules that was put together by a commentator, in the Middle Ages the glossators put their own spin on this text. In the nineteenth century, the French *Code Civil* was followed by important commentaries, as was the German *Bürgerliches Gesetzbuch* in the twentieth century.[46] It is a classic task of lawyers to write commentaries. At this moment we seem to be living in a time when we need to concentrate, as long as no new treaties are concluded, on what lawyers have done traditionally: to comment on the existing law. During the 1990s international lawyers saw many new treaties concluded. For IHL, the Statute of the International Criminal Court is an important element to reinforce compliance with its most fundamental rules.[47] One could even have the impression that a process of world legislation had set in. But today, if we accept Denise Garcia's observations and discount the Arms Trade Treaty,[48] there has not been an important treaty concluded in this field, or a treaty amendment, for a number of years. So we see a slump. But existing treaties must be administered and lawyers are the servants of these treaties. They need to nurture them, to keep them alive, and to elucidate them for our time. This is the function of manuals and commentaries.

Yet lawyers, as servants of treaties, should not overestimate themselves. They can only do so much in regard to treaties and they cannot themselves go back to the drawing board. Their authority to interpret a treaty is limited.[49] Maybe their role as interpreters has changed somewhat; in the 1990s they could feel more encouraged to be activist in their approach. But we can see from national contexts that there are times when lawyers can be generally more activist and that there are times when lawyers have been generally less activist. In the United States, for example, there have been more and less activist times in the field of constitutional interpretation.[50] Lawyers cannot easily determine when the time is ripe for evolutive or activist approaches, but they should try to sense the changes in the general receptivity for evolutive interpretation. Antonio Cassese was a lawyer who had such a sense when he authored famous and innovative decisions, such as the ICTY decision in *Tadić*[51] and the decision of the Special

---

45 Heike Krieger and Jonas Püschmann, 'Legitimacy and Law-Making in International Humanitarian Law', Chapter 1 in this book, 9–10.

46 David Kästle-Lamparter, *Welt der Kommentare: Struktur, Funktion und Stellenwert juristischer Kommentare in Geschichte und Gegenwart* (Mohr Siebeck 2016) 66–69, 101–102; Randall Lesaffer, *European Legal History: A Cultural and Political Perspective* (CUP 2009) 254–61; Franz Wieacker, *Privatrechtsgeschichte der Neuzeit unter besonderer Berücksichtigung der deutschen Entwicklung* (Vandenhoeck & Ruprecht Verlag 1967) 58–59, 133–34.

47 Rome Statute of the International Criminal Court (adopted 17 July 1998, entered into force 1 July 2002) 2187 UNTS 90 (ICC-Statute).

48 Denise Garcia, 'Global Norms Governing the Protection of Civilians, Conflict and Weapons: Formal or Informal Law-Making?', Chapter 5 in this book, 78.

49 James Crawford, 'Subsequent Agreements and Practice from a Consensualist Perspective' in Georg Nolte (ed), *Treaties and Subsequent Practice* (OUP 2013) 29–34.

50 See eg Dennis J. Goldford, *The American Constitution and the Debate Over Originalism* (CUP 2005) 61–65.

51 *Prosecutor v Tadić (Appeal Judgment)* ICTY-94-1-A (15 July 1999).

Tribunal for Lebanon on the definition of terrorism.[52] But the time today seems to be less conducive for such decisions.

The degree of activism or restraint which is appropriate in the interpretation and identification of international law is not merely a technical legal question. It also involves the exercise of reasonable judgment. The Vienna Convention on the Law of Treaties provides for a range of interpretative possibilities, but these possibilities are not unlimited. The Convention contains rules which force lawyers to argue hard. It is not enough to point to the ordinary meaning of the text and to invoke the object in purpose. It is also necessary to look at the subsequent practice of the parties and to review each of these means of interpretation in light of the others. After this 'single combined operation, which places appropriate emphasis on the various means of interpretation indicated, respectively, in articles 31 and 32'[53] has been loyally pursued, the options should be reasonably narrowed down, thereby enabling a persuasive interpretation.[54]

52 *Interlocutory Decision on Applicable Law: Terrorism, Conspiracy, Homicide, Perpetration, Cumulative Charging* (Appeals Chamber) Case number STL-11-01/I/AC/R176bis (16 February 2011).

53 ILC, 'Report of the International Law Commission on the 70th session' (30 April – 1 June and 2 July – 10 August 2018) UN Doc A/73/10 ch IV, 22.

54 ILC, 'Report of the International Law Commission on the 70th session' (30 April – 1 June and 2 July – 10 August 2018) UN Doc A/73/10 ch IV, 22.

16. Manuals and courts: International humanitarian law, informal law-making and normativity

Dale Stephens[1]

Modern international humanitarian law (IHL) can be characterized by its long historical pedigree, its broad scope and its unparalleled density of regulation. The ceaseless cascade of treaties,[2] protocols and additional protocols[3] to international conventions regulating warfare,[4] in conjunction with the continuing effervescence of customary law,[5] articulates through sheer volume a sense of hope that military violence may be somehow understood, controlled and ameliorated.

The regulation of bloodshed in armed conflict and its goal of pragmatic amelioration of violence is surely a worthwhile goal, but its normative ambition infuses a sense of order and

---

[1] The author would like to acknowledge the research assistance provided by Mr Simon Guthrie, Ms Sarah Brown and Mr Thomas Wooden.

[2] Most significantly in this context are the four 1949 Geneva Conventions: Geneva Convention for the Amelioration of the Condition of the Wounded and Sick in Armed Forces in the Field (opened for signature 12 August 1949, entered into force 21 October 1950) 75 UNTS 31 (GC I); Geneva Convention for the Amelioration of the Condition of Wounded, Sick and Shipwrecked Members of Armed Forces at Sea (opened for signature 12 August 1949, entered into force 21 October 1950) 75 UNTS 85 (GC II); Geneva Convention relative to the Treatment of Prisoners of War of August 12, 1949 (opened for signature 12 August 1949, entered into force 21 October 1950) 75 UNTS 135 (GC III); Geneva Convention relative to the Protection of Civilian Persons in Time of War (opened for signature 12 August 1949, entered into force 21 October 1950) 75 UNTS 287 (GC IV).

[3] Most relevantly, Protocol Additional to the Geneva Conventions of 12 August 1949, and relating to the Protection of Victims of International Armed Conflicts (opened for signature 8 June 1977, entered into force 7 December 1978) 1125 UNTS 3 (AP I); Protocol Additional to the Geneva Conventions of 12 August 1949, and relating to the Protection of Victims of Non-International Armed Conflicts (opened for signature 8 June 1977, entered into force 7 December 1978) 1125 UNTS 609 (AP II); Protocol Additional to the Geneva Conventions of 12 August 1949, and relating to the Adoption of an Additional Distinctive Emblem (opened for signature 8 December 2005, entered into force 14 January 2007) 2404 UNTS 261 (AP III).

[4] See for example Convention on Prohibitions or Restrictions on the Use of Certain Conventional Weapons which may be deemed to be Excessively Injurious or to have Indiscriminate Effects (opened for signature 10 April 1981, entered into force 01 December 1983) 1342 UNTS 137; and the numerous annexed Protocols that are established under the head Convention: Protocol I on Non-Detectable Fragments, Protocol II on Prohibitions or Restrictions on the Use of Mines, Booby Traps and other Devices; Protocol III on Prohibitions or Restrictions on the Use of Incendiary Weapons, Protocol IV on Blinding Laser Weapons and Protocol V on Explosive Remnants of War.

[5] Most significantly, Jean-Marie Henckaerts and Louise Doswald-Beck, *Customary International Humanitarian Law, Vol 1: Rules* (CUP 2005).

rational deliberation within a universe of chaos that is often hard to reconcile with the reality of the battlefield. Because of its internal architecture and associated modalities of ordering, there is much within warfare that is not caught by the formal sources of IHL. Deep doubts about law's capacity to restrain are never fully resolved, which is partly due to the intrinsically political nature of conflict and the unknowable capacity for extreme violence by the state, especially when faced with a perceived existential threat. It was always going to be a difficult task to reconcile reasoned deliberation with the contemplated possibility of annihilation.

Despite the extent of the formal regulation of armed conflict, there is much that is missed or not even contemplated in the growing universe of means and methods of warfare. Hence, added to the current formal legal framework that underpins armed conflict is the growing presence of more informal and dynamic deliberative processes that vie for legitimacy in shaping the development and application of the law. Such processes seek to make normative contribution to the law through the development and publication of respective international operational law manuals. Such manuals, prepared not by states but by private experts, are becoming more frequent and precise in their focus, ranging from collating rules applicable to naval warfare ('San Remo Manual'),[6] air and missile warfare ('Harvard AMW Manual'),[7] cyber warfare (Tallinn Manual 2.0'),[8] and on the horizon, warfare conducted in, through and from outer space ('Woomera Manual').[9] In addition to this emerging phenomenon, there has been a corresponding rise in the number and types of international judicial and quasi-judicial bodies adjudicating law in the field of IHL and also contributing to the corpus of normative content that applies and shapes the legal regulation of armed conflict.

This chapter will analyse the effect of these deliberative processes and examine the methodological approaches adopted when locating and identifying relevant rules and principles of IHL. Suffice to say, it is becoming clear that international operational law manuals and decisions of courts and tribunals are finding their normative place within the practice of operational law. Governments and military commanders (and their lawyers) are influenced by these indirect sources in the drafting of Rules of Engagement and other legal operational tools for setting the boundaries surrounding the application of force. It is the rise of international operational law manuals, in particular, that heralds perhaps the most significant contribution to contemporary military legal decision-making. The rise of international operation law manuals has necessarily resulted in a developing academic critique regarding the legitimacy of such manuals and has in turn ignited a vigorous defence of the procedural integrity of the manual-drafting process. This attention has been partially fuelled by the realization that such manuals do inform operational decision-making in the battlespace and have also been confidently used and invoked by courts, tribunals and quasi-judicial bodies in their adjudicative and/or inquiry roles. Within the highly decentralized world of military legal practice, therefore, the role and place of informal sources of authority are becoming well entrenched. The

6 Louise Doswald-Beck, *San Remo Manual on International Law Applicable to Armed Conflicts at Sea* (CUP 1994) (San Remo Manual).

7 Program on Humanitarian Policy and Conflict Research at Harvard University, *HPCR Manual on International Law Applicable to Air and Missile Warfare* (CUP 2013) (Harvard AMW Manual).

8 Michael Schmitt, *Tallinn Manual 2.0 On The International Law Applicable to Cyber Operations* (2nd ed, CUP 2017) (Tallinn Manual 2.0).

9 See University of Adelaide and others, 'The Woomera Manual' (*University of Adelaide*, 2019) <https://law.adelaide.edu.au/woomera> accessed 31 January 2021 ('Woomera Manual').

invocation of apparently informal prescriptions in such formal circumstances naturally draws attention to the integrity that underpins the manual process as well as the impact of court and tribunal decisions on military legal operational planning. Thus, an examination of the place and methodological agency these two contributions have within the firmament of IHL is a critical undertaking and one that this chapter will address.

1. MANUALS AND INTERNATIONAL HUMANITARIAN LAW

Over approximately the last 100 years, there have broadly been three historic moments where IHL has undergone general transformative development. These moments relate to the 1899/1907 Hague Conventions,[10] the 1949 Geneva Conventions (GC I–IV), and the 1977 Additional Protocols to the Geneva Conventions (AP I–III). While there have been a number of weapons treaties negotiated since 1977,[11] there has not been a major re-examination of the general body of IHL since this time.

There are some possible explanations for why this re-examination has not been undertaken. It may be that the prospect of states being able to agree to a comprehensive redesign of the current legal regime is unlikely. When the idea of negotiating a treaty regarding the placement of weapons in outer space was recently proposed, it offered an opportunity to grapple with an emerging area of possible armed conflict. The idea did not, however, receive much support.[12] Another explanation may be that the growing technologies which contribute to contemporary military capability such as cyber weaponry, trusted machine autonomy and the weaponization of outer space represent too dramatic a turn from traditional conceptions of military legal focus and that states are not yet clear on their position of how the law can or should apply. Alternatively, it may be that the general principles of IHL are so well established that there is no need to further develop broad principles or general rules. This last point is one that has been particularly advanced by Duncan Hollis, who opined that 'the corpus of IHL is now largely

---

[10] For example, Hague Convention (II) with Respect to the Laws and Customs of War on Land and its annex: Regulations concerning the Laws and Customs of War on Land (opened for signature 19 July 1899, entered into force 04 September 1900); Hague Convention (III) relative to the Opening of Hostilities (opened for signature 18 October 1907, entered into force 26 January 1910); Hague Convention (IV) respecting the Laws and Customs of War on Land and its annex: Regulations concerning the Laws and Customs of War on Land (opened for signature 18 October 1907, entered into force 26 January 1910).

[11] Convention on Prohibitions or Restrictions on the Use of Certain Conventional Weapons Which May be Deemed to be Excessively Injurious or to Have Indiscriminate Effects (opened for signature 10 April 1981, entered into force 2 December 1983) 1342 UNTS 137; Convention on the prohibition of the development, production, stockpiling and use of chemical weapons and on their destruction (opened for signature 13 January 1993, entered into force 29 April 1997) 1015 UNTS 163; Convention on Cluster Munitions (opened for signature 3 December 2008, entered into force 1 August 2010) 2688 UNTS 39.

[12] The Representative of the Russian Federation and the Representative of China presented to the Conference on Disarmament on 10 June 2014. Their revised draft is called Treaty on Prevention of the Placement of Weapons in Outer Space and of the Threat or Use of Force against Outer Space Objects (PPWT). This proposal has not been further advanced and there appears minimal likelihood of negotiation and adoption of a treaty instrument on this topic. The text of the Draft Treaty is available online <https://digitallibrary.un.org/record/633470> accessed 31 January 2021.

complete'[13] and that we are now in an 'era of application'[14] which focuses less on establishing grand general principles, and more on the exacting task of their specialized application to a widening array of differing contexts and circumstances.

There is merit to this last suggestion, but it should not be overstated. Throughout the past 100 years, there have been numerous examples of manuals relating to the law applicable in armed conflict being prepared by private experts. Such manuals are designed to restate the law, as then understood, in a coherent and concise manner to a particular topic of warfare. Hence, such manuals have included the 1880 *Oxford Manual of the Law on Land* by the Institute of International Law,[15] the 1913 *Oxford Manual of Laws of Naval Warfare Governing the Relations Between Belligerents* by the Institute of International Law,[16] and the 1923 *Hague Draft Rules of Aerial Warfare* prepared by a Commission of Jurists.[17] As already indicated above, these older manuals have found their contemporary equivalents in the form of the 1994 *San Remo Manual on International Law Applicable to Armed Conflicts at Sea*, the 2005 ICRC *Customary International Humanitarian Law Vol 1: Rules*, the 2009 *Interpretative Guidance on the Notion of Direct Participation in Hostilities under International Humanitarian Law* by the International Committee of the Red Cross (ICRC),[18] the 2013 *Harvard Manual on International Law Applicable to Air and Missile Warfare*, and the 2017 *Tallinn Manual 2.0 on the International Law Applicable to Cyber Operations* by the NATO Cooperative Cyber Defence Centre of Excellence.

These manuals articulate what was understood to be the prevailing *lex lata* and applied such law through a series of rules and supporting commentary in a coherent and practical manner. It is clear, though, that new paradigms were encountered in these areas and that the law is not always so prescriptive that it can be axiomatically applied. Rather, legal principles were also invoked and fashioned in a manner to apply to the contexts anticipated in each survey in a way that does necessarily carry with it a progressive tone. To that end, the process is not entirely one of application of a kind imagined by Hollis, but rather a combination of application and reworking.

The term 'manual' may have an ambiguous connotation, suggesting it is a 'how to' instruction guide. Manuals are more significant than this. Their authority, and therefore their traction, derives from the quality of their scholarship and the persuasiveness of the positions reached. The manual represents the views of highly qualified experts in the field and seeks to establish a level of certainty and stability in the context of locating and applying prevailing rules of IHL to the theatres of selected warfare. It is clear that these written compendiums of rules have significant influence within government legal decision-making circles.

---

13 Duncan Hollis, 'IHL's Era of Application' (*Opinio Juris*, 22 August 2014) <http://opiniojuris.org/2014/08/22/ihls-era-application/> accessed 31 January 2021.

14 ibid.

15 Institute of International Law, 'The Laws of War on Land', Oxford, 9 September 1880 <https://www.icrc.org/ihl/INTRO/140?OpenDocument> accessed 31 January 2021.

16 Institute of International Law, 'Manual of the Laws of Naval War', Oxford, 9 August 1913 <https://www.icrc.org/ihl/INTRO/265?OpenDocument> accessed 31 January 2021.

17 Commission of Jurists, 'Rules concerning the Control of Wireless Telegraphy in Time of War and Air Warfare. Drafted by a Commission of Jurists at The Hague, December 1922 – February 1923', 19 February 1923 <https://www.icrc.org/ihl.nsf/INTRO/275> accessed 31 January 2021.

18 See Nils Melzer, ICRC, *Interpretative Guidance on the Notion of Direct Participation in Hostilities under International Humanitarian Law* (ICRC 2009) (ICRC DPH Study).

1.1 Manuals and Motivation

There has long been a sense that the law applicable to armed conflict represents a rather insular field of legal practice and thinking. IHL seemed dominated by its heavy reliance upon positivist method[19] and its somewhat niche specialization. There arose an epistemic professional community of practitioners, military legal officers and academic specialists that engaged exclusively in this field. From this professional culture, concepts were developed, tested, applied, and defended. Refinements to processes were constantly made as a result of experience or deeper theoretical analysis to ensure proper coverage and ongoing viability of this field. Alliances of sorts were developed between adherents of IHL and separate professional international bodies, such as the ICRC, to advance common understandings of this convulsive body of law.[20] Hence, while vibrant, the area also seemed opaque and objectively inaccessible to other international legal scholars. This was more a result of its perceived specialized technical framework and implicitly privileged practice, than any overt professional boundary. IHL was nonetheless considered by some to be an area of anticipated forbidden trespass.

Despite this relative insularity, decisions emerging from bodies such as the International Court of Justice (ICJ) regarding the intersection between IHL and international human rights law,[21] coupled with the growing reach and application of broader principles and topics of international law, forced a realization that IHL was potentially vulnerable to 'side winds' of unanticipated and divergent legal design. This realization was being acknowledged by all in the field as a growing feature of the intersections of professional commitments within international law more broadly.

By the late 20th century, the imprecise relationships between legal forms, law and policy and the disquiet expressed regarding the realization of particularized interpretative tropes came to illustrate the disaggregated nature of the practice of international law generally and IHL specifically. Indeed, the reach for a unifying metanarrative that provided a foundation for international humanitarian law in the face of these challenges seemed to be increasingly elusive. The 2006 International Law Commission (ILC) Fragmentation Study made pointedly clear that the general international legal structure had grown much more pluralistic and com-

---

[19] Naz K. Modirzadeh, 'Folk International Law: 9/11 Lawyering and the Transformation of the Law of Armed Conflict to Human Rights Policy and Human Rights Law to War Governance' (2014) 4 Harvard National Security Journal 225, 235: 'IHL lawyers, as a whole, are very fond of rules and rules-talk. For other international lawyers, IHL lawyers often seem remarkably positivist. They spend a great deal of time debating and discussing black-letter rules, their interpretation, their manifestation, and the consequences of their violation. They take such talk very seriously, and it has fuelled, for many decades, the vast bulk of scholarship and debate within this relatively insular field.'

[20] David Kennedy, *The Dark Sides of Virtue: Reassessing International Humanitarianism* (Princeton University Press 2004) 237, 271.

[21] *Legality of the Threat or Use of Nuclear Weapons* (Advisory Opinion) [1996] ICJ Rep 226; *Legal Consequences of the Construction of a Wall in the Occupied Palestinian Territory* (Advisory Opinion) [2004] ICJ Rep 136; *Armed Activities on the Territory of the Congo (Democratic Republic of the Congo v Uganda)* (Judgment) [2005] ICJ Rep 168.

prised numerous 'rule-complexes'[22] that came with their own 'ethos'.[23] Different caucuses of lawyers with different constituencies and different projects all competed for ascendency. In the face of these inexorable developments, highly respected voices in the field called for others to 'keep off the grass' of IHL.[24] Such calls were not heeded.

It was becoming increasingly clear that old certainties might no longer apply. Decisions by the European Court of Human Rights (ECtHR) regarding the application and apparent precedence of international human rights norms in contrast to rights and obligations under the law applicable to armed conflict created growing anxiety in the field.[25] The ILC Fragmentation Study correctly observed that resolving apparent contradictions and unanticipated imposts required an exercise of both interpretative art and science.[26] This is a product not only of the nature and subject matters of these bodies of law, but is a result of the emerging legal cultures, needs for specialization, and activities of particular caucuses that promote the objectives of 'their' areas of international law.[27]

At the same time, IHL development and application was preoccupied with its own enduring internal discourse relating to the perennial balance between military and humanitarian goals in armed conflict. Both goals are recognized as constituting integral components of this body of law but are sensitive to particularized modes of interpretative commitment.[28] Accepting this, the practice of IHL is one that is therefore undertaken within a highly pluralist field of interpretation. IHL is a field where the realization of a unified and coherent structure proves largely illusory. Within this realm, Kennedy notes that 'lines are now harder to draw, both because the world of war has become more mixed up and because ambiguities, and contradictions in the materials we use to draw the lines have become more pronounced'.[29] In addition, the emergence of new technologies in the cyber, aerial and outer space fields presented new challenges for military legal thinking and demanded immediate attention.

It is against this background that the impetus for the drafting of these international operational law manuals might best be understood. Both perceived external 'threats' to the integrity of the IHL project as well as reconciling the constant internal balance between military and humanitarian priorities underpin the motivation for the manuals. This is especially so in the new and dynamic contexts of armed conflict. Such inputs to motivation in turn provide a telling explanation for the methodologies employed in the development of the manuals.

---

22 ILC, 'Fragmentation of International Law: Difficulties Arising from the Diversification and Expansion of International Law – Report of the Study Group of the International Law Commission' (13 April 2006) UN Doc A/CN.4/L.682, as corrected (11 August 2006) UN Doc A/CN.4/L.682/Corr. (finalized by Martti Koskenniemi) 11 (ILC Fragmentation Study).

23 ibid 14.

24 David Luban, 'Military Necessity and the Cultures of Military Law' (2013) 26 Leiden Journal of International Law 315, 315–17 quoting Professor Yoram Dinstein.

25 The following examples are illustrative of these phenomena: *Al-Jeddah v United Kingdom* App no 27021/08 (ECtHR, 7 July 2011); *Hassan v United Kingdom* App no 29750/09 (ECtHR, 16 September 2014).

26 ILC (n 22) 234.

27 ibid 85.

28 Luban (n 24) 315 and the deployment of his heuristic taxonomy of 'international humanitarian law' and 'law of armed conflict' perspectives of this body of law illustrate this point.

29 David Kennedy, 'Lawfare and Warfare' in James Crawford and Martti Koskenniemi (eds), *The Cambridge Companion to International Law* (CUP 2012) 167–71.

1.2 Manuals and Methodology

It is dangerous to attribute too much commonality to the methodological practice and frameworks that underpinned modern-day manuals. The San Remo Manual, the Harvard AMW Manual and the Tallinn Manual 2.0 were the products of different policy and institutional inputs. Despite this, there are some commonalities worth surveying.

It is the stated goal of all the manuals that their respective projects are confined to restating the *lex lata.* To this end, the respective projects do not seek to create new boundaries and otherwise develop or create new law, but rather are dedicated to providing a workable taxonomy of rules and commentary that restates, or otherwise situates the law at the time of publication. In introducing the finished product of the Harvard AMW Manual, Director Claude Bruderlein notes 'that the AMW Manual will facilitate the dissemination of an authoritative set of rules reflecting international law as perceived and discussed among these experts' and that the significance of the AMW Manual is that it represents

> the best opinion of a group of leading experts about the existing rules of international law applicable to air and missile warfare, as gathered and reviewed by its members from a vast array of national and international sources. The goal of the (...) Manual, in this context, is not to serve as a definite source of international law, but to facilitate the process of identification of these rules and to support professional exchanges on their interpretation.[30]

Similarly, Henderson notes that the purpose of the Harvard AMW Manual 'is to restate the current customary international law governing air and missile warfare. It purports to be neither a draft treaty nor an attempt to develop the law.'[31] Indeed, the drafters of the Harvard AMW Manual anticipated that the work would inform debate about the nature of the law applicable to air and missile warfare and would contribute to the shaping of operational rules of engagement and the crystallization of state positions on the law.[32] The stated emphasis of the Harvard AMW Manual is to provide an 'agreed version of the law',[33] to reflect the 'consensus of some of the most respected *jus in bello* scholars in the world on how existing law of armed conflict rules and norms apply to this type of warfare'.[34]

The statements made by the editors and commentators regarding the status of the manuals reveal a hesitancy regarding the place of these manuals. While legal and technical experts were all used in the production of the rules and commentaries in each, there has been no overt claim by any of the editors and/or contributors that these works constitute any kind of collective expression of 'highly qualified publicists' for the purposes of attributing a status reflected in Article 38(1)(d) of the Statute of the ICJ.[35] Nonetheless, the views expressed by those partic-

---

[30] Claude Bruderlein, 'Introduction' (2012) 47 Texas International Law Journal 261, 262.

[31] Ian Henderson, 'Manual on International Law Applicable to Air and Missile Warfare: A Review' (2010) 49 Military Law and the Law of War Review 169, 170.

[32] ibid.

[33] Charles Garraway, 'The Use and Abuse of Military Manuals' (2004) 7 Yearbook of International Humanitarian Law 425, 431.

[34] Geoffrey S. Corn and Gary P. Corn, 'The Law of Operational Targeting: Viewing the LOAC Through an Operational Lens' (2012) 47 Texas International Law Journal 337, 338.

[35] Statute of the International Court of Justice (adopted 26 June 1945, entered into force 24 October 1945) 33 UNTS 993.

ipating may well qualify under that banner. However, they do not obviously represent treaty or customary international law in their own right, nor do they claim to be definitive. They do, however, seek to reflect international law applicable to their fields of focus. Henderson has cogently noted that:

> While the rules cannot, and do not claim to be, authoritative, the depth and breadth of scholarship is arguably sufficient to in effect set up a rebuttable presumption. It may not be the law merely because it is in the Manual, but there would have to be a cogent argument as to why something that the Manual claims to be a rule should not be treated as such.[36]

In respect of the first Tallinn Manual, general editor Michael Schmitt notes that the manual reflects the views of scholarly opinions of the independent experts and that the 'results from expert-driven process [are] designed to produce a non-binding document applying existing law to cyber warfare. The Manual does not set forth *lex ferenda*, best practice or preferred policy.'[37]

The ambition of the manuals speaks to their intended purpose and therefore their status. They are not intended to be rarefied academic accounts of deconstructive legal analysis, but rather are fully intended to be accessible and operationally relevant. Hence, according to Bruderlein, 'the (…) Manual is intended for "front end" use, as an operational or training document. A statement in "less-than lawyer" mode to make it accessible and operational.'[38]

1.3 *Lex Lata* and Progressive Development

It is a general feature of all the international operational law manuals that they are expressed to be no more than a restatement of existing law. External commentary largely acknowledges that they have achieved their goals of 'clarifying'[39] or providing 'an agreed version of the law'.[40] Invariably, though, there is some level of progressive development that will be necessarily included in any project of restatement. In respect of the San Remo Manual the experts were dedicated to the task of clarifying the law of naval warfare that had largely been prescribed under treaty law 100 years earlier and they needed to reconcile that law with the adoption of the Geneva Conventions and Protocols (that, with the possible exception of aspects of GC II, do not directly regulate naval warfare) along with almost 100 years of naval operations state practice.[41] To that end, legal concepts necessarily had to be adapted to contemporary practice. The same is true for the Harvard AMW Manual that needed to deal with developing technol-

---

36 Henderson (n 31) 180.

37 Schmitt (n 8) 5.

38 As paraphrased in Kenneth Anderson, 'The Model Air and Missile Warfare Manual' (*Opinio Juris*, 12 February 2011) <http://opiniojuris.org/2011/02/12/the-model-air-and-missile-warfare-manual/ > accessed 31 January 2021.

39 Wolff Heintschel von Heinegg, 'The Current State of the Law of Naval Warfare: A Fresh Look at the San Remo Manual' (2006) 82 International Law Studies 269, 270.

40 Garraway (n 33) 431.

41 Doswald-Beck (n 6) Introductory Note: 'The purpose of the Manual is to provide a contemporary restatement of international law applicable to armed conflicts at sea. The Manual includes a few provisions which might be considered progressive developments in the law but most of its provisions are considered to state the law which is currently applicable.'

ogies and the reflected experience of the two Gulf Wars and the war in Afghanistan, which deployed these new aerial technologies. Moreover, the closest model upon which air warfare could reference were the 1923 draft Hague Rules on Air Warfare. As Sassoli and Quintin observe:

> The [Harvard AMW Manual's] added value lies in the field of air-to-air warfare, for it provides numerous precisions and adaptations of general principles to the specificities of the air environment. This is essential considering that Protocol I does not formally cover air-to-air warfare, which remains governed by rather ill-defined customary rules.[42]

Similarly, the Tallinn Manual was largely seen as a necessary response to the reality of cyber operations that struck countries such as Estonia and Georgia in recent times under a legal framework that was very unclear.

This progressive development element must necessarily be cautious if the integrity of the restatement goal is to be met. It seems evident that the experts and editing staff of these manuals needed to tread carefully in claiming the existence of any new or substantially modified new paradigm. One clear example of that approach is the legal issue concerning cryptographic equipment on board hospital ships and aircraft and the rules that apply to such equipment. Article 34(2) GC II implicitly prohibits the use of cryptographic equipment on hospital ships. The rationale, as explained in the San Remo Manual, is that the prohibition ensured that such protected ships cannot betray that protection through the transmission of military information. Despite this, the San Remo Manual struck an equivocal stance on such equipment by concluding that '[i]n order to fulfill most effectively their humanitarian mission, hospital ships *should* be permitted to use cryptographic equipment. The equipment shall not be used in any circumstance to transmit intelligence data nor in any other way to acquire any military advantage.'[43]

This position was guarded in its choice of the word 'should'. All commentators understood this position as a sound reading of the true purpose of the existing rule, but one that potentially was contrary to existing law.[44] It was equally recognized that the use of the word 'should' accurately reflected changing customary international law that had developed since 1949 as a result of modern military communication practices.[45]

The Harvard AMW Manual expands upon this equivocation and takes a more definitive position by stating that 'Medical aircraft must not possess or employ equipment to collect intelligence harmful to the enemy. It may, however, be equipped with encrypted communications equipment intended solely for navigation, identification and communication consistent with the execution of its humanitarian mission.'[46] The commentary on the revised position taken in the Harvard AMW Manual concerning the qualified lawfulness of using encrypted

---

[42] Marco Sassoli and Anne Quintin, 'Active and Passive Precautions in Air and Missile Warfare' (2014) 44 Israel Yearbook on Human Rights 69, 123.

[43] Doswald-Beck (n 6) Rule 171 (emphasis mine).

[44] Richard J. Grunawalt, 'Hospital Ships in the War on Terror: Sanctuaries or Targets?' (2005) 58 War College Review 89, 101–102.

[45] Garraway (n 33) 430.

[46] Harvard AMW Manual (n 7) rule 81.

communications reflects, by majority, an expression of contemporary operational practice and legal understanding.[47]

It remains a matter for states to determine whether or not this position on customary international law is correct. It is states which make international law, not experts or any other non-state actor, but such a conclusion by experts may allow states the opportunity to publicly accept or reject this reading of customary international law. The manuals deal with numerous other issues that have required greater clarity. These are issues not only resident within general customary international law, but also issues that appear over time in the course of the development of the manuals themselves. Hence, topics concerning the definition of airspace, the role of the Security Council in times of armed conflict, of definitions of military objectives and rights of blockade and visit and search, *inter alia*, all received refined assessment in the Harvard AMW Manual from what was contained in the San Remo Manual.

To this end, the goals of the manual editors and contributors in fostering reflection on the cogency of the rules and commentary are most pronounced. The positions reached in the manuals are designed to generate debate and to encourage consistency in legal positions reached by identifying the gaps, ambiguities and contradictions in the law and providing means for ensuring a level of coverage that is internally consistent. As to the specific methodological means taken when establishing rules or providing justificatory commentary, it is evident that inductive, deductive and analogical methods of analysis are all applied at various points through the manuals in the construction of rules and their supporting commentary. Each approach necessarily carries its own advantage/disadvantage regarding performative accuracy.

These manuals therefore seek to create a kind of 'normative feedback loop', whereby they express norms that already exist as customary international law (with or without a level of fine-tuned progressive adjustment), but also encourage states to consider these, resolve these and hopefully adhere to these and incorporate them more fully into their state practice and *opinio juris*, which in turn has the effect of strengthening the authority of the rules identified in the manuals.

1.4 Critique

Inevitably, the manual phenomenon has received academic criticism, relating largely to the representative nature of the experts selected to participate in the creation of such manuals through to the methodological imprecision of the projects themselves.

The Tallinn Manual seems to have received the most criticism. Lauri Mälksoo, for example, has observed that the Tallinn Manual was very Western in composition, noting that the contributing experts 'have distinctly American and Old European backgrounds'[48] with no contribution, for example, from China, the Russian Federation or even Eastern Europe.

Such criticism is not without force. Self-selection of 'experts' necessarily carries the risk that such contributors are not well established enough in their fields, or otherwise do not fully

---

47 ibid 235.

48 Lauri Mälksoo, 'The Tallinn Manual as an International Event' (*International Centre for Defence and Security*, 8 August 2013) <https://icds.ee/en/the-tallinn-manual-as-an-international-event/> accessed 31 January 2021.

represent the range of views held on particular issues because they do not attract broad geographical representation that enables differing views to be proffered and tested.

In relation to the Harvard AMW Manual process, it is evident that the directing staff of that project did seek broad geographical input with meetings held on all five continents in the review phase of the rules and commentary. Interestingly, in respect of the first expert draft of the manual's rules to be considered by the Asia-Pacific forum that met in Sydney in 2007 to consider the draft, an overwhelming sentiment was that it did indeed represent both an overtly academic and 'European' perspective.[49] The resulting Sydney meeting that was attended by representatives from Australia, Cambodia, the People's Republic of China, Indonesia, Japan, the Republic of Korea, Malaysia, New Zealand, Pakistan, the Philippines, Singapore and Thailand, reworked the manual and over 100 substantive changes were made. There was subsequently significant state engagement with over 50 governments[50] and particular emphasis on the engagement with the permanent five members of the Security Council. All engagements were undertaken on a non-attribution basis, allowing greater freedom of expression and interaction on the issues contained within the Harvard AMW Manual.

It is a matter for the coordinators of these projects to anticipate the level of inevitable criticism if there is a lack of broad representation. It is equally clear, however, that the quality of the publication and the level of credibility it generates will turn more on the quality of the analysis than merely including representatives from a wide range of states who have nothing to add. It is equally clear that while all participants in these projects participate in their 'private' capacities, there are many representatives from governments and militaries whose 'private' views echo that of their state. To this end, it can be a useful 'track 1.5' mechanism for states to advance and test views without the issue of attribution providing a restraint to open and frank discussion.

Similarly, in respect of cyber war, other critiques of the manual phenomenon have revolved around the capacity for international humanitarian rules to be clarified in circumstances where state practice and expressions of *opinio juris* are yet unformulated, at least publicly. Hence, Kessler and Werner observe:

> The Manual's focus on armed conflict/military action represents a less than comprehensive achievement. The level of action regulated in the Tallinn Manual has hardly occurred, with known cyber attacks implemented below the level of an armed conflict. Cyber attacks to date have had relatively benign consequences – inconvenience and offence (…) There is a lack of historical experience (…) excluding Stuxnet, there has been no cyberwar incident associated with the widespread devastation and damage associated with 'war' (…) thus evaluating legality of responses remains a matter of speculation and hypothetical reasoning.[51]

In respect of the issue of tracking state practice and locating *opinio juris*, there is necessarily difficulty in a field where technology is developing exponentially and where tactics, techniques and procedures are not readily revealed. Indeed, with respect to the Tallinn Manual, such challenges were acknowledged at the outset. General editor of the Tallinn Manual,

---

[49] The author's own notes reflected this observation during the proceedings.

[50] Bruderlein (n 30) 262.

[51] Oliver Kessler and Wouter Werner, 'Expertise, Uncertainty, and International Law: A Study of the Tallinn Manual on Cyberwarfare' (2013) 26 Leiden Journal of International Law 793, 800.

Michael Schmitt, observed that cyber space is not a lawless firmament but is governed by established norms,[52] but that such norms needed to be located (not developed) and faithfully articulated. This necessarily requires that well-accepted principles of customary international law need to be applied within new realms of operational experience, and to that end, informed hypothetical testing is an acceptable way to deliver the required level of clarity. Such a position is consistent with the role of advisory opinions of international courts. Indeed, in the ICJ's *Nuclear Weapons Advisory Opinion*, it was observed that IHL 'applies to all forms of warfare and to all kinds of weapons, those of the past, those of the present and those of the future'.[53] The lack of publicly declared attacks and defences in the cyber realm should not constrain thinking and the development of rules that are viewed as having application in reasonably anticipated, albeit hypothetical, circumstances.

In such methodological circumstances, it is imperative that the manual be transparent and reflect any conflicting views. Hence, it is usual that international operational law manual working processes mandate that all experts agree on rule composition, but that any disagreements in legal positions in arriving to this consensus be recorded in the associated commentary to the relevant rule. Invariably, this promotes higher abstraction in rule articulation, but ensures that the commentary becomes critical to understanding underlying strengths of positions taken.[54] This, in turn, enables the intended audiences of the manuals, especially states, to arrive at their own views regarding the cogency of the legal positions finally adopted.

1.4.1 The impact of manuals

There is evidence that international operational law manuals are having their intended effect within targeted audiences, principally military legal officers and government officials. Not surprisingly perhaps, given its historical longevity, the San Remo Manual has probably had the most impact. Its content has found faithful expression in Chapter 13 of the UK Ministry of Defence Joint Service Manual of the Law of Armed Conflict[55] as well as the German Navy Commander's Handbook.[56] As for the Harvard AMW and Tallinn Manuals, there has not been the same reproduction of text within national manuals yet, but they are of more recent vintage.

It is also becoming increasingly evident that courts, tribunals and other quasi-judicial bodies are using international operational manuals as useful references to assist in deliberative or advocacy projects. In respect of modern manuals this has been most pronounced in the case of the San Remo Manual. It has been cited with approval by the International Criminal Court (ICC) Pre-Trial Chamber in the case of *Situation of the Registered Vessels of Comoros, Greece,*

---

52 Michael Schmitt, 'Cyberspace and International Law: The Penumbral Mist of Uncertainty' (2013) 126 Harvard Law Journal Forum 176.

53 *Legality of the Threat or Use of Nuclear Weapons* (Advisory Opinion) [1996] ICJ Rep 226, 259 para 86.

54 International Humanitarian Law Research Institute: IHL in Air and Missile Warfare, 'About the Project – Overview' (Program on Humanitarian Policy and Conflict Research) <http://www.ihlresearch.org/amw/about-project> accessed 22 April 2016.

55 UK Ministry of Defence, 'Joint Service Manual of the Law of Armed Conflict' (Joint Service Publication 2004) 383 <https://www.gov.uk/government/uploads/system/uploads/attachment_data/file/27874/JSP3832004Edition.pdf> accessed 31 January 2021.

56 von Heinegg (n 39) 269.

and Cambodia.[57] Similarly, it was referenced by the quasi-judicial national and international bodies that were commissioned to inquire into the Gaza Maritime Incident of 31 May 2010 between Israel and non-government groups seeking to breach a blockade off the Gaza coast. In respect of that incident, the Human Rights Council,[58] the Turkel Commission (Israel),[59] the Turkish Government National Commission[60] and the UN Secretary General Panel of Inquiry[61] all referred to the rules and commentary of the San Remo Manual in their final reports. Such reference implicitly endorses the manual's authoritative status, even if each body arrived at different conclusions regarding the factual and legal conclusions to be drawn in respect of the incident under consideration.

Similarly, the San Remo Manual has been referenced with approval in a judgment by the International Criminal Tribunal for the Former Yugoslavia (ICTY)[62] and also a report prepared by the ICC's Office of the Prosecutor concerning incidents between North and South Korea occurring in early 2011.[63]

To date there have been no references to the Harvard AMW Manual nor the Tallinn Manual within international court or tribunal decisions; however, there have been non-governmental organization reports that have authoritatively cited the Harvard AMW Manual.[64] There is also evidence that the Harvard AMW Manual is being used in international courses to train operational commanders and personnel.[65]

There is a difference of opinion on whether manuals such as these should form the basis of judicial or quasi-judicial decision-making. There is a line of argument that international operational law manuals are not designed for use in legal proceedings and should not be used

---

57 *Situation on Registered Vessels of Comoros, Greece and Cambodia* (Article 53(1) Report) ICC-01/13-6-AnxA (6 November 2014) 18, 31 (*Situation on Registered Vessels*).

58 Human Rights Council, 'Report of the international fact-finding mission to investigate violations of international law, including international humanitarian and human rights law, resulting from the Israeli attacks on the flotilla of ships carrying humanitarian assistance' (27 September 2010) UN Doc A/HRC/15/21, 50.

59 The Public Commission to Examine the Maritime Incident of 31 May 2010, 'The Turkel Commission Report: Part 1' (January 2011) para 33 <https://www.gov.il/BlobFolder/generalpage/downloads_eng1/en/ENG_turkel_eng_a.pdf> accessed 31 January 2021.

60 Turkish National Commission of Inquiry, 'Report on the Israeli Attack on the Humanitarian Aid Convoy to Gaza on 31 May 2010' (February 2011) para 61 <http://www.mfa.gov.tr/data/Turkish%20Report%20Final%20-%20UN%20Copy.pdf> accessed 31 January 2021.

61 'Report of the Secretary-General's Panel of Inquiry on the 31 May 2010 Flotilla Incident' (2 September 2011) para 28 <http://www.un.org/News/dh/infocus/middle_east/Gaza_Flotilla_Panel_Report.pdf> accessed 31 January 2021.

62 *Prosecutor v Mile Mrkšić et al* (Judgment) ICTY-95-13 (27 September 2007) 192, 457.

63 ICC, *Situation in the Republic of Korea* (Article 5 Report) (June 2014) para 51 <https://www.icc-cpi.int/iccdocs/otp/SAS-KOR-Article-5-Public-Report-ENG-05Jun2014.pdf> accessed 31 January 2021.

64 Physicians for Human Rights, 'Overview of Principles and Rules of International Humanitarian Law Applicable to Conduct of Hostilities with a Focus on Targeting of Hospitals and Medical Units', fns 17, 41 and 67 <https://s3.amazonaws.com/PHR_syria_map/ihl-methodology-appendix.pdf> accessed 31 January 2021; Nathaniel A. Raymond, Brittany Card and Ziad Al Achkar, 'The Case Against International Drones' (*Canadian International Council*, 12 December 2012) <https://opencanada.org/the-case-against-humanitarian-drones/> accessed 31 January 2021.

65 One example is the Geneva Centre for Security Policy that runs courses for military professionals based around the Harvard AMW Manual.

by judicial bodies.[66] This argument seems to represent something of a sub-set of argument that relates more broadly to national military law manuals and their intended purpose. On the one hand, they are intended to provide guidance to military members and are generally drafted in a manner that ensures that they are concise and accessible. Such brevity may not capture nuanced or more comprehensive government positions on key legal issues. On the other hand, such articulations as contained within international operational law manuals are written without any particular national perspective in mind and might be used to assist a judicial decision-maker in understanding the legal context of a particular issue. Much as Article 38(1)(d) of the Statute of the ICJ permits recourse to secondary sources such as the views of the most highly qualified publicists, international operational law manuals can, on the basis of their persuasiveness and cogency, assist a judicial decision-maker in confirming the existence or application of a legal rule. Importantly, though, Garraway observes that 'Manuals can indeed be used as part of the law-making process but their evidential value should not be overstated. Their purpose is ultimately practical – to assist the soldiers, sailors and airman on the front line to "temper the harshness and cruelty of combat" by abiding by the law.'[67]

1.4.2 Conclusion – manuals

It is evident that this is the age of the manual and that manual-drafting by experts continues unabated. The status of these international operational law manuals is self-declared to not be binding. The manuals' target audiences are principally military professionals and government advisors. The authority of the manuals derives entirely from their persuasiveness and integrity of their legal form. They are different from national military legal manuals in that they do not purport to represent a particular national perspective but rather seek to provide an agreed neutral version of the law applicable to operations. They are designed and are written in a manner that seeks to be accessible to all operational decision-makers. To this end, the strategy of the drafters and editors of these manuals is reflective of particular goals of normative legal reach.

It remains an enduring truism that law is 'done' daily in the thousands upon thousands of transactions that take place between practitioners and clients across the globe. While review of judicial decisions forms the corpus of most external assessments of law's social role, a truer sense of the sociology of law is resident within the dispensation of advice that occurs in the multiple venues and contexts in everyday life. This is what Weber identifies with his prosaic observation that law is what lawyers do.[68] This was also the motivating intuition of legal realism[69] and finds enduring contemporary expression today; Luban notes, for example, 'legal advising is the most important thing that lawyers do, and lawyer advice, rather than judicial decisions, defines the law'.[70] Similarly, he notes '[a] better standpoint for jurisprudence is that of the lawyer, not of the judge (…). The lawyer-client consultation is the primary point of

---

66 Anderson (n 38).

67 Garraway (n 33) 440.

68 Martti Koskenniemi, *From Apology to Utopia: The Structure of International Legal Argument* (CUP 2006) 478.

69 Mauro Zamboni, *Law and Politics: A Dilemma for Contemporary Legal Thinking* (Springer 2008) 90.

70 Luban (n 24) 319.

intersection between "The Law" and the people it governs.'[71] It is this end and this audience that the manuals speak to and it is here that they may have their most durable impact in the construction and dispensation of legal advice in hundreds, if not thousands, of operational legal transactions occurring daily.

2. THE ROLE OF COURTS AND MILITARY OPERATIONAL DECISION-MAKING

While international operational legal manuals are intended to apply directly to relevant audiences to advance the development and application of the law, the role of international courts, tribunals and quasi-judicial agencies has been more diffuse. This is partly attributable to the decentralized nature of the international adjudicative system, but is also partly attributable to the social role of courts, especially those exercising international criminal jurisdiction.

Courts such as the ICTY, the Special Tribunal for Lebanon (STL) and the ICC seek to establish the criminal accountability of defendants subject to their jurisdiction. To that end they do not all speak with the same voice as they exist under different authorities, with different crimes, modes of liability, defences, and procedures, albeit with similarities. Their task is, moreover, to establish criminal liability, a threshold that obviously must not be breached but is plainly set too low for modern professional military forces in the broader ambition of ensuring compliance with IHL. Merely ensuring that criminal breaches do not occur is the minimum standard of legal compliance that must be achieved, but professional armed forces are generally committed to higher standards of battlefield practice than that.

These courts, along with the ECtHR when it is dealing with military issues and the intersection of IHL and international human rights law, are not always binding in their reach, but military legal officers and government officials, even of countries that are not subject to their jurisdiction, nonetheless routinely analyse their decisions. This is done in a manner that seeks to predict whether a particular concept or paradigm represented in a judgment may impact more broadly on thinking and planning in the field. It is clear that these judicial bodies have made constructive contribution to the corpus of law underpinning armed conflict. Decisions have been reached that confirm many understandings of the rules applicable to armed conflict of the type included within international operational law manuals described in section 1 above. Understandings of command/superior responsibility,[72] of available defences,[73] of particular provisions relating to the prohibitions on spreading terror[74] and the limits of military necessity[75] are all useful contributions to understanding in the field.

Despite these positive contributions, it is equally clear that sometimes judicial outcomes have also been inconsistent with generally accepted understandings of practice within the operational law field. While risking extraordinary oversimplification, a view will be advanced that in recent years, the courts, when dealing with operational law issues, have made contributions that are too little, too far and too prescriptive to be helpful to shaping military practice.

---

[71] David Luban, *Legal Ethics and Human Dignity* (CUP 2009) 131.

[72] *The Prosecutor v Tihomir Blaškić* (Judgment) ICTY-95-14 (3 March 2000); *Prosecutor v Delalić et al.* (Judgment) ICTY-96-21 (16 November 1998).

[73] *The Prosecutor v Drazen Erdemović* (Judgment) ICTY-96-22 (29 November 1996).

[74] *Prosecutor v Stanislav Galić* (Judgment and Opinion) ICTY-98-29 (5 December 2003).

[75] *Prosecutor v Pavle Strugar* (Judgment) ICTY-01-42 (31 January 2005).

2.1 Too Little

The principle of proportionality is a fundamental concept within operational legal decision-making. The principle, which finds expression in Article 51(5)(b) AP I, provides 'An attack which may be expected to cause incidental loss of civilian life, injury to civilians, damage to civilian objects, or a combination thereof, which would be excessive in relation to the concrete and direct military advantage anticipated'.

Proportionality creates an evaluative standard that requires that anticipated military advantage be weighed against incidental loss of civilian life and damage to civilian objects. While broader socio-political gains may not be factored into any determination, it nonetheless leaves an open discretion of how to balance two competing ideas. Numerous states parties to the AP I have made declarations seeking to assure a more expansive (and militarily advantageous) formalist architecture, including for example declarations that the security of the attacking force may be a factor that may be taken into account when balancing against 'excessive' civilian loss.[76] Similarly, proportionality assessments should be undertaken with respect to the 'attack as a whole and not individualized aspects of the attack'.[77]

Dinstein acknowledges the criticism levelled at the principle as elaborated within the AP I as permitting possibly too great a subjective assessment by military commanders when undertaking the balancing requirement.[78] As with the principle of distinction, a somewhat linear formulation of assessment is undertaken. Hence civilians and civilian objects are accorded a 'value' and an exchange is processed along consequentialist lines, whereby an attack may proceed on the basis that 'anticipated concrete and direct military advantage' is not 'excessive' in relation to civilian loss. Some texts also pointedly remind audiences that the term is 'excessive' and not 'extensive'.[79] The type of judgment to be exercised is an evaluative one, where broader policy-type considerations may be given effect in determining whether

---

[76] An example of this is found in the Australian Declaration to AP I: 'In relation to paragraph 5(b) of Article 51 and to paragraph 2(a)(iii) of Article 57, it is the understanding of Australia that (...) the term "military advantage" involves a variety of considerations including the security of attacking forces,' International Committee of the Red Cross, 'Declarations Made at the Time of Ratification: Australia' <https://ihl-databases.icrc.org/applic/ihl/ihl.nsf/Notification.xsp?action=openDocument&documentId=10312B4E9047086EC1256402003FB253> accessed 31 January 2021.

[77] See for example the following declarations to AP I by Australia: 'In relation to paragraph 5(b) of Article 51 and to paragraph 2(a)(iii) of Article 57, it is the understanding of Australia that references to the "military advantage" are intended to mean the advantage anticipated from the military attack considered as a whole and not only from isolated or particular parts of that attack,' International Committee of the Red Cross, 'Declarations Made at the Time of Ratification: Australia' <https://ihl-databases.icrc.org/applic/ihl/ihl.nsf/Notification.xsp?action=openDocument&documentId=10312B4E9047086EC1256402003FB253> accessed 31 January 2021; and the United Kingdom: 'In relation to paragraph 5(b) of Article 51 and paragraph (2)(a)(iii) of Article 57, that the military advantage anticipated from an attack is intended to refer to the advantage anticipated from the attack considered as a whole and not only from isolated or particular parts of the attack,' International Committee of the Red Cross, 'Declarations Made at the Time of Ratification: United Kingdom of Great Britain and Northern Ireland' <https://www.icrc.org/applic/ihl/ihl.nsf/Notification.xsp?action=openDocument&documentId=0A9E03F0F2EE757CC1256402003FB6D2> accessed 31 January 2021.

[78] Yoram Dinstein, *The Conduct of Hostilities Under the Law of International Armed Conflict* (CUP 2004) 122.

[79] ibid 120.

an 'anticipated military advantage' is or isn't proportionate to the incidental civilian loss or damage to civilian objects (or a combination thereof) expected. An assessment is to be made as to military significance of an attack in terms that invite a wide, but bound, level of discretion. While not expressed in mathematical terms, there is nonetheless a quality of calibrated judgment as to whether a bridge, road, or military barracks is worth a loss of 5, 50, or 500 civilians in any particular circumstance.

Given the significant nuance that underpins this concept, it would be hoped for that a court or tribunal might provide relevantly sophisticated formula for assessment. In the case of *Galić*, however, the ICTY determined that '[i]n determining whether an attack was proportionate it is necessary to examine whether a reasonably well-informed person in the circumstances of the actual perpetrator, making reasonable use of the information available to him or her, could have expected excessive civilian casualties to result from the attack'.[80]

Such a finding in this case that 'reasonableness' is the governing standard is not problematic *per se*, but of course provides little definitive guidance and conceptually operates to elevate the subjective to the objective so as to appear as a 'natural' outcome with relative ease.[81]

2.2 Too Far

In contrast to the open-ended test formulated by the ICTY regarding proportionality, the Tribunal erred in going too far with its prescription when assessing the principle of distinction in the case of *Gotovina*.

The principle of distinction has been described as a 'cardinal' principle of the law of armed conflict by the ICJ.[82] While expressed in general language as a principle, the concept of distinction has been resolutely textualized within IHL in terms of a paradigmatic rule. Indeed, as reflected in Article 48 AP I, it is self-identified as the 'Basic Rule' of the Protocol and states: 'In order to ensure respect for and protection of the civilian population and civilian objects, the Parties to the conflict shall at all times distinguish between the civilian population and combatants and between civilian objects and military objectives and accordingly shall direct their operations only against military objectives.'

In the case of *Gotovina*,[83] the ICTY dealt with the question of artillery shelling by Croatia military forces within the Krajina region of Croatia. The Trial Chamber determined that given the types of artillery used in that instance, a 200-metre radius zone around the target was a sufficient basis for assessing the lawfulness of the attacks. Accordingly, in applying a quantitative approach, it was determined to be open by the Trial Chamber to conclude that any artillery shells landing outside this 200-metre impact zone were indiscriminate and thus unlawful. In the event, the Trial Chamber determined that a small percentage of the shells did in fact land

---

80 *Prosecutor v Stanislav Galić* (Judgment and Opinion) ICTY-98-29 (5 December 2003) 58.

81 Koskenniemi (n 68) 597.

82 *Legality of the Threat or Use of Nuclear Weapons* (Advisory Opinion) [1996] ICJ Rep 226 para 78: 'The cardinal principles contained in the texts constituting the fabric of humanitarian law are the following. The first is aimed at the protection of the civilian population and civilian objects and establishes the distinction between combatants and non-combatants; States must never make civilians the object of attack.'

83 *Prosecutor v Ante Gotovina et al.* (Judgment) ICTY-06-90 (15 April 2011).

outside this radius. Hence the defendants, Gotovina and Markac, were found guilty on the basis of this formulation.

Such a conclusion was highly specific in its mathematical formulation. In reply to this proportionality decision, a group of military operational law experts met within the International Humanitarian Law Clinic at Emory Law School to analyse the legal implications of the *Gotovina* Trial Judgment. The group then submitted an Amicus Curiæ Brief to the ICTY Appeals Chamber to provide 'the insights of military and civilian IHL experts who have studied, and in many cases applied, this complex process [targeting in a populated area] in hostilities'.[84]

On appeal, the ICTY Appeals Chamber took account of the evidence presented by the Amicus Curiæ Brief and rejected the self-imposed constructed 200-metre zone, noting that there had been little to no justification for its imposition and that the evidence of the expert witnesses on this matter had been equivocal. Such a zone, while allowing for ostensibly objective assessments of guilt under the distinction formulation, required substantial justification that simply was not provided by the Trial Chamber. Indeed, the vagaries of military action, including environmental conditions, the mechanical functioning of particular weapons pieces, the possibility of individual negligence/careless use of the systems, the possibility of targets of opportunity and so on, all required that a more thorough regime be established. This was a 'highly technical'[85] area, which the Appeals Chamber demanded that any kind of court-imposed target zone be fully explained and justified, especially when determining criminal guilt. Such prescription demanded by the Trial Chamber was too far a reach for meaningful compliance.

2.3 Too Prescriptive

In one of the few cases arising from the ICTY that did address the question of the principle of distinction directly, the question of breach was so palpable that it sets the bar too high, at least in the manner in which the model used by the ICTY was subsequently used. Hence, in the *Martić* trial,[86] a legal defence regarding an alleged violation of the proportionality standard was advanced as to the shelling of locations within Zagreb by M87 Orkan rockets in May 1995. In essence, the facts were that cluster munitions were fired at maximum range into a civilian area with the ostensible purpose of targeting a military objective. The Chamber reviewed the weapon system used, noting that the M87 Orkan rocket was a non-guided cluster munition, with each submunition consisting of 420 pellets of 3mm size and had a dispersal area of 2 hectares. The Trial Chamber held, with the Appeals Chamber agreeing, the determination that the M87 Orkan rocket was an indiscriminate weapon and hence a requisite criminal intention could be manifested by virtue of the weapons system used. This conclusion seems inevitable on the facts presented. What is problematic is the subsequent reference to this case as setting some kind of standard for determining the application of the principle of distinction.

---

[84] *Prosecutor v Ante Gotovina et al.* (Application and Proposed Amicus Brief concerning the 15 April Trial Chamber Judgment and Requesting that the Appeals Chamber Reconsider the Findings of Unlawful Artillery Attacks During Operation Storm) ICTY-06-90 (12 January 2012) 1.

[85] *Prosecutor v Ante Gotovina et al.* (Judgment) ICTY-06-90 (16 November 2012) 21, 61.

[86] *Prosecutor v Milan Martić* (Judgment) ICTY-95-11 (12 June 2007).

This test was referred to in the *Final Report to the Prosecutor by the Committee Established to Review the NATO Bombing Campaign Against the Federal Republic of Yugoslavia*[87] that was commissioned to review the use of force employed by NATO during *Operation Allied Force.* Such reliance is unfortunate as it seems to establish a reference point for distinction that sets a standard far in excess of what a professional military force would tolerate regarding compliance with the rules relating to distinction in armed conflict. No professional force would ever countenance using cluster munitions in a crowded civilian area where a military objective may be co-located. Yet the egregious violation expressed in the case of *Martić* was being used as a kind of international measure. As such this case offers very little in terms of future planning under this critical principle.

2.4 Conclusion – Courts and Methodology

It is almost certainly unfair to criticize the impact of court and tribunal decisions on the development of operational law processes given their specific social role. Maintaining professional military standards, on the one hand, and judging criminal guilt according to prescribed criteria and enumerated modes of liability under governing international criminal law statutes, are two different things. Nonetheless, despite the decentralized and diffuse nature of international criminal law in the context of war crimes, decisions of international adjudicative bodies do carry with them unavoidable normative impact. The professional international military legal reaction to the trial decision of *Gotovina* was palpable. The Amicus Curiæ brief that was prepared, received wide international reporting and considerable support. This occurred not because the ICTY determination had any direct bearing on countries outside the former Yugoslavia, but because it was recognized that the modalities of legal decision-making might be impacted through indirect means of influence. This is manifested through concepts of liberalism and social agency (public opinion) as well as ideas of constructivism and identity formation.

In recent years, many have proclaimed, in non-pejorative terms, how legally compliant their military operations have been.[88] This emphasis reflects a contemporary realization of the connection between legal validity and legitimacy. It is also a product of the reactions by professional military forces to the loss of credibility that comes from a sense of social and professional rupture occasioned by too far a departure from values underpinning contemporary international humanitarian law. Hence, despite the formalist objections that can be easily mounted to blocking reasoning employed in particular judgments ever directly impacting professional military forces outside the jurisdiction of the ICTY, there is a realization that military

---

[87] ICTY, 'Final Report to the Prosecutor by the Committee Established to Review the NATO Bombing Campaign Against the Federal Republic of Yugoslavia' (2000) 39 International Legal Material 1264, para 27.

[88] Roger Normand and Chris Jochnick, 'The Legitimation of Violence: A Critical Analysis of the Gulf War' (1994) 35 Harvard International Law Journal 387, 395 citing, *inter alia*, General Colin Powell: 'decisions were impacted by legal considerations at every level. Lawyers proved invaluable in the decision-making process.' At the war's conclusion, the Pentagon boasted that Coalition forces had 'scrupulously adhered to fundamental law of war proscriptions' in conducting 'the most discriminate military campaign in history'. Quoting a Pentagon spokesman, a leading American law journal called the Gulf War the 'most legalistic war ever fought'.

legal culture may not be so immune, hence the anxiety experienced in the particular instance of the *Gotovina* trial judgment.

On the other hand, it is not surprising that judicial bodies have been reluctant to be overly prescriptive in setting the thresholds of violations of the concepts of distinction and proportionality. Beyond the well-worn examples at the extremes,[89] such a decision is necessarily a relative one. It is also clear that there is no universally acknowledged military advantage 'unit' of exchange in proportionality assessments under the law, nor is there one for 'civilian loss'; indeed, there is an intrinsic relativity as to how civilian loss is rated as 'excessive' by different military forces based upon particular socio-political preferences.[90] However, in some cases there may well be a consensus or 'reasonable certitude about what the right answer is'.[91] Destroying a village to target a soldier on leave is a paradigmatic example of a disproportionate attack.[92] Beyond such paradigmatic cases, 'demonstrable certainty is not to be had' and decision-makers are, in fact, in a quandary of human fallibility.[93]

The law applicable to armed conflict may be attempting to reconcile what may be irreconcilable. Yet as Dinstein observes, there really is no alternative to the formulations of distinction and proportionality as presently outlined,[94] with all the attendant risks of subjectivity and competing visions that these tests provide. By deploying an inductive or analogical reasoning to these concepts one might approximate a kind of consistency, yet the vagaries of fact patterns, the measurement of 'anticipated' military advantage, of assessing what is 'excessive' in the particular circumstances at the time make this a fraught exercise. Deductive reasoning offers a firmer base for determination, yet such reasoning itself has been subject to withering critique for over a century.[95] The problem is not the creation of a viable syllogistic form, but the inevitable backwards reasoning that actually operates to draft a premise from a desired conclusion. Because it is the premise that underpins such reasoning and provides the touchstone for accuracy, it is here that subjective reasoning necessarily applies in the first place.[96]

Warfare sits at the edge of law. There is a consensus that the concepts of distinction and proportionality provide a necessary framework for lawfully ameliorating violent excess, yet at

---

89 Dinstein (n 78) 122: 'An obvious breach of the principle of proportionality would be the destruction of a whole village – with hundreds of civilian casualties – in order to eliminate a single enemy sniper. In contrast, if – instead of a single enemy sniper – an artillery battery would operate from within the village, such destruction may be warranted.'

90 Michael Schmitt, 'The Principle of Discrimination in 21st Century Warfare' (1998) 2 Yale Human Rights and Development Law Journal 143, 151.

91 Lloyd Weinreb, 'Law's Quest for Objectivity' (2006) 55 Catholic University Law Review 711, 727.

92 Yves Sandoz, Christophe Swinarski and Bruno Zimmerman, *Commentary on the Additional Protocols of 8 June 1977 to the Geneva Conventions of 12 August 1949* (International Committee of the Red Cross 1987) 684.

93 Weinreb (n 91) 727.

94 Dinstein (n 78) 122.

95 Oliver Wendell Holmes, 'The Path of the Law' (1997) 110 Harvard Law Review 991, 994: 'The prophecies of what the courts will do in fact, and nothing more pretentious, are what I mean by the law.'

96 John Dewey, 'Logical Method and Law' (1924) 33 Philosophical Law Review 560, 567 noted: 'The problem is to find statements, of general principle and of particular fact, which are worthy to serve as premises. As a matter of actual fact, we generally begin with some vague anticipation of a conclusion (or at least of alternative conclusions), and then we look around for principles and data which will substantiate it or which will enable us to choose intelligently between rival conclusions.'

the same time a hesitancy that being too prescriptive may impose too high a burden on law's purchase of warfare. War is an elusive subject, one that necessarily demands law's attention, but under which standard modes of interpretation seem impermeable. This necessarily generates criticism from those who are suspicious of law's claims in practice. However, when given the opportunity, judicial bodies themselves are equally anxious about the veracity of law's logic and the right vision to be adopted in applying the law in practice. Decisions are either banal in their conclusions or seek structural change either to assert military priorities or vice versa with humanitarian preferences. Either way, the notion of the clean application of inductive or deductive reasoning and neutral rules to unassailable facts exists as an aspirational goal. Yet decisions are made in armed conflict and the law complied with. Despite its practical indeterminacy, guidance is routinely delivered to military forces that contextualize such guidance to ground decision-making under the law. Contemporary approaches presume that the law provides a bounded space of rationality that permits calibrated decision-making where everything is properly balanced. This can be attained in practice, but the premise of such decision-making is often a result of considerable policy infiltration. The bounded reality is a product of a policy–legal interface where conditions have been created to allow for the sense of neutrality, where a type of legal automaticity seems possible, largely due to the heavy work being undertaken beforehand by infusing a policy orientation that acts to create a range of seemingly self-evident facts.

3. CONCLUSION

War remains international law's most intractable challenge[97] and has been subject to a dizzying array of regulative genres over the centuries. Contemporary techniques have seen an unprecedented density of international legal prescription, all conditioned upon tropes of validity to shape behaviour. The steady legal proceduralization of force to realize high strategic and humanitarian goals might certainly be counted a success by most measures, but it also reveals many ambiguities, blind spots and uncertainties.[98] Doubts about international law's methodological consistency[99] add to the disquiet regarding its effectiveness. There remain many sites of contest in the legal regulation of armed conflict. Military, governmental, humanitarian, public and private voices all engage in ongoing and intense dialogue over the nature of legal regimes created and imposed.

Law is routinely invoked, defended, derided and proselytized to secure military outcomes while seeking to preserve humanitarian priorities. Throughout the 20th century, but particularly after the Second World War, the modern alliance between political liberalism and legal positivism was seen to possess enormous emancipatory promise for the development of international law generally, but particularly in relation to the regulation of warfare.[100] Notwithstanding this promise, the capacity of states to make new law seems diminished in recent times. The development of new technologies and new tactics by non-state actors has

---

[97] Kennedy (n 29) 158.

[98] I have co-opted these terms from David Kennedy's use of this phraseology, which he employs throughout his scholarship as one heuristic mechanism to query the efficacy of legal propositions.

[99] ILC (n 22) 11, 493.

[100] See generally Howard N. Meyer, *The World Court in Action: Judging Among the Nations* (Rowman and Littlefield Publishers 2002).

added pressure to interpretative approaches of the law governing armed conflict. It seems unlikely that any kind of transformative moment with respect to core issues relating to the regulation of means and methods of warfare, as occurred in the three transformative moments of 1899/1907, 1949, and 1977, will occur any time soon. Yet the gaps remain.

In addition, the old certainties regarding the exclusivity of IHL began to erode as inroads were made from the field of international human rights law and broader notions of other interweaving law. Such developments exposed vulnerabilities in method and doctrinal commitment.

These vulnerabilities and gaps are filled by practitioners as well as military and academic experts in the field who have initiated the various projects dedicated to the drafting of international operational law manuals to facilitate meaningful guidance to the conduct of armed conflict. The status of these manuals is a matter of much debate. Their audiences are broad. They seek to provide meaningful direction to decision-makers in the field and yet retain a level of sophistication to ensure a coherency with settled paradigms. Such sophistication is seen as a bulwark against encroachment by allied fields of international law.

These international operational law manuals are in many ways something new within this field, a restatement of law pertaining to armed conflict in selected areas. Such restatements are well known within the legal tradition of the United States. Justice Cardozo of the US Supreme Court described elegantly the significance of such restatements when describing the somewhat analogous American Law Institute's Restatements in 1923:

> When, finally, it goes out under the name and with the sanction of the Institute, after all this testing and retesting, it will be something less than a code and something more than a treatise (…) It will be invested with unique authority, not to command, but to persuade (…). I have great faith in the power of such a restatement to unify our law.[101]

The analogy between the US Restatement project as described by Cardozo and the international operational law manual process is apt. The practice of international law and IHL in particular is a variegated process of input and reaction from relevant constituencies. Persuasion often has greater traction than arguments made under assertions of formal validity. This phenomenon represents a victory for the humanitarian strategy to permanently render law's imprint upon political and military decision-making, but of course comes with a price concerning legitimacy. International operational law manuals seek to preserve that legitimacy by relying upon the strength of their construction, methodology and argument to advance reasoned elaboration in this field.

Sharing a similar role are the judgments and views of courts, tribunals and quasi-judicial bodies who routinely dispense their verdicts and views on IHL and in turn necessarily impact the substance of the law as they do so. While highly decentralized and offering no general formal hierarchy, the decisions of such bodies are scrutinized and internalized by military legal officers and others. Within the pluralist universe that is international law, such inputs can carry significant normative weight. Constituencies of IHL lawyers and military legal officers react to such decisions, irrespective if formally bound, given the potential for such decisions to shape expectations and concepts of legitimacy within both the professional and general populations.

---

[101] Benjamin N. Cardozo, *The Growth of the Law* (Yale University Press 1924) 9.

The modern military force is one that does not only seek to act legitimately in accordance with external standards, but also one that 'aspires to be legitimate in its own eyes'.[102] To this end, the role of international operational law manuals and the decisions of courts and tribunals will continue to have significant normative effects in the modern era and thus assessment of the methodological ordering of such inputs is critical if informal law-making and questions of legitimacy are going to be meaningfully understood.

[102] Kennedy (n 29) 292.

PART VI

Legitimacy and participation

17. International humanitarian law-making in Latin America: Between the international community, humanity, and extreme violence

Alejandro Rodiles[1]

1. INTRODUCTION

This chapter identifies different phases of international humanitarian law-making in Latin America. However, I do not aim to present a comprehensive historical account of the development that international humanitarian law (IHL) has experienced in the region from the independence wars in the early nineteenth century until the present day. Instead, I will comment on the relationship between Latin America and IHL. This relationship includes the overall approach to *ius in bello*, and, more importantly, how this body of law has been perceived and conceived by Latin American diplomats, scholars, and judges, as well as the aims which are pursued through the participation of the region in its development. How are the rules of IHL interpreted? Which role is attributed to the law of war within national legal systems, and how is it conceived in relation to general international law? How far and in what sense is its development promoted? And why is there a sense that IHL matters in the region? These are the kind of questions that I will address in the following pages. The picture that will emerge from these lines is a particular interpretation of the said relationship, based on historical data and contemporary tendencies regarding the creation, application, and interpretation of IHL norms in Latin America, i.e., law-making in a broad sense.[2]

In certain instances, the relationship that I will describe goes beyond the specific principles and norms of IHL, and touches upon the relationship between the region and international law more broadly. In other cases, it only concerns a few countries, or certain national or regional actors, like domestic courts and the institutions of the Inter-American human rights system. It must be mentioned that this chapter does not intend to erase the many and important differences in the approach to the law of war in the various countries of the region. However, there is a common thread to this narrative: legitimacy. Indeed, the overall approach, perception, and

---

[1] My gratitude goes to Pablo Kalmanovitz (CIDE) and Tatiana Alfonso (ITAM) for most helpful comments and suggestions. I also thank Daniel García (ITAM) for technical assistance. The usual disclaimer applies.

[2] In a way, thus, this chapter can be seen as partly informed by the comparative international law project, see Anthea Roberts and others, 'Conceptualizing Comparative International Law' in Anthea Roberts and others, *Comparative International Law* (OUP 2018) 3–31.

conception of IHL imply an understanding of the legitimacy underlying it. As I will argue in the following sections, in each of the historical contexts identified in this chapter, a particular conception of international humanitarian law's legitimacy is discernible, which in turn helps to explain the degrees and ways Latin America has participated in its making – the legitimacy of participation from the internal perspective. An understanding of the legitimacy of this body of law should be read here as the perception of it within the broader fabric of international law. IHL's role is therefore at times indistinguishable from the overall relationship between Latin America and international law – as well as its role in the conduct of international relations, and in the articulation of the universal. It is in this sense that understandings of legitimacy can be described as the driving force in the participation of the region in IHL's evolution.

The conceptions of IHL's legitimacy in Latin America have changed over time. In section 2, I will refer to the wars of independence in the first half of the nineteenth century. During this period, law-making expressed itself mainly through treaty-making between the leaders of the independence movements and the Spanish governors of the Americas. During this initial phase, the legitimacy of the law of war was strongly related to the search for a Latin American identity and the desire to meet the standard of civilization at the same time: international humanitarian law-making was seen as a vehicle of independence and an entry point to the community of civilized nations.

From the mid-nineteenth century on, Latin American participation in the making of IHL has become a matter of diplomatic tradition. I will argue in section 3 that this tradition has favoured constructive engagement by Latin American diplomats in the codification and progressive development of the law of war, precisely because this body of law is (still) viewed as a crucial component of the broader law of the international community. This stands in line with the codification tradition of Latin America. The relationship between Latin America and IHL that can be underscored for this period, and which actually continues until this day, is part and parcel of the region's relationship with the international legal system *qua* order. Participation is seen as legitimate because IHL is itself a legitimizing force of the broader legal order of the international community.

The picture of Latin America's relationship with IHL would not be complete without understanding the role of the new key players in the region when it comes to international law-making: courts. This is the third and last phase identified here (section 4). The more recently significant role of judiciaries, regional and national, has been motivated by various factors, but two are of particular interest in the present context. First, IHL is viewed as part of a broader legal project for the region, i.e., *ius constitutionale commune* in Latin America (ICCLA), as it is called among legal scholars and the Inter-American Court of Human Rights (IACHR).[3] Thus, IHL's legitimacy stems from the same source as that which provides the basis for ICCLA: human dignity. The second factor motivating and justifying this participation is related to a very different story: the cruel realities of extreme violence present in parts of the region. Manifestations of extreme violence are forcing courts to dwell on the linkages between IHL and international human rights law, thereby developing innovative and

3 For an overview, see Armin von Bogdandy and others (eds), *Transformative Constitutionalism in Latin America – The Emergence of a New Ius Commune* (OUP 2017); for a critical appraisal of this project, see Alejandro Rodiles, 'The Great Promise of Comparative Public Law for Latin America: Toward *Ius Commune Americanum*?' in Roberts (n 2) 501–23.

far-reaching interpretations which amount to actual legislation on matters related to complex situations of internal conflict. Taken together, these jurisprudential developments form part of an emerging 'law of violence', as I will argue, in which the boundaries between the law of peace and the law of war are increasingly difficult to trace.

2. FROM 'WAR TO DEATH' TO 'HOSTILITIES CARRIED OUT BY CIVILIZED PEOPLE': INDEPENDENCE AND THE REGULATION OF WAR

Latin America and the Caribbean have a long and often ignored tradition in the making of the law of war, anchored in their emergence as a subcontinent of independent states. The creation of *Gran Colombia* between 1819 and 1820, which comprised much of the northern part of South America (Colombia, Ecuador, and Venezuela, as well as parts of northern Peru, western Guyana, and north-western Brazil), and today's Panama, was accompanied by negotiations between the *Libertador*, Simón Bolívar, and the Spanish Governor of the Captaincy General of Venezuela, Pablo Morillo, on two treaties: the Treaty of Armistice and the Treaty of the Regulation of the War. These are known as the 'treaties of Trujillo', because they were signed in the city of Trujillo, in today's Venezuela, on 25 and 26 November 1820, respectively.[4]

The Treaty of Armistice between the Kingdom of Spain and Colombia was thought to put an end to a particularly bloody episode in the wars of independence that took place in New Granada (today's Colombia) and in the Captaincy General of Venezuela, between 1812 and 1820, known as the 'war to death'.[5] In 1813, Simón Bolívar officialized this war of destruction with the 'Decree of War to Death' ('*Decreto de Guerra a Muerte*'), which called for the destruction of the 'barbaric Spaniards' who had 'violated the sacred law of the peoples' by committing 'all crimes' in the conduction of hostilities. This decree declared 'every Spaniard who [did] not conspire against the tyranny and in favour of the just cause' a traitor who should be killed. Americans (i.e., those born in the Western hemisphere), on the other hand, who had conspired against independence, 'misguided by error or perfidy', should be forgiven because Americans could not be guilty in this war.[6] Although the 'war to death' was officially declared only by one side, it was practised by independence fighters and Royal loyalists alike, turning the rebellion into a war marked by racial conflict and a 'theatre of blood'.[7] The Treaty of Armistice provided for a ceasefire of six months. In the case that the war was resumed after that period, or that the ceasefire was broken before it (what eventually occurred, in January 1821), Article 14 stipulated that a treaty regulating the conduct of hostilities 'in conformity

---

[4] On the history of these treaties, see Marcos Ruben Carrillo, 'Los Tratados de Trujillo' (1969) 32 Boletín de la Academia de Ciencias Políticas y Sociales 21.

[5] Anthony McFarlane, *War and Independence in Spanish America* (Routledge 2014) 111ff.

[6] Brigadier of the Union, Chief General of the Army of the North and the Liberator of Venezuela, Simón Bolívar, 'Decree of War to the Death', 15 June 1813, reproduced in Ideario político del libertador Simón Bolívar (Monografías, January 2013) <https://www.monografias.com/trabajos96/ideario-politico-del-libertador-simon-bolivar/ideario-politico-del-libertador-simon-bolivar.shtml> accessed 31 January 2021.

[7] Treaty of the Regulation of the War between the Governments of Colombia and Spain of 26 November 1820 (adopted and entered into force 26 November 1820), Gaceta de Caracas N° 19, Caracas, 6 December 1820, 95, preamble <www.cervantesvirtual.com/obra-visor/tratado-de-regularizacion-de-guerra-1820--0/html/ff86d340-82b1-11df-acc7-002185ce6064_2.html> accessed 31 January 2021.

with the law of civilized nations' should govern between the same parties.[8] As mentioned, the Treaty of the Regulation of the War was signed only a day after the armistice convention.

The second Trujillo treaty is not only significant for the history of Latin American independence, but it also plays an important and often ignored role in the history of universal international law. The French international lawyer and one of the inaugural judges of the International Court of Justice (ICJ), Jules Basdevant, was one of the first and remains one of the few who have recognized the relevance of the Treaty of the Regulation of the War,[9] including in Latin American legal scholarship.[10] This avant-garde convention included far-reaching provisions on the protection of the wounded and the sick, establishing that 'these disgraceful' should not be considered prisoners of war but treated with double consideration and respect, and afforded the same treatment as that received by the wounded and the sick of one's own army (Article 4). This provision clearly influenced later developments of *ius in bello*, in particular the First Geneva Convention of 1864,[11] often considered the starting point of 'modern, codified International Humanitarian Law'.[12] The second Trujillo agreement can also be seen as a pioneering treaty in regards to the codification of the rights of prisoners of war (POWs).[13] Articles 5 to 10 contained several provisions ranging from the obligatory exchange of POWs, to the recognition of POW status being applied to spies, to the allowance of *in situ* visits by commissioners appointed by the chiefs of armies in order to supervise the treatment of POWs and to ameliorate their condition.[14]

According to Basdevant, the most innovative aspect of the Trujillo agreement on the regulation of war is that it applied and codified the customary law of international armed conflict of that time to an internal armed conflict, a civil war, and that it did so guided by the spirit of progress and liberalism:

> (…) si l'on observe le but essentiel poursuivi, à savoir la régulation de la guerre, et le fait par les deux parties en lutte de s'entendre pour limiter les horreurs d'une guerre civile par les règles de la guerre

---

[8] Treaty of Armistice between Colombia and the Kingdom of Spain (adopted and entered into force 25 November 1820), Gaceta de Caracas N° 19, Caracas, 6 December 1820, 95 <www.cervantesvirtual.com/obra-visor/tratado-de-armisticio-1820--0/html/ff6c3062-82b1-11df-acc7-002185ce6064_2.html> accessed 31 January 2021.

[9] Jules Basdevant, 'Deux Conventions Peu Connues sur le Droit de la Guerre (Etats-Unies d'Amérique et Grand-Bretagne, 12 mai 1813, Colombie et Espagne, 26 novembre 1820)' (1914) 21 Revue Générale de Droit International Public 5; see also Julio Jorge Urbina, 'La aportación latinoamericana al desarrollo del derecho internacional humanitario' in Eduardo Rey Tristán and Patricia Calvo González (eds), *200 años de Iberoamérica (1810–2010). Congreso Internacional: Actas del XIV Encuentro de Lationoamericanistas Españoles, Santiago de Compostela, 15–18 de septiembre de 2010* (Universidad de Santiago de Compostela 2010) 2237–58.

[10] But see Hernando Valencia Villa, 'El derecho de los conflictos armados y su aplicación en Colombia' (1990) 15 Revista International de la Cruz Roja 5.

[11] Convention for the Amelioration of the Condition of the Wounded in Armies in the Field (adopted 22 August 1864, entered into force 22 June 1865) <http://hrlibrary.umn.edu/instree/1864a.htm> accessed 31 January 2021.

[12] Marco Sassòli and others (eds), *How does Law Protect in War? Cases, Documents and Teaching Materials on Contemporary Practice in International Humanitarian Law* vol. 1 (3rd edn, ICRC 2011).

[13] See also Villa (n 10) 5–6.

[14] Treaty of the Regulation of the War between the Governments of Colombia and Spain of 26 November 1820 (n 7) arts 5–10.

internationale, comprises d'ailleurs dans un esprit progressif et libéral, on reconnaitra que par là un grand exemple a été donné.[15]

It should be noted that the classification of the independence struggles in Spanish America as civil wars was questioned by Alejandro Álvarez. For the former Chilean judge of the ICJ, European powers, with the exception of Britain who supported emancipation, viewed Latin American independence struggles as revolts that had to be suppressed as they were an affront to the integrity of the metropole, whereas the former Spanish colonies in the Americas understood that they were exercising their legitimate right, a consequence of individual freedom, to become independent states. Thus, according to Álvarez, the latter upheld the view that '*la lutte avait les caràcteres non d'une guerre civile, mais d'une guerre internationale*'.[16] Writing in 1909, Álvarez took this issue very seriously, as for him it was related to the role younger American states would hold vis-à-vis their European counterparts in the new international order, which was crucial for the assurance over time of their independence and the non-intervention of the European powers in their affairs. As such, the classification of the independence wars as international armed conflicts was, in the mind of Álvarez, related to the Monroe doctrine, and played an important role in the foundations of his Western hemispheric (and by no means exclusively Latin American) *droit international américain*.[17]

Álvarez's claim about the international character of these wars remains rather isolated. But this is not out of a sense of negation of the right of the former colonies to fight for their independence. Mexican philosopher Luis Villoro explains how the Creole elite in Mexico City, i.e., those born in the colony but of Spanish origin, started to question the legitimacy of Spanish rule after the Abdications of Bayonne of 1808 by which Charles IV of Spain and his son Ferdinand VII handed power over to Napoleon, giving way to Spain's own war of independence, also known as the 'Peninsular war'.[18] The vacuum of power that followed in the Iberian Peninsula gave the local elites in the American centres of knowledge and power reason to question not the legitimacy of the Crown itself, but of those who ruled on behalf of an absent king. For the Creole forerunners of independence, the delegated power of the Spanish Crown exercised by colonial authorities was broken and sovereignty resided now in the inhabitants of the new world – the war was against the delegated colonial authorities, not the Crown. Although Villoro refers to the 'revolution of independence' in Novohispana and the subsequent declaration of Mexican independence in 1821, the war and political crisis in the Kingdom of Spain played as important a role in the struggles against colonial authorities in New Spain as in New Granada and Venezuela.

The second aspect emphasized by Basdevant is the 'liberal and progressive spirit' which guided the negotiations of the Trujillo conventions, and which is clearly reflected in their text.

---

15 Basdevant (n 9) 27.

16 Alejandro Álvarez, *Le Droit International Américain: Son Fondement – Sa Nature d'après l'Histoire diplomatique des Etats du Nouveau Monde et leur Vie Politique et Économique* (Pedone 1910) 39.

17 ibid 39–40. For a differentiated treatment of Álvarez's oeuvre, which at times was too much focused on the United States and less concerned with the sovereignty of Latin American states, see Juan Pablo Scarfi, *The Hidden History of International Law in the Americas: Empire and Legal Networks* (OUP 2017) 74ff.

18 Luis Villoro, 'La Revolución de Independencia' in Daniel Cossío Villegas (ed), *Historia General de México* vol 1 (3rd edn, El Colegio de México 1981) 591, 604–605.

Article 14 of the Treaty of Armistice provided for the adoption of 'a treaty regulating war in conformity with the law of nations, and *the most liberal, wise and humane practices of the civilized nations*',[19] and the Preamble of the Treaty of the Regulation of the War expressed the desire to regulate the war 'in conformity with *the laws of cultured nations, and the most liberal and philanthropic principles*'.[20] The usage of the term 'cultured nations' is emblematic indeed. A synonym of 'civilized nations', 'cultured nations' was often employed in colonial legislation on sanitation and disease control, for instance, serving as a reminder of the example to be followed in the conquered territories, i.e., the laws and regulations of learned European nations.[21] The tension cannot be overlooked: a few years after declaring war to death against the 'barbaric Spaniards', the *Libertador* felt the need to make it crystal clear that the emerging independent nations of the Americas embraced the highest standards in the conduct of hostilities as dictated by the old world. This paradox, however, became the defining characteristic of the Creole elite of the Spanish colonies as well as of the newly created Latin American states.

Independence struggles and state-formation in Spanish America were led by the Creole elite across the continent. As explained by Liliana Obregón in her seminal essay on the emergence of the Latin American legal consciousness, the term 'Creole' ('*criollo*') refers to 'the American-born élite of Spanish descent'.[22] Creoles distinguished themselves from Spanish rulers and merchants in that they were socially and culturally attached to the locales where they were born and lived, and which they regarded as their land, thus developing a feeling of national allegiance to the 'new world'. Especially in the urban centres of the colonies, an accommodated class of Spanish descent emerged which was highly educated, often in Europe, and which embraced the ideas of *les philosophes*, or of other thinkers of the *Abendland*.[23]

Enlightenment, that period of European thought and culture which 'ushered in our modern western world',[24] was the cultural standard of the Creole, Simón Bolívar,[25] who had been

---

19 Treaty of Armistice between Colombia and the Kingdom of Spain (n 8) art 14 (emphasis added).

20 Treaty of the Regulation of the War between the Governments of Colombia and Spain of 26 November 1820 (n 7) Preamble (emphasis added).

21 See, for instance, Adriana Maria Alzate Echeverri, *Suciedad y Orden: Reformas Sanitarias Borbónicas en la Nueva Granada 1760–1810* (Universidad del Rosario 2007) 235.

22 Liliana Obregón, 'Completing Civilization: Creole consciousness and international law in nineteenth-century Latin America' in Anne Orford, *International Law and Its Others* (CUP 2006) 247, 249.

23 Luis Villoro mentions that in Novohispana (today's Mexico) the real influence on the Creole elite came not from *les philosophes* but from naturalist legal thinkers. He underlines the importance of the Jesuit, Francisco Javier Alegre, born in Veracruz and a Professor of Canon law in Mérida, and his *Institutionum Teologicarum* of 1789 as being crucial in the formation of the ideas that justified the insurgency against the authorities of New Spain. Alegre relied mainly on Suárez and Puffendorf; see Villoro (n 18) 606–607. For the vita and work of Alegre, see Mauricio Beuchot, 'Algunas Doctrinas Filosóficas de Francisco Xavier Alegre sobre el Hombre, el Derecho y la Guerra Justa' in Leon Olivé and Luis Villoro, *Filosofía Moral, Educación e Historia: Homenaje a Fernando Salmerón* (Universidad Nacional Autónoma de México 1996) 507.

24 William Bristow, 'Enlightenment' (*The Stanford Encyclopedia of Philosophy*, 10 August 2011) <www.plato.stanford.edu/archives/sum2011/entries/enlightenment/> accessed 31 January 2021.

25 See for example the *Discourse of Angostura of 15 February 1819* held by Bolívar at the inauguration of the Second Constitutional Congress of Venezuela where he clearly relied on Rousseau; see Bolívar (n 6).

a pupil of one of the most influential liberal intellectuals in the region, Andrés Bello.[26] This influence, specifically on the making of the Trujillo treaties, is underlined by Basdevant:

> En proposant cette convention [i.e., the second Trujillo convention], Bolívar a peut-être agi sous l'influence des idées philosophiques du XVIIIe siècle : il avait des séjours en Europe et était un admirateur de Rousseau. L'esprit de cette convention est en harmonie et avec la formule de Montesquieu, reprise par Blackstone, l'abbé Grégoire, lord Stanhope et Talleyrand, et devenue courante, que, dans la guerre, les nations doivent se faire le moins de mal qu'il est possible, et avec le principe de Rousseau, adopté par Portalis, que la guerre est une relation d'État à État.[27]

There is probably no way of understanding the approach to, and the overall conception of international law in Latin America in the nineteenth and early twentieth centuries without referring to Liliana Obregón's notion of 'Creole legal consciousness'. Obregón's work is also crucial for understanding the legitimacy conception underlying the law regulating war at that time in the region, and, with it, the motivation of Latin American participation in its making. Although Obregón refers mainly to the post-independence era and to jurists like the Argentinean, Carlos Calvo, or the Chilean, Alejandro Álvarez, she also makes it clear that this consciousness of the Creole literati emerged during Spanish rule,[28] and men like Bello and Bolívar were crucial in this regard. She refers the concept of 'legal consciousness' back to Duncan Kennedy, for whom this represents that which 'characterizes the legal profession as a social group (…) and the constellation of ideals and goals current in the profession at a given moment'.[29] 'Creole legal consciousness' thus refers to the dominant and recurrent ideas and ideals about law within that accommodated class of Spanish descent which came to lead the independence struggles and the processes of state-formation in the post-independence era.[30]

As for the goals inherent to this particular representation of the function of law, Creole legal consciousness reflects an inner tension, or even paradox, surrounding the aspiration of constructing a Latin American legal and political identity by trying to reach the European standard of civilization (differentiation through identification). The law of nations embodied that 'standard of civilization', while at the same time represented an articulation of the need for independence. In the context of the ongoing armed conflicts, the laws and customs of war provided the means for showing the world that the aspirant nations of the new world

---

26 On this 'Venezuelan-born polymath, educator, writer and diplomat', see 'Relearning Old Lessons' (*The Economist*, 1 February 2014) <www.economist.com/news/americas/21595478-latin-americas-enduring-need-rule-law-education-and-openness-relearning-old-lessons> accessed 31 January 2021. On the relationship between Bello and Bolívar, see Mariano Picón-Salas, *De la Conquista a la Independencia* (Fondo de Cultura Económica 1975) 231–33. It should be noted that Bello and Bolívar spent time together in Europe.

27 Basdevant (n 9) 18.

28 Obregón (n 22) 251.

29 Duncan Kennedy, *The Rise and Fall of Classical Legal Thought* (Beard Books 1975) 27; Liliana Obregón, 'Between Civilization and Barbarism: Creole interventions in international law' (2006) 27 Third World Quarterly 815, 819.

30 These ideas, as acknowledged by Obregón, varied across time and space, relying in some instances on *les philosophes*, in others on Jeremy Bentham, and yet in others on the late scholasticism of Francisco Suárez. A constant thread was, however, the sense of a common heritage of a Roman legal tradition, still very much present in today's self-comprehension of legal culture in the region; see Obregón (n 22) 249–50.

were perfectly capable of joining the family of the civilized, precisely by demonstrating their willingness and ability to obey with such laws and customs, and, what is more, to codify and develop them. And here, the critique of Alejandro Álvarez on the usual classification of the independence struggles in Spanish America as civil wars calls for re-evaluation. The application of the rules of war among (civilized) nations via its codification in the second Trujillo convention was already an act of independence: a way of placing Great Colombia vis-à-vis its European counterpart in the international system. However, this was only possible by assimilating the rules of the European system. But it is important to underline that the laws of war of the 'cultured nations' were clearly conceived as legitimate by the Creole independence leaders since they represented 'the most liberal and philanthropic principles'.[31] So, participation in the making of such laws was seen as legitimate on both grounds: due to their inherent goodness (something very European), as well as on the basis of contributing to the independence of the new world and the forging of a nation's own identity (something, *prima facie*, opposed to Europe).

3. FROM THE ANXIETY OF BELONGING TO THE INTERNATIONAL COMMUNITY TO THE PROMOTION OF THE INTERNATIONAL RULE OF LAW: INTERNATIONAL HUMANITARIAN LAW-MAKING BY DIPLOMATS

In his *General Introduction* to *International Law: Achievements and Prospects*, Mohammed Bedjaoui mentions the following in relation to the integration of Latin American states to the international community:

> [t]he admission of otherwise new members to this system thus depended on the will of the European States that were already part of it. In fact, only those countries that had officially embraced European institutions and culture, such as the United States and the States of Latin America, were accepted into the 'club'.[32]

Bedjaoui situates his remarks in the second half of the nineteenth century. This would seem to confirm that by showing themselves willing to assimilate to the standard of civilization, as expressed *inter alia* in the declarations to comply with, codify and develop the laws regulating war among 'cultured nations', the young independent states of Latin America were successfully admitted to the family of the civilized: the realization of the Creole dream. However, in the footnote corresponding to this passage, Bedjaoui, himself referring to Paul Guggenheim, mentions that this admission 'was not achieved without difficulty'.[33] These remarks relate to the fact that Latin American states were not admitted to the Brussels Conference of 1874, where a Russian draft on an agreement on the laws and customs of war was discussed.[34] In

---

31 Treaty of the Regulation of the War between the Governments of Colombia and Spain (n 7), Preamble.

32 Mohammed Bedjaoui, *International Law: Achievements and Prospects*, Part I (UNESCO/ Martinus Nijhoff 1991) 1, 7–8.

33 ibid.

34 See 'Project of an International Declaration concerning the Laws and Customs of War', Brussels, 27 August 1874 <www.ihl-databases.icrc.org/ihl/INTRO/135> accessed 31 January 2021. The draft was not accepted as a binding treaty but only as a declaration.

addition, no Latin American country had been invited to initial discussions of the First Geneva Convention for the Amelioration of the Condition of the Wounded in Armies in the Field, held in August 1864, of which the second Trujillo treaty of 1820 can be considered to be a forerunner. As documented by José María Ruda, an Argentinean diplomat, former member of the International Law Commission (ILC), and judge at the ICJ, the invitation to attend the 1864 Conference in Geneva was extended '"to all civilized powers" and no Latin American country was included'.[35] This was to become the history of Latin American participation in 'universal' international humanitarian law-making from the early days of independence until the end of the nineteenth century, all the willingness expressed to honour the laws and customs of war according to the 'cultured nations' notwithstanding.[36] It was not until 1907, at the second Peace Conference at The Hague, that most Latin American states participated in a conference on IHL at the universal level.[37] In fact, 1907 should mark 'the debut at the world level of the South American States in international political life. For most of them, this was the first meeting of that sort.'[38]

But the rejection suffered during the nineteenth century would not become a reason to lessen the interest in *ius in bello* within the region. As far as Latin American international legal scholarship of that epoch is concerned, it is noteworthy that Simón Bolívar's teacher, Andrés Bello, devoted more than 140 pages (of 257) to the law applicable to 'the state of war' in his *Principios de Derecho de Jentes* of 1832, considered the first modern book on general international law in the region.[39] Likewise, Carlos Calvo devoted one of the six volumes of his classic oeuvre, *Le Droit International Théorique et Practique*, to the state of war and the state of neutrality.[40] It is interesting to observe the importance that Calvo gave to the treatment of POWs, relying, like Bolívar during his time, on Rousseau.[41]

Interest in *ius in bello* in the region did not remain constrained to academia.[42] Although Mexico was the sole Latin American country present at The Hague Peace Conference of 1899,[43] during the second Pan-American Conference, held in Mexico City in 1901, several countries of the Western Hemisphere, including the United States (the other country on the continent which took part in the First Peace Conference) adopted a Protocol on Adherence to

---

35 Jose Maria Ruda, 'The Latin American Concept of Humanitarian Law' in Henry Dunant Institute (ed), *International Dimensions of Humanitarian Law* (UNESCO/Henri Dunant Institute/Martinus Nijhoff 1998) 45.

36 In 1899, Mexico was the sole Latin American country that took part in the Conference at The Hague; see ibid.

37 See Antonio Augusto Cançado Trindade, 'The Presence and Participation of Latin America at the Second Hague Peace Conference of 1907' in Yves Daudet (ed), *Topicality of the 1907 Hague Conference, the Second Peace Conference: Proceedings of the Workshop held in The Hague on 6–7 September 2007* (Martinus Nijhoff 2008) 51, 52ff.

38 Ruda (n 35) 46.

39 Andres Bello, *Principios de Derecho de Jentes* (Viuda de Calleja e Hijos 1844).

40 Carlos Calvo, *Le Droit International Théorique et Practique Précédé d'un Exposé Historique des Progrès de la Science du Droit des Gens* vol 4 (4th edn, Pedone-Lauriel/Puttkammer und Mühlbrecht 1888).

41 ibid 191.

42 For further references surrounding the role of international humanitarian law in early Latin American legal scholarship, see Ruda (n 35) 41–44.

43 Brazil was invited, but declined to participate, see Alan E. Boyle and Christine M. Chinkin, *The Making of International Law* (OUP 2007) 66.

the Conventions of The Hague. The first Article of this instrument, through which each party agreed to initiate the corresponding process of adherence to the three treaties of 1889,[44] is worth reproducing:

> *The American Republics, represented at the International Conference of American States in Mexico, which have not subscribed to the three Conventions signed at The Hague on 29th. of July, 1889, hereby recognize as part of Public International American Law the principles set forth therein.*[45]

This article is significant mainly for two reasons. First, it portrays the image of a region that was willing and able to participate in the development of *ius in bello* even if it was not invited to take part in its original making; in concert and including those two countries which seemed to enjoy a different status vis-à-vis European powers, they were sending a signal to the rest of the world that they did not accept being left out of the 'club'. In this sense, the Mexico City Protocol of 1901 is a fine example of Pan-Americanism, that highly interesting period in the history of international law and diplomacy which marked an attempt by Latin America and the United States (US) to counter the old international hierarchies as defined by European powers. As Mark Mazower mentions, Pan-Americanism can be described as a 'hemispheric counterdiplomacy that unified North and South in a common if uneasy embrace against European diplomatic hegemony'.[46] Second, by recognizing The Hague Conventions of 1889 as part of the international public law of the Americas, the Latin American states which signed this Protocol were showing that they 'did not perceive international law as foreign and distant model imposed by Europe',[47] but as their own, or, better framed: as a universal body of law to which they felt connected – i.e., entitled to benefit from its virtues and to participate in its creation. Note that here the paradox of the Creole legal consciousness is at its best: one sees the assertion of regional law[48] through the confirmation of universal law, and the self-awareness of a region articulated through the anxiety of being part of the universal. In a sense, the struggle for independence, in the Creole tradition, went on well into the twentieth century. Let me recall in this context the words of a motion introduced by the hosts of the Second Pan-American Conference in which living tribute to Carlos Calvo was paid:

> This motion is in harmony with the purposes of the congress, and is a significant proof of the spirit which unites the countries represented therein; more than a glory for the Argentine Republic, a glory for all America is this sage, who consecrated his strenuous, and fortunately long, life to repair an omission of the writers on international law 'who', as he himself says, 'left this vast American continent in the dark, although its power and influence are increasing from one day to another, and whose people in equality with those of Europe, are advancing on the road of civilization and enlightenment'.[49]

---

[44] Practically all nations represented in Mexico City in 1901 adhered to the said conventions; see James Brown Scott (ed), *The International Conferences of American States 1889–1928. A Collection of the Conventions, Recommendations, Resolutions, Reports, and Motions adopted by the First Six International Conferences of the American States, and Documents relating to the Organization of the Conferences* (Carnegie Endowment for International Peace/OUP 1931) 62–63.

[45] ibid.

[46] Mark Mazower, *Governing the World. The History of an Idea* (Penguin Books 2012) 9.

[47] Obregón (n 22) 263.

[48] In this case beyond Latin America, but the role of the US in 'American international law' is a complex matter which deserves attention in its own right; see Scarfi (n 17).

[49] Reprinted in Scott (n 44) 108.

This passage obviously goes beyond *ius in bello*, as The Hague 1889 conventions and the 1901 Mexico City Protocol did, but it reveals the inherent legitimacy that is ascribed to international humanitarian law as part of the broader project of the law of the international community to which Latin Americans, at that time, were eager to fully take part in. What followed was the participation of the region in international humanitarian law-making on two different fronts, so to speak. These two fronts, already signalled to at the Second International Conference of American States, comprise the codification of laws and customs of war at the regional level, and the participation at conferences on the subject at the universal level. These two fronts do not oppose each other, but are rather complementary: mutually reinforcing efforts of the region in the making of universal international law. As the Mexican scholar and diplomat, César Sepúlveda, made clear in the case of Inter-American human rights law: the regional and universal human rights systems have been conceived within the region as harmonically complementing each other under the ultimate goal of strengthening the universal protection of this unified body of law.[50] Antônio Augusto Cançado Trindade has also emphasized that the whole regional codification enterprise of international law, public and private,[51] is 'the Latin American legacy to international law and justice'.[52]

At the regional level, several resolutions were adopted at different international conferences of American states during the interwar period, ranging from the protection of cultural property in the event of armed conflict (1933); to the humanization of warfare (calling for the prohibition of the use of chemicals which cause unnecessary harm, in 1936); to the respect of human rights in times of war for those not participating in hostilities (1938).[53] These developments took place under the spirit of 'civilization' and 'Christian morality', as expressly mentioned in a resolution on the humanization of warfare, adopted in an extraordinary meeting of foreign ministers, held on the occasion of the beginning of the Second World War.[54] It should be recalled that Resolution XIII of the Seventh International Conference held in Montevideo (1933), i.e., the same conference in which the Montevideo Convention on the Rights and Duties of States was adopted, led to the Roerich Pact of 1935,[55] signed in Washington, DC,

---

50 Cesar Sepúlveda, *Derecho Internacional* (26th edn, Editorial Porrúa 2013) 531–34.

51 On Latin America's great codification project, see Alejandro Álvarez, *La Conférence de Juristes de Rio de Janeiro et la Codification du Droit International Américain* (Pedone 1913); Alejandro Álvarez, *Le Continent Américain et la Codification du Droit International: Une Nouvelle 'École' du Droit des Gens* (Pedone 1938). For a comprehensive analysis of this period of the history of international law, see Arnulf Becker Lorca, *Mestizo International Law: A Global Intellectual History 1842–1933* (CUP 2014) 305ff. Mention must be made that for Becker, this codification project embodied an effort to shift 'from a universal international law to regional international legal orders, from the standard of civilization to formal statehood and a declarative doctrine of recognition, and from intervention to non-intervention' (ibid 306). While I do not question the importance of the move to formal statehood and non-intervention as principal motivations behind the codification project, I regard the regional codification efforts as complementary to the advancement of universal international law.

52 Antonio Augusto Cançado Trindade, 'Los Aportes Latinoamericanos al Derecho y la Justicia Internacionales' in Antonio Augusto Cançado Trindade and Alfredo Martinez Moreno, *Doctrina Latinoamericana del Derecho Internacional* (Corte IDH 2003) 33, 38.

53 For a comprehensive account of regional developments on international humanitarian law during this period, see Ruda (n 35) 49–50; Urbina (n 9) 2246–50.

54 See Ruda (n 35) 50.

55 Treaty on the Protection of Artistic and Scientific and Historical Monuments (signed 15 April 1935, entered into force 26 August 1935) 167 LNTS 289.

among 11 states of the Americas, which would become the first comprehensive treaty on the protection of cultural property in war, and thus a forerunner of the 1954 Hague Convention.[56]

However, the most important regional development in regards to IHL came after 1945, within the Cold War context. In 1967, the Treaty for the Prohibition of Nuclear Weapons in Latin America and the Caribbean, better known as the 'Treaty of Tlatelolco',[57] was adopted in Mexico City, declaring Latin America the first region in the world free of nuclear weapons (NWFZ). The move gained Mexico's Foreign Minister at that time and principal promoter of that treaty, Alfonso García Robles, the Nobel Peace Prize in 1982. The Treaty of Tlatelolco set up an international organization in order to monitor its compliance, the Agency for the Prohibition of Nuclear Weapons in Latin America and the Caribbean (OPANAL). Two additional Protocols were adopted on the very same day as the treaty itself. Through Additional Protocol I, those states with overseas territories on the subcontinent (territories *de jure* or *de facto* under their responsibility, according to Article 1) commit to honour the NWFZ. France, the US, the Netherlands, and the United Kingdom are parties to it. By virtue of Additional Protocol II, nuclear powers commit to not carry out any activity prohibited under Article 1 of the Treaty, such as nuclear testing, as well as not to employ nuclear weapons nor to threaten their use against any state of Latin America and the Caribbean. All permanent members of the United Nations Security Council have signed and ratified the second protocol to the Tlatelolco Treaty.[58]

At the universal level, broad Latin American attendance at international conferences on the law of war began, as mentioned, with the Second Hague Peace Conference. In his meticulous account of Latin American participation in the making of the law of war, Ruda explains that the role of diplomats of the region during the first conferences of the twentieth century was a rather modest one, limiting themselves to general and supportive statements, and to presenting minor proposals here and there. This gradually changed over the years, particularly after the Second World War, where participation in treaty-making by states from the 'third world' increased considerably in number and substance.[59]

For sure, one can observe certain alignment in positions among Latin American states, in the sense that proposals from one state tend to be supported by other states of the region. In addition to regional solidarity, there are a number of common themes and cherished topics among Latin American nations, like the protection of the wounded and the sick, the regulation of POWs (that traditional Latin American preoccupation since Bolívar), and a great deal of support for the work of the International Committee of the Red Cross (ICRC). But this does not translate easily into a Latin American 'block' in international humanitarian law-making.

---

56 Dietrich Schindler and Jiri Toman, *The Laws of Armed Conflicts* (Martinus Nijhoff 1998) 737–39; Knut Dörmann, 'The Protection of Cultural Property as laid down in the Roerich Pact of 15 April 1935' (1993) 6 Humanitäres Völkerrecht 230.

57 Treaty for the Prohibition of Nuclear Weapons in Latin America and the Caribbean (signed 14 February 1967, entered into force 22 April 1968) 634 UNTS 281. After Argentina (1994) and Cuba (1995) adhered to the treaty, all 33 countries of Latin America and the Caribbean became parties to this convention.

58 Information available at the website of the OPANAL <http://www.opanal.org/protocolos-adicionales> accessed 31 January 2021.

59 On this, see Michael Bothe, 'Sovereign Equality and Law-Making: How do States from the Global South Shape International Humanitarian Law? – A Comment to Alejandro Rodiles and Balingene Kahombo', Chapter 19 in this book, 326.

Moreover, negotiation-alliances often show no predetermined geography at all, or at least none that is ubiquitous along the different themes of the international agenda. In matters surrounding *ius in bello*, what brings delegations together is often the lack of arsenal, resources, and, perhaps, even interest in developing certain weaponry of their respective states. Therefore, some Latin American states, like Mexico, have built a strong partnership with Northern European countries, Austria, Switzerland, and the so-called CANZ (Australia, Canada, and New Zealand) on issues concerning the use of certain weapons. For instance, the long struggle to ban anti-personnel mines has important precedence in the Geneva Conference of 1974–1977, where Mexico and Switzerland – the two delegations had worked closely together since the Lugano Conference of 1976[60] – presented an initiative on a draft article on the issue.[61] As the negotiations in the mid-1990s on the Ottawa Anti-Personnel Mine Ban Convention of 1997 revealed, the role of Mexico, along with Austria, Belgium, Canada, Denmark, Germany, Ireland, Norway, the Philippines, South Africa, and Switzerland, is widely acknowledged. This core group of states, together with a coalition of NGOs, was instrumental in bringing this treaty into existence.[62] These countries thereby helped to set important precedence in the history of diplomatic negotiations concerning the law of war, which from that moment on has not been a matter for states alone.[63] The successful negotiations on the Dublin Convention on Cluster Munitions of 2008 is another example of this, whereby Mexico and Peru were part of the core group of states, together with Austria, Ireland, New Zealand, Norway, and the Holy See.[64]

The same can be said of the participation of Latin American states in newer arenas of law-making, like the adoption of standards and non-binding, but effective, commitments through informal and flexible coalitions of the willing.[65] Latin American states and others

---

[60] Two conferences of government experts on the use of certain conventional weapons were held, the first in Lucerne, from 24 September to 18 October 1974, and the second in Lugano, from 28 January to 26 February 1976. On the Mexican–Swiss initiatives on non-detectable fragments and time-fused weapons, see ICRC, *Conference of Government Experts on the Use of Certain Conventional Weapons. Second Session—Lugano 28.1–26.2.1976* (ICRC 1976) 188–89. On the Lugano Conference, see Frits Kalshoven, 'The conference of government experts on the use of certain conventional weapons (Second session, Lugano, 28 January – 26 February 1976)' (1996) 7 Netherlands Yearbook of International Law 197.

[61] *Official Records of the Diplomatic Conference on the Reaffirmation and Development of International Humanitarian Law Applicable in Armed Conflicts, Geneva 1974–1977*, vol 16, CCDH/IV/211 (Federal Political Department 1978) 585–87. Together with Yugoslavia, the two countries also presented a draft on booby-traps; see *Official Records of the Diplomatic Conference on the Reaffirmation and Development of International Humanitarian Law Applicable in Armed Conflicts, Geneva 1974–1977*, vol XVI, CCDH/IV/209 (Federal Political Department 1978) 583. Venezuela introduced a different proposal on the same subject; see *Official Records of the Diplomatic Conference on the Reaffirmation and Development of International Humanitarian Law Applicable in Armed Conflicts, Geneva 1974–1977*, vol XVI, CCDH/IV/212 (Federal Political Department 1978) 587.

[62] Alan Bryden, *International Law, Politics and Inhumane Weapons. The Effectiveness of Global Landmine Regimes* (Routledge 2013) 53.

[63] See Rob McRae and Don Hubert (eds), *Human Security and the New Diplomacy. Protecting People, Promoting Peace* (McGill-Queens University Press 2001).

[64] Virgil Wiebe, John Borrie and Declan Smyth, 'Introduction' in Gro Nystuen and Stuart Maslen (eds), *The Convention on Cluster Munitions: A Commentary* (OUP 2010) 1, 11–36.

[65] See Alejandro Rodiles, *Coalitions of the Willing and International Law – The Interplay between Formality and Informality* (CUP 2018).

from the so-called 'global south' participate in informal venues and seek to shape the law through these means, just as those from the 'north', to a greater or lesser degree. In fact, the selection of formal or informal fora on IHL, like on other topics of the global agenda, is determined by the issues at hand, and other factors, such as whether a nation is a nuclear power or not. For instance, the *Initiative on the Humanitarian Impact of Nuclear Weapons* is a north–south coalition, or just a coalition of like-minded nations from the 'south' and 'north' alike, including Japan and Guatemala, Norway and Venezuela, as well as the strong involvement of international organizations and global multi-stakeholder networks, such as the *International Campaign to Abolish Nuclear Weapons* (ICAN). States and other actors from this coalition pursued the creation of a binding instrument banning nuclear weapons, actually succeeding with the adoption of the Treaty on the Prohibition of Nuclear Weapons, on 7 July 2017.[66] Because no nuclear power has signed it so far and probably will not do so in the foreseeable future, it could be thought of as an ineffective law-making exercise, arguably even as a case of reverse codification. However, the whole process that led to its adoption represents an important effort of modifying the law of war through a change in narrative. The states of the Initiative have endorsed the view that a world free of these weapons of mass destruction (WMD) 'is consistent with [their] obligations under international law, including those derived from the NPT [1968 Treaty on the Non-Proliferation of Nuclear Weapons] as well as from Common Article 1 to the Geneva Conventions'.[67] Beyond an expression of *opinio iuris*, these states rely on scientific information in order to promote a new collective sensibility in this regard, emphasizing that '[t]he new evidence that has emerged [...] about the humanitarian impact of nuclear weapons casts further doubt on whether these weapons could ever be used in conformity with international humanitarian law'.[68] Through the Humanitarian Pledge of 2015, participants in this informal forum 'call to fill the legal gap for the prohibition and elimination of nuclear weapons', and call on nuclear powers to diminish the role of these weapons in military doctrines.[69]

---

[66] On 24 October 2020, Honduras became the 50th state to ratify this treaty, which accordingly entered into force on 22 January 2021 (90 days after Honduras deposited its instrument of ratification). See, <disarmament.un.org/treaties/t/tpnw> accessed 31 January 2021.

[67] See 'Chair's Summary of the Second Meeting', Nayarit, Mexico, 13–14 February 2014 <https://www.reachingcriticalwill.org/images/documents/Disarmament-fora/nayarit-2014/chairs-summary.pdf> accessed 31 January 2021.

[68] See 'Chair's Summary of the Third Meeting', Vienna, Austria, 8–9 December 2014 <https://www.bmeia.gv.at/fileadmin/user_upload/Zentrale/Aussenpolitik/Abruestung/HINW14/HINW14_Chair_s_Summary.pdf> accessed 31 January 2021. A similar move in narration can be observed in the framework of the Global Compact for Safe, Orderly and Regular Migration, the negotiations of which have been facilitated by Mexico and Switzerland. This non-binding instrument and the whole negotiation process surrounding it have been structured around the idea of changing the description and perception of the migration phenomenon by consciously and consistently avoiding terms such as 'illegal migration'; for information on the Global Compact, see <https://refugeesmigrants.un.org/migration-compact> accessed 31 January 2021. On the role of narration and collective sense-making in international law, see Wouter Werner, 'Godot was Always There: Repetition and the Formation of Customary International Law' (*Global Cooperation Research Papers* 22, Duisburg 2019) <www.gcr21.org/publications/gcr/research-papers/godot-was-always-there-repetition-and-the-formation-of-customary-international-law> accessed 31 January 2021.

[69] 'Humanitarian Pledge' <www.bmeia.gv.at/fileadmin/user_upload/Zentrale/Aussenpolitik/Abruestung/HINW14/HINW14vienna_Pledge_Document.pdf> accessed 31 January 2021. For the role of pledges in contemporary international law-making, see Rodiles, *Coalitions of the Willing* (n 65) 196ff.

The narrative that the use of nuclear weapons is not in accordance with IHL, in particular with the fundamental principles of distinction and proportionality, is consistent with the discourse underlying the negotiations that led to the Treaty of Tlatelolco. Thus, the fact that Mexico continues to play such an active role in promoting the ban on nuclear weapons in multiple fora, formal and informal, is only in line with its diplomatic tradition.[70] In this context, it is important to underline Mexico's amendment proposal to the Rome Statute of the International Criminal Court in order to typify the use of nuclear weapons as war crimes.[71] As Balingene Kahombo explains in this book, the position on the illegality of nuclear weapons remains controversial on the global plane, and Mexico's initiative regarding the Rome Statute has received little support. Nonetheless, interesting developments in Africa are heading towards a similar direction.[72]

The preceding lines show that regional and universal efforts have been deployed as a mutually reinforcing enterprise aimed at strengthening the global IHL regime. Universal efforts include coalition-building with like-minded actors from the south and north alike, and if the most appropriate venue for an issue at hand is considered to be a flexible one, Latin American diplomats play this informal game as well. The IHL regime has not been perceived by Latin American international legal elites (diplomats and scholars – for a long time the very same people) with the suspicion of a European construct, but as a universal project: a highly valuable one, which significantly contributes to the consolidation of the post-War international legal order. It is in this sense that Latin American (diplomatic) participation in international humanitarian law-making, from the late 1940s until our present day, is linked to a perception of the legitimizing force that this body of law plays within the broader fabric of international law. And this force is related to the goal of submitting the most powerful, during the most extreme situations, where the national interest is most at stake, to the same rules. Participation in international humanitarian law-making becomes thus part of a more ambitious legal and political project of the region, of the third world, and of other less powerful states from the north and south alike: the promotion of the international rule of law.[73] This also explains the important role attributed to IHL by the former Group of Rio[74] during the debate on the rule of

---

[70] On Mexico's consistent practice on the illegality of the use of nuclear weapons, see ICRC, 'Customary IHL Database, Mexico: Practice Relating to Nuclear Weapons' <https://ihl-databases.icrc.org/customary-ihl/eng/docs/v2_cou_mx_nuwea> accessed 31 January 2021.

[71] The proposal suggests adding to art 8, para 2 b), the following: 'Employing nuclear weapons', see ICC-ASP/10/32 (9 December 2011), Annex II.

[72] Balingene Kahombo, 'Sovereign Equality and Law-Making: How do States from the Global South Shape International Humanitarian Law? – An African Perspective', Chapter 18 in this book, 310–11.

[73] On the promotion of the rule of law at the international level as a major project of the third world, see Sundhya Pahuja, *Decolonising International Law: Development, Economic Growth and the Politics of Universality* (CUP 2011) 173–79; and as a project of the less powerful, from north and south alike, see Alejandro Rodiles, 'Non-Permanent Members of the United Nations Security Council and the Promotion of the International Rule of Law' (2013) 5 Goettingen Journal of International Law 333.

[74] The Rio Group is the predecessor of the Community of Latin American and Caribbean States (CELAC), a mechanism of political consultation which tries to unify the position of these 33 states on the different themes of the multilateral agenda. CELAC is the closest which exists to a 'Latin American block' of multilateral diplomacy.

law at the international level, held in the Sixth Committee of the UN General Assembly, in autumn 2009.[75]

4. FROM THE LAW OF HUMANITY TO THE LAW OF VIOLENCE: INTERNATIONAL HUMANITARIAN LAW-MAKING BY LATIN AMERICAN COURTS

Any picture that intends to portray the relationship of Latin America with IHL would be missing an important component if it failed to address the perception, approach, and interpretation of *ius in bello* by another important actor, which does not comprise national leaders and diplomats. While the constructive engagement of diplomats continues to be an important expression of the region's participation in the making of this body of law, I do not hesitate to state that the real innovative actors of today's Latin America regarding international law-making, including but not limited to the law of war, are courts and tribunals. This is a rather familiar story as far as the IACHR is concerned. This international, and very activist, tribunal has been one of the main promoters worldwide of the merger of IHL and international human rights law. Indeed, this has been widely commented on as the most notable characteristic of the Latin American approach to international humanitarian law, and arguably as the most significant 'contribution' of the region to law-making in this area.[76]

Since *La Tablada* case of 1997,[77] the work of the Inter-American Commission on Human Rights has been well known for this suggested merger.[78] While the IACHR was first a little hesitant to follow the path of the Commission, today it embraces this approach too. Since *Las Palmeras* decision of 2000, the San José Court has made it clear that it 'is competent to determine whether any norm of domestic or international law applied by a state, in times of peace or armed conflict, is compatible or not with the American Convention'.[79]

75 UNGA, 'Summary Record of the 8th meeting on 14 October 2009' (2009) UN Doc A/C.6/64/SR.8, 3.

76 See Urbina (n 9) 2250 ff.; Fanny Martin, 'Application du Droit International Humanitaire par la Cour Interaméricaine des Droits de l'Homme' (2001) 83 International Review of the Red Cross 1039–66; Emiliano J. Buis, 'The Implementation of International Humanitarian Law by Human Rights Courts: The Example of the Inter-American Human Rights System' in Roberta Arnold and Noelle Quénivet (eds), *International Humanitarian Law and Human Rights Law: Towards a New Merger in International Law* (Martinus Nijhoff, 2008) 269; Alejandro Ramelli Arteaga, 'El Derecho Internacional Humanitario ante la Corte Interamericana de Derechos Humanos' (2009) 9 Anuario Mexicano de Derecho Internacional 35; Laurence Burgorgue-Larsen and Amaya Úbeda de Torres, '"War" in the Jurisprudence of the Inter-American Court of Human Rights' (2011) 33 Human Rights Quarterly 148.

77 *Juan Carlos Abella v Argentina*, Case 11.137, Inter-American Court of Human Rights Report No. 55/97, OEA/Ser/L/V/II.97, doc. 38 (October 30 1997); on this case, see Liesbeth Zegveld, 'The Inter-American Commission on Human Rights and international humanitarian law: A comment on the Tablada Case' (1989) 38 International Review of the Red Cross 505.

78 *Avila v Colombia*, Case 11.142, Inter-American Commission of Human Rights Report No. 26/97, OEA/Ser.L/V/II.95, doc 7 rev at 444 (30 September 1997); see also Inter-American Commission of Human Rights, 'The Report on Terrorism and Human Rights' OEA/Ser.L/V/II.116 (22 October 2002).

79 *Las Palmeras v Colombia* (Judgment) Inter-American Court on Human Rights Series C No 67 (4 February 2000) para 32.

From *Las Palmeras* on, the IACHR has interpreted a series of provisions of the American Convention of Human Rights of 1969[80] in light of the Geneva Conventions, in particular Common Article 3,[81] as well as in light of Additional Protocol II.[82] This approach was deeply influenced by the former President of the San José Court, Antônio Augusto Cançado Trindade. For today's Brazilian judge of the ICJ, the 'coextensive interpretation and application of Article 4 of the American Convention on Human Rights [right to life] and of Article 3 [of the Geneva Conventions]', sustained by the IACHR in *Las Palmeras*, did not go far enough to converge both regimes. Cançado Trindade, therefore, has constantly promoted, through his academic writings as well as from the bench,[83] a position which favours 'the identification of, and compliance with, the general obligation of guarantee of the exercise of the rights of the human person, common to the American Convention and the Geneva Conventions'.[84] He further considers this merger as crucial for the purposes of developing the *erga omnes* character of obligations of protection of the human person.[85]

The promotion of the synergy between IHL and international human rights law by this regional tribunal has many reasons. For sure, it is, on the one hand, a strategic move by the IACHR in order to augment its own powers, something it has pursued since its early days and through many avenues.[86] It is, at the same time, and closely related to the former, a manifestation of a legal trend in the region, the so-called *ius constitutionale commune* in Latin America (ICCLA). According to this project, a Latin American common constitutional law is emerging primarily through judicial dialogue between the San José Court, and national constitutional and highest tribunals.[87] The protection of human dignity and the correlated humanization of international and constitutional law lie at the core of this project, which endows the regional court, as well as national tribunals, with broad discretion in the protection and indeed construction of the most favourable rights for persons.[88] According to this rationale, human dignity and its judicial protection cannot depend on the separation between the law of peace and the law

---

80 American Convention on Human Rights ('Pact of San José') (signed 22 November 1969, entered into force 18 July 1978) 1144 UNTS 123.

81 *Bámaca Velásquez v Guatemala* (Judgment on the Merits) Inter-American Court on Human Rights Series C No 70 (25 November 2000) paras 203–14.

82 *'Masacre de Mapiripán' v Colombia* (Judgment on the Merits), Inter-American Court on Human Rights Series C No 134 (15 September 2005) paras 114–15, 153, 172; *'Masacres de Ituango' v Colombia* (Judgment) Inter-American Court on Human Rights Series C No 148 (1 July 2006) paras 179–80, 209.

83 See Antonio Augusto Cançado Trindade, Gerard Peytrignet, and Jaime Ruiz de Santiago, *Las Tres Vertientes de la Protección Internacional de los Derechos de la Persona Humana: Derechos Humanos, Derecho Humanitario, Derecho de los Refugiados* (Editorial Porrúa 2003). For an updated version of this thesis, see Antonio Augusto Cançado Trindade, *La Humanización del Derecho Internacional Contemporáneo* (Editorial Porrúa 2014).

84 *Las Palmeras v Colombia* (Separate Opinion of Judge Antonio Augusto Cançado Trindade) Inter-American Court on Human Rights Series C No 67 (4 February 2000) para 7.

85 ibid.

86 *Other Treaties Subject to the Consultative Jurisdiction of the Court*, Advisory Opinion OC-1/82, Inter-American Court on Human Rights Series A No 1 (24 September 1982) para 32.

87 See Bogdandy and others (n 3).

88 For a critical appraisal of this interpretive method, see Alejandro Rodiles, 'The Law and Politics of the *Pro Persona* Principle in Latin America' in Helmut Philipp Aust and Georg Nolte (eds), *The Interpretation of International Law by Domestic Courts: Uniformity, Diversity, Convergence* (OUP 2016) 170.

of war; instead a comprehensive *corpus iuris* of both legal regimes has to be promoted for the sake of the protection of human dignity.[89] Note that here the legitimacy conception underlying the participation of the region in the development of IHL has shifted from the international community to humanity, in the sense of Cançado Trindade's new *ius gentium*.[90] In other words, while diplomatic engagement in the progressive development, codification, and other (informal) means of normative evolution of the IHL regime has been largely motivated by the reaffirmation of Latin America's belonging to the international community and the strengthening of the law of that community, the relationship of Latin American courts with IHL is characterized by two beliefs: a) that IHL is an intrinsic component of a global law centred on the individual (which makes it legitimate), and b) that the promotion of this law within the region (as another building block of ICCLA) is part of the global enterprise of public law in the post-national era – the latter being a sort of postmodern expression of the Creole paradox of differentiation through identification.[91]

As mentioned, ICCLA is said to emerge through communication processes among the IACHR and the national courts of the region. In the present context, it is thus interesting to observe that the merger of IHL and international human rights law promoted by the international tribunal in San José has been echoed in the benches of Bogotá and Lima, at least to a certain extent. The Constitutional Court of Colombia (CCC), which during the 1990s proclaimed the *ius cogens* character of IHL *tout court*,[92] has declared that the norms of IHL, together with those of international human rights law, form part of the constitutional bloc which protects human dignity in times of internal armed conflict.[93] The 'constitutional bloc' (*bloque de constitucionalidad*) is a judicial technique developed by the CCC according to which human rights and related principles and rules, which are not expressly established in the national constitution, are to be integrated into it, whenever they are deemed relevant for concrete instances of constitutional control or judicial review.[94] Thus, according to the Bogotá

---

89 '*Masacre de Mapiripán' v Colombia* (n 82) para 153 (although referring to the protection of the rights of the child, human dignity is the underlying rationale in the integrative approach of the San José tribunal).

90 See Antonio Augusto Cançado Trindade, *International Law for Humankind: Towards a New Jus Gentium* (Brill 2010).

91 On this, see Rodiles, 'The Great Promise of Comparative Public Law for Latin America' (n 3) 522–23.

92 *Sentencia C-574/92*, Constitutional Court of Colombia (28 October 1992); *Sentencia C-088/93*, Constitutional Court of Colombia (26 February 1993); *Sentencia C-225/95*, Constitutional Court of Colombia (18 May 1995). This strong assessment was softened in a decision of 2007 whereby the Court determined the *ius cogens* status of certain fundamental principles of international humanitarian law, like the principles of distinction, precaution, and humanity, relying more on the 2005 ICRC Study on Customary International Humanitarian Law than on the jurisprudence of the San José tribunal. See *Sentencia C-291/07*, Constitutional Court of Colombia (25 April 2007). This criterion has been reiterated, although with less clarity, in *Sentencia C-084/16*, Constitutional Court of Colombia (24 February 2016). I thank Pablo Kalmanovitz for drawing my attention to this.

93 *Sentencia C-225/95*, Constitutional Court of Colombia (18 May 1995).

94 On the *bloque de constitucionalidad*, see further Rodiles, '*Pro Persona* Principle in Latin America' (n 88) 153, 166 (with further references).

jurisprudence, IHL norms and international human rights law converge in a constitutional bloc in favour of the protection of the vulnerable during armed conflict.[95]

The constitutional bloc plays a significant role in the construction of ICCLA, and other courts in the region have mimicked this interpretive method. It should come as no surprise that the *bloque constitucional* has also been used in relation to IHL by the Constitutional Tribunal of Peru, a country which experienced internal armed conflicts in the 1980s and 1990s. By making express reference to the jurisprudence of the IACHR, the court in Lima has declared that IHL and international human rights law share the same goals and that their norms are guided by complementarity, hence declaring them part of the 'international constitutional bloc' that establishes a parameter of interpretation and of normative development of internal law.[96]

This particular approach to the *ius in bello* taken by some Latin American national courts has led to quite innovative interpretations. In a ruling which comes quite close to actual legislation, the CCC has established a 'charter of basic rights of the displaced', affording elementary rights to those who, as a consequence of Colombia's long struggle amongst guerrilla organizations, drug cartels, paramilitary militias, and the government, have become internally displaced persons (IDP). These rights range from the provision of humanitarian assistance and housing to education for those under 15 years of age.[97]

What is perhaps most interesting is the jurisprudence of the CCC in relation to Colombia's Law of Victims and Land Restitution of 2011 (Law 1448), by which the government of Juan Manuel Santos recognized the existence of an NIAC in his country and prepared the ground for the peace process with the *Fuerzas Armadas Revolucionarias de Colombia* (FARC). According to article 3 of Law 1448, a 'victim' is a person who has suffered harm 'as a consequence of breaches of international humanitarian law or grave and manifest violations of international norms of human rights *occurred on the occasion of the internal armed conflict*'.[98] The last part of this norm has opened the door for a broad interpretation by the CCC on the very nature of Colombia's violence. First, the Court has clarified that 'on the occasion of' encompasses the harm caused by violations of IHL and international human rights law that derive from situations of violence which take place 'in the context of the internal armed conflict', i.e., those which have 'a close and sufficient relation with the development of the armed conflict'.[99]

---

95 See, most recently, *Sentencia C-084/16* (n 92). On the self-comprehension of Colombia's Constitutional Court as the protector of those who are vulnerable to violence and poverty, see Manuel Jose Cepeda-Espinosa, 'Judicial Activism in a Violent Context: The Origin, Role, and Impact of the Colombian Constitutional Court' (2004) 3 Washington University Global Studies Law Review 529. It must be mentioned, though, that the convergence thesis has experienced ambivalent evolutions in Colombia in more recent times. As Pablo Kalmanovitz explains, from 2006 on, the Colombian armed forces have pushed, including through its 2009 Operational Law Manual, for the differentiation of these two bodies of law; see Pablo Kalmanovitz, 'Entre el Deber de Protección y la Necesidad Militar: Oscilaciones del Discurso Humanitario en Colombia, 1991–2006' (2018) 1 Latin American Law Review 33; see also Pablo Kalmanowitz, '*Ius Post Bellum* and the Imperative to Supersede IHL' (2016) 110 AJIL Unbound 193, 196–97.

96 *Sentencia Exp. 00022/2011/PI/TC*, Constitutional Tribunal of Peru (2015).

97 *Sentencia T-025/04,* Constitutional Court of Colombia (22 January 2004); *Sentencia T-068/10*, Constitutional Court of Colombia (4 February 2010).

98 Ley 1448 de Víctimas y Restitución de Tierras 2011 (emphasis added).

99 *Sentencia C-253A/12*, Constitutional Court of Colombia (29 March 2012), section 6.3.3.

And second, it has clarified that this reading is in harmony with its own broad interpretation of the notion of 'armed conflict', which 'far from a restrictive optic (…) has been interpreted in a wide sense that includes all the complexity, as well as factual and historical evolution of Colombia's internal armed conflict'.[100]

The wide notion of NIAC embraced by the Bogotá jurisprudence is a case in point for the increasing difficulties of differentiating between the law of war and the law of peace in a region plagued with situations of extreme violence derived from chronic conflicts that are to a great extent economically driven. The failed 'wars on drugs' in Brazil, Colombia, Mexico, and large parts of Central America are pushing the elements and requirements for the classification of internal armed conflicts to their limits.[101] What is more, these situations in which 'the boundaries between such things as war, crime and peace appear increasingly vague and blurred'[102] are putting the very category of NIAC under strain, giving rise to the difficult question: how far can postmodern conflicts of this sort still be captured by this category, and by IHL altogether? National courts in Latin America increasingly have to dwell on the differentiation of the law applicable in times of peace and times of war,[103] and to create innovative theses on the contextual nature of armed conflicts and of violence more broadly, as well as on the rights of victims of violence. Taken together, these evolutions are producing what might be called an emerging 'law of violence' in Latin America, which I believe to be the hallmark of contemporary Latin American participation in the making of IHL – provided that one conceives law-making as also encompassing those normative evolutions which have the potential of turning established legal categories upside down.

It is not difficult to see that, this time, participation is driven by necessity: the need to respond to crude violence legitimates the involvement of Latin American national courts in this normative enterprise. The reasons for the protagonist role of courts in these recent evo-

---

100 *Sentencia C-781/12*, Constitutional Court of Colombia (10 October 2012), section 7.

101 For a general overview, see Pierre Hauck and Sven Peterke, 'Organized Crime and Gang Violence in National and International Law' (2010) 92 International Review of the Red Cross 433; with special reference to Brazil, see Sven Peterke, *Rio de Janeiros „Drogenkrieg" im Lichte der Konfliktforschung und des Völkerrechts. Eine Fallstudie zur Behandlung organisierter bewaffneter Gewalt* (Berliner Wissenschaftsverlag 2009); on Mexico's 'narco-war' and the classification problem, see Alejandro Rodiles, 'Law and Violence in the Global South: The Legal Framing of Mexico's "Narco War"' (2018) 23 Journal of Conflict & Security Law 269; see also Alejandro Roemer, 'Between War and Peace: A Study on the Instrumentalization of International Law in "Mexico's Drug War"' (Master thesis submitted to ITAM, International Relations Department, and SciencePo, Paris School of International Affairs, March 2018).

102 Mark Duffield, 'Post-modern conflict: Warlords, post-adjustment states and private protection' (1998) 1 Civil Wars 65, 67.

103 The remarks of former Justice José Ramón Cossío during the deliberations on a ruling of the Mexican Supreme Court on military jurisdiction in 2012 are emblematic in this regard. While Cossío dwells extensively on the need to maintain the distinction between times of peace and war, his remarks clearly show the difficulties of this in the context of Mexico's struggle against major drug cartels; see 'Official records of the public session of the Court's Plenum' (*Suprema Corte de Justicia de Nacion*, 7 August 2012) <www.scjn.gob.mx/PLENO/ver_taquigraficas/07082012POsn.pdf> accessed 31 January 2021; for the judgment, see 'Conflicto Competencial', Suprema Corte de Justicia de Nacion 38/2012, 9 August 2012. On these judicial developments, particularly in Colombia, Mexico, and Peru, see Julio Ríos-Figueroa, *Constitutional Courts as Mediators: Armed Conflict, Civil-Military Relations, and the Rule of Law in Latin America* (CUP 2016).

lutions are related to their increased importance in the public life of many of these countries, but also to the discourse of ICCLA and the corresponding expansive methods of interpretation which allow them to stretch otherwise rigid legal categories and to merge those which have traditionally fallen under schemata of separation: building 'constitutional blocs' of national and international norms, and promoting the merger of IHL and international human rights law whenever it may favour the protection of human dignity. If human dignity is vulnerable to forms of violence which are not comprehensible under the traditional dichotomy between times of war and times of peace, the legal responses must adapt to these changing and messy circumstances. This eventually leads to deconstruction. However, I am not suggesting that Latin American courts and tribunals are consciously promoting deconstruction of the IHL regime, something I seriously doubt. What I suggest is that the legal discourse of ICCLA and the methods of interpretation developed within its framework facilitate the sort of flexible legal innovations which the postmodern conflicts of the region are making necessary. In the end, the paths of an academic project of global public law for the region are determined by the actual situations of conflict in quite unpredictable ways.

5. CONCLUSION

The picture I have presented of the role of Latin America in the codification, progressive development, and other forms of normative evolution of the IHL regime denotes a more or less recurrent pattern along the different phases identified here, with the exception of the current evolutions by national courts. The rules on *ius in bello* were first considered a crucial component in the civilizing mission of international law: abiding by them and contributing to their development were conceived as powerful means for showing that the new world was ready to enter into the family of the civilized. Participation in the law regulating war was conducive to emancipation and representative of an anxiety of belonging at the same time – a characteristic of the 'Creole legal consciousness'.[104] As newly created sovereign states, representatives of the countries of the region sought, from the beginning, to demonstrate their readiness to honour these rules. Even as most nations of the region would still experience marginalization from the 'universal' conferences held until the early twentieth century, these countries relied, together with the US, on the great regional codification project in order to signal to the world their willingness and ability to take part in the development of the laws of war, and by that means to advance, 'in equality with those of Europe (...) on the road of civilization and enlightenment'.[105] As such, participation in international humanitarian law-making continued to be driven during the early years of the new republics of the Americas by the underlying idea of the inherent legitimacy of this body of law, which regulates war according the most philanthropic of values, and, at the same time, by a rather pragmatic conception of its enabling potential for Latin American countries to become full participants in the community of the civilized.

Once these states gained accession to the club, their diplomatic representatives began to play a productive role in the construction of the universal IHL regime. The degree of this participation has varied over time and from country to country, evolving from a rather modest

---

[104] See Obregón (n 22) 249.
[105] Reprinted in Scott (n 44) 108.

role to a more active one over the years – in part as a consequence of tectonic shifts in world affairs, such as the emergence of the post-war order – and in part simply due to the learning processes which they inevitably had to undergo as new members. Here, too, participation has been, until this very day, motivated by the conviction of the inherent value of the norms and principles regulating war, which by making the world a more human place, are perceived as a significant contribution to the function of law in the international community, i.e., in the sense of 'the subjection of the totality of international relations to the rule of law',[106] including war. Note that here an important shift from the law of the 'civilized' or 'cultured' to the law of the 'international community' took place. And here lies the key for understanding Latin American diplomatic participation in international humanitarian law-making. The shift from the standard of civilization to the international community is not just a cosmetic change but a complex one that involves continuity and disruption at once. Continuity as the old European standard of civilization did indeed come into crisis after the Second World War, but never disappeared completely from the image of international law. Disruption since the nominal expansion of the community of nations, with all its hypocrisies, paradoxes and illusions, helped to construe among the nations of the new world – and later of the third world – a self-awareness as members of the international community, accompanied by a notion of shared ownership of what holds that community together: international law. This has profound consequences for the comprehension and approach to international law by the third world, or, as we say today, the global south, until the present day. In the Latin American case, it could be said that the anxiety of belonging mutated into a preoccupation of conservation; of defending what allows this community (to which Latin American states now belonged under the banner of sovereign equality) to exist in the first place, i.e., the international legal order.[107] Hence, IHL's legitimacy is inherently linked to that of the law of the international community, and Latin America's participation in its making is part of the endeavours of the region to promote the rule of law at the international level. This is also consistent with the general perception of the law of armed conflict in Latin America as one which is not a European or northern imposition, but one which has its roots in a common legal heritage (of Roman law, and of the legal and political thinkers of natural law and the Enlightenment period, which Creoles made their own), and which has developed as part of the law of the international community. Feelings surrounding the limitation of sovereignty as a consequence of the law of war do not figure into this picture – quite to the contrary: the law of war has been conceived as a powerful tool, first in achieving sovereignty, and second in preserving it by helping to constrain even the most powerful, in the most extreme situations, and where the national interest is most at stake.

The role of Latin American courts and tribunals in international humanitarian law-making is quite clear in respect to the promotion of the merger of IHL and international human rights law, consistently advanced by the regional human rights tribunal. This has been a strategic move by

---

106 Hersch Lauterpacht, 'The Grotian Tradition in International Law' (1946) 23 British Yearbook of International Law 19.

107 This would support Arnulf Becker's argument that the appropriation of (European) international law by jurists in the periphery – in our case the Creole intellectual leaders of independence – was crucial in making international law universal. In this sense, the defence of the international legal order by Latin American diplomats is not only a twentieth-century rule-of-law idea but a consequential move in their own history of participation in the making of the law that governs in times of peace and in times of war; see Becker Lorca (n 51) 51ff.

the San José Court in order to augment its powers but also consistent with the neo-natural legal philosophy of one of its most, if not the most, influential judge, Antônio Augusto Cançado Trindade. The basic idea is that the separation between the law of peace and the law of war cannot stand in the way of an effective and broad judicial protection of human dignity. Hence, a comprehensive *corpus iuris* of both legal regimes is the best means to advance towards a new *ius gentium*. These ideas have been replicated by some Latin American national courts in the framework of the judicial dialogue they hold with the IACHR, which is said to contribute to an emergent common constitutional law in the region (ICCLA). The participation of Latin America in this instance of international humanitarian law-making, which has been widely commented as the most significant 'contribution' of the region to the *ius in bello*,[108] is thus driven by the law of humanity.

National courts in the region are key players in the construction of ICCLA. The constitutional tribunals in Bogotá and Lima have been particularly active in the integration of IHL into the 'blocs' of public law that are supposed to build the new common law of the Americas. As such, the law of war has become part of this project, which in turn is a regional manifestation (or experiment) of global constitutionalism. So, humanity instead of the international community, and global constitutionalism, in the place of the international rule of law, seem to be the values and aspirations guiding the newer and most visible modes of the region's participation in the evolution of IHL through its courts – the legitimacy conception underlying and motivating this participation. However, the most significant instances of innovative international humanitarian law-making in today's Latin America are those which correspond to what I have termed the 'law of violence'. Here, participation is driven and legitimated by strict necessity to react to extreme violence caused by postmodern conflicts like the failed wars on drugs which have put the notion of non-international armed conflict under strain. In contrast to former modes of participation, this is potentially deconstructing as it challenges the categories on which IHL rests.[109]

---

[108] Note that I otherwise avoid the notion of 'regional contribution' as this somehow presupposes that there is a core universal to which the peripheries may add something to; in a similar vein, see Becker Lorca (n 51) 13.

[109] See Rodiles, 'Law and Violence in the Global South' (n 101) 280–81.

18. Sovereign equality and law-making: How do states from the Global South shape international humanitarian law? An African perspective

Balingene Kahombo[1]

1. INTRODUCTION

Current international humanitarian law (IHL) is a European production. Since the adoption of the initial Geneva Convention of 1864, multilateral forums dedicated to the law's progressive development were held without African states' participation. Only Ethiopia had acceded to the 1907 Hague Conventions in 1935,[2] except Conventions I, II and XII concerning the peaceful resolution of interstate disputes.[3] Again, Ethiopia and Libya were the only African countries present at the time the four Geneva Conventions of 12 August 1949 were adopted.[4] Until accession to independence by most African states in the 1960s, IHL extended to Africa by the will of colonial powers through treaty ratifications and implementation measures such as legislative acts applicable to domestic repression which constituted grave breaches of the Geneva Conventions.[5] It is self-evident that such non-participation of independent African states in

---

1 This chapter is a revised version of the article Balingene Kahombo, 'Regionalism and International Humanitarian Law in Africa: Progress and Challenges' (2020) 93 Friedenswarte 96 (DOI 10.35998/fw-2020-0006). I am grateful to the publisher for the permission to reprint this amended version of the article.

2 Dietrich Schindler and Jiři Toman, *The Law of Armed Conflicts* (Martinus Nijhoff Publishers/Henry Dunant Institute 1988) 57–59.

3 Convention (I) for the Pacific Settlement of International Disputes (opened for signature 29 July 1899, entered into force 04 September 1900) 187 CTS 410; Convention (II) respecting the Limitation of the Employment of Force for the Recovery of Contract Debts (opened for signature 29 July 1899, entered into force 04 September 1900) 187 CTS 429; Convention (XII) relative to the Creation of an International Prize Court (opened for signature 18 October 1907, entered into force 26 January 1910) 105 CTS 381. See James Brown Scott, *The Proceedings of the Hague Peace Conferences: the Conference of 1907, Volume I: Plenary Meetings of the Conference* (OUP 1920).

4 Seydou Nourou Tall, *Théories et réalités du droit international humanitaire: contribution à l'étude de l'application du droit des conflits armés en Afrique noire contemporaine* (University Cheik Anta Diop 2001) 70.

5 After independence, succession to these treaties and laws of former colonial powers by African states was not automatic. The latter either notified to the depositary state that they accepted succession or, in most of the cases, sent their new instruments of accession to the treaties concerned as independent

these law-making processes affected the legitimacy of IHL in Africa. The fact is that the law of armed conflict negatively appeared as a sort of 'foreign law' which had not taken into account a number of humanitarian problems which were particular to African states. For instance, disagreements were perceptible on issues surrounding which situations could be regarded as an (international) armed conflict and the legal status of combatants, including local resistance fighters against regimes of domination. Additional problems emerged owing to the growth and the diversification of armed conflicts across the continent. Most of these conflicts were, and continue to be, civil wars which are linked to the challenges posed by the process of building democratized, politically stable and coherent post-colonial nations and states. Issues such as mercenarism and the crisis of internal displacement of persons affected by armed conflict thus required specific regional legal responses.

The contribution of African states to the development of IHL has taken various forms.[6] On the one hand, they did not reject pre-existing multilateral humanitarian conventions and principles. Consent and adherence to the law of armed conflict was provided under the main empirical explanation that most of the rules and values it conveyed were already firmly rooted in African culture of humanity in time of crises.[7] In addition, African states continued to attend diverse forums in order to contribute to the progressive development of IHL at the universal level. A prominent example includes the diplomatic conferences held between 1974 and 1977 for the adoption of both Additional Protocols of 7 June 1977 to the Geneva Conventions of 1949. On the other hand, African states have undertaken law-making efforts aiming to regionalize the law of armed conflict. Regionalization here refers to the process by which states transform norms and principles of IHL into a sort of law made in Africa; develop its substantive rules and/or procedural as well as enforcement mechanisms; and also regulate, within the regional framework, those humanitarian problems of specific concern to the continent. It is therefore a process of 'Africanization of international humanitarian law'[8] following the activation of the particular policy of regionalism which represents, for the International Law Commission (ILC), another privileged forum for international law-making 'because

---

and sovereign countries. As a consequence, new Geneva Conventions Acts were to be adopted domestically. For example, Uganda acceded to these treaties in 1964. Section 7 (1) of its Geneva Conventions Act (1964) provides that 'the Geneva Convention Act, 1911, the Geneva Convention Act, 1937, and the Geneva Conventions Act, 1957, of the United Kingdom in so far as they form part of the law of Uganda are hereby repealed'. See International Committee of the Red Cross (ICRC), *Respect of the Geneva Conventions: Measures Taken to Repress Violations – Report Submitted at the XXth International Conference of the Red Cross* (ICRC 1965) 113.

6 See Dino Kritsiotis, 'Humanitarian Warfare: Towards an African Appreciation' in Jeremy I Levitt, *Africa: Mapping New Boundaries in International Law* (Hart Publishing 2008) 150; Frans Viljoen, 'Africa's Contribution to the Development of International Human Rights and Humanitarian Law' (2001) 1 African Human Rights Law Journal 31–38.

7 Michel-Cyr Djiena Wembou and Daouda Fall, *Droit international humanitaire: théorie générale et réalités africaines* (L'Harmattan 2000) 168; Yolande Diallo, 'Traditions africaines et droit humanitaire' (1976) 58 International Review of the Red Cross 451; Yolande Diallo, *Les traditions africaines et le droit humanitaire: similitudes et divergences – Tome 2* (ICRC 1978).

8 Churchill Ewumbue-Monono and Carlo Von Flue, 'Promotion of International Humanitarian Law through Cooperation between the ICRC and the African Union' (2003) 85 International Review of the Red Cross 762.

of the relative homogeneity of the interests and actors concerned'.[9] This process enables complementary, rather than contradictory, universal law-making efforts. This process of legal regionalization is likely the most important contribution of African states to law-making processes in IHL. Further, it is expected that regional rules developed on this basis may have an impact, even in the long term, on the progressive development of this body of law at the global level. As the ILC has underscored, 'much of international law has developed in this way, as the gradual extension of originally regional rules to areas outside the region'.[10]

In view of such a regional perspective, the current study will not examine African participation in law-making processes within universal forums. It will only focus on the law-making efforts that reflect the regionalization of the law of armed conflict in Africa, which is essentially an interstate process. It is argued that African states have various opportunities at their disposal to ascertain the law, either through incorporation of pre-existing humanitarian norms into African legal instruments or through codification of new rules peculiar to the continent. Each opportunity encompasses advantages and practical problems. The latter is illustrated through the experience of states of the African great lakes region. However, the main challenge to this 'regional legal development' seems to be the lack of reach of an effective normative order. Numerous problems in this respect pertain to the participation of addressees of legal norms in the regionalization process of IHL; the law's implementation by states at the domestic level; and the lack of efficient regional enforcement mechanisms to ensure respect for the law so laid down. In order to exemplify the matter, a number of mechanisms established by African states will be selected for short analysis, namely the possibility of establishing an international commission of enquiry to investigate serious violations of IHL; the regional criminalization of the law of armed conflict; and the right of the African Union to intervene in a member state.

2. AFRICAN REGIONAL LAW-MAKING OPPORTUNITIES

Two opportunities must be distinguished here, that is to say, the incorporation of humanitarian norms into African legal instruments (2.1) and the codification of new rules which are specific to the continent (2.2).

2.1 Incorporation of Universal Humanitarian Norms into African Legal Instruments

Multiple African legal instruments have incorporated pre-existing humanitarian legal norms. Among these instruments, the most important are the African international treaties adopted at the regional or sub-regional levels. Within the Organization of African Unity (OAU) and the African Union (AU), its continental successor, the following treaties may be highlighted: the OAU Convention and Protocol on the Prevention and Combating of Terrorism,[11] the

---

9 ILC, 'Report of the International Law Commission on the Work of its 57th Session' (2 May–3 June and 11 July–5 August 2005) UN Doc A/60/10, 207, 209.

10 ibid.

11 OAU Convention on the Prevention and Combating of Terrorism (adopted 14 July 1999, entered into force 6 December 2002) 2219 UNTS 179 and the Protocol to the OAU Convention on the Prevention and Combating of Terrorism (adopted 8 July 2004, entered into force 26 February 2014) <https://au.int/en/treaties/protocol-oau-convention-prevention-and-combating-terrorism> accessed 31 January 2021.

Protocol relating to the Establishment of the AU Peace and Security Council (PSC),[12] the African Convention on the Conservation of Nature and Natural Resources,[13] the Protocol to the African Charter on Human and Peoples' Rights on the Rights of Women in Africa,[14] and the African Nuclear Weapon-free Zone Treaty (Pelindaba Treaty).[15] Within the International Conference on the Great Lakes Region (ICGLR), founded in 2004,[16] the main instrument is the Nairobi Pact on Security, Stability and Development in the Great Lakes Region.[17] The Nairobi Pact is complemented by several protocols,[18] notably the Protocol on the Prevention and Suppression of Sexual Violence Against Women and Children[19] and the Protocol for the Prevention and the Punishment of the Crime of Genocide, War Crimes and Crimes Against Humanity, and all forms of Discrimination.[20]

None of these treaties are exclusively devoted to the law of armed conflict. However, they reflect two tendencies in regards to the technical expression of humanitarian legal norms.

First, some treaties recall the obligation to respect IHL. Various language is used to this effect and the obligation applies to states parties,[21] extends to the AU (namely in the case

---

[12] (adopted on 9 July 2002 and entered into force on 26 December 2003) <https://au.int/en/treaties/protocol-relating-establishment-peace-and-security-council-african-union> accessed 31 January 2021.

[13] Revised African Convention on the Conservation of Nature and Natural Resources (adopted 11 July 2003, entered into force 23 July 2016) <https://au.int/en/treaties/african-convention-conservation-nature-and-natural-resources-revised-version> accessed 31 January 2021.

[14] (adopted on 11 July 2003, entered into force on 25 November 2005) <https://au.int/en/treaties/protocol-african-charter-human-and-peoples-rights-rights-women-africa> accessed 31 January 2021.

[15] Organization of African Unity, African Nuclear Weapon-Free Zone Treaty (Pelindaba Treaty) (adopted on 11 April 1996, entered into force 15 July 2009) (1996) 35 ILM 698.

[16] See Dar es Salaam Declaration of 20 November 2004 on Peace, Security, Democracy and Development in the Great Lakes Region <http://icglr.org/images/Dar_Es_Salaam_Declaration_on_Peace_Security_Democracy_and_Development.pdf> accessed 31 January 2021.

[17] (adopted on 15 December 2006, entered into force 21 June 2008) <http://www.icglr.org/images/Pact%20ICGLR%20Amended%2020122.pdf> accessed 31 January 2021.

[18] All these protocols are part of the Pact and have automatically entered into force at the same date as the Pact on 21 June 2008.

[19] (adopted on 30 November 2006, entered into force 21 June 2008) <http://library.icglr-lmrc.org/index.php/publications/2-pact-protocols/9-icglr-2006-protocol-on-the-prevention-and-suppression-of-sexual-violence-against-women-and-children> accessed 31 January 2021.

[20] (adopted 29 November 2006, entered into force 21 June 2008) <https://www.icglr-rtf.org/publication/view/protocol-for-the-prevention-of-the-crime-of-genocide-war-crimes-and-crimes-against-humanity-and-all-forms-of-discrimination> accessed 31 January 2021.

[21] See for example art 11 of the Protocol to the African Charter on Human and Peoples' Rights on the Rights of Women in Africa (n 14) relating to the 'protection of women in armed conflict', which recalls that 'states parties undertake to respect and ensure respect for the rules of international humanitarian law applicable in armed conflict situations, which affect the population, particularly women'. They shall also, 'in accordance with the obligations incumbent upon them under international humanitarian law, protect civilians including women, irrespective of the population to which they belong, in the event of armed conflict'. The Protocol to the OAU Convention on the Prevention and Combating of Terrorism (n 11) also stresses 'the imperative for all member states of the African Union to take all necessary measures to protect their populations from acts of terrorism and to implement all relevant continental and international humanitarian and human rights instruments' (Preamble, para 15). See also the Nairobi Pact on Security, Stability and Development in the Great Lakes Region (n 17), Preamble, para 5.

of peace support operations or military humanitarian interventions in member states),[22] and binds non-state actors like armed opposition groups taking part in a conflict.[23] The same obligation has been recalled in international peace agreements, such as the Lusaka Peace Accord of 10 July 1999, to which three states of the African great lakes region are parties, together with rebel groups in conflict against the government of the Democratic Republic of Congo (DRC). The obligation to respect certain elements of IHL can also be found in AU unilateral acts which are indeed promoted and voted on by member states. For example, the Kigali Declaration of 8 May 2003, adopted by the AU Ministerial Conference on Human Rights in Africa, calls upon member states 'to fulfill their obligations under international law and, in particular, to take the necessary measures to put an end to the practice of child-soldiers and to ensure the protection of civilian populations, particularly children, women, elderly persons and persons with disability in situations of armed conflict'.[24] Another important example is the AU Executive Council's decision of July 2003 on the situation of refugees, returnees and displaced persons, in which the Council condemns the serious acts of violence committed against civilians (including refugees and displaced persons) before urging 'the parties in conflict to scrupulously observe the international humanitarian law'.[25] It seems that these recalls and restatements of the obligation to respect the law of armed conflict are part of the Common African Defense and Security Policy of which one of the objectives is to 'provide a framework for humanitarian action to ensure that international humanitarian law is applied during conflicts between and among African states'.[26] To borrow the words of the International Court of Justice used in its advisory opinion in *Certain Expenses of the United Nations* in 1962, these AU unilateral acts are not merely hortatory.[27] Even if they may not be necessarily regarded as constituting state practices for the formation of customary IHL in Africa, they can rather contribute to its consolidation. A number of these acts are binding on AU member states, for example, having obtained binding character through their introduction in regional conven-

---

22 For example, the African Union, Protocol relating to the Establishment of the Peace and Security Council of the African Union (n 12) provides that this body must promote and be guided itself, among others, by the principle of 'respect for the rule of law, fundamental human rights and freedoms, the sanctity of human life and international humanitarian law' (arts 3(f) and 4(c)).

23 For instance, the ICGLR, Protocol for the Prevention of Genocide (n 20), reaffirms 'the obligations from United Nations principles and directives under the terms of which all parties to an armed conflict are obliged to fully observe the international law applicable to the rights and protection of women and young girls, in particular as civil persons' and notes 'the obligations under the Geneva Conventions of 1949 and the related Additional Protocols of 1977 (…)' (Preamble, para 4).

24 African Union, 'Kigali Declaration' adopted at the First Ministerial Conference of Human Rights in Africa (8 May 2003) AU Doc MIN/CONF/HRA/Decl.1 (1) para 17.

25 'Decision on the Situation of Refugees, Returnees and Displaced Persons' (8 July 2003) Doc. EX/CL/44 (III) para 7.

26 African Union, 'Solemn Declaration on a Common African Defense and Security Policy' (28 February 2004) Ext/Assembly/AU/Decl. 1(II) para 3 (v).

27 Certain Expenses of the United Nations (Article 17, paragraph 2, of the Charter) (Advisory Opinion) [1962] ICJ Rep 151, 163.

tional arrangements.[28] Moreover, each AU member state remains under a general threat of sanctions in the case of non-compliance with regional humanitarian policies.[29]

Further, some humanitarian legal norms have been simply rewritten into African treaties and therefore bring clarity in the applicable law. For example, in relation to the methods and means of conducting hostilities, the Pelindaba Treaty restates the prohibition of armed attacks by conventional or other means against (civil) nuclear installations in Africa,[30] because these installations are non-military objectives. Furthermore, Article XV of the African Convention on the conservation of nature and natural resources, which deals with 'military and hostile activities [against the environment]', provides that states parties must:

> b) refrain from employing or threatening to employ methods or means of combat which are intended or may be expected to cause widespread, long-term, or severe harm to the environment and ensure that such means and methods of warfare are not developed, produced, tested or transferred; c) refrain from using the destruction or modification of the environment as a means of combat or reprisal.

These rules are now likely part of customary IHL in international and non-international armed conflicts.[31]

Concerning the protection of civilians, the OAU Convention on the prevention and combating of terrorism confirms that terrorist acts may be committed during armed conflicts of any kind,[32] since states are 'determined to eliminate terrorism in all its forms of manifestation'[33] within the continent. The Convention further indicates that the [mere] struggle waged by peoples in accordance with the principles of international law for their liberation or self-determination, including armed struggle against colonialism, occupation, aggression and domination by foreign forces does not amount to terrorism.[34] This provision is clearer than that contained within Additional Protocol I to the Geneva Conventions, which only stipulates that

---

28 Such is the case for the African Union, Solemn Declaration on a Common African Defense and Security Policy (n 26). See African Union Non-Aggression and Common Defence Pact (adopted 31 January 2005, entered into force 18 December 2009) 2656 UNTS 285, arts 1(f), 2(b) and 4(d). For instance, art 2(b) stipulates that '(…) this Pact seeks to define a framework under which the Union may intervene or authorize intervention, in preventing or addressing situations of aggression, in conformity with the Constitutive Act, the Protocol [relating to the establishment of the AU Peace and Security Council] and the Common African Defence and Security Policy'.

29 Organization of the African Unity, Constitutive Act of the African Union (opened for signature 11 July 2000, entered into force 26 May 2001) 2158 UNTS 3, art 23(2): '(…) any member state that fails to comply with the decisions and policies of the Union may be subjected to (…) sanctions, such as the denial of transport and communications links with other member states, and other measures of a political and economic nature to be determined by the Assembly'.

30 Pelindaba Treaty (n 15), art 11.

31 Jean-Marie Henckaerts and Louise Doswald-Beck (eds), *Customary International Humanitarian Law, Vol I: Rules* (CUP 2005) 143–58 (Rule 43).

32 See ICRC, Protocol Additional to the Geneva Conventions of 12 August 1949, and relating to the Protection of Victims of International Armed Conflicts (Protocol I) (adopted on 08 July 1977, entered into force 07 December 1978) 1125 UNTS 3, art 51(2); ICRC, Protocol Additional to the Geneva Conventions of 12 August 1949, and relating to the Protection of Victims of Non-International Armed Conflicts (Protocol II) (adopted on 08 July 1977, entered into force 07 December 1978) 1125 UNTS 609, arts 4(2)(d) and 13(2).

33 OAU Convention on the Prevention and Combating of Terrorism (n 11) Preamble, para 13.

34 ibid art 3.

'armed conflicts in which peoples are fighting against colonial domination and alien occupation and against racist regimes in the exercise of their right of self-determination (...)'[35] are international armed conflicts. The problem with Additional Protocol I is that a controversial interpretation may arise as to the magnitude required for a given struggle, referred to in the African Convention on the prevention and combating of terrorism, in order to be treated as an armed conflict. Likewise, acts covered by IHL are not acts of terrorism.[36] The clarification is worthy of concern given the danger of confusion at the domestic level. For example, in its judgment of 29 October 2014, a local court in the DRC unconvincingly held that the killing of the commander of the national army in operation in the region of Beni (North Kivu Province) by rebels amounted to the crime of terrorism.[37]

In the same vein, clarity in law relates to the obligation to establish universal jurisdiction for the repression of war crimes. Article 10 of the Protocol for the prevention and the punishment of the crime of genocide, war crimes and crimes against humanity, and all forms of discrimination in the African great lakes region prescribes the following grounds of conditional jurisdiction in favor of any state party: 'a) when these crimes are or were committed on its territory: b) when the presumed offender is a national of the said state or is ordinarily resident in its territory; and c) when the victim is a national of the said state.' These provisions are clearer, and considerably different from the Geneva Conventions and their Additional Protocol I, which only provides for the obligation to prosecute or extradite perpetrators of their grave breaches, and only in relation to international armed conflicts.[38] Thus, the African provision seems to be noticeably innovative, rather than just replicating the applicable law. More innovation can be found in the codification of humanitarian norms specific to Africa.

2.2 Codification of Regional African Humanitarian Rules

Various humanitarian challenges are now regulated by specific regional African rules. These rules cover the protection of vulnerable persons and the limitation of means or methods of warfare during African conflicts. Three of these challenges deserve comment in order to illustrate how decisions at the regional level have led advancement of the law and inspired regulation at the global level on controversial issues over which no agreement existed or

---

35 See Protocol I (n 32) art 1(4).

36 African Union, Protocol on Amendments to the Protocol on the Statute of the African Court of Justice and Human Rights (Protocol on Amendments) (adopted on 27 June 2014, not yet entered into force) <https://au.int/en/treaties/protocol-amendments-protocol-statute-african-court-justice-and-human-rights> accessed 31 January 2021 (Annex) art 28G(D).

37 Operational Military Court of the North Kivu Province, Colonel Mamadou Ndala case, judgment, 29 October 2014, RP n°015, 017 and 018/014 (not published). The judgment was delivered in application of art 6, 157 and 158 of the DRC's Military Penal Code (2002).

38 See Geneva Convention for the Amelioration of the Condition of the Wounded and Sick in Armed Forces in the Field (opened for signature 12 August 1949, entered into force 21 October 1950) 75 UNTS 31, art 49(2); ICRC, Geneva Convention for the Amelioration of the Condition of Wounded, Sick and Shipwrecked Members of Armed Forces at Sea (opened for signature 12 August 1949, entered into force 21 October 1950) 75 UNTS 85, art 50(2); Geneva Convention relative to the Treatment of Prisoners of War of August 12, 1949 (opened for signature 12 August 1949, entered into force 21 October 1950) 75 UNTS 135, art 129(2); Geneva Convention relative to the Protection of Civilian Persons in Time of War (opened for signature 12 August 1949, entered into force 21 October 1950) 75 UNTS 287, art 146(2).

remains yet to be found. Challenges relate to the prohibition of mercenarism (2.2.1); the ban of the use of nuclear weapons (2.2.2); and the protection of internally displaced persons affected by armed conflict (2.2.3).

2.2.1 The prohibition of mercenarism

Mercenarism, or the state of being a mercenary, has been a severe, long-time sore for African international relations. While the use of mercenaries during armed conflict was still quite a normal phenomenon around the time the southern states were being decolonized,[39] the legality of mercenary recruitment, use, financing and training became particularly problematic during this time. Former colonial powers were suspected of resorting to the use of mercenaries since it had become politically difficult to use their regular armed forces in order to hinder the process of decolonization or, at least, of self-determination after independence.[40] In Africa, the phenomenon is best illustrated by the crisis of mercenaries during the Katanga Congolese secession (1960–1962), the Biafra secession in Nigeria (1968–1969), the civil wars in Sudan (1970) and Angola (1975–1976), or the war for the decolonization of Zimbabwe (1970).[41] Beyond these examples, mercenaries have been associated with almost all contemporary African armed conflicts, including those which occurred in Liberia, Sierra Leone, Ivory Coast, Central African Republic, and the DRC.[42] Outside the realm of armed conflicts, mercenaries have been involved in many military *coups d'état* across the continent, notably in Benin and Comoros.

Several United Nations resolutions, adopted by the Security Council or the General Assembly, have condemned mercenarism or held that mercenaries are criminals to be prosecuted and tried as such under domestic law. General Assembly resolution 3314 of 14 December 1974 even assimilated the sending by a state, or on its behalf, of mercenaries in order to perpetrate armed activities against another state as an act of aggression.[43] However, these United Nations resolutions are problematic for several reasons. First, some are contextualized to specific cases (e.g., Katanga or Biafra sessions) and cannot be relied upon to imply a general prohibition against mercenarism during any armed conflict. Second, these resolu-

---

[39] Stephen John Gordon Clarke, *The Congo Mercenary: a History and Analysis* (South African Institute of International Affairs 1968) 9–10; Josiane Tercinet, 'Les mercenaires et le droit international' (1977) 23 Annuaire français de droit international 269, 270. See also Charles Calvert Bayley, *Mercenaries for the Crimea: The German, Swiss and Italian Legions in British Service, 1854–1856*, (McGill-Queens University Press 1977).

[40] Lyal S. Sunga, *The Emerging System of International Criminal Law: Developments in Codification and Implementation* (Martinus Nijhoff Publishers, Kluwer Law International 1997) 184; John Riley and Michael Gambone, 'Men with Guns' (2010) 28 Wisconsin International Law Journal 40, 56; Juan Carlos Zarate, 'The Emergence of a New Dog of War: Private International Security Companies, International Law and the New World Disorder' (1998) 34 Stanford Journal of International Law 75, 86–90.

[41] See Eric David, 'Les mercenaires en droit international (développements récents)' (1977) 13 Revue belge de droit international 197, 200–201; Clarke (n 39) 9–10.

[42] See Jean-Paul Segihobe, *Le Congo en droit international: essai d'histoire agonistique d'un Etat multinational* (Presses universitaires Ryckmans 2011) 208; Khareen Pech, 'The Hand of War: Mercenaries in the Former Zaïre 1996–97' in Abdel-Fatau Musah and John Kayode Fayemi (eds), *Mercenaries: An African Security Dilemma* (Sterling, Pluto Press 2000) 117–54.

[43] UNGA Res 3314 (XXIX) (29 November 1974) art 3(g).

tions have been drafted as non-binding recommendations to member states. Third, and more importantly, they have not provided any definition of the term 'mercenary'.

This justifies why African states, Nigeria taking the lead,[44] raised the matter at the diplomatic conferences dedicated to the adoption of the Additional Protocols (to the Geneva Conventions of 1949) of 7 June 1977. However, due to a lack of consensus among negotiating states, no general prohibition against mercenarism was reached.[45] Only a minor compromise was found within the framework of Article 47 of Additional Protocol I in four ways. First, this treaty does not prohibit as such the recourse by states to use of mercenaries as a wrongful act at international law. Second, Article 47 stipulates that a mercenary shall not enjoy the right to be a combatant or a prisoner of war. This means that they could be prosecuted, if caught by the adverse party, solely on the ground of being a mercenary, without having committed any other crime, provided that the incrimination does exist under domestic law as required by the principle of legality. This denial of the status of combatant to mercenaries was strategic in order to advance the cause of peace. In fact, putting a mercenary in a position whereby they could be 'less tempted to shoot his way out of a situation in order to avoid capture'[46] must be avoided, because 'he is more likely to abide by his obligations as a combatant if he can also expect to benefit from the rights attaching to the status'.[47] Third, Article 47 conventionally defines a mercenary as being any person who:

> a) is specially recruited locally or abroad in order to fight in an armed conflict; b) does, in fact, take a direct part in the hostilities; c) is motivated to take part in the hostilities essentially by the desire for private gain and, in fact, is promised, by or on behalf of a party to the conflict, material compensation substantially in excess of that promised or paid to combatants of similar ranks and functions in the armed forces of that party; d) is neither a national of a party to the conflict nor a resident of territory controlled by a party to the conflict; e) is not a member of the armed forces of a party to the conflict; and (f) has not been sent by a state which is not a party to the conflict on official duty as a member of its armed forces.

Fourth, Article 47 applies only to international armed conflicts.

This deficiency of Additional Protocol I strengthened the necessity for the adoption of the OAU Convention for the Elimination of Mercenarism in Africa on 3 July 1977. The drafting process was boosted by three African precedents, namely: i) the OAU Convention governing the specific aspects of refugee problems in Africa which had excluded any mercenary from enjoying refugee status in African states since 1969 inasmuch as they were guilty of acts contrary to the purposes and principles of the OAU, now the AU;[48] ii) the OAU Committee of Experts which had proposed the first draft convention on mercenarism in Rabat (Morocco)

---

[44] See David (n 41) 204.

[45] Tall (n 4) 89–90.

[46] Françoise J. Hampson, 'Mercenaries: Diagnosis Before Prescription' (1991) 22 Netherlands Yearbook of International Law 4, 15–16.

[47] ibid.

[48] Organization of African Unity, Convention Governing the Specific Aspects of Refugee Problems in Africa, (adopted 10 September 1969, entered into force 20 June 1974) 1001 UNTS 45, art 1(5)(c). See also Mutoy Mubiala, 'La protection des réfugiés et des personnes déplacés en Afrique' in Oswald Ndeshyo (ed), *Mélanges Célestin Nguya-Ndila– La République démocratique du Congo: les défis récurrents de décolonisation, de l'Etat de droit et de développement économique et social* (Cedesurk 2012) 705.

in June 1972; and iii) the Luanda (Angola) trial,[49] conducted from 11–19 June 1976, whereby 13 individuals (nine British, three Americans and one Irish) who were caught by the Angola government's forces during the civil war were prosecuted 'for the crime of being mercenaries and for crimes against peace (…) in a mercenary war of aggression'.[50] They were all convicted of mercenarism: four were sentenced with the death penalty and nine sentenced to prison.[51] Following this event, the International Commission of Enquiry on Mercenaries (ICEM), which was convened by Angola to observe the trial and to make recommendations for an international action to deal with such problems in the future, produced a new draft convention on mercenarism.[52] This second draft treaty, together with the one which was proposed by the OAU Committee of Experts in 1972, constituted the principal materials upon which the OAU Convention for the elimination of mercenarism in Africa was elaborated.

The OAU Convention differs from Additional Protocol I on three major points. First, it applies to armed conflicts of any kind. Second, the OAU Convention criminalizes mercenarism and considers that it is 'a crime against peace and security in Africa'.[53] Third, the crime of mercenarism may be committed by any person, natural (individual) or legal/juridical (corporation or association, or representative of a state or the state itself).[54] This development joined efforts to ascertain corporate criminal liability under international law, as illustrated by the International Convention on the Suppression and Punishment of the crime of Apartheid, adopted in November 1973. But it came far before the adoption of the UN Convention against Transnational Organized Crime (Palermo Convention) of 15 November 2000,[55] the ICGLR's Protocol against Illegal Exploitation of Natural Resources of 30 November 2006[56] and of course the Malabo Protocol of 27 June 2014. Fourth, the OAU Convention indicates that the crime of mercenarism is committed by any of the following acts – when the offender:

> a) shelters, organises, finances, assists, equips, trains, promotes, supports or in any manner employs bands of mercenaries; b) enlists, enrolls or tries to enroll in the said bands; c) allows the activities mentioned in paragraph (a) to be carried out in any territory under its jurisdiction or in any place under its control or affords facilities for transit, transport or other operations of the above mentioned forces.[57]

---

49 Tall (n 4) 272.

50 Mike J. Hoover, 'The Laws of War and the Angolan Trial of Mercenaries: Death to the Dogs of War' (1977) 9 Case Western Reserve Journal of International Law 323, 327, 353.

51 ibid 323.

52 See David (n 41) 204; Segihobe (n 42) 206.

53 Organization of African Unity, OAU Convention for the Elimination of Mercenarism in Africa (adopted on 3 July 1977, entered into force 22 April 1985) <https://au.int/en/treaties/convention-elimination-mercenarism-africa> accessed 31 January 2021, art 1(3).

54 ibid art 1(2).

55 Art 10 of the UN Convention against Transnational Organized Crime (adopted 15 November 2000, entered into force 29 September 2003) 2225 UNTS 209 obliges states parties to establish the liability of legal persons for participation in serious crimes involving an organized criminal group or for the laundering of proceeds of crime, corruption and obstruction to justice.

56 Art 17(1) and (2) of the ICGLR's Protocol <https://ungreatlakes.unmissions.org/sites/default/files/icglr_protocol_against_the_illegal_exploitation_of_natural_resourcess.pdf> accessed 31 January 2021 provides: '1. Each Member State shall adopt measures to establish the liability of legal entities for participating in the illegal exploitation of natural resources. 2. Subject to the legal principles of the Member State, the liability of legal entities may be criminal, civil or administrative.'

57 OAU Convention on the Prevention and Combating of Terrorism (n 11) art 1(2).

In terms of legal impact, most of the provisions of the OAU Convention were introduced into the United Nations Convention Against the Recruitment, Use, Financing and Training of Mercenaries whose adoption followed on 4 December 1989. Further, this universal convention extended the definition of mercenarism to mercenaries used to perpetrate military coups in other independent states.[58] Both treaties have led to the consolidation of the definition of the crime of mercenarism as enshrined in the Protocol on amendments to the Protocol on the Statute of the African Court of Justice and Human Rights (Annex) of 27 June 2014.[59]

Next, the prohibition of the use of nuclear weapons is discussed.

2.2.2 The ban on the use of nuclear weapons

It is well known that nuclear weapons are not prohibited nor authorized under general international law. In its Advisory Opinion of 8 July 1996, the ICJ even stated that it cannot 'conclude definitively whether the threat or use of nuclear weapons would be lawful or unlawful in an extreme circumstance of self-defence, in which the very survival of a state would be at stake'.[60]

In general, efforts have been focused on nuclear disarmament. In Africa, denuclearization policy dates back to the United Nations resolution of 24 November 1961, which was endorsed by African states during the first ordinary session of the OAU Assembly in July 1964.[61] This policy continued until it achieved regional codification by the Pelindaba Treaty establishing the 'African nuclear-weapon-free-zone' in 1996.[62] This zone comprises 'the territory of the continent of Africa, islands states members of OAU and all islands considered by the Organization of African Unity in its resolutions to be part of Africa'.[63] States are hereby forbidden to possess, develop, manufacture, test, or allow transit of nuclear weapons or explosive devices within this zone. Only peaceful nuclear activities for non-military purposes are permitted.

However, the Pelindaba Treaty did not prohibit as such the use of nuclear weapons in African conflicts. A step forward was made by the Protocol on Amendments to the Protocol on the Statute of the African Court of Justice and Human Rights (Annex), which holds that the fact of 'using nuclear weapons or other weapons of mass destruction'[64] amounts to a war crime, irrespective of the type of armed conflict within which such weapons are deployed. Despite the lack of a clear definition as to what may be regarded as 'other weapons of mass destruction', it appears that the African continent is taking the lead on a controversial issue on which states have not yet found a compromise at the global level. This explains why the use of

---

58 International Convention against the Recruitment, Use, Financing and Training of Mercenaries (adopted 4 December 1989, entered into force 20 October 2001) 2163 UNTS 75, art 1(1).

59 Protocol on Amendments (n 36) Annex, art 28H. It must be noted that the UN Commission on International Law drafted a Code of crimes against peace and security of the humanity containing the crime of mercenarism in 1991. However, disagreements appeared upon its universal relevance in this category of crimes to the extent that it was omitted in the Draft Code of 1996.

60 Legality of the Threat or Use of Nuclear Weapons (Advisory Opinion) [1996] ICJ Rep 226, 266.

61 Balingene Kahombo, *La politique africaine commune de défense et de sécurité: fondement et cadre de mise en œuvre du pouvoir d'intervention de l'Union africaine dans les Etats membres* (Université de Kinshasa 2011) 38–40; Oswald Ndeshyo, *L'héritage de l'OUA à l'UA: la quête permanente de l'unité africaine* (Editions universitaires africaines 2010) 410.

62 Pelindaba Treaty (n 15) Preamble, para 14.

63 Pelindaba Treaty (n 15) art 1(a).

64 Protocol on Amendments (n 36) (Annex), art 28D(g).

nuclear weapons has not been criminalized in the Statute of the International Criminal Court (ICC) of 17 July 1998 despite advocacy by several states from the global south, including India.[65] A proposal to amend the ICC Statute has been introduced by Mexico in this regard.[66] There is an expectation that the combination of all these developments from the global south may act as an incentive to reforming the law at the global level. One of the positive effects of this development is the adoption of the UN Treaty on the Prohibition of Nuclear Weapons on 7 July 2017, even though it is opposed by nuclear state powers (USA, Russia, China, United Kingdom, France, India, Pakistan, Israel and North Korea) and other countries which benefit from the American nuclear umbrella, such as Germany and The Netherlands. Their opposition is a clear indication likely that they will not *a fortiori* adhere to the criminalization of the use of nuclear weapons in the context of armed conflict.

2.2.3 The protection of internally displaced persons affected by armed conflict

The displacement of people gives rise to two different phenomena: the displacement of persons 1) within their own country and 2) across international borders in order to find shelter in a foreign state.[67] In the latter case, the displaced are referred to as refugees (a subject not under examination here), while in the former case the phenomenon refers to internally displaced persons (IDPs).

The internal displacement of persons is not unknown in the law of armed conflict. Various provisions protect IDPs – by granting them the rights enjoyed by the local civil population – offering protections against discrimination and forced displacement, and safeguarding their right to life, dignity and freedom. However, there is no overall binding legal instrument dealing with IDPs at the universal level. The United Nations has only endorsed the 'Guiding Principles on Internal Displacement' of 1998. These guidelines were prepared by Francis M. Deng, acting as the Representative of the UN Secretary General on the human rights issues related to internally displaced persons.[68] Arguably, this soft document was preferred to a formal treaty because of concerns of the International Committee of the Red Cross (ICRC) surrounding 'the negative potential of reopening the door on already accepted rights, thereby

---

65 Garima Tiwari, 'Why India Continues to Stay out of ICC?' (*A Contrario International Criminal Law,* 27 April 2013) <http.//acontrarioicl.com/2013/04/27/why-india-continues-to-stay-out-of-icc/> accessed 31 January 2021.

66 See Secretariat of the Assembly of the States Parties, 'Informal Compilation of Proposals to Amend the Rome Statute' (23 January 2015) <www.icc-cpi.int/iccdocs/asp_docs/Publications/WGA-Inf-Comp-RS-amendments-ENG.pdf> accessed 31 January 2021.

67 Sikiru Taiwo Kassim, 'Civil Wars and the Refugee Crisis in West Africa: a Case Study of Liberian Refugees in Nigeria' in W. Alade Fawole and Charles Ukeje (eds), *The Crisis of State and Regionalism in West Africa: Identity, Citizenship and Conflict* (Codesria 2005) 175–90.

68 See Francis M. Deng, 'Frontiers of Sovereignty: A Framework of Protection, Assistance and Development for the Internally Displaced' (1995) 8 Leiden Journal of International Law 249; Jean-Philippe Lavoyer, 'Guiding Principles on Internal Displacement: A Few Concerns on the Contribution of International Law' (1998) 324 International Review of the Red Cross 467; Thomas G. Weiss and David A. Korn, *Internal Displacement: Conceptualization and Its Consequences* (Routledge 2006).

undermining them',[69] and also 'the desire to avoid the delay inherent in state negotiations on such a potentially contentious issue in light of the urgent need for action on the ground'.[70]

Consequently, by adopting the AU Convention for the Protection and Assistance of IDPs in Africa in 2010 (Kampala Convention), AU member states have taken the lead to offer the continent's first innovative and binding regional instrument on the issue.[71] This Convention goes far beyond the Protocol on the Protection and Assistance to IDPs, which is part of the Nairobi Pact on Security, Stability and Development in the African great lakes region. The latter constitutes a mere sub-regional conventional codification of the said UN Guiding Principles on Internal Displacement, with the advantage of making them binding on states concerned in this part of Africa. It seems that the continuing and severe crisis of IDPs across the continent, particularly due to non-international armed conflict, was the major impetus behind the adoption of the AU Convention: in order to find a solution to what appears to be more of a regional problem, rather than a national or a sub-regional one,[72] and to establish a proper enforcement mechanism for the protection of IDPs.[73]

The Kampala Convention applies to the AU, both state parties and non-state actors (armed groups, international organizations and humanitarian agencies), irrespective of the type of armed conflict and even in times of peace, in regards to matters not related to war, such as displacement induced by development projects.[74] Among other important substantive provisions, the Kampala Convention recognizes that the right of IDPs to humanitarian assistance should not be impeded. It also prohibits: violation of the civil and humanitarian character of places where IDPs are sheltered; the recruitment, request or permission of children to take part in hostilities; as well as any serious violations of humanitarian law, including war crimes, crimes against humanity and genocide. The Kampala Convention particularly insists on the prohibition against the 'arbitrary displacement of persons',[75] that include but are not limited to: i) displacement based on policies of racial discrimination or other similar practices aimed at/or resulting in altering the ethnic, religious or racial composition of the population; ii) the individual or mass displacement of civilians in situations of armed conflict, unless the security of the civilians involved or imperative military reasons so demand, in accordance with IHL; iii) displacement intentionally used as a method of warfare or due to other violations of IHL in situations of armed conflict; iv) displacement caused by generalized violence or violations of human rights; v) displacement as a result of harmful practices; vi) forced evacuations in cases of natural or human-made disasters or other causes, if the evacuations are not required in order

---

69 Franis M. Deng, 'Africa's Internally Displaced and the Development of International Norms: Standards versus Implementation' in Levitt (n 6) 93.

70 ibid.

71 See Abdulqawi Ahmed Yusuf, 'Pan-Africanism and International Law' (2013) 369 Recueil des Cours de l'Académie de Droit International 161, 315–16.

72 Leslie Claire Bailey, 'Out of Africa: Toward a Regional Solution for Internal Displacement' (2014) 39 Brooklyn Journal of International Law 353, 381; Mubiala (n 48) 713.

73 See below, section 3.1 on the 'Development of efficient regional enforcement mechanisms'.

74 African Union Convention for the Protection and Assistance of Internally Displaced Persons in Africa (Kampala Convention) (adopted 22 October 2009, entered into force 06 December 2012) <https://au.int/sites/default/files/treaties/36846-treaty-0039_-_kampala_convention_african_union_convention_for_the_protection_and_assistance_of_internally_displaced_persons_in_africa_e.pdf> accessed 31 January 2021, art 10.

75 ibid arts 1(d) and 4(4)(a) to (h).

to ensure the safety and health of those affected; vii) displacement used as a form of collective punishment; viii) displacement caused by any act, event, factor, or phenomenon of comparable gravity to all of the above and which is not justified under international law, including human rights and IHL.[76] States parties are obliged to ensure 'the accountability of non-state actors concerned, including multinational companies and private military or security companies, for acts of arbitrary displacement or complicity in such acts'.[77] This obligation includes 'individual responsibility (…), in accordance with applicable domestic and international criminal law'.[78] In addition, individual members of armed groups must be held criminally responsible for their acts which violate other rights of IDPs under international law and national law.[79] In this regard, the Kampala Convention has contributed to the development of the international legal regime in regards to the accountability of non-state actors.[80]

It has been argued that this legal development may have a positive impact outside of Africa, and particularly in the Middle East region. Arab states may adopt an analogous treaty because they are confronted with problems surrounding IDPs, comparable to those occurring on the African continent, notably for reasons of armed conflict.[81] A similar impact at the global level is not impossible. It is even desirable in order to fill the current vacuum stemming from the lack of an overall global binding instrument on the issue in respect of states from all regions. The Kampala Convention could also help develop (universal) IHL and enhance the chance for ensuring respect for obligations provided for, since enforcement mechanisms would potentially involve broader elements of the international community, rather than being restricted to the region of the state where the rights of IDPs have been disregarded. In any event, still in Africa, a number of challenges must be surmounted so as to achieve effective implementation of those humanitarian rules already laid down.

3. CHALLENGES TO EFFECTIVE INTERNATIONAL HUMANITARIAN LAW IN AFRICA

Though numerous, the main challenges relate to the development of efficient regional enforcement mechanisms (3.1); the question of participation in the regionalization process of the law of armed conflict on the continent (3.2); and practical difficulties surrounding implementation at the domestic level (3.3).

3.1 Development of Efficient Regional Enforcement Mechanisms

In most African humanitarian treaties it is common to find enforcement mechanisms specific to each treaty. For example, the Kampala Convention established the Conference of States Parties, to be regularly convened for the discussion of the Convention's implementation.[82] Further, the Convention relies on the system of states' reports under Article 62 of the African

---

76 ibid.
77 ibid art 3(1)(h).
78 ibid art 3(1)(g).
79 ibid arts 7(4) and (5)(a) – (i).
80 Mubiala (n 48) 724; Yusuf (n 71) 319.
81 Bailey (n 72) 360–61.
82 Kampala Convention (n 74) art 14(1) – (3).

Charter on Human and Peoples' Rights, as well as monitoring through the African Peer Review Mechanism (APRM), established within the framework of the New Partnership for Africa's Development (NEPAD).[83] The problem with these kinds of enforcement mechanisms is that they are often confined to a limited number of states which accept the obligation to submit reports to the regional body or to allow for their level of compliance to be monitored from the outside. Moreover, other addressees of legal norms, namely non-state actors, remain outside of such enforcement mechanisms, given that they only target states. Finally, these enforcement mechanisms offer little results, beyond recommendations that can be officially published – a policy of sanctions which can be introduced against those states which are deemed, after examination, to be in breach of their obligations or to have systematically disregarded regional treaties to which they have consented. Thus, emphasis must be put on three other distinct enforcement mechanisms, due to their applicability towards African states and non-states actors, as well as the policy of sanctions they imply.

3.1.1 The criminalization of international humanitarian law in Africa

This first mechanism indicates that some humanitarian prohibitions have been transformed into regional criminal offenses (crimes against peace and security in Africa) in order to ensure that perpetrators are held criminally responsible for their acts. Two observations deserve mention in this respect.

On the one hand, and in comparison to general international law, the Protocol on Amendments to the Protocol on the Statute of the African Court of Justice and Human Rights (Annex) has extended the definition of war crimes. Its Article 28D contains additional acts of war crimes that cannot be found in the ICC Statute. An example, among such innovative regional incriminations, is the criminal prohibition against 'using nuclear weapons or other weapons of mass destruction' during armed conflict in Africa. Another innovation is the broadening of the meaning of a child referred to in the definition of war crimes. While the ICC Statute takes into account the yardstick of 15 years old,[84] the Amendments Protocol (Annex) incriminates acts of 'conscripting or enlisting children under [the age of eighteen years] into the [national] armed forces or using them to participate actively in hostilities'.[85] It appears that this age prescription comes from the African Charter on the rights and welfare of the child, which refers to a child as being 'every human being below the age of 18 years'.[86] This means that all children, not just a category of them, as stems from the ICC Statute and both Additional Protocols[87] to the Geneva Conventions of 1949 which inspired it, are covered by that incrimination. Positively, this regional prescription possesses the advantage of having corrected the internal contradiction of the ICC Statute, in that this international instrument does not prohibit the practice of child soldiers over the age of 15 years, including their participation in hostili-

---

[83] ibid, art 14(4). See also UNGA 'New Partnership for Africa's Development: progress in implementation and international support: resolution/ adopted by the General Assembly' 65th Session (2011) UN Doc A/Res/65/284.

[84] Rome Statute of the International Criminal Court (Rome Statute) (opened for signature 17 July 1998, entered into force 1 July 2002) 2187 UNTS 90 art 8(2)(b)(xxvi) and (e)(vii).

[85] Protocol on Amendments (n 35) Annex, art 28D (b)(xxvii) and (e)(vii).

[86] African Charter on the Rights and Welfare of the Child (adopted 1 July 1990, entered into force 29 November 1999) CAB/LEG/24.9/49 (1990) art 2.

[87] Protocol I (n 32) art 77(2); Protocol II (n 32) art 4(3)(c).

ties, while such persons are also excluded from the Court's jurisdiction, for they are persons under 18 years old.[88]

On the other hand, there is still a degree of ambiguity which surrounds the criminalization of some anti-humanitarian behaviors such as 'acts of arbitrary displacement of persons' in times of armed conflict. Most of these acts are not targeted by the Amendments Protocol (Annex), which was adopted in 2014, almost five years after the Kampala Convention. Under the incrimination of war crimes, only a number of acts are mentioned, such as 'ordering the displacement of civilian population for reasons related to the conflict, unless the security of the civilians involved or imperative military reasons so demand'[89] during a non-international armed conflict, or 'the transfer, directly or indirectly, by the Occupying Power of parts of its own civilian population into the territory it occupies, or the deportation or transfer of all or parts of the population of the occupied territory within or outside this territory'[90] in time of an international armed conflict. It is true that another act contributing to the arbitrary displacement of persons may be caught under the category of crimes against humanity, namely the 'deportation or forcible transfer of population'.[91] However, the status of regional positive law remains lower than what has been determined by the Kampala Convention, irrespective of the nature of armed conflict.

Second, criminalizing aspects of humanitarian law also signifies the development of a regional institutional approach to prosecute those perpetrators who may be responsible for serious violations of the law. In this regard, the AU and its member states have established an International Criminal Section within the African Court of Justice and Human Rights.[92] If well managed, this approach could alleviate and efficiently complement the work of universal institutions such as the ICC within the continent.[93]

3.1.2 The right of the African Union to intervene in the affairs of member states

The AU Constitutive Act stipulates, 'the right of the (African) Union to intervene in a member state pursuant to a decision of the Assembly in respect of grave circumstances, namely: war crimes, genocide and crimes against humanity'.[94] This mechanism is the first ever provision of such magnitude to be expressly mentioned in an international treaty. It is also expressly relied upon for the purpose of enforcing the Kampala Convention for the protection and assistance of IDPs in Africa.[95] Any state party can also request the intervention of the AU 'in order to restore peace and security (...) and thus contribute to the creation of favourable conditions for finding durable solutions to the problem of internal displacement'.[96]

---

88 Rome Statute (n 84) art 26: 'The Court shall have no jurisdiction over any person who was under the age of 18 at the time of the alleged commission of a crime.'

89 ibid art 28D(e)(viii).

90 ibid art 28D(b)(ix).

91 ibid art 28C(1)(d).

92 Protocol on Amendments (n 36) Annex art 16 and 28A.

93 See Balingene Kahombo, 'Africa within the Justice System of the International Criminal Court: the Need for a Reform' (Berlin Potsdam Research Group' – KFG – International Rule of Law: Rise or Decline? 2016) <https://ssrn.com/abstract=3129009> accessed 31 January 2021.

94 Constitutive Act of the African Union (n 29) art 4(h).

95 Kampala Convention (n 74) art 1(e).

96 ibid art 8(2); Constitutive Act of the African Union (n 29) art 4(j).

In practice, the right of the AU to intervene may imply the need to engage in military operations to halt gross violations of IHL in a member state. In 2015 it was invoked as such by the AU PSC as the last resort, should Burundi not accept the deployment on its territory of a peace support operation, called the African Prevention and Protection Mission in Burundi (MAPROBU).[97] Moreover, the AU right to intervene took on a quasi-judicial interpretation when it resulted in the trial of the former Chadian President, Hissène Habré,[98] prosecuted for torture, war crimes and crimes against humanity, before the African Extraordinary Chambers, which were created in 2012.[99] Broadly, this practice illustrates that the AU is entitled to establish a special regional criminal court with the mandate to prosecute crimes that would normally fall under the criminal domestic jurisdiction of one or more member state(s).

The problem with this mechanism is that it is not anticipatory nor preventive, as is the United Nations doctrine of the responsibility to protect (R2P).[100] One must deplore the fact that the AU may intervene only within the course of the commission of serious crimes, after their perpetration or the rupturing of peace. The mechanism is also very difficult to activate. The decision must be taken by the AU Assembly, which is not a permanent body, when in reality such issues presumably require swift action. Extraordinary sessions of the AU Assembly are subject to strict procedural conditions. For example, any demand by a member state for an extraordinary session of the AU Assembly must be approved by a two-thirds majority of all members, in order to succeed.[101] Meanwhile, the matter on the ground could be exacerbating. Thus, in such conditions, it is better that the competence to take a decision surrounding intervention is allocated to the PSC, for example, a permanent body under the supervision of the AU Assembly.[102]

3.1.3 The regional commission of enquiry on violations of international humanitarian law

The last mechanism to mention stems from the possibility to establish, where necessary, a regional commission of enquiry on allegations of serious violations of humanitarian and human rights law. Such an enquiry may be undertaken by the African Commission on Human and Peoples' Rights mandated by the OAU Assembly (now AU Assembly) pursuant to Article

---

97 African Union (Peace and Security Council), 'Communique' (Addis Ababa 17 December 2015) PSC/PR/COMM (DLXV), para 13 (c) (iv).

98 See Assembly/AU/Dec.127 (VII): Decision on the Hissène Habré case and the African Union (2 July 2006) Doc.Assembly/AU/3 (VII) para 3. In this paragraph, 'the Assembly observes that, according to the terms of Articles 3(h), 4(h) and 4(o) of the Constitutive Act of the African Union, the crimes of which Hissène Habré is accused fall within the competence of the African Union'.

99 See Agreement on the Establishment of the Extraordinary African Chambers within the Courts of Senegal between the Government of the Republic of Senegal and the African Union (adopted on 22 August 2012, entered into force 30 January 2013) (2013) 52 International Legal Material 1024. The Extraordinary African Chambers are based in Dakar (Senegal).

100 ICISS, *The Responsibility to Protect: Report of the International Commission on Intervention and State Sovereignty* (International Development Research Center 2001); United Nations, 'A More Secure World: Our Shared Responsibility – Report of the Secretary General's High-Level Panel on Threats, Challenges and Changes' (2004) paras 199–203 <www.un.org/en/peacebuilding/pdf/historical/hlp_more_secure_world.pdf> accessed 31 January 2021.

101 African Union (Assembly of the African Union), 'Rules of Procedure of the Assembly of the Union' (Addis Ababa 9 July 2002) ASS/AU/2(I), Rule 11 (1).

102 Kahombo, *La politique africaine commune de défense et de sécurité* (n 61) 172–73.

58 of the African Charter on Human and Peoples' Rights. The result of such an enquiry is a detailed report, with conclusions and recommendations, which is submitted to the Assembly.

However, in the past, the mechanism failed to some extent.[103] In fact, the OAU Assembly was reluctant to authorize the African Commission on Human and Peoples' Rights to enquire into situations where atrocities were being committed in member states where leaders of these states were likely significantly implicated.[104] This was due not only to the trend of auto-protection between peers, but also in the absence of state consent in most of cases, the safety of the African Commission on Human and Peoples' Rights' personnel and assets could not be guaranteed on the ground by non-consenting home governments.[105] Moreover, the mechanism is confined only to states parties to the African Charter on Human and Peoples' Rights. As a consequence, two different developments have followed.

First, the AU PSC has been permitted to work in close cooperation with the African Commission on Human and Peoples' Rights. The PSC is a political body having the mandate to undertake a mission of inquiry within a state party in accordance with its broad powers concerning issues relating to peace and security in Africa and the principles governing its functioning, namely, 'respect for the rule of law, fundamental human rights and freedoms, the sanctity of human life and international humanitarian law'.[106] The best example here concerns the commission of enquiry which was tasked with investigating atrocities committed in South Sudan in 2014 following the PSC's Communiqué of 30 December 2013.[107]

The second development concerns the fact that the African Commission on Human and Peoples' Rights has decided, outside the framework of Article 58, but generally with the consent of territorial states, to undertake missions of fact-finding in states that are subject to serious political instability or armed conflict. A precedent in this regard surrounds the report the Commission delivered following its mission in Darfur (Sudan) in 2004,[108] which recommended the setting up of an international commission of enquiry to investigate alleged violations of human rights and IHL by all belligerent parties.[109] All these developments are relevant and should be consolidated in practice for African states, given the disuse of the International Fact-Finding Commission established under Article 90 of Additional Protocol I to the Geneva Conventions of 1949, despite the recognition of its competence by a number of countries such as Rwanda in 1993, the DRC in 2002, and Uganda in 2008. In fact, the International

---

[103] Chidi Anselm Odinkalu, 'International Criminal Justice, Peace and Reconciliation in Africa: Re-imagining an Agenda beyond the ICC' (2015) 40 Africa Development 257, 271–72.

[104] ibid 271.

[105] ibid.

[106] See Protocol Relating to the Establishment of the Peace and Security Council of the African Union (n 22) arts 3(f) and 4(c).

[107] See African Union, 'Final Report of the African Union Commission of Inquiry on South Sudan', Addis Ababa, 15 October 2014 <www.peaceau.org/uploads/auciss.final.report.pdf> accessed 31 January 2021.

[108] See AComHPR, 'Report of the African Commission on Human and Peoples' Rights' Fact-Finding Mission to the Republic of Sudan in the Darfur Region' (08 to 18 July 2004) EX.CL/364 (XI), Annex III <www.achpr.org/files/sessions/41st/mission-reports/sudan/misrep_factfind_sudan_2004_eng.pdf> accessed 31 January 2021.

[109] See Thabo Mbeki and others, 'Darfur: the Quest for Peace and Reconciliation. Report of the African Union High-Level Panel on Darfur (AUPD)' (October 2009), PSC/AHG/2(CCVII) Peace and Security Council, Abuja (Nigeria) 29 October 2009.

Fact-Finding Commission is irrelevant for African non-international armed conflicts, by far the most recurrent on the continent. Further, African fact-finding missions are more flexible and adaptable to circumstances because they are not permanent mechanisms. They are constituted on a case-by-case basis in the form of delegations of the African Commission on Human and Peoples' Rights, funded by the AU, rather than consenting states, as may be the case for the Fact-Finding Commission based on Additional Protocol I to the Geneva Conventions of 1949.

3.2 Participation in the Process of Regionalization of International Humanitarian Law

How can we ensure that state and non-state actors voluntarily comply with humanitarian obligations they are subjected to? This question raises the issue of legitimacy of regional humanitarian law when it comes to the extent to which addressees of legal norms are included for participation in the process of regionalization of the law of armed conflict. Normally, participation is one of the prerequisite criteria for the promotion of voluntary compliance with obligations under international law. However, a distinction must be drawn between participation in the regional law-making process and participation in terms of ratification of, or accession to, regional/sub-regional humanitarian treaties. In both cases, the interests of non-state actors come far behind that of states, which remain the principal interested players.

Concerning the process of law-making (in relation to humanitarian treaties), regional rules are elaborated through formal interstate forums in which non-state actors, namely international non-governmental organizations (NGOs), have limited participation. The procedure is dominated by the primacy of the Assembly of Heads of States (for the AU or any other African interstate organization), which takes the final decision surrounding the adoption of text which has been negotiated by intergovernmental experts or committees of independent experts and at the ministerial level. NGOs may only be called upon to produce their views on draft text when it is still on the table of negotiating states' experts. As soon as drafting moves to the institutional arena of the concerned African interstate organization, the procedure becomes exclusionary for non-state actors, including within the AU Commission on International Law (AUCIL).[110]

Armed groups, i.e., 'dissident armed forces or other organized armed groups that are distinct from the armed forces of the state',[111] cannot participate in this process of regional law-making given the fact that they are denied legitimacy, recognition, or legal status across the conti-

---

[110] See Statute of the African Union Commission on International Law (adopted and entered into force on 4 February 2009) <https://au.int/en/treaties/statute-african-union-commission-international-law-aucil> accessed 31 January 2021. The AUCIL is an African Union independent advisory organ. Art 4 of its Statute provides that the AUCIL's mission is, among others, 'to undertake activities relating to codification and progressive development of international law in the African continent with particular attention to the laws of the Union as embodied in the treaties of the Union, in the decisions of the policy organs of the Union and in African customary international law arising from the practice of Member States' and 'to encourage the teaching, study, publication and dissemination of literature on international law in particular the laws of the Union with a view to promoting acceptance of and respect for the principles of international law, the peaceful resolution of conflicts, respect for the Union and recourse to its Organs, when necessary'.

[111] Kampala Convention (n 74) art 1(e).

nent.[112] Similarly, and like NGOs, they cannot become parties to African humanitarian treaties insofar as, under international law, this faculty (via ratification or accession) is chiefly a state prerogative and a right which stems from bodies of their creation: interstate organizations.

It follows that this lack of participation raises the problem of legitimacy surrounding legal norms as they apply to non-state actors rather than vis-à-vis states themselves. Concerning armed groups, a double strategy can be used to promote their voluntary compliance in relation to obligations with which these armed groups have had no part in shaping. On the one hand, there is the criminalization strategy: where states ensure the criminal responsibility of armed groups under international or domestic law. In general, this strategy requires amendments to applicable positive law, for example in order to recognize the criminal liability of such groups. On the other hand, humanitarian obligations can be recalled in documents relating to military doctrines of armed groups or in peace agreements in any state where a process of reconciliation has been undertaken.[113] However, peace agreements may also falter in terms of their implementation mechanisms. In the African great lakes region, for example, it is remarkable that atrocities have continued after long processes of peace negotiations, as illustrated by the situation in the DRC following the conclusion of the Lusaka Peace Accord of 10 July 1999. In fact, while the United Nations constituted its peacekeeping operation on 30 November 1999, the latter was deprived of sufficient personnel to efficiently monitor application of the agreement. Initially, the operation consisted of only 90 military personnel,[114] whereas the gravity of the conflict (since August 1998) was such that it had directly involved eight African countries, several rebellions, and numerous other armed groups (Congolese and foreigner) propagating the culture of violence and terror.[115] Moreover, parties to the conflict did not trust each other. In particular, the government of the DRC, under president Laurent-Désiré Kabila's regime, did not believe in peace via an agreement and so refused, until the end of 2000, to allow for substantial UN military deployment within the country, except arguably on the borders with state aggressors.

A closely related problem may be raised in regards to the AU itself. The AU cannot accede to treaties adopted under its own aegis and as a result of which it is granted several rights and obligations. Enforcement of these treaties becomes therefore problematic for two principal reasons. First, in *Femi Falana's case*, the African Court on Human and Peoples' Rights held that it could not examine a judicial claim against the AU concerning a treaty to which it was not a party.[116] This jurisprudence has been confirmed in the *Atabong Denis Atemnkeng case*.[117] Second, there is no regime of criminal responsibility which applies to the continental organi-

---

[112] ibid art 7(1).

[113] Churchill Ewumbue-Monono, 'Respect for International Humanitarian Law by Armed Non-State Actors in Africa' (2006) 88 International Review of the Red Cross 905, 915–16.

[114] UNSC Res 1258 (6 August 1999) UN Doc S/RES/1258, para 8.

[115] Rwanda, Uganda and Burundi (and their Congolese rebel allies) against the DRC, Angola, Namibia, Zimbabwe and Chad.

[116] ACtHPR, *Femi Falana v The African Union, Application No.001/2011*, Judgment of 26 June 2012, paras 71–72. See also Adelardus Kilangi, 'Legal Personality, Responsibility and Immunity of the African Union: Reflection on the Decision of the African Court on Human and Peoples' Rights in the Femi Falana Case' (2013) 1 AUCIL Journal of International Law 95.

[117] ACtHPR, *Atabong Denis Atemnkeng v The African Union*, Application No.014/2011, Judgment of 15 March 2013, paras 39 and 46 (a).

zation,[118] except that which potentially binds its agents. Hence, the promotion of compliance with humanitarian law on the part of the AU side rests on other initiatives. One such initiative is the development of 'Guidelines for the protection of civilians in African peace support operations'[119] which aim

> to improve the security of the population and people at risk and to ensure the full respect for the rights of groups and the individual recognised under regional instruments including the African Charter of Human and Peoples' Rights, the AU Convention for the Protection and Assistance of Internally Displaced Persons, and the Convention Governing the Specific Aspects of Refugee Problems in Africa, and international law, including humanitarian, human rights and refugee law.[120]

Furthermore, the AU has adopted the 'Policy on Prevention and Response to Sexual Exploitation and Abuse for Peace Support Operations'.[121] Another initiative concerns AU partnerships with humanitarian organizations and agencies, such as the ICRC, which mainly focus on the dissemination of IHL in Africa and the training of diplomats, military and security officers, state armed forces and contingents deployed within the framework of AU peace support operations.[122] Both initiatives are complemented by 'the African humanitarian framework policy' stressing the AU's central role in humanitarian action across the continent. This role includes supporting 'effective delivery of protection and assistance to affected populations (refugees, returnees, IDPs and host populations)'[123] and contribution to 'the putting in place of durable solutions to situations of forced displacements and effective response to natural and man-made disasters'.[124] While it can be suggested that accession to regional treaties by the AU is potentially a good thing in the sense that it may enhance the AU's accountability for obligations and rights that are stipulated on its behalf, it also remains important that member states play their role at the domestic level.

---

118 Even if the Protocol on Amendments (n 36) (Annex) provides that this Court 'shall have jurisdiction over legal persons, with the exception of states' (art 46C (1)), nothing enables to imply criminal responsibility of the AU which is an interstate organization.

119 See African Union Peace and Security Council, 'Progress Report of the Chairperson of the Commission on the Development of Guidelines for the Protection of Civilians in African Peace Support Operations', 18 May 2011, PSC/PR/2(CCLXXIX) <www.peaceau.org/uploads/progress-report-protection-of-civilians-eng-.pdf> accessed 31 January 2021.

120 African Union, 'Proposed Guidelines for the Protection of Civilians in African Peace Support Operations for Considerations by the African Union' <www.operationspaix.net/DATA/DOCUMENTTEXTE/8763.pdf> accessed 31 January 2021.

121 Assembly/AU/Decl.5(XXXII), African Union Policy on Prevention and Response to Sexual Exploitation and Abuse for Peace Support Operations (Annex), 32nd Ordinary Session of the AU Assembly, Addis Ababa (Ethiopia), 10–11 February 2019 <https://au.int/sites/default/files/decisions/36461-assembly_au_dec_713_-_748_xxxii_e.pdf> accessed 31 January 2021.

122 Ewumbue-Monono and von Flue (n 8) 753–58.

123 African Union, 'African Humanitarian Policy Framework – Initial Draft', 11 March 2010, 3 <www.peaceau.org/uploads/africanhumanitarian-policy-1st-draft.pdf> accessed 31 January 2021.

124 ibid 3–4.

3.3 Advantages of Regional Law-Making Efforts and Challenges to Implementation by States at the Domestic Level

It has already been argued that beyond the advantage of bringing clarity surrounding applicable law, the aforementioned technique of incorporating humanitarian norms into African legal instruments has the potential to extend the ambit of application of the law of armed conflict in Africa. This is true for non-state actors, including armed groups. It is also true in regards to the AU. In the same vein, certain states that do not ratify universal instruments may still be bound by regional or sub-regional treaties on the same matter. For example, Rwanda is bound by the Protocol for the prevention and the punishment of the crime of genocide, war crimes and crimes against humanity, and all forms of discrimination within the African great lakes region, which incorporates several provisions of the ICC Statute to which it is not a state party: notably the definition of war crimes and the principle regarding the irrelevance of official capacity as a bar to criminal prosecution. Codification of new regional rules is an impetus to this approach of extending the scope of application of the law of armed conflict in Africa.

Despite all these advantages, incorporation and codification of humanitarian norms in African legal instruments face two pivotal challenges. The first relates to the ratification of African treaties. Within the great lakes region, for example, the DRC has not yet acceded to the Protocol relating to the Establishment of the AU Peace and Security Council nor the African Convention on the prevention and combating of terrorism, whilst both treaties are already in force in Burundi, Uganda and Rwanda.[125] Similarly, Uganda and the DRC have not yet ratified the Pelindaba Treaty (which came into force on 15 July 2009) nor the African Convention on the Conservation of Nature and Natural Resources (which came into force on 23 July 2016), contrary to Burundi and Rwanda, which have ratified both.[126] The same disparity applies to the Kampala Convention (which came into force on 6 December 2012), which is binding on Rwanda and Uganda, but not on Burundi and the DRC.[127] Likewise, the OAU Convention for the Elimination of Mercenarism in Africa has been ratified only by Rwanda and the DRC.[128] Such disparity surrounding ratification may lead to fragmented application of humanitarian norms in this part of Africa, at least in respect to continental treaties.

The second challenge, which tends to exacerbate the first, is the deficient and/or diverging domestication of regional and sub-regional obligations. This challenge concerns the lack of national legislation implementing IHL or, even when the latter does exist, a lack of sufficient

[125] See the lists of ratifications <https://au.int/sites/default/files/treaties/37293-sl-protocol_relating_to_the_establishment_of_the_peace_and_security_council_of_the_african_union_1.pdf> and <https://au.int/sites/default/files/treaties/37289-sl-oau_convention_on_the_prevention_and_combating_of_terrorism_1.pdf> accessed 31 January 2021.

[126] See the lists of ratifications <au.int/sites/default/files/treaties/37288-sl-the_african_nuclear-weapon-free_zone_treaty_the_treaty_of_pelindaba_3.pdf>; <https://au.int/sites/default/files/treaties/7782-sl-revised_african_convention_on_the_conservation_of_nature_and_natural_resources.pdf> accessed 31 January 2021.

[127] See list of ratifications <https://au.int/sites/default/files/treaties/36846-sl-AFRICAN%20UNION%20CONVENTION%20FOR%20THE%20PROTECTION%20AND%20ASSISTANCE%20OF%20INTERNALLY%20DISPLACED%20PERSONS%20IN%20AFRICA%20%28KAMPALA%20CONVENTION%29.pdf> accessed 31 January 2021.

[128] See list of ratifications <https://au.int/sites/default/files/treaties/37287-sl-oau_convention_for_the_elimination_of_mercenarism_in_africa_1.pdf> accessed 31 January 2021.

harmonization with international rules. An empirical investigation of this matter within the African great lakes region could confirm this assumption. Meanwhile, the AU has undertaken efforts to fill the gap by suggesting model laws to be adopted in member states by national parliaments in order to harmonize domestic positive law. Two of these model laws are already relevant to the body of IHL, namely the African Union's model national law on universal jurisdiction over international crimes (genocide, crimes against humanity, war crimes, piracy, trafficking in drugs and terrorism),[129] and the African model anti-terrorist law.[130]

4. CONCLUSION

This study has shown that the harmonization of national legislation, incorporation of (universal) humanitarian rules within African legal instruments, and codification of specific regional norms are the principal channels through which the law of armed conflict has been shaped and indeed becomes law made in Africa. This body of law is expressed in a multitude of regional and sub-regional instruments. The situation has led to complexity in the normative system, simplification of which may be promoted by the unification of scattered provisions into one African humanitarian instrument, at least as far as treaty law is concerned. Three major substantive lessons can be drawn from regional developments in this regard.

First, it appears that the classic categorization of armed conflict – international, non-international and new conflicts – tends to be of limited relevance within African treaties. The OAU Convention for the elimination of mercenarism in Africa and the Kampala Convention for the protection and assistance of internally displaced persons provide the clearest examples of this. Neither of them refers to the nature of armed conflict as reducing their applicability. The empirical explanation for this development may lay in 'crises dynamics', which show that interstate armed conflicts have receded in the region, while those of a non-international character and the so-called 'new conflicts' or 'conflicts of mixed nature' have become the principal features of violence within the continent.[131] It is predictable that, going forward, the classic categorization of armed conflict under IHL will be progressively relinquished.

Second, efforts to shape the law of armed conflict in Africa are supposed to produce the following three positive results: i) bringing clarity in law for state and non-state actors with regard to the set of obligations they should comply with; ii) extending the ambit of application of IHL; iii) serving as a leading yardstick in law-making processes at the regional level so as to potentially induce legal reform and to advance the law at the universal level.

It remains to be seen how states and other addressees of the normative order comply with their obligations. For states, particularly, fragmentation in the application of humanitarian

---

129 African Union Executive Council, African Union Model National Law on Universal Jurisdiction over International Crimes (EX.CL/731(XXI)), 13 July 2012 <http://legal.au.int/en/sites/default/files/MODEL%20LAW%20FINAL-EN_0.pdf> accessed 31 January 2021.

130 African Union Assembly, African Model Anti-Terrorist Law, Final Draft as Endorsed by the 17th Ordinary Session of the Assembly of the Union, 1 July 2011 <http://caert.org.dz/official-documents/african-model-law-en.pdf> accessed 31 January 2021.

131 See Jakkie Cilliers, 'Future (im)perfect? Mapping Conflict, Violence and Extremism in Africa' (ISS Paper 287, October 2015) 4, 9–10 <https://issafrica.org/research/papers/future-im-perfect-mapping-conflict-violence-and-extremism-in-africa> accessed 31 January 2021

rules as a result of the disparity of treaty ratifications, the domestication of international obligations, and the lack of harmony of national legislations should be avoided. Criminalization of breaches of IHL should also be strengthened, including categories of inhumane acts such as the 'arbitrary displacement of persons', for which further incrimination is required regionally and domestically. All these measures could better contribute to the development of legitimate and effective IHL in Africa.

19. Sovereign equality and law-making: How do states from the Global South shape international humanitarian law? A comment to Alejandro Rodiles and Balingene Kahombo

Michael Bothe

One of the conflict lines which characterizes the current international order still is that between what, for the sake of abbreviation or simplification, is called the Global South and the Global North. The term is not really used in the geographic sense; it denotes different historic positions of economic development and society. The question thus is whether and to what extent that specific historic position determines the participation of the states belonging to the Global South in shaping the international legal order. This comment deals with a particular part of that question, namely the formation and development of international humanitarian law (IHL). It is based on the two elaborate chapters submitted by Alejandro Rodiles and Balingene Kahombo dealing with two regions of the South, Latin America and Africa. It expands consideration of the question as a matter of both geography and content.

There are occasions where the states of the Global South seem to be united in their position concerning law-making processes, in the field of IHL as well as in other fields. There are issues which are of common concern for next to all members of the Global South because they contain special significance for the specific position of these states. Examples related to IHL include the question of wars of national liberation[1] or the prohibition of nuclear weapons.[2] Yet at a closer look, the position of the Global South is regionally fragmented and the same holds true for the Global North. As to the Global South, it is necessary to distinguish five groups: Latin America, Africa, the Middle East (the Arab countries and Iran), the Indian Sub-Continent and South-East Asia. The position of China is peculiar. Differences and commonalities are to a great extent explained by different histories of colonization and decolonization.

IHL, as we know it today, is to a large extent the offspring of the European system of states in the 18th and 19th century.[3] Its intellectual origins lie in the philosophy of the age of enlight-

1 Jean-Marie Henckaerts and Louise Doswald-Beck, *Customary International Humanitarian Law, Vol 1: Rules* (CUP 2005) 392; David Glazier, 'Wars of National Liberation' (May 2009) in Rüdiger Wolfrum (ed), *Max Planck Encyclopedia of Public International Law* (online edn).

2 See eg the similar voting behaviour of the states of the Global South in favour of the request for an Advisory Opinion transmitted to the ICJ under the UN GA 'Legality of the Threat or Use of Nuclear Weapons' Res. 49/75 K (15 December 1994) UN Doc A/RES/49/75.

3 Geneva Convention for the Amelioration of the Condition of the Wounded in Armies in the Field (adopted 22 August 1864, entered into force 22 June 1865) in Dietrich Schindler and Jiří Toman,

enment, as they were formulated by Rousseau in his 'Contrat social',[4] which characterizes war as a conflict between states, conducted by their military organs against the military effort of another state. This is the source of two basic principles of IHL: the principle of distinction[5] and the protection of those who are *hors de combat.*[6] Today, this law of armed conflict is a universal system, and law-making in that system has become universal. It has become universal by the progressive entry of non-European states into the essentially European club of law-makers which existed in the 18th and 19th century.[7] This was a slow process. The first multilateral law-making event was the Paris Peace Conference of 1856, which adopted the Declaration Respecting Maritime Law.[8] Turkey had been a party to the war which was ended by the Paris Peace, thus becoming, to a certain degree, part of the European system. At the behest of France and Great Britain, a number of Latin American states and Japan acceded to the declaration. No non-European state (not even Turkey) was invited to the Geneva Conference of 1864, which was the starting point of the Geneva Conventions treaty system. Persia and Turkey took part in the 1868 St Petersburg conference which adopted the declaration on expanding bullets.[9] No non-European state (except Turkey) participated with the Brussels Conference of 1874, which adopted the first codification of the laws and customs of war.[10] At the first Hague Peace Conference of 1899, six non-European states participated: from the Americas –

The Laws of Armed Conflicts (Martinus Nijhoff Publishers 1988) 280–81; Institute of International Law, 'The Laws of War on Land', Oxford, 9 September 1880 <https://www.icrc.org/ihl/INTRO/140?OpenDocument> accessed 31 January 2021. See Martti Koskenniemi, *The Gentle Civilizer of Nations: The Rise and Fall of International Law 1870–1960* (CUP 2008) 84–88; Hans-Peter Gasser, 'Humanitarian Law, International' (December 2015) in Rüdiger Wolfrum (ed), *Max Planck Encyclopedia of Public International Law* (online edn).

4 Jean-Jacques Rousseau, *Du contrat social ou Principes du droit public* (Amsterdam 1762).

5 Nils Melzer, *Targeted Killing in International Law* (OUP 2008) 300–66; Henckaerts and Doswald-Beck (n 1) 3–8.

6 Dorota Banaszewska, 'Hors de combat' (November 2015) in Rüdiger Wolfrum (ed), *Max Planck Encyclopedia of Public International Law* (online edn).

7 Bardo Fassbender and Anne Peters (eds), *The Oxford Handbook of the History of International Law* (OUP 2012); Stephan Verosta, 'History of International Law, 1648 to 1815' (June 2007) in Rüdiger Wolfrum (ed), *Max Planck Encyclopedia of Public International Law* (online edn); Hans-Ulrich Scupin, 'History of International Law, 1815 to World War I' (May 2011) in Rüdiger Wolfrum (ed), *Max Planck Encyclopedia of Public International Law* (online edn).

8 'Declaration Respecting Maritime Law, Paris, 16 April 1856' in Dirk Roland Haupt and others (eds), *Documents on International Humanitarian Law* (3rd edn, Academia Verlag 2016) 5. The seven powers who signed the Declaration were: France, Great Britain, Ottoman Empire, Sardinia, Russia, Austria and Prussia.

9 Declaration Renouncing the Use, in Time of War, of Explosive Projectiles Under 400 Grammes in Weight, St Petersburg (11 December 1868) reprinted in Dietrich Schindler and Jiří Toman (n 3) 102. Nations represented were Austria-Hungary, Bavaria, Belgium, Denmark, France, Great Britain, Greece, Italy, Netherlands, Persia, Portugal, Prussia and the North German Confederation, Russia, Sweden-Norway, Switzerland, the Ottoman Empire and Württemberg.

10 'The Brussels International Declaration of 1874 concerning the Laws and Customs of War' (1974) 14 International Review of the Red Cross 616. On 27 July 1874, delegates of 15 European states met in Brussels to examine the Russian draft of an international agreement concerning the laws and customs of war. The Convention was never ratified, nevertheless it constituted an important step towards codification of the law.

Mexico and the United States; from Asia – China, Japan, Persia and Siam.[11] It was only at the Second Hague Conference in 1907 that the scope of participation was considerably enlarged by a number of Latin American states, bringing the total number of Latin American states' participation to 18.[12] In the interwar period, further states joined the club: two states having a special status in the British colonial empire, namely India and South Africa, the only then independent African states, namely Ethiopia and Liberia, of which only Ethiopia became a party to the Geneva Conventions of 1929,[13] and Egypt.[14] Participation in the negotiations of the 1949 Geneva Conventions was not much broader. More Asian states were included (Afghanistan, Pakistan [after the partition of India], the Philippines, Sri Lanka, and Syria). It was only at the 1974/77 Diplomatic Conference which adopted the two Protocols Additional to the Geneva Conventions that IHL law-making became truly universal. It included the newly independent states of Africa (after the wave of decolonization which took place in the 1960s) and South-East Asia (with its diverse and sometime violent decolonization processes).[15]

As to the attitude of the Global South towards IHL law-making, three questions have to be distinguished:

- Did an autonomous development of IHL and human rights law evolve within these countries before their entry into the club and/or after that entry?
- What is the position of the states of the Global South, after their entry into the club, in respect of global or universal law-making?
- Have the autonomous concepts and specific interests of the Global South had an impact on the global development of IHL?

As to the first question, Latin America has the oldest tradition. Its wars of independence were led by persons of European descent, to name only Simon Bolivar. He had internalized the teachings of the age of enlightenment, and Latin American practice during the wars of

11 Signatory states: 'Final Act of the International Peace Conference. The Hague, 29 July 1899' (ICRC) <https://ihl-databases.icrc.org/applic/ihl/ihl.nsf/States.xsp?xp_viewStates=XPages_NORMStatesSign&xp_treatySelected=145> accessed 31 January 2021.

12 State Parties to the Convention (III) relative to the Opening of Hostilities (18 October 1907) <https://ihl-databases.icrc.org/applic/ihl/ihl.nsf/States.xsp?xp_viewStates=XPages_NORMStatesParties&xp_treatySelected=190> accessed 31 January 2021.

13 Geneva Convention for the Amelioration of the Condition of the Wounded and Sick in Armies in the Field (adopted 27 July 1929) in Schindler and Toman (n 3) 326–34; Convention relative to the Treatment of Prisoners of War (adopted 27 July 1929) in Schindler and Toman (n 3) 341–64.

14 Ethiopia became only a party to the 1929 Geneva Convention concerning the Wounded and Sick, see 'Ethiopia, Historical Documents' (International Committee of the Red Cross) <https://ihl-databases.icrc.org/applic/ihl/ihl.nsf/vwTreatiesHistoricalByCountrySelected.xsp?xp_countrySelected=ET&nv=8> accessed 31 January 2021. Egypt became a party to both 1929 Geneva Conventions, see 'Egypt, Historical Documents' (International Committee of the Red Cross) <https://ihl-databases.icrc.org/applic/ihl/ihl.nsf/vwTreatiesHistoricalByCountrySelected.xsp?xp_countrySelected=EG&nv=8> accessed 31 January 2021.

15 The list of participating states is contained in the Final Act of the Diplomatic conference on the Reaffirmation and Development of International Humanitarian Law Applicable in Armed Conflict, in *Official Records of the Diplomatic Conference on the Reaffirmation and Development of International Humanitarian Law Applicable in Armed Conflicts, Geneva 1974–1977*, vol 1 (Federal Political Department 1978) 3; Hans-Peter Gasser, 'Geneva Conventions I–IV (1949)' (December 2015) in Rüdiger Wolfrum (ed), *Max Planck Encyclopedia of Public International Law* (online edn).

independence, at least during their latter phase, can be seen as one of the earliest examples of modern IHL law-making in the spirit of the enlightenment. Later in the 19th and in the earlier decades of the 20th century, the Americas developed Pan-American rules on the law of armed conflict. The Roerich Treaty of 1935 is the outstanding example.[16] After the Second World War, the practice of the American institutions tasked with ensuring respect for human rights also became relevant for IHL. These include the Inter-American Commission on Human Rights, created by the Organization of American States (OAS) in 1959,[17] and the Inter-American Court of Human Rights, established in 1979 pursuant to the 1969 American Convention on Human Rights.[18] Both institutions were instrumental in developing a concept of human rights serving as a restraint on military activities even in situations of armed conflict, IHL and human rights thus being applied in parallel (see cases *Palmera*[19] and *Tablada*[20]).

As for Africa, the essential IHL developments took place after independence under the auspices of the newly created African political and human rights institutions: the Organization of African Unity (OAU),[21] since 2001 the African Union[22] as a political institution, and the African Commission on Human and Peoples' Rights established pursuant to the (Banjul) Charter on Human and Peoples' Rights (1981)[23] – later the African Court of Human and Peoples' Rights established in 2006 under a Protocol Additional to the Banjul Charter.[24] The latter court has now been merged with the AU Court of Justice, leading to the establishment of the African Court of Justice and Human Rights.

An example of specific African treaty-making is the 2009 Kampala Convention on Internally Displaced Persons in Africa.[25] International and non-international conflicts in Africa have displaced hundreds of thousands of people. Technically, they are not refugees if and

---

16 The Roerich Pact or 'Treaty on the Protection of Artistic and Scientific Institutions and Historic Monuments' is an inter-American treaty signed by the representatives of American states in the Oval Office of the White House on the initiative of Nicholas Roerich (1874–1947) (adopted 15 April 1935, entered into force 26 August 1935) in Haupt and others (n 8) 109.

17 The Charter of the Organization of American States (OAS) (adopted 30 April 1948, entered into force 13 December 1951) 119 UNTS 48, art 106.

18 The American Convention on Human Rights (adopted 22 November 1969, entered into force 18 July 1978) 1144 UNTS 144.

19 *Las Palmeras v Colombia* (Judgment) Inter-American Court of Human Rights Series C No 90, 33 (6 December 2001).

20 *Juan Carlos Abella v Argentina*, Case 11.137, Inter-American Court of Human Rights Report No. 55/97, OEA/Ser/L/V/II.97, doc. 38 (30 October 1997).

21 The organization was established on 25 May 1963 pursuant to art 1(1) of the Charter of the Organization of African Unity (adopted 25 May 1963, entered into force 13 September 1963) 479 UNTS 70.

22 The African Union was established on 26 May 2001 in Addis Ababa pursuant to art 2 of the Constitutive Act of the African Union (adopted 11 July 2000, entered into force 26 May 2001) 2158 UNTS 3.

23 The African Charter on Human and Peoples' Rights (adopted 27 June 1981, entered into force 21 October 1986) 1520 UNTS 217.

24 The Protocol to the African Charter on Human and Peoples' Rights on the Establishment of an African Court on Human and Peoples' Rights (adopted 9 June 1998, entered into force 25 January 2004) OAU Doc OAU/LEG/EXP/AFCHPR/ PROT (III) 681, 683, 753, 902.

25 African Union Convention for the Protection and Assistance of Internally Displaced Persons in Africa (Kampala Convention) (adopted 22 October 2009, entered into force 06 December 2012) <https://au.int/sites/default/files/treaties/36846-treaty-0039_-_kampala_convention_african_union_convention

where they do not leave their countries. The ICRC, in its study on issues where IHL needs to be developed, has singled out the protection of internally displaced persons as one of four issues to be considered.[26] However, in the ensuing consultations, states refused to give priority to this problem. Thus, the Kampala Convention still stands out as an African example of IHL law-making on an issue which also deserves universal treatment.

The African Court of Human and Peoples' Rights issued a judgment on human rights implications of the prosecution of war crimes.[27] The African Human Rights institutions have also dealt with the question of human rights in armed conflicts.[28] This has led to jurisprudence on human rights as a restraint on military action in both international and non-international armed conflicts, leading to attitudes which are similar to those pursued by Latin American human rights bodies.

It must be emphasized as a common element of IHL development in both Latin America and Africa that regional human rights institutions have recently played an important role.

As to Asia, modern IHL is often related to earlier spiritual sources of the countries of the region: for example, Islam, Buddhism, Hinduism, and Confucianism. These religions or social philosophies may indeed provide additional foundations for respect of IHL within these countries. However, it would be an exaggeration to construe a line of development between these sources and modern international humanitarian law. Two Asian subgroups have created human rights treaties and institutions which might have the potential to address armed conflict and IHL law-making and, therefore, be considered as development of practice similar to that of the institutions in Latin America and Africa. However, due to the recent origins of these institutions, no such practice has had the chance to develop so far. The League of Arab States provides the framework for the Arab Charter on Human Rights (introduced originally in 1994 with a new version in 2004)[29] and the Association of Southeast Asian Nations (ASEAN) the Human Rights Declaration of 2012.[30] The institutions established by these organizations are the Arab Commission on Human Rights (or Arab Permanent Committee on Human Rights)[31] and the Arab Court of Human Rights,[32] which is, however, subject to severe critique con-

_for_the_protection_and_assistance_of_internally_displaced_persons_in_africa_e.pdf> accessed 31 January 2021.

26 ICRC, *International Humanitarian Law and the challenges of contemporary armed conflicts, Report 33IC/19/9.7* (ICRC October 2019); *International Humanitarian Law and the challenges of contemporary armed conflicts, Report 32IC/15/11* (ICRC October 2015); *International Humanitarian Law and the challenges of contemporary armed conflicts, Report 31IC/11/5.1.2* (ICRC October 2011).

27 The African Court on Human and Peoples' Rights, *African Commission on Human and Peoples' Rights v Libya* (3 June 2016).

28 See eg the African Commission on Human and Peoples' Rights, *'General Comment No. 3 on the African Charter on Human and Peoples' Rights'* 57th Ordinary Session (18 November 2015); African Commission on Human and Peoples' Rights, *'Resolution on the Promotion and Respect of International Humanitarian Law and Human and Peoples' Rights'* 14th Ordinary Session (10 December 1993).

29 The Arab Charter on Human Rights (adopted 15 September 1994, updated 22 May 2004, entered into force 24 January 2008) (2005) 12 International Human Rights Reports 893.

30 The Association of Southeast Asian Nations Human Rights Declaration (adopted on 18 November 2012) <http://www.asean.or/ew/sean-statement-communique/te/sean-human-rights-declaration ?category_id=26> accessed 31 January 2021.

31 Art 40 of the Arab Charter on Human Rights (n 29).

32 The League of Arab States, Ministerial Council approved on 1 September 2013 a decision (Decision No.7656) to establish the Arab Court of Human Rights with its seat in Bahrain. The Statute of

cerning its ability to effectively protect individual rights.[33] In 2009, ASEAN established an ASEAN Intergovernmental Commission on Human Rights.[34]

As to the second question, a first specific input of the Global South into the universal development of IHL related to the rules on the use of the emblem. In reservations to the Geneva Convention of 1906 and to the 1907 Hague Convention for the Adaptation to Maritime Warfare of the Principles of the Geneva Convention, Turkey and Egypt reserved the right to use the red crescent and Persia the right to use the red lion and sun, as the emblems protecting their medical services.[35] These emblems were then recognized in the text of the Geneva Convention of 1929.[36]

Yet the first major input of states of the Global South in regard to universal IHL law-making took place at the Geneva Conference of 1974/77, where several issues of particular interest for the Global South were raised. The first related to the status of wars of national liberation and of liberation movements and was of common concern to states of the Global South, whereas Western states first strongly resisted. The first phase of the negotiations was difficult; however, finally the recognition of wars of national liberation as international armed conflicts was no longer controversial, at least as far as the great majority of states was concerned.[37] As a result of this victory, a majority of the Global South states not only lost any interest in the approximation of the law of non-international conflicts to that of international, which had been a major goal for many states of the Global North, although not only for them. A considerable number of the states of the Global South adamantly resisted the very idea of an increased protection of the victims of non-international armed conflicts as they considered it as detrimental for their sovereignty. That increase, however, had been an essential point on the part of efforts of the ICRC to improve the situation of the victims of all armed conflicts. After the negotiations of the first three years had resulted in a text of AP II which would have led to far-reaching approximation of NIAC law to IAC law, strong resistance by many states of the Global South, mainly led by delegates from certain (not all) Arab states and the Indian

---

the Arab Court of Human Rights (adopted 7 September 2014) Res. No. 7790 E.A (142) C 3, at the time of writing, only Saudi Arabia has ratified the Statute.

33 See International Commission of Jurists, 'The Arab Court of Human Rights: A flawed Statute for an Ineffective Court' (*International Commission of Jurists*, 2015) <www.icj.org/wp-content/uploads/2015/04/MENA-Arab-Court-of-Human-Rights-Publications-Report-2015-ENG.pdf> accessed 31 January 2021; Joe Stark, 'New Arab Human Rights Court is Doomed from the Start' (*Human Rights Watch*, 26 November 2020) <www.hrw.org/news/2014/11/26/new-arab-human-rights-court-doomed-start> accessed 31 January 2021.

34 The ASEAN Intergovernmental Commission on Human Rights was established in October 2009, 'About AICHR' (ASEAN Intergovernmental Commission on Human Rights) <http://aichr.org/about/> accessed 31 January 2021.

35 The International Federation of Red Cross and Red Crescent Societies, 'The emblem debate' (*International Federation of Red Cross and Red Crescent Societies*, 22 March 2018) <http://www.ifrc.org/en/who-we-are/the-movement/emblems/the-emblem-debate> accessed 31 January 2021; International Committee of the Red Cross, 'The history of the emblems' (*International Committee of the Red Cross*, 22 March 2018) <https://www.icrc.org/eng/resources/documents/misc/emblem-history.htm> accessed 31 January 2021.

36 Art 19 of the 1929 Geneva Convention for the Amelioration of the Condition of the Wounded and Sick in Armies in the Field (n 13).

37 See Michael Bothe and Karl Josef Partsch, 'General Introduction' in Michael Bothe, Karl Josef Partsch and Waldemar A. Solf, *New Rules for Victims of Armed Conflicts* (2nd edn, Nijhoff 2013) 7–8.

Sub-Continent, appeared. The idea of a simplified version of AP II, i.e., a version which provided far less protection for the victims of non-international armed conflicts and was more respectful of state sovereignty, was finally accepted by all participating states after a number of difficult negotiations over important details (e.g., starvation as a means of warfare, relief operations). The ICRC customary law study published in 2005, however, found that the differences between NIAC and IAC had by that time been reduced as a result of customary law development.[38] Thus, the 'Southern' refusal regarding treaty-making of 1977 had been overcome. One of the reasons may be found in the corresponding developments in Latin America and Africa described earlier.

As to methods and means of warfare, a major issue was the tactics of freedom fighters. The position of many (not all) states of the Global South was to pursue an approach which favoured guerrilla tactics and therefore tried to water down the obligation of combatants to distinguish themselves in the course of fighting. A difficult compromise was found in Article 44 AP I, which until this day is the major reason for the United States refusing to ratify AP I. Another important concern, mainly for African countries, was the problem of mercenaries. The solution found in AP I did not satisfy all of the demands which came from African states. An African answer to this challenge is the 1977 OAU Convention on Mercenaries,[39] to which currently 32 African states are party.[40] The UN Convention on Mercenaries of 1989[41] only has 36 parties, and only five from the Global North, with major military powers from both the North and the South (and next to all Asian states) lacking.[42]

The impact of these problems, in particular of the split between the Global South and the Global North on some issues, on ratification is limited. From the Global North, only the US and Israel have not ratified AP I. For these countries, the major stumbling block is indeed the question of guerrilla tactics,[43] i.e., a North–South issue. Additional non-ratifying states range from Turkey to Indonesia (Turkey, Iran, Pakistan, India, Myanmar, Malaysia, Indonesia and Iraq until 2010, the Philippines until 2012) and require a more elaborate analysis which is beyond the scope of this chapter.

An issue which unites the Global South and many states of the Global North is the prohibition on nuclear weapons.[44] It must be noted that Nuclear Weapons Free Zones have mainly

---

38 Henckaerts and Doswald-Beck (n 1) 35.

39 Organization of African Unity, OAU Convention for the Elimination of Mercenarism in Africa (adopted on 3 July 1977, entered into force 22 April 1985) <https://au.int/en/treaties/convention-elimination-mercenarism-africa> accessed 31 January 2021.

40 Organization of African Unity Convention for the Elimination of Mercenarism in Africa (n 39).

41 The International Convention against the Recruitment, Use, Financing and Training of Mercenaries (adopted on 4 December 1989, entered into force on 20 October 2001) 2163 UNTS 75.

42 ibid.

43 Abraham D. Sofaer, 'Agora: The U.S. Decision not to Ratify Protocol I to the Geneva Conventions on the Protection of War Victims. The Rationale for the United States Decision' (1988) 82 American Journal of International Law 784–87; Emily Crawford, 'Geneva Conventions Additional Protocol I (1977)' (June 2015) in Rüdiger Wolfrum (ed), *Max Planck Encyclopedia of Public International Law* (online edn).

44 Sarah Johanna Swart, 'An African contribution to the nuclear weapons debate' (2015) 97 International Review of the Red Cross (2015) 753–73.

been created in the Global South: the 1967 Treaty of Tlatelolco[45] in Latin America being the first of its kind. Later came the South Pacific Nuclear Free Zone Treaty (Rarotonga 1985),[46] the Southeast Asian Nuclear-Weapon-Free Zone Treaty (Bangkok 1995),[47] the African Nuclear-Weapon-Free Zone Treaty (Pelindaba 1996)[48] and the Central Asian Nuclear Weapon Free Zone Treaty (Semipalatinsk 2006).[49]

As to conventional weapons, the UN Convention[50] has from the beginning enjoyed broad participation from all parts of the world. Lively controversies exist, on the other hand, concerning the two important weapons conventions adopted outside of UN processes: the 1997 Ottawa Convention on Antipersonnel Mines[51] (non-parties *inter alia* US, Russia, China, India, and Pakistan) and the 2008 Dublin Convention on Cluster Munitions[52] (with the same non-parties). In these two cases, the conflict lines rather exist between states of the Global North. Many states from the Global South have supported and even actively promoted these treaties.

The problem of non-state personnel involved in armed conflicts still is on the international agenda.[53] It has played a role in more recent conflicts in the African region, too. The General Assembly (GA) and the Human Rights Council (HRC) have it on their agenda, recently dealing with the use of mercenaries in the Central African Republic. The 'Working Group on the use of mercenaries as a means of violating human rights and impeding the exercise of the right of peoples to self-determination' regularly delivers reports to the HRC and to the GA. A modern related problem (which, however, must be distinguished) is the question of private organizations fulfilling certain tasks traditionally performed by state agents in relation to armed conflicts, so-called private military and security companies (PMSC). An attempt to render the rules applicable to this practice more concrete, the 2008 'Montreux Document' on

---

45 Treaty for the Prohibition of Nuclear Weapons in Latin America and the Caribbean (signed 14 February 1967, entered into force 22 April 1968) 634 UNTS 281.

46 The South Pacific Nuclear Free Zone Treaty (signed 6 August 1985, entered into force 11 December 1986) <https://www.state.gov/t/isn/5189.htm> accessed 31 January 2021.

47 The Southeast Asian Nuclear-Weapon-Free Zone Treaty (opened for signature 15 December 1995, entered into force 28 March 1997) 1981 UNTS 129.

48 Organization of African Unity, African Nuclear Weapon-Free Zone Treaty (Pelindaba Treaty) (adopted on 11 April 1996, entered into force 15 July 2009) (1996) 35 ILM 698.

49 The Central Asian Nuclear Weapon Free Zone Treaty (opened for signature 8 September 2006, entered into force 21 March 2009) <http://www.nti.org/learn/treaties-and-regimes/central-asia-nuclear-weapon-free-zone-canwz> accessed 31 January 2021.

50 The Convention on Prohibitions or Restrictions on the Use of Certain Conventional Weapons which may be deemed to be Excessively Injurious or to have Indiscriminate Effects (adopted 10 October 1980, entered into force 2 December 1983) 1342 UNTS 137.

51 The Convention on the Prohibition of the Use, Stockpiling, Production and Transfer of Anti-Personnel Mines and on their Destruction (adopted 18 September 1997, entered into force 1 March 1999) 2056 UNTS 211.

52 The Convention on Cluster Munitions (adopted on 30 May 2008, entered into force 1 August 2010) (2009) 48 ILM 357.

53 *International Humanitarian Law and the challenges of contemporary armed conflicts, Report 33IC/19/9.7* (ICRC October 2019); *International Humanitarian Law and the challenges of contemporary armed conflicts, Report 32IC/15/11* (ICRC October 2015); *International Humanitarian Law and the challenges of contemporary armed conflicts, Report 31IC/11/5.1.2* (ICRC October 2011); *International Humanitarian Law and the challenges of contemporary armed conflicts, Report 30IC/07/8.4* (ICRC November 2007).

pertinent legal obligations and good practice relating to private military and security companies,[54] resulting from a joint Swiss/ICRC initiative, has received a lukewarm reaction within the United Nations – in other words by the majority of the Global South nations – although experts from some states of the Global South participated in its elaboration. The HRC mandated the UN Working Group on Mercenaries to discuss the growing practice of the use of PMSCs by the UN.[55] It would be an incorrect statement of the conflict lines existing on this issue to claim it is only a North–South controversy.

Finally, a word must be said on ensuring respect of IHL. As to criminal law and in particular the ICC, there is also no conflict between nations of the Global North and the Global South. Among the opponents of the ICC, one finds in particular the US, China and the Russian Federation, which has recently withdrawn its signature. There also is the block of non-ratifying states from Turkey to Indonesia similar to that related to AP I. On the other hand, a considerable part of the Global South has ratified the Statute, states from Latin America and Africa, although not from Asia. The recent withdrawals of African states, executed or announced (with announcements revoked and revived), are, first, due to a turn of events considered unfortunate by many African politicians, namely the issuing of an arrest warrant against an African head of state, which seemed to excessively violate African concepts of state dignity, and, second, the fact that there was a certain concentration of the Court's prosecutorial activities on African countries – a development, however, largely due to the fact that African states themselves submitted their situations to the Court, which made claims that the ICC was anti-African somewhat unconvincing. The position of the Arab states is inconsistent. On the one hand, they share the African states' misgivings about heads of state being prosecuted by the ICC Prosecutor, but on the other hand they support the Palestinian move to use the ICC as a means of pressure against Israel.

The most challenging current controversy on IHL law-making relates to the creation of a new compliance mechanism. The Swiss/ICRC initiative on this issue did not yield the desired result at the International Red Cross/Red Crescent Conference in December 2015.[56] The consultations and negotiations on this question which followed with a view to achieving a solution at the next Conference in 2019 were terminated without a result in late 2018. The ICRC commented diplomatically: '(…) it became clear that, in the current international environment, the time was not ripe for reaching a consensual agreement among States on ways to strengthen respect for IHL within the intergovernmental process.' [57] In this controversy, the dividing line does not run along the North–South frontier. The major opponents of the new

---

[54] UNGA 'The Montreux Document: On pertinent international legal obligations and good practices for States related to operations of private military and security companies during armed conflict' (6 October 2008) UN Doc A/63/467–S/2008/636, 7.

[55] UN Human Rights Council Resolution 7/21, 'Mandate of the Working Group on the use of mercenaries as a means of violating human rights and impeding the exercise of the right of peoples to self-determination' (28 March 2008) UN Doc A/HRC/RES/7/21; UN Commission on Human Rights, 'The Use of Mercenaries As a Means of Violating Human Rights and Impeding the Exercise of the Right of Peoples to Self-determination' (7 April 2005) UN Doc E/CN.4/RES/2005/2.

[56] See the statement of the ICRC 'No agreement by States on mechanism to strengthen compliance with rules of war' (*ICRC*, 10 December 2015) <https://www.icrc.org/en/document/no-agreement-states-mechanism-strengthen-compliance-rules-war> accessed 31 January 2021.

[57] See 'Factual Report on the Proceedings of the Intergovernmental Process on Strengthening Respect for IHL – Progress report' (ICRC and the Swiss Federal Department of Foreign Affairs, October

mechanism were the Russian Federation and India; the major promoters came from Western countries.

A traditional means of ensuring compliance, in the field of IHL as well as in others, is fact-finding. In the debate concerning a new compliance mechanism, considerable resistance against any form of fact-finding was felt, and as a consequence, already the Swiss/ICRC proposal submitted to the 2015 International Conference made no reference to it.[58] This, as already stated, is not a North–South controversy. As to existing fact-finding procedures, the Global South favours the fact-finding procedures used by the HRC also in relation to IHL (for example cases of Lebanon,[59] Gaza,[60] Libya[61] and Syria[62]), which is explained by the fact that there is a Third World majority in the Council.[63] This practice has been criticized as being 'politicized', which constitutes a valid critique to the extent that the Council indeed predetermined results in the way that it framed the questions. It must at least be conceded that this practice of the HRC is far from being generally accepted. But also on this question, it would be an oversimplification to consider this controversy as a North–South issue. On the other hand, the said practice of the HRC would not have been possible without strong support from the Global South.

The existing fact-finding institution, namely the International Humanitarian Fact-finding Commission established pursuant to Article 90 AP I, derives its obligatory competence from declarations made by parties to that treaty. Most states of the Global North and of Latin America have made such a declaration, some states of the African continent, too, yet next to no state of Asia (Japan belonging to the Global North).[64] There thus seems to be a kind of alliance between North and South on this fact-finding procedure. The reality, however, is somewhat different. The procedure has only been used once in the nearly 30 years of its existence, and the reasons lie in the widespread aversion of governments to independent and impartial fact-finding, mentioned above. This aversion is reflected in the withdrawal of the Article 90 Declaration by the Russian Federation in October 2019.

As to the third question, the impact of Global South positions in the process of universal IHL law-making, a differentiated approach is indicated. It has been shown in the answer to the

2019) 11 <https://rcrcconference.org/app/uploads/2019/10/33IC-IHL-Compliance-factual-report-_en.pdf> accessed 31 January 2021.

[58] ICRC and Swiss Federal Department of Foreign Affairs, 'Strengthening compliance with international humanitarian law: Draft resolution and concluding report' (October 2015) 32IC/15/19.2.

[59] UN Security Council Res 1595 (7 April 2005) UN Doc S/RES/1595.

[60] UN Human Rights Council, 'Ensuring respect for international law in the Occupied Palestinian Territory, including East Jerusalem' (23 July 2014) UN Doc A/HRC/RES/S-21/1.

[61] UN Human Rights Council, 'Technical assistance and capacity-building to improve human rights in Libya' (6 April 2015) UN Doc A/HRC/RES/28/30; UN Human Rights Council, 'Technical assistance and capacity-building to improve human rights in Libya' (22 March 2016) UN Doc A/HRC/31/L.20.

[62] UN Human Rights Council, 'The deteriorating situation of human rights in the Syrian Arab Republic, and the recent situation in Aleppo' (25 October 2016) UN Doc A/HRC/RES/S-25/1.

[63] The seats in the Council are distributed as follows: African states: 13 seats, Asia-Pacific states: 13 seats, Latin American and Caribbean states: 8 seats, Western European and other states: 7 seats, Eastern European states: 6 seats, see 'Membership of the Human Rights Council' (UN Human Rights Council) <http://www.ohchr.org/EN/HRBodies/HRC/Pages/Membership.aspx> accessed 31 January 2021.

[64] An up-to-date list of states having recognized the competence of the Commission is found on the Commission's website: 'State Parties' (International Humanitarian Fact-Finding Commission) <https://www.ihffc.org/index.asp?page=statesparties_list> accessed 31 January 2021.

second question that some of the concepts developed and put forward by states of the Global South have indeed been successful, but only some of them.

In conclusion, it can be said that the impact of the Global South on IHL law-making is a complex issue. The numeric majority of the states of the Global South makes it impossible to achieve any international consensus without the South concurring. Yet this voting superiority is counterbalanced by the economic and military superiority of the North. Together with the fact that both North and South are divided on a number of issues, this accounts for diverse negotiating processes. These processes are slow, as a consensus is difficult to achieve. It is not the North–South divide alone which makes the international problem-solving process inadequately slow. However, it is part of the problem.

20. Between war and peace: Negotiating and implementing legitimate ceasefire agreements

Cindy Wittke[1]

1. INTRODUCTION

This chapter focuses on contemporary practices of negotiating and implementing ceasefire agreements. Usually, these agreements constitute forms of politico-legal elite-driven settlements between the main parties to ongoing asymmetric violent conflicts. The negotiation and implementation of these agreements frequently include external actors, who often become effective third parties to these processes, e.g., international organizations or so-called 'groups of friends'. The challenges that arise during the negotiation, monitoring, and implementation of internationalized and legalized ceasefire agreements are at the centre of debates amongst practitioners and scholars of international politics and law alike.

Since the end of the Cold War at least 303 ceasefire agreements have been negotiated to address intra-state conflicts between state and non-state parties.[2] Recent examples include the protracted negotiation processes to reach a lasting ceasefire agreement for Syria and the debated Minsk I and II Agreements mediated by the so-called Normandy-Format addressing the conflict in the eastern regions of Ukraine.[3] These two example processes point us to the

[1] The author wants to thank Cedric Ryngaert, Astrid Jamar, and Lars Müller for their comments on earlier drafts of this chapter as well as the participants of the 'Legitimacy and Law-Making in International Humanitarian Law' conference, held at the Freie Universität Berlin, DFG Collaborative Research Centre 700, 26–28 November 2015, for inspiring comments and discussions.

[2] 'Language of Peace', a collaborative project of United Nations Peacemaker and the University of Cambridge's Legal Tools of Peacemaking project lists 303 ceasefire agreements under the combined search categories 'ceasefire/cessation of hostilities' and 'intra-state' <languageofpeace.org> accessed 31 January 2021.

[3] Christine Bell and others, 'PA-X Peace Agreement Database' (Political Settlements Research Programme University of Edinburgh 2019) <https://www.peaceagreements.org/search> accessed 31 January 2021 currently lists 46 documents that entail ceasefire provisions for Syria. UN Peacemaker lists the following documents addressing the conflict in the Eastern regions of Ukraine: Unilateral Plan of Peaceful Settlement of Situation in the Eastern Regions, President Petro Poroshenko, 20 June 2014; Memorandum on the Implementation of the Provisions of the Protocol on the Outcome of Consultations of the Trilateral Contact Group on Joint Steps Aimed at the Implementation of the Peace Plan (Implementation of the Minsk Agreement), 19 September 2014; Protocol on the results of consultations of the Trilateral Contact Group with respect to the joint steps aimed at the implementation of the Peace Plan of the President of Ukraine, P. Poroshenko, and the initiatives of the President of Russia, V. Putin, 5 September 2014 (date of signature) (quoted as: Minsk I Agreement); Package of measures for the

complex substantial as well as procedural dimensions of the negotiation, monitoring, and implementation processes of contemporary ceasefire agreements. Debates surrounding these processes are *inter alia* shaped by challenging questions concerning the inclusion and exclusion of different kinds of actor, the legal status and legitimacy of the direct parties to ceasefire agreements, the legal nature and status of obligations written into ceasefire agreements, the role of external actors as effective third parties in these processes, and the effects of ceasefire agreements on the regulation and/or sustainable settlement of ongoing intra-state conflicts.[4] The politico-legal debates around these questions are framed by what Christine Bell calls a 'lack of fit' of ceasefire and peace agreements. The expression 'lack of fit' illustrates the fact that ceasefire agreements 1) are negotiated in the grey zones between ongoing violent conflict, the end of violence, and the initiation of a sustainable peace process; that they 2) cannot easily be divided into legally binding and non-binding arrangements; and that they also 3) cannot be clearly accommodated by the spheres of either domestic or international law.[5] For all these reasons it is urgent to further investigate challenges of legitimacy in transitional post-conflict law-making focusing on the negotiation and implementation of ceasefire agreements as significant formalized events on the long continuum from regulating the ongoing conduct of a violent conflict to sustainable peace. To this end, the analysis will address mechanisms of inclusion and exclusion of actors, the status, mandate, legitimacy, and accountability of actors involved in the negotiation and implementation of ceasefire agreements, as well as legalized practices and internationalizing effects when negotiating and implementing ceasefire agreements from two broader perspectives. The first perspective comprises a discussion about the accommodation of ceasefire agreements between state and non-state parties into categories of international humanitarian law (IHL) and general international law. It focuses on the normative regulation of the ongoing violent intra-state conflict in which ceasefire

---

Implementation of the Minsk agreements, 12 February 2015 (quoted as: Minsk II Agreements or Minsk Package) <https://peacemaker.un.org/document-search> accessed 31 January 2021; see also Cindy Wittke, 'The Minsk Agreements: More than "Scraps of Paper"?' (2019) 35 East European Politics 264.

4 For example: Jean Arnault, 'Good Agreement? Bad Agreement? An Implementation Perspective' (Center of International Studies Princeton University 2006) <https://gsdrc.org/document-library/good-agreement-bad-agreement-an-implementation-perspective> accessed 31 January 2021; Roy Licklider, 'The Consequences of Negotiated Settlements in Civil Wars, 1945–1993' (1995) 89 American Political Science Review 681; Pieter Hendrik Kooijmans, 'The Security Council and Non-State Entities as Parties to Conflicts' in Karel Wellens (ed), *International Law, Theory and Practice, Essays in Honour of Eric Suy* (Martinus Nijhoff 1998); Fionnuala Ni Aolain, 'The Fractured Soul of the Dayton Peace Agreement: A Legal Analysis' (1998) 19 Michigan Journal of International Law 957; Christine Bell, *Peace Agreements and Human Rights* (OUP 2000); Roy Licklider, 'Obstacles to Peace Settlements' in Chester A. Crocker and others (eds), *Turbulent Peace, The Challenges of Managing International Conflict* (United States Institute of Peace Press 2001) 697; Virginia Page Fortna, 'Scraps of Paper? Agreements and the Durability of Peace' (2003) 57 International Organization 337; Christine Bell 'Peace Agreements: Their Nature and Legal Status' (2006) 100 American Journal of International Law 373; Ira William Zartman, 'The Timing of Peace Initiatives: Hurting Stalemates and Ripe Moments' in John Darby and Roger Mac Ginty (eds), *Contemporary Peacemaking: Conflict, Violence and Peace Processes* (Palgrave Macmillan 2003); Gabriella Blum, *Island of Agreement, Managing Enduring Armed Rivalries* (Harvard University Press 2007); Cindy Wittke, *Law in the Twilight: International Courts and Tribunals, the Security Council and the Internationalisation of Peace Agreements between State and Non-State Parties* (CUP 2018).

5 Bell, 'Peace Agreements: Their Nature and Legal Status' (n 4) 392; Christine Bell, *On the Law of Peace, Peace Agreements and the Lex Pacificatoria* (OUP 2008) 22.

agreements are negotiated and implemented as well as on the status of their direct state and non-state parties. The second perspective turns the focus towards the role of external actors in promoting and even effectively enforcing substantive and procedural standards for the negotiation and implementation of ceasefire agreements between state and non-state parties. The elaborations on both perspectives are framed by theoretically and empirically informed discussions about legality and legitimacy challenges that arise in the course of the negotiation, monitoring, and implementation of ceasefire agreements. Therewith the chapter will also connect to debates about the functional authority developed and exercised by the United Nations (UN) Security Council (UNSC) as norm-promoter and standard-setter in the transition from ongoing violent conflict to peace *inter alia* through so-called *ceasefire resolutions*. This international functional authority covers both the UNSC's practice to call upon, recommend, and demand ceasefires from the parties in its resolutions, as well as the UNSC's role as effective third party during the negotiation and implementation of ceasefire agreements through its resolutions. Thus, the involvement of the UN, and especially of the UNSC, in such complex peace processes can serve as a leading example for an international organization that acquired global functionalist authority, which it exercises during the negotiation and implementation of ceasefire agreements in order to regulate and terminate complex violent conflict settings involving state and non-state actors.[6] In the focus of the analysis, from a more general perspective, is the engagement of an international organization in the governance of peace and post-conflict law-making, based on its developed and practised functionalist and executive authority in conflict and post-conflict settings in which local actors do not have the capacity to agree on or implement a politico-legal settlement in terms of how to govern themselves on the long continuum from ongoing conflict to sustainable peace.[7] Moreover, focusing on global functionalist authority also raises the question: on which level can law-making, interpretation, and enforcement be located in the outlined settings? This question puts at the centre whether the direct parties to the agreement make, interpret, and enforce their ceasefire agreements, i.e., whether they are 'masters of the treaties' ('Herren der Verträge')? Or under which conditions the interpretation and enforcement of ceasefire agreements is elevated to the international level and in the end maybe even effectively appropriated by the UNSC through Chapter VII resolutions.

[6] Comment: Initially, legal research focused mostly on the UN's good office, and its role as mediator and facilitator of internationalized peace processes. This chapter's account of the role of international organizations like the UN in the negotiation and implementation of ceasefire agreements and the making of law in the transition from ongoing violent conflict to sustainable peace goes beyond perspectives on the UN's good office and its putative 'neutral' mediation and facilitation role as 'global guardian of peace'; see also: Cindy Daase, 'The Law of the Peacemaker: The Role of Mediators in Peace Negotiations and Lawmaking' (2012) 1 (3) Cambridge Journal of International and Comparative Law 107; Cindy Daase, 'The United Nations and the Secretary-General as Mediators and Norm-Promoters, Global Norms and Standards in the Mediation of Intra-State Conflicts' in Werner Gephart (ed), *Rechtsanalyse als Kulturforschung* (Verlag Vittorio Klostermann 2012); Wittke, *Law in the Twilight* (n 4).

[7] The term global functionalist authority is used in reference to Anne Orford, who states '(...) international executive rule works through local laws where possible, trumping them with administrative regulations and decrees where necessary to achieve the goals determined centrally', Anne Orford, *International Authority and the Responsibility to Protect* (CUP 2011) 203.

In order to address the above-raised question and to implement the outlined agenda, we will first discuss shared characteristics of contemporary ceasefire agreements between state and non-state parties (2). Next, we will contextualize the negotiation and implementation of ceasefire agreements by focusing especially on the classification of the ongoing violent conflict as intra-state and/or non-international armed conflict according to the Geneva Conventions (3). After concluding this section with an argument in favour of obtaining a broad understanding of complex intra-state conflicts as contexts of the negotiation and implementation of ceasefire agreements, we will turn to the challenge of whether or not internationalized ceasefire agreements can be considered international treaties, and thus sources of international law (4). In the last section (5), the chapter analyses the role of the UNSC when recommending and demanding ceasefires in UNSC resolutions; and when referring to the implementation of already established ceasefire agreements. This section will also investigate the effects of these forms of involvement on the internationalization and legalization of ceasefire agreements between state and non-state parties. These discussions will also address challenges surrounding legitimacy as well as questions around the localization of (transitional) post-conflict law-making and enforcement in ceasefire agreements in domestic and/or international law. The analysis concludes that the UNSC's involvement essentially contributes to an internationalized status of the non-state parties to ceasefire agreements and the obligations created by them for the purpose of the advancement of a peace process (6). In sum, the chapter puts a spotlight on the broader research agenda on internationalized and legalized peace agreements and political settlements between state and non-state parties. It underlines that contemporary ceasefire agreements are part of creating new spaces and forms of transitional law-making and governance in so-called areas of limited statehood in the struggle between ongoing conflict and reaching sustainable peace.

2. CONTEMPORARY CEASEFIRE AGREEMENTS ADDRESSING INTRA-STATE CONFLICTS

What are common characteristics of contemporary internationalized and legalized ceasefire agreements between state and non-state parties? How can we approach the legality and legitimacy of ceasefire agreements analytically?

First of all, there is no fixed legal definition of the term ceasefire.[8] Bell considers a contemporary ceasefire as a '(...) suspension of acts of violence by military and paramilitary forces, usually resulting from the intervention of a third party'.[9] Bell and O'Rourke additionally find

---

[8] 'Ceasefires are by no means a new concept within the international community and were traditionally used to denote an agreed temporary halt to armed hostilities so that each of the belligerent parties suspended their aggressive actions,' see Christian Henderson and Noam Lubell, 'The Contemporary Legal Nature of UN Security Council Ceasefire Resolutions' (2013) 26 Leiden Journal of International Law 369.

[9] Christine Bell, 'Ceasefire' (December 2009) in Rüdiger Wolfrum (ed), *Max Planck Encyclopedia of Public International Law* (online edn) para 1. See also Henderson and Lubell (n 8) 369; Comment: Taking a systematically different perspective, the Uppsala database defined a ceasefire agreement as an agreement that is regulating the behaviour of the warring parties without addressing the incompatibility. A ceasefire agreement that in fact addresses the incompatibility between the parties is considered to be a peace agreement in the context of the database, Department of Peace and Conflict Research, Uppsala Conflict Data Program (UCDP) (Uppsala University) <http://www.pcr.uu.se/research/ucdp/definitions>

that ceasefire agreements will often be connected to comprehensive framework peace agreements. Framework agreements can include and extend ceasefires, linking them effectively to new political and legal structures, through what is considered as a constitutional framework or new 'power map'.[10] Bell and O'Rourke's understanding finds empirical support.[11] The Peace Agreement Access Tool (PA-X) Database of the Political Settlements Research Program takes a first immanent empirical step in addressing the above outlined politico-legal challenges. The PA-X Database categorizes and codes more than 1,700 documents according to a refined politico-legal codebook informed by the broader understanding of the political settlement concept.[12] Broadly speaking, the PA-X divides ceasefires into two formal categories: 1) ceasefires as a type of agreements of their own, i.e., 'pure' ceasefire agreements, and 2) ceasefires that are included in another type of agreement, e.g., as part of a framework agreement listed for instance under the headline of 'security'. The database also enables the user to search for ceasefires and ceasefire provisions included in pre-negotiation, framework and implementation agreements. For the purpose of this chapter we can sum up that ceasefire agreements both stand alone in regulating ongoing violent intra-state conflicts, and constitute parts of other, for instance broader, framework agreements. Moreover, a ceasefire agreement can be between one or more state and non-state parties, recommended and imposed by the UNSC; they can be local – limited to certain geographic regions – or addressing a conflict across a broader territorial area; and they can be permanent or limited in their duration. When it comes to their substance, contemporary ceasefire agreements can amongst others include provisions addressing the withdrawal of forces to agreed-upon positions; disarmament; demobilization of fighters; rehabilitation and reintegration programmes for fighters; the restructuring of the entire police and security sector, including the identification of military and non-military prohibited acts, enforcement and monitoring mechanisms; and ad hoc provisions.[13] Thus, ceasefire agreements

---

accessed 31 January 2021; Bell, 'Ceasefire' (above) para 6, addressing the distinction between cessation of hostilities and ceasefire agreements.

10 For a definition of Framework Agreements that also informed the categorization of UN Peacemaker and of PA-X, see Bell, *Peace Agreements and Human Rights* (n 4) 25–26; Bell, *On the Law of Peace, Peace Agreements and the Lex Pacificatoria* (n 5) 60–61.

11 Christine Bell and Catherine O'Rourke, 'The People's Peace? Peace Agreements, Civil Society, and Participatory Democracy' (2007) 28 International Political Science Review 293; Bell, 'Ceasefire' (n 9) para 15: 'Non-international armed conflicts (…) tend to be resolved by negotiated settlements which aim to reach compromises that will put a permanent end to protracted social conflict. Ceasefire agreements in this context often operate not just to halt the violence but as pre-negotiation agreements which serve to frame and shape substantive negotiations.' Solomou finds that 'Peace agreements are agreements between parties to a violent conflict, which are designed to formally end a conflict. They are different from an armistice, which is an agreement to stop hostilities, or a ceasefire, in which parties agree to temporarily stop fighting. Contemporary peace agreements frequently go beyond the purpose of bringing a conflict to an end, encompassing provisions of increasing complexity covering a multiplicity of areas. For example, some peace agreements include governance provisions, aiming to set up a government of national unity. Other peace agreements are extensive and comprehensive to the point of providing the framework for the (re-)building of a state.' Alexia Solomou, 'Comparing the Impact of the Interpretation of Peace Agreements by International Courts and Tribunals on Legal Accountability and Legal Certainty in Post-Conflict Societies' (2014) 27 Leiden Journal of International Law 495, 498.

12 Christine Bell and others (n 3).

13 Bell, 'Ceasefire' (n 9) paras 16–17; see also Peace Agreements Database Search, UN Peacemaker <http://peacemaker.un.org/document-search?keys=&field_padate_value%5Bvalue%5D%5Bdate%5D

can be extensive, detailed and comprehensive in terms of outlining obligations they seek to establish for their parties.

In sum, ceasefire agreements under consideration in this chapter are agreements between at least one state and non-state party in written form. Often they are or become an integral part of a comprehensive or framework peace agreement.[14] Furthermore, ceasefire agreements of the outlined nature will in most cases constitute more than *modi operandi*. A *modus operandus* would only determine factual situations and give a framework for the actors' conduct in them, rather than being a result of the parties' consent and intent to negotiate a legally binding contractual arrangement, aiming for creating new obligations, or to settle legal disputes.[15] Consequently, legitimacy plays a less important role in the context of *modi operandi* compared to the negotiation and implementation of transitional arrangements like ceasefire agreements. Putting it differently, ceasefire agreements are formal politico-legal settlements that institutionalize ongoing dialogues between elites on the continuum between the regulation of a violent intra-state conflict and the transition towards a sustainable peace process.

These initial observations correspond with the assumption that internationalized ceasefire agreements between state and non-state parties share common procedural, structural, and formal features. First, ceasefire agreements between state and non-state parties are usually negotiated and implemented during ongoing violent intra-state conflicts, as well as against the background of a partly or fully collapsed intra-state politico-legal order, i.e., in what are considered *areas of limited statehood*.[16] Consequently, ceasefire agreements are extra-constitutional agreements. Conflict parties also use or instrumentalize the negotiation and implementation processes of such agreements to optimize their situation, e.g., for reaching concessions at the negotiation table.[17] These characteristics of the negotiation and implementation of ceasefire agreements come also with the risk of not clearly outlining and/or starting the political and legal settlement of a conflict. Instead, parties tend to inscribe what could be considered formalized politico-legal *un*settlements into these agreements. These *un*settlements

=&field_pacountry_tid=&field_paconflict_tid%5B%5D=1&field_pathematic_tid%5B%5D=35> accessed 31 January 2021.

14 Bell finds 'The term ceasefire, however, also finds a widespread usage in the context of non-international armed conflict, where ceasefires tend to be negotiated between State and non-State parties, and implemented by international actors including regional forces and the UN. These ceasefire agreements can be stand-alone as part of a peace process, or can be arrived at as part of a broader settlement, where the military agreement to halt violence is tied to provision of substantive new constitutional structures. Often parties will not agree to halt the military violence without some of the substance of the dispute being addressed.' See Bell, 'Ceasefire' (n 9) para 27.

15 Andrej Lang, 'Modus operandi and the ICJ's appraisal of the Lusaka Ceasefire Agreement in the Armed Activities Case: The Role of Peace Agreements in International Conflict Resolution' (2008) 40 New York University Journal of International Law & Politics 107; Margaret E. McGuinness, 'Case Concerning Armed Activities on the Territory of the Congo: The ICJ Finds Uganda Acted Unlawfully and Orders Reparations' (*American Society of International Law Insights*, 9 January 2006) <https://www.asil.org/insights/volume/10/issue/1/case-concerning-armed-activities-territory-congo-icj-finds-uganda-acted> accessed 31 January 2021; *Armed Activities on the Territory of the Congo (Democratic Republic of the Congo v Uganda)* (Judgment) [2005] ICJ Rep 168.

16 Concerning the definition and research on 'areas of limited statehood' see for instance: Stephen D. Krasner and Thomas Risse, 'External Actors, State-Building, and Service Provision in Areas of Limited Statehood: Introduction' (2014) 27 Governance 539.

17 Bell, 'Ceasefire' (n 9) paras 16–17.

frame and constrain future politico-legal settlement processes by effectively institutionalizing the conflict constellations and the incompatibilities between the parties into those continuous dialogue processes.[18] Second, throughout its practice, the UN has established a set of emerging authoritative norms and common elements influencing the negotiation of ceasefire agreements. Especially the UNSC has been involved as an active third party. Its involvement is based on its authority granted by the UN Charter and decades of executive practice. It frames the negotiation, drafting, and implementation of ceasefire agreements within a set of assumed and promoted international standards, norms, and rules. Moreover, the UNSC's involvement practice also leads to the regulation of the conflict, in case the UNSC finds that the parties to the conflict are not willing or not able to effectively negotiate and/or implement a lasting ceasefire agreement.[19] In all outlined settings, IHL, and international law in general, could provide legitimacy guidelines and yardsticks for the varying negotiation, drafting, and implementation processes of ceasefire agreements. A ceasefire may also be guided, externally decided upon, or even imposed on the parties to a protracted intra-state violent conflict by third parties with strong functional and executive authority. The most relevant examples for such a practice are resolutions of the UNSC addressing the negotiation and implementation of ceasefire agreements and so-called UNSC Ceasefires that call upon, recommend, demand, or endorse a ceasefire or that take recourse to the implementation of an already established ceasefire.[20] Hence, the UNSC's engagement constitutes the clearest form of international involvement and internationalization of ceasefire, or may even amount to legal interventionism. Third, reference to international law can be considered as one way in which the direct conflict parties and third parties seek to remedy objections concerning the legitimacy and even the legality of the negotiating state and non-state parties, their lacking direct accountability to constituencies, as well as regarding the legitimacy of institutions and processes written into formalized ceasefire agreements.[21]

---

[18] Christine Bell and Jan Posposil, 'Navigating Inclusion in Transitions from Conflict: The Formalised Political Unsettlement' (2017) 29 Journal of International Development 576.

[19] Bell, 'Ceasefire' (n 9) para 24.

[20] See also Olivier Corten and Anne Lagerwall, 'La violation d'un cessez-le-feu constitue-t-elle nécessairement une violation de l'article 2 § 4 de la charte des Nations Unies?' (2008) 61 Revue Hellénique de Droit International 87; There are very early examples of SC Ceasefires, and since the end of the Cold War the SC has additionally endorsed and pushed the establishment of ceasefires, in particular in *intra-state* violent conflict situations, addressing both state as well as non-state parties; see for instance UNSC Res 752 (15 May 1992) UN Doc S/RES/752; UNSC Res 941 (23 September 1994) UN Doc S/RES/941; UNSC Res 924 (1 June 1994) UN Doc S/RES/924; UNSC Res 1701 (11 August 2006) UN Doc S/RES/1701; see also Olivier Corten and Pierre Klein, 'Are Agreements between States and Non-State Entities Rooted in the International Legal Order?' in Enzo Cannizzaro (ed), *The Law of Treaties, Beyond the Vienna Convention* (OUP 2011) 3, 17; Nico Krisch, 'Art. 40' in Bruno Simma and others (eds), *The Charter of the United Nations, A Commentary*, vol 2 (3rd edn, OUP 2012) 1300, paras 8–9; Jochen A. Frowein, 'Art. 40' in Bruno Simma and others, *The Charter of the United Nations, A Commentary* (OUP 1994) 619, paras 9–10; 'Security Council Action Under Chapter VII: Myths and Realities no. 1' (*Security Council Report*, 23 June 2008) <https://www.securitycouncilreport.org/research-reports/lookup-c-glkwlemtisg-b-4202671.php> accessed 31 January 2021.

[21] More on this issue: Michal Saliternik, 'Reducing the Price of Peace: The Human Rights Responsibilities of Third-Party Facilitators' (2014) Global Trust Working Paper 2/2014 <http://globaltrust.tau.ac.il/publicationsISSN2309-7248> accessed 31 January 2021; Michal Saliternik, 'Perpetuating Democratic Peace: Procedural Justice in Peace Negotiations' (2016) 27 European Journal

These considerations raise the question of how to approach the concept of legitimacy within the context of contemporary ceasefire agreements' negotiation and implementation. Legitimacy can be understood as a multi-dimensional concept in which legal, normative, and empirical aspects of accepted and unaccepted uses of power can be differentiated. What can be considered as legitimate power?[22] We assume that those in power, i.e., the elite, who are the parties to ceasefire agreements in the given context, will seek to secure some consent concerning the legitimacy of their power and politico-legal agreements from at least the most important actors and groups among their subordinates or of the constituency they claim to represent.[23] According to Beetham, power can be considered to be legitimate to the extent that: 1) it is exercised in line with established rules; 2) that these rules can be justified by reference to beliefs, especially those shared by both dominants and subordinates; and 3) that there is evidence of consent by the subordinate to the particular power relation. Additionally, what counts as consent is a culturally specific matter, determined by the conventions of a given society. At the same time, no society can be characterized by a complete uniformity of beliefs.[24] Furthermore, both legitimacy and illegitimacy can materialize in all three outlined dimensions. They can also be realized to different degrees in ceasefire agreements' negotiation and implementation processes. In the end, Beetham finds '(…) the social scientist, in concluding that a given power relationship is legitimate, is making a *judgment*, not delivering a *report* about people's belief in legitimacy.'[25] Applying this perspective on legitimacy to the negotiation and implementation of ceasefire agreements leads to the concern that negotiation and implementation processes can be considered elite-driven institution-making processes that have to be in line with established rules that are shared and considered legitimate by all parties. Further, that these processes are capable of establishing mutually acceptable power relations, not only between the parties, but also among the subjects of the agreements. Given the abovementioned observations and the common characteristics of ceasefire agreements, these considerations indicate an assumed form of trust and belief in the legitimacy of international law and the functional authority of third parties in supporting and guiding the making of transformative law in, and through, ceasefire agreements. Consequently, legitimacy is aligned with the effective exercise of functional international public authority, which will be discussed in section 4

---

of International Law 617; Saliternik explores to whom, how, and by whom parties to peace negotiations can be held accountable; Levitt is in general sceptical when it comes to extra-constitutional arrangements between the state and what he labels 'warlords': Jeremy Levitt, 'Illegal Peace: An Inquiry into the Legality of Power-Sharing with Warlords and Rebels in Africa' (2006) 27 Michigan Journal of International Law 495; Jeremy Levitt, *Illegal Peace in Africa: An Inquiry into the Legality of Power Sharing with Warlords, Rebels, and Junta* (CUP 2012).

22 See from a general perspective David Beetham, *The Legitimation of Power* (Palgrave Macmillan 1991) 4–5.

23 See from a general perspective, ibid 3.

24 Beetham is highly critical when it comes to Weber's definition of legitimacy as 'belief in legitimacy' (Legitimitätsglauben) on the part of the relevant social agents; Beetham referring to Weber, ibid 6–7, 17. Additionally, legal validity is insufficient to secure legitimacy, since the rules through which power is acquired and exercised stand in need of justification (rightful source of authority). This is the second level of legitimacy: power is legitimate to the extent that the rules of power can be justified in term of beliefs shared by both dominant and subordinate, ibid 16–17, 19.

25 ibid 13.

of this chapter with the example of the engagement of the UNSC during the negotiation and implementation of ceasefire agreements.

In sum, the discussion of common characteristics of ceasefire agreements leads to the preliminary conclusion that the context surrounding the conflict between the parties to ceasefire agreements and/or locating political settlement processes between parties of intra-state conflicts on the continuum from conflict to a lasting peace, could prove crucial for evaluating the status of a ceasefire agreement as well as of the parties to ceasefire agreements, and in the end the obligations created by them with ceasefire agreements. Hence, the negotiation and implementation context of ceasefire agreements will be central to discussions in the following section.

3. CONTEXTUALIZING THE NEGOTIATION AND IMPLEMENTATION OF CEASEFIRE AGREEMENTS

What effect has the evaluation of the context in which ceasefire agreements are negotiated, for instance from an IHL perspective, on the legal status of the agreements; the parties of the agreements; and thus the transitional legal rules, rights and obligations created through them?

First of all, the negotiation and implementation of a ceasefire agreement does not effectively end an ongoing violent intra-state conflict. Nonetheless, it can frame the negotiation of a substantive and comprehensive peace agreement that seeks to terminate the violent conflict. The International Tribunal for the Former Yugoslavia (ICTY) found in *Prosecutor v Tadić* concerning the duration of armed conflicts, the application of IHL, and the point in time in which a situation of armed conflict is considered to have ended after the conclusion of an agreement:

> (…) an armed conflict exists whenever there is a resort to armed force between States or protracted armed violence between governmental authorities and organized armed groups or between such groups within a State. International humanitarian law applies from the initiation of such armed conflicts and extends beyond the cessation of hostilities until a general conclusion of peace is reached; or, in the case of internal conflicts, a peaceful settlement is achieved. Until that moment, international humanitarian law continues to apply in the whole territory of the warring States or, in the case of internal conflicts, the whole territory under the control of a party, whether or not actual combat takes place there.[26]

Hence, the ICTY appears to consider only a framework or comprehensive peace agreement that addresses the roots of a conflict aiming to terminate it as the moment in time in which the application of IHL should end. In the reverse conclusion ceasefire agreements are most likely to be negotiated in and addressing the context of the transformative grey zone between ongoing violent conflict and an effective peace process, in which IHL continues to apply.

Remaining within the context of IHL, Common Article 3 of the Geneva Conventions as well as Additional Protocols I and II seem to be of natural relevance for contextualizing the legal framework for the negotiation and implementation of ceasefire agreements between state and non-state parties and their potential law-making character. However, considering the possible variety of non-state parties to ceasefires, an exclusive IHL perspective could effectively limit the analysis to ceasefire agreements between state and non-state parties that seek

---

[26] *Prosecutor v Dusko Tadić* (Jurisdiction) ICTY IT-94-1-AR72 (2 October 1995) para 70.

self-determination and/or non-state parties that have a form of organization compatible with the military-like command structure. Nevertheless, it is opportune to discuss whether ceasefire agreements between parties in intra-state conflict constellations that could be categorized as non-international armed conflicts can be considered a form of *special agreements* in accordance with Common Article 3(3) of the Geneva Conventions. The notion of special agreements is broad and covers any agreement that brings into force (additional) humanitarian law norms. Special agreements are, for instance, agreements between the conflicting state/*de iure* government and non-state party through which humanitarian law norms other than those contained in Common Article 3 are brought into force. However, when it comes to the international legal or law-making nature of these agreements, Common Article 3 clearly states that the application of the provisions of Article 3(3) 'shall not affect the legal status of the parties to the conflict'. Moreover, the International Committee of the Red Cross' Commentary states that 'special agreements' '(...) will generally only be concluded because of an existing situation which neither of the parties can deny'.[27] According to this perspective, *special agreements* rather appear to have the character of *modi operandi*. Thus, they would not constitute consent-based treaties and forms of consensual law-making between the conflicting parties, which would create new and extend binding rules and obligations for the parties to govern their future relations. Zegveld, however, considers *special agreements* concluded between the state and armed opposition groups, as well as between different armed opposition groups, as binding agreements in accordance with Article 3 of the Vienna Convention on the Law of Treaties (VCLT), referring in particular to 'the practice of international bodies' in concluding such agreements. Consequently, Zegveld also must assume at least a certain limited legal subjectivity and treaty-making capacity for armed groups in relation to non-international armed conflicts in the scope of Common Article 3 of the Geneva Conventions. Yet, to base this blanket assumption concerning the legal subjectivity and treaty-making capacity of armed opposition groups on Common Article 3 would ignore that Common Article 3 'shall not affect the legal status of the parties to the conflict'. Zegveld's standpoint is, nevertheless, confirmed by Moir, who finds that this formula was a false attempt 'to safeguard the legal status of the *de iure* government', because the inclusion of a provision like Common Article 3 in an international convention would automatically give the insurgents a status as high as the legal status which is denied to them.[28] Moreover, Moir and Zegveld are confirmed by Sivakumaran, who comes to the conclusion that '[b]ilateral agreements concluded between the warring parties are particularly important given the equality of obligation that arises through the agreement.'[29] Yet, Sivakumaran convincingly adds that '[t]he language used in these agreements is of particular interest. The parties "reiterate", "reconfirm", and "reaffirm" their obligations, all of which suggest that the relevant human rights obligations are not being created by the agreement but existed even prior to the conclusion of the agreement.'[30] In sum, from a broader ceasefire and

---

27 Jean Pictet (ed), *Commentary to Convention (III) relative to the Treatment of Prisoners of War. Geneva, 12 August 1949* (ICRC 1960), commentary on art 3, 43.

28 Lindsay Moir, *The Law of Internal Armed Conflict* (CUP 2002) 65.

29 Liesbeth Zegveld, *Accountability of Armed Opposition Groups in International Law* (CUP 2002) 28, 30; Sandesh Sivakumaran, *The Law of Non-International Armed Conflict* (OUP 2012) 133.

30 Sivakumaran (n 29) 132; additionally, concerning the categorization of peace agreements and ceasefires as domestic agreements that refer to international law (human rights, IHL) but are not governed by international law, see Corten and Klein (n 20) 13.

peace agreement perspective, Common Article 3 as well as the Protocols I and II can only serve as one possible reference point for the analysis of their legality and legitimacy, as well as for the localization of consensual law-making by parties of ceasefire agreements. Additionally, the limitation of a synonymous usage of the terms 'intra-state' with 'non-international armed conflict' would lead to overlooking the role that third parties play for the establishment, negotiation, and implementation of ceasefire agreements between state and non-state parties and the implications on (consensual) law-making, especially by the direct state and non-state parties to the conflict and ceasefire agreement. In conclusion, the chapter does not use the terms intra-state conflict and non-international armed conflict interchangeably. Instead, the analysis is guided by post-modern and post-national understandings of intra-state conflict constellations that are distinctive of the inter- and intra-state conflicts/wars of classical modernity. This perspective is additionally closely related to questions regarding the (functional) authority to make ceasefire agreements and regarding who can make authoritative decisions concerning their interpretation and implementation.

Current debates in social sciences use terms like 'new wars',[31] 'asymmetric conflict', 'extra-systemic conflict', 'civil war' or 'internal conflict' to address the outlined conflict constellations.[32] These categories for describing and analysing post-modern conflict constellations from an international relations perspective have in common that these conflicts are characterized as having their core at the local, domestic level while having at the same time an internationalized transnational dimension. They acknowledge international and transnational connections and the involvement of external actors in the outlined processes so that the 'distinctions' between internal and external aggression (attacks from abroad) and repression (attacks from inside the country), or even between local, domestic, regional and international spheres are impossible to draw or sustain.[33] Thus, in post-modern/post-national conflict con-

---

[31] Kaldor claims in her seminal book *New and Old Wars* that in the course of the past decades after the end of the Cold War a new type of 'organized violence developed', especially in Africa and Eastern Europe, which she calls 'new wars'. The term is used to distinguish these conflicts from prevailing perceptions of war drawn from earlier times. Yet, Kaldor also acknowledges certain validity in the arguments raised by critics of the 'new era argument' who have suggested that many features of the so-called 'new wars' can be equally identified in earlier wars and additionally that the dominance of the Cold War between the two superpowers overshadowed the number and significance of small wars or 'low-intensity conflicts', Mary Kaldor, *New and Old Wars, Organized Violence in a Global Era* (2nd edn, Stanford University Press 2007) 1–3.

[32] Bell on the use the term 'civil war', see Bell, *On the Law of Peace, Peace Agreements and the Lex Pacificatoria* (n 6) 49–50; for broad overviews on civil wars from various perspectives see: Paul Collier and Anke Hoeffler 'On Economic Causes of Civil War' (1998) 50 Oxford Economic Papers 563; Christopher Daase, *Kleine Kriege – Große Wirkung, Wie unkonventionelle Kriegsführung die internationale Politik verändert* (Nomos 1999); Samuel P. Huntington, *The Clash of Civilizations and the Remaking of World Order* (Simon & Schuster 2002); Herfried Münkler, *Die neuen Kriege* (Rowohlt 2002); Monika Heupel and Bernhard Zangl 'Vom „alten" zum „neuen" Krieg – Zum Gestaltwandel kriegerischer Gewalt' (2004) 45 Politische Vierteljahresschrift 346; Sven Chojnacki, 'Wandel der Kriegsformen? Ein kritischer Literaturbericht' (2004) 32 Leviathan 402; Ulrich Schneckener, 'Fragile Staatlichkeit als globales Sicherheitsrisiko' (2005) 26 Aus Politik und Zeitgeschichte 28–9; Sven Chojnacki, 'Auf der Suche nach des Pudels Kern: Alte und neue Typologien in der Kriegsforschung' in Dietrich Beyrau and others (eds), *Formen des Krieges: von der Antike bis zur Gegenwart* (Schöningh 2007) 479; Sabina Ferhadbegović and Brigitte Weiffen, 'Erleben – Darstellen – Bewältigen: Eine kulturwissenschaftliche Perspektive auf den Bürgerkrieg' (2012) 1 Zeitschrift für Friedens- und Konfliktforschung 187, 188–89.

[33] Kaldor (n 31) 2–3.

stellations, the classic distinctions between internal and external, war and peace, aggression and repression seem to be blurred legally and to break down politically.[34]

For Kaldor, the key to the regulation as well as termination of *new wars* is the reconstruction of legitimacy. Partly resonating with Beetham's conceptualization outlined above, Kaldor understands legitimacy as a form of consent concerning the support of political institutions that acquire their authority on the basis of operating within an agreed set of rules.[35] Pushing this assumption one step further, ceasefire agreements, and especially peace agreements between state and non-state parties, can be considered as seeking to re-create or newly establish this kind of legitimacy through the codified consent of direct and third parties. Through mutually agreed authoritative standards and rules, the parties of the ongoing conflict strive to create new (transitional) law as well as to reinvoke existing law in extra-constitutional arrangements. In sum, ceasefire and peace agreements could be considered as creating a form of agreed rule of law on the continuum from ongoing armed conflict to sustainable peace. What remains opaque, though, is the source of the imagined legitimacy of the direct parties to conflicts and ceasefire agreements. It also remains opaque who the parties' constituency is, which they are assumed to represent as well as to whom the parties are accountable in negotiation and implementation processes. Consequently it also remains opaque what kind of obligations the parties create based on which legal regime(s). The outlined puzzle leads to two interrelated questions: what kind of contractual arrangements and laws are created by ceasefire agreements? And could the law-making capacity and practice of ceasefire agreements and their state and non-state parties be located in the realm of international treaty law?

4. CEASEFIRE AGREEMENTS AS INTERNATIONAL TREATIES?

Can contemporary internationalized and legalized ceasefire agreements be considered international treaties and thus, sources of international law in accordance with Article 38 of the International Court of Justice's (ICJ) Statute?[36] To put it shortly, ceasefire agreements between state and non-state parties are not treaties according to Article 2(1)(a) of the Vienna Convention on the Law of Treaties.[37] The 1969 VCLT applies only to treaties between states, concluded after its entry into force in 1980.[38] Moreover, the expressed intent of the state party to enter into a binding agreement – governed by international law – could be considered as a determinant of the legal status of an agreement, of its parties, and the nature of the obligations created by it. This intent can also be expressed in the factual choice of using strongly

---

34 ibid 2, 122–23; see again overview by Ferhadbegović and Weiffen (n 32) 188–89.

35 Kaldor (n 31) 122–23.

36 Statute of the International Court of Justice (adopted 26 June 1945, entered into force 24 October 1945) 33 UNTS 993.

37 '(…) "treaty" means an international agreement concluded between States in written form and governed by international law, whether embodied in a single instrument or in two or more related instruments and whatever its particular designation; (…)', art 2(1)(a) VCLT.

38 Kirsten Schmalenbach, 'Article 3' in Oliver Dörr and Kirsten Schmalenbach (eds), *Vienna Convention on the Law of Treaties, A Commentary* (Springer 2012) 50, para 3; Philippe Gautier, 'Art. 2, 1969 Vienna Convention', in Olivier Corten and Pierre Klein (eds), *The Vienna Conventions on the Law of Treaties, A Commentary* (OUP 2011) 36, paras 10, 37, 12.

legalized – obligatory and precise – language and form.[39] Yet, to be more than a one-sided declaration of the state party to a ceasefire agreement, the non-state party must also have a certain treaty-making capacity. Thus, a non-state party should be able to be held accountable for its expressed intent to be bound by, and to enforce, a ceasefire agreement and/or peace agreement whose negotiation and implementation is governed by international law. Article 3 of the VCLT opens the door for a discussion as to whether a ceasefire agreement between state and non-state parties that are (partly) subjects of international law with a treaty-making capacity can be accommodated under customary international treaty law. Yet, Article 3 does not provide for a definition or concrete list of what it calls 'other subjects of international law'.[40] In sum, the developing practice of negotiating, monitoring, and implementing internationalized and legalized ceasefire agreements as part of the broader context of peace agreements between state and non-state parties indicates that the circle of actors whose interactions are relevant on the domestic and international plane for the creation and making of (transitional) law is broadening. Moreover, even if ceasefire or peace agreements between state and non-state parties will mostly not constitute international treaties and thus sources of international law, their factual existence constitutes new practices of transitional post-conflict law-making, posing new challenges of legality and legitimacy evaluation, which can be, in one form or another, governed by international (treaty) law. In other words, international law is shaping the practice of different actors involved in the negotiation and implementation of ceasefire and peace agreements in intra-state post-conflict settings. Hence, ceasefire agreements are hybrid politico-legal sources of law 'floating' in the twilight between domestic and international law without becoming a clear source of international law in accordance with Article 38 ICJ Statute. These practices lead to the phenomenon that internationalized ceasefire agreements between state and non-state parties, like comprehensive internationalized peace agreements, are *de facto* interpreted in accordance with the rules of interpretation of international treaty law.[41]

---

[39] See also the literature on the concept of legalization and its adaptation by Bell for approaching peace agreements: Kenneth W. Abbott and others, 'The Concept of Legalization' (2000) 54 International Organization 401; Bell, *Peace Agreements and Human Rights* (n 4) 79–80; Bell, *On the Law of Peace, Peace Agreements and the Lex Pacificatoria* (n 5) 144–45.

[40] Schmalenbach (n 38) 50 para 3; Yves Le Bouthillier and Jean-Francois Bonin, 'Art. 3, 1969 Vienna Convention', in Olivier Corten and Pierre Klein (eds), *The Vienna Conventions on the Law of Treaties, A Commentary* (OUP 2011) 3–24, 66–67 paras 1–2, 68 para 6; Comment: Obviously, also the Vienna Convention on the Law of Treaties between States and International Organizations or between International Organizations (VCLTO) would not be directly applicable to peace agreements between state and non-state parties, as these non-state parties are not international organizations like the UN. The UN for instance is often a third party to those agreements if not a direct party. Hence, a search for an analogy in the VCLTO would be weak. Additionally, art 3 VCLTO would have similar implications for the discussion as art 3 VCLT, cf Bouthillier and Bonin, 'Art. 3, 1969 Vienna Convention' (cited above) 71–75 paras 15–25.

[41] See for instance the Abyei Award in which the arbitral tribunal applied the Vienna Convention's rules of treaty interpretation to the Comprehensive Peace Agreements between Sudan and the Sudanese People's Liberation Movement/Army (SPLM/A) of 2005, Comprehensive Peace Agreement between the Government of Sudan and the SPLM/SPLA (with Annexes) (09 January 2005) <http://peacemaker.un.org/node/1369> accessed 31 January 2021; Cindy Daase, 'The Abyei Dispute Between Sudan and South Sudan, The Role of Arbitration in Peace and Secession Processes' in Thilo Marauhn and Hatem Elliesie (eds), *Legal Transformation in Northern Africa and the South Sudan* (Eleven International Publishing 2015) 149; Cindy Daase, 'Peace Agreements between State and Non-State Parties and Alternative

This argumentation underlines the abovementioned legitimacy perspective of international law's factual authority and guiding role in the negotiation, interpretation, and implementation of ceasefire agreements. In sum, the outlined practice, again, points to the analytical challenge of where we can localize the practised authority of this international guidance and interpretation and therewith of who has the authority for creating ceasefire agreements, as well as the authority for deciding who interprets and implements them.

5. SECURITY COUNCIL RESOLUTIONS AND CEASEFIRE AGREEMENTS

As pointed out above, the UN, and especially the UNSC, have developed a form of international authority when it comes to their involvement during the negotiation and implementation of ceasefire agreements to settle intra-state conflicts. This involvement can take the form of 1) UNSC resolutions addressing the negotiation and implementation processes of ceasefire agreements, and 2) UNSC resolutions actually entailing the ceasefire or ceasefire arrangements themselves as a form of obligation addressing the parties to the conflict. Thus, which effects do the two forms of involvement of the UNSC have on the nature and status of ceasefire agreements, their parties, and the legal obligations created through them? How does the functional authority, which the UNSC exercises during its involvement in the negotiation, monitoring, and implementation of ceasefire agreements, affect the legal status and perceived legitimacy of ceasefire agreements and ongoing political settlements? There are two possible forms of UNSC involvement that could affect law-making through ceasefire agreements between state and non-state parties. Since the formation of the UN, and especially since the end of the Cold War, the UN, and especially the UNSC, has developed a practice of what could be called Security Council Ceasefire Resolutions.[42] UNSC resolutions *call upon*, *recommend*, or *demand* the relevant parties involved in a violent intra-state conflict to come to a ceasefire that is directly or implicitly outlined by the UNSC's resolution, and resolutions that decide on measures to effectively implement or enforce ceasefires and ceasefire agreements.[43] The outlined forms of involvement of the UNSC raise the question of whether the UNSC – as an organ of the UN with the main responsibility for international peace and security – exercises a functional authority, in particular through Chapter VII resolutions, that take partly or entirely the *de facto* and *de iure* function of a negotiated ceasefire between the direct parties

---

Dispute Settlement, Lessons Learned from the Abyei Arbitration' (2013) 46 Verfassung und Recht in Übersee 152.

[42] Henderson and Lubell (n 8) 369.

[43] The chapter follows Henderson and Lubell, who argue that: '[...] the term "ceasefire" does not necessarily specifically need to be expressly mentioned in the particular resolution for it to be classed as a "ceasefire resolution". Furthermore the resolution does not need to have the provision regarding the ceasefire as its primary purpose, ie, included in the first operative paragraph of the resolution. It may equally be included later in the resolution. In addition, some ceasefire resolutions require that the parties abide by a particular ceasefire that has already been agreed to by the parties, whereas others might include a general urge for the parties to lay down their arms. Lastly, the UNSC employs different ways of expressing that it requires a ceasefire; most commonly it "calls for" or "calls upon" the parties concerned to cease their fire, but it also "urges", "appeals", and "demands" for such a ceasefire to be implemented. The important characteristic, however, is that there is a clear message by the UNSC that the warring parties should indeed cease their fire.' See ibid 370.

to an intra-state conflict and ceasefire agreement. These observations consequently lead to the question of what is then the relationship between UNSC resolutions outlining a ceasefire and an actual ceasefire agreement that was concluded as a contractual arrangement by state and non-state parties themselves? Where can the effective authority and binding act of law-making and the obligations created for the actors involved be located, i.e., who has the authority to make ceasefire agreements/create obligations through and based on ceasefire agreements, and who has the authority to interpret and enforce these agreements throughout the multi-layered processes?

First of all, the UNSC developed a practice to refer to existing ceasefire agreements to address threats of peace through intra-state conflict situations. The UNSC refers to the compliance of the parties, finds violations, and takes sanction measures that in fact eventuate as enforcement measures. Both forms of UNSC involvement that are presented as two distinct forms of involvement can come together in one conflict setting; they cannot be entirely separated from each other and trigger the same set of questions as outlined above. Nevertheless, it remains to be seen whether the answers to these questions are the same for both scenarios and forms of UNSC involvement. Addressing the above raised questions demands examining the authority, mandate and competency of the UNSC to get involved in these processes.

Within the UN system, the UNSC's primary responsibility is to maintain international peace and security. For peacefully settling inter-state and increasingly also intra-state conflicts, the UNSC developed a practice to call upon, recommend, and demand the parties to a conflict to maintain or agree upon a ceasefire.[44] Often this has been used as an emergency appeal by the UNSC in a situation that either 'endangered' or 'threatened' peace.[45] There are early examples in which the UNSC became active in putting an end to fighting and creating a ceasefire. The earliest and maybe most prominent example was the attempt of the UNSC to end the fighting in the Palestine War of 1948.[46]

If the UNSC determines a 'threat to peace', 'breach of the peace', or 'act of aggression' is occurring in accordance with Article 39 UN Charter, it can *inter alia* make recommendations, order provisional measures, or take non-military or military sanction and effective enforcement measures according to the particular situation. It is also widely assumed that those measures are not only binding for the Member States of the UN, but that they can also bind or at least affect the behaviour of other actors, as for instance non-state parties to conflicts

---

[44] Sydney D. Bailey, 'Cease-Fires, Truces, and Armistices in the Practice of the UN Security Council' (1997) 71 American Journal of International Law 461, 463; Henderson and Lubell (n 8) 369–70; see for instance Ceasefire Agreement between the Government of Sierra Leone and RUF, Abuja/Nigeria (10 November 2000) <http://www.sierra-leone.org/ceasefire1100.html> accessed 31 January 2021; and UNSC Res 1334 (22 December 2000) UN Doc S/RES/1334; Peace Agreement between the Government of Liberia, the Liberians United for Reconciliation and Democracy, the Movement for Democracy in Liberia and the Political Parties, Accra/Ghana (18 August 2003), UN Doc S/2003/850 (29 August 2003).

[45] These 'calls' are often accompanied, or quickly followed, by a request to a subsidiary organ or mandate for a Special Envoy or Representative to try to mediate a more sustainable, comprehensive and durable peace agreement between the parties (of inter- and intra-state conflicts); see Bailey (n 44) 463–64; Daase, 'The Law of the Peacemaker' (n 4) 107.

[46] Back then the SC used various terms and formulations when calling for a cessation of violent and military actions, eg UNSC Res 42 (5 March 1948) UN Doc S/RES/42; UNSC Res 43 (1 April 1948) UN Doc S/RES/43; UNSC Res 53 (15 July 1948) UN Doc S/RES/54; UNSC Res 62 (16 November 1948) UN Doc S/RES/62; Bailey (n 44) 463–66; Kooijmans (n 4) 334.

and peace agreements.[47] The UNSC has also developed the practice to determine intra-state conflict situations to be threats to peace under Article 39 UN Charter, especially since the end of the Cold War.[48] Furthermore, so-called UNSC Ceasefire resolutions under Chapter VII UN Charter are passed when the parties to a conflict are so entrenched in their position, or there is such a high level of distrust, that direct negotiations either cannot be sustained or are not achievable.[49] With these measures the UNSC apparently seeks to create – based on its mandate and authoritative practice – a situation in which the peaceful settlement and the transformation from conflict to a peace process becomes binding and obligatory for the parties.

These intensive forms of involvement of the UNSC raise concerns as to whether an exclusively externally initiated ceasefire can lead to a negotiated comprehensive agreement between the direct parties to an intra-state conflict and then to a sustainable peace process through the implementation of such an agreement. Authors ranging in their analytical perspectives have even blamed the UNSC of having prolonged and fuelled fighting with its ceasefire resolutions in some instances.[50] They argue that an externally created, ordered, or imposed ceasefire can, in some situations, grant the parties time to rest to prepare new attacks and acts of aggression,[51] instead of fulfilling the UNSC's expressed desire to avoid further human suffering and violations of IHL.[52] Hence, the assumption seems opportune that an effective ceasefire – following

---

47 Arts 40, 41, 42 UN Charter, for an overview: Krisch, 'Art. 40' (n 20) (2012) 1297; Krisch, 'Art. 41' in Simma and others (n 20) (2012) 1305; Krisch, 'Art. 42' in Simma and others (n 20) (2012) 1330.

48 It remains disputed as to whether and how the SC has to at least indicate that an intra-state conflict has implications for the regional/international level. In the early 1990s Frowein saw that at least the indicated internationalized dimension of a violent conflict as a prerequisite for the application of art 39 UN Charter. However, when it came to the determination of a 'threat to peace', he admitted that: 'With the end of the Cold War, the opportunities open to the SC under Art. 39 UN Charter have become much greater. It seems now to be accepted that extreme violence within a state can generally be qualified as a threat to peace.' See Frowein, 'Art. 39' in Simma and others (n 20) (1994) 608–609 paras 5–8, 611 para 19 (with examples); the 'double strategy' of combining an intra-state conflict and an international/regional threat to peace was also visible in the cases of Angola, Liberia and Sierra Leone, Erika de Wet, *The Chapter VII Powers of the United Nations Security Council* (Hart Publishing 2004) 155; and Nolte finds: 'Since the adoption under Chapter VII of S/RES/792 on Somalia, it has been generally accepted that even a situation which causes no physical repercussions abroad may nonetheless constitute as threat to the peace in the sense of Art. 39.' Georg Nolte, 'Purposes and Principles, Art. 2 (7)' in Bruno Simma and others (eds), *The Charter of the United Nations, A Commentary,* vol 1 (3rd edn, OUP 2012) 301 para 51; Nolte also added: 'Some States, however, have insisted that sanctions should not be tools for interventions in matters within the domestic jurisdiction of States or "should not become a method – more or less covert – of intervening in affairs that fall essentially within the domestic jurisdiction of States."' Nolte, ibid 310–11, paras 73–75. Altogether, this reflects the ambiguities of the SC's involvement in intra-state conflict and post-conflict settings which constitute a 'threat to peace'; in her book de Wet sees the 'double strategy' and 'negative peace concept' confirmed, which also means that the SC's powers to determine a threat to peace are not unlimited, and also no *ultra vires* actions, see de Wet (cited above) 175; Niels M. Blokker and Marieke Kleiboer, 'The Internationalization of Domestic Conflict: The Role of the UN Security Council' (1996) 9 Leiden Journal of International Law 7, 32–33.

49 For example, UNSC Res 1701 (11 August 2006) UN Doc S/RES/1701; Security Council Report (n 20).

50 Rather extreme example: Edward Luttwak, 'Give War a Chance' (1999) 78 (4) Foreign Affairs 36; Henderson and Lubell (n 8) 369–70.

51 Luttwak (n 50) 36–44.

52 See for instance UNSC 752 (15 May 1992) UN Doc S/RES/752; UNSC Res 941 (23 September 1994) UN Doc S/RES/941; UNSC Res 924 (1 June 1994) UN Doc S/RES/924; UNSC Res 1701 (11

a contractual idea – would still require a certain degree of mutual agreement. Such a consensus between the conflict parties on the terms of the ceasefire could also include the mandate and the composition of a UN Mission, which usually goes hand in hand with such a UNSC resolution to monitor the implementation of the ceasefire and the support of negotiating a more comprehensive agreement that terminates the conflict. This is, of course, an idealized and, thus, simplified scenario. On the ground, in intra-state conflict situations which endanger or 'threaten the peace', the UNSC faces much more complicated constellations between the conflicting state and non-state parties, which decisively influence whether a UNSC ceasefire is effectively implemented and the negotiation process of a durable and comprehensive peace agreement and peace process commenced.[53]

In sum, in its practice of dealing with intra-state conflicts and ceasefire agreements between state and non-state parties, the UNSC tends to guide, supervise, govern, and even effectively enforce the implementation of ceasefire agreements between state and non-state parties and certain obligations created by them. Thus, the UNSC acts as a rule-promoter and norm-proliferator during the implementation of peace agreements with a view to guarantee and advance the peace process.[54] All in all, when it comes to ceasefire and peace agreements between state and non-state parties, the UNSC takes part in the broader law-making and law-enforcing exercise in intra-state post-conflict settings in the form of executive regulations relying on its functional and executive authority based on its Chapter VII practice.

It still remains to be discussed whether Chapter VII resolutions are binding for the non-state parties to conflicts and ceasefire agreements, in particular whether they can in fact affect the status and behaviour of non-state parties in violent intra-state conflicts and during the negotiation and implementation of internationalized ceasefire agreements between state and non-state parties. As shown earlier, since its establishment and increasingly since the end of the Cold War, the UNSC has addressed not only inter- but also intra-state conflicts as a threat to international and regional peace and has taken measures under Chapter VII UN Charter. With respect to entities other than states, there are numerous examples in which the UNSC has addressed its demands and targeted its sanction and enforcement measures directly to non-state actors and individuals in endangered peace processes, especially by referring to

---

August 2006) UN Doc S/RES/1701; Ceasefire Agreement between the Government of Sierra Leone and RUF, Abuja/Nigeria (10 November 2000) <http://www.sierra-leone.org/ceasefire1100.html> accessed 31 January 2021; and UNSC Res 1334 (22 December 2000) UN Doc S/RES/1334; Peace Agreement between the Government of Liberia, the Liberians United for Reconciliation and Democracy, the Movement for Democracy in Liberia and the Political Parties, Accra/Ghana (18 August 2003), UN Doc S/2003/850 (29 August 2003).

[53] This analysis echoes some points of Henderson and Lubell (n 8) 369–70, which complements and confirms the here presented line of argumentation and developed positions in most parts; see also Michael Wood, 'The Law of Treaties and the UN Security Council: Some Reflections' in Enzo Cannizzaro (ed), *The Law of Treaties Beyond the Vienna Convention* (OUP 2011) 244, 245–46.

[54] At the same time the SC protected or respectively reaffirmed the sovereignty of the state, for instance by referring to the establishment of authority of the government to control the exploitation of natural resources; a government, which usually was established in the course of the implementation of an internationalized peace agreement, see Jeremy Farrall, *United Nations Sanctions and the Rule of Law* (CUP 2007) 33; concerning the tendency of the SC to contribute through its measures to long-term institution-building, see Krisch, 'Art. 41' (n 47) 1313–14 para 17, 1322–24 paras 30–33, 1328 para 42; Krisch 'Art. 42' (n 47) 1346–48 paras 29–32.

ceasefire and peace agreements. This includes armed groups, *de facto* governments and political factions. Confronted with defiance to its demands from such actors, the UNSC has, in some cases, decided to impose sanctions.[55] There are clear cases in which the UNSC has addressed intra-state conflict situations and the non-state parties involved. Still, uncertainty remains regarding the binding effect of Chapter VII resolutions on the non-state parties: are UNSC demands directed at them binding for them? The language used by the UNSC in different cases seems to suggest this.[56] Already in the 1994 UN Charter Commentary, Frowein finds that: 'In the situation of civil war the SC has addressed resolutions under Chapter VII to the parties of the dispute. It would seem that parties fighting a civil war within a member state are subject to the jurisdiction of the SC.'[57] Other authors argue that non-state entities/parties to peace agreements who are clearly neither states nor members of the UN could be considered as bound by those UNSC measures under Chapter VII because they are located (in one form or another) in a member state. Hence, they would be also subject to Chapter VII enforcement mechanisms in an all-inclusive manner. From this perspective the UNSC could adopt more refined and targeted sanction and enforcement measures that only affect part of the member state's territory and/or certain entities located therein.[58]

There is an established debate about whether or not UNSC resolutions, which cannot be considered as adopted under Chapter VII, either for lack of necessary determination or for failure to spell out their enforcement character, create binding decisions. It is beyond the scope of this chapter to present and discuss this debate in depth. The focus will be rather on the finding that the 'Chapter VII chapeau' seems not so much applied by the UNSC for the purpose of giving clear evidence of its intent to make certain parts of a resolution binding and obligatory under Chapter VII, but rather for mainly political and rhetorical purposes, i.e., in the attempt to first of all create political pressure for the targeted actors to change their undesired behaviour, and to hint at possibly more intensive measures in case of non-compliance.[59] This perspective turns our focus to the question of how to interpret UNSC resolutions, and whether all UNSC resolutions, and not necessarily only those under Chapter VII, can include obligatory

---

55 The SC has in various cases targeted individuals as well. In some instances, this occurred through the freezing of bank accounts or travel bans on specific individuals, sometimes through explicit demands to surrender named persons. The SC thereby subjected them to enforcement measures through intermediary state action. In the context of peace agreements between state and non-state parties, this is especially relevant when it comes to the leadership of the state and non-state parties to the agreement, see Krisch, 'Introduction to Chapter VII, The General Framework' in Simma and others (n 20) (2012) 1249–51 paras 27–30, 1270–71 paras 68–69; Whether emerging states or breakaway territories continue to be non-state entities or whether they could be treated like states remains a 'grey zone' of discussion. Such questions may emerge in the future, particularly in light of the status of Kosovo or Palestine, see also Security Council Report (n 20) 13.

56 Krisch, 'Introduction to Chapter VII, The General Framework' (n 55) 1270–71 paras 68–69.

57 Frowein, 'Art. 39' (n 20) 616 para 38; Farrall (n 54) 334–35, 357–68; de Wet concerning the Angolan example: '(…) it was the first time that the Security Council took sides in a domestic conflict, by imposing mandatory sanctions against a specific group within a state, as opposed to against the state itself.', de Wet (n 48) 164, 182.

58 de Wet (n 48) 182; see also 164, 254; additionally concerning 'smart' and 'targeted' sanctions, see Krisch, 'Art. 41' (n 47) 1308–309 paras 4–6.

59 Security Council Report (n 20) 4, 29; UNSC Res 1782 (29 October 2007) UN Doc S/RES/1782 could serve as an example.

provisions.[60] Legal practitioners and scholars alike have been seeking to identify a set of criteria in order to help identify when a UNSC resolution is normally intended to contain binding provisions and whether the UNSC takes actions under Chapter VII. These criteria include: (1) a determination of the existence of a 'threat to (international) peace', a 'breach of the peace', or an 'act of aggression' in accordance with Article 39; (2) the chapeau 'acting under Chapter VII'; and (3) the verb 'decide' in the resolution's relevant operative paragraphs pointing to the binding effect of the measures.[61] Moreover, when it comes to ceasefires between state and non-state parties, the UNSC seems to float between acting under Chapter VI – calling for a peaceful settlement of conflicts, framing the negotiation and endorsing the negotiation and implementation of a ceasefire agreement by calling its parties to comply with their obligations under the agreement – and deepening its involvement through Chapter VII measures by either recommending or demanding a ceasefire from the parties to a violent intra-state conflict.

In the end, to come to a conclusion concerning the localization of law-making and the creation of obligations through ceasefire agreements between state and non-state parties in the illustrated scenarios, it is essential to discuss the challenges of the synchronic interpretation of UNSC resolutions and ceasefire agreements between state and non-state parties. According to which rules and set of criteria UNSC resolutions and obligations created by them could be interpreted is again a complex question. It is even more so from a ceasefire agreement perspective, when UNSC resolutions frame the negotiation; and refer to, support and enforce a ceasefire agreement and obligations deriving from it, i.e., when the interpretation of UNSC resolutions addressing a particular intra-state conflict situation has to be considered jointly with the interpretation of ceasefire agreements. It seems opportune to conclude that when the UNSC quasi adjudicates, interprets, and enforces ceasefire agreements, acting under Chapter VII, this form of interpretation is also binding for all the parties of the agreement.[62]

Furthermore, in order to determine under which powers the UNSC acts in a particular resolution, it seems necessary to analyse the overall context of a resolution's creation and adoption; the precise wording used by the UNSC; and subsequent discussions in the UNSC during the resolution's implementation and endorsement by subsequent UNSC resolutions.[63] The previous resolutions that a present resolution is evoking and referring to can also play

---

[60] For example, UNSC Res 54 (15 July 1948) UN Doc S/RES/54 determined that the situation in Palestine was a threat to international peace and security and ordered a cessation of hostilities referring explicitly to arts 39 and 40 of the UN Charter. Although the chapeau 'Acting under Chapter VII' was not mentioned as a basis for the action then taken, the chapter's authority was being used. Over time a similar practice evolved around art 39 and the determination and usage of 'threat to peace', 'breach of the peace' or act of aggression, thus, taking the language of art 39 to indicate the SC's intent to use its Chapter VII powers, see UNSC Res 54 (15 July 1948) UN Doc S/RES/54 paras 1–2.

[61] Security Council Report (n 20) 4, 17; similar Michael Wood, 'The United Nations Security Council and International Law: The Legal Framework of the Security Council' (Hersch Lauterpacht Memorial Lectures 2006) 14 para 38 <https://www.lcil.cam.ac.uk/sites/www.law.cam.ac.uk/files/images/www.lcil.law.cam.ac.uk/Image/Publications/2006_hersch_lecture_1.pdf> accessed 31 January 2021.

[62] Hence, the chapter seeks to give a first answer to Wood's inquiry how far the practice of the SC to address ceasefire agreements between state and non-state parties has clarified legal issues surrounding these agreements, see Wood, 'The Law of Treaties and the UN Security Council: Some Reflections' (n 53) 245.

[63] For a comprehensive overview see: Michael Wood, 'The Interpretation of Security Council Resolutions' (1998) 2 Max Planck Yearbook of United Nations Law 73; see also: Anne Peters, 'Art. 25' in Bruno Simma and others (eds), *The Charter of the United Nations, A Commentary*, vol 1 (3rd edn,

a decisive role in determining the UNSC's intent to create a binding resolution, acting under Chapter VII. Since Chapter VII measures usually form part of a series of actions undertaken by the UNSC, a UNSC resolution has to be considered in this series of resolutions outlining actions and measures addressing a particular conflict, ceasefire, peace process, and peace agreement(s).[64] Moreover, in contrast to treaties, which are based on the idea of creating rights and obligations amongst two or more parties based on mutual consent, and which seek consistency and long-term commitment, the drafting of UNSC resolutions, including legally binding resolutions under Chapter VII, is first and foremost a political struggle and decision-making process in the ranks of the UN's 'executive organ', the UNSC.[65] Moreover, the legal effects and obligations created by Chapter VII resolutions can be created without explicit consent of the addressee and even against it.[66] Thus, both the original intention and the subsequent practice of the states involved in the creation of a UNSC resolution acquire less weight than in treaty interpretation.[67] Subsequent practice will be relevant only if it is expressed by the UNSC – in the form of authoritative interpretation, endorsement and continued action, and especially in the form of new UNSC resolutions – or by all member states of the UN. In the particular context of UNSC resolutions addressing the establishment of a ceasefire and/or the negotiation and implementation of ceasefire agreements, the preamble of an individual UNSC resolution may assist in its interpretation next to the wording and language used in its operative part addressing the parties to peace agreements and making them targets of sanction and enforcement measures.[68] Furthermore, the text of UNSC resolutions should be interpreted in good faith in accordance with the ordinary meaning to be given to the terms used in the context and in light of its object and purpose.[69] Parallel to Article 32 VCLT, supplementary means of interpretation can be the preparatory works of the UNSC sessions as well as reports of the Secretary-General (SG) to the UNSC and other documents of the UNSC, such as presidential statements.[70] UNSC resolutions are accessible and relevant for a wide range of authorities and

---

OUP 2012) 797–99 paras 24–28; Krisch, 'Introduction to Chapter VII, The General Framework' (n 55) 1264–66 paras 55–59; see also Security Council Report (n 20) 9.

[64] Wood, for instance, identified three crucial points for the interpretation of SC resolutions: to understand (1) the role of the SC under the Charter, (2) the particular working and drafting process of an SC resolution, and (3) the background of a resolution, ie the legal, political context as well as related SC actions and reports, Wood, 'The Law of Treaties and the UN Security Council: Some Reflections' (n 53) 244–55; and Stefan Talmon, 'Security Council Treaty Action' (2010) 30 Oxford University Legal Research Paper Series 22.

[65] Concerning the drafting process of SC resolutions and implications on the interpretation of SC resolutions, see Wood, 'The Interpretation of Security Council Resolutions' (n 63) 80–81; see also Talmon (n 64) 22.

[66] Peters (n 63) 797–99 paras 24–28; Krisch, 'Introduction to Chapter VII, The General Framework' (n 55) 1264–66 paras 55–59.

[67] Krisch, 'Introduction to Chapter VII, The General Framework' (n 55) 1265 para 55; Peters (n 63) 798–99 paras 26–28.

[68] Wood, 'The Interpretation of Security Council Resolutions' (n 63) 86 (terms of the resolution), 87 (preamble may assist in interpretation), 87 (SC resolutions often not self-contained unlike treaties; S/RES often can just be understood as a series of SC resolutions).

[69] ibid 88.

[70] According to Wood, the value of provisions in SC resolutions recalling past resolutions should be carefully looked upon on a case-by-case basis, see ibid 83, 91–92; Krisch, 'Introduction to Chapter VII, The General Framework' (n 55) 1264–66 paras 55–59.

individuals. Their interpretation, however, is, above all, up to the UNSC and its subsidiary organs. Only the UNSC, or somebody authorized to do so by the UNSC, may give authoritative interpretation.[71] Hence, subsequent UNSC resolutions could play an important role for the interpretation of a particular past UNSC resolution and the continuation of measures.[72] Yet, there is also a blurred line between subsequent resolutions, interpretations and amendment, which is connected to the question of whether a Chapter VII measure and Chapter VII resolution can only be terminated and amended by another Chapter VII measure and Chapter VII resolution.[73] The outlined constellations and relations of ceasefire agreements and UNSC resolutions could lead to an authority and legitimacy challenge and even dilemma when it comes to the effective implementation of ceasefires. The authority and practice of the parties to intra-state conflicts and ceasefires could collide with, and be challenged by, the authority of the UNSC, which presumably overrides the authority of the parties, but which also lacks the perceived legitimacy and effective compliance according to the conflict parties.

Hence, a mixed approach seems to be the best modus of interpretation to explore the 'legal' and 'law making nature' of UNSC resolutions.[74] This means a combination of a Charter-focused approach[75] and a general textual approach, focusing on the wording and language (authoritative, mandatory) employed in consecutive UNSC resolutions.[76] Concerning the interpretation of UNSC ceasefire resolutions, Henderson and Lubell summarize as follows: '(...) whether employing the "Charter", "textual", or "fully contextual" approaches, there will always be a struggle to discern a consistent pattern or unearth an interpretative method to provide clarity as to the binding nature of UNSC ceasefire resolutions.'[77]

In the end, these findings reveal the challenges of a double dimension of 'interpretation' when it comes to relations between UNSC resolutions that are so-called ceasefire resolutions and ceasefire agreements between state and non-state parties that are referred to by UNSC resolutions. Only the latter could be considered as consensual agreements. On the other hand, UNSC ceasefire resolutions can be followed by ceasefire agreements between state and non-state parties. These constellations lead us back to the question of where the law-making and creation of obligations for the parties can be located, i.e., in which 'legal sphere'? The allegedly structurally clearest answer is to point out that in both cases the UNSC in fact internationalizes the ceasefire and the relevant actors of an intra-state conflict by 'imposing' a ceasefire on them or enforcing a ceasefire agreed upon by them. In both constellations, the obligations are based, in the end, on the UNSC's binding resolutions. The created obligations

---

71 Peters (n 63) 798 para 25; Wood, 'The Interpretation of Security Council Resolutions' (n 63) 82–83.

72 Wood, 'The Interpretation of Security Council Resolutions' (n 63) 83.

73 This was especially discussed concerning UNSC Res 1244 (10 June 1999) UN Doc S/RES/1244, during the Kosovo Advisory Opinion; Michael C. Wood, 'The Interpretation of Security Council Resolutions' (n 63) 82; Wood finds: 'The importance which lawyers attach to consistency of drafting has to be balanced against the need for flexibility if general agreement is to be reached, and as often as not reached swiftly.'

74 Henderson and Lubell (n 8) 371.

75 ibid 371.

76 Language practice two-fold: aim of resolutions and language to reach votes ibid 371, 381–82.

77 Ibid 396.

are transferred or appropriated by the UNSC's measures that can in a reverse conclusion risk 'disowning' the parties to an agreement.[78]

Yet, again, this is only part of the picture, as many authors would agree that an imposed UNSC ceasefire might create clear obligations for the parties to an intra-state conflict but might not be effective on the ground as this act would not be perceived as legitimate and not be based on the interest and consent of the parties. Therefore, it is the double dimension of the interpretation of UNSC resolutions and ceasefire agreements between state and non-state parties that should guide future investigations concerning rules and obligations created by ceasefires for state and non-state parties.

6. CONCLUSION

This chapter's exploration of the extent to which the negotiation and implementation of legitimate ceasefire agreements and ceasefires as consensual law-making could be considered as pointing to an emerging form of 'globalized governance' (regulation, administration and constitutionalization) within the grey zone of ongoing intra-state conflict and peace processes.

The negotiation and implementation of post-Cold War ceasefires between state and non-state parties to settle intra-state conflicts suggest and even demand new perspectives on how and by whom domestic, international (humanitarian) and transitional law can be created and enforced on the long-stretched continuum from ongoing conflict to sustainable peace. The chapter also revealed a tendency not only to internationalize but also in effect to denationalize their negotiation and implementation, and in effect law-making.

---

78 '(…) many ceasefires are ordained by the Security Council, the more imposed a ceasefire the less likely it may be to work, precisely because it will lack the agreement between parties necessary to implementation. This explains why even Security Council resolutions under Chapter VII usually take place against a backdrop of negotiation and agreement,' Bell, 'Ceasefire' (n 9) para 20.

21. Law-making participation by non-state armed groups: The prerequisite of law's legitimacy?

Hyeran Jo

1. INTRODUCTION

Non-state armed groups (NSAGs) are active players in the international scene. In contemporary global conflict scenes, we have observed the Islamic State's destruction of cultural properties in Syria, Boko Haram's kidnapping of schoolgirls in Nigeria, the influence of al-Qaeda in the Middle East and Africa, just to name a few. Sexual violence in the Democratic Republic of Congo, and negotiations between the FARC (Fuerzas Armadas Revolucionarias de Colombia) and Colombian government are also imprints of NSAGs in the global context.

At face value, NSAGs and international law appear as incompatible as oil and water. Traditionally, only nation-states or delegations of states have been the sole negotiators of international law. In practice, NSAGs militarily fight against the existing state order. So, the baseline expectation is that NSAGs would be averse to international law that states created.

On the international law side, its legitimacy has always been in flux, and some scholars have observed that international law faces a 'legitimacy crisis'.[1] The statement is especially true for the recent status of international humanitarian law (IHL), partly due to the rule violation of violent and salient actors such as NSAGs, and the fluid and varied nature of modern conflicts. In addition, the belief that IHL is not adequate to face contemporary problems of internal conflicts[2] seems to be eroding the legitimacy of IHL.

Would the NSAGs' participation in the law-making process increase the legitimacy of IHL? If so, on what grounds and under what conditions would this occur? The question is difficult to answer partly because of the global political structure. In international politics, major power-wielders are sovereign nation-states, and they are the traditional law-makers of public

[1] See in Rein Müllerson, 'Aspects of Legitimacy of Decisions of International Courts and Tribunals: Comments' in Rüdiger Wolfrum and Volker Röben (eds), *Legitimacy in International Law* (Springer 2008) 194, roundtable discussions for the representative works regarding the debate on international law's legitimacy. See Thomas Franck, 'Legitimacy in the International System' (1988) 82 American Journal of International Law 705, 711, a seminal work that analyses international law's legitimacy (adherence, congruence). See Mattias Kumm, 'The Legitimacy of International Law: A Constitutionalist Framework of Analysis' (2004) 15 European Journal of International Law 907, for the discussion of 'legitimacy crisis' and a proposal of a constitutionalist view in light of recent developments in international politics, involving new actors and new circumstances.

[2] In this chapter, conflicts of 'non-international character' or 'non-international armed conflicts' or 'internal conflicts' are used interchangeably.

international law. Also, there are no global demos that can approve clear delegation structures as within national systems.[3] With this 'gatekeeper structure' of international law, whether and how NSAGs should participate in international law-making is not straightforward.[4]

However, the question on the connection between NSAG participation and IHL's legitimacy is an important one. First and foremost, the 'moral force of international law' is at stake.[5] Support for and compliance with IHL depends on the perception of law as legitimate. If the users of IHL consider it illegitimate in terms of its content and process, the law's raison d'être will diminish. Additionally, the issue of NSAGs and IHL legitimacy speaks to the fundamental questions of legal studies and social/political studies: who makes the law, with what influence, based on what rights, and with what consequences?

One might question whether IHL needs legitimacy *at all*. Some might argue that other criteria – accountability, for example – might be more important desiderata for legal rules. Why might simple legality not be enough? Why should we consider *legitimacy* as an important end goal for IHL? In regard to this debate, this author takes the position that IHL's success ultimately depends on the behaviour of main stakeholders and rule participants, that is, 'conflict actors' including governments and NSAGs, and how legitimate *they* perceive the rules to be. Those perceptions are critical to their compliance behaviour and whether rules are ultimately adhered to. Especially when the legality of IHL is less certain, more restricted, and more controversial with respect to NSAGs, the consideration of legitimacy becomes even more important for the law to remain relevant and meaningful.

International law, in order to be relevant and meaningful, needs support from the rule addressee, who has the perception that international law has the 'right to govern' (the definition of legitimacy). Without the law's legitimacy, legality itself does not guarantee adherence. Legitimacy of IHL is crucial in part because subjects' perceptions about legitimacy of rules enhance their sense of responsibility, accountability, and compliance with laws. It is generally understood that the goal for legitimacy in international law lies in 'compliance pull'.[6] Legitimacy is important because it elicits the sense that IHL is 'worthy of support', ultimately having the power and authority to bring about compliance and govern the conflict behaviour. At a higher level, legitimacy can confer a 'duty to obey' and a 'moral obligation'. For these reasons, in order for IHL to be embedded in conflict actors' modes of fighting, legitimacy beyond legality becomes crucial.

Noting the importance of IHL's legitimacy, this chapter develops the following core argument: the law-making participation by NSAGs may not be necessary for IHL to achieve its legitimacy but has the potential to contribute to the law's legitimacy. The NSAGs' law-making participation may not be necessary because other multiple paths exist to enhance the law's legitimacy, such as states' compliance. However, the law-making participation by NSAGs,

---

3 See Ruth Grant and Robert Keohane, 'Accountability and Abuses of Power in World Politics' (2005) 99 American Political Science Review 29, for the discussion on global accountability.

4 On the state doctrine in international law in relation to NSAGs, see Jan Klabbers, '(I Can't Get No) Recognition: Subjects Doctrine and the Emergence of Non-State Actors' in Jarna Petman and Jan Klabbers (eds), *Nordic Cosmopolitanism: Essays in International Law for Martti Koskenniemi* (Martinus Nijhoff Publishers 2003) 354–55.

5 See Kumm (n 1) 907–31 for the discussion of importance of legitimacy question.

6 See Franck (n 1) 711 on the notion of compliance pull. See Rein Müllerson (n 1) 194 on legitimacy of international law.

especially in the form of self-legal commitment, could enhance the law's legitimacy by improving the normative value of the law as well as the prospect of compliance with the law.

Excellent legal analyses on NSAGs' law-making participation have been done by many legal scholars.[7] As a political scientist studying international relations, my approach is more empirical. This means less reliance on case law and jurisprudence than international lawyers would expect and more emphasis on the social science logic of the international legal system, as well as empirical and behavioural records of NSAGs' practices. Consequently, my discussion will bring political constraints and opportunities centrally into the discussion of international law.[8] What I hope to add is a presentation of empirical patterns and clarification of the link between the NSAGs' law-making participation and the legitimacy of IHL.

This chapter first sets the conceptual terrain by defining key terms, reviews the history and practice of NSAGs' law-making participation, and analyses the relationship between NSAG law-making participation and IHL legitimacy. The conclusion addresses broad policy implications, with a reflection on what NSAGs' law-making participation might mean for the law's legitimacy, both in legal and policy realms.

2. DEFINITIONS

By defining the key terms – non-state armed groups, legitimacy, and participation – I set the conceptual bounds of this chapter. First, NSAGs comprise opposition groups that are fighting against national governments militarily.[9] These sometimes include groups that use terror tactics, if those groups have clear political goals with military presence with some level of organization.[10] Other NSAGs – paramilitaries, militias, armed gangs, or private contractors, for example – are also active players in the current international system,[11] but they operate under a different logic, and thus are excluded from the inquiry of this chapter. Unlike NSAGs, paramilitaries fight on behalf of the government. Similarly, unlike NSAGs with political goals,

---

7 I cannot do full justice to this literature due to space constraints, but for representative works see Sandesh Sivakumaran, 'Binding Armed Opposition Groups' (2006) 55 International and Comparative Law Quarterly 369; Marco Sassoli, 'Taking Armed Groups Seriously: Ways to Improve Their Compliance with International Humanitarian Law' (2010) 1 Journal of International Humanitarian Legal Studies 5; Cedric Ryngaert, 'Non-state Actors in International Humanitarian Law' in Jean d'Aspremont (ed), *Participants in the International Legal System: Multiple Perspectives on Non-State Actors in International Law* (Taylor and Francis 2011) 284ff; Anthea Roberts and Sandesh Sivakumaran, 'Lawmaking by Non-state Actors: Engaging Armed Groups in the Creation of International Humanitarian Law' (2012) 37 Yale Journal of International Law 107.

8 See Jeffrey Dunoff and Mark Pollack, *Interdisciplinary Perspectives on International Law and International Relations: The State of the Art* (CUP 2013) on the bridge between international law and international relations.

9 According to legal definitions, these groups include members of irregular forces that meet Geneva Convention III or Additional Protocol II criteria. For the background, see Ryan Goodman, 'The Detention of Civilians in Armed Conflict' (2009) 103 American Journal of International Law 48.

10 For the recent debate on the legal criteria of NSAGs, see Katharine Fortin, *The Accountability of Armed Groups under Human Rights Law* (OUP 2017).

11 On paramilitaries, see the review by Sabine Carey, 'Pro-Government Militias' (2017) 20 Annual Review of Political Science 127. On private security, see the recent data effort in Deborah Avant and Kara Kingma Neu, 'The Private Security Events Database' (2019) 63 Journal of Conflict Resolution 1986.

private contractors are normally driven by profit motives. These differing goals of NSAGs and other types of armed groups necessitate distinct discussions in terms of participation in law-making. Note, as well, that I will consider non-state armed 'groups' as requiring a certain level of organization to be considered.[12] As such I will not consider NSAGs that are relatively unorganized, such as roving bandits.

Legitimacy is the perception about authority or the 'right to rule'.[13] Following the conventional definition, this chapter is concerned with the legitimacy of international rules – how users or subjects of the law perceive the law to be legitimate and authoritative. I will refer to this as 'rule legitimacy'.[14] The source and origin of legitimacy is critical. Where law comes from and how it is made affects whether it is accepted as lawful and legitimate. Often, just and fair procedure confers rule legitimacy; other times, long-term adherence to the binding character of substantive rules result in rule legitimacy. I will call the former 'procedural legitimacy' and the latter 'substantive legitimacy'. Procedural legitimacy, based on fair and just procedure or decision-making processes of rules, illustrates that the creation of those rules is not altered for the benefit of the few. Substantive legitimacy comes from the rules reflecting a widely held view.[15] If the affected subjects stand by the rules, even if the rules might disadvantage them, we can say that the rules have substantive legitimacy. For IHL to be legitimate, sufficient levels of perception that the rules are fair and just in procedure and substance must exist. Without one or the other, the law's legitimacy would not be complete.

Participation in law-making is defined as the provision of input in the creation or development of law. Laws relevant to NSAGs fall within three main areas of international law, namely IHL, international human rights law (IHRL), and international criminal law (ICL). Although this chapter's main focus is on IHL, IHRL and ICL are also discussed as relevant.[16]

In all three areas of law, the density of codification is thin when dealing with NSAGs. In the realm of IHL, the laws governing internal conflicts are confined to the Article 3 common to the Geneva Conventions as well as customary rules. IHRL is applicable to ordinary individuals and confers obligations to states, but whether this body of law applies directly to NSAGs or to each individual within the NSAG is debatable. The application of ICL to NSAGs is developing

---

12 See the case law of the International Criminal Tribunal for the Former Yugoslavia (ICTY), especially *Prosecutor v Tadić* (Decision on the Defence Motion for Interlocutory Appeal on Jurisdiction) IT-94-1-T (2 October 1995); See also Annyssa Bellal, Giacca Gilles and Stuart Casey-Maslen, 'International Law and Armed Non-State Actors in Afghanistan' (2011) 93 International Review of the Red Cross 47.

13 Allen Buchanan and Robert Keohane, 'The Legitimacy of Global Governance Institutions' (2006) 20 Ethics and International Affairs 405.

14 This concept of rule legitimacy is in line with Franck's definition of legitimacy that emphasizes the procedural aspect of legitimacy: 'quality of a rule *which derives from a perception on the part of those to whom it is addressed that it has come into being in accordance with right process*' in Franck (n 1) 706.

15 See Ryngaert (n 7) for detailed discussion on substantive legitimacy in the context of non-state actors.

16 There is some overlap between international humanitarian and human rights law, as both bodies of law share the belief in the fundamental respect for life. Also, IHL overlaps with international criminal law (ICL), especially after the establishment of the International Criminal Court (ICC) in 2002 based on the 1998 Rome Treaty, which has jurisdiction over the crimes against humanity, war crimes and genocide. See David Scheffer, *All the Missing Souls: A Personal History of the War Crimes Tribunals* (Princeton University Press 2013) for these discussions.

with case law from international tribunals and the operations of the International Criminal Court.

Law-making participation can be conceptualized as occurring on a spectrum: from passive (indirect participation in law-making) to active (direct participation in law-making), legislative (involvement in drafting activities) to interpretative (engaging in interpreting activities), inclusive (inviting all groups) to exclusive (inviting only a few armed groups), and informal (including armed groups as observers) to formal participation (including armed groups as negotiators). The multiple dimensions of participation have different consequences on the development of law and the subsequent legitimacy of rules.

Two categories of law-making approaches provide useful distinctions for NSAGs' law-making participation. The first is the *hard-law approach* that emphasizes the legislative role of NSAGs in codifying and formalizing the rules. Producing this hard law[17] requires formal negotiation and a deliberation process. NSAGs have some experience (e.g., liberation movements during the Additional Protocols' negotiation), but the development of hard law has remained in the domain of state delegations for centuries. The second potential form of NSAGs' law-making is the *soft-law approach*, which takes place via unilateral declarations, bilateral agreements with states or international organizations, or accumulating customs.

Now, take the above three terms together: 'non-state armed groups', 'legitimacy', and 'participation in law-making', and we arrive at specific questions to ponder. First, consider the combination: 'non-state armed groups' and 'participation'. NSAGs are subjects of international law and rule addressees of IHL. Should NSAGs participate in the law-making, or is the status quo with state doctrine best? Second, take the combination of 'non-state armed groups' and 'legitimacy', which leads to the following question: under what conditions can NSAGs' law-making participation enhance the law's legitimacy?

3. ARMED GROUPS' LAW-MAKING PARTICIPATION IN PRACTICE – HISTORY AND CONTEMPORARY PRACTICE

Contrary to the popular belief that NSAGs are outlaws, some *have* participated in the drafting of international law in practice. During the negotiation of the 1977 Additional Protocols to the Geneva Conventions, several dozen national liberation movement groups participated as observers. Among these non-state actor participants, three groups – the Palestine Liberation Organization (PLO), the Pan-Africanist Congress (PAC), and the South West Africa People's Organization (SWAPO) – signed the Final Act of the Diplomatic Conference.[18]

---

[17] Kenneth Abbott and Duncan Snidal, 'Hard and Soft Law in International Governance' (2000) 54 International Organization 421.

[18] Jean-Marie Henckaerts, 'Binding Armed Opposition Groups through Humanitarian Treaty Law and Customary Law' in *Proceedings of the Bruges Colloquium: 25th–26th October 2002: Relevance of International Humanitarian Law to Non-State Actors* (College of Europe 2003) 123–37, 128; Giovanni Mantilla, 'The Political Origins of the Geneva Conventions of 1949 and the Additional Protocols of 1977' in Matthew Evangelista and Nina Tannenwald (eds), *Do the Geneva Conventions Matter?* (OUP 2017); Emma Stone Mackinnon, 'Contingencies of Context: Legacies of the Algerian Revolution in the 1977 Additional Protocols to the Geneva Conventions' in Ingo Venzke and Kevin Jon Heller (eds), *Situating Contingency in International Law: On the Possibility of a Different Law* (OUP 2020).

In the contemporary period, as well, some NSAGs *are* contributing to international law-making. For example, some commit to IHL by expressing their intent to abide by the rules and making agreements with governments that include IHL components.[19] However, the legal force of these commitments is uncertain. They can be considered a form of 'hybrid treaties', as Roberts and Sivakumaran suggest,[20] or as shaping customary international law, which is more controversial. At worst, these expressions may be little more than empty signals with no direct connection to compliance behaviours. However, one thing is certain: those instruments are NSAGs' expressions of consent, some of which can be counted as the intent to be bound by IHL or at least recognizing the existence and applicability of IHL. This respect and recognition of rules is important for the law's legitimacy. Such acceptance is in stark contrast to the silence of some NSAGs or wholesale rejection of other NSAGs. Without acceptance, law's legitimacy cannot hold or take roots.

The Rebel Groups and International Law (RGIL) database is a collection of information about armed opposition groups' commitments to and compliance with international law.[21] The commitment part of the RGIL dataset was constructed using Geneva Call's Directory of Armed Non-State Actor Humanitarian Commitments terms as 'Their Words'.[22] The list of armed group commitments is not an exhaustive one, but it reveals some interesting patterns.

First, the database reveals that more than 100 NSAGs have committed to international law in some form, with many committing through multiple channels – either by unilateral declarations or in the form of bilateral agreements with international organizations or non-governmental organizations. Second, these commitments cover issues ranging from technical issues such as the use of anti-personnel mines to social issues such as child protection and sexual violence.[23] The database's typology and examples are demonstrated in Table 21.1. As the RGIL database illustrates, NSAGs are participating in law-making already. Although they cannot conclude or ratify international treaties or conventions, they are already making bilateral agreements or expressing unilateral declarations. About 20 per cent of contemporary NSAGs have expressed their commitment to IHL in some form.[24] Some do follow the rules of war, exhibiting restraints in regard to: the killing of civilians, use of child soldiers, and use of anti-personnel mines that maim and kill people indiscriminately.[25] Various NSAGs have set

---

[19] For the examples and analysis of these rebel expressions, see Sandesh Sivakumaran, *The Law of Non-International Armed Conflict* (OUP 2012).

[20] Roberts and Sivakumaran (n 7) 144.

[21] Hyeran Jo and others, 'Rebel Groups & International Law Database' <http://hyeranjo.wix.com/compliantrebels> accessed 31 January 2021. The database is the basis of the following book, Hyeran Jo, *Compliant Rebels: Rebel Groups and International Law in World Politics* (CUP 2015).

[22] 'Their Words. Directory of Armed Non-State Actor Humanitarian Commitments' (Geneva Call) <http://theirwords.org/pages/geneva-call> accessed 31 January 2021.

[23] Compared to issues surrounding child protection and sexual violence, which are often laden with cultural complexities, the anti-personnel mines issue was more specific (focusing on the specific type of mines, namely, mines that cause unnecessary human suffering) and more actionable (ie assisting mine-clearing actions is more straightforward, partly due to its technical nature, than ending sexual violence).

[24] Hyeran Jo and others, 'Signaling Restraints: International Engagement and Rebel Groups' Commitment to International Law' (2021) International Interactions (forthcoming).

[25] Kristian Gleditsch, Simon Hug, Livia Schubiger and Julian Wucherpfennig, 'International Conventions and Non-State Actors: Selection, Signaling, and Reputation Effects' (2018) 62 Journal of Conflict Resolution 346.

Table 21.1 Patterns of legal commitments by non-state armed groups

By issues	Number of instances of commitments by armed opposition groups	Example
Anti-personnel mines	85	Democratic Party of Iranian Kurdistan (PDKI) Deed of Commitment
Child protection	36	Karen National Union (Myanmar) UN Action Plans
Civilian protection	54	Mouvement pour la Justice et la Paix (MJP) (Côte D'Ivoire)
General human rights	172	Ejército de Liberación Nacional (ELN) (Colombia)
By Types		
Unilateral declaration	223	National Socialist Council of Nagalim (NSCN) (India) Statement against Terrorism (2008)
Bilateral agreement	470	Lusaka Ceasefire Agreement between the Congolese Government and Mouvement de Libération du Congo (MLC), Rassemblement Congolais pour la Democratie (RCD) (1999), calling for respect for human rights and civilian protection
Internal code of conduct	70	Irish Republican Army (IRA) (Northern Ireland) Handbook for Volunteers of the Irish Republican Army – Notes on Guerrilla Warfare (1956)

Note: The total number of commitments recorded by Geneva Call's, Their Words database, is 574 (as of 30 November 2020).
Source: Rebel Groups and International Law Database; Their Words (Directory of Armed Non-State Actor Humanitarian Commitments) by Geneva Call.

up and run their own courts. These include CPN-M (Nepal), the FMLN (El Salvador), and the LTTE (Sri Lanka). Opinions surrounding these practices are divided among IHL scholars,[26] though these initiatives by NSAGs are claimed to be based on IHL. These aforementioned groups contribute to rule legitimacy implicitly without actively participating in the legislative law-making process. By demonstrating compliance or accepting the fact that the rule applies to them, those groups implicitly agree that IHL principles are legitimate and worthy of following. These instances of NSAGs' legal commitments have the possibility to enhance the rule legitimacy in the sense that we would expect that the number and extent of rule-committers and rule-compliers increases.

[26] While Sandesh Sivakumaran, 'Courts of Armed Opposition Groups: Fair Trials or Summary Justice?' (2009) 7 Journal of International Criminal Justice 489 and Jonathan Somer, 'Jungle Justice: Passing Sentence on the Equality of Belligerents in Non-International Armed Conflict' (2007) 89 International Review of the Red Cross 655, allow room for insurgent courts to contribute to international humanitarian law-making; Parth S. Gejji, 'Can Insurgent Courts Be Legitimate Within International Humanitarian Law?' (2009) 91 Texas Law Review 1525 disagrees on the grounds that insurgent courts result in negative consequences, such as loosening the standards of IHL.

The RGIL dataset presents the following typology of NSAGs' law-making participation, as summarized in Table 21.2: quasi-legislators, committers, custom-makers, judges, regulators, and rejectionists. 'Quasi-legislator/observer' armed groups actively participate in the traditional treaty law-making or hard-law processes. Examples include national liberation movements being present as observers during the drafting of the Additional Protocols in 1977. 'Soft-law-maker' armed groups can be further classified into several sub-categories: committers, custom-makers, judges, and regulators. 'Committer' armed groups express commitment to international law through various instruments, such as unilateral declarations and bilateral agreements with states and international organizations. There are activist armed groups that proactively interact with other types of informal international law-makers, such as international organizations or non-governmental organizations. The nine armed groups that have signed United Nations Action Plans to stop the use of child soldiers are examples of such activist armed groups. 'Custom-makers' are armed groups that contribute to customary international law by complying with IHL. Whether or not armed groups can contribute to customary international law can be debated. But as long as their behaviour is consistent with law, it could be beneficial to the development of IHL, if not harmful. 'Judge' armed groups run courts to conduct trials according to IHL, or so they claim. The actual utility of rebel courts has not been fully determined[27] but it is a notable development in IHL that observes judicial roles within rebel ranks. Finally, 'regulator' armed groups include IHL elements into their own military regulation using an internal code of conduct. Again, whether the insurgent leadership uses internal code of conduct as instruments to discipline rank-and-file soldiers, or govern their army following IHL, the motivation is not clear. Also, how NSAG leaders interpret IHL can be often problematic.[28] However, internal codes consistent with IHL principles can arguably enhance the rule legitimacy. The last category considered is a 'rejectionist' type. Participation in law-making does not have to have a positive influence on norm development. In fact, some NSAGs break, not make, the law, undermining the rule legitimacy, invoking the debates and revealing contentions in IHL.

The distribution of each type of rebel group in the law-making process is also interesting to note. 'Quasi-legislators' have difficulty coming into being because of government opposition. 'Committers' constitute about 20 per cent of rebel groups, which is a bit of a surprise given our common feeling that NSAGs might not know, nor care, about international law at all. 'Custom-makers' usually arise when local customs are aligned with international rules. When local practices and beliefs are consistent with IHL, in this particular typology, rule-compliance could lead to the accumulation of customs. The last category of 'rejectionists' usually consists of some extremists and/or jihadists, where no norm overlap exists. All these examples illustrate that law-making participation by NSAGs is *not* a rare event. Also, these current practices imply that the various participation episodes have the potential to enhance/debase the IHL's legitimacy, because they add conforming practice (adding to 'widespread practice') and/or present the instances of 'consent' or rule-acceptance via legal commitments.

---

27 See the debate in Sivakumaran, 'Courts of Armed Opposition Groups' (n 26) and Gejji (n 26).

28 See the example of Taleban's Layeha, as discussed in Hyeran Jo and John Niehaus, 'Through Rebel Eyes: Rebel Groups, Human Rights, and Humanitarian Law' (2018) 81 Law and Contemporary Problems 101.

Table 21.2 Armed opposition groups and international law-making participation: a typology

Types	Description	Examples
Quasi-legislators	Participate as observers in treaty negotiation	Liberation movements during 1977 Additional Protocol negotiation
Committers	Expressing commitment via unilateral declaration or bilateral agreements	Sudan People's Liberation Army (Sudan) Operation Lifeline Sudan
Custom-makers	Adding to 'widespread practice'	FMLN (El Salvador)
Judges	Running insurgent courts based on IHL	CPN-M (Nepal), LTTE (Sri Lanka)
Regulators	Developing internal code of conduct consistent with IHL	Moro Islamic Liberation Front (Philippines)
Rejectionists	Debasing IHL	Islamic State (Syria)

The different types of NSAG participation contribute to rule legitimacy in varying degrees. 'Quasi-legislator' groups will have direct involvement and input in drafting treaties, which will enhance 'procedural legitimacy' as well as 'substantive legitimacy', as they will participate in and contribute to the content of the rules. 'Committer' groups are more likely to enhance rule legitimacy by signalling their intent to commit, by adding legal instruments so as to demonstrate commitment, and consequently expanding the IHL's base. 'Custom-maker' groups will contribute to rule legitimacy in the long run. 'Judge' groups, although controversial, will enhance legitimacy, only if the insurgent trials are fair and in accordance with IHL. 'Rejectionist' groups will debase rule legitimacy through their disregard for IHL, although such challenge, if properly met, could strengthen the IHL's legitimacy after all. None of these NSAG participation roles guarantees rule legitimacy, but each has the potential to impact the legitimacy of IHL. I explore this participation–legitimacy nexus in more depth in the next section.

4. NSAGS' LAW-MAKING PARTICIPATION AND RULE LEGITIMACY – PREREQUISITE OR RECOMMENDED?

Now that I have examined the current state of armed groups' law-making participation, I circle back to the central question of this chapter: is NSAGs' law-making participation a prerequisite[29] for law's legitimacy?[30] To find an answer, we have to examine whether armed group participation leads to legitimacy and, if so, via what mechanisms. In particular, it is important to ask the following: to what extent, through which kinds of participation, through which processes, and with what political and legal weight might NSAG participation impact rule

[29] Synonyms of 'prerequisite' include precondition, essential, requirement, necessity, compulsory or obligatory. Therefore, the question essentially is, whether NSAGs' participation is a must condition for IHL's legitimacy.

[30] The literature that examines the connection between armed group participation and the law's legitimacy is thin. One exception is Ryngaert (n 7). This author presents a view that is consistent with Ryngaert's 'consent-based approach' to bring about procedural and substantive legitimacy of IHL. This chapter is different in its method and explication to answer the connection between law-making participation and law's legitimacy in a more direct fashion.

legitimacy. In this vein, this section analyses the general relationship between participation and legitimacy and then proposes a conditional theory of NSAGs' law-making participation and IHL's legitimacy. The theory will posit that different modes of NSAG law-making participation are likely to enhance IHL's rule legitimacy in different ways and at varying levels. Ultimately, it is submitted that NSAGs' law-making participation is not necessarily a prerequisite of rule legitimacy, but that such participation is cautiously recommended, depending on the modes of participation.

4.1 Existing Approaches to Armed Group Participation

Existing approaches on the participation–legitimacy nexus can fall broadly into two camps. One is the 'traditional' approach, which favours maintaining the centrality of states in international law-making. The other can be characterized as the 'progressive' approach, which includes armed group participation. The scholars in the first camp take a traditional view of law-making by states. For example, Anderson contends that the rules of war should be owned by democratic states.[31] Gejji opposes the idea of giving any international law-making, judicial role to rebel courts, arguing this remains within the domain of nation-states, as evinced by the history of the Geneva Conventions and the Additional Protocols.[32] Legal rules regarding internal armed conflicts grow out of the rules governing international conflicts, and the trend seems to be entrenched in the making of IHL.

The progressive camp includes the views of Clapham, Sassoli, and Sivakumaran.[33] Sassoli writes: 'how could [armed] groups be expected to abide by a special set of laws designed to govern conflicts if they are not, however, involved in the law-making process?'[34] Sivakumaran argues that 'in order to increase the degree of legitimacy of and foster a sense of respect for the laws governing internal armed conflict, participation of armed opposition groups in the formation of the rules is vital'.[35] In a similar vein, Roberts and Sivakumaran find middle ground to argue that certain forms of participation should be allowed (and are politically feasible).[36] The authors advocate for the inclusion of mechanisms such as unilateral declarations, hybrid treaties, and possibly quasi-custom to allow participation of NSAGs, while moderating states' opposition to such participation.[37]

These existing approaches submit normative evaluations on armed groups' participation – whether it is beneficial or not for IHL in general – but do not provide a concrete and specific

---

31 Kenneth Anderson, 'Who Owns the Rules of War?' (*New York Times Magazine*, 13 April 2003) <www.nytimes.com/2003/04/13/magazine/who-owns-the-rules-of-war.html?> accessed 31 January 2021.

32 Gejji (n 26).

33 Andrew Clapham, *Human Rights Obligations of Non-State Actors* (OUP 2006); Sassoli, 'Taking Armed Groups Seriously' (n 7); Sivakumaran, 'Binding Armed Opposition Groups' (n 7).

34 Marco Sassoli, 'Transnational Armed Groups and International Humanitarian Law' (Winter 2006) HPCR Occasional Paper Series 6, 40 <https://www.hpcrresearch.org/sites/default/files/publications/OccasionalPaper6.pdf> accessed 31 January 2021.

35 Sivakumaran, 'Binding Armed Opposition Groups' (n 7).

36 Roberts and Sivakumaran (n 7).

37 More recently, Tanisha Fazal recognizes the need for armed groups' law-making participation in her book, *Wars of Law: Unintended Consequences in the Regulation of Armed Conflict* (Cornell University Press 2018).

answer as to whether armed group law-making participation contributes to the law's legitimacy. The next section deliberates on the said question of NSAG participation and IHL rule legitimacy.

4.2 Participation–Legitimacy Nexus

In legal and political studies, participation is generally understood to enhance legitimacy.[38] The logic is that legitimacy is constructed by the key audiences' belief and, therefore, participatory actions naturally affect the belief of those participants. I argue that NSAGs' participation may contribute in part to the legitimacy of IHL, but this contribution does not comprise a 'critical' component of legitimacy. The primary reason for this contention is that *there are multiple ways to enhance IHL's legitimacy* besides NSAGs' law-making participation. Among them, enhancing states' compliance records is one way to boost IHL's legitimacy. Let's suppose that the logic of reciprocity holds. If states comply, armed groups are also expected to comply and respect the law. The end result will be enhanced compliance, thus increased legitimacy. Of course, the asymmetric nature of non-international conflict will inhibit the operation of direct reciprocity, but some examples show that state compliance might enhance NSAGs' compliance. For example, the ban on anti-personnel mines prompted many states to reconsider the use of the explosive mines that unnecessarily caused human suffering. Eschewing a potential military advantage, about 60 NSAGs have committed to ending the use of anti-personnel mines, either through the signing of Geneva Call's Deed of Commitment or unilateral declaration. Prioritizing an increase in NSAGs' actual compliance will ultimately enhance IHL's legitimacy.[39]

In a similar fashion, other institutions associated with IHL can enhance the law's legitimacy. With the ICC having jurisdiction over crimes against humanity, IHL's legitimacy could be increased as well via the operation of the ICC. The same is true for the International Committee of the Red Cross. As an institution bestowed by the Geneva Conventions to assist victims of conflict and to disseminate IHL, its legitimacy is also an important contributor to IHL's legitimacy. The existence of multiple ways of enhancing legitimacy demonstrates that IHL will not gain more legitimacy simply because NSAGs participate in law-making processes. There are many other ways to enhance legitimacy[40] and compliance, so direct par-

[38] See John A. Booth and Mitchell A. Seligson, *The Legitimacy Puzzle in Latin America: Political Support and Democracy in Eight Nations* (CUP 2006) for recent empirical work in political science.

[39] There is a bit of twist here. Since Krieger cautions for the use of legitimacy as political leverage on the part of the NSAGs, we want to cautiously draw conclusions on the net effect on the law's legitimacy. See Heike Krieger, 'International Law and Governance by Armed Groups: Caught in the Legitimacy Trap?' (2018) 12 Journal of Intervention and Statebuilding 563.

[40] Franck (n 1) 711, 744–48 suggests several ways rules can take legitimacy: 'literary structure, origins, internal consistency, reasonableness, utility in achieving stated ends and connection to the overall rule system, and the extent to which their origins and application comport with the international community's "rules about rules".' Franck proposed four indicators of rule legitimacy: determinacy (clear message), symbolic validation (through rule-making processes and institutions, pedigree or ritual), coherence (over time and internally), and adherence (to a rule hierarchy). Internal consistency and reasonableness, for example, can be set by states, not necessarily by armed groups. The international community can enhance rule determinacy, meaning that rules may become more specific than existing rules pertaining to armed groups (beyond the common art 3 and Additional Protocols). Armed group participa-

ticipation by armed groups may not be essential. For example, states' compliance, through the mechanism of reciprocity, could influence armed groups' compliance.[41] Although it is difficult to expect the same level of reciprocity in internal conflicts as in international conflicts, reciprocal behaviour on both sides would ultimately enhance the legitimacy of rules.[42] In this sense, armed groups' direct participation may not be a prerequisite of legitimacy.

4.3 Two Logics on Participation and Rule Legitimacy

Two different logics can be presented with regard to armed groups' law-making participation as a means of enhancing the law's legitimacy. One is direct-participation logic; the other is delegation logic.

Direct-participation logic proposes that the democratic principle of direct participation of *demos*, or key stakeholders, is important and that deliberation is necessary to produce law. The argument holds that direct deliberation produces ownership of rules and ultimately contributes to a positive outcome. This logic is related to procedural legitimacy – a sense that the process is 'fair and adequate'.[43] The logic of democratic legitimacy tells us that democratic process, involving open deliberation and participation without exclusion, enhances legitimacy, especially procedural legitimacy.[44] According to this logic, we can expect that NSAG participation, simply for the sake of participation, would enhance legitimacy. This view would hold that participation is a necessary component for rule legitimacy.

However, direct-participation logic suffers a fatal flaw. International law does not hold a natural constituency in the same way that a national/local government does. Without referenda and voting systems, international law can never be truly democratic in the direct-democracy sense.[45] Although non-governmental organizations often bring their voices to the arena of international law-making, mimicking global demos, this form of civil society participation often suffers from an absence of the core structures of democracy, such as accountability.[46]

Also, we have to answer another difficult question: do armed groups have the right to participate? The question is still debated among legal scholars, as mentioned above. In this regard we must consider practical questions as to who should be invited to participate in law-making.

---

tion would certainly pose problems regarding coherence because of the evolving nature of norms regarding internal conflict (as Franck's example about the norm of self-determination suggests).

41 Gabriella Blum, 'On a Differential Law of War' (2011) 52 Harvard International Law Journal 164, 202–204 also considers this possibility of self-restraint on the part of the stronger party (ie states) with the aim of decreasing the incentive to defect from IHL obligations. Blum calls it 'raising the bar for stronger powers'.

42 See Mark Osiel, *The End of Reciprocity: Terror, Torture, and the Law of War* (CUP 2009) on reciprocity in internal wars. John Morrow, *Order within Anarchy: The Laws of War as an International Institution* (CUP 2014) finds that in the case of some norms (eg POW treatment or civilian killing), reciprocity operates more often in comparison to others (eg chemical and biological weapons use). Future research should address the question: in which areas of law does reciprocity operate more frequently, in the case of internal conflict.

43 Wolfrum and Röben (n 1) 6, 194.

44 Grant and Keohane (n 3).

45 See Allen Buchanan 'The Legitimacy of International Law' in Samantha Besson and John Tasioulas (eds) *The Philosophy of International Law* (OUP 2010) ch 3, 79–97 on this very point.

46 See Grant and Keohane (n 3) on this point of global accountability.

Politically, the invitation of only prominent armed opposition groups will irk their national governments. What about weak groups that are highly fragmented and would likely demand different standards of warfare? Additionally, we have to be mindful of the potential cost of pursuing broad participation that includes armed groups. To align ourselves with the lowest common denominator means that the rules will be less detailed, more ambiguous, and thus more uncertain.[47] More participation has the potential for broader disagreement and therefore increased levels of negotiation, which might often result in debilitating consequences in terms of the content of the rules. In this sense, direct participation logic based on democratic ideals might enhance procedural legitimacy, but risk debasing substantive legitimacy.

Delegation logic focuses on the political structure of international law-making. National delegations are given the power to make laws by national governments, and in turn, national governments are bestowed with power to negotiate and make international laws by their populace, which includes NSAGs. Delegation logic would therefore hold that NSAG law-making participation is not a necessary component for rule legitimacy. Since law-making power is delegated, direct deliberation that is inclusive of NSAGs is not necessary to secure procedural or substantive legitimacy. Rules will be made by delegated powers and state-centric rules will be consequently binding upon NSAGs.

International law is generally regarded as 'lacking procedural legitimacy' partly because it is founded on two levels of delegation. An individual delegates the law-making function to a national government at the domestic level, and international law is made by a collection of national governments worldwide at the international level. The delegation at the domestic level is direct and it can therefore be easily argued that an individual consented to such political and legislative delegation. With respect to the delegation at the international level, it is not clear whether an ordinary individual would regard international law as relevant and directly binding on them.

As with ordinary individuals, NSAG members did not explicitly delegate the authority to negotiate international laws to states. At the national level, individuals do not actively participate in law-making, but nevertheless, laws are considered to be legitimate because delegation is assumed in the national political and legal system. Similarly, members of NSAGs (as a collection of ordinary citizens of a state) have delegated functions to a state by virtue of being citizens. If we consider NSAG members as individuals as part of the state, they implicitly authorized states to enact international laws. With this logic, NSAGs are not entitled to participate because states, and only states, have delegated law-making powers.

Delegation logic, however, ignores the nature of NSAGs and their political motivations. NSAGs generally oppose government policies, which might include a government's commitment to international rules. Also, the delegation model excludes any form of participation by NSAGs, risking the alienation of this important stakeholder. If IHL bestows only obligations on NSAGs, but not rights, NSAGs might not perceive IHL as legitimate.

How do we reconcile these two seemingly different logics in understanding IHL legitimacy? I offer a conditional theory of non-state armed group participation and rule legitimacy building the middle ground between the two logics. My conditional theory of NSAG participation and IHL legitimacy proposes that *different modes of participation generate different levels of rule*

---

47 See Roberts and Sivakumaran (n 7) for the rebuttal on this point.

legitimacy. Recognizing the heterogeneity among NSAGs will help us better understand the nexus between law-making participation and legitimacy.

4.4 Participation Challenges

Political constraints and legal challenges abound with respect to NSAG participation in international law-making. The first challenge is political: NSAGs' law-making participation might *increase* rule legitimacy of international law but might *decrease* political legitimacy of national governments. Giving participatory roles to NSAGs would enhance their perception about rule legitimacy. But the unavoidable risk is that rules may be de-legitimized as far as states are concerned. This is partly why governments sometimes erect rules to ban the interaction between NSAGs and external entities like international organizations.[48] Also, some NSAGs strategically use international law to boost their political legitimacy and debase the opposing government's legitimacy. Darfuri groups took such an action when they appeared at the ICC while the Sudanese president Omar al-Bashir did not.[49]

The problem then can be viewed as a legitimacy battle between the traditional power-wielders/international legislators (nation-states) and new up-and-comers (NSAGs). This perspective demonstrates the difficulty of achieving rule legitimacy by simply encouraging NSAGs' participation. For example, Common Article 3 and the Additional Protocols are widely accepted, but not by all states. Several states did not sign on to the Additional Protocols, concerned that doing so might confer legitimacy on opposition groups.[50] Governments are in general wary of opposition groups gaining political legitimacy, because they perceive the legitimacy battle as a zero-sum game: if NSAGs have it, governments lose it. This dichotomous formulation might limit the potential for international law to become legitimate in the eyes of both sets of warring parties in internal conflicts.

NSAGs' participation was controversial back in 1974–77 during the negotiation of the Additional Protocols to the Geneva Conventions.[51] History tells us that more diverse contemporary armed groups (warlords, roving bandits, ethnic groups, militias or paramilitaries) would complicate the picture even more. Back in 1977, liberation movements were the dominant forces of armed groups. Fast forward to the 2010s and the contemporary nature of armed groups is a lot more diverse. States might not be opposed to accept or listen to the opinions of some organized NSAGs, but they would be averse to the participation of *any* armed group (which could amount to between 100 and 500 groups at present, depending on how you count them).

---

48 Take, for example, the material support law (18 US Code § 2339A) by the United States that bans the interaction with terrorist organizations. Sudan's al-Bashir government expelling dozens of humanitarian NGOs is another example.

49 See *The Prosecutor v Omar Hassan Ahmad Al Bashir*, ICC-02/05-01/09; *The Prosecutor v Bahar Idriss Abu Garda* ICC-02/05-02/09 (2009); and *The Prosecutor v Abdallah Banda Abakaer Nourain*, ICC-02/05-03/09 (2014). Abu Garda, the Chairman and General Coordinator of Military Operations of the United Resistance Front (URF) appeared at the Court on 18 May 2009. Banda, the Commander-in-Chief of Justice and Equality Movement (JEM), appeared at the Court on 17 June 2010.

50 Reputational concerns of national governments in civil conflicts have empirical support. Barbara Walter, *Reputation and Civil War: Why Separatist Conflicts Are So Violent* (CUP 2009).

51 Anderson (n 31).

The second challenge relates to substantive legal rules, particularly thin legal density of rules which apply to NSAGs. While the Additional Protocols are applicable to internal conflicts, drafters purposefully left ambiguity in laws pertaining to internal conflicts. As a consequence, many legal issues are subject to interpretations, including the proportionality principle and civilian immunity. For example, legal determination of which armed groups would be subject to the Additional Protocols or how NSAG conduct should be accountable is not entirely clear.[52] Such uncertainty inhibits further participation of some NSAGs, which might not be even aware of IHL.[53]

Interpretative tension also arises in regard to law. The legal interpretations of NSAGs are often different from state entities.[54] Local customs or religions often colour the interpretation of IHL, meaning that the way in which NSAGs understand the law may be different from state interpretations.[55] NSAGs' understanding of IHL can look more like a fusion of local norms and international customs. For example, some NSAGs understand that international rules prohibit children under 18 in their ranks, but since Islamic cultures consider children over 15 as adults, this tension can naturally arise.[56]

A related challenge is the design of substantive legal rules. How one should reform IHL, including adding to the existing Geneva Conventions, is a hotly debated topic.[57] The critical questions that should be answered with respect to NSAGs' law-making participation are: whether and to what extent the conduct of NSAGs should be actively regulated, as well as whether they should be held to a different level of accountability than states.[58]

The third problem is the issue of obstinate rejectionists. To some NSAGs, international law is fundamentally illegitimate. They view international law as a Western production and refuse to abide by it. Some jihad armed groups refuse to accept basic principles of IHL, as having a too narrow definition of civilians. The justification offered by the Islamic State for killing civilians of different beliefs is one such example. Although the core principles of Shari'a law are not far from IHL proscriptions, varying strands of Islamic armed groups interpret or justify their acts differently.[59] This is not healthy for the legitimacy consolidation of international law. Those firm rejectionists would not participate because of fundamental differences in beliefs;

---

52 Katharine Fortin and Jann Kleffner, 'Responsibility of Organized Armed Groups Controlling Territory: Attributing Conduct to ISIS' in Rogier Bartels and others (eds), *Military Operations and the Notion of Control Under International Law* (T.M.C. Asser Press 2021) 306–28.

53 On the awareness and interpretations of IHL by NSAGs, see Tanisha Fazal, 'Rebellion, War Aims and the Laws of War' (2017) 146 Daedalus 71.

54 Hyeran Jo, 'International Humanitarian Law on the Periphery: Case of Non-State Armed Actors' (2020) 11 Journal of International Humanitarian Legal Studies 97.

55 Hyeran Jo, 'International Legal Argumentation by Non-State Armed Actors: Patterns, Processes, and Putative Effects' in Steven Ratner and Ian Johnstone, *International Legal Argumentation Outside the Courtroom* (OUP 2021).

56 See the problem with the Moro Islamic Liberation Front (MILF) as described in IRIN, 'Philippines: Child Soldiers in Spotlight as Mindanao Battle Rages' (*IRIN news*, 21 October 2008) <https://reliefweb.int/report/philippines/philippines-child-soldiers-spotlight-mindanao-battle-rages> accessed 31 January 2021.

57 Steven Ratner, 'International vs. Internal Armed Conflict' (*Crimes of War*, 2011) <http://www.crimesofwar.org/a-z-guide/international-vs-internal-armed-conflict/> accessed 31 January 2021.

58 Blum (n 41).

59 Sheikh Wahbeh Al-Zuhili, 'Islam and International Law' (2005) 87 International Review of Red Cross 269.

they cannot participate in law-making because of the presumed strong opposition by state actors.

The political risks and legal difficulties as well as institutional design ambiguity associated with NSAGs' law-making participation suggest that rule legitimacy does not necessarily require NSAGs' participation as a precondition. The difficulties, however, should be balanced with the important aspects of participation that have the potential to enhance the law's legitimacy.

4.5 Conditional Theory of Armed Group Participation and Legitimacy

The enhancement of IHL legitimacy may be conditioned by different modes of armed group participation, whether the participation is direct or not.

Direct participation, such as partaking in treaty-making with observer status, would not necessarily enhance rule legitimacy: it would enlarge the participation pool, so demos or relevant conflict actors might view IHL as legitimate. However, this direct participation approach carries a big political cost, because states might view such a drafting process as *illegitimate*, especially if the substantive rules agreed upon are perceived as being against their interests.

Indirect participation, such as the signing of unilateral declarations or other forms of commitment made by NSAGs, has the potential to enhance rule legitimacy. Without such participation, IHL might lose the ability to generate a 'compliance pull'. However, indirect participation can turn out to be nothing more than empty statements, propaganda, or cheap talk if NSAGs do not follow through and comply in practice. NSAGs' behaviours are difficult to monitor, and it is quite possible that these quasi-legal commitments turn out to be meaningless. These legal and political troubles mean that indirect participation is not a necessary condition for legitimacy of IHL, but a potentially enabling condition, if and only if encouraging this mode of participation is carefully crafted and monitored. Without the mechanism of following up or enforcement,[60] NSAGs' legal commitments could end up as scraps of paper, only to deepen the rift between states and NSAGs. Another form of indirect participation is the inclusion of accumulated practice and compliance behaviours.[61] Treaties are important as the key traditional source of international law, but customs are increasingly important. Although the question as to whether armed groups' practice constitutes custom is controversial, the accumulation of compliance over time will ultimately greatly enhance IHL's legitimacy by demonstrating rule-adherence among key addresses.

Based on the above considerations, Table 21.3 presents the provisional links between the participatory roles of NSAGs and the legitimacy of IHL.

First, 'quasi-legislator' NSAG participation will have ambiguous effects on legitimacy. State opposition, a political roadblock, will *decrease* IHL's legitimacy, although such participation might have the potential to *increase* some procedural legitimacy by including key participants/rule addressees, namely NSAGs.

---

[60] Examples include the Monitoring and Reporting Mechanism in the United Nations Action Plans to reduce the number of child soldiers among armed groups, or the follow-up visits by the Geneva Call in the issue of anti-personnel mines issue.

[61] See Gauthier De Beco, 'Compliance with International Humanitarian Law by Non-State Actors' (2005) 18 Journal of International Law of Peace and Armed Conflict 190 on compliance mechanisms.

Second, 'committer' NSAG participation, through the issuing of unilateral declarations and agreements, has the potential to increase the law's legitimacy. States do not strongly object to such legal commitments by NSAGs, and such commitments can be a vehicle for armed groups' compliance, especially if NSAGs make conscious efforts to enforce those commitments within their organizational ranks. But, this mode of participation can create opportunities on the part of the NSAGs to selectively apply IHL and, thus, it should be clear to NSAGs that they are bound by all IHL rules applicable to them (i.e., Geneva Conventions Common Article 3 and the Additional Protocol II).[62]

Third, 'regulator' NSAGs might enforce IHL through an internal code of conduct. The General Order of the Moro Islamic Liberation Front (MILF) in the Philippines is one such example. The group tried to implement a ban on child soldiering through a code within their ranks.[63] If well enforced and consistent with IHL, these internal rules and regulations can potentially increase the law's legitimacy. However, many NSAGs have fractionalized and disarrayed organizational structures with weak command-and-control structures. Even MILF's commander had difficulty enforcing the ban on child soldiering, because of his weak control over regional commanders who ignored instructions when faced with troop shortages. Therefore, the 'regulator' role of NSAGs has minimal, but potentially beneficial, effects on legitimacy by increasing NSAG-level compliance.

Fourth, 'judge' NSAGs run their own courts to try rule violations. Several scholars have vetted the practice of these rebel courts and find that there are cases of misuse[64] and strategic use of justice as a tool for civilian control and mobilization.[65] NSAGs often use these functions as propaganda, but the political purpose of these bodies cannot be ignored. This mode of participation therefore would not increase IHL legitimacy, having the potential to undermine the substantive and procedural aspects of legitimacy.

Fifth, 'custom-maker' NSAGs include those which comply with IHL rules. Their increasing practice and compliance records will ultimately benefit the IHL regime. When key conflict actors comply, despite the fact that they have inherent interests and a strong incentive to violate the law, they give law legitimacy via accumulated compliance. Thus, I expect that this custom-making practice would increase IHL's legitimacy. However, as noted before, the legal status of accumulating compliance behaviours as customs has not been settled.[66]

The above analysis of the potential mechanisms linking participation and legitimacy tells us that the net effects of NSAG participation might be positive under restricted circumstances. As summarized in Table 21.3, we learn that many cases of participation have ambiguous effects,

---

[62] See Ryngaert (n 7) on the consent-based approach. He writes 'it is the requirement of consent, on which the entire edifice of international law is based after all, that should be addressed head-on, if the legitimacy of IHL and, hence, the effective compliance with it by non-state actors is to be secured.'

[63] See, in particular, Supplemental General Order for General Order Nos. 1 & 2; and in support of the Action Plan between the MILF and the United Nations in the Philippines Regarding the Issue of Recruitment and Use of Child Soldiers in the Armed Conflict in Mindanao by the Bangsamoro Islamic Armed Forces, the armed wing of the Moro Islamic Liberation Front. Geneva Call (n 22).

[64] Gejji (n 26).

[65] Cyanne Loyle, 'Rebel Justice During Armed Conflict' (2020) 65 Journal of Conflict Resolution 108.

[66] Jean-Marie Henckaerts and Louise Doswald-Beck, *Customary International Humanitarian Law* (CUP 2005); Roberts and Sivakumaran (n 7).

Table 21.3 Modes of NSAG law-making participation and rule legitimacy: links

NSAG participation types	Mechanism and effects	Legitimacy of IHL
Quasi-legislators	Political roadblock (state opposition)	Legitimacy effect ambiguous
Committers	Increased acceptance and recognition of rules; adding consent and custom (via compliance): ownership of rules	Potentially increase legitimacy
Regulators	Internal monitoring: internalization	Increase legitimacy
Judges	Judicial decisions	Legitimacy effect suspect
Custom-makers	Increased compliance	Potentially increase legitimacy

which warrant a cautious approach when choosing a particular armed group's participation in the making of IHL.

5. CONCLUSION

International law is ever evolving in the sense that laws and norms are constantly interpreted and practised by users of the law. Substantive and interpretative participation is already occurring among some non-state armed actors. In some cases, the participation of NSAGs in international law-making may prove helpful to the law's legitimacy to the extent that such participation incentivizes acceptance of law and compliance with law. For the sake of the legitimacy of rules and of international law, indirect law-making participation in the form of humanitarian law engagement should be encouraged as long as it changes the perceptions of NSAGs, with the potential to increase compliance as a consequence. After all, legitimacy is based on perception and accompanied behaviours. Already compliant NSAGs will need little attention, as they will strive to contribute to international law-making, through unilateral declarations or by making human-rights-based peace treaties. Switchover compliers, who have the potential to switch from non-compliance to compliance, will need a nudge towards knowledge surrounding the rules, and getting accustomed to the mode of informal participation through interactions with international humanitarian actors.

I dealt with the question of rule legitimacy in the context of non-international armed conflicts and NSAGs. However, I hope this chapter partly touched upon a deeper question in international law, namely, how we judge the legitimacy of international law, and on what criteria. The analysis of the evolving nature of armed conflicts in the world, and the consideration of the actual practice of NSAGs, reveals the following: our traditional thinking that state consent gives international law rule legitimacy might be outdated, and new perspectives on how to build rule legitimacy might be needed. Future research should address whether NSAGs' commitments *actually* increase compliance for the benefit of IHL's legitimacy, or whether NSAGs' expressed legal commitments amount simply to cheap talk or empty promises. These are empirical questions that should be answered more rigorously in order for IHL to remain relevant and legitimate.

22. Non-state armed groups and international humanitarian law-making – the challenge of legitimacy: A reply to Cindy Wittke and Hyeran Jo

Cedric Ryngaert[1]

1. INTRODUCTION

In this comment I engage with Cindy Wittke and Hyeran Jo's contributions, focusing specifically on the legitimacy challenges with which the imposition of international humanitarian law (IHL) on non-state armed groups is confronted.

Taking first the perspective of *international executive norm-direction* developed by Wittke, legitimacy may notably be in doubt when external actors, such as the United Nations Security Council (UNSC), impose – via resolutions – ceasefire agreements and their attendant norms on armed actors, including non-state actors, embroiled in intra-state conflict. Such a directive process may well be lawful given the broad executive powers of the UNSC, but possibly have insufficient regard for norm-support in the field by the actors called on to execute the agreement. In section 2, therefore, I plead for adequate ownership – a key parameter of legitimacy – of ceasefire agreements by the parties to the conflict. In section 3, I take the perspective of *the imposition of IHL on non-state armed groups via treaties* – the Geneva Conventions and their Additional Protocols in particular – to which those groups have not formally consented. To counter the legitimacy deficit from which such imposition suffers, and engaging with Hyeran Jo's arguments, I critically appraise alternative methods of legitimacy-enhancement that are based on procedural and substantive justice. I argue that securing non-state actor consent is desirable from a legitimacy and eventually effectiveness perspective, but that a failure to secure such consent should not be an argument to cast doubt on the binding character of IHL for non-state armed groups.

[1] The author appreciates the financial support from the European Research Council (Proposal 336230 – UNIJURIS) and the Dutch Organization for Scientific Research (No. 016.135.322).

2. LEGITIMACY AND THE TOP–DOWN IMPOSITION OF NORMS ON NON-STATE ARMED GROUPS BY THE UN SECURITY COUNCIL

Cindy Wittke's chapter highlights an international process that has been under way for some time in different areas of limited governance, namely the exercise of what Anne Orford has termed 'international functionalist authority' or 'international executive rule': where local actors do not have the capacity to govern effectively themselves, jurisdiction and authority shifts to international actors, who centrally determine the goals to be achieved while relying on local law-making where useful for implementation purposes.[2] Wittke's account of the UNSC *imposing* ceasefires on governments and non-state armed groups fits this pattern. As peace and security are global public goods,[3] even if their disturbance might seem to be localized within just one state (in the form of an intra-state conflict), the international community, represented by the UNSC, has an interest in their protection. This is not just because intra-state conflicts have transnational connections these days, but also because state sovereignty has become conditional on the ability of states to protect their own citizens,[4] and because humanity-centred, cosmopolitan thinking has made the individual the ultimate unit of legal and moral concern.[5] This means that, to the extent that states and non-state actors fail to end an armed conflict, fail to agree on rules that provide short- and long-term human security,[6] and/or fail to agree on power division and institution-(re-)building, they risk intervention by the international community and loss of ownership over national transitional processes. Thus, ceasefire agreements and their substantive provisions, including IHL provisions, may be imposed on the warring parties by binding UNSC resolutions. UNSC intervention concerning ceasefire agreements inevitably raises the question: where is law-making precisely located? For the ultimate legal source of an 'imposed' ceasefire is the UN Security Council resolution, i.e., a decision of an international organization that could, in some circumstances, be legally binding and thus a source of international law. These questions have been raised in similar contexts in the past, e.g., when the UNSC 'imposed' a bilateral treaty between the UN and Lebanon on the estab-

---

2 Anne Orford, *International Authority and the Responsibility to Protect* (CUP 2011) 203 ('International executive rule works through local laws where possible, trumping them with administrative regulations and decrees where necessary to achieve the goals determined centrally.').

3 Scott Barrett, *Why Cooperate?: The Incentive to Supply Global Public Goods* (OUP 2007).

4 See for a philosophical exploration: Jens Bartelson, *Sovereignty as Symbolic Form* (Routledge 2014).

5 See Ruti G. Teitel, *Humanity's Law* (OUP 2011); Roland Pierik and Wouter Werner (eds), *Cosmopolitanism in Context: Perspectives from International Law and Political Theory* (CUP 2010) 1.

6 The Commission on Human Security defines human security as 'protect[ing] the vital core of all human lives in ways that enhance human freedoms and human fulfilment. Human security means protecting fundamental freedoms – freedoms that are the essence of life. It means protecting people from critical (severe) and pervasive (widespread) threats and situations. It means using processes that build on people's strengths and aspirations. It means creating political, social, environmental, economic, military and cultural systems that together give people the building blocks of survival, livelihood and dignity.' See Commission on Human Security, *Human Security Now. Protecting and Empowering People* (2003).

lishment of the Special Tribunal for Lebanon on the latter country when it failed to approve the treaty text.[7]

2.1 Legality

Few would doubt that, under the UN Charter, the UNSC has the authority for such action, either as a provisional measure under Article 40, or as a more extended measure under Article 41. It just remains to be examined whether the relevant UNSC resolution is indeed binding, or was meant to be binding. Wittke engages at length with this issue, which requires some serious interpretative work with respect to the relevant resolution, also in light of previous resolutions on the same subject matter. There is merit in her argument – which harks back to the *Namibia* Advisory Opinion of the International Court of Justice[8] – that UNSC resolutions could also be binding if not (explicitly) adopted under Chapter VII, even if there is no consensus on this in the literature. In order to determine whether such resolutions are actually binding, teleological techniques of interpreting UNSC resolutions, which emphasize the substantive goals of the international community, may be called for, as international law is currently moving from formalist to non-formalist approaches, especially where it comes to the protection of such global public goods as peace and security.[9] The 'Charter'-focus approach – advanced by Wittke and inspired by the work of Henderson and Lubell,[10] and which puts a premium on the primary goal of the drafters of the UN Charter to maintain international peace and security supposedly articulated in the resolution – is such a technique. This approach still finds its roots in the 'object and purpose' language of Article 31 of the Vienna Convention on the Law of Treaties.[11] However, as the Convention does not technically govern the interpretation of UNSC resolutions,[12] even more innovative approaches could be resorted to, e.g., consequentialist ones that base the interpretation of a text on its anticipated beneficial *effects* on global justice.[13] Thus, in case of uncertainty as to the binding character of a UNSC resolution imposing a ceasefire on

---

[7] UNSC Res 1757 (30 May 2007) UN Doc S/RES/1757; *The Prosecutor v Ayyash et al* STL 11/01/PT/TC (27 July 2012); *Prosecutor v Dusko Tadić* (Jurisdiction) ICTY IT-94-1-AR72 (2 October 1995).

[8] *Legal Consequences for States of the Continued Presence of South Africa in Namibia (South West Africa) notwithstanding Security Council Resolution 276 (1970)* (Advisory Opinion) [1971] ICJ Rep 16 paras 114–16.

[9] eg Nico Krisch, 'The Decay of Consent: International Law in an Age of Global Public Goods' (2014) 108 American Journal of International Law 1 on the decline of consent with respect to the protection of global public goods by international law.

[10] Christian Henderson and Noam Lubell, 'The Contemporary Legal Nature of UN Security Council Ceasefire Resolutions' (2013) 26 Leiden Journal of International Law 369, 371.

[11] Vienna Convention on the Law of Treaties (adopted 23 May 1969, entered into force 27 January 1980) 1155 UNTS 331 art 31(1) 'A treaty shall be interpreted in good faith (…) in the light of its object and purpose.'

[12] Wittke concedes this, but nevertheless goes on to apply the rather classic principles of treaty law to the interpretation of UNSC resolutions – while de-emphasizing the role of the original intention and the subsequent practice of states.

[13] See for a consequentialist assessment of the justice of international law Steven Ratner, *The Thin Justice of International Law* (OUP 2015) 62 stating that 'in evaluating the justice of individual legal norms, we should similarly be concerned with the extent to which compliance with the rule will contribute to a state of affairs associated with a just world.' Note that Ratner does, as such, not propose consequentialism as a technique of interpreting documents.

the warring parties, the scales may tip in favour of 'bindingness' where important beneficial effects in terms of human security, including compliance with international humanitarian and human rights law, could be expected.

2.2 Legitimacy

On the basis of Chapter VII of the UN Charter, and in case of uncertainty when using various techniques of interpretation, an argument could thus be made (1) that UNSC resolutions could legally force a ceasefire agreement, including specific obligations, on a state and a non-state actor, and (2) that both actors are bound by law to implement such an agreement and its obligations. However, as Hyeran Jo also observes, legality in itself does not guarantee adherence. Adherence depends on legitimacy, which in turn may be a function of participation of, and ownership by, the norm-addressees. Wittke is certainly right when stating that 'an effective ceasefire would still require a certain degree of mutual agreement, *i.e.* consensus, between the conflict parties'. This holds true even where the international community would take more forcible action by intervening to enforce the ceasefire. While such action may in the short run ensure effectiveness, in the long run, the use of force cannot displace the consent of the stakeholders as the basis for governance and compliance.

In light of concerns over legitimacy, and the attendant problems of effectiveness, it can be argued that, when the chances of a decent agreement between the parties are limited, the UNSC may want to refrain from imposing ceasefire agreements, as such agreements are unlikely to be complied with. UNSC intervention appears to be much more legitimate where it supports and facilitates existing and burgeoning agreements between the parties, and thus does not disown them.[14] One could assume that parties may even welcome such intervention when the UNSC makes available additional resources to monitor and verify compliance with the respective parties' commitments, and when, by sharing best practices, it demonstrates that ceasefire agreements may be in the best interests of the parties and have led to a more durable peace, reconciliation and reconstruction.

3. LEGITIMACY AND THE BINDING CHARACTER OF INTERNATIONAL HUMANITARIAN LAW CONVENTIONS

A concern over the legitimacy and effectiveness of external imposition of norms in non-international armed conflicts is also at the heart of Hyeran Jo's contribution. While Wittke focuses on the imposition of *particular (ceasefire) agreements and obligations* on both states and non-state actors through international executive action (UNSC intervention), Jo concentrates on the imposition of *general obligations* – especially obligations under IHL – on non-state armed groups through conventions addressed to both states and non-state actors. There is obviously some overlap between these processes – otherwise they would not

[14] Darryl Robinson, 'Inescapable Dyads: Why the International Criminal Court Cannot Win' (2015) 28 Leiden Journal of International Law 323, 328 discussing UNSC referrals of situations to the ICC, and citing in this respect the criticism that in this case 'the ICC is intervening without international or local support, it will be ineffective, it will raise hopes that will be disappointed, and it will muddy the waters of other important processes'.

be discussed together here. Not only do they both raise legitimacy concerns which pertain to non-state armed groups, but also questions as to whether the relevant obligations have the same content: the obligations to which non-state armed groups are subject under general international law (IHL or even international human rights law)[15] may indeed be redeployed or 'recalled' in particular agreements. The processes are nevertheless analytically distinct, as their formal legal sources differ: the former is based on a UN Security Council resolution, whereas the latter is based on a convention (treaty).

3.1 Participation

Jo starts from the well-known logical inconsistency that, under positive IHL applicable in non-international armed conflicts, non-state armed groups are required to abide by the rules, and only rules containing obligations for that matter,[16] which their opponents – states – created.[17] Such a normative solution was obviously informed by the desire to create a level playing field, in which both states and non-state actors would be subject to the same legal constraints. The question as to why the latter are bound by obligations without having given their consent to be bound, does not dissipate, however. In earlier publications, I have signalled this problem, and, on grounds of both legitimacy and effectiveness, advocated the securing of consent of non-state armed groups.[18] Similarly, Jo is of the view that, for reasons of legitimacy, armed groups' participation in law-making is advisable. She advances a number of participatory techniques to this effect, which I would almost unflinchingly support. Just like Jo, I attach great weight to non-state actors' issuance of unilateral declarations, conclusion of agreements,

---

15 There is a large debate going on regarding whether, and if so, under what circumstances, non-state armed groups are bound by international human rights law. See for a thorough investigation Katharine Fortin, *Accountability of Armed Groups under Human Rights Law* (OUP 2017). See also an earlier publication of mine: Cedric Ryngaert, 'Human Rights Obligations of Armed Groups' (2008) 41 Revue belge de droit international 355.

16 See on this Veronika Bilkova, 'Treat Them as They Deserve!? Three Approaches to Armed Opposition Groups under Current International Law' (2010) 4 Human Rights and International Legal Discourse 111.

17 See Geneva Convention for the Amelioration of the Condition of the Wounded and Sick in Armed Forces in the Field (opened for signature 12 August 1949, entered into force 21 October 1950) 75 UNTS 31 (GC I); Geneva Convention for the Amelioration of the Condition of Wounded, Sick and Shipwrecked Members of Armed Forces at Sea (opened for signature 12 August 1949, entered into force 21 October 1950) 75 UNTS 85 (GC II); Geneva Convention relative to the Treatment of Prisoners of War of August 12, 1949 (opened for signature 12 August 1949, entered into force 21 October 1950) 75 UNTS 135 (GC III); Geneva Convention relative to the Protection of Civilian Persons in Time of War (opened for signature 12 August 1949, entered into force 21 October 1950) 75 UNTS 287 (GC IV), common art 3; Protocol Additional to the Geneva Conventions of 12 August 1949, and relating to the Protection of Victims of International Armed Conflicts (opened for signature 8 June 1977, entered into force 7 December 1978) 1125 UNTS 3 (AP I).

18 Cedric Ryngaert, 'Imposing International Duties on Non-State Actors and the Legitimacy of International Law' in Math Noortmann and Cedric Ryngaert (eds), *Non-State Actor Dynamics in International Law: From Law-Takers to Law-Makers* (Routledge 2010); idem, 'Non-State Actors in International Humanitarian Law' in Jean d'Aspremont (ed), *Participants in the International Legal System* (Routledge 2011); Cedric Ryngaert and Anneleen Van de Meulebroucke, 'Enhancing and Enforcing Compliance with International Humanitarian Law by Non-State Armed Groups: An Inquiry into some Mechanisms' (2011) 16 Journal of Conflict and Security Law 443.

and promulgation of internal codes of conduct (in her taxonomy, Jo usefully calls such non-state actors 'committers' and 'regulators', as subcategories of indirect participation in IHL-making).[19] Just like Jo, given practical and political obstacles, I expect little from direct participation of armed groups in international humanitarian law-making. And just like Jo, echoing the publication of Roberts and Sivakumaran,[20] I would cautiously support non-state actors' participation in the formation of 'quasi-custom'.[21]

3.2 Substantive Legitimacy

However, I may not fully agree with the underlying theoretical reasons for enhanced participation in law-making, namely Jo's understanding of the concept of legitimacy. Jo argues basically that such participation enhances the procedural and substantive legitimacy of IHL norms. Procedural legitimacy is, in essence, a Habermasian notion pursuant to which only processes of true deliberative democracy, which represent the relevant stakeholders and potential norm-addressees, are likely to yield legitimate law.[22] This notion forms the theoretical backbone for the direct and indirect involvement of non-state armed groups in international humanitarian law-making. In addition, Jo employs the notion of *substantive legitimacy*. In my own work, I have used this notion to refer to the *quality of the norm* at issue, and argued that the requirement of procedural legitimacy – in particular the consent of a non-state actor – need not strictly apply to *fundamental* legal norms, with the content of which no reasonable actor would, or is supposed to, take issue (e.g., IHL norms that rise to the level of *jus cogens*).[23] Jo, for her part, submits that substantive legitimacy comes from 'accumulated practices' or 'widespread compliance'.[24] One may wonder, in this respect, whether using this notion of substantive legitimacy does not lead to circular reasoning, in that norm-compliance informs the legitimacy of IHL, whereas at the same time legitimacy informs compliance. Thus, it is argued that because armed groups comply with most IHL rules, IHL's legitimacy increases. *Why* precisely these groups would comply remains somewhat of a mystery, but an informed guess is that they do so because there is an intermediate cause for them to do so, namely a perception that these norms (at least their underlying rationales) are legitimate, if not because they have come into being through a genuine participatory process, then at least because of the substantive quality of these norms ('output legitimacy' may possibly be used in this context).

---

19 A failure to commit to international humanitarian law norms – which may well occur as committing is a voluntary act – does not, however, detract from the continuing validity of these norms with respect to non-state actor conduct, even if the theoretical basis of this validity remains opaque.

20 Anthea Roberts and Sandesh Sivakumaran, 'Lawmaking by Non-State Actors: Engaging Armed Groups in the Creation of International Humanitarian Law' (2012) 37 Yale Journal of International Law 107.

21 See also ILA Committee on Non-State Actors, 'Second Report of the Committee: Non-State Actors in International Law: Lawmaking and Participation Rights' (International Law Association 2012) 6 of which I was the co-rapporteur.

22 Jürgen Habermas, *Between Facts and Norms: Contributions to a Discourse Theory of Law and Democracy* (MIT Press 1996).

23 See Ryngaert, 'Imposing International Duties on Non-State Actors' (n 18).

24 Hyeran Jo, 'Law-Participation by Non-State Armed Groups: The Prerequisite of Law's Legitimacy?', Chapter 21 in this book, 364, 372–73.

Various actors may well have different opinions on the 'substantive justice' of a given norm, so that this line of legitimacy reasoning may only take us so far. Jo mentions in this respect armed groups that would reject even basic norms of IHL regarding the distinction between civilians and combatants. Allowing such armed groups to have a voice in international humanitarian law-making may then well risk debasing the substantive legitimacy of IHL. This fear may be overblown in that, in the dominant understanding of how customary law norms crystallize, quasi-uniform practice, including the practice of *states*, is required. Accordingly, one need not be particularly concerned about the potential regression of existing norms of customary IHL. However, there is admittedly some risk that emerging, more progressive IHL norms that may be supported by states never actually crystallize because of the opposition of non-state armed groups afraid of losing their tactical advantage in the asymmetrical warfare often characterizing non-international armed conflicts.[25]

3.3 Differential Treatment

On a somewhat related note, there is the vexed issue of whether armed groups should be held to a different (more relaxed) standard than states in terms of IHL compliance – an issue earlier addressed by Gabriella Blum.[26] There is little doubt that such a principle will be supported by armed groups as it takes into account the reality of asymmetrical warfare, but it remains to be seen which armed groups are entitled to 'preferential treatment', and in what circumstances. It is, in any event, of note that in respect of state obligations, the European Court of Human Rights has recognized, in an armed conflicts context, that convention rights can be 'divided and tailored'[27] – which opens possibilities for various international actors to incur different obligations, depending on the context and their respective capacities to comply. An argument can surely be made that at least with respect to positive obligations, some armed groups might be held to a lower standard, simply because they have limited resources.[28] Differential treatment of non-state armed groups can enhance the legitimacy of IHL in the latter's eyes, and may possibly also draw support from weaker states who might be bound by similarly relaxed standards. However, too explicit an acknowledgment of differential treatment may draw the ire of other states, and risks decreasing the legitimacy of, and state compliance with, IHL.

3.4 Government Compliance

This brings me to another important point raised by Jo, namely that government compliance with IHL boosts the legitimacy of IHL, and encourages non-state actors to comply in turn, as

---

[25] Think, for instance, entirely hypothetically, of an international humanitarian law rule, inspired by the human right to life, that requires that lethal force be used only as a last resort.

[26] Gabriella Blum, 'On a Differential Law of War' (2011) 52 Harvard International Law Journal 164.

[27] *Al-Skeini and ors, Bar Human Rights Committee (intervening) and ors (intervening) v United Kingdom,* 53 EHRR 18 ECtHR (2011) para 137 in the context of the extraterritorial application of the European Convention on Human Rights; as also highlighted by Fortin (n 15) 154.

[28] eg Protocol Additional to the Geneva Conventions of 12 August 1949, and relating to the Protection of Victims of Non-International Armed Conflicts (adopted 8 June 1977, entered into force 7 December 1978) 1125 UNTS 609 art 5(1)(c) providing that persons whose liberty has been restricted 'shall be allowed to receive individual or collective relief' by all parties to the non-international armed conflict.

a matter of reciprocity, with IHL norms. In fact, Jo considers this strategy to enjoy a higher priority, in terms of IHL legitimacy enhancement, than bringing about armed groups' participation in law-making. Surely, the power of example has a major impact on non-state actors' willingness to comply with IHL, as non-state actors are typically quick to condemn government incidents and deflect criticism of their own record. That said, analytically speaking, the exact link with the legitimacy of IHL may not readily be seen. It seems that non-state armed groups, confronted with lacklustre compliance of governments with IHL, do no more than criticize the governments' compliance records, and do not necessarily cast doubt on the legitimacy of the relevant norms. In fact, precisely because they criticize governments for the transgression of IHL norms, they vindicate the existence and legitimacy of these rules. Now obviously, transgressions by the government may limit the appetite of the non-state armed group to comply with IHL, but this is arguably not a matter of legitimacy, but rather an aspect of the – admittedly wrong – characterization of IHL conventions as bilateral, synallagmatic contracts, in which each party to the contract is bound to provide something to the other.[29] The above comment obviously does not detract from the importance of shoring up government compliance with IHL.

3.5 Enforcement

Apart from government compliance, Jo also identifies other priorities in terms of IHL legitimacy enhancement, notably strengthening enforcement, by the International Criminal Court (ICC) in particular. In the abstract, enforcement of IHL adds to its legitimacy and even enhances its legal character. Indeed, the unavailability of enforcement mechanisms is sometimes cited as evidence of the immature character of the international legal system. As far as the ICC's legitimacy in the eyes of non-state armed groups is concerned, it is surely desirable for the ICC to also go after government representatives, and not only after rebels – a criticism that has for instance been levelled at the ICC's actions with respect to Uganda.[30] Nonetheless, one may wonder whether more vigorous enforcement by the ICC contributes, as a matter of course, to its legitimacy. Going by African reactions against the ICC's vigorous enforcement of IHL – including some states' threats to leave the Court[31] – enforcement and legitimacy

29 In reality, currently applicable international humanitarian law is an *objective regime* that no longer allows one party to invoke non-compliance by another party to justify or excuse its own non-compliance. See ICRC, *30th International Conference of the Red Cross and Red Crescent: Resolution 3, Reaffirmation and implementation of international humanitarian law: Preserving human life and dignity in armed conflict* (ICRC 2007), Preamble 'recalling that the obligation to respect international humanitarian law binds all parties to an armed conflict, and emphasising that this obligation is not based on reciprocity'; see also *Prosecutor v Kupreškić et al.* (Judgment) ICTY IT-95-16-T (14 January 2000) para 517. On countermeasures see International Law Commission, 'Draft articles on Responsibility of States for Internationally Wrongful Acts, with Commentaries' (2001) UN Doc A/56/10 art 22.

30 Robinson (n 14) 327 referring to the 'apology' criticism that the Court is being used as a tool to further the interests of the territorial state party to the conflict.

31 'African Union summit on ICC pull-out over Ruto trial' (*BBC*, 20 September 2013) <https://www.bbc.com/news/world-africa-24173557> accessed on 31 January 2021; Michael Pizzi, 'South Africa threatens to withdraw from ICC, alleging anti-African bias' (*Al-Jazeera America*, 12 October 2015) <http://america.aljazeera.com/articles/2015/10/12/south-africa-threatens-to-withdraw-from-icc-alleging-anti-african-bias.html> accessed on 31 January 2021; 'African Union members back Kenyan plan to

appear to be inversely related. It is uncertain whether this institutional criticism will also yield doubts over substantive norms, but there is definitely reason to be concerned over institutional overreach. If institutions start interpreting norms in a manner that is not attuned to the realities on the battlefield, the legitimacy of both the institution and the IHL norm may suffer.[32]

3.6 International Committee of the Red Cross (ICRC)

A third strategy advanced by Jo as an IHL legitimacy-enhancer is the strengthening of the legitimacy of the ICRC, the guardian of IHL. It is not entirely clear to what extent the ICRC is currently seen as illegitimate, on what grounds, and how this should be remedied. One could think, however, of the ICRC's practice of, in some situations, preferring IHL compliance over IHL obedience: when engaging with states or armed groups, the ICRC sometimes uses non-legal discourses (e.g., morality, tradition, international recognition, reciprocity…) when trying to persuade its interlocutors to comply with IHL.[33] Such a strategy may well be successful in its net results as the normative pull for compliance may not work for all parties, but inevitably the legitimacy of IHL as a system of norms that should be complied with because of its legal character may suffer.[34] It is not clear, however, whether Jo would indeed cite this practice in her critique of the ICRC.

4. CONCLUDING OBSERVATIONS

Despite the critique formulated in this comment, Jo, Wittke and I agree that norm imposition through international executive action or generally applicable treaties or customary norms is considered as problematic from a legitimacy perspective. The solution is to deprive the addressees of the norm-illegitimacy argument by giving them sufficient agency and ownership over the shaping of norms, and thus to widen the circle of primary law-makers.[35] This strategy, which has obvious compliance advantages, will however only work when the addressees also want to own the norms. My reading is that we also all agree that, therefore, a fallback option should remain of simply imposing obligations on the parties to the conflict, or recalling their existing obligations, regardless of the legitimacy losses thus incurred.

leave ICC' (*The Guardian*, 1 February 2016) <https://www.theguardian.com/world/2016/feb/01/african-union-kenyan-plan-leave-international-criminal-court> accessed on 31 January 2021.

[32] This also explains why art 124 of the Rome Statute of the International Criminal Court (adopted 7 July 1998, entered into force 1 July 2002) 2187 UNTS 3 provides that a state 'on becoming a party to this Statute, may declare that, for a period of seven years after the entry into force of this Statute for the State concerned, it does not accept the jurisdiction of the Court with respect to the category of crimes referred to in article 8', *ie*, the provision on war crimes.

[33] This has been documented by Steven R. Ratner, 'Law Promotion Beyond Law Talk: The Red Cross, Persuasion, and the Laws of War' (2011) 22 European Journal of International Law 459.

[34] ibid 500 'For lawyers, a persuasive process oriented toward compliance might represent a poor substitute for the rule of law.'; Ratner himself is, however, supportive of the ICRC's approach: 'Legal scholars obsessed with the ideal of internalization are missing the true picture of advocacy in the international arena, where actors concerned with norms argue – and settle – for action merely in conformity with them.'

[35] See also Teitel (n 5) 171, 203.

PART VII

Legitimacy and norm entrepreneurs

23. The impact of human rights advocacy: Between (mis)stating the law and pursuing humanitarian policies?

Robert Cryer

1. INTRODUCTION

International humanitarian law (IHL) – or the law of armed conflict (LOAC), depending on the preferred terminology (and the choice can be one that can be indicative of deeper commitments)[1] – is a topic that has, over the past two decades, become a ground of considerable contestation. This is, in part, owing to the fact that human rights bodies, in particular non-governmental organizations (NGOs), have increasingly turned to it to refer to its protective aspects in armed conflict. It is probably fair to say that such NGOs have been more comfortable with the 'Geneva' aspects of IHL than its 'Hague' counterpart. To some extent there is a level of ambivalence about the latter aspect of law of the armed conflict amongst the NGO community – after all, the law here permits status-based killing, which is something that is an anathema to many in the human rights community. Nonetheless, there are protections in the law here to which many in the human rights community seek to refer. Perhaps on the other side, those involved in the practical application of IHL/LOAC seek to invoke experience/expertise, in a manner that Foucault would have more than understood. As Janina Dill has said, 'different professional angles generate distinct emphases in the assessment of war'.[2]

It is the purpose of this chapter to look into these issues, and discuss how they have played out in a number of contexts. It will begin by discussing aspects of the various professions and their interpretations of the law in the area, and how the law in the area is perhaps particularly susceptible to what, more than 50 years ago, Judge Radhabinodh Pal described (in a slightly different context) as 'interested interpretation'.[3] As such, the chapter will also discuss the senses of identity that inform such interpretations of the law, and those which are taken to be those identities by others. It will also critique the idea that any one identity can easily be

---

1 See David Luban, 'Military Necessity and the Cultures of Military Law' (2013) 26 Leiden Journal of International Law 315; Robert Cryer, 'Review of A.P.V. Rogers, *Law on The Battlefield*' (2013) 10 Journal of Conflict and Security Law 121. In this piece I will use the terms interchangeably. Deliberately.

2 Janina Dill, *Legitimate Targets: Social Construction, International Law and US Targeting* (CUP 2015) 2.

3 Dissenting Opinion of the Member from India, reprinted in Neil Boister and Robert Cryer (eds), *Documents on the Tokyo International Military Tribunal* (OUP 2008) 907.

attributed to any one particular interpreter, as it would be reductionist to ascribe one identity to any person. It is the case that there are polarized positions, and they will be emphasized, but the position is more often nuanced.

This is perhaps to be expected, as the LOAC is itself torn between military necessity and humanity, and so views are certain to differ. To instantiate its points, and to further the debate, the chapter then discusses two areas where this has been at issue: unnecessary suffering and proportionality. It concludes with a plea for debate between the various parties without some of the rancour that has sometimes characterized the debate, with actors on many sides of the debate caricaturing the views of whom they disagree.

2. IDENTITIES IN INTERNATIONAL HUMANITARIAN LAW

First, however, some conceptual ground-clearing needs to be engaged in.

It is tempting to deal with military lawyers and human rights lawyers who discuss the LOAC as two diametrically opposed groups that can simply be put in contradistinction to one another.[4] It is easy to do, as Yoram Dinstein has done (perhaps for rhetorical effect, and not without caveats) to speak in a binary fashion of military lawyers and 'human rights-niks' (with a clear preference for the former).[5] In an analogous, albeit more subtle, manner, David Luban has spoken of two different cultures of 'military law'.[6] The first being the LOAC concept, which provides a primary role for the utilitarian role of the *jus in bello* in authorizing that which is required with military necessity. As the second culture, he describes the humanitarian (IHL) vision of the law. This 'begins with humanitarianism, and assigns human dignity and human rights primary status (…) [it] (…) regards peace as the normal condition for human life (…) but it is not pacifist'.[7]

In many ways I adopt Luban's frame for the purposes of this chapter, although, as he accepts, it is somewhat Manichean,[8] as both supposed groups are far more diverse than might be thought. I will also, with some caveats, use Koskenniemi's quadripartite distinction between the roles of judge, adviser, activist, and academic.[9] Although, the roles can change, overlap, and may be temporally focused (not a position I would expect Koskenniemi to disagree with).

---

4 For these ideal types see Luban (n 1) 317.

5 Yoram Dinstein, 'Concluding Remarks: LOAC and Attempts to Abuse or Subvert It' in Raul Pedrozo and Daria Wollshlager (eds), *International Law and the Changing Character of War* (US Naval War College 2013) 488.

6 The term is one with which some exception may be taken as military law, at least in the UK context, means something rather different from the *jus in bello*.

7 See Luban (n 1) 316. For a piece that puts the distinction into question on practical, sociological and historical grounds see David Kennedy, 'War and International Law: Distinguishing Military and Humanitarian Professions' in Anthony Helm (ed), *The Law of War in the 21st Century: Weaponry and the Use of Force* (US Naval War College 2006) 3.

8 It could also be thought to trace the insider/outsider perspectives outlined by Thomas Franck, 'An Outsider Looks at the Foreign Office Culture' (2005) 23 Wisconsin International Law Journal 1.

9 Martti Koskenniemi, 'Between Commitment and Cynicism: Outline for a Theory of International Law as Practice' in Jean d'Aspremont and others (eds), *International Law as Practice* (CUP 2017) 38, this was initially drawn by Koskenniemi in 1999 (under the same title in United Nations (ed), *Collection of Essays by Legal Advisers of States, Legal Advisers of International Organisations and Practitioners in the Field of International Law* (UN 1999) 495). The former may now be easier to find.

Similarly, it is also not to treat all such groups as monolithic. To return to Luban's armed conflict/humanitarian distinction, for example, on the military side of things, even within the West (indeed within NATO) very clear differences can be seen between the thought of the late Brigadier General APV Rogers and, for example, Colonel W Hays Parks.[10] Furthermore, it is salutary to note that some, such as the very well-respected (and rightly) commentator on the law of the armed conflict, Professor Michael Schmitt, an ex-military lawyer who now also has an academic position, are perhaps seen differently by different audiences, as something of a hawk in Europe, but often thought of as a dove on the other side of the proverbial pond.[11]

It is also important to distinguish between non-governmental actors,[12] who are by no means all the same. All they share is that they are non-governmental actors,[13] they 'follow their own stars',[14] have different goals, agendas, and levels of expertise. So, for example, at one end there is Human Rights Watch's very careful analysis of the Kosovo Conflict, which was informed by the very well-respected LOAC (and human rights) lawyer François Hampson,[15] at the other are comments by human rights bodies that have no expertise in the area, and quite clearly are not legitimate actors in the area (one example would be the 'National' Red Cross Society of the *Republika Sprksa*, the head of which was one Mr Karadžić).[16] Naturally many organizations fall between these two poles, and both notional 'sides' can be guilty of caricaturing those with whom they disagree. What is 'lawfare' for some lawyers is appropriate advocacy for others.[17] Similarly, what may be seen as a pragmatic, militarily legitimate interpretation to some, may appear self-interested militarism to others.[18] The International Committee of the Red Cross (ICRC) obviously has a special role in both developing and improving respect for humanitarian law, and guards it carefully.[19]

This can be linked to state-based and broader approaches to international law-making. States have traditionally asserted a monopoly over the creation, application, and interpretation of international law. As Sandesh Sivakumaran has argued: 'Contrary to orthodox positivist accounts (…) it is the community of international humanitarian lawyers that makes and shapes international humanitarian law and it does so through dialogue between its members.'[20]

---

10 Anthony P.V. Rogers, *Law on the Battlefield* (2nd edn, MUP 2004); cf William Hays Parks, 'Air War and the Law of War' (1990) 32 Air Force Law Review 1.

11 This comment comes from discussions with Professor Schmitt; and, it ought to be said that anything in this chapter that may not be taken as being *ad hominem*, my comments are not intended as such.

12 Steve Charnovitz, 'Nongovernmental Organizations and International Law' (2006) 100 American Journal of International Law 348, 350.

13 See Stefan Hobe, 'Non-Governmental Actors' in Rüdiger Wolfrum (ed), *Max Planck Encyclopaedia of Public International Law*, vol 7 (OUP 2012) 716.

14 Charnovitz (n 12) 348.

15 Human Rights Watch, *Under Orders: War Crimes in Kosovo* (Human Rights Watch 2001).

16 Taylor Baines, 'Profile: "Radovan Karadzic"' (*Global Policy Forum*, 11 August 2000) <https://www.globalpolicy.org/component/content/article/165/29445.html> accessed 31 January 2021.

17 See generally Charles S. Dunlap, 'Lawfare Today: A Perspective' (2008) 3 Yale Journal of International Affairs 146.

18 See Luban (n 1) 317.

19 Robin Geiβ and others (eds), *Humanizing the Laws of War: The Red Cross and the Development of International Humanitarian Law* (CUP 2017).

20 Sandesh Sivakumaran, 'Making and Shaping the Law of Armed Conflict' (2018) 71 Current Legal Problems 119, 120; see also Michael Schmitt and Sean Watts, 'State Opinio Juris and International Humanitarian Law Pluralism' (2015) 91 International Security Studies 198.

What is interesting to note is that Sivakumaran and others have pointed out that states have been slow or reticent to act in response to the views of others.[21] There are various institutional, practical, and legal concerns that have led states to do this, but it does mean that others have rushed in where states fear to tread. As a result it is no real surprise that it has been asserted that NGOs 'have exerted a profound influence on the scope and dictates of international law'.[22] This has been abundantly documented in international law more generally,[23] and IHL in particular. The ICRC's role in this is singular,[24] but is beyond the full scope of this chapter.[25] The participation of non-state actors in this process of law-formation, though, has not gone without critical comment,[26] even in relation to the ICRC.[27]

2.1 Identities in International Law

As mentioned above, in addition to the armed conflict/humanitarian distinction, Koskenniemi has attempted to categorize international lawyers. The different categories of international lawyers, as well, play out differently and do play a role in the interpretation of the LOAC, as we shall see. The different actors seek to further, consciously or not, through their various roles and identities, agendas. These may be military focused or more motivated by humanitarian concerns. Nonetheless, it is also the contention of this chapter that whilst there are examples of those who fall clearly on one side or the other, most have a mixture of both, and that their roles/identities can also be mutually constitutive. In other words, the roles that are adopted to promote agendas on either side of the equation can also feed back into how the various actors look at the law, and see themselves. It is also part of this chapter's argument that this mutual constitution may lead to the relevant actors having both mutual roles and identities that overlap. Thus, *grosso modo*, the military/humanitarian divide needs not to be treated as truly binary, and it is important to understand the participants in the debate as complex, and at times conflicted, personalities.

2.1.1 The judge

Although Koskenniemi notes that most international lawyers never become judges, and formal dispute mechanisms are not the norm, judging remains the cynosure of a great deal of legal attention.[28] He identifies as the main characteristic of the role of 'the judge', the commitment

---

21 Sivakumaran (ibid) 156–57.

22 Charnovitz (n 12) 348.

23 ibid 350 and the literature cited therein.

24 See eg Ved Nanda, 'Nongovernmental Organizations and International Humanitarian Law' (1998) 71 International Law Studies 71 (1998) 337; and Geiβ and others (n 19).

25 In part as it is an example of what Sandesh Sivakumaran calls a 'state-empowered entity' in that it gains its mandate from state consent, unlike NGOs in the traditional sense, cf Sandesh Sivakumaran, 'Beyond States and non-State Actors: The Role of State Empowered Entities in the Making and Shaping of International Law' (2017) 55 Columbia Journal of Transnational Law 343.

26 Charnovitz (n 12) 368.

27 eg Burrus Carnahan, who accused the ICRC of 'making exaggerated claims for the destructiveness of lasers', the ICRC has 'helped lay the basis for false war crimes charges', Burrus Carnahan, 'Unnecessary Suffering, the Red Cross and Tactical Laser Weapons' (1996) 18 Loyola of Los Angeles International and Comparative Law Journal 705, 731.

28 Koskenniemi (n 9) 54–55.

to impartial decision-making and being committed to 'the rules', but, for Koskenniemi here, that commitment is undermined by the indeterminacy of the rules, and thus the necessity of making a call that cannot be utterly neutral.[29] It would be difficult to read Antonio Cassese's *oeuvre*, especially in his last illness, and not see that ambivalence: his commitment to humanitarianism,[30] and the realization that to push it forward it would have to be framed in a manner that I have described elsewhere as 'presentational positivism'.[31] Less subtly, few could doubt that Judge Cançado-Trindade has used his position both as a judge on the Inter-American Court of Human Rights and latterly on the ICJ to promote a naturalist agenda that looks closer to the activist position explained below. It is also the case, though, that the judges' reasoning is shaped to a certain extent by their national training, so even with the best will in the world, it may not be possible to reach the Olympian heights that the role seeks to reach.[32]

2.1.2 The adviser

The adviser is the role of a lawyer acting, particularly, although by no means only, in governmental service (including legal advisers to the armed force). Koskenniemi notes that this may be thought of as the embodiment of cynicism. According to him, the aporia of advisers is that not only their academic colleagues will critique their work, but also their political ones in their ministries and departments.[33] This leads to a tendency, in spite of some level of constraint, that advisers still consider themselves to be guardians of the law, also sensitive to activists' complaints about abdication of that role, whilst also finding that the academic shows 'easy moralism, that is an irresponsible indulgence in self-aggrandisement', whilst simultaneously finding private faith and public commitment to the state is difficult, which can also change over time. For example, it must be said that different advisers have different approaches, to the philosophical, and idiosyncratic.[34] As Stephen Schwebel has said, the role of a government legal adviser is 'a function not solely of structure but also of personality'.[35]

Again, though, it must be said that legal advisers often differ. So, for instance, on one hand there are those such as John Yoo, who, during his time as a legal adviser in the US government, appeared to take the view that his role was to provide legal 'cover' for the policies adopted by the George W. Bush administration rather than provide external critical review of it.[36] On

---

29 ibid 55.

30 Antonio Cassese, 'Soliloquy' in Cassese and others (eds), *The Human Dimension of International Law* (OUP 2008) lxx.

31 Robert Cryer, 'International Criminal Tribunals and the Sources of International Law: Cassese's Contribution to the Canon' (2012) 10 Journal of International Criminal Justice 1045, 1048.

32 Lyndell Prott, *The Latent Power of Culture and the International Judge* (Professional Books 1979).

33 Koskenniemi (n 9) 60.

34 For a notable example see Phillip Allott, 'The International Lawyer in Government Service' (2005) 25 Wisconsin International Law Journal 13. His 'The Language, Nature and Method of International Law' (1971) 45 British Yearbook of International Law 79, was memorably described to me by a senior (now retired) colleague as the longest resignation note the Foreign and Commonwealth Office had ever received; it was published whilst Allott was still, at the time, in the employ of the FCO.

35 Stephen Schwebel, 'Remarks on the Role of the Legal Adviser of the US State Department' (1991) 2 European Journal of International Law 131, 131.

36 For a detailed and comprehensive rebuttal see David Luban, *Torture, Power and Law* (CUP 2014), especially ch 8. On the debate more generally see Karen Greenberg (ed), *The Torture Debate in America* (CUP 2006).

the other hand, a more nuanced view of the role of the legal adviser in what in the UK is the Foreign and Commonwealth Office (FCO) has been provided by Sir Arthur Watts, who notes that it is the role of such an adviser to:

> [s]trike the right balance between the objective legal position and the more partisan function of advocacy (...) once the policy has been decided, however, the role of the legal advisor consists in putting forward the best legal case he[[37]] can in support of that policy. In this respect he is very much an advocate, not a judge. Even so as an advocate he is still constrained by his professional sense of responsibility.[38]

This may differ in changing circumstances, and it is the case that different government legal advisers will draw the line at different points, up to, and including, resigning where they cannot continue to accept a government position, as occurred in relation, for example, to the legality of the use of force against Iraq in 2003.[39]

Within the specific context of government legal systems, we may wish to query whether or not military lawyers have a particular role, straddling the divide between the adviser, the lawyer, and, on at least some accounts, someone who feels a commitment to military culture, which is meant to inculcate discipline, knowledge of facts on the ground, and higher values that are at least meant to inform military activity.[40]

Not that they always do, and individuals in different militaries may be as different as those in any organisation, structured or not. Furthermore, it is far from a secret that different military cultures and doctrines often diverge even between close allies.[41] At a more abstract level, David Kennedy has the self-image of the law and legal adviser that deformalism, flexibility, and providing facilitative approaches allows the adviser here to present the decision to kill as a judgment call.[42]

2.1.3 The activist

The activist, on the other hand, would fall, at least at first glance, on the other end of the scale. With a project to advance, which may be humanitarian or not, the aporia of the activist lies in the realization that to do so involves reducing matters to legal argumentation, where something is always lost, and they are arguing against someone with greater argumentative legal expertise.[43] Arguing within the law causes a slippery slide towards adopting lawyerly forms and ways of thinking that are an anathema to those with 'causes', but also wish to be a large

---

37 The use of the masculine pronoun is notable here.

38 Arthur Watts, 'International Law and International Relations: United Kingdom Practice' (1991) 2 European Journal of International Law 157, 164.

39 The legality of which has been deeply contended, see Vaughan Lowe, 'The Iraq Crisis: What Now?' (2003) 52 International and Comparative Law Quarterly 859, and led to resignations in the UK of members of the security services and legal advisers in the FCO.

40 This is argued forcefully by Yishai Beer, *Military Professionalism and Humanitarianism: The Struggle to Reduce the Hazards of War* (OUP 2018) ch 1.

41 United States Department of Defense, *DoD Manual on the Law of War* (Department of Defense 2015); Danish Department of Defence, *Military Manual on International Law Relevant to Danish Armed Forces in International Operations* (Danish Department of Defence 2015, English translation 2018).

42 David Kennedy, 'Speaking Law to Power: International Law and Foreign Policy: Final Remarks' (2005) 23 Wisconsin International Law Journal 173, 180.

43 Koskenniemi (n 9) 61.

part of the debate.[44] However, there are risks here, of academic colleagues believing that they have sold their academic rigour for a seat at the far end of the table, whilst activists consider the academic to be disinterested in the causes they seek to promote.

Perhaps this is most notable with the approach taken by the 'people's tribunals'.[45] These began largely with the Russell Tribunal on the Vietnam War and are avowedly unofficial bodies asserting their legitimacy from their separation from official authority. In addition, in terms of the standards they apply, they do not only apply the law, and therefore also include moral and political standards, or, in the terms of one of the major advocates for, and participants in, such tribunals, Richard Falk, apply a 'Jurisprudence of Conscience'[46] rather than the strictures of just the law. Their views of the law, though, are filtered through the commitment that they adopt.

2.1.4 The academic

For Koskenniemi, the academic's position is the least stable, as it requires a commitment to sound argumentation, but also seeks influence with advisers. The two, whilst they often overlap, again, create tension. To some extent 'the academic' looks down from their ivory tower on both the activist and the adviser for different reasons, but in part from a disciplinary insecurity.[47] This is particularly the case for international lawyers, who are often criticized by their colleagues as dealing with an area that is not 'really law'.[48] It also ought to be said that academics are a diverse group, bounded culturally,[49] and often come from various parts of the political spectrum. For example, few would consider China Miéville anything other than a person of the left.[50] Carl Schmitt, on the other hand, was a card-carrying and avowed Nazi.[51]

In addition, academics can influence the development of the law in various ways, be it through their writings, their teaching, or the advice that they provide, either formally or informally, to state actors.[52] It would be simplistic to lump together the various academics who work in the area of international law, both more generally and in the area of armed conflict. As will be seen, they differ in beliefs and approaches, and come from various backgrounds. The possibility that ideology may skew the views of authors cannot be ignored.[53]

---

44 ibid 61.

45 On which generally see Andrew Byrnes and Gabrielle Simm (eds), *Peoples' Tribunals and International Law* (CUP 2018).

46 Richard Falk, 'War, War Crimes, Power, and Justice: Towards A Jurisprudence of Conscience' (2013) 21 Transnational Law and Contemporary Problems 667, 684.

47 Koskenniemi (n 9) 64.

48 David Harris summed it up very nicely as being a 'standard sherry party question' whether international law is really law. David J. Harris, *Cases and Materials on International Law* (6th edn, Stevens 2004) 4.

49 See eg Anthea Roberts, *Is International Law International?* (OUP 2017).

50 China Miéville, *Between Equal Rights: A Marxist Theory of International Law* (Pluto Press 2006).

51 Carl Schmitt, *The Nomos of the Earth in the International Law of the Jus Publicum Europaeum* (Telos 2003); Carl Schmitt, 'The Führer Protects Justice' translated in Detlev Vagts 'Carl Schmitt's Ultimate Emergency: The Night of the Long Knives' (2012) 87 The Germanic Review 203.

52 On the role of academics in the development of international law see Sandesh Sivakumaran, 'The Influence of Teaching of Publicists on the Development of International Law' (2017) 66 International and Comparative Law Quarterly 1.

53 See for example Myres S. McDougal and Florentine Feliciano, *The International Law of War: Transnational Coercion and World Public Order* (New Haven Press 1994).

2.2 Multiple Identities

We are all used to multiple identities in our lives: mother, son, father, daughter, aunt, uncle, brother, sister, consumer, carer, critic, reader, writer, artist, technician, and so on. All of these together make up who we are, but they are not hermetically sealed. A son may be a carer for his mother, a daughter may mend her brother's bicycle, or a child may make a birthday card for their aunt or uncle at school. The roles may wax and wane, or otherwise change over time. But, consciously or otherwise, such roles underlie the way in which we consider issues.

The same is also true of the roles above, and so if Koskenniemi could be criticized, it would be on the basis that the roles he identifies could be seen as separate categories, and perhaps a bit stereotyped. As mentioned above, there are different types of each of the above characters, but also people may have more than one role, both consecutively or sequentially, depending on context, career opportunity, political commitment or personal circumstance. It is the purpose of this part to briefly canvas the careers of some international lawyers to see how they have adopted multiple roles throughout their careers, which often cross or transcend the descriptions offered above.

The first of these is Herman Mosler, the inaugural head of the legal department of the German Foreign Office. He had been appointed to this post from his job at a chair in Frankfurt. After his role in the Foreign Office, he became the director of the Max-Planck Institute in Heidelberg, before taking up a position as a well-regarded judge of the ICJ.[54] As such, he had at least, academic, advisory, and judicial functions.

The second (very) mini-case study is of a lawyer whose name will be known to most, if not all, of the readership of this chapter: Sir Hersch Lauterpacht. His life is well documented, not least by the lengthy biography written by his son,[55] and various other pieces on his life and work.[56] Having come to the UK as a refugee in the 1920s, Lauterpacht went up through the academic ranks quickly, becoming the Whewell Chair of International Law in Cambridge (perhaps the most 'academic' of roles) in 1938. During the Second World War and after he advised the UK government on various issues, including the Nuremberg War Crimes Trials.[57] After the war he also co-authored the influential 1958 UK Manual of Military Law with ex-Army lawyer cum academic Professor Colonel Gerald IAD Draper.[58] He was a strong advocate for the genocide convention, and for human rights more generally, producing arguably the first monograph on the subject in 1950.[59]

In 1954, having previously been appointed to the International Law Commission, Lauterpacht was appointed as the British judge on the ICJ, a role which he undertook until his

---

54 See Jochen Frowein, 'Legal Advice on Foreign Policy in Germany' (2005) 23 Wisconsin International Law Journal 25, 26. The summary of Mosler's career is largely based on this piece.

55 Elihu Lauterpacht, *The Life of Hersch Lauterpacht: A Life* (CUP 2010).

56 Martti Koskenniemi, 'Lauterpacht: The Victorian Tradition in International Law' (1997) 8 European Journal of International Law 215; Brian Simpson, 'Hersch Lauterpacht and the Genesis of the Age of Human Rights' (2004) 120 Law Quarterly Review 49.

57 See Martti Koskenniemi, 'Hersch Lauterpacht and the Development of International Criminal Law' (2004) 2 Journal of International Criminal Justice 810.

58 Hersch Lauterpacht and Gerald Draper, *The Law of War on Land, Being Part III of the Manual of Military Law* (HMSO 1958). Lauterpacht acknowledges his role in the foreword, iv.

59 Ana Filipa Vrdoljak, 'Human Rights and Genocide: The Work of Lauterpacht and Lemkin in Modern International Criminal Law' (2009) 20 European Journal of International Law 1163.

untimely death in 1960. He used this position to push forward on causes he believed in, albeit with careful reasoning.[60] The multiple nature of Lauterpacht's contributions, across his various professional roles and personal commitments, can perhaps be most succinctly encapsulated by the pieces published in the *British Yearbook of International Law* after his death, the titles of which were 'The Scholar as Prophet' and the three-part 'The Scholar as Judge'.[61] A larger mixing of the various identities could hardly be more evident.

Other names could easily abound of those who have either simultaneously adopted various roles, civilian, military, activist, judicial and other roles,[62] but space prevents their detailed development here. Suffice it to say that international lawyers (or members of the famous 'invisible college'[63] of them (whatever that may be)) are perceived as being, or consider themselves as engaged, in far more than one role – a matter that does not make identifying positions as clear as lying in any one of them. Nonetheless, the next section will attempt to use them as a frame to help understand the structure of argument, and reasons behind them in the area of IHL/LOAC.

3. EVALUATING APPROACHES TO THE LAW

It is perhaps no surprise that the issue of identities, and their implications for interpretation have arisen in the area of IHL/LOAC. This is especially the case in what is traditionally called 'Hague' Law, where the treaty and customary law on point is often frustratingly ambiguous. In Allott's words, treaties 'are reminiscent of the national legislation of the worst kind, in which compromises are enacted in formulae which are known to be, and may be intended to be, ambiguous or even meaningless'.[64] Therefore, even more than elsewhere, what is required are judgment calls,[65] which occur against the, conscious or otherwise, personal and professional senses of identity of the interpreters.[66]

---

60 Shabtai Rosenne, 'Sir Hersch Lauterpacht's Concept of the Task of the International Judge' (1961) 55 American Journal of International Law 825.

61 cf Wilfred Jenks, 'Hersch Lauterpacht: The Scholar as Prophet' (1960) 36 British Yearbook of International Law 1; Gerald Fitzmaurice, 'Hersch Lauterpacht – The Scholar as Judge: Part I' (1961) 37 British Yearbook of International Law 1; 'Part II' (1962) 38 British Yearbook of International Law 1; 'Part III' (1963) 39 British Yearbook of International Law 133. There was a later tribute in 1979, Gerald Fitzmaurice, 'Hersch Lauterpacht and His Attitude to the Judicial Function' (1979) 50 British Yearbook of International Law 1.

62 Examples could include Richard Baxter, military lawyer, academic and judge, Pieter Kooijmans, diplomat, minister and judge, Theodor Meron, diplomat, government lawyer, academic and judge, and Rosalyn Higgins, academic, advocate and judge.

63 Oscar Schachter, 'The Invisible College of International Lawyers' (1977) 72 North-Western Law Review 217.

64 Allott (n 34) 15, 18.

65 Kennedy (n 7) 20.

66 On which, see generally David Kennedy, *Of Law and War* (Harvard University Press 2006).

3.1 Unnecessary Suffering

So, for example, the principle of unnecessary suffering is embodied by the balance between military necessity and the principle of humanity. It received its classical formulation in the 1868 Declaration on the Prohibition of the Use of Explosive Projectiles, which reads:

> Considering: That the progress of civilization should have the effect of alleviating as much as possible the calamities of war; That the only legitimate object which States should endeavour to accomplish during war is to weaken the military forces of the enemy; That for this purpose it is sufficient to disable the greatest possible number of men; That this object would be exceeded by the employment of arms which uselessly aggravate the sufferings of disabled men, or render their death inevitable; That the employment of such arms would, therefore, be contrary to the laws of humanity.[67]

The principle receives its modern, customary[68] formulation in Article 35 of Additional Protocol I to the Geneva Conventions. This provides that:

> (1) In any Armed Conflict the Right of the Parties to the conflict to choose methods or means of warfare is not unlimited.
> (2) It is prohibited to employ weapons, projectiles and material and methods of warfare of a nature to cause superfluous injury or unnecessary suffering.[69]

This is brought into useful focus by paragraph 402 of the German Joint Services Regulations: '"Superfluous injury" and "unnecessary suffering" are caused by the use of weapons and methods of combat whose foreseeable harm would be clearly excessive in relation to the lawful military advantage intended.'[70]

However, as is frequently noted, although the principle is well established, its interpretation is not. As a committee discussing the 1980 Conventional Weapons Convention noted:

> Unnecessary suffering is a term implying numerous medical parameters. From a strictly medical standpoint, it seems impossible at the present stage of medical knowledge to objectively define suffering or to give absolute values permitting comparisons between human individuals. Pain, for instance, which is but one of many components of suffering, is subject to enormous individual variations.[71]

---

67 LXIV UKPP (1869) 659.

68 Jean-Marie Henckaerts and Louise Doswald-Beck, *Customary International Humanitarian Law* (CUP 2005) 237. Although see Henri Meyrowitz, 'The Principle of Superfluous Injury or Unnecessary Suffering' (1994) 34 International Review of the Red Cross 98, 103. The ICJ has described it as one of the 'cardinal principles of humanitarian law', *Legality of the Threat or Use of Nuclear Weapons* (Advisory Opinion) [1996] ICJ Rep 66 para 238.

69 See eg Yves Sandoz and others, *Commentary on the Additional Protocols of 8 June 1977* (ICRC 1987) 389–420; Michael Bothe and others, *New Rules for Victims of Armed Conflicts* (Martinus Nijhoff 1982) 192–198.

70 Quoted and commented upon in Stefan Oeter, 'Means and Methods of Combat' in Dieter Fleck (ed), *The Handbook of International Humanitarian Law* (2nd edn, OUP 2008) 119, 130–31.

71 Quoted in Sandoz and others (n 69) 408.

An attempt by the ICRC to quantify suffering, through its SIrUS project,[72] floundered, not least owing to state opposition.[73] But this is only part of the problem. As the German Regulations note, there has to be a balance between the contested concept of suffering, and military necessity. There are two aspects to this: the first is that necessity is a 'relational' concept. As Bothe, Partsch, and Solf note: '[t]o speak of necessity (or lack of necessity) is simultaneously to raise the question of "Necessary (or unnecessary) for what".'[74] The second is the balancing exercise, which is one that cannot be reduced to mechanistic approaches any one of which ought not to claim to be authoritative. Hence, in the ICJ's *Nuclear Weapons* opinion, on one hand Judge Schwebel thought such munitions were not prohibited by the principle of unnecessary suffering, but Judge Shahabuddeen took the opposite view.[75] In spite of possible assertions that Judge Shahabuddeen may have stretched the law to make sure that he put his foot down on the illegality of nuclear weapons, thus being an activist as well as a judge, it might also be said that Judge Schwebel was, as a judge, equally an activist in favour of the policies of states that owned such munitions.

Taking a middle ground, Judge Rosalyn Higgins said in this regard in the *Nuclear Weapons* Opinion: '[the balancing exercise] explains why (…) [t]he status of incendiary projectiles, flamethrowers, napalm, high velocity weapons – all especially repugnant means of conducting hostilities – have thus remained contested.'[76]

This is, in some ways, reflected also in the plurality opinion, which states that:

> The Court [cannot] make a determination on the validity of the view that the recourse to nuclear weapons would be illegal in any circumstance owing to their inherent and total incompatibility with the law applicable in armed conflict. (…) In view of the unique characteristics of nuclear weapons, to which the Court has referred above, the use of such weapons in fact seems scarcely reconcilable with respect for such requirements. Nevertheless, the Court considers that it does not have sufficient elements to enable it to conclude with certainty that the use of nuclear weapons would necessarily be at variance with the principles and rules of law applicable in armed conflict in any circumstance.[77]

Here we can see activist judges, more conservative lawyers, some of whom have acted as legal adviser (Schwebel) – probably more on the conservative end, but also Mohamed Shahabuddeen, a more activist judge, who had very strong, to say the least, links to the Guyanese government, having been a crown lawyer, attorney general, minister of justice, vice prime minister and vice president of that state prior to his career as an international judge. Writing extra-curially has

---

[72] The SIrUS Project takes its name from the term 'Superfluous Injury or Unnecessary Suffering' and originated after a symposium on 'The medical profession and the effects of weapons' organized by the ICRC (Montreux, March 1996).

[73] See eg William Boothby, *Weapons and the Law of Armed Conflict* (OUP 2009) 65–66, but see Steven Haines, 'The Developing Law of Weaponry' in Andrew Clapham and Paula Gaeta (eds), *The Oxford Handbook of International Law in Armed Conflict* (OUP 2014) 285.

[74] Bothe and others (n 69) 196.

[75] *Legality of the Threat or Use of Nuclear Weapons* (Dissenting Opinion of Schwebel) [1996] ICJ Rep 66 para 836; and Shahabuddeen para 871.

[76] ibid 586 (para 16).

[77] ibid para 95.

made clear that he believes that judges have a role in the development of the law.[78] Hence it is wrong to treat any group or person as adopting one overarching view.

That said, and rather inconsistently with the general regulation of incendiary weapons contained in Optional Protocol III to the 1980 Conventional Weapons Convention, when discussing the legality of barrel bombs, the Independent International Commission on Syria (which is decidedly a human rights body, which has been set up by the Human Rights Council) took a rather stern view. This was that '[w]here barrel bombs were built as de facto incendiary weapons, they also violated rules of international humanitarian law prohibiting the use of weapons that cause superfluous injury, unnecessary suffering or that are indiscriminate by nature'.[79] In fairness, this discussion occurred in the context of the indiscriminate use of such weapons. There is essentially no legal reasoning undertaken in the report on the point on incendiary weapons. The point is very strong, and correct, but the lack of explanation does not increase its authority.

In part owing to this, it is difficult to see that the approach of the Independent International Commission on Syria would receive general acceptance amongst military lawyers, particularly from those states that use incendiary weapons. They may have a point, but there is also something of a turf war amongst the various actors involved in interpreting IHL. The dilemma is well expressed by Air Commodore (Ret) William Boothby:

> There are contextual and cultural dimensions to this rule. The value to be attached to a given amount of military advantage may well be in part determined by the geo-strategic situation of a particular State *remembering as we must, that the implementation of this principle, and the problems related to it falls exclusively within the competence of States*. (…) The value placed on human life and injury may be subject to culturally-based appreciations, so different States may well reach different conclusions when applying this principle to apparently similar facts. (…) *Any suggestion that the cultural difference point should justify taking these decisions out of the hands of States* fails to recognise this area of public international law is the *property of States* (…) to seek to impose interpretations with which States may differ is a recipe for conflict over legal interpretation and application, and risk side-lining the very law we are discussing.[80]

This is a full-throated defence of not only the primary, but exclusive, authority of states to interpret and apply IHL. This, of course, relies on the idea that only states have any authority to interpret international law, something which is now somewhat antediluvian.[81] It is a very

---

78 Mohamed Shahabuddeen, 'Does the Principle of Legality Stand in the Way of Progressive Development of Law' (2004) 2 Journal of International Criminal Justice 1007.

79 UN Human Rights Council, 'Report of the Independent International Commission of Inquiry on the Syrian Arab Republic' (12 February 2014) UN Doc A/HRC/25/65 Annex VI 54 para 42.

80 Boothby (n 73) 64–65 [emphasis added].

81 The precise extent to which, though, is contentious, see Antonio Cassese, 'The Martens Clause: Half a Loaf or Simply Pie in the Sky?' (2000) 11 European Journal of International Law 187; Theodor Meron, 'The Martens Clause, Principles of Humanity and the Dictates of Public Conscience' (2000) 94 American Journal of International Law 78.

different vision of the dialogical process discussed by Sivakumaran, and perhaps might be best explained by Koskenniemi, that

> There is no externally introduced distortion (…) [it] (…) follows from the fluid character of international legal rules and principles: one is bound to make a choice and it is hardly unnatural that one's choice is for the alternative that is closest to oneself.[82]

3.2 Targeting

The law of targeting is a huge area of IHL, and some of its provisions are deeply controversial, especially in their application.[83] It is also immensely important, particularly for Western states who, post-Kosovo, have tended to prefer to limit their major engagements to engagements from the air.[84] It would be impossible to cover all of the aspects of it here, so I will concentrate on only one aspect – the prohibition of indiscriminate attacks – and debate between different actors in relation to the Kosovo conflict.

The prohibition of indiscriminate attacks is a long-standing principle of the LOAC, given voice in Additional Protocol I, Article 51, which is generally accepted as being customary:[85]

> 4. Indiscriminate attacks are prohibited. Indiscriminate attacks are:
>   (a) those which are not directed at a specific military objective;
>   (b) those which employ a method or means of combat which cannot be directed at a specific objective (…)
>
> and consequently, are of a nature to strike military objectives or civilian objects without distinction.

There are other aspects to the ban on indiscriminate attacks, Article 51(5) gives them:

> Among others, the following types of attacks are to be considered as indiscriminate:
> (a) an attack by bombardment which treats as a single military objective a number of clearly separated and distinct military objectives located in a city, town, village or other area containing a similar concentration of civilians or civilian objects; and
> (b) an attack which may be expected to cause incidental loss of civilian life, injury to civilians, damage to civilian objects, or a combination thereof, which would be excessive in relation to the concrete and direct military advantage anticipated.

It is an aspect of the protection of civilians. Not only should they not be deliberately targeted, but nor should they be the victim of attacks which are launched not caring if they are there or

---

82 Koskenniemi (n 9) 51.

83 See generally Leslie C. Green, *The Contemporary Law of Armed Conflict* (3rd edn, MUP 2008) 169–187; Rogers (n 10) chs 1–7; UK Ministry of Defence, *The Manual of the Law of Armed Conflict* (OUP 2004) ch 5; Gary D. Solis, *The Law of Armed Conflict: International Humanitarian Law in War* (CUP 2010) chs 11, 14.

84 Anthony P.V. Rogers, 'Zero Casualty Warfare' (2000) 82 International Review of the Red Cross 164; Robert Cryer, 'The Fine Art of Friendship: *Jus in Bello* in Afghanistan' (2002) 7 Journal of Conflict and Security Law 37, 47–56, 62–67.

85 Ove Bring, 'International Humanitarian Law After Kosovo: Is the *lex lata* Sufficient?' (2002) 71 Nordic Journal of International Law 39.

not, or by methods that cannot distinguish them from military objectives. There is obviously a link here to the duties on attackers to take measures to ensure they do not attack civilians.

Hence, it is not the case that there can never be civilian deaths in armed conflict. Although it remains the case that civilians can never be deliberately targeted as such, incidental civilian deaths are acceptable when targeting a military objective if it is not 'excessive in relation to the concrete and direct military advantage anticipated'. If it is excessive, though, the attack cannot proceed (Article 57(2)(a)(iii)).

Although it is only one aspect of the prohibition of indiscriminate attacks, this chapter will next concentrate on proportionality. The reason for this focus was well described by Enzo Cannizzaro, as being 'mysterious'.[86] In other words, the relevant rules are not what Thomas Franck described as sophist, rather than idiot rules. As such, they are not self-applying, but rather than providing bright lines, they provide a framework for discussion,[87] and perhaps, in the end, dissensus. This is inevitable, as most of the actors involved accept, at least at the rhetorical level.

Attempting to clarify this, a case study of NATO in former Yugoslavia/Kosovo will be examined. The practice of NATO states here was subject of extensive comment and critique from NGOs, such as Human Rights Watch (which concluded, after a fairly close analysis, that there were violations of IHL, but not rising to the level of war crimes),[88] Amnesty International (which considered war crimes to have been committed), as well as a number of academic commentaries, which came to various conclusions, albeit most of them critical.[89] Importantly, and certainly at the time unique in that an international criminal tribunal, the International Criminal Tribunal for former Yugoslavia (ICTY), issued a report written at the behest of the Prosecutor determining whether a full investigation into Operation Allied Force (the name for the NATO bombings) ought to be opened.[90] Again academic response was, in the main, negative.[91] Perhaps tellingly, one of the most thoughtful of the NATO report, Michael Bothe asked for the matter of NATO practices to be subject to review by the European Court of Human Rights.[92]

3.3 Proportionality

The difficulty with application of the principle of proportionality also requires balancing of the expected military advantage and the, perhaps incommensurable, civilian casualties and

---

86 Enzo Cannizzaro, 'Proportionality in the Law of Armed Conflict' in Andrew Clapham and Paula Gaeta (eds), *The Oxford Handbook of International Law in Armed Conflict* (OUP 2014) 332.

87 Thomas Franck, *The Power of Legitimacy Among Nations* (OUP 1990) ch 5.

88 See Human Rights Watch, *Under Orders: War Crimes in Kosovo* (Human Rights Watch 2001) 39–40.

89 For an overview see Anne-Sophie Massa, 'NATO's Intervention in Kosovo and the ICTY's decision not to Prosecute: An Abuse of Prosecutorial Discretion' (2006) 24 Berkeley Journal of International Law 610.

90 ICTY, 'Final Report to the Prosecutor by the Committee Established to Review the NATO Bombing Campaign Against the Federal Republic of Yugoslavia' (2000) 39 International Legal Material 1257.

91 Massa (n 89) 610.

92 Paulo Vevenuti, 'The ICTY Prosecutor and the Review of the NATO Bombing Campaign against the Federal Republic of Yugoslavia' (2001) 12 European Journal of International Law 503, 527–29.

damage. As William Fenrick said in relation to the Kosovo Conflict in the (not uncontroversial) Report to the Prosecutor:

> The main problem with the principle of proportionality is not whether or not it exists but what it means and how it is to be applied. It is relatively simple to state that there must be an acceptable relation between the legitimate destructive effect and undesirable collateral effects. For example bombing a refugee camp is obviously prohibited if its only military significance is that people in the camp are knitting socks for soldiers. Conversely an air strike on an ammunition dump should not be prohibited merely because a farmer is ploughing a field in the area. Unfortunately, most applications of the principle are not so clear cut (…) because the comparison is often between unlike quantities and values. One cannot easily assess the value of innocent human lives as opposed to capturing a particular military objective (…).[93]

As Cannizzaro has said, the critics of the principle tend to foreground the subjectivity of applying such an indeterminate standard, but notes that it is an accepted part of 'the international legal landscape (…). The reasons for this success are manifold (…) the model applies to situations in which a number of different interests entitled to legal protection can be identified but cannot be *a priori* composed in a predetermined behavioural scheme.'[94]

However, the ICTY's Prosecutor Report relies on incommensurability to move to make a normative commitment:

> The answers to these questions are not simple. It may be necessary to resolve them on a case by case basis, and the answers may differ depending on the background and values of the decision maker. It is unlikely that a human rights lawyer and an experienced combat commander would assign the same relative values to military advantage and to injury to non-combatants. Further, it is unlikely that military commanders with different doctrinal backgrounds and differing degrees of combat experience or national military histories would always agree in close cases. It is suggested that the determination of relative values must be that of the 'reasonable military commander'. Although there will be room for argument in close cases, there will be many cases where reasonable military commanders will agree that the injury to non-combatants or the damage to civilian objects was clearly disproportionate to the military advantage gained.[95]

It is, *inter alia*, this uncertainty about the principle that led the drafters of the Rome Statute of the International Criminal Court to draft the relevant provision of that treaty (Article 8(2)(b)(iv)) in a deliberately narrow fashion, to prevent the Court from second-guessing decisions taken on the ground.[96] However, in doing so, it has to be said, the drafters of that crime, and the elements of crimes made it exceptionally difficult to prosecute, such that it will be difficult to prosecute indiscriminate attacks. It is likely, for example, that in spite of all the discussion of the possibility of sending the situation in Syria to the ICC, many of the attacks, such as those with barrel bombs, will be exceptionally difficult to prosecute.

Suffice it to say, the approach taken in the ICTY Prosecutor Report drew both credit and critique from both sides of the armed conflict/humanitarian spectrum. Some of those have

---

93 ICTY, 'Final Report' (n 90) para 48.

94 Cannizzaro (n 86) 332–33.

95 ICTY, 'Final Report' (n 90) para 50.

96 For critique of this see Robert Cryer, *Prosecuting International Crimes: Selectivity and the International Criminal Law Regime* (CUP 2005) ch 5.

been decidedly lawyerly and very much from the academic milieu.[97] There were criticisms of William Fenrick, who is generally considered the author of the report (a designation he would probably not actively disagree with), which were vituperative and *ad hominem*.

The most extraordinary of these is a piece by Michael Mandel, an academic (a professor at Osgoode Hall Law School in Toronto) and activist, in particular involved with Kosovo. He describes the report as being an 'amateur whitewash', and a 'fraud'.[98] He continues in this frame, saying 'it seems like it was written by a NATO lawyer rather than a judge, this should not be surprising because there is little doubt that the brief was in fact by a NATO lawyer, if only an ex-NATO lawyer Canadian Armed Forces Frigate Captain William J. Fenrick',[99] and that he 'cannot help wondering whether the authors had spent too much time in the Hague's famous "coffee shops"'.[100] This is the language of an activist, although there is also legal garb in which some of its other discussions are framed, and are shared by others.[101] Here, though, we see an academic as an activist, and the two roles rather clashing.

I think what is notable, though, in spite of the tone of Mandel's remarks, is that Fenrick, an experienced Canadian Army lawyer prior to working for the ICTY,[102] when discussing proportionality, suggests the relevant test is that of the view of the reasonable military commander, an evaluative frame which does not have any formal status in *jus in bello* treaties. However, this is increasingly sedimented in discussions of the law in the area which sets the frame for discussion that without questioning its formal status, and the fact that many targeting decisions may now have to be signed off at the political/civilian level. What is also relevant is that Fenrick notes that even within the military context, there may well be considerable disagreement. To this we ought to add another factor: that targeting is done on the basis of protocols that tend to be arranged outside of the actual theatre.

Fenrick's approach here was non-accidental. As he finishes his piece, Fenrick expresses his view that if the law in the area is

> to become more transparent, and one hope, more humane, outsiders, including military experts and advisers not directly involved in particular conflicts, should learn from the military planning process (…). As with military case studies, case studies may require reliance on arbitrary assumptions. If, however they are accepted as such and open to revision, the case studies will be useful and have a relative validity. The law applicable to targeting and proportionality must be brought down to Earth.[103]

---

97 See eg Paolo Benvenuti, 'The ICTY Prosecutor and the Review of the NATO Bombing against the Federal Republic of Yugoslavia' (2001) 12 European Journal of International Law 503; Eric David, 'Respect for the Principle in the Kosovo War' (2001) 3 Yearbook of International Humanitarian Law 81.

98 Michael Mandel, 'Politics and Human Rights in International Criminal Law: Our Case Against NATO and the Lessons to be Learned from it' (2001) 25 Fordham International Law Journal 95, 95–96.

99 ibid 117.

100 ibid 118.

101 See Benvenuti (n 97) 527–29 and Massa (n 89) 610.

102 William Fenrick, 'The Law Applicable to Targeting and Proportionality after Operation Allied Force: A View from the Outside' (2003) 3 Yearbook of International Humanitarian Law 53 (53 fn 2 explains: Senior Legal Adviser, OTP, ICTY. 'The views expressed in this article do not necessarily reflect the views of the Office of the Prosecutor or of the United Nations. The author was involved in the preparation of the OTP ICTY review of Operation Allied Force and is a retired Canadian Military Lawyer'). After retiring from the ICTY, Fenrick took up a chair in Dalhousie University. He has truly had multiple roles.

103 ibid 80.

In addition to the fact that no irony could be detected by him in the final sentence, there seems to be few of those who are not at one level or another military. Fenrick's point is less strident than Boothby's but comes from a similar place. It also questions who Fenrick's 'outsiders' are.

An outstanding counterpoint comes from Michael Bothe, who argues that whilst the military may have the 'boots on the ground' experience, there needs to be civilian control over the armed forces: 'In democratic systems, the values pursued by the military and those by society cannot be far apart. The value system on the basis of which the military is operating has to conform to that of the civil society and not *vice versa*.'[104] After all, what is done by the military is done in the name of the state, and therefore the name of its citizens, who have a right to a say in the laws that govern those who at some level act for or are representing them.

It is against this background that discussions of IHL ought to be seen as an embodiment of the life of law, and indeed its meaning. This is because, at least here, the meaning of the law is embodied in the use that is made of the skeletal, evaluative rules that exist more than the rules themselves. As Carlo Focarelli has said,

> [i]f law is a social construct ultimately founded in mythic belief, there must be a constant struggle engaged by different groups to control the generation and prevalence about its belief and reality. While science looks for truth in the world 'before us', like mountains, law is 'among us'. Scientists are not part of the process of creating mountains but jurists and people do participate in the making and unmaking of law. Law is mythic because we are a part thereof. When dealing with law 'observers' become 'agents' whether they like it or not. The 'we' who make or unmake law is in constant struggle, whether actively or tacitly, to shape the law one way or another.[105]

In a cognate part of IHL, some of the military critics of the ICRC *DPH Guidance*[106] show this in no short order. For example, Corn and others make such a commitment open, stating that

> We are under no illusion that we will persuade proponents of this least harmful means rule to reconsider their position. Nor are we insensitive to the profound human consequences of a rule that legally authorises attack with methods and means of warfare that are likely to cause death as a measure of first resort with no obligation to consider lesser means to incapacitate the target – even against an individual who may in fact pose little or no threat to an attacking force at that precise moment. If anything, the combined sixty-two years of military experience shared by three of the authors – experience that required a very personal sensitivity to the human dimension of warfare – makes it impossible for us not to appreciate these consequences. But this experience, and our continued collective experience of working closely with those who remain engaged in the physically, mentally, and morally demanding business of fighting our nations' wars, also informs our view that the LOAC must, as it historically has, remain rationally grounded in the realities of warfare. We are confident that anyone grappling with this issue understands that decisions related to the employment of combat power are not resolved

---

[104] Michael Bothe, 'The Protection of the Civilian Population and the NATO Bombing of Yugoslavia: Comments on a Report to the ICTY Prosecutor' (2001) 12 European Journal of International Law 531, 535.

[105] Carlo Focarelli, *International Law as Social Construct: The Struggle for Global Justice* (OUP 2012) 55–56.

[106] See Robert Cryer, 'The International Committee of the Red Cross' "Interpretive Guidance on the Notion of Direct Participation in Hostilities": See a Little Light' in Robin Geiß and others (n 19) 113–40, which this part draws upon, and develops.

> in the quiet and safe confines of law libraries, academic conferences, or even courtrooms, they are resolved in the intensely demanding situations which our nation thrusts our armed forces.[107]

Their approach, which mixes paternalism, more than hints of the technocratic and self-referential, is not an isolated one.[108] It can, with little extension, be seen as an attempt to create or maintain an interpretative hegemony over IHL, by the assertion of special expertise, relying on a form of military 'common sense' approach to IHL which cannot go unchallenged. As Bonaventura de Sousa Santos has shown, legal 'common sense' is as constructed as any other form of knowledge,[109] and, as Cemenceau famously put it, war is far too important to be left to the military on their own.

This leads to a more general point: that IHL is not simply the purview of the military/ government lawyer. There is a risk, if the interpretation of IHL is left entirely to military practitioners (although, again, experience shows that many are *bona fide* supporters of what they may call law of the armed conflict, and human rights), that IHL becomes simply a meek form of self-regulation. The banking crisis has shown us that, although expertise in the area is very important for ensuring that the law is relevant, it cannot be the sole source of reference.

4. CONCLUSION

As Koskenniemi has commented, 'international law is what international lawyers do and think'.[110] It also relates to ideas of self-image, and roles that are fluid. It is also the case that there has been a risk of caricaturing of others in the debate on sometimes simplistic lines. As we have seen there can be multiple identities, even within one person or community.

The legitimacy of all the actors involved and their interpretations of what can be drawn from what are often frustratingly Delphic, negotiated texts on the law relating, especially, although not only,[111] when they relate to Hague law, that only received anything approaching codification with Additional Protocol I in 1977. From the early 1990s onwards, there has been increasing discussion about the lawfulness or otherwise of various combat-related issues, with a plurality of voices on point. From the military perspective, there have been increasing calls for explanation and justification of decisions made with respect to the *jus in bello*, not least as it is only on this basis that activities in armed conflict (which are increasingly being subject to human rights scrutiny, especially post the *Al-Skeini* case[112]), and involve conduct that, other than the existence of an armed conflict, would amount to domestic criminal activity,[113] as has been said sufficiently frequently that it is a cliché, 'war is about killing people and breaking stuff'.

---

[107] Geoffrey Corn and others, 'Belligerent Targeting and the Invalidity of a Least Harmful Means Rule' (2013) 89 International Law Studies 536, 541, the use of 'our' in the quote further shows the specific context in which the authors write, and who their intended audience is.

[108] See also, eg Hays Parks (n 10), and Boothby (n 73).

[109] Bonaventura de Sousa Santos, *Towards a New Legal Common Sense* (2nd edn, CUP 2002).

[110] Koskenniemi (n 9) 65.

[111] Here is not the place to go further into the issue of constructed ambiguity that has characterized the now infamous torture memoranda, on which see Luban (n 36).

[112] *Al-Skeini v UK* App No 55721/97 (ECtHR, 7 July 2011).

[113] Chris af Jochnick and Roger Normand, 'The Legitimation of Violence: A Critical History of the Laws of War' (1994) 35 Harvard International Law Journal 49.

There is truth in this, and it is not the intention of this chapter to traduce military lawyers, or 'humanitarian' lawyers, who also need to accept that the *jus in bello* is not a means to an end of fighting, which, whilst an understandable aim, is not something that is likely to come about any time soon. It is to encourage a debate between them, in which both sides ought to engage in a genuine conversation.

Indeed, it is possible to go further to say that IHL, of necessity, has to have an external evaluative element if it is to be law worthy of the name, in that it is not simply a system of self-regulation. Bothe's point, made about proportionality, is a more general one. It has been more than 40 years since the end of the Vietnam War, and it is a salutary lesson that if the interpretation of the *jus in bello*, which is, in the first instance, a matter which a considerable voice ought to be given to those with expertise in the area, no one person or constituency's call on this can be considered authoritative.

There is a reason that domestically there is judicial review of executive action. The same considerations require that the *jus in bello* should be subject to similar standards. Sometimes this will lead to overturning of particular judgments, at times it will lead to support for them. I remain ecumenical on the different interpretations of the law, but would ask that others take the same position on how interpretation is approached. No human being has final authority, and we can at least be polite in our discussions, and respect the fact that good faith interpretations of the law in the area may differ but ought not to be dismissed without evaluation. It is too easy to stereotype those arguing with their thumb on the humanity side as engaged in lawfare, or at least noble cause corruption,[114] misstating the law for bad or good reasons.

Perhaps it is fitting to remind ourselves, to close, that, as Allott has said:

> Lawyers – all lawyers – belong to a surreptitious priesthood whose allegiance is not only to the client, the corporation, or the government that they serve. They have a second allegiance, an ideal allegiance, as servants of the Law. Lawyers are special agents of the general will, confidential ministers of the social superego, guides on the perilous ascent from the State of Nature to the Rule of Law. Theirs is the still small voice of the universal within the cacophony of the particular.[115]

If nothing else, the various actors ought to speak to one another, with respect and not by reference to presumed, fixed, determinative identities. Many do not but some do; they may do so on bases conscious or otherwise. If this plea for open discussion, on the basis of full respect for all voices, sounds Habermasian,[116] so be it.

---

114 See, on the latter eg John Kleining, 'Rethinking Noble Cause Corruption' (2002) 4 International Journal of Police Science and Management 295.

115 Allott (n 34) 223.

116 On which see, eg Mathieu Deflem, 'The Legal Theory of Jürgen Habermas: Between the Philosophy and the Sociology of Law' in Reza Banakar and Max Travers, *Law and Social Theory* (2nd edn, Hart 2013) ch 4.

24. From the Martens clause to the CNN factor: Is the impact of media and public opinion on law-making discernible?

Daniel Joyce

1. INTRODUCTION

In this chapter I begin to analyze the impact of media and public opinion on law-making.[1] To do so I draw upon ongoing research charting the complex relationship between the media and international law. The media and the public are configured as objects for protection within conflict, though much work still needs to be done to ensure adequate protection for both.[2] This chapter considers the media question at a different level, in terms of the media's role in generating public concern and attention, and consequently examines their role as actors in law-making itself.

First, I provide an overview of the topic, looking at shifts in our understanding of the significance of the media and public opinion and also pointing to their special significance in areas like international humanitarian law (IHL). Second, I move to discuss the limitations and critiques made of this significance – examining the question of discernibility and the difficulty associated with quantification of media effects. Third, I turn to consider three examples of international legal scholarship considering the role for the media in international law and IHL. I begin with the work of Monica Hakimi, who looks at the media as a participant in international law more broadly, and then examine scholarship focusing specifically on the media, public opinion and IHL by David Kennedy, Frédéric Mégret and Frederick Pinto. Fourth, I conclude by evaluating the CNN effect and its perceived role in international decision-making; and also consider how the 'media question' is shifting given digitalization. Should we now be focusing more directly on the internet's role and exploring whether this has shaped and driven the mediatization of international law, or whether in fact it points to its demise and the rise instead of social media, big data and decision-making?

1 An example of important earlier scholarship addressing some of these questions through the frame of customary law is Achilles Skordas, 'Hegemonic custom?' in Michael Byers and Georg Nolte (eds), *United States Hegemony and the Foundations of International Law* (CUP 2003) 317–47.

2 Nina Burri, *Bravery or Bravado? The Protection of News Providers in Armed Conflict* (Brill-Nijhoff 2015). See also 'Pen and Sword – Journalism and IHL' (Australian Red Cross) <https://www.redcross.org.au/stories/podcasts/laws-of-war/pen-and-sword-journalism-and-ihl> accessed 31 January 2021.

2. INTERNATIONAL HUMANITARIAN LAW, THE MEDIA AND PUBLIC OPINION

The influence and power of the media in international law and relations is receiving greater attention as global governance develops alongside technologies and communicative platforms such as the internet.[3] In fact, as with globalization itself, while its current forms may be 'new', the topic and its significance has been of interest since a much earlier time. Where today we speak of clicktivism and digital activism as significant levers within international norm communication,[4] at the beginning of the twentieth century writers such as Elihu Root explored the role of public opinion in international affairs and in generating hope for the ever-slippery area of compliance.[5] This theme remains, with notions of public participation now central to discussions of international legal frameworks and their legitimacy in fields as disparate as trade law, international commercial arbitration, international criminal law and, of course, IHL.

In some sense, IHL and law-making was a critical exemplar leading in this direction. The Martens clause and its focus upon 'the dictates of the public conscience' provides an early, if contested, conception of public opinion's place within IHL.[6] Theodor Meron, in writing of the Martens clause and its significance in terms of 'progress in humanizing IHL', notes the role and influence of 'the ICRC, NGOs, the media, and public opinion' along with the wider resonance which the wording of the clause has had.[7] It is contained in the majority of significant IHL treaties and in military manuals, it has featured in case law, and it continues to influence thinking and provoke debate within IHL scholarship.[8] Emily Crawford views the Martens clause as a 'more generalized statement of policy which argues that, where the law is silent, parties to an armed conflict are not free to act in ways contrary to customary international law and the more generalized principles of humanity and public conscience'.[9] Antonio Cassese provided an authoritative account of debates over the clause and its interpretation in case law. He saw the clause as a diplomatic tool in its time ('an expedient way out of a diplomatic deadlock'), but while skeptical of arguments that it represented new sources of

---

[3] Achilles Skordas, 'Mass Media, Influence on International Relations' (April 2014) in Rüdiger Wolfrum (ed), *Max Planck Encyclopedia of Public International Law* (online edn); Daniel Joyce, 'Human Rights and the Mediatization of International Law' (2010) 23 Leiden Journal of International Law 507.

[4] See further, Daniel Joyce, 'Media Witnesses: Human Rights in an Age of Digital Media' (2013) 8 Intercultural Human Rights Law Review 232; Zeynep Tufekci, *Twitter and Tear Gas: The Power and Fragility of Networked Protest* (Yale University Press 2017).

[5] Elihu Root, 'The Sanction of International Law' (1908) 2 American Journal of International Law 451.

[6] Tetsuya Toyoda, 'Influence of Public Opinion on International Law in the Nineteenth Century' (2009) 46 Alberta Law Review 1099; Sienho Yee, 'Public Opinion' (January 2013) in Wolfrum (n 3).

[7] Theodor Meron, 'The Martens Clause, Principles of Humanity, and Dictates of Public Conscience' (2000) 94 American Journal of International Law 78.

[8] For analysis of the case law and scholarship see: Meron (n 7); Antonio Cassese, 'The Martens Clause: Half a Loaf or Simply Pie in the Sky?' (2011) 11 European Journal of International Law 187; Rotem Giladi, 'The Enactment of Irony: Reflections on the Origins of the Martens Clause' (2014) 25 European Journal of International Law 847.

[9] Emily Crawford, 'Unequal before the Law: The Case for the Elimination of the Distinction between International and Non-International Armed Conflicts' (2007) 20 Leiden Journal of International Law 441, 461–462, fn 107.

international law, Cassese did see it as having lasting interpretive significance, as relevant for a potential general principle concerning considerations of humanity, as well as providing some inspiration – 'the clause has implicitly or explicitly been used as a sort of general instruction concerning the *interpretation* of certain international rules or as a means of better understanding the thrust of modern humanitarian law'.[10] Its significance has echoed beyond IHL,[11] with Stephen Hopgood's critique of the human rights industry reflecting that Martens, 'whose preamble to the Hague Conventions of 1899 and 1907 is an iconic statement of the underlying moral narrative of humanism, believed that there was but one law running through the history of nations, "the principle of respect for the human person"'.[12] But Hopgood is more skeptical when it comes to viewing dominant NGOs such as Human Rights Watch as the product of purely public engagement and participation, rather than 'elite mobilization' and American hegemony.[13]

The Martens clause in some sense also points to the deeper connections between law, media and violence that have become central to some understandings of the way modern warfare is now structured and fought – the 'battle for hearts and minds' in Iraq and the revival of counter-propaganda in the conflicts associated with global terrorism. This also reflects the 'moral internationalism' of which Anne Orford has written, arguing that the rise of the responsibility to protect concept 'is evidence of the increased influence of moral argument as a force in international relations, manifested particularly through the powerful role played by international civil society networks in shaping the language and focus of foreign relations'.[14] An example of this trend is the blending of discourses of humanitarianism and human rights and their discursive and also technical influence across areas as seemingly distinct as IHL, human rights, environmental law, trade law, refugee law, terrorism, investor arbitration, rule of law initiatives and international criminal law.

Normative communication, which is associated with media power and the management, even manipulation, of public opinion, lies at the heart of international relations and, as Orford argues, it matters whether crises are characterized as humanitarian or in national security terms.[15] Equally the 'worldly effects' of idealist humanitarian discourse need greater attention.[16] This is something that David Kennedy has highlighted painfully in relation to the human rights movement and the laws of war.[17] Orford warns further that '[w]hile human rights activists and cosmopolitans may challenge the authority and unity of states in the name of humanity, the claim to be representing humanity strengthens the authority of new actors and justifies their resort to force.'[18]

---

10 Cassese (n 8) 193, 198, 201–202, 208, 213.

11 Cassese (n 8) 212.

12 Stephen Hopgood, *The End Times of Human Rights* (Cornell University Press 2013) xiv.

13 ibid xi.

14 Anne Orford, 'Moral Internationalism and the Responsibility to Protect' (2013) 24 European Journal of International Law 83, 103. See Orford's reflection at 104 that Michael Walzer's earlier argument that the '"important thing is the conscience and moral convictions of ordinary people" seems vindicated'.

15 Orford (n 14) 107.

16 ibid 106.

17 David Kennedy, 'The international human rights regime: still part of the problem?' in Rob Dickinson and others (eds) *Examining Critical Perspectives on Human Rights* (CUP 2012) 19–34.

18 Orford (n 14) 104.

In her revisionist history of IHL Amanda Alexander argues (as does Samuel Moyn regarding human rights[19]) that its transformation has been largely contemporary.[20] For Alexander this was partly the result of a 'general embrace' of humanitarian values in the 1990s in the context of new forms of conflict and institutions like the international criminal tribunals, along with a more diverse and less 'pessimistic' approach to scholarship, the advocacy of key NGOs and the International Red Cross (ICRC). Another factor was the role of the antecedent era of the 1970s with its emerging decolonized international law.[21] Alexander suggests that 'the correct understanding of the *ius in bello* by the end of the 20th century was that it was a truly IHL, a law in which considerations of humanity trumped military necessity'.[22] This involved a pluralist approach to the making of IHL, its mediatization and engagement with global forms of public opinion. As Alexander reflects, '[t]he varied cast of actors who have played a role in this history of international humanitarian law shows that (...) [it] (...) is not a code managed and shaped by states alone. It shows that it is a broader practice, which can comprehend contributions by conventional and unconventional participants.'[23]

When we think here of the role for the media, we should appreciate that the media is both a distinct set of actors, with many journalists now trying to engage with concepts of IHL and human rights in their reporting on conflict,[24] but also a process of communication which with the advent of digital media has become crucial to ways in which NGOs themselves pursue their strategic advocacy.[25] Nick Couldry suggests that mediatization requires a media strategy from all political participants, including 'humanitarian NGOs'.[26] Communication, since at least the time of Thucydides and his re-telling of the Melian Dialogues, has been central to the waging of war, but the possibilities of communication have extended across time, space and genre, with James Der Derian writing that '[g]lobal political actors daily force-multiply their influence in war and diplomacy through networked multiple media'.[27] Our contemporary concern with drones, robots and cyberwarfare reflects the broader connection between communication, conflict and technology.

---

19 Samuel Moyn, *The Last Utopia: Human Rights in History* (CUP 2012).

20 Amanda Alexander, 'A Short History of International Humanitarian Law' (2015) 26 European Journal of International Law 109, especially at 135–138.

21 ibid 130–135.

22 ibid 135.

23 ibid 136.

24 See for example the work of the Committee to Protect Journalists as a media-focused NGO, <https://www.cpj.org/> accessed 31 January 2021.

25 For scholarship on NGO engagement with digital media and the connections between the media and human rights see: Sarah Joseph, 'Social Media, Political Change, and Human Rights' (2012) 35 Boston College International & Comparative Law Review 145; Lindsey N Kingston and Kathryn R Stam, 'Online Advocacy: Analysis of Human Rights NGO Websites' (2013) 5 Journal of Human Rights Practice 75; Philip Alston and Colin Gillespie, 'Global Human Rights Monitoring, New Technologies, and the Politics of Information' (2012) 23 European Journal of International Law 1089; Matthew Powers, *NGOs as Newsmakers: The Changing Landscape of International News* (Columbia University Press 2018).

26 Nick Couldry, *Media, Society, World: Social Theory and Digital Media Practice* (Polity 2012) 146.

27 James Der Derian, *Virtuous War: Mapping the Military-Industrial Media-Entertainment Network* (2nd edn, Routledge 2009) 253.

At its heart the issue of public opinion points both to the increasing mediatization of international law[28] and also to the significance of international law's customary and normative basis. It also highlights both the weaknesses of international law and its ongoing dynamism. For attention to the rhetorical and communicative character of law-making also reminds us of its failures, its indeterminacy and the possibility of argument on either side of a brief. This has been especially evident in recurring debates about the legality of intervention and conflict, the second Iraq War being an illustrative example, but also more recent conflicts as in Syria.[29]

The media is beginning to be understood as a participant in legal processes and in law-making.[30] The traditional mass media has been an important mechanism by which such categories and norms have been framed and distributed. Digital media networks, and especially social media platforms such as Facebook and Twitter, now supplement the traditional media, compete with them for influence, attention and advertising, and also contribute more broadly to the construction of global publics, thereby helping to frame international agendas and shape transnational activism. Hilary Charlesworth writes of modern international law-making as 'being the product of the behaviour and agreement of states, and to some extent the product of abstract values such as "humanity" (…), "fairness" (…), or "communitarian values"'.[31] Charlesworth also points to 'unease about whether international law should reflect the behaviour of states or a system of deeper human values'.[32] As our conception of the relevant subjects of international law expands, so too must our thinking about a range of potential actors involved within law-making. Emerging forms of social and citizen media reflect this concern with countering state-centric communicative forms and outcomes on the international plane. However, social media is not a panacea for deeper problems concerning hierarchy, concentration of power, inequality of arms and participation in international law-making. Despite these important limitations, social media advocacy and co-ordination, especially in a civil society context, does represent a significant tool for public engagement, notwithstanding the digital divide that continues to shape access to communications technologies and the internet.[33]

While much of the modern development of international law has prioritized institution-building, treaty-making and tribunal creation, its consensual and customary character remains central to its creative force and reach. Custom will always invite disagreement, but IHL law-making would be much poorer without it. The ground-breaking customary studies initiated by the ICRC have made a significant contribution to the field's development. And popular engagement with notions of humanitarianism and the role played by the Geneva Conventions have increased with the role now played by law as a popular discourse in debating the merits of the *ius ad bello* and the *ius in bello*.

---

28 Joyce, 'Human Rights and the Mediatization of International Law' (n 3); idem, *Informed Publics, Media and International Law* (Hart Publishing 2020).

29 Catriona Drew and Matt Craven, 'Invoking the language of "savagery" and "barbarism" in international law debates' (*OUP Blog*, 3 February 2014) <http://blog.oup.com/2014/02/colonial-warfare-humanitarian-intervention-international-law/> accessed 31 January 2021.

30 Monica Hakimi, 'The Media as Participants in the International Legal Process' (2006) 16 Duke Journal of Comparative and International Law 1; Alan Boyle and Christine Chinkin, *The Making of International Law* (OUP 2007) 20.

31 Hilary Charlesworth, 'Law-making and sources' in James Crawford and Martti Koskenniemi (eds), *The Cambridge Companion to International Law* (CUP 2012) 187.

32 ibid 200.

33 Joyce, 'Media Witnesses: Human Rights in an Age of Digital Media' (n 4).

The Martens clause, though rather enigmatic, plays an enduring part in the standard narrative of IHL's development and in the broader arc of humanitarianism's rise to prominence within international legal thinking. The familiar history of the development of the Red Cross and the figure of Henri Dunant as its founder, shocked by what he saw on the battlefield, and determined to bring greater regulation and public awareness of the horrors of war, is a driving influence in the field's self-understanding.[34] In this way, whatever the ongoing formal significance of the Martens clause, it plays a deeper and more emotive, even legitimizing role, as a touchstone for the field's connection to a more participatory and engaged law, with roots in the popular conscience and in a wider conception of international public opinion.

IHL on this account is not a set of rather outdated, overly formalistic and inadequate rules which seek to do the unthinkable in civilizing the barbaric and in balancing the incommensurable. It is, rather, a practical and increasingly transparent and popularly legitimated mechanism to restrain and regulate the worst excesses of warfare. On this latter and contrasting view, IHL typifies a newer form of international law which is both soft and hard, utopian and realist, and which places the human civilian subject at the center of international concern and protection, aiming to move beyond the positive project of international law as a purely interstate realm.[35]

3. LIMITATIONS OF MEDIA POWER AND PUBLIC OPINION – IS THEIR INFLUENCE DISCERNIBLE?

While there is increasing recognition of both the historical and contemporary influence of the media and public opinion in international law-making and in the field of international relations, both are challenging concepts to define, and the task is made all the more difficult on the international plane. Is there a global media? Can it be anything but hegemonic, partial and concentrated in the hands of too few? Is there an identifiable international community or global public whose influence and participation can be harnessed to revive the field and enhance its legitimacy and effect? Can media power, while clearly discernible, be effectively measured and analyzed? These are just some of the difficulties that any analysis of media power and public opinion face in this area. And they are also broader issues for an analysis of the impact of newer participants in international law-making.[36]

Walter Lippmann wrote of the dangers of conflating public opinion with the media, and similar issues arise when looking for an 'international community' or in trying to discern accurately a global public opinion or consensus.[37] Nevertheless the media's role in influencing public opinion and consequently in shaping international decision-making and enforcement of humanitarian law is discernible, and derives ultimately from the media's power in representing and shaping the social reality of life. As Carlo Focarelli notes, in discussing the role of the media and communication in international law: '[t]here can be little hope for international law

---

[34] See Alexander (n 20) 62–64.

[35] See the analysis of international humanitarian law from a 'protection' perspective in Crawford (n 9).

[36] Boyle and Chinkin (n 30) 44–45.

[37] Walter Lippmann, *Public Opinion* (Free Press Paperbacks 1997, first published in 1922) 19.

to be "true" law if most people do not believe this to be the case, and the media are today the key tools that make people form their beliefs.'[38]

This contemporary view of the necessity of international law's foundation in and engagement with public opinion has antecedents.[39] So while the ideal of informed public opinion may link to notions of legitimacy, transparency and participation as significant values within modern international law, it is an ideal that remains elusive in terms of quantification. Often it is substituted for media coverage or morality or democratic notions. Some, like Michael Ignatieff, worry that in what he views as the 'new world disorder' (with its revival of Cold War resonant blocs and divisions), '[a]uthoritarian oligarchies can make decisions rapidly, while democratic societies struggle to overcome opposition in the courts, a free press, and public opinion'.[40] In this rather pessimistic variant of liberal internationalism, its values and institutions can also hamper the ability to play the game.

Public opinion is linked to the modernization of diplomacy and international law, and is associated with forms of liberal internationalism that emphasize democratic values, transparency and participation. It is also understood to be influential in terms of policy and decision-formation. It is linked to enforcement in the mode of naming and shaming and other behavioral accounts of international law and it is said to thicken in the context of digital forms of global media and the internet. Its influence is felt in law-making. As Sienho Yee argues, the Martens clause is a clear example of this influence, with the role of civil society in the form of NGOs and their participation in law-making settings another example given.[41] But Yee also points to the limitations and dangers which plague public opinion and its (at times overbearing) relative, the mass media.[42]

The central paradox underlying any analysis of media and public opinion's role within law-making and international legal process more generally is that most observers now acknowledge such power and call for greater attention to be given to it but are unsure of how to proceed in terms of deeper analysis. There is a methodological challenge which has yet to be overcome, even in the field of media studies itself with its techniques of ethnography, sociology, framing and discourse analysis and now big data analytics. The media theorist Nick Couldry, while pointing to this broader methodological challenge, has written that '[f]or all the uncertainties about how media will develop in the next decade, our relations to contemporary media configurations help shape the social worlds we inhabit and our possibilities for due recognition within them'.[43]

Often for international lawyers there are associated fears regarding the media's implication in spectacle,[44] in commodification and in a kind of industry-wide attention deficit disorder. This has been one associated problem in developing a richer account of the CNN effect, which

---

38 Carlo Focarelli, *International Law as a Social Construct: The Struggle for Global Justice* (OUP 2012) 135.

39 See, for example, Henri E. A. M. Rolin, 'Public Opinion and International Law' (1942) 9 Social Research 169, 181.

40 Michael Ignatieff, 'The New World Disorder' (*The New York Review*, 25 September 2014) <https://www.nybooks.com/articles/2014/09/25/new-world-disorder/> accessed 31 January 2021.

41 Yee (n 6) paras 18, 22.

42 ibid 25–31.

43 Couldry (n 26) 180.

44 ibid 147.

more broadly looks to the role played by mainstream global media coverage and the pressure of continuous news cycles in filtering and shaping foreign policy and decision-making. As Boyle and Chinkin conclude, '[w]hile the "CNN Factor" in the making of international law should not be discounted, it must be remembered that media attention is selective and often short-lived.'[45]

These criticisms endure in scholarship regarding the CNN effect. Virgil Hawkins goes so far as to argue that one major consequence of the CNN effect is not in fact the successful leveraging of public pressure via the established media to influence and shape foreign policy decision-making, but rather the resulting effects from the Western media not paying enough attention to conflict or in doing so in a highly selective and disproportionate manner.[46] On this account, the majority of conflicts receive little or no mainstream Western media coverage due to 'entrenched perceptions of newsworthiness and commercial considerations'.[47] Hawkins writes that the scholarship 'has generally not been supportive of a strong CNN effect, with much of it serving to debunk claims of media power'.[48] But this may result from focusing on a particular category of cases involving decision-making regarding military intervention, missing other dimensions of media power such as agenda-setting.[49] It is itself simplistic to view the CNN effect only in terms of US foreign policy decision-making regarding intervention and a narrow category of media outlets. But it is useful to think, as Hawkins does, about the biases, absences and limitations of mainstream coverage in a global power such as the US.

Hawkins focuses on US media and its coverage of conflict in 2009, illustrating that a small number of conflicts (Afghanistan, Iraq, Israel-Palestine and Pakistan) completely dominated coverage, with the majority of conflicts elsewhere forgotten.[50] Hawkins also reminds us that perceptions of parochial and national interests often play a significant role in the editorial decisions regarding the newsworthiness of conflicts.[51] For example, forgotten conflicts in Africa may continue to be deadly and protracted but are largely ignored in the US media.[52] Hawkins does point to some more positive potential consequences of coverage, including conflict prevention, more informed policy-making and even the collection of evidence for litigation purposes, but concludes that '[l]ack of media coverage contributes to a lack of policy, and a lack of policy contributes to deadlier conflicts'.[53]

Peter Viggo Jakobsen considers some earlier examples where the CNN effect did appear to be influential in Iraq in 1991, in Somalia in 1992 and in Rwanda in 1994.[54] But Jakobsen shares the concerns of Hawkins, Boyle and Chinkin, and points to problems with media coverage also before and after conflict, or in covering good news stories where conflict is avoided.[55]

---

45 Boyle and Chinkin (n 30) 20.

46 Virgil Hawkins, 'Media Selectivity and the Other Side of the CNN Effect: The Consequences of Not Paying Attention to Conflict' (2011) 4 Media, War & Conflict 55.

47 ibid 56.

48 ibid.

49 ibid.

50 ibid 57–59.

51 ibid 61–62.

52 ibid 61.

53 ibid 62–65.

54 Peter Viggo Jakobsen, 'Focus on the CNN Effect Misses the Point: The Real Media Impact on Conflict Management is Invisible and Indirect' (2000) 37 Journal of Peace Research 131, 134.

55 ibid 131–41.

Jakobsen points to instances where media coverage can interfere with conflict management in detrimental ways and can distort peace processes, concluding that 'the media is probably more of a hindrance than a help for Western conflict management at the general level'.[56]

Audrey Lustgarten and François Debrix continue in the mode of critical analysis of the media's role in the specific case of monitoring IHL during the military intervention in Kosovo.[57] To some extent their argument inverts the traditional view of the CNN effect by illustrating that in Kosovo it was the media coverage which was shaped by military command. They ask whether the media and through them the public can act as an IHL watchdog, to fill what they call 'the humanitarian gap', 'this space of normative incompatibility between humanitarian law and state-sponsored military interventions'.[58] Lustgarten and Debrix argue, by reference to the case of Kosovo in 1999, that the media fail in their public duty as 'humanitarian mediators'.[59] Again they criticize the short attention spans of Western politicians and the media.[60] Furthermore they argue that the media-generated 'humanitarian spectacle provides a moral buffer that (…) legitimizes the continued apathy of the Western spectator'.[61] In analyzing media coverage of Kosovo at the time, they find that much of it traded in generic themes of bad Serbs and good NATO forces intervening to save the victims. The media narratives which emerged rarely diverged from these common types, which they argue were in fact provided by NATO and their spin doctors, with journalists even failing to independently investigate instances of NATO violations.[62] According to Lustgarten and Debrix:

> investigative reporting and watchdog journalism were not at their finest in Kosovo. While NATO forces violated IHL on at least nine occasions, directly resulting in the death of 500 civilians, the media failed to even mention many of these incidents, let alone engage in any type of meaningful, independent reporting.[63]

Despite these important criticisms and empirical analysis, there is a perception held amongst the media and decision-makers that the CNN effect continues to have some purchase. Important factors here include the role played by the internet, live and constant news coverage, and increasing efforts by governments and the military to influence public opinion and to manage and control media coverage of conflicts. As Jakobsen writes, '[t]here is a general feeling that media coverage, especially television, has had an increased influence on Western conflict management since the collapse of the Soviet Union.'[64] This effect may be both positive and negative, and we must also think about ways in which the power of traditional media has been supplemented or perhaps superseded by digital media, much of it interactive and citizen-generated. Here too hopes for a digital media revival of participation and democracy may be overblown. Couldry warns that in 'developing a broader account of media's role in

---

56 ibid 138–41.
57 Audrey Lustgarten and François Debrix, 'The Role of the Media in Monitoring International Humanitarian Law during Military Interventions: The Case of Kosovo' (2005) 30 Peace & Change 359.
58 ibid 362.
59 ibid 387–89.
60 ibid 368.
61 ibid 369.
62 ibid 375–85.
63 ibid 385.
64 Jakobsen (n 54) 131.

social change, we must always be suspicious of linear accounts of how media change, how people respond to those technologies and how effects flow from those responses'.[65] Indeed, during the Trump presidency concerns about the dominance of mainstream media coverage have shifted to anxieties regarding the prevalence of 'fake' news and digital disinformation.

4. INTERNATIONAL LEGAL THEORY REGARDING THE MEDIA'S EFFECT

As examined above, it is very difficult to quantify the influence of the media and to fully ascertain the public in international law terms. Nevertheless, there is increasing interest in doing so. Here I examine and present three significant and contrasting accounts of the media's power in shaping international law, by reference to the scholarship of Monica Hakimi, David Kennedy, Frédéric Mégret and Frederick Pinto.

4.1 The Media as Participants in International Legal Process

I begin with Monica Hakimi's important article, 'The Media as Participants in International Legal Process'.[66] It adopts a New Haven School approach with its emphasis on process and attention to international law as communication.[67] From this perspective, the media can be viewed as either a significant actor in its own right in terms of the role of journalists and media organizations, or else in exemplary terms as a messenger and means for communication. International law is seen as total, in the sense that law is a complete social system, but also as limited, especially from the perspective of the narrower conception of law as a system of rules. This approach to international law can be critical of media which strays from liberal democratic conceptions of its role as a watchdog. However, by idealizing communication as a central and facilitative value and process, this perspective can tend to idealize the media itself, and put great stock in its role (some would argue overvaluing the media). The posture taken as regards international law emphasizes participation and, in certain guises, the development of a shared world view. Again, all areas of life are potentially the domain of law, though law is seen as part of broader constitutive social processes.

Hakimi sees law in terms of processes of decision grounded in a normative context and emphasizes the democratic watchdog potential of the media.[68] Hakimi also notes that there is a striking lack of scholarship in this area, which she attributes in part to the fact that the media are 'unconventional participants', lacking a defined institutional role, and working as 'messengers' or 'behind the scenes'.[69] The media, she argues, 'fill the communicative gaps in the international legal process'.[70] As an example, Hakimi discusses the media's 'critical role in disseminating intelligence about Abu Ghraib, in invoking and applying the relevant inter-

---

65 Couldry (n 26) 29.
66 Hakimi (n 30).
67 ibid 3. See further an earlier example, W. Michael Reisman, 'International Lawmaking: A Process of Communication' (1981) 75 American Society of International Law Proceedings 101.
68 ibid 1.
69 ibid 2.
70 ibid 4.

national legal norms, and in communicating the responses of the relevant actors'.[71] Indeed, Hakimi elaborates further, providing a list of positive functions which the media plays within the various stages of the international legal process. These include prescription (law-making), codification, invocation, application and termination (where a norm ceases to be binding as law). In terms of prescription, Hakimi notes that the media identify decision-makers, disperse intelligence, specify substantive policies and allocate communal values. Here, though, she recognizes that the media 'shape' knowledge and public consciousness rather than simply communicating 'raw information'. Her image of the media thus tends to hover between that of messenger and watchdog, though she later considers fewer positive aspects of the media.[72]

Hakimi's is a useful and wide-ranging contribution, but risks seeing the media only through the lens of the New Haven School's categories and value system.[73] Hakimi ascribes to the media a unique and facilitative role within the international legal system, but then moves to consider the bad media dimension and 'factors that impede the media's performance in the international legal process'.[74] These limiting factors are familiar from general critiques of the media and include: simplification and inaccurate reporting, pressures for instant news, the possibility for capture by propaganda and state control, bias and distortion due to commercial interests and advertising and cultural bias. For Hakimi, propaganda 'may be desirable, for example, to the extent that it can be used to peacefully bring about positive changes in the world arena'.[75] But who is to determine what is positive and what is negative? When will propaganda be viewed in good media terms as public diplomacy? This is an enduring criticism of the New Haven approach, and a weakness of this contribution. While viewing international law and the media in relatively dynamic terms, politics remain static. To avoid the 'corruption' of international legal process, Hakimi contends that it is necessary to identify and foster an optimal media environment. The image of international law as communication is then burdened by an underlying end goal of liberal media environments, sometimes requiring international legal intervention (in the form of development, coercion or privatization of markets), while obscuring any responsibility of the international community for what results.[76] The resulting tension for Hakimi is how to balance the interests of state sovereignty with the free flow of communication.[77] Law is communication in a rather functional way. And the media is significant insofar as it is instrumentally useful and a practical reality. Another significant, though quite different and more critical, view of the media's role can be found in the work of David Kennedy on war and law.

4.2 The Media's Role in Lawfare

David Kennedy is a prominent international lawyer whose scholarship has begun to treat the media's significance in greater depth, especially in his contribution to the *Cambridge*

71 ibid 7.
72 ibid 11–13, 19.
73 ibid 14.
74 ibid 21.
75 ibid 26.
76 Hakimi (n 30) 29.
77 ibid 30.

Companion to International Law[78] and his earlier book, *Of War and Law*.[79] Kennedy's intention is to first present war analytically as a historical and contemporary institution, before then providing a historical sweep of the engagement of international law in war-making. Finally, he argues that war in the contemporary era is waged by law, what he terms lawfare. International law has become the central discourse for decision-making during war in particular and 'the vocabulary for international politics and diplomacy', which itself begs the question of the discipline's engagement in advocacy and its own ethical responsibility for and in war.[80] However, he also counters the widely advocated view that international law acts only to limit war; in fact, argues Kennedy, international law is central to war – so much so that it has begun to structure and legitimize it. He provocatively suggests that law is implicated in violence and carries a darker side.[81] Indeed Kennedy, in a variety of fields, has done much to show that rather than offering a set of rules, the discipline is politics, necessitating a turn to an explicit, critical intervention in the world of policy and decision-making.[82] A key contribution here is not to focus on finding what are the rules to apply, but rather in asking how do they operate, what effects do they have, and what could they be? Without an ultimate source of interpretative authority, the emphasis turns to persuasion and strategy, and here Kennedy has much to say about media spectacles, audiences for mediated decision-making, the court of world public opinion and legitimacy.[83] Further he writes of the way in which perception has become significant in determining legitimacy, drawing into view the role for the media and public relations.[84]

Kennedy has connected the media's influence with the rise of a 'global policy class of experts who respond to the same media and speak the same language'.[85] He also points to the connection between law, media and violence.[86] The danger here is for Kennedy to oversubscribe influence to these shadowy elites at the expense of real investigation of citizen challenges to their power, through more interactive forms of social media. The media, though open to manipulation and perhaps less representative of the citizenry than claimed through projections of witnessing global public audiences, are still given an important role in agenda-setting.[87] I agree that audiences are used by the powerful as a discursive legitimizing tool, but, as Kennedy acknowledges, different audiences will receive and interpret messages in different ways.[88] He also recognizes the active nature of some audiences for international law, as 'participants, with their own strategies'.[89] This is an important point. Ultimately public opinion is a double-edged sword, with the potential to both empower and unseat elites.

---

[78] David Kennedy, 'Lawfare and Warfare' in James Crawford and Martti Koskenniemi (eds), *The Cambridge Companion to International Law* (CUP 2012) 158–83.

[79] David Kennedy, *Of War and Law* (Princeton University Press 2006).

[80] Kennedy, *Of War and Law* (n 79) 5.

[81] ibid 22, 167.

[82] Unfortunately for reasons of space it is not possible to discuss here Kennedy's contributions in other fields such as human rights law and development, see further Stephen Humphreys, 'The Emptiness of Empire and Other Hazards of Theory' (2008) 57 International and Comparative Law Quarterly 225.

[83] Kennedy, *Of War and Law* (n 79) 26, 28–29, 39–41, 45, 91–92, 96, 125–26, 159, 161.

[84] ibid 156.

[85] ibid 7.

[86] ibid 15.

[87] ibid 18.

[88] ibid 124–25.

[89] ibid 126.

Kennedy emphasizes the communicative dimension of both war and law.[90] He argues that '[c]ommunicating the war is fighting the war, and law – legal categorization – is a communication tool'.[91] In this mediatized context for war, audience is a recurring theme and a strategic necessity. But on this account, there is a danger that law becomes driven by its strategic and persuasive power, rather than its moral or ethical force. The message becomes law.

In his more recent analysis Kennedy remains concerned with the changing nature of warfare. He is preoccupied with a dynamic and largely rhetorical conception of international law-making which draws media and argument into view, and which 'places legal distinction in strategic play as a part of war itself, further proliferating and fragmenting the sites of its doctrinal and institutional operation'.[92] On this view, debates over law and war cannot be fully resolved doctrinally and must engage ethics and politics.[93] Law becomes communicative as its internal arguments are externalized for audiences – 'the battlefield is not only a matter of deployed force – it is also a rhetorical and legal claim.'[94] According to Kennedy, law is dynamic and is changed by its interactions and usage by a range of actors such as the Red Cross, humanitarian activists and global media such as CNN or Al Jazeera, as of course it is shaped still by states, their domestic political debates and institutions of government.[95]

This is a sophisticated and thoroughly contemporary understanding of the dynamic nature of international law-making, but it is also bewildering in its scope and possibility, which in turn creates problems in terms of discernibility and predictability. But while Kennedy is ready to acknowledge these uncomfortable truths about international law, he remains clear that '[t]here is no court of world public opinion on the international stage to adjudicate such claims.'[96] This is a powerful and critical insight, which cuts through much of the empty rhetoric surrounding the concept of the 'international community'. But are we willing to let go of such a possibility or ideal? Could not global publics offer much to the field of law-making, if we acknowledge their limitations and potential for manipulation?[97] Though there is critical force in certainty, there can also be underestimation of potential benefits. While incapable of finite calculability, in the era of digitalization and the internet it seems dangerous also to discount, at least conceptually, the force and varied forms of global public opinion.

This, in part, takes us back to the role of the Martens clause and ongoing efforts to humanize international law and to better take account of its political dimensions. Here Kennedy's insight is provocative and pragmatic. He argues that '[w]e should think of international law as a set of arguments and counter-arguments, rhetorical performances and counter-performances, deployed by people pursuing projects of various kinds.'[98] This is the plural, dynamic and com-

---

90 ibid 45, 97.
91 ibid 122.
92 Kennedy, 'Lawfare and Warfare' (n 78) 161.
93 ibid 161.
94 ibid 166.
95 ibid 166.
96 ibid 167.
97 Joyce, 'Media Witnesses: Human Rights in an Age of Digital Media' (n 4) 272–78.
98 Kennedy, 'Lawfare and Warfare' (n 78) 173.

municative international law of the present. This is also international law-making as advocacy, strategy and as externalized professional practice. As Kennedy argues:

> We must recognize that neither humanitarian idealism nor military necessity provides a standpoint outside the ebbs and flows of political and strategic debate about how to achieve objectives on the battlefield. Conversing before the court of world public opinion, statesmen not only assert their prerogatives – they also test and establish those prerogatives through action. Political assertions come armed with little packets of legal legitimacy – just as legal assertions carry a small backpack of political corroboration.[99]

This provides an important and nuanced account of international law as argument and strategy, all made in the glare of publicity, but with layered and often conflictual audiences and constituencies. Kennedy alludes to the CNN effect, but also seeks to unsettle its oversimplification, as he does usefully with IHL itself.[100]

4.3 International Humanitarian Law as Image

A further approach looks at IHL itself in terms of image. It foregrounds the visual and the virtual, which is useful for international lawyers and a system faced with mediated globalization and interactive forms of visual connection. This approach perceives law's agendas as open to manipulation, spectacularizing – but also contestation. The media's role is seen in aesthetic and ideological terms. Law's power is held to lie not in its stability of meaning, but in its symbolic reach and potential for cultural re-interpretation. This shifts attention from meaning to the process and politics of meaning construction, to open the possibility for critical evaluation of our consumption of international law and its imagery. Law appears as no longer solely textual or deliberative, and fresh cultural territory for international legal theory draws into view.

Here, an important contribution to international legal scholarship has been made by Frédéric Mégret and Frederick Pinto. In their article, '"Prisoners' Dilemmas": The Potemkin Villages of International Law?', they investigate the mediatization of international law in the context of the war against terrorism, revealing the ways in which the media can distort and shape the production of law by reference to IHL, where they focus on the resulting 'virtualization of human suffering' and the complicity of law.[101] Mégret and Pinto argue that violence has become legitimized in the context of mediatization, which they summarize as 'the transformation of the signals of the living world into codified bits of information for mass consumption'.[102] They argue that the law is generally blind to its own representation through the media: 'lawyers are trained to think of the law and the representation of the law as two distinct things.'[103] The authors focus on virtuality (a phenomenon related to mediatization), which they see as

---

[99] ibid 179.

[100] ibid 179, 181–82.

[101] Frédéric Mégret and Frederick Pinto, '"Prisoners' Dilemmas": The Potemkin Villages of International Law?' (2003) 16 Leiden Journal of International Law 467, 469.

[102] ibid 467, 468.

[103] ibid 468.

'the predominance of signs over meaning through the saturation of public space by the mass media'.[104]

To make their argument, Mégret and Pinto focus on three cases with associated images and visual narratives: an image from 2002 at the US military base in Guantanamo Bay where detainees from the war on terror have been controversially held; the showing on Al-Jazeera of captured Coalition prisoners of war from the Iraq War in 2003; and the 2002 reporting of conditions at a prison near the site of the destruction of the Buddhas of Bamiyan in Afghanistan.[105] They discuss the 'huge impact' of an early image of Guantanamo prisoners handcuffed in orange suits, which has become iconic of the war against terror.[106] The authors consider the image as both voyeuristic and pornographic, and examine the subsequent speculation, as with the images from Abu Ghraib, that either this was a public relations blunder or a sinister diversion from something else. Mégret and Pinto argue that, despite the law's difficulty in recognizing the power of images, this picture 'very much *defined* the legal debate, in that it delimited the legal terrain upon which it unfolded'.[107] In some senses audiences have subsequently fetishized these images as representative of the worst conditions possible, when in fact similar and possibly worse violations occur invisibly elsewhere, for example in the domestic context. By framing the issue solely through a conventional IHL perspective, other ways of protesting about Guantanamo are muffled, a point made also by David Kennedy. Ultimately mediatization can trivialize our experience of war, reducing the complexity of life to a simplified image or set of manageable representations.[108] Yet the liberal narrative of the media society presented is one of redemption in the shape of bringing attention to violations – providing the impetus for reform and an outlet for indignation. As such, the law reasserts its own position on the high ground and the violation is distanced and corrected.

The second case considered relates to the broadcasting by Al-Jazeera of captured US and UK soldiers during the 2003 invasion of Iraq. The images showed the soldiers disoriented and were criticized by the US and UK governments as violating protections afforded to prisoners under IHL. Mégret and Pinto contend that the images may in fact reveal the weakness of the Iraqi government and the unevenness of the war and publicity machines of both sides. This argument is further strengthened when the images are contrasted with Guantanamo, where the possibility of torture haunts the few images that emerged (or even Abu Ghraib, where explicit images of degradation may ironically have concealed even more serious violations held in secret). The authors also point to the need to consider the agenda-setting role for the media and the ways in which both the media and international law depend on typologies of victims and perpetrators, resulting in 'hyper-individualization' which afflicts fields such as human rights, humanitarian law and international criminal law.[109] While their criticism of the Western media is more familiar, the connection with international law's own responsibility is important. Media audiences elsewhere, such as in the Middle East, would have received and interpreted these images in different ways, impacting the image of international law in such contexts.

---

104 ibid 467, 468.

105 This article appears to have been written before photographs of prisoners at Abu Ghraib led to another media scandal.

106 ibid 469–70.

107 ibid 471.

108 ibid 473.

109 ibid 481.

Another aspect highlighted is the 'media's appetite for the visible' and poor treatment of the invisible.[110] Mégret and Pinto help to show that the media's role in 'shaping the production of law' is underexplored and of particular significance in times of war and violence. They also argue that the media relies upon an 'unambiguous' conception of international law as discipline rather than advocacy.[111]

The article finishes with a third illustration of the 'complex relationship of law, politics, and the media' by recalling a French media report from Afghanistan in 2002.[112] In this story a French reporter visits a prison at the symbolic site once occupied by the Buddha statues before their destruction by the Taliban. The veteran correspondent is mistakenly shown ordinary detainees in one part of the prison in terrible conditions, when he should have been taken by the jailer to inspect the model prison, which exists as a symbol of IHL's narrative of progress and protection. These model prisoners seem better fed and housed than local civilians, not to mention the ordinary prisoners. As the authors reflect, 'thanks to the incorporation of IHL in various public relations strategies, it may be infinitely better to be caught as a member of a fundamentalist militia in the course of fighting than as a simple thief.'[113] Respect for international law here is part of the '*staging of reality itself*' and international law is revealed itself as an image, 'a mediatization of violence'.[114] Ultimately Mégret and Pinto warn that virtualization threatens law and that the media may replace humanitarianism with endless representation of violence, thereby undermining the international order.[115]

These varied and significant conceptions of the media's role in international law-making and in IHL push us to think further about media and public opinion. In doing so we need to acknowledge historical developments from the Martens clause through to the debate regarding the CNN effect in the post-Cold War moment. But we also need to begin to evaluate these questions in light of digital media and the internet.

5. BEYOND THE CNN EFFECT – DIGITAL FUTURES?

Kenneth Keith has written that we need to question the state-centric view of international law, its structures and processes.[116] This chapter's focus on the role of the media and of public opinion in international law-making has also pointed in this direction and argued for a more complex view of law-making that encompasses a role for the media and that views the media in a broader frame. This will at times involve aspirational overreach, but there is also a danger of underreach. We can widen our view of actors in international law to include non-state actors such as civil society, but then focus on NGOs to the exclusion of other players like the media.[117]

---

110 ibid 482.

111 ibid 484.

112 ibid 486.

113 ibid 488.

114 ibid 488–489.

115 ibid 490.

116 Kenneth Keith, 'Stepping Away from the State' (2014) 3 Cambridge Journal of International and Comparative Law 628.

117 While I am interested in analyzing the underexplored connections between the media and NGOs (especially in terms of method and form), I am grateful to Janina Dill for also pointing to their distinc-

Part of my challenge here then has been to widen our collective sense of a role for the media within international law-making and within IHL. But as international law grapples with change, so too does the transforming media landscape. It remains a danger, then, that in widening our view to include the traditional media, we neglect the rise of digital media. Many of my examples above are either historical or were generated by the era of humanitarian intervention in the 1990s which coincided with moves towards a more global experience of the media. The idea of the CNN effect can be traced to that time.

The CNN effect and earlier debates over the role of public opinion within international relations and foreign policymaking remain important in the present day. But it is clear that we now also need to begin to think beyond the CNN effect to an increasingly digital future. It is not possible to give a comprehensive or final analysis of the present. But we need to analyze these changes and to consider examples such as social media effects alongside more traditional media.

For example, digital media platforms bring greater interactivity, connection and distribution, but they also bring spectacle, simplification and commodification. From one perspective, social media engagement revives connection and empathy; from another, it is largely about performance and commodification of the self, at the expense of the other. Mediatization of conflict may not in fact result in greater public engagement with IHL and its normative role. So in large part many of the early debates discussed will retain significance and many of the dangers signaled remain live, perhaps even intensified, with digital media. Another consideration is that the competition for attention and advertising has also damaged the traditional media's economic model, meaning that in certain contexts their ability to perform a watchdog role is weakened.

Digital media and the internet bring into view new areas to think about – the significance of search engines and their editorial function, the challenge of maintaining trust and an ethical framework for the media in a de-professionalizing context, the reach of technology and developing notions of presence and co-presence which may yet transform our ability to witness and respond to conflict in real time, the possibility of open-source fact-finding and evidentiary models emerging online. Here we can think of Wikileaks and online whistleblowing, social media advocacy for humanitarianism, digital witnessing, and the enhanced capacities that new technologies and applications may bring as evidenced by the Harvard Humanitarian Initiative or the Ushahidi crowd-sourcing platform.[118] Such developments bring both praise and critique, useful and damaging effects. At times the claims for technological progress can be viewed as old wine in new bottles, but the internet and digital media can also be seen as paradigm-shifting. We need then to begin to evaluate whether our normative frameworks can adjust or will need further tinkering. Such questions arise within IHL as it considers the

---

tiveness and for questioning whether the media act as norm entrepreneurs in the way that, say, an activist human rights NGO may.

118 See further: <https://wikileaks.org/>; <http://hhi.harvard.edu/>; <https://www.ushahidi.com/> all accessed 31 January 2021; Sam Dubberley, Alexa Koenig and Daragh Murray (eds) *Digital Witness: Using Open Source Information for Human Rights Investigation, Documentation, and Accountability* (OUP 2020); Eyal Weizman, *Forensic Architecture: Violence at the Threshold of Detectability* (Zone Books 2017).

examples of cyber security and warfare, of robots, autonomous weapons systems, drones and the like.[119]

Social media may act in part to multiply the effect of the media more broadly,[120] to assist in bridging geographies and limiting the dominance of the Western media. But darker possibilities also exist – of viral deception, misinformation and propaganda, which return us to historical fears relating to the public in international law. There exists the real possibility that in the field of IHL, social media pressure may intensify aspects of the CNN effect, such as its emphasis on real-time decision-making and oversimplification. Our thinking about these effects is necessarily tentative, but it must deepen. Equally more thought should be given to the increasing role that big data and data associations will play in global governance and in decision-making.[121]

6. CONCLUSION

This chapter has begun to map out some distinctive ways in which the media and public opinion affect processes of international law-making. In beginning to consider the specific example of IHL, I have analyzed both historical understandings of this role, as evidenced in the Martens clause, and more contemporary debates regarding the CNN effect and the rise of social media. I have also examined three relatively rare accounts within international legal scholarship of the media's role within international law and specifically IHL. Finally, I have begun to move beyond these accounts and the role of the traditional media and towards the digital media landscape, the internet and big data.

These developments, and the mediatization of international law more broadly, herald new ways of thinking about the relevant actors in our field and point to shifting dynamics within law-making. And yet serious challenges remain in moving beyond the question of discernibility and confronting the complexity of media power and its worldly effects, both upon public opinion and in constituting our sense of the international and the human. What is clear, as Achilles Skordas notes, is that:

> Mass media organizations have become influential participants in international relations, and shape the world public's perceptions by selectively focusing on, or framing, issues with relevance for international law (facts, or assessments of situations).[122]

What remains to be seen is whether this mediatization can thicken our relations and deliver on the promise of a participatory international law.

---

[119] Nehal Bhuta and others (eds), *Autonomous Weapons Systems: Law, Ethics, Policy* (CUP 2016); Rain Liivoja, Kobi Leins, Tim McCormack, 'Emerging Technologies of Warfare' in Rain Liivoja and Tim McCormack (eds), *Routledge Handbook of the Law of Armed Conflict* (Routledge 2016).

[120] I am indebted to William Boothby for this point.

[121] See further: Fleur Johns, 'Data, Detection, and the Redistribution of the Sensible in International Law' (2017) 111 American Journal of International Law 57; Eyal Benvenisti, 'Upholding Democracy Amid the Challenges of New Technology: What Role for the Law of Global Governance?' (2018) 29 European Journal of International Law 9.

[122] Skordas (n 3) para 61.

25. Media, public opinion and humanitarian advocacy

William Boothby

One can only agree with Daniel Joyce that the notion of moral argument as a force within international law, and indeed as the inspiration of much of the development of that law over the last century and a half, is incontestable. The sentiments expressed in the preambular language of the 1868 St Petersburg Declaration,[1] the uplifting, even poetic, language of the Martens Clause,[2] the sometimes workmanlike but always ethically centric introductory words of some modern arms control treaties[3] all attest to the strong link between the collective moral compass of the negotiators, ideas of the role of public conscience and the texts that emerged from their deliberations.

The perhaps interesting question is whether negotiators of the past held some kind of common appreciation of morality, some generally accepted concept of the distinction between the acceptable and the unacceptable. The St Petersburg and Hague Convention language rather suggests that they did. Even more interesting is the question whether any such common ethical yardstick exists today. There are undoubtedly those who reject contemporary humanitarian law norms, either because they consider them to be born of what they see as an alien set of moral values or simply because the prosecution of a conflict grounded in terror presupposes a rejectionist stance, whether as an expedient or because the individuals concerned have assessed Western moral values and find them wanting. So the modern question seems to be: whose moral values should hold sway and how do we deal with their rejection?

A development of that question is whether emerging norms are in fact global, and if so, should claims that those norms have Western origins and are thus of limited general relevance and acceptability be simply cast aside as unacceptable? That would certainly be the present author's position. The principles of distinction, discrimination, humanity, military necessity, superfluous injury and neutrality are the critical defences against a descent by humanity into

---

1 Declaration Renouncing the Use, in Time of War, of Explosive Projectiles Under 400 Grammes in Weight, St. Petersburg (11 December 1868) reprinted in Dietrich Schindler and Jiří Toman, *The Laws of Armed Conflicts* (3rd edn, Martinus Nijhoff Publisher 1988) 102.

2 Hague Convention (IV) Respecting the Laws and Customs of War on Land and Its Annex: Regulations Concerning the Laws and Customs of War on Land (adopted 18 October 1907, entered into force 26 January 1919) <http://www.refworld.org/docid/4374cae64.html> accessed 31 January 2021 preambular para 8.

3 See for example Convention on the Prohibition of the Use, Stockpiling, Production and Transfer of Anti-Personnel Mines and on Their Destruction (adopted 18 September 1997, entered into force 1 March 1999) 2056 UNTS 211 preambular para 8.

widespread, unrestrained, long-lasting and brutal violence in which victims and the innocent become the chosen targets; such a development would have the inevitable consequence that peace becomes ever harder to maintain or re-establish. So while recognizing that customary law norms are fewer and less prescriptive than some individuals of a more optimistic disposition would have us believe, nevertheless there are powerful arguments to be made for recognition of the core customary law principles and many of the customary and treaty law rules that flow from them as the legal construct that is critical to maintenance of humanity and, thus, of significant swathes of the human race.

The argument that legal development is or should be based, at least in part, on the practice of non-state actors raises all sorts of practical difficulty. Which non-state actors would be acceptable participants in such a process; what would be the baseline for assessing their acceptability; should, for example, their record of compliance with existing norms be a factor here; would it be easy to identify their 'practice'; and how does one assess the generality of such 'practice' among a population of such non-state actors that it is going to be hard to list? The argument that their practice should at least be considered is undoubtedly well made. It is the practicality that is troublesome, and one worries that law established by practice of and/or input from non-state actors may prove unacceptable to states.

It is, however, clearly correct that modern conflicts put civilians at the centre of the hostilities, whether as direct participants, victims, medical personnel, religious personnel, hostages, journalists, or in a variety of other capacities. One capacity that would seem to the present author to have major implications for how future wars will be fought and how future war crimes will be detected, prosecuted and punished is the role of civilians as witnesses. A witness who is limited to speaking long after the event of atrocities the perpetrators of which have long disappeared may have value to subsequent legal proceedings if the guilty are found and brought to court. Too often this has not happened. The guilty too frequently escape the scene, avoid justice and the victims are left to suffer with little prospect of securing justice.

It seems just possible that modern technology may be changing this, at least to a degree. The advent of smartphone technologies, the possibility for events on the battlefield to be recorded by observers, the increasingly widespread connectivity between the ordinary citizen and the mass media – these and other developments are making it more possible to put the actions of war criminals on record. The day before this text was written, a Russian fighter aircraft was shot down reportedly by a Turkish aircraft. The fiery descent to earth of the victim aircraft was recorded, presumably on a smartphone, was communicated to the mass media and was transmitted by the television news channels of the world on the same day.[4] It is the ability of the ordinary citizen to combine cameraman, sound recordist and commentator as events unfold that radically broadens and deepens the mass media coverage of events. If 'a picture tells a thousand words', a minute of video footage with accompanying sound and contemporary comment and reaction will provide the most persuasive, indeed compelling, evidence of what happened, of who acted in which way, of the pertinent facts of an incident and of the consequences and so on.

The implications are clear. The march of digital technology will potentially make it harder for war criminals to maintain their impunity for their inhumane deeds. It may make it possible

---

[4] 'Turkey "shoot down warplane on Syria border"' (*BBC News*, 24 November 2015) <https://www.youtube.com/watch?v=IzLhJeByjRE> accessed 31 January 2021.

to identify evil-doers long after the event, and, with painstaking and careful investigation, justice may become a more realistic prospect.

There are, however, wider implications for states and, indeed, for commanders. The Rome Statute of the International Criminal Court (ICC) addresses the responsibility of commanders and of those in positions analogous to command in the following terms:

> (a) A military commander or a person effectively acting as a military commander shall be criminally responsible for crimes within the jurisdiction of the Court committed by forces under his or her effective command and control, or effective authority and control as the case may be, as a result of his or her failure to exercise control properly over such forces, where:
> (i) That military commander or person either knew or, owing to the circumstances at the time, should have known that the forces were committing or about to commit such crimes; and
> (ii) That military commander or person failed to take all necessary and reasonable measures within his or her power to prevent or repress their commission or to submit the matter to the competent authorities for investigation and prosecution.

The ICC Statute provision then goes on to address responsibility arising from superior and subordinate relationships other than those involving military command. It allocates responsibility to such superiors where the superior either knew, or consciously disregarded, information which clearly indicated that the subordinates were committing or about to commit such crimes, where the crimes concerned activities that are within the effective responsibility and control of the superior, and where the superior failed to take all necessary and reasonable measures within his or her power to repress or prevent them or to submit the matter for investigation and prosecution.[5]

Self-evidently, the advent of social media reporting is going to make it very much more difficult in the future for a commander to argue that they neither knew nor should have known what was going on. If footage of indiscipline and of criminal behaviour is circulating within social media, a commander ought to be correspondingly aware, and a failure by them to take timely action will tend to render the commander criminally liable. It follows logically from this that any information of this nature detected on social media will need to be passed immediately to responsible commanders for effective action to be taken.

There is of course another aspect of social media that is vital to the conduct of future military operations, namely its use as the medium of choice for the members of non-state groups to communicate with one another, for elements within the group to coordinate their activities, for the conduct of hostilities to be arranged, even choreographed, for operational instructions to be issued and for other purposes. Correspondingly, national security agencies are keen to penetrate these communication webs in order to gain intelligence as to the activities of groups, as to their membership, as to their future plans, all with a view to countering the threat they pose to the society and to individual citizens. So social media is not just a medium for the recording and reporting of hostile and other acts associated with armed conflict; it also facilitates the organization, control, coordination and conduct of the group. Indeed, it is the environment in which the battle for the maintenance of internal security will increasingly be fought.

---

[5] Rome Statute of the International Criminal Court (adopted 17 July 1998, entered into force 1 July 2002) 2187 UNTS 90 (ICC-Statute) art 28.

These are essentially the practical implications of the social media revolution that we have witnessed in recent years. There is, however, a more general observation to be made. It is that it is no longer sensible to speak of public opinion and the mass media, respectively, as discrete phenomena. Social media increasingly acts as a vitally important link between the individual and the mass media. Whereas in former times the mass media broadcasted, and the citizen received, now the citizen interacts with the mass media. In the future the citizen will provide increasing input to what it transmits, they will provide comment on what they see on mass media, they will correct or update mass media versions of events, and the picture the mass media is able to present will be increasingly a synthesis of what reporters, commentators and experts discover and what the citizen provides. This is essentially a democratization process that will influence a broad range of social intercourse, by no means limited to war, conflict and crisis reporting. The media magnates will retain power to influence the story, or at least to influence its presentation, but citizen witnesses may improve the objective accuracy and timeliness of what is presented.

There is sometimes a tendency to consider in isolation the effect on the conduct of warfare of a single development in technology, doctrine, law or some other relevant field. Such analysis may or may not produce an accurate, indeed a realistic, vision of the way ahead. So perhaps as technology, society and human behaviour all change over time, it would be more profitable to consider the effect of social media developments on, say, the role of civilians and of the media in armed conflict in the context of other relevant changes. There can be little doubt that the law itself has become an increasingly important factor in influencing battlefield behaviour. Legal activity can take a considerable number of forms. As the author has discussed elsewhere,[6] commanders, planners, decision-makers and the armed forces in general must increasingly act in a spotlight to which the mass and social media certainly contribute, but which also comprises a variety of kinds of legal challenge.

Coroners' courts in England and Wales inquire into the circumstances leading to a death where the body of the relevant individual is, or is brought, within the coroner's jurisdiction.[7] If the death arose from military activity, the proceedings may be expected to inquire into their nature, how they were conducted, whether expected precautions were taken and other relevant matters. Other countries will have similar procedures.[8] Other inquiries may be established under domestic law procedures to inquire into events specified in their terms of reference. For the UK, section 343 of the Armed Forces Act 2006[9] provides for the holding of service inquiries into any matter involving the armed forces that it is considered should be the subject of an inquiry, while the Inquiries Act 2005[10] enables the holding of public inquiries to look into matters of major public concern. States are obliged to repress breaches of the Geneva

---

[6] William H. Boothby, *Conflict Law: The Influence of New Weapons Technology, Human Rights and Emerging Actors* (T.M.C. Asser Press 2014) ch 11.

[7] Coroners and Justice Act 2009 (UK) ch 25.

[8] Consider for example the Fatal Accidents and Sudden Deaths Inquiry Act 1976 (Scotland) (repealed) ch 15.

[9] See also the Armed Forces (Service Inquiries) Regulations 2008, SI 2008/1651 (UK).

[10] See Inquiries Act 2005 (UK) ch 12. The al-Sweady Public Inquiry was established under this Act pursuant to a statement on 25 November 2009 by the then UK Secretary of State for Defence with regard to allegations that Iraqi nationals were detained by British soldiers in Iraq in 2004 and were unlawfully killed at a British camp and that others were mistreated at that camp and at a detention facility.

Conventions and of Additional Protocol I.[11] Moreover such offences as war crimes, crimes against humanity, genocide and, in due course, the crime of aggression are subject to the potential jurisdiction of the ICC.[12] It will also be recalled that ad hoc tribunals and similar arrangements have been established to address the serious breaches of international law perpetrated in the former Yugoslavia,[13] in Rwanda,[14] in Sierra Leone[15] and in certain other conflicts. So breaches of IHL can potentially be dealt with by national courts, by ad hoc tribunals and special courts, or by the ICC.

Proceedings linked to past conflicts have also been pursued before the civil courts by way of judicial review of procurement or other decisions,[16] before human rights courts, and there have been political challenges, for example as to the lawfulness of the resort to the use of force.[17]

It therefore seems clear that there are nowadays numerous legal avenues where the citizen can challenge some of the decisions made by commanders, senior officials, the executive and others in authority in connection with the conduct of military operations. The important point from the perspective of this short chapter is, however, that the citizen who has available to them this broader range of challenge options is the same citizen as has the greater possibility of recording what happened, of getting that record into the public domain and of accordingly influencing public understanding of the particular event and, perhaps, public appreciations as to the way the war is being fought. Indeed, it is the same citizen who, as a member of an organized armed group, may be using social media to communicate with other members of the group and to facilitate violent activities aimed at destabilizing the state. Social media constitute not only a fact of modern life but also a fact of modern warfare, and this is so from a number of perspectives.

We should not underestimate the importance of the immediacy of communication that social media afford. Events that, at the genesis of the modern law of armed conflict in the 1860s,

---

11 See Geneva Convention for the Amelioration of the Condition of the Wounded and Sick in Armed Forces in the Field (adopted 21 August 1949, entered into force 21 October 1950) 75 UNTS 31, common art 1; Geneva Convention for the Amelioration of the Condition of Wounded, Sick and Shipwrecked Members of Armed Forces at Sea (adopted 21 August 1949, entered into force 21 October 1950) 75 UNTS 85; Geneva Convention relative to the Treatment of Prisoners of War (adopted 12 August 1949, entered into force 21 October 1950) 75 UNTS 135; Geneva Convention Relative to the Protection of Civilian Persons in Time of War (adopted on 12 August 1949, entered into force 21 October 1950) 75 UNTS 287; Protocol Additional to the Geneva Conventions of 12 August 1949, and relating the Protection of Victims of International Armed Conflicts (adopted 8 June 1977, entered into force 7 December 1978) 1125 UNTS 3 art 1. For the UK, this has been reflected in the Geneva Conventions Act 1957 (UK) ch 52 and the Geneva Conventions (Amendment) Act 1995 (UK) ch 27.

12 ICC-Statute (n 5) arts 5–8.

13 Statute of the International Criminal Tribunal for the Former Yugoslavia (as amended on 17 May 2002) (adopted 25 October 1993 by SC Resolution 827/1993) (ICTY-Statute).

14 Statute of the International Criminal Tribunal for Rwanda (as last amended on 13 October 2006) (adopted 8 November 1994 by SC Res 955/1994) (ICTR-Statute).

15 The Special Court for Sierra Leone was established in 2002 by virtue of an agreement between the Government of Sierra Leone and the United Nations; Statute of the Special Court for Sierra Leone (entered into force 16 January 2002), pursuant to UNSC Res 1315 (14 August 2000) UN Doc S/RES/1315.

16 Consider for example *Smith and others (FC), Ellis (FC), Allbutt and others (FC) v Ministry of Defence* [2013] UKSC 41.

17 *R (on the application of Gentle and another) v Prime Minister and others* [2008] UKHL 20.

would, at best, achieve scant treatment in a couple of column inches on an inside page days if not weeks after the event, are now liable to become 'breaking news' on 24-hour television, reported instantly from the locus in quo, discussed almost instantly by media-recruited experts and known by the public at large within hours or even minutes of the particular happening.

If this is the context in which current and future wars will be fought, it is pertinent to ask whether reasonably well-trained troops seeking to comply with applicable law will be able to operate effectively and successfully under such multifaceted and intrusive scrutiny. Will such coverage have the effect that the watching public has unrealistic expectations of perfect performance by the armed forces that are acting in their name? Will there be space in this high-speed communication medium for sensible realism to intrude? While the prevention of egregious criminal activity on the battlefield is to be applauded, the imposition of unrealistic constraints on the ability of the armed forces of democratic states to operate effectively is liable to have longer-term consequences that we may live to regret. In short, reporting and analysis must maintain the balance between military necessity and humanity that many commentators, including the author, recognize as vital elements underpinning the current law of armed conflict. If that balance is abandoned, it is respect for the law itself that is liable to suffer and that is an outcome that all involved must strive to avoid.

PART VIII

Conclusion

26. A legitimacy crisis of international humanitarian law?

Heike Krieger and Jonas Püschmann

1. THE COMPETING NARRATIVES OF INTERNATIONAL HUMANITARIAN LAW'S LEGITIMACY

This book's title, *Law-Making and Legitimacy in International Humanitarian Law*, may raise an eyebrow. This is because there is still a widespread tendency to view international humanitarian law (IHL) as a legal regime whose legitimacy is beyond doubt. So why question it? Underneath the surface of narratives proclaiming humanitarian progress, a competing, and critical, view of IHL's function and purpose has long become established. This alternative narrative seems to reach a certain peak in light of the reappraisal of US legal policies in response to the so-called War on Terror and other forms of military interventionism.[1] Evaluating law-making in IHL therefore requires us to dissect diverging agendas.

1.1 The High Degree of Legitimacy of International Humanitarian Law on its Surface

The very purpose of IHL evokes an impression of an intrinsic normative legitimacy.[2] IHL protects against and restricts the effects of warfare and aims to alleviate the suffering in wartime. Accordingly, the International Court of Justice (ICJ) has repeatedly described its rules and principles as enshrining 'elementary considerations of humanity'[3] and claims that 'overriding consideration[s] of humanity' lie 'at the heart' of IHL.[4] Specific legal effects follow from this

---

1 Among others Naz Modirzadeh, 'Cut These Words: Passion and International Law of War Scholarship' (2020) 61 Harvard International Law Journal 1; Samuel Moyn, *Humane: How the United States Abandoned Peace and Reinvented War* (Macmillan 2021).

2 See, for example on the website of the ICRC, 'What is international humanitarian law?' (ICRC, 31 December 2014) <https://www.icrc.org/en/document/what-international-humanitarian-law> accessed 31 January 2021: 'International humanitarian law is a set of rules that seek to limit the effects of armed conflict. It protects people who are not or are no longer participating in hostilities and restricts the means and methods of warfare.'

3 Stefan Kadelbach, 'The Role of Legitimacy in International Humanitarian Law – A Comment', Chapter 3 in this book, 37; ICJ, *Military and Paramilitary Activities. in and against Nicaragua* (*Nicaragua v United States of America*) (Merits) [1986] ICJ Rep 14, para 218.

4 ICJ, *Legality of the Threat or Use of Nuclear Weapons* (Advisory Opinion) [1996] ICJ Rep 253, para 95.

characterization. Reference to the ethic ideals of humanity and humanitarianism bestows upon IHL a specific form of legitimacy which seems to exceed other branches of international law. This is the reason why IHL is still broadly accepted as the main yardstick for measuring the legitimacy and acceptability of behaviour in warfare.[5] Where this legitimacy is endangered, the International Committee of the Red Cross (ICRC), in its role as a guardian of IHL, attempts to protect it. For example, as a response to the perception that 'IHL is more often violated than respected', the ICRC has established an explicit initiative to change 'the narrative' on IHL in an attempt to 'engender further compliance with the law' through a more positive focus on 'success stories'.[6] The interrelatedness between effectiveness and legitimacy lurks behind such attempts.[7] Indeed, if IHL is considered illegitimate, there is a strong likelihood that 'its raison d'etre will diminish'.[8]

1.2 The Humanitarian Nature of International Humanitarian Law: Contestations of the Prevalent Narrative

This rather positive narrative that surrounds IHL, however, has never existed as wholly uncontested, and criticism sometimes even goes so far as to imply that IHL might just be a 'sham'.[9] Indeed, an exclusive focus on the humanitarian objectives of IHL only tells half of the story. From a radical pacifist perspective, IHL may be seen as an instrument to enable war because it creates the impression that war could be conducted in a humane way and 'that legal war is more humane than an illegal war'.[10] Thus, the very existence of IHL is considered to imply that it is legitimate or at least legal to differentiate between necessary and unnecessary forms of dying or suffering, within the context of armed conflicts. Thereby, 'the basic fact that nations purport to respect the rule of law helps protect the entire structure of war-making from more fundamental challenges.'[11] Approaches within the field of critical legal studies question

---

[5] Jean d'Aspremont, 'The Roles of Legitimacy in International Legal Discourses: Legitimizing Law vs Legalizing Legitimacy', Chapter 2 in this book, section 3; David Kennedy, *A World of Struggle: How Power, Law, and Expertise Shape Global Political Economy* (Princeton University Press 2016) 258.

[6] Juliane Garcia Ravel and Vincent Bernard, 'Changing the narrative on international humanitarian law' (ICRC, 4 November 2017) <https://blogs.icrc.org/law-and-policy/2017/11/24/changing-the-narrative-on-international-humanitarian-law/> accessed 31 January 2021.

[7] On the interrelatedness between effectiveness and legitimacy see: Cord Schmelzle, 'Evaluating Governance. Effectiveness and Legitimacy in Areas of Limited Statehood' (2011) SFB-Governance Working Paper Series, No. 26, Research Center (SFB) 700, Berlin <https://www.sfb-governance.de/publikationen/sfb-700-working_papers/wp26/SFB-Governance-Working-Paper-26.pdf> accessed 31 January 2021; Cedric Ryngaert, 'Non-State Armed Groups and International Humanitarian Law-Making: The Challenge of Legitimacy – A Reply to Cindy Wittke and Hyeran Jo', Chapter 22 in this book, 378.

[8] Hyeran Jo, 'Law-Making Participation by Non-State Armed Groups: The Pre-Requisite of Law's Legitimacy?', Chapter 21 in this book, 358.

[9] Jochen von Bernstorff, 'Is IHL a Sham? A Reply to Eyal Benvenisti and Doreen Lustig' 31 European Journal of International Law 709.

[10] Chris af Jochnick and Roger Normand, 'The Legitimation of Violence: A Critical History of the Laws of War', (1994) 35 Harvard International Law Journal 49, 50; see also David Kennedy, *Of War and Law* (Princeton University Press 2006).

[11] Jochnick and Normand (n 10) 58.

the prevailing narrative[12] that IHL has become more and more humane and assume thereby that the 'modern view falsely promotes the present laws of war as a humanitarian break from the "savage" past'.[13] This rhetoric is seen to conceal the sense that states have deliberately designed IHL to favour considerations of military necessity over humanitarian concerns.[14]

Other criticisms claim that law-making in the field of weapons also suffers from 'cynical window dressing' because only those weapons are banned which have become futile or because the states that benefit from forbidden weapons do not participate in the pertinent treaties.[15] The Treaty on the Prohibition of Nuclear Weapons[16] may be seen as a case in point:[17] while no state possessing nuclear weapons has joined the treaty,[18] the ICRC characterizes the entry into force of the treaty as a 'victory for humanity'.[19]

Above all, a sense of unease regarding the conceptual dialectic underpinning IHL norms can be felt within these writings. This dialectic goes back to developments of the 19th century, where jurists articulated 'legal claims of humanity as conditions of legitimacy on the use of force, and demanded that they be weighed against statist considerations of military necessity',[20] establishing the juxtaposition of military necessity with humanity, and thereby creating the legal dilemma of today's 'laws of war' balancing exercise. While humanitarian considerations represent an ethical value in themselves, the concept of military necessity represents a more pragmatic or utilitarian concern. From an ethical perspective,[21] any attempt to achieve a balance between these two concepts is – at least prima facie – principally flawed.[22]

---

12 For this narrative see eg Michael Schmitt, 'Military Necessity and Humanity in International Humanitarian Law: Preserving the Delicate Balance' (2009–2010) 50 Virginia Journal of International Law 795 or ICTY, *Prosecutor v Tadić* (Decision on the Defence Motion for Interlocutory Appeal on Jurisdiction) IT-94-1 (2 October 1995) para 97: 'A State-sovereignty-oriented approach has been gradually supplanted by a human-being-oriented approach'; *Prosecutor v Kupreškić et al* (Judgment) ICTY-95-16-T (14 January 2000) para 518: 'norms of international humanitarian law were not intended to protect State interests; they were primarily designed to benefit individuals *qua* human beings.'

13 Jochnick and Normand (n 10) 60.

14 ibid 50.

15 von Bernstorff (n 9) 715.

16 Treaty on the Prohibition of Nuclear Weapons (adopted 7 July 2017, entered into force 22 January 2021) <https://treaties.unoda.org/t/tpnw> accessed 31 January 2021.

17 For arguments why this is not a form of window dressing but part of norm-creating process longue-durée see Harald Müller and Carmen Wunderlich, 'Nuclear Disarmament without the Nuclear Weapon States: The Nuclear Ban Treaty' (2020) 149 (2) Daedalus 171.

18 See for the list of state parties to the treaty <disarmament.un.org/treaties/t/tpnw> accessed 31 January 2021.

19 Peter Maurer and Yoshiharu Otsaki, 'A victory for humanity' (ICRC, 21 January 2021) <https://blogs.icrc.org/law-and-policy/2021/01/21/victory-humanity/> accessed 31 January 2021.

20 Pablo Kalmanovitz, *The Laws of War in International Thought* (OUP 2020) 141.

21 For philosophical justifications of the rationale of IHL see: Janina Dill and Henry Shue, 'Limiting the Killing in War: Military Necessity and the St. Petersburg Assumption' (2012) 26 Ethics and International Affairs 311; Janina Dill, 'Should International Law Ensure the Moral Acceptability of War?' (2013) 26 Leiden Journal of International Law 253; Henry Shue, 'Laws of War, Morality, and International Politics: Compliance, Stringency, and Limits' (2013) 26 Leiden Journal of International Law 271; Jeff McMahan, 'The Ethics of Killing in War' (2004) 114 Ethics 693.

22 For approaches to (re-)emphasize the limiting role of necessity see Yishai Beer, 'Humanity Considerations Cannot Reduce Wars Hazards Alone: Revitalizing the Concept of Military Necessity' (2016) 26 European Journal of International Law 801.

However, most authors who take an outspokenly critical stance towards IHL do not aim to completely deconstruct the laws of war. Instead, they aim to warn against a conception of IHL as the 'embodiment (…) of rescue, amelioration, and humanity'[23] and strive to offer arguments as to why the balance between considerations of necessity and humanity, as defined by the mainstream interpretation of IHL, favours the state and negatively affects individuals.[24] For example, Benvenisti and Lustig argue that the judicious interpreter needs 'to adopt a critical attitude towards existing treaties and to take into account the interests of the underrepresented in the process of construing it' because the pertinent treaties 'grant priority to military necessity over humanitarian concerns'.[25]

Irrespective of whether authors support the prevailing narrative or advocate that, given the so far dubious record of IHL, a turn in favour of stronger humanization must occur from now onwards, they all attribute desired change for the better to the increasing impact of civil society and courts on law-making.[26] In particular, non-governmental organizations (NGOs) such as Amnesty International (AI) and Human Rights Watch (HRW) or the International Campaign to Ban Landmines, have been influential in this respect. A further factor challenging the foundational underpinnings of IHL is seen to lie in a general increase of interest in IHL among scholars, widening the epistemic community from military lawyers to lawyers with a background in general international law or human rights law.[27] In terms of methodological preconditions for bringing about such a change, literature has identified reliance on

> effective and acceptable methods for interpreting the law creatively and introducing change. These strategies include a restatement of the law, a reinterpretation of laws, a reference to custom and the construction of new histories (…). By deploying these strategies, practitioners are able to not only change the law but also to erase its former incarnations and the moment of change itself.[28]

1.3 Preserving the Military Nature of International Humanitarian Law: Contestation in Favour of the Status Quo

Simultaneously, a competing counter-narrative has emerged promoted by the epistemic community of mainstream IHL/military lawyers. This counter-narrative emphasizes the adverse effects of the abovementioned methodological approaches. By assuming the role and functions of states in the law-making process, courts, such as the International Criminal Tribunal for the former Yugoslavia (ICTY), are seen by these scholars as endangering the appropriate balance between military necessity and humanity. The same argument is applied to the impact of NGOs. Their role is seen as unfettered lobbyism for humanitarian considerations since these actors do not have to 'bear the consequences' of their interpretative claims on the battlefield. In contrast, it is claimed that states which actually conduct warfare are in a better position and

---

23 Kalmanovitz (n 20) 151.

24 Jochnick and Normand (n 10) 51.

25 Eyal Benvenisti and Doreen Lustig, 'Beyond the "Sham" Critique and the Narrative of Humanitarianism: A Rejoinder to Jochen von Bernstorff' (2020) 31 European Journal of International Law 721, 724–25.

26 Amanda Alexander, 'A Short History of International Humanitarian Law' (2015) 26 European Journal of International Law 109, 110.

27 ibid 131.

28 ibid 137.

have a greater incentive to appropriately weigh military necessity against considerations of humanity. This balance is considered to be enshrined in the provisions of treaty law through the treaty-making process in which states participate and which eventually allows for opting out in case of disagreement. Since states remain the decisive actors for creating and interpreting international law, supplanting state-driven law-making processes entails the danger that the existing consensus on the law becomes hard to identify and that these processes become distorted. This, in turn, contributes to uncertainty about the *lex lata*. Therefore, authors such as Thilo Marauhn or Michael Schmitt strongly criticize that NGOs raise claims about *lex ferenda* in the disguise of *lex lata* or do not apply the *lex lata* standards, for instance in relation to the principle of proportionality, to the factual situation on the ground in an appropriately well-argued manner. Thereby, the involvement of NGOs is said to weaken the international rule of law.[29] Thus, from the perspective of military lawyers the paradigm shift is far from settled, rather an ongoing tug-of-war between different participants within the law-making process continues even challenging the underlying consensus of IHL.

1.4 The Plurality of Agendas and Actors and Their Impact on Law-Making

Even though, as Cryer argues, one should not consider the abovementioned positions as monolithic,[30] the chapters show that such diverging agendas within various law-making processes create ambivalences in the interpretation of IHL that go beyond the standard dispute about the appropriate denomination of this area of law as 'international humanitarian law' or 'law of war'.[31] Such ambivalences may also not be sufficiently captured by a mere formalist view of international law.[32] According to the still dominant formal account of international law, with its focus on the formal sources of international law, states remain the gatekeepers, since eventually no rule of international law can be created without their consent, as reflected in the *Lotus* Judgment.[33] Moreover, despite claims to the contrary, this has not changed much until today if one regards courts as state-empowered institutions endowed with the implicit consent of states. Nevertheless, in light of the increasing importance of non-state actors, some states may have lost 'some of their political autonomy to national and transnational social forces

[29] Thilo Marauhn, 'The International Rule of Law in Light of Legitimacy Claims' in Heike Krieger, Georg Nolte and Andreas Zimmermann (eds), *The International Rule of Law – Rise or Decline?* (OUP 2019) 293–300; Schmitt (n 12) 816–839, in particular 838.

[30] Robert Cryer, 'The Impact of Human Rights Advocacy: Between (Mis)Stating the Law and Pursuing Humanitarian Policies?', Chapter 23 in this book, 387.

[31] For instance, when the ICRC used the term 'international humanitarian law' in its study on customary international humanitarian law, the US response was quick to criticize the usage of the term itself and preferred the term 'law of war'; see Jean-Marie Henckaerts and Louise Doswald-Beck, *Customary International Humanitarian Law* (ICRC/CUP 2005) and John B. Bellinger III and William J. Haynes II, 'A US government response to the International Committee of the Red Cross Study Customary International Humanitarian Law' (2007) 89 International Review of the Red Cross 443, 443. See also Page Wilson, 'The Myth of International Humanitarian Law' (2017) 93 (3) International Affairs 563.

[32] Kadelbach (n 3), 40.

[33] PCIJ, *S.S. 'Lotus' (France v Turkey)* (Judgment) PCIJ Series A No. 10 (1927) 18: 'The rules of law binding upon States (…) emanate from their own free will'.

which would then give such social forces relevant influence and turns such states into merely formally competent actors'.[34]

There is, therefore, a need to take a broader look at law-making at large, as the book demonstrates. It is apparent that discourses on new challenges in IHL are shaped mainly by actors other than states. The scene is dominated by competing authorities – sometimes even based in other legal fields, such as international criminal law or human rights law – which all claim to legitimately interpret the law, albeit with diverging agendas. Doubts about normative certainty are particularly problematic for IHL, since this legal regime needs to be practical on the ground within the circumstances of ongoing hostilities: 'If institutions start interpreting norms in a manner that is not attuned to the realities on the battlefield, the legitimacy of both the institution and the IHL norm may suffer.'[35] Moreover, the increasing relevance of human rights actors and discourses (by human rights treaty bodies and courts as well as non-state actors with a human rights mandate) questions the dominant, or previously even exclusive, role of IHL in measuring the legitimacy of behaviour and actors engaged in armed conflict. Instead, human rights law and the enforcement procedures that it offers may have replaced IHL to a large extent, thereby questioning the very purpose and foundation of IHL.[36] Thus, it would be problematic for the consensus underlying the whole framework of IHL if it would increasingly turn from a *jus in bello* framework into a *jus contra bellum*,[37] as it inherently and originally, in a certain manner, accepts armed conflict by regulating it. IHL was once thought of as restrictive in its setting out of clear rules for the exceptional case of wars that typically had not been regulated by international law. In the current contemporary setting, the diversity in agenda and increasing number of interpretative communities becoming involved, results in IHL appearing increasingly rather permissive in light of conflicting norms of human rights law that may be abrogated by IHL. This perception may explain the strong criticism voiced[38] against the 2021 judgment of the European Court of Human Rights (ECtHR) in the case of *Georgia v Russia (II)* in which the court refused to extend the concept of 'jurisdiction' in Article 1 of the European Convention on Human Rights (ECHR) to the conduct of active hostilities in an international armed conflict.[39]

---

34 Georg Nolte, 'Interpretation and Identification of International Humanitarian Law: Responses of the International Law Commission', Chapter 15 in this book, 246.

35 Cedric Ryngaert, 'Non-State Armed Groups and International Humanitarian Law-Making' (n 7) 383.

36 cf Jann Kleffner, 'A Bird's-Eye View on Compliance with the Law of Armed Conflict 70 Years After the Adoption of the Geneva Conventions' (2021) 22 Yearbook of International Humanitarian Law 2019 107, 119: 'The (…) steady process of "human-rights-ization" of the LoAC [law of armed conflict] entails that a focus on individual rights replaces the considered and delicate balance between humanitarian considerations and military necessity that informs LoAC in its entirety.'

37 cf Björnstjern Baade, Linus Mührel and Anton Petrov, 'Concluding Observations: how International Humanitarian Law is Shaped to Meet the Challenges Arising from Areas of Limited Statehood' in idem, *International Humanitarian Law in Areas of Limited Statehood* (Nomos 2018) 217, 226.

38 Helen Duffy, 'Georgia v. Russia: Jurisdiction, Chaos and Conflict at the European Court of Human Rights' (*Just Security*, 2 February 2021) <https://www.justsecurity.org/74465/georgia-v-russia-jurisdiction-chaos-and-conflict-at-the-european-court-of-human-rights/> accessed 22 February 2021; Marko Milanovic, 'Georgia v. Russia No. 2: The European Court's Resurrection of Bankovic in the Contexts of Chaos' (*EJIL:Talk!*, 25 January 2021) <https://www.ejiltalk.org/georgia-v-russia-no-2-the-european-courts-resurrection-of-bankovic-in-the-contexts-of-chaos/> accessed 31 January 2021.

39 *Georgia v Russia (II)* App no 38263/08 (ECtHR, 21 January 2021) paras 141–144.

On the other side of the coin, the input of such diverse interpretative communities is important for the legal regime because there is also a risk that 'if the interpretation of international humanitarian law is left entirely to military practitioners (…) IHL becomes simply a meek form of self-regulation'.[40] Broadened engagement with rules of IHL on the part of different communities ranging from civil society, international organizations as well as non-state armed groups and human rights communities may thus be seen as strengthening IHL by pluralizing and democratizing law-making processes. A certain pluralism of perspective may help to further enhance the legitimacy of the regime. As had been noted by Thomas Franck, 'logical deduction suggests (…) that rules which are perceived to have a high degree of determinacy – that is, readily ascertainable normative content – would seem to have a better chance of actually regulating conduct in the real world than those which are less determinate.' But where rules are less determined, the rule 'may overcome that deficit if it is open to a process of clarification by an authority recognized as legitimate by those to whom the rule is addressed'.[41] Therefore, a broad interpretative community consisting of domestic and international courts, quasi-judicial bodies and manual processes may help to overcome interpretive uncertainties in the application of IHL and enhance the legitimacy belief by engaging with the regime. Nevertheless, in order to have such effects, such law-making processes need to be legitimate in themselves.

2. INDICATORS POINTING TOWARDS A PERCEIVED LACK OF LEGITIMACY OF INTERNATIONAL HUMANITARIAN LAW

The chapters of this book present many overarching issues that contribute to a perceived lack of legitimacy regarding the law-making processes in IHL. These include the exclusion of armed groups (2.1), the (limited) inclusion of states from the Global South (2.2), the ambivalent role of international courts and expert bodies in the interpretation or creation of rules (2.3), and finally, the growing influence of norm entrepreneurs and evaluations external to the law (2.4).

2.1 The Exclusion of Armed Groups from Formal Law-Making

Armed groups are mostly excluded from IHL law-making and have traditionally been delegitimized in IHL rather than legitimized, because states fear that any engagement with armed groups by international actors could strengthen their political or even legal status. Therefore, states have deliberately framed international law in such a way as to favour existing governments and state structures over armed groups.[42] Nonetheless, over time, the legal regime has expanded in scope in order to impose obligations on non-state actors. Starting with concepts of belligerency through Common Article 3 of the Geneva Convention and Additional Protocol II, the expansion has widened through the imposition of particular obligations. Cases in point

---

40 Cryer (n 30) 402.

41 Thomas Franck, *The Power of Legitimacy among Nations* (OUP 1990) 52.

42 For further details, see Heike Krieger, 'International Law and Governance by Armed Groups: Caught in the Legitimacy Trap?' (2018) 12 Journal of Intervention and State Building 563, 574–77.

are top–down decisions by the UN Security Council, as Wittke has shown,[43] or an increasing tendency of new treaties in the field of IHL to equally apply to international as well as non-international armed conflicts and thereby also impose general obligations on non-state actors, i.e., armed opposition groups, as noted by Garcia and Jo.[44] Recent developments in this regard can be seen, in particular, in the aspects of IHL that govern the choice of weapons and prohibit or restrict the use of certain weapons, and UN Security Council Resolutions dealing with ceasefires.

With such broadened application, what remains questionable is whether these rules can still exert compliance pull over non-state armed groups because, as noted by Ryngaert, '[i]f states create international legal duties for non-state actors without the latter's consent, the legitimacy of the international legal system may potentially come under strain.' This is the case irrespective of questions of legality of such an extended application as '[l]egality in itself does not guarantee adherence'[45] but adherence depends on legitimacy. Traditional approaches to the legitimacy of IHL either rely on the overall legitimacy of existing sanctioning regimes, such as international criminal law, or on the substantive legitimacy distinct to IHL norms.[46] This may nevertheless not be enough to address armed groups' lack of compliance with IHL.[47] Franck's conception of legitimacy suggests as a minimum that, 'the perception of those addressed by a rule or a rule-making institution that the rule or institution has come into being and operates in accordance with generally accepted principles of right process', be met.[48] An important part of such a process is the symbolic validation of a rule, for example its 'ability to communicate (…) the voluntarily acknowledged authenticity of a rule or a rule-maker, or, sometimes, the authenticity (validity) bestowed on a symbolic communication's recipient'.[49] In the same vein, the interactional account of legitimacy offered by Brunnée and Toope underlines that '[t]o be effective, ambitious substantive norms require deeper shared understandings of the right ordering of society'[50] and therefore 'influential norms will not emerge in the absence of processes that allow for the active participation of relevant social actors'.[51]

---

[43] Cindy Wittke, 'Between War and Peace: Negotiating and Implementing Legitimate Ceasefire Agreements', Chapter 20 in this book, 348ff.

[44] Denise Garcia, 'Global Norms Governing the Protection of Civilians, Conflict, and Weapons: Formal or Informal Law-Making?', Chapter 5 in this book, 65; Jo, 'Law-Making Participation by Non-State Armed Groups' (n 8).

[45] Cedric Ryngaert, 'Imposing International Duties on Non-State Actors and the Legitimacy of International Law' in Math Noortmann and Cedric Ryngaert, *Non-State Actor Dynamics in International Law* (Ashgate 2010) 71; Ryngaert, 'Non-State Armed Groups and International Humanitarian Law-Making' (n 7) 378; Jo, 'Law-Making Participation by Non-State Armed Groups' (n 8) 358.

[46] See eg Heike Krieger, 'Where States Fail, Non-state Actors Rise? Inducing Compliance with International Humanitarian Law in Areas of Limited Statehood' in eadem, *Inducing Compliance with International Humanitarian Law: Lessons from the African Great Lakes Region* (CUP 2015) 504, 514; Ryngaert, 'Non-State Armed Groups and International Humanitarian Law-Making' (n 7) 380.

[47] Ryngaert, 'Imposing International Duties on Non-State Actors and the Legitimacy of International Law' (n 45).

[48] Franck (n 41) 19.

[49] ibid 91.

[50] Jutta Brunnée and Stephen Toope, *Legitimacy and Legality in International Law: An Interactional Account* (CUP 2010) 32.

[51] ibid 54.

The necessity for a more inclusive law-making process has also been expressed by armed groups themselves,[52] for instance at the Third Meeting of Signatories to Geneva Call's Deeds of Commitment, where several actors stressed 'that awareness and ownership of international humanitarian norms by all parties to armed conflict are critical in efforts to improve compliance'.[53] Research on armed groups also demonstrates that compliance with IHL may increase if non-state armed groups actively engage with IHL.[54] Especially for groups with long-term political goals, engagement with IHL acts as a form of 'rebel governance or diplomacy'[55] which can be utilized in order to increase their own legitimacy in the eyes of their supporters or national and international audiences, irrespective of the limiting legal framework:

> Benefits resulting from conducting diplomacy based on an engagement with international humanitarian law may range from recognition by or observer status within international organisations or expressions of political sympathy from states, to the supply of material support, for example in the form of money or weapons.[56]

This may bring broader and more visible acceptance of IHL generally, as is exemplified by Jo's chapter. Jo argues around 20 per cent of armed groups are committed to respecting IHL; some even aim to ensure compliance via their own courts,[57] through the translation of IHL norms within their own codes of conduct[58] or via agreements concluded with states, such as ceasefire agreements.[59] Accordingly, Wittke, in the case of top–down imposition of obliga-

---

52 For more examples of such pronouncements, see further Lars Müller, *Die Rolle nicht-internationaler Waffenstillstandsabkommen im humanitären Völkerrecht* (Nomos 2019) 47 (especially the references in fn 103).

53 'Declaration of the Third Meeting of Signatories to Geneva Call's Deeds of Commitment' (*Geneva Call*, 20 November 2014) 21 <https://www.genevacall.org/wp-content/uploads/2020/09/3rd-Meeting-of-Signatories-Report-1.pdf> accessed 31 January 2021.

54 cf Hyeran Jo, *Compliant Rebels* (CUP 2015) 256; Anthea Roberts and Sandesh Sivakumaran, 'Lawmaking by Non-State Actors: Engaging Armed Groups in the Creation of International Humanitarian Law' (2012) 37 Yale Journal of International Law 107, 126–29; International Council on Human Rights, 'Ends & means: Human Rights Approaches to Armed Groups' (ICHR 2010) 51 <http://www.international-council.org/download/ends-and-means-human-rights-approaches-to-armed-groups/> accessed 31 January 2021. This remains nevertheless only valid in the case that such groups are generally open to law-making itself. For instance, in recent declarations of religious armed groups, one can also find a general rejection of law that does not derive from god, on this see Jo, 'Law-Making Participation by Non-State Armed Groups' (n 8) 371f; and Olivier Bangerter, 'Reasons Why Armed Groups Choose to Respect International Humanitarian Law or Not' (2011) 93 International Review of the Red Cross 353, 381.

55 For the term rebel diplomacy see Bridget Coggins, 'Rebel Diplomacy: Theorizing Violent Non-State Actors' Strategic Use of Talk' in Ana Arjona, Nelson Kasfir and Zachariah Mampilly, *Rebel Governance in Civil War* (CUP 2015) 98, 105; Reyko Huang, 'Rebel Diplomacy in Civil War' (2016) 40 (4) International Security 89, 90.

56 Krieger, 'International Law and Governance by Armed Groups' (n 42) 573 with reference to Huang (n 55) 102. In this regard, see also Alicia de la Cour Venning, 'Revolutionary Law Abidance: Kachin Rebel Governance and the Adoption of IHL in Resistance to Myanmar State Violence' (2019) 19 International Criminal Law Review 872.

57 Jo, 'Law-Making Participation by Non-State Armed Groups' (n 8) 362. The percentage is based on a statistical analysis of international law commitments by rebel groups between 1974 and 2010.

58 Sandesh Sivakumaran, 'Implementing Humanitarian Norms' in Krieger (n 46) 133ff.

59 Wittke (n 43) and Müller (n 52).

tions by the UN Security Council, also calls for a certain ownership and therefore a 'certain degree of mutual agreement (…) between the conflict parties' to be effective. According to her approach, it would be preferable if conflict parties could agree on a mandate and composition of a UN mission that goes hand in hand with a UNSC resolution, within a ceasefire agreement, notwithstanding that such a scenario might be 'idealized and, thus, simplified'.[60]

For these abovementioned reasons, when it comes to general treaty obligations, Jo and Ryngaert both call for a greater (at least indirect) involvement of armed groups in formal IHL law-making, in order to enhance its procedural legitimacy. Nevertheless, as Jo argues, whereas law-making participation in IHL may enhance the regime's legitimacy, this is not the only factor and therefore not a definite prerequisite for the legitimacy of IHL.[61]

2.2 Inclusion of States from the Global South

As set out in the chapters by Bothe, Kahombo and Rodiles, many states, especially of the Global South, were – for a long time – not involved in the process of IHL law-making. Moreover, not only was the Global South excluded from law-making, in the early phase of IHL's evolution, its norms were not even deemed applicable in colonial wars.[62] It is against this backdrop that states of the Global South, for various reasons, later acceded to the relevant international treaties and why in the late 1960s Third World and socialist states mobilized to push for the formal revision of IHL, which led to the negotiation of the two Additional Protocols of 1977.[63]

Nevertheless, attempts to exclude states from the Global South from IHL law-making processes continue. For example, for the purpose of ascertaining norms of IHL, some states argue in favour of a hierarchy of relevance of pertinent state practice. The most obvious example is the US response to the ICRC Study on Customary IHL, where the US criticized the lack of consideration of specially affected states because

> the Study tends to regard as equivalent the practice of States that have relatively little history of participation in armed conflict and the practice of States that have had a greater extent and depth of experience or that have otherwise had significant opportunities to develop a carefully considered military doctrine.[64]

This, together with other similar statements made by US representatives,[65] points towards a doctrine of special affected states that would vest almost complete control over customary

---

60 Wittke (n 43) 351.

61 Jo, 'Law-Making Participation by Non-State Armed Groups' (n 8) section 4.

62 von Bernstorff (n 9) 719. See also Tom Ruys, 'Actor Legitimacy and the Application of IHL – A Rejoinder to d'Aspremont', Chapter 4 in this book, section 2.

63 Helen M Kinsella and Giovanni Mantilla, 'Contestation before Compliance: History, Politics, and Power in International Humanitarian Law' (2020) 64 International Studies Quarterly 649, 651.

64 Bellinger, III and Haynes II (n 31) 445–46.

65 Among others, see US Department of Defense, *Law of War Manual* (US Department of Defense 2016) 32: '"specially affected States" could include, depending upon the relevant matter, the nuclear powers, other major military powers, and occupying or occupied States.'

law-making in militarily powerful states.[66] Despite this, it is clear that such an approach not only challenges the universality of IHL from an input-legitimacy perspective, but it also represents a deviation from the specially affected doctrine. It would largely exclude the practice of those states that may have an interest in the regulation of armed conflict on the basis of being affected by the conduct of militarily powerful states.[67] Additionally, from a humanitarian perspective, the doctrine of specially affected states becomes blurry as eventually virtually all states may have an interest in most of the rules of a more humanitarian character even if they are not party to a conflict. Such an interest is also exemplified in IHL treaty law: Common Article 1 of the Geneva Conventions states that all state parties ensure respect for the Convention.[68] At the same time, methodologically, the doctrine of specially affected states also does not hinder one from taking into account the interests of other more generally affected states. This is because the doctrine does not per se declare that the practice of those specially affected states weighs more, but only considers such practices as indispensable in the determination of customary international law.[69]

Whereas the corresponding engagement of the Global South with IHL can be seen as a way to 'potentially induce legal reform and to advance the law at the universal level',[70] such developments may also question the relevance of IHL as a global framework and the sole yardstick for legitimate behaviour in armed conflict. For example, there seems to be a tendency to dissolve distinctions and categorizations central to the traditional conceptions of IHL within these states. The approach taken by Latin-American states and courts (with the Inter-American Court of Human Rights at the forefront) apparently blurs the distinction between a law of peace and a law of war that increasingly emphasizes the role of IHL as a law of humanity and provides more 'flexible legal innovations' that may eventually lead to a deconstruction of IHL by creating a 'law of violence'.[71] A similar tendency may be seen from an African perspective, where law-making also aimed to address the challenges of novel dynamics and forms of violence. Responses to these challenges have affected the classic categorization of armed conflicts (international, non-international and new kinds of conflicts) that tends to decline in African treaty-making. At the same time, such initiatives complement and widen general

---

[66] Kevin Jon Heller, 'Specially-Affected States and the Formation of Custom' (2018) 112 American Journal of International Law 191, 203ff and 241.

[67] cf Michael Wood, 'The Evolution and Identification of the Customary International Law of Armed Conflict' (2018) 51 Vanderbilt Journal of Transnational Law 727, 734: 'It is perhaps difficult to say in all cases that only those states that are fighting are specially affected; again, depending on the specifics, other involved states may also be affected, for example, by a use of nuclear weapons.' Similarly, Jean-Marie Henckaerts, 'Customary International Humanitarian Law: A Response to US Comments' (2007) 89 International Review of the Red Cross 473, 482: 'Unlike the law of the sea, where a state either has or does not have a coast, with respect to humanitarian law any state can potentially become involved in armed conflict and become "specially affected".'

[68] In this regard, cf Jean-Marie Henckaerts and Louise Doswald-Beck (n 31) xlv; see also: ILC, 'Second report on identification of customary international law' (22 May 2014) UN Doc A/CN.4/672, 39.

[69] Wood (n 67) 734.

[70] Balingene Kahombo, 'Sovereign Equality and Law-Making: How do States from the Global South Shape International Humanitarian Law? An African Perspective', Chapter 18 in this book, 322.

[71] Alejandro Rodiles, 'International Humanitarian Law-Making in Latin America: Between the International Community, Humanity, and Extreme Violence', Chapter 17 in this book, 297.

concepts of IHL with regional specificity.[72] Regional efforts contribute to a clarification of the law for state and non-state actors with regard to their obligations in different contexts and situations. Examples provided in this book range from the prohibition of armed attacks against nuclear installations[73] to the merger of IHL and human rights law.[74] The historical absence of African states in traditional IHL law-making increases the legitimacy of these regional codifications and clarifications of the rules of IHL.

A tendency for stronger regionalism or particularism in IHL may be seen as an ambivalent development entailing considerations of both effectiveness and legitimacy. On the one hand, it may eventually indicate the inability of 'one' IHL to exist as the main yardstick for assessing legitimate behaviour in armed conflict due to its failure to adequately account for regional specifics.[75] Thus, IHL regionalism may contribute to the development of norms that concisely address and guide behaviour on the ground, thereby making rules more effective. At the same time, in view of numerous international or internationalized conflicts with parties from many regions of the world, a process of decoupling from the standards included in the Geneva Conventions may endanger their effectiveness.

In terms of legitimacy, any evaluation may depend on framing. The idea of 'one' universal body of IHL is entangled with its ambivalent 19th-century roots and impaired by the limited number of original state parties in 1949. It thereby feeds into the criticism that IHL is a 'sham'. From such a perspective, the idea that there is a universal core to which the peripheries may now add could be seen as an argument that would perpetuate historical power asymmetries. According to this argument there is no genuine consensus on the universality of IHL's underlying values if states from the Global South can only engage with a pre-existing idea of IHL.[76] At the same time, such criticism could be turned upside down. Contributing to a universal IHL 'core' may also be seen as the only way to substantively realize state equality, to push back against the dominance of certain states in the law-making process and thereby enhance the overall legitimacy of IHL. What is required, however, to realize such a vision is to increase the capabilities and safeguards for a genuinely open discursive law-making process that in itself does not replicate old hierarchies and European or US dominance.[77]

---

72 Kahombo (n 70).

73 ibid 305. With reference to the Pelindaba Treaty.

74 Rodiles (n 71) 296. With reference to a new law of violence.

75 Michael Bothe, 'Sovereign Equality and Law-Making: How do States from the Global South Shape International Humanitarian Law? – A Comment to Alejandro Rodiles and Balingene Kahombo', Chapter 19 in this book, 330.

76 For a sharp criticism of 'the illusion of proclaimed universality' and a call to conceive of international law as comprising 'several centres of impetus and proposal for international law' Apollin Koagne Zouapet, 'Regional Approaches to International Law: Rise or Decline of International Law?' (2021) KFG Working Paper Series, n 46 at 66 https://ssrn.com/abstract=3804733 accessed 31 January.

77 On the omission of actors and ideas from the Global South international law's discursive practices: James Gathii, 'The Promise of International Law: A Third World View' (Grotius Lecture presented at the 2020 Virtual Annual Meeting of the American Society of International Law) 3–16 <https://papers.ssrn.com/sol3/papers.cfm?abstract_id=3635509> accessed 31 January 2021.

2.3 Law-Making in Disguise: The Authoritative Interpretation of International Humanitarian Law by Non-State Actors

Many observers assume that non-state actors could play a decisive role in enabling and safeguarding a fairer law-making process.[78] Indeed, the main thrust of modern IHL development comes from state-empowered courts and expert processes. One can even go as far as to claim that we are living in an 'age of manuals'.[79] This may be due to the reason that, according to Nolte, in the absence of new treaties, lawyers typically concentrate on their traditional role of commenting on existing law.[80] However, in view of the general plurality of actors in international law 'the question is who among those, and under what conditions, can legitimately claim to intervene in them [the current processes of international law-making], or, in other words, who among these authorities in the descriptive sense are also authorities in a normative sense'.[81] One therefore needs to assess the empirical legitimacy of these developments – in other words, the degree to which relevant actors feel bound by the pronouncements and judgments of courts as well as expert manuals.

The main IHL developments from courts come from international criminal courts and bodies. In general, such courts may enhance legitimacy in the sense that enforcement of the law via their judgments may encourage compliance, which in turn adds to legitimacy.[82] On the other hand, discussions about withdrawals from the ICC[83] and other contestations of its authority may impair this ability to boost compliance and effectively enforce the law. This impacts the law's legitimacy because it casts doubt to what extent courts are able to provide an authoritative account of the law and facts.

Moreover, international courts may create law 'when judges refer to modern and progressive approaches to customary international law'.[84] For IHL, such an approach entails specific problems because such courts are not set up as universal adjudicators of this legal regime but merely to take it into account under a different and more limited mandate.[85] The ICC, for example, is not an 'IHL court', as such; nevertheless, it interprets certain IHL norms in a limited manner in its assessment of war crimes. Moreover, any pronouncement on matters of IHL would be expected to 'remain on the bottom line' because criminal courts follow the general principle of *nulla poena sine lega certa* and confusion with regard to the content of the

[78] This seems to be the underlying claim of Eyal Benvenisti and Doreen Lustig, 'Monopolizing War: Codifying the Laws of War to Reassert Governmental Authority, 1856–1874' (2020) 31 European Journal of International Law 127; for criticism of certain NGO argumentative practices in relation to human rights law: Zouapet (n 76) 46.

[79] cf Dale Stephens, 'Manuals and Courts – International Humanitarian Law, Informal Law-Making and Normativity', Chapter 16 in this book, 266.

[80] Nolte (n 34), 251.

[81] Samantha Besson and José Luis Martí, 'Legitimate Actors of International Law-Making: Towards a Theory of International Democratic Representation' (2018) 9 Jurisprudence 504, 506.

[82] Jo, 'Law-Making Participation by Non-State Armed Groups' (n 8) 367.

[83] Bothe (n 75) 332; Ryngaert, 'Non-State Armed Groups and International Humanitarian Law-Making' (n 7) 382f.

[84] Thomas Rauter, 'Judicial Practice in International Criminal Law – Law-Making in Disguise?', Chapter 12 in this book, 216.

[85] cf *Georgia v Russia (II)* App no 38263/08 (ECtHR, 21 January 2021) para 142.

applicable law would generally lead to a more cautious approach to any interpretation.[86] At the same time, international criminal courts, as Rauter pointed out, when faced with the problem of not being equipped with 'precise international criminal norms adequate to fulfil their task to deliver justice [… ,] turned to the flexibility and doctrinal confusion surrounding customary international law as a source of law'.[87] This has implications for the legitimacy as laid down in Franck's account of adherence to the law as an indicator of legitimacy: 'A rule has greater legitimacy if it is validated by having been made in accordance with secondary rules about rule-making.'[88] Methodological divergence in determining rules of customary international law calls into question this adherence to secondary rules or such uniform rules itself and thereby undermines the perceived legitimacy of such law-making efforts.[89]

In contrast to courts which are state-empowered institutions, expert processes leading to the development of manuals are, in principle, enacted by private individuals, although states occasionally exert an indirect influence, such as in the case of the NATO-supported Tallinn Manuals. The legitimacy of manuals as law-making tools may be dubious. On the one hand, in an international legal system where states have a monopoly over treaty-making but no monopoly over accounting for and interpreting the law, manuals may, as Nolte argues, be considered 'classic legal techniques' and a natural exercise of lawyerly administration of treaties to 'nurture them, to keep them alive, and to elucidate them for our time'.[90] On the other hand, Wouter shows that it is the particular form and design of manuals that differentiates them from classic legal commentary. Manuals are 'more likely to be used *instead* of primary legal sources' by their 'users' and are not just informing legal analysis.[91] They, in other words, 'put their products in place of the law'.[92] Manuals also 'explicitly deny that they are engaged in law-making in the formal sense'.[93] They claim to embody a certain form of legitimacy as they are 'engendering a belief in the acceptability of the manual because its arguments are fixed by and in line with existing international law'.[94] *De lege ferenda* interpretations contained within manuals may therefore be disguised behind the claim that they are merely restating the law. It is especially in light of the treaty-making deadlock that manuals signal that existing rules suffice and only need to be understood properly for the purposes of regulating new wars or technologies. Thus, they may actually hamper efforts for law reform. This is especially crucial in new contexts, such as cyberspace, where their results 'unavoidably venture into the political domain'.[95]

Contrary to other manual processes which navigate historically evolved and established domains, in new areas of exploration, contestations are to be expected. This is due to the knowledge gap that naturally exists where a matter is still evolving and therefore still open to

---

86 cf Dominik Steiger, 'Enforcing IHL Through Human Rights Bodies' in Krieger (n 46) 271.
87 Rauter (n 84) 213.
88 Franck (n 41) 193.
89 cf Rauter (n 84) 212.
90 Nolte (n 34) 251.
91 Wouter Werner, 'The Law at Hand – Paratext in Manuals on International Humanitarian Law', Chapter 13 in this book, 224.
92 Anton Petrov, *Expert Laws of War* (Edward Elgar 2020) 23.
93 Werner (n 91) 220.
94 ibid.
95 Robin Geiß and Anni Pues, 'International Manuals in International Humanitarian Law – A Rejoinder to Wouter G. Werner', Chapter 14 in this book, 238.

discussions and practical implementation. For this reason, it is hard to draw the line between politics and law where a restatement itself cannot draw upon sufficient practice and precedent. Generally, the authority of experts in such manual processes derives from the quality of experts' individual scholarship and the persuasiveness of their position in the process. But where such an authority is impaired insofar as they venture into new spaces of enquiry, additional sources of legitimacy become a relevant factor for the compliance pull they aim to exert on practitioners on the ground in their function as gap-filler and therefore law-maker. Geiß and Pues show that actors involved in those processes are increasingly aware of their need to be inclusive and representative in order to be considered relevant on the ground. If manuals are as inclusive as possible, they will probably be regarded as less interest driven. This eventually enhances their legitimacy from an outcome-legitimacy perspective. Nevertheless, as Stephens contends, the self-selection mechanisms inherent to manual processes always carry the risk that their contributors are not well established or representative enough. Thus, expert processes risk replicating or even augmenting power asymmetries in law-making. What applies to state-driven law-making processes is also of concern for scholarly efforts. Ultimately, only the inclusiveness of expert processes can ensure that such processes do not unilaterally foster specific interests and forestall political debates in arguing that the law suffices but inform a necessary broader political debate and are in the end perceived as legitimate.

Overall, whereas court decisions and manual processes may strengthen understanding of IHL by providing more certainty, these exercises come with the risk of provoking contestations and uncertainties on the future direction of the regime. 'Viewed as a whole, there is a risk of overregulation, overly detailed regulation and resultant incoherence that is at odds with the original idea of keeping the rules of armed conflicts as simple and realistic as possible.'[96] Moreover, Geiß and Pues, as well as Wouter, argue that manual processes blur the line between law and non-law and may enable a 'pick and choose' attitude for the convenient set of law, which eventually may lead to a loss in IHL's normative power.[97] In hiding their law-making attributes behind a mere restatement, manuals offer states a way to follow them without going through established law-making procedures. The existence of manual processes therefore tends to conceal the gaps in the existing bodies of IHL in the era of 'new wars' and may therefore contribute to a further stagnation of necessary state-driven processes.[98] This can be illustrated in a remarkable way by the German position on the application of international law in cyberspace. Here, the Tallinn Manual 2.0 is cited along courts and states, blurring the line between expert processes and official government positions, deligitimizing the latter.[99]

---

[96] Robin Geiß and Andreas Zimmermann, 'The International Committee of the Red Cross: A Unique Actor in the Field of International Humanitarian Law Creation and Progressive Development' in Robin Geiß, Andreas Zimmermann and Stefanie Haumer (eds), *Humanizing the Laws of War: The Red Cross and the Development of International Humanitarian Law* (CUP 2017) 253.

[97] Geiß and Pues (n 95) 236.

[98] ibid 239.

[99] Germany, The Federal Government, 'On the Application of International Law in Cyberspace' (March 2021) <https://www.auswaertiges-amt.de/blob/2446304/32e7b2498e10b74fb17204c54665bdf0/on-the-application-of-international-law-in-cyberspace-data.pdf> accessed 15 July 2021.

2.4 The Increasing Influence of Public Opinion and Introduction of External Moral Expectations

The media and other relevant norm entrepreneurs are becoming increasingly visible participants in legal processes and even in law-making. This development has deeper implications for considerations about IHL's legitimacy.[100] With the help of traditional media, as well as social media platforms, citizens themselves become witnesses and commentators of armed conflict. As such, the media as representatives of the 'public conscience' in terms of the Martens clause already contributed to shifts in IHL in the 19th century[101] and may well continue to contribute to further processes of 'humanizing' IHL. Traditionalists therefore fear that the increasing pressure exerted by media and especially social media[102] creates a kind of 'public concern' in the field of IHL that may question the ability of armed forces to operate effectively. For them, this development risks maintenance of the 'balance between military necessity and humanity (…) underpinning the current law of armed conflict'.[103] Such an involvement may lead to an oversimplification and increasingly focuses on real-time decision-making which had largely been absent from IHL, where assessments typically rest on ex-ante decisions on the ground. Moreover, from a legitimacy perspective, the influence exerted by media is often guided by principles such as newsworthiness and selectiveness, and can therefore barely be seen as representative of global public opinion.

Partly replicating the discourses of the 19th century, the way armed conflicts are covered today may show declining support for the moral claims inherent in IHL[104] and instead assess conduct on different moral terms external to the law. In particular, media reports critical of state behaviour in armed conflict that actually conforms with dominant interpretations of IHL contributes to a process of a decoupling of legal standards and other normative assessments in the public sphere. For example, one of ABC's Middle East correspondents in an interview, when asked about the inherent tension of IHL and the balancing of military necessity and humanity, responded that

> NATO powers are prepared to kill 30 civilians for one moderately high value target, and (…) everybody involved in the game privately nods their head and agrees that it was legitimate to wipe all of these women and children off the face of the earth. That's another thing that undermines perceptions of IHL. How can this happen? Look at this blasted apart child? How can this be legitimate?[105]

---

[100] Daniel Joyce, 'From the Martens Clause to the CNN Factor: Is the Impact of Media and Public Opinion on Law-Making Discernible?', Chapter 24 in this book.

[101] Kalmanovitz (n 20) 149.

[102] See Rosine Faucher, 'Social Media and Change in International Humanitarian Law Dynamics' (2019) 2 Inter Gentes 48.

[103] William Boothby, 'Media, Public Opinion and Humanitarian Advocacy', Chapter 25 in this book, 427.

[104] For an understanding of IHL norms as a moral system with moral demands: Hilly Moodrick-Even Khen, '*Aidōs* and *Dikē* in International Humanitarian Law: Is IHL a Legal or a Moral System?' (2016) 99 The Monist 26; see, however, for a more differentiated approach Adil Haque, *Law and Morality at War* (OUP 2017).

[105] 'Q & A with Matt Brown, ABC's Middle East Correspondent and Tara Gutman, Deputy National Manager of IHL, Australian Red Cross' (2015) 12 International Humanitarian Law magazine 5, 7 <https://www.redcross.org.au/getmedia/80c27d1f-f7ca-4631-a83e-0349f704316f/IHL-Magazine-Edition-12-Journalism.pdf.aspx> accessed 31 January 2021.

Such forms of decoupling may be strong drivers of legal change. Social science literature argues that the creation of cognitive dissonance pushes actors to reduce such dissonances through law reform.[106] In this sense, the multiple indications within public and academic discourse about IHL that demonstrate a widespread unease with the fundamental structure and the moral basis of current IHL can be interpreted as claims for law reform. However, even law reform on the basis of interpretation continues to face the ultimate limit of state consent. In view of the decentralized nature of IHL, law-making without any recognized authority that could clarify the ascertainable normative content for all addressees, may increasingly suffer from normative uncertainty. This makes the call for a more proactive role of states in the law-making process – at least not outside of the realm of weapon treaties[107] or more recently with regard to cyberspace – even more important.

3. THE RELUCTANCE OF STATES TO ACT AS PRIMARY LAW-MAKERS IN INTERNATIONAL LAW

Obviously, one should not overemphasize a certain reluctance of states to act as primary law-makers in IHL. To some extent, the current widespread research focus on non-state actors may simply distort the perception of the role of states and conceal their ongoing impact. A case in point is the ECtHR's jurisprudence on the extraterritorial application of the ECHR and the Conventions in relation to IHL. While the Court's restrictive interpretation of 'jurisdiction' in Article 1 ECHR in the *Bankovic* case tended to preserve a distinction between IHL and international human rights law, later cases have pushed for an application of the ECHR to situations of armed conflict. Still, states continued to contest the competence of the Court to judge at least on certain constellations in military missions abroad and continue to emphasize the prevalent role of IHL in situations of armed conflict. An instrument for these claims and contestations are third party interventions in proceedings before the ECtHR and, in appropriate cases, like-minded states organize and coordinate such interventions aiming to increase their impact.[108] While it is difficult to prove any direct effect, these interventions seem to – at least partly – have been influential. In the *Hassan* case, the ECtHR held that 'the Court considers that, even in situations of international armed conflict, the safeguards under the Convention continue to apply, albeit interpreted against the background of the provisions of international humanitarian law'.[109] On the basis of these findings, it interpreted Article 5(1) ECHR against its explicit wording and relied on member states' practice to arrive at its conclusion.[110] In the case of *Georgia v Russia (II)*, the court upheld its *Bankovic* approach and excluded ongoing hostilities in an international armed conflict from the sphere of application of the ECHR by

---

[106] Teresa Reinold and Michael Zürn, '"Rules about Rules" and the Endogenous Dynamics of International Law: Dissonance Reduction as a Mechanism of Secondary Rule-Making' (2014) 3 Global Constitutionalism 236.

[107] See on recent developments in this field, Garcia (n 44).

[108] eg third party interventions by Denmark, Estonia, Greece, Poland, Portugal and the United Kingdom as well as Germany in ECtHR, *Behrami and Saramati* App nos 71412/01 and 78166/01 (ECtHR, 2 May 2007) paras 96–120; third party interventions by Denmark, France, Norway, Sweden, and the United Kingdom in *Hanan* App no 4871/16 (ECtHR, 16 February 2021) paras 123–28.

[109] *Hassan* App no 29750/09 (ECtHR, 16 September 2014) para 104.

[110] ibid paras 101–103.

explicitly referring to the consent of the Contracting Parties.[111] The example underlines the process-like character of law-making that evolves over time, consists of ongoing discursive exchanges[112] and entails a stop-and-go element. States remain a, if not the, decisive voice in such processes.

However, in other fora states are less outspoken. The reasons for this reluctance are manifold. On the one hand, states claim and recall their 'primary responsibility (…) in the development of IHL'[113] and advocate for state-driven processes to solve existing problems. On the other hand, the inter-state environment currently does not seem to enable consensual agreements, as observed at the 33rd International Conference of the Red Cross and Red Crescent.[114] This may be a reflection of current geopolitical shifts in the international legal order and the general crisis of multilateralism,[115] where certain states are eager to demonstrate that they are (still) relevant or are becoming more relevant in international negotiations, if alone, by hindering the successful outcome of negotiations. It is also likely that particular states' reluctance to promote certain multilateral efforts is in turn directly connected to the multiplication of law-making institutions and persons in the field of IHL, so that we are actually faced with a kind of vicious circle: in light of the divergent agendas, states may simply want to maintain the possibility to choose and also do not want to highlight a certain position, where they would generally disagree.[116] This may be further aggravated by an environment where most of the articulations on IHL tend to favour the humanitarian aspect of the legal regime, whereas states may generally tend to argue in favour of a position that leaves them enough operational freedom in warfare.[117]

Another observation points to manual processes and finds that it is unlikely that there will be a normative development where an issue had been covered by expert process, but where there had been new treaties (such as weapon law) there has not been an expert process beforehand.[118] Therefore, with widespread manual processes that signal that existing norms suffice, there is also a retreat of state action, arguably due to the additional argumentative burden that such negotiations would place on them.

---

[111] *Georgia v Russia (II)* App no 38263/08 (ECtHR, 21 January 2021) paras 141–144.

[112] See Hans-Joachim Cremer, 'Regeln der Konventionsinterpretation' in Oliver Dörr, Thilo Marauhn and Rainer Grote (eds), *EMRK/GG Konkordanzkommentar* (2nd ed, Mohr Siebeck 2013) para 58.

[113] cf Resolution 1 'Strengthening legal protection for victims of armed conflicts' in ICRC and IFRC, *Report of the 31st International Conference of the Red Cross and Red Crescent* (ICRC 2011) 24–25 <https://www.icrc.org/en/publication/1129-report-31st-international-conference-red-cross-and-red-crescent-including-summary> accessed 31 January 2021.

[114] International Committee of the Red Cross and the Swiss Federal Department of Foreign Affairs, 'Factual Report on the Proceedings of the Intergovernmental Process on Strengthening Respect for IHL – Progress report' (October 2019) 11 <https://rcrcconference.org/app/uploads/2019/10/33IC-IHL-Compliance-factual-report-_en.pdf> accessed 31 January 2021.

[115] On this, see Heike Krieger, Georg Nolte and Andreas Zimmermann (eds) (n 29).

[116] Sandesh Sivakumaran, 'Making and Shaping the Law of Armed Conflict' (2018) 71 Current Legal Problems 119, 153.

[117] ibid 156 with reference to Sean Watts, 'The Updated First Geneva Convention Commentary, DOD's Law of War Manual, and a More Perfect Law of War: Part II' (*Just Security*, 29 July 2016) <https://www.justsecurity.org/32194/updated-geneva-convention-commentary-dods-law-war-manual-perfect-law-war-part-ii/> accessed 31 January 2021; Eyal Benvenisti, 'The Legal Battle to Define the Law on Transnational Asymmetric Warfare' (2010) 20 Duke Journal of Comparative & International Law 339, 358f.

[118] Petrov (n 92) 13.

In light of the multiplication of actors involved in law-making and the high moral expectations that are attributed to this field of law, as has been shown in the chapters of this book, one might well add another reason for this deadlock in treaty-making and normative clarification. In addition to the legal arguments in favour of humanitarian interpretations, there are also high moral expectations that developed externally to the legal regime. Such expectations are predominantly influenced by human rights law and follow an increasingly broad media coverage of armed conflicts and a significant place of public opinion. In light of such expectations, states may not feel able to openly argue against a more humanitarian legal framework in favour of military necessity or even less regulation and may be hampered in the revision of existing law to allow the flexibility they consider as necessary to efficiently conduct armed operations. They may therefore simply opt for less transparent and informal methods of law-making, which may well explain why a turn to informality, as has been described in this book, can be observed. Informality entails an inherently less traceable legal outcome avoiding, to a large extent, public scrutiny at the cost of clearly applicable rules, and, in the end legitimacy. That this is not a far-fetched argument can be exemplified in states' reactions to the various non-binding, human rights-informed and morally laden initiatives that states join while carefully excluding language of binding commitments that would actually restrain their options. A case in point is the Oslo Safe Schools declaration.[119] Australia, Canada, France, Japan, South Korea and the UK were among those states that were reluctant to commit to the non-binding declaration because it contained statements beyond what the applicable IHL would require. The harsh criticism that Germany was confronted with when deciding not to sign the declaration[120] led later – presumably due to the moral and political pressure – to its support.[121] At the same time, such examples should not be overstated, as such initiatives largely focus on selective practices within armed conflict and do not question entirely the operational freedom of states and the legal regime. Therefore, states may be more willing to concede to such moral pressures as long as their relative freedom in the overall framework remains generally intact. For those reasons, it may be argued that if an open negotiation for a new normative framework would take place today, the likely result would be a regime different from the existing relatively 'unconstrained regime'.[122] As a result, such an open negotiation of the overall legal framework is generally avoided.

Of course, in light of growing outputs by a plethora of actors, states might also simply feel practically overburdened to respond to each and every pronouncement with the additional process of finding an internally consistent position beforehand. While this may be indeed the case for states that lack sufficient material or personal capacity to strategically engage with

---

[119] Global Coalition to Protect Education from Attack, 'Safe Schools Declaration' (29 May 2015) <http://protectingeducation.org/sites/default/files/documents/safe_schools_declaration-final.pdf> accessed 31 January 2021.

[120] Ulrike Scheffer, 'Menschenrechtler empört über Deutschland' (*Tagesspiegel*, 17 May 2015) <https://www.tagesspiegel.de/politik/deklaration-zum-schutz-von-schulen-menschenrechtler-empoert-ueber-deutschland/11787154.html> accessed 31 January 2021.

[121] For an activist perspective on the Oslo Safe School declaration, cf Article 36, *Reflections from the Safe Schools Declaration process for future international political commitments on civilian protection*, Discussion Paper (August 2019) <http://www.article36.org/wp-content/uploads/2019/08/SSD-process-reflections.pdf> accessed 31 January 2021.

[122] Petrov (n 92) 223.

the increasing number of actors, for states with sufficient capabilities, this might also point towards an increasing lack of interest in taking part in such a debate.

4. CONCLUSION: THE FRAYING CONSENSUS OF INTERNATIONAL HUMANITARIAN LAW

Hidden beyond stagnation, informal law-making and the abstinence of states from law-making, we observe a more far-reaching disagreement about the direction into which IHL should be developed. The legitimacy challenges in the law-making process in IHL signal that its underlying consensus is fraying.[123] As the contributions within this book show, IHL is currently undergoing a deeper process of norm change, the outcome of which remains open. Various established and new actors compete for reform and 'right' understanding of the legal corpus and its rules and how they are ought to be applied on the ground. This struggle for legal development contributes to current turbulences and ambivalences within the law and its application. It had been noted elsewhere that

> [l]egitimacy strengthens legality when laws meet and reflect public expectations and are largely accepted. Legality and legitimacy should be, and often are, in a harmony. However, when the existing laws are seen as paralyzing the progress, states can undertake legally uncertain actions, while claiming legitimacy and challenging the existing status of law.[124]

In that sense, it appears that with a plurality of actors, contestations around the legal structure and values that underpin IHL become more visible – in particular because of diverging interpretations by actors that had formerly existed outside the regime, for example non-state armed actors and members of human rights communities as well as civil society actors including the media.[125] Of course, one may argue that IHL has always been a site of intensive political contestation,[126] and while previous dynamics may have also contributed to an ambiguous state of IHL, they eventually furthered new rules. Still, it is the variance of voices and fora as a result of a deepened process of globalization[127] that makes the current environment qualitatively and quantitatively different from previous challenges to IHL.

Accordingly, IHL is also challenged from within established categories, i.e., by states in regional law-making and expert processes which – albeit involving traditional IHL practitioners and academics that sometimes resist changes on the basis of their traditional under-

---

123 cf on the fraying of the social bargain that led to the creation of the regime, Ian Clark and others, 'Crisis in the Laws of War? Beyond Compliance and Effectiveness' (2017) 24 European Journal of International Relations 319.

124 Vesselin Popovski, 'Legality and Legitimacy of International Criminal Tribunals' in Richard Falk, Mark Juergensmeyer, and Vesselin Popovski, *Legality and Legitimacy in Global Affairs* (OUP 2012) 407.

125 cf on the CNN effect, Joyce (n 99).

126 Kinsella and Mantilla (n 63) 655.

127 See for this argument Andrew Hurrell, 'Cultural Diversity within Global International Society' in Andrew Phillips and Christian Reus-Smit (eds), *Culture and Order in World Politics* (CUP 2020) 117: 'a decisive momentum lies rather in the increased capacity of a far wider range of states and social actors to become active subjects and agents in the politics and practices of international law and society. It is the diffusion of agency and of political consciousness that has been the most important feature of the globalization of international society.'

standings – also push for development in areas not historically covered by the regime. The various agendas in the law-making of the growingly diverse participants of the 'humanitarian community'[128] show that they do not aim to inform IHL or simply comment on existing law, but to develop it in the direction that appears to be most suitable. This concerns basic questions of IHL, as had been noted elsewhere,[129] such as the consensus on the balancing of military necessity and humanity, but also the distinction between international and non-international armed conflicts, the normative addressees and even the act of killing itself.

This process eventually affects the degree of determinacy of IHL's norms as a precondition of its compliance pull. The uncertainties of law reform in international law are especially problematic in the field of IHL because, as Geiß and Pues point out, it is an area of law that 'needs to be particularly user-friendly to increase the potential for compliance in the inherently dire circumstances of armed conflict'.[130] Where rules are less determined, they should be subject to a process of clarification by a competent authority.[131] This clarification depends on who is doing the interpretation, the pedigree of authority to interpret and the coherence of principles the interpreters apply.[132] In a legal regime where states are both subject to and the source of international law, the legitimizing community would be seen in states. Nevertheless, as the book shows, IHL *de facto* consists of a wider community that judges the legitimacy of the regime. Together with the absence of states' formal engagement with the regime, this reality finally leads to a decline in the power of states over the laws they created because states can no longer ignore the different ideas of legitimacy resembled in the various law-making efforts by state and non-state actors.[133]

In general, legal methodology – from a positivist perspective – demands that in order for a rule or interpretation to be perceived legitimate, it has to follow a certain accepted and inherent rule-making process leading to normatively correct outcomes. Nevertheless, the book shows that even though most actors do generally follow the accepted legal methodology in norm interpretation, the outcomes vary significantly, blurring the difference between norm interpretation and norm creation. Therefore, legal methodology as an internal discourse-structuring device may not even be able to fully grasp those developments. As can be seen in the various contributions to this book, there is a deep divergence of understanding of the right interpretation of IHL and the identification of customary international law. When, for instance, the objective state practice element of the two elements test of customary international law is negligible in light of the demands of public conscience and humanity,[134] the outcome may become rather dependent on the moral persuasion of the interpreter and blurs the distinction between a purposive interpretation of a rule and subsequent practice. This is problematic, as eventually it is the methodological foundation that secures structural developments

---

[128] Petrov (n 92) 165.

[129] ibid.

[130] Geiß and Pues (n 95) 237.

[131] Franck (n 41) 61.

[132] ibid.

[133] cf Christopher Thomas, 'Uses and Abuses of Legitimacy in International Law' (2014) 34 Oxford Journal of Legal Studies 729, 747–49.

[134] cf Robert Heinsch, 'Methodological Challenges in Ascertaining Customary International Humanitarian Law: Can Customary International Law Respond to Changing Circumstances in Warfare?', Chapter 11 in this book, section 6.

and serves to distinguish law from non-law against an emerging 'alternative international law'.[135] It is therefore problematic that IHL appears to be developing anyway even in absence of states' involvement through the various modes of law-making. As states nevertheless are still the main addressees of IHL and through their involvement in armed conflicts also the main actors in the application of this body of law, further engagement with the legal discourse is warranted. In its absence, legal development will largely be based on the competing legitimacy of the various actors in the law-making arena of IHL, filling this vacuum with uncertain outcomes for the legal regime itself.

---

[135] Nolte (n 34) section 2.

Index